EDITION **8**

DEVELOPING AND ADMINISTERING

A CHILD CARE *and* EDUCATION PROGRAM

Dorothy June Sciarra
Professor Emerita, University of Cincinnati

Anne G. Dorsey
Professor Emerita, University of Cincinnati

Ellen M. Lynch
Associate Professor, University of Cincinnati

Shauna M. Adams
Associate Professor, University of Dayton

D0149010

WADSWORTH
CENGAGE Learning·

Australia • Brazil • Japan • Korea • Mexico • Singapore • Spain • United Kingdom • United States

WADSWORTH
CENGAGE Learning·

Developing and Administering a Child Care and Education Program, Eighth Edition

Dorothy June Sciarra, Anne G. Dorsey, Ellen M. Lynch, Shauna M. Adams

Editor-in-Chief: Linda Ganster-Schreiber

Executive Editor: Mark D. Kerr

Development Editor: Kate Scheinman

Editorial Assistant: Greta Lindquist

Assistant Editor: Genevieve Allen

Media Editor: Elizabeth Momb

Senior Art Director: Jennifer Wahi

Marketing Manager: Kara Kindstrom

Marketing Program Manager: Klaira Markenzon

Senior Marketing Communications Manager: Heather Baxley

Manufacturing Planner: Rebecca Cross

Rights Acquisitions Specialist: Roberta Broyer

Design Direction, Production Management, and Composition: PreMediaGlobal

Cover Designer: Jeff Bane

Cover Image: Cover photograph by Jessica R. Pike

For product information and technology assistance, contact us at **Cengage Learning Customer & Sales Support, 1-800-354-9706.**

For permission to use material from this text or product, submit all requests online at **www.cengage.com/permissions**. Further permissions questions can be e-mailed to **permissionrequest@cengage.com**.

Library of Congress Control Number: 2012933741

ISBN-13: 978-1-111-83338-1

ISBN-10: 1-111-83338-9

Advantage Edition:

ISBN-13: 978-1-133-52549-3

ISBN-10: 1-133-52549-0

Wadsworth
20 Davis Drive
Belmont, CA 94002-3098
USA

Cengage Learning is a leading provider of customized learning solutions with office locations around the globe, including Singapore, the United Kingdom, Australia, Mexico, Brazil, and Japan. Locate your local office at **www.cengage.com/global**.

Cengage Learning products are represented in Canada by Nelson Education, Ltd.

To learn more about Wadsworth, visit **www.cengage.com/wadsworth**.

Purchase any of our products at your local college store or at our preferred online store **www.cengagebrain.com**.

Printed in the United States of America
2 3 4 5 6 7 16 15 14 13 12

To my colleagues and former students who continue to offer support and an inspiration to me, and also to my co-author and dear friend, Anne G. Dorsey, without whom this edition as well as all the previous editions could not have been written. Thanks Anne.   D.J.S.

To Robert Frost, without whom I may never have met Robert W. Dorsey.   A.G.D.

To Dennis, whose unending patience and support never cease to amaze and support me; to Kaitlyn and Taylor, whose spirits continue to change my life so powerfully, absolutely, and unexpectedly; and to my mother, whose life has been a model of strength and spirit.   E.M.L.

To Stan, my husband, partner, and best friend, who inspires me to see the glass as half full—without your love and support I would be truly lost. To my daughters, Meredith and Jillian, who add much joy to my life—thank you for allowing me to share your stories in my teaching and my writing. To my colleagues Joni Baldwin, Joy Comingore, Diana Smith, and the teachers, staff, and children of the Bombeck Family Learning Center, whose work inspired my contributions to this book. To my co-authors—thank you for allowing me to add my voice to your sagacious work. S.M.A.

BRIEF CONTENTS

CONTENTS

CHAPTER 8
Equipping the Center   147

CHAPTER 9
Staffing the Center   171

CHAPTER 10
Recruiting Children   219

CHAPTER 15
Evaluating Center Components   347

CHAPTER 16
Marketing the Program   375

PREFACE

In our fast-paced world, we were not at all surprised to see that it was time to prepare the eighth edition of our text *Developing and Administering a Child Care and Education Program* focusing on the director's role in early childhood education programs. Nor should you be surprised to see that we have added to our team by bringing together authors with a variety of backgrounds in early childhood education. Together we provide the best and most current information for you and your students. Our goal is to provide professors of early childhood education and their students an understanding of the need for well-prepared directors who come to their role with a background in child development, appreciation of how learning occurs, and knowledge of basic business practices—particularly those involving finance and staff and client relations.

STATE OF THE DIRECTORSHIP

As more attention is given to the importance of the early years of child development and growth, additional scrutiny of early childhood programs is occurring. What's going on? And who is in charge? Educators, legislators, funders, program administrators, staff, and parents all want the best for children. But, of course, wanting the best, knowing what children need, and being able to provide it don't come easily. Yet strong standards for directors of programs for young children are not fully developed in many areas. Progress is evident based on the work of individuals such as Paula Jorde Bloom, who for many years has written about leadership and provided programs in support of directors' development. Roger and Bonnie Neugebauer have for more than 30 years provided bimonthly information specifically for directors in their *Exchange* publication. A number of states now have some requirements, although the required rigorous ones may not be fully in place as yet.

We recognize that one book alone will not prepare directors for their role. Our goal is to help future

teachers and directors understand the importance of the director's role for early childhood staff, children, their families, and the community. We hope that our text will also help those who are designing director licensure move more quickly to that goal.

OUR AUDIENCE

The eighth edition of *Developing and Administering a Child Care and Education Program* was written for college students at all levels interested in early childhood development. They may be preparing to be teachers of young children or they may be planning ahead to becoming administrators. Our intention is to depict the role of director, whether starting a new center or administering one already in operation. When teachers understand this role, they are more likely to recognize why their director has certain expectations of teachers, and what teachers' responsibilities are as they plan and implement a flexible, interesting program for the young children in their group. Students in associate, baccalaureate, and masters programs need this information. As they study these chapters, they begin to realize in an early childhood education career, none of the roles is independent of all the aspects that a director leads.

CONCEPTUAL APPROACH

When the director is competent to engage in a wide range of human interactions as well as in managing the center's business components, the center will function well. When the director's background in one or both of these components is weak, the center is likely to close, or even more disturbing, the program will continue in a way that is not productive for the children it serves.

Above all, we see the director as a well-prepared, ethical person who is authoritative and dedicated to meeting the needs of young children and their families. We emphasize adopting and using the National Association for the Education of Young Children's Statement of Commitment, Code of Ethical Conduct, and the Supplement for Early Childhood Program Administrators whenever puzzling situations arise that may be of an ethical nature. We see the director's responsibility as educating staff and families about the Code and how it can be used appropriately.

SUPPORTIVE MATERIALS FOR INSTRUCTORS AND STUDENTS

Within the chapters, we include boxes that illustrate the points discussed in that section of the chapter. Called "Director's Corner," these vignettes clarify the material with examples described from a director's experiences. Throughout the text are features called "Reflections." Designed to give readers an opportunity to pause and consider their understanding of the points being made in the text, these boxes often relate to an experience a student may have or have had. Each chapter ends with a summary followed by one or more activities labeled "Try It Out!" Directions for individual, partner, or small group activities are included. When the student is directed to respond in writing, a form may be provided in the text and on the book's Education CourseMate website.

Appendices in our book provide a wealth of updated lists for both instructors and students. These include Sources of Materials, Equipment and Supplies, Early Childhood Professional Organizations, Early Childhood Periodicals and information sources, and copies of many NAEYC Standards.

WHAT'S NEW IN THIS EDITION—AN OVERVIEW

The eighth edition of *Developing and Administering a Child Care and Education Program* presents completely updated and expanded content. Here are some of the major revisions to both the text as a whole as well as those for each chapter:

- A new chapter addressing administrator concerns and issues related to curriculum has been added.
- Student learning objectives at the beginning of each chapter have been revised.

- Relevant NAEYC Standards have been provided at the beginning of each chapter and the NAEYC icon within the text indicates where content related to the standards is addressed.
- A standards correlation chart has been added inside the front and back covers of the text to highlight which standards are covered in each chapter.
- Updated and expanded *Try It Out!* end-of-chapter activities have been provided to give students opportunities to apply what they have learned.
- New TeachSource Video Vignettes have been integrated into chapters to provide additional background information as well as to illustrate best practices.
- Photographs, references, and websites have been revised and updated.
- The Appendices have been completely updated and expanded. Additions include the NAEYC Code of Ethical Conduct, NAEYC Standards for Early Childhood Professional Preparation Programs, the NAEYC Program Administrator Definition and Competencies, and the NAEYC Accreditation Standards for Early Childhood Programs.
- Completely updated and expanded online materials and resources, including *Expanding Your Learning* exercises, challenge students to "dig deeper" as they learn and apply content.

Key Revisions and Additions to Each Chapter

Chapter 1—The Working Director
- Additional focus on the use of a systems approach to administration in light of the current economy.

Chapter 2—Assessing Community Need and Establishing a Program
- New information on the use of technology in conducting a needs assessment provided.
- Revised strategies provided for developing mission and values statements.

Chapter 3—Licensing and Certification
- Updated and expanded information regarding accreditation of programs.
- Expanded information related to Quality Rating Improvement Systems.

- Updated information about the various types of credentialing and credentialing bodies.
- Inclusion of new information related to career pathways in early childhood.

Chapter 4—Organizing Center Structure and Working with a Board

- Information about the roles of director and board chairman and members.
- Discussion of the recognition of home-based programs.
- More information about franchising based on its current popularity in early childhood business plans.

Chapter 5—Handling Financial Matters

- Additional support for students who experience frustration when mathematics is introduced.
- Further attention to the requirement that *all* directors understand center finances, even when someone else is handling the financial component.

Chapter 6—Funding the Program

- New focus on funding beyond what is needed for a current year's operation.
- Discussion of approaches to obtaining funds needed for major projects.

Chapter 7—Developing a Center Facility

- New information about "going green."
- Focus on the effect of the components of a facility on the child.

Chapter 8—Equipping the Center

- Additional discussion related to the needs of teachers in equipping the center.

Chapter 9—Staffing the Center

- The relationship of center climate is represented more extensively throughout the content on staffing.
- New emphasis on updated human resources principles.
- Expanded examples of human resources documents.
- Conflict resolution policy is now included.

- New information on interviewing and checking references.
- New information on the exit interview.

Chapter 10—Recruiting Children

- Updated information on including children with special learning needs in early care and education.
- New information on continuity of care for infants and toddlers.
- Multiage grouping and differentiated instruction with new graphics.

Chapter 11—Supporting Quality Curriculum

- Includes a comprehensive definition of curriculum and its impact on the whole program.
- Provides an overview of the principles of developmentally appropriate practices and other curriculum-related position statements and standards.
- Explains the role of the director as curriculum mentor.
- Includes in-depth discussion of curriculum planning models.
- Describes how directors can support intentional teaching.
- Includes a framework for creating a program-wide assessment system that supports instructional decision making, tracks children's progress, and informs program evaluation.
- Explains effective strategies for integrating content standards and developmental skills.
- Describes how to support school readiness within a seamless birth to age 3 system.

Chapter 12—Managing the Food and the Health and Safety Programs

- Inclusion of the United States Department of Agriculture's MyPlate icon and information.
- Updated information related to the USDA Child and Adult Care Food Program.
- Updated information related to exclusion policies.
- Updated information regarding the use of standard precautions.

Chapter 13—Working with Families, Volunteers, and the Community

- Describes the impact of the revised NAEYC standards on establishing reciprocal relationships with families.

- Expanded section on parent communication.
- Addition of new family support programs.

Chapter 14—Providing for Personal and Professional Staff Development

- New information on the early childhood career lattice.
- Includes information on meeting the needs of professionals with a variety of levels of expertise.

Chapter 15—Evaluating Center Components

- Discussion of the role of screening in early childhood programs.
- Discussion of the value of QRIS involvement in evaluation of the center as well as in staff development based on need.

Chapter 16—Marketing the Program

- Connections between a strategic plan and a marketing plan.
- How to use a SWOT Analysis Chart to develop a marketing plan.
- How best to market to Generation X-ers and Millennials.
- Updated information on how technology and new media can support marketing.

USING THE TEXT

When presenting material from *Developing and Administering a Child Care and Education Program*, instructors may choose to follow the existing order of chapters, or they may decide to depart from that order. Every chapter is self-contained, so either approach works well. Some instructors use the content as the basis of lectures, adding examples from their own experiences or inviting local directors to meet with the class to discuss a particular topic. Others assign students to interview directors on topics addressed in the text.

Many students enrolled in an administration class are involved in or will have completed an early childhood field experience. Many may be working in early childhood programs. Because the focus of college-level students may be primarily on the classroom, instructors may have students reflect on those experiences to determine how a director influences a program. For example, in your center, how does the

director's work affect the health, safety, and nutrition of the children?

Some instructors use the Reflections feature found throughout the text as a starting point for class discussions or as a topic for writing assignments. The Director's Corner feature, which presents quotes from directors on the chapter topic, can also be used this way. Other instructors use the Try It Out! exercises to stimulate discussion or reflection on personal experiences or feelings. These activities may take the form of role-playing or debates.

Most students are comfortable with the reading level of our book. Terms that may be new are explained in context. The activities on our Education CourseMate website are also supportive.

Developing and Administering a Child Care and Education Program lends itself well to related field experiences. Advanced students may be assigned as interns to work with directors, much as student teachers work with mentor teachers. Other instructors may assign students to form teams to create their own center on paper. This assignment may include creating an imaginary site, a mission statement, a funding plan, a tuition schedule, a budget, a marketing plan, a staffing plan, a policy and procedures manual, and a salary schedule. The assignment may be limited to one or more of these components. Instructors may assign students to write a paper or prepare a class presentation on one of the topics discussed in the text, using related resources listed in the appendices or at the end of each chapter.

ANCILLARY MATERIAL

Online Instructor's Manual with Test Bank

The Online Instructor's Manual contains resources designed to streamline and maximize the effectiveness of your course preparation. The Instructor's Manual contains information to assist the instructor in designing the course, including case studies, learning objectives, teaching and learning activities, and additional print and online resources. For assessment support, the updated Test Bank includes true/false, multiple-choice, and short answer questions for each chapter.

Online Exam View

Available for download from the instructor website, ExamView® testing software includes all the test items from the printed Test Bank in electronic format, enabling you to create customized tests in print or online.

Online PowerPoints

Preassembled Microsoft® PowerPoint® lecture slides for each chapter cover content from the book.

Professional Enhancement Booklet

The Administration and Supervision booklet for students, which is part of Cengage Learning's Early Childhood Education Professional Enhancement series, focuses on key topics of interest to future early childhood directors, teachers, and caregivers. Students will keep this informational supplement and use it for years to come in their early childhood practices.

Education CourseMate

Cengage Learning's Education CourseMate brings course concepts to life with interactive learning, study, and exam preparation tools that support the printed textbook. CourseMate includes an integrated eBook, quizzes, flashcards, downloadable and customizable forms from your book, videos, and more, and EngagementTracker, a first-of-its-kind tool that monitors student engagement in the course. The accompanying instructor website offers access to password-protected resources such as an electronic version of the instructor's manual, test bank, and PowerPoint® slides.

WebTutor™ for BlackBoard and WebCT

Jumpstart your course with customizable, rich, text-specific content within your Course Management System. Whether you want to Web-enable your class or put an entire course online, WebTutor™ delivers. WebTutor™ offers a wide array of resources including media assets, access to the eBook, quizzes, web links, exercises, and more.

ABOUT THE AUTHORS

Dorothy June Sciarra continues to be an active early childhood educator in a diverse variety of situations. She has served as director of the child development laboratory center at the University of Cincinnati, serving children and families from a wide range of backgrounds. Her work as director set the standard throughout the area for taking a stand for appropriate practice whether or not it was popular. Teachers who work with her understand their responsibility to the children and families and develop a clear understanding of early childhood education under her guidance.

Dr. Sciarra's work as professor of child development/early childhood education has been highly praised. Former students still talk about her child development courses and her deep understanding of childhood. Dr. Sciarra served as department head with responsibility for early childhood associate, bachelor's, and master's degree programs and pioneered a system for career development as capable students were enabled to move seamlessly from the CDA to the associate and then on to the baccalaureate degree level. Currently she is involved in several community early childhood efforts including board membership on the University of Cincinnati Early Learning Center. She is active in 4C, a National Association of Child Care Resource and Referral Agency, and has participated tirelessly on many of its Agency training committees. Dr. Sciarra is a recipient of the 4C Early Childhood Award and was the first recipient of the Ohio Association for the Education of Young Children's Early Childhood Teacher Educator Award. In 2007, 4C again recognized Dr. Sciarra's work at a statewide luncheon where it was announced that the 4C library would be named in her honor. Dr. Sciarra has mentored many early childhood educators, including coauthor Anne Dorsey. Together they also wrote *Leaders and Supervisors in Child Care Programs* published by Thomson Delmar Learning. In 2010, Dr. Sciarra and Professor Dorsey were honored with the United Way Impact Award for their work in promoting appropriate early childhood education.

Anne G. Dorsey began her ECE career working in the Child Life Department at Cincinnati Children's Hospital. Three sons later, she taught both preschool and college courses while attending graduate school. When she received a full-time faculty position, Dr. Dorothy June Sciarra convinced her that she should be her co-author and, years later, that she should become leader of the lab school and the ECE college programs. Professor Dorsey's interests in the broader community were and are based on her belief that working together, the University child development and early childhood education program could benefit from coordination with local agencies such as United Way, 4C, and Cincinnati Association for the Education of Young Children. Agencies could also benefit from the collaboration with faculty and college students.

Locally, Professor Dorsey has served on the Committee of Management of YMCA Child Development and continues to serve on the UC Early Learning Center Board, the Promoting Resilient Children Advisory Board, and the SPARK Advisory Board of the Children's Home. She has been a member of the NAEYC Ethics Panel, the NAEYC Professional Practice Panel, and the Ohio Association for the Education of Young Children Board. Professor Dorsey has visited many colleges and universities as a member of the National Council for Accreditation of Teacher Education Board of Examiners. As a strong supporter of the National Association of Early Childhood Teacher Educators, she has been secretary, program chair, president, and editor of the *Journal of Early Childhood Teacher Education* in its very early format, and served as president of the NAECTE Foundation. She received the OAEYC Teacher Education Award and the NAECTE Outstanding Early Childhood Teacher Educator Award. Traveling with her husband, she has visited 24 countries over the years and focused on early childhood education in each country, except, of course, Antarctica, where she waded among hundreds of penguins and their young. Currently, Professor Emeritus Dorsey enjoys volunteering as Data Manager for NAECTE and as an assessor of kindergarten and preschool children for the schools and for the United Way Collaborative Partners Committee, of which she is a member. Her favorite child comment came from a preschooler whom she had assessed several times during the child's years in an early learning center. "Well Anne, I guess we won't see each other anymore; I'm going to kindergarten!"

Ellen M. Lynch is associate professor of early childhood education at the University of Cincinnati. Her doctorate is in special education with a focus on early childhood special education. She has been active in local and state early childhood organizations, including the Ohio Association for the Education of Young Children (OAEYC), for which she served as chair of the Children with Special Needs Committee; the state Board of Directors; and the Division for Early Childhood of the Council for Exceptional Children. Additionally, she served as president of the Ohio Coalition of Associate Degree Early Childhood Programs. Dr. Lynch's current scholarly interests include engaging in the scholarship of teaching and learning (SoTL) and exploring the use of technology to support learning among preservice teachers. She is both an editor and reviewer for several problem-based learning journals. She has presented widely at local, state, national, and international levels on a variety of aspects of teaching young children, teacher education, and best practices for teaching in higher education.

Shauna M. Adams is an associate professor of early childhood at the University of Dayton, where she also serves as the executive director of the Center for Early Learning. Dr. Adams has taught graduate and undergraduate students in such courses as child development, preschool methods, primary methods and early childhood advocacy, research, and leadership. In her role as the director of the Center for Early Learning, Dr. Adams promotes opportunities for the Bombeck Family Learning Center to serve pre-service and in-service early childhood professionals as a demonstration school and forum for professional development. She also advocates for children and families by serving on local and state committees that support quality early care and education and serves the University's mission by providing support to Catholic Early Childhood programming.

After teaching special education in public schools for ten years, Dr. Adams became a school psychologist, working with children in preschool and the primary grades. She earned her doctorate in Early Childhood and Special Education from the University of Cincinnati. Dr. Adams became immersed in early care and education through her work with the Bombeck Family Learning Center and has established partnerships with Head Start, Public School Preschool, Early Care and Education, and a variety of agencies that support young children and families. Additionally, Dr. Adams worked with community partners to develop the University of Dayton's online Early Childhood Leadership and Advocacy programs, which were designed to address the need for leadership in early childhood while also supporting the early childhood career lattice. She is also the lead author of the *ACCESS Curriculum Framework* and has produced a number of articles, conducted presentations, developed websites, and pursued other outlets to share this framework with the field of early care and education.

ACKNOWLEDGMENTS

Our book is the result of continuous support from friends and colleagues who have helped us immeasurably, even when they didn't realize the contributions they were making. We particularly want to thank the directors, many of whom are former students, who helped us understand their day-to-day work from a wide variety of situations and perspectives. Special thanks go to Kelly Bigham, whose insights on moving up to directing your center added reality to these chapters; to Kathleen Bryan, who explained the popular year-long Developing Early Childhood Leaders Program; to Dr. Paula Jorde Bloom who generously shared information related to adminstrator credentialing; and to Patricia Gleason, Lisa Garofalo, Julie Hermes, Cindy Sherding, and Linda Jenner, who know and shared a wide range of agency and government rules and expectations. We are indebted to our photographers, Jessica Pike, who is responsible for the majority of the photographs including the cover shot, and Meredith Adams, whose work included many of the outdoors photographs, and to the teachers, staff, children, and families of the Bombeck Family Learning Center, where many of the new photos in this eighth edition were taken. We appreciate the guidance and encouragement given to us by our Cengage editor, Kate Scheinman.

We also would like to express our gratitude to the following reviewers, who offered numerous, valuable suggestions:

Jeanne Barker,
Tallahassee Community College

Evia Davis,
Langston University

Dede Dunst,
Mitchell Community College

Belinda Hammond,
Cuesta College

Jill Harrison,
Delta College

Mernie Rosenberg,
Colorado Community Colleges Online

Reginald Williams,
South Carolina State University

Diane Wolter,
College of Lake County

We hope our readers will find here the technical information they need to direct a viable program. Our greater desire is that they will recognize the significance of the leadership role of the director and the challenge and personal satisfaction derived from creating and implementing an excellent early care and education program for young children and their families.

Dorothy June Sciarra, Anne G. Dorsey, Ellen M. Lynch, and Shauna M. Adams

1

The WORKING DIRECTOR

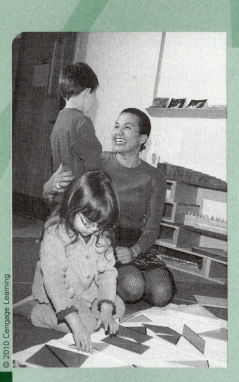

© 2010 Cengage Learning

The successful director and center personnel together work to learn to build their organization in a way that is satisfying to them and to their clients and creates a true system of learning.

Objectives

After reading this chapter, you should be able to:

- Identify administrative styles and roles.
- Describe the purpose of the NAEYC Code of Ethical Conduct: Supplement for Early Childhood Program Administrators.
- List four subsystems with which an early childhood program system interacts.
- Describe two tools that enable the director to blend program management and people leadership.

Standard Addressed in this Chapter

naeyc Accreditation Standard 10

Learning about the management and leadership of early childhood programs is important for staff and for current and prospective directors. The role of administrator requires knowledge and skills both in early childhood education and development and in business practices. With expertise in both of these areas, whether demonstrated by an individual or by a team, the program is likely to be successful for children, families, staff, and investors.

An effective director of an early childhood education center is involved in all the jobs that will be described in this text, from enrolling children to evaluating staff, from budgeting to taking inventory, and from maintaining a physical plant to bandaging a child's scraped knee. The director's job includes doing or overseeing all aspects of program management and leadership. To do any one of these tasks, a director must have skills and knowledge; to do all of them requires stamina, understanding, and organization; and to do all of them effectively demands exceptional interpersonal skills as will be emphasized throughout this text. These characteristics and abilities enable the director to bring the best to parents, children, staff members, board members, and the community. In turn, serving as a model of these skills encourages those same people to give their best to the center. The effective director realizes that an early childhood education center can never be a one-person operation. There is a network of caring and learning together that transcends the day-to-day chores and makes being part of a center worthwhile.

MAKING A COMMITMENT naeyc

Leadership and Management

When you agree to become a director, you take on tremendous responsibility to numerous stakeholders. These include the following:

1 children enrolled in the center (and those seeking enrollment)

2 families of those children

3 all center personnel (and those who apply for positions)

4 the center's board, funders, and other agencies and administrators to whom you report or with whom you interact

5 the community

6 yourself

How can you possibly make a commitment to all these individuals and groups? Perhaps you believed that you would be responsible for seeing that the teachers at your center did what they were supposed to do. Perhaps you thought there might be a problem with one or two of them—but you felt confident to handle that type of situation. Maybe you thought there would be one or two parents who expected special treatment, or a child who frequently hurt other children. And maybe you thought, "Sure, I can handle that."

Being an administrator entails much more than *handling* people and situations. The director must recognize that her constituency consists of the six components just listed. She must become familiar enough with all of them to know what is important to each.

You may be wondering why the director's constituency includes those *applying* for enrollment or positions at the center. Policies, procedures, and interactions in *every* aspect of the organization's work are included. Therefore, although the director may not have an opening for a child or may find that a job applicant is not appropriate for the role, she is expected to treat each of them in accordance with the center's philosophy.

Meeting Challenging Situations   naeyc

Any individual who assumes responsibility must recognize that challenges will arise. Some of these are easily met. Quite often the solution is not clear-cut. As you ponder what to do in such situations, you may be wondering, "Is this a policy issue, one for which I, as director, should take action and maintain the policy, or are there other factors that make this a moral or an ethical issue?"

You can expect to be challenged by ethical issues as you work to meet the needs of the wide range of constituents. Fortunately, you have valuable tools at your fingertips: The National Association for the Education of Young Children (NAEYC) Code of Ethical Conduct and the Statement of Commitment as well as the Supplement to the Code for Early Childhood Program Administrators (NAEYC, 2005; 2006) are on the NAEYC website and are included in Appendix A parts 1 and 2. Becoming familiar with the Code and the Supplement now will help you when you are faced with a dilemma.

Both the Code and the Supplement begin with statements of core values. All individuals who work with young children should be expected to be committed to holding and acting on those values. For example, directors should value and be committed to the belief that "the well-being of the children in our care is our primary responsibility, above our obligations to other constituents" (NAEYC, 2006).

Both the Code and the Supplement contain ideals, which "reflect the aspirations of practitioners," and principles, which "guide conduct and assist practitioners in resolving ethical dilemmas" (NAEYC, 2006). Note that the documents do not purport to provide specific answers; rather, they serve as guides for decision makers who are facing unique situations.

Once the director is familiar with the Code and the Supplement, she can begin to help staff and families understand their importance. Distributing copies to staff and families as part of their handbooks and then holding discussion sessions enables everyone to become familiar with why the center espouses the use of the Code and the Supplement. Be sure to include in the dialogue the importance of *reflecting* on an ethical dilemma and seeking guidance from a trusted professional when that is needed. As in all other aspects of early childhood work, confidentiality is essential.

REFLECTION

After you have read and thought about the Code of Ethical Content: Supplement for Early Childhood Program Administrators, reflect on situations you think would be most challenging for you. Have you encountered any ethical dilemmas for which using the Code might have been helpful?

CONSIDERING THE CENTER'S SYSTEMS   naeyc

Leaders of new or redeveloping businesses often begin their work by calling personnel together to create a vision. But only when everyone in the organization is committed to that vision is it achieved. Often what is missing is the realization that all businesses, whether operated to design and sell automobiles or to support children's well-being, operate as systems. We know that each of our bodies is a system, and we are usually well aware when something goes wrong with our bodily system. We know, too, that this system is composed of many systems: the digestive system, the respiratory system, and so forth. We can see patterns emerging. For example, a pattern of overeating and lack of exercise affects one or more systems and can lead to obesity. Most of us are becoming more aware of environmental systems. Destroying the habitats of various species can lead to their extinction. To work effectively in any business, including the early childhood education business, we must recognize that each of us plays a role in that system. Each of us must engage in systems thinking.

Senge defines systems thinking as "a conceptual framework, a body of knowledge and tools that has been developed over the past 50 years, to make the full patterns clearer, and to help us see how to change them effectively" (2006, p. 7). In each early childhood program, a body of knowledge and tools for working together exists. New members join that program with many of the beliefs, theories, and practices common to the field, but they must grow together with their colleagues to create the unique system that enables their program to function successfully.

Because each early childhood program operates as a system, whether the system is visible or not, the director and staff must work together to recognize the characteristics of that system. Periodically, a review must be conducted of the overall system on which a program's operation is based. Who are we as a center? What is it that makes us the XYZ Center? What premises do we hold that guide us in our work? Are those premises valid? Are some of the center's operating methods still in place simply out of habit? Today, some centers are curtailing or eliminating independent playtime for preschoolers and substituting group instruction. Center personnel need to discuss the reasons for these actions and ensure that such changes support the center's vision.

DIRECTOR'S CORNER

"We have six centers within our corporation, widely spread over the local area. Each center has its own identity. The populations we serve at each site differ. However, everyone who works here shares the same basic beliefs about children's learning and development.

"I meet with the six directors as a group every month. We all look forward to that, and each of us benefits. Each of the directors is at a different stage in her development as a director, yet as a group we share our thinking and support one another. Each director goes back to her center and has a meeting of her staff. Together they learn how to create the kind of program that we and they believe is supportive of children and families.

"Several schools and companies have asked us to create and operate centers at their sites. We're choosing carefully where we'll expand and under what circumstances. We must follow the principles that we have agreed on in order to operate."

—Executive director, not-for-profit, multisite corporation

Systems in Early Childhood Programs

The system for an early childhood center consists of a number of subsystems. Some of these subsystems, which will be addressed in other chapters, include the finance system, the systems for securing and managing facilities and equipment, and the system related to personnel. The subsystems each make a contribution to the whole, and together they create a whole greater than the sum of the parts.

Those who create systems base them on what they believe to be important. For example, presumably you have a system for planning curriculum. As center personnel gather to review curriculum, you may find that a teacher says, "We have always had our own way of doing things. Let's just leave it at that." However, in systems thinking, the willingness of each group member to meet and share thinking, to be open to each other's ideas, and to be willing to search for the best solution enables the group to learn together. Establishing such group openness takes time, willingness of the leader to be open also, and commitment to implement the plan to which the group agrees.

© 2010 Cengage Learning

The director and staff find ways to support each child's development and to help each child learn.

In an early childhood education center, several key systems are external to the organization and beyond the direct control of center personnel. Consider that family systems affect the operation of the center. Family members want what is best for their children. Family members interact with other systems, such as those at their place of employment. Those systems affect family members' ability to participate at the center and how the center views the role of families. For example, family members may not be free to attend conferences and programs at the center.

The regulatory system, whether required (such as licensing) or optional (such as accreditation or a state Quality program), is another external system that interfaces with early childhood programs. Regulatory systems have different requirements, some of which coincide with the way the center wants to function and some of which may not.

An important aspect of the director's role in working with the overall system and the related

subsystems is emphasis on establishing an understanding among all personnel (including the director) that they are colleagues rather than a hierarchy. This process is challenging because the difference in daily responsibilities is quite apparent and necessary. However, when all personnel have developed trust in one another, they can learn to suspend the hierarchy for the sake of discussion. The challenge is to learn how to learn together (Senge, 2006).

ADMINISTRATIVE STYLES AND ROLES   naeyc

Although all directors are responsible for administering a program, their administrative styles are unique and, therefore, the outcomes of their programs differ. Some of the differences are based on the roles assigned to the directors, while others are based on the personalities, knowledge, skills, and attitudes of the directors. Their effectiveness in supporting the development of a "we" feeling—group spirit—is a key factor in the success of the organization. Each member of the team must be ready to work in a manner that will contribute to the overall organization. Other early childhood programs may follow trends, real or imagined, such as, "Kindergarten teachers expect us to have these children prepared to read knowing how to print all the letters and able to sit and complete worksheets for a half-hour or more." While that may be the case in some schools, many kindergarten teachers will see each child as an individual and work with her accordingly. The administrator plays an important role is helping teachers, children, and families recognize the role of the present system and how it relates to future systems in kindergartens and above.

Styles

Individuals who head an organization often start out using a managerial approach. They determine what has to be done, how it is to be done, and who should do whatever the task requires. The assigned staff member is expected to report back to the manager when the task is completed or at intervals along the way. If that does not happen, the manager takes responsibility for checking up on the staff member and commenting on the staff member's work or lack of success. This style may be appropriate in situations in which many staff members are relatively new in the field and have little background to draw upon. Even in that situation, however, when given

(A)

(B)

(C)

(D)

Making room to learn together. Children do it. Do we?

opportunities, staff members often exceed expectations. Or they may begin to feel like a cog in a wheel, going round and round and never really having an opportunity to be involved.

Other managers use a more laissez-faire approach, leaving much of the decision making to the staff. Little or no overall structure may leave staff members with no support for decisions they make and with confusion about how the many independent decisions fit together. The administrator's interest may be directed more toward building relations beyond the center for the benefit of the center. Although building relations beyond a business locale is essential, building a knowledgeable staff who understand the vision and goals cannot be minimized. This approach certainly does not support the development of a centerwide system, although staff may develop an effective system on their own. There is such a variety of managerial styles that it is impossible to describe each one.

Some directors are natural leaders rather than managers. Others, over time and with mentoring, reading, and studying, become leaders. The director, who is a leader, looks to the staff for ideas, initiative, and implementation. Certainly, the leader does not turn over the running of the center to any staff member who steps forward. Rather, the leader supports and encourages staff to become part of the team that will help the center and its programs thrive. Directors realize that they must balance day-to-day reality with the vision that the center's stakeholders have prepared. The director whose leadership skills include the ability to accept and welcome ideas from others demonstrates competence and confidence. (To read more about becoming a leader, see Covey, 2004; Lambert, 1998; McCrea, 2002; Sciarra & Dorsey, 2002.)

DIRECTOR'S CORNER

"I had no idea how complex my role as director would be. Such a wide variety of people seem to need me immediately for such a wide variety of reasons. Meeting them all would probably be impossible (and maybe not even wise), but at the end of the day—most days—I know the challenges have been worthwhile. All it takes is one little pair of arms hugging me or one teacher smiling and saying on her way out, 'See you tomorrow, Chris!'"

—Director, large suburban preschool

Roles

If all the directors of centers in one state or county were to gather and discuss their roles, the job descriptions would undoubtedly cover a very wide range of categories. Some directors teach, perhaps spending half of every day in their own classrooms. Others never teach but are responsible for several centers; they travel between the centers, keeping abreast of two or more sets of circumstances, staff members, children, families, equipment lists, and so forth. Some may be responsible to an industry, a corporate system, a public school principal, or a parent cooperative association, while others are proprietors and owners.

Some directors make all the policy and procedure decisions; others are in settings where some policy is set by a school system or corporate management team. In other situations, every procedural detail is administered by a board. A director in a large center may have an assistant director, secretary, receptionist, and a cook; however, a director of a small center often does all the record keeping, supervising, answering of telephones, and meal preparation. Directors work with half-day programs, full-day programs, or perhaps even 24-hour care programs. The programs may offer care for infants and toddlers, or for older children, both before and after school. Sick child care or care of children with major special needs also may be provided.

The financial plan may involve proprietary or agency operations and may or may not be organized to make a profit. Program goals range from providing a safe place where children are cared for to furnishing total developmental services for children, including medical and dental care; social services; screening and therapy; as well as activities that promote intellectual, motor, emotional, social, and moral development.

Both the expectations of the clients served by the program and the expectations of the community will affect the center director's role. Some communities appreciate a director who is active in participating in the affairs of their community council, in lobbying for legislative reform, and in seeing that the cultural backgrounds of the children are preserved. Others prefer a director who focuses strictly on center business or on preparing children to deal with the demands of the elementary school. Directors must blend their personal philosophies with those of the community to achieve a balance. This blending can occur only if a potential director and a board explore each other's philosophies before agreeing on the responsibility for administering a particular program. If the philosophies of the director and those of the

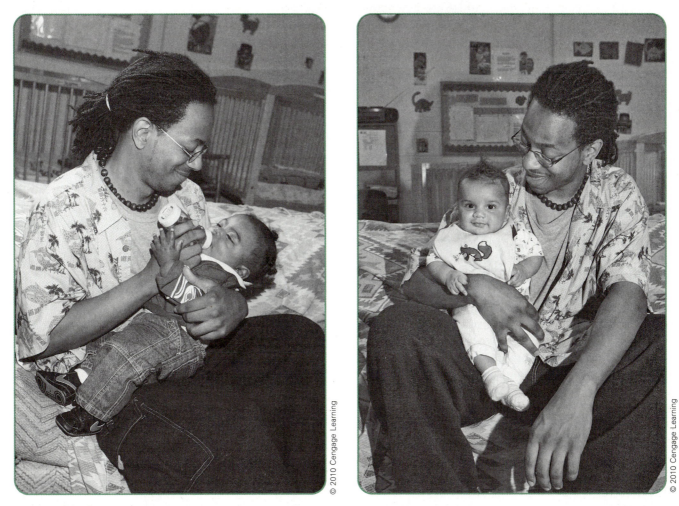

While visiting an infant room, the director may comment to a staff member about the caring support provided for infants during feeding time and afterwards.

center truly are incompatible, one or the other must be changed.

Sometimes, the director is confronted with a conflict between the two roles. The job description and the expectations of the people connected with the center may dictate that the director be present to greet teachers, parents, and children each day and to bid them good-bye each evening. In between, the director may be expected to be present in case an emergency arises. Simultaneously, however, there are obligations to the profession and to the community that must be met. The director may be asked to speak at a luncheon meeting of a community group that is ready to make a contribution to the center, to attend a board meeting of a local professional association, or to provide information at a session called by the diagnostic clinic to plan for one of the children with special needs who attends the early childhood education center.

Directors, especially those with experience, also have a responsibility to serve as child advocates. Although the NAEYC Code of Ethical Conduct calls on all who work with young children to "acknowledge an obligation to serve as a voice for children everywhere" (NAEYC, 2005), directors are more likely to have opportunities to see the broader picture of events in the community and beyond. They can keep informed about important legislative issues and about conditions affecting children and families by reading professional journals and newsletters and by being knowledgeable about local and national news. Many advocates are working for an all-encompassing system of early childhood programs. For example, when you type NAEYC on a search engine, you will receive a list of NAEYC sites with a wide range of information about the organization. You can also subscribe to Educators Online Exchange as well as Exchange

Everyday sponsored by the Child Care Exchange (www.childcareexchange.com). Children's Defense Fund (www.childrensdefense.org) will add you to its email list if you request legislative updates. Share your findings with others interested in early childhood and you will quickly find dozens of sources of related information. As with any website, it is important to check legitimacy.

Because directors are leaders and models, not only in their own centers but also throughout the community, staff, parents, and others often look to them for information about advocacy issues. Some directors may post information for staff and parents; others may make a concerted effort to involve people in an action plan. Some may write letters to the editors or to legislators, while others may testify before various governmental groups. In determining participation in advocacy efforts, each director must weigh responsibility to be an advocate against responsibility to the center, as well as consider personal time.

Although many directors work more than a 40-hour week, it is unreasonable and unwise to expect them to devote evening and weekend hours to their jobs on a regular basis. Directors who spend too much time on the job may become physically and emotionally exhausted, leading to ineffectiveness. As models for staff members, directors must demonstrate that they can balance personal and center needs. As you study this text, you may wonder how directors do it all. Knowledge, disposition, organization, and support all contribute to directors' success.

Personal Qualities

Directors may become enmeshed in unreasonable workloads because they have become personally involved in the center's work. An effective director should be involved closely with the activities of the center while maintaining distance, a difficult combination to attain. The primary reason for the difficulty in achieving this balance is that good directors assume their roles largely because they care about people. Caring is apparent when the director assumes the role of learner as well as teacher and keeps abreast of current research while providing this information to staff when it is relevant. Caring is demonstrated by paying attention to detail, such as spelling an unusual name correctly, ordering the special food a teacher would like for a project, and seeing that each board and staff member is notified of an early childhood lecture that is being held in the community. Caring is regarding the operation of the center in a serious manner, yet maintaining a sense of humor.

For some people, caring is shown in an exuberant manner with lots of enthusiastic conversation, hugging, and facial animation. Others who are just as caring are quiet, seem somewhat reserved, and perhaps move into relationships more slowly. Directors may have other combinations of personal qualities, but the genuine and essential ability to care is the one that makes the difference.

An interesting aspect of caring is that it may be misunderstood. Because they are concerned for others, directors sometimes may have to adjust the style in which they relate to people. For example, some individuals may be uncomfortable about being touched; if the director unknowingly puts an arm around people who feel this way, they may be annoyed or insulted and be unable to accept the care and concern that is intended.

Being a caring person in the face of all the responsibilities of directing a center can be difficult. At times a director may feel overwhelmed. The caring director is constantly helping others by listening and providing emotional support for both children and adults and may well need people to respond in kind. Those individuals who become effective directors usually enjoy giving to others; they seem to thrive on it. However, because they are seen at the center as the source of so much giving, they must seek sustenance from either the caring network at the center, or a relative or friend outside the center. Even those people who freely and happily give of themselves need, at times, to receive support and encouragement through recognition and understanding.

Directing can be stressful because the director, although surrounded by people, is in a very real sense an isolate. She has no peers in the center and, no matter how loved and respected, is "the boss." This feeling can prevail even when all personnel, including the director, have come together to form a learning system. Overdoing the caring component of the director's role can be damaging to staff, children, and families. The director's role is to support others, rather than to take over for their comfort. Furthermore, the director is still ultimately responsible to the owner, the board, the main office, funders, and others.

It would be inappropriate for the director to confide in one particular staff member because some of the information with which she works cannot be shared with anyone at the center. Some directors have established a network of directors. They meet, perhaps monthly, for a relaxing lunch and conversation. There is reassurance in knowing that other directors have to report child abuse, experience staff turnover, have too many forms to fill out, and have considered quitting. As a group, directors can create ways to solve problems, to support one another, and to heighten community awareness regarding the needs of young children and their caregivers while maintaining confidentiality.

Directors realize they have the power to create healthy, supportive communities for children, families, and staff but also recognize that their early childhood training and classroom experiences have not prepared them to carry the vast array of responsibilities of running a center. Until relatively recently, little attention was paid to credentialing directors. Depending on the size, scope, and type of program, directors find they have duties that are as varied and complex as those of major corporate leaders. Yet they have had little or no preparation and often have no opportunity to prepare for the job. Limited mentoring is available.

To be effective leaders, directors must ensure that their own needs are met. Being a martyr, even a cheerful martyr, who never takes vacation or sick days may, in fact, lead staff to feel somewhat guilty when they recognize and meet their own needs. Competent directors serve as models of balance.

DIRECTOR'S CORNER

Although I had been assistant director at the center, my role did not go beyond visiting the classrooms to see that all was well. When our director and her family moved to another state, I was offered the director's position. Little did I know how much I had to learn! Where is there a copy of the budget? Do we have enough money? What is expected of me? Do we have to pay taxes? What if someone doesn't pay tuition? Uh, oh, my computer isn't working. How can I get it fixed?

NOTE TO SELF: 1. BEGIN CREATING A CENTER MANUAL.
2. RECRUIT AND TRAIN ASSISTANT DIRECTOR.

—Director, nonprofit center

MANAGING THE PROGRAM   naeyc

Although directors may have a broad range of roles, and although they may bring a variety of personal qualities to these roles, every director is responsible for program maintenance. This task, whatever its parameters, is possible only when the director is skilled and knowledgeable. Throughout this text, the information essential to doing the work of a center director is discussed. This information, when combined with some teaching and administrative experience, should help you meet the responsibilities that are required for appropriate program maintenance and enhancement. As with every other professional role, directors need to continue learning and developing. A list of typical responsibilities is included here.

Depending on the organizational structure of your center, some of these responsibilities may be carried out by other personnel. However, the director is

© 2010 Cengage Learning

Directors and staff work together to welcome children and families.

responsible for ensuring that they are carried out appropriately.

1 Develop goals and objectives in relation to the center's philosophy, placing emphasis on the needs of clients.

2 Develop and maintain knowledge of standards created by professional and regulatory groups. Ensure that standards are being addressed appropriately throughout the center.

3 Work with staff to plan a curriculum to meet the objectives of the center.

4 Visit each classroom frequently, preferably daily.

5 Develop a positive working relationship with the board of directors and its committees, placing emphasis on communicating the center's accomplishments and needs to the board.

6 Establish policies for center operation, or become familiar with policies established by the center board, parent corporation, board of education, or other sponsor.

7 Draw up procedures for implementation of policies.

8 Prepare and maintain a manual for board and staff members.

9 Work with licensing agents to meet applicable licensing regulations.

10 Provide adequate insurance coverage.

11 Comply with all local, state, and federal laws relating to the center's operation.

12 Establish and operate within a workable budget.

13 Keep accurate financial records.

14 Pay bills and prepare payroll.

15 Collect tuition.

16 Write proposals and seek other funds for operation of the center.

17 Locate and maintain suitable physical facilities for the center's program.

18 Order and maintain equipment.

19 Develop and maintain a marketing plan.

20 Enroll and group the children.

21 Employ appropriate staff.

22 Orient staff.

23 Coach staff.

24 Develop knowledge levels and skills of staff so that upward mobility within the profession is feasible.

25 Evaluate the program, the staff members, and the children's progress.

26 Develop an effective communication system among staff members through regular staff meetings, conferences, and informal conversations.

27 Provide in-service training for staff and volunteers.

28 Fill roles of other staff members in emergency situations.

29 Plan and implement a family program that is responsive to needs and interests.

30 Explain the center's program to the community.

31 Participate in professional organizations.

32 Become an advocate for children.

33 Continue professional development through reading and attending pertinent courses such as workshops, conferences, and lectures.

Program maintenance requires that the director be organized. Just as the director expects teachers to have a plan for the year, month, week, and day, so too must the director have plans. Whether the plans are on a handheld device or on paper, they must be followed to a reasonable degree. Organization of documents is also essential. Although some paper forms are necessary, computerized systems often simplify documentation. If backed up and stored appropriately, they can be easy to locate, use, and modify. At the same time, discarding items that are no longer needed will make it easier to find working documents.

As you read other chapters of this text, you will notice the many types of files directors are expected to keep. These include policy manuals, staff records, child records, financial data, as well as numerous others. Most, if not all of these, can be made available online if access is restricted to those who have a right to see them. As with all important documents, it is essential to have a backup copy in a safe place.

SERVING AS CURRICULUM LEADER   naeyc

Many of these program management jobs will be discussed in subsequent chapters. However, a key aspect of the center director's role to which this text gives limited attention is that of developing curriculum. The director is the curriculum leader. Early childhood teacher preparation programs have at least one course devoted to curriculum. Directors who do not have an adequate early childhood background should expect to complete at least one course in early childhood curriculum. A section in an administration textbook and course could leave the false impression that that would suffice, but directors as well as teachers must continue to develop their understanding of curriculum and its relation to child development. Read the chapter on the director's role in leading curriculum to learn more about the importance of this topic.

To aid in updating curriculum information, numerous books are available. Directors must assume responsibility for becoming familiar with curriculum for the young child, its sources, goals, and implementation approaches (see the Director's Library in Appendix H for suggested reading).

The director is responsible for instituting and maintaining a good-quality curriculum. Consulting with the teachers is expected, but the director must ensure that the goals and philosophy of the program are reflected in the curriculum. Directors who employ new teachers or teachers with little or no background in child development and early childhood education will need to provide detailed coaching (Sciarra & Dorsey, 2002).

The director must recognize that it is highly unlikely that a curriculum that purports to have already done all the planning and provided all the necessary materials will be effective. Such programs are usually costly. They may also be unaesthetic, with "art" that should not appear in classrooms. Most important, it is impossible for the best teacher to plan every day's curriculum a year in advance. Such a plan cannot take into account the changing needs of the children. Nor can such a plan address the children's specific cultures, individual backgrounds, or current interests. In short, a preplanned commercial curriculum should be examined carefully to determine whether it addresses the outcomes and uses a theoretical base that fits your organization's mission and that will be significant for children's learning. Recall that when developmentally appropriate practice was first being discussed, hundreds of manufacturers labeled their products, books, and curriculum kits "developmentally appropriate." Today, with the emphasis on research or evidence-based curricula, curricula are being labeled "research based." Before adopting a curriculum on the strength of that claim, make sure you see the research. Find out who the subjects were, what was done, and what the results were. Determine whether the results relate to your center's mission and goals.

Carter and Curtis (2010) remind directors of the importance of having a vision—a vision that goes beyond a high score on a state or national evaluation or getting new equipment. They encourage directors to envision how the program and experiences of staff and children *could* be. Directors can help staff, children, and families go beyond "cookie cutter" environments, equipment, and activities. But first the director and staff must reflect, read, and believe in the goal of becoming what they would really like to be, going beyond today's criteria for success. As directors get mired down in day-to-day tasks, turning to resources that focus on *what should be* can renew their delight in the roles of director, staff member, and child.

LEADING PEOPLE

Directors sometimes acquire program management skills and stop there, failing to realize the importance of the skills of leading people. Centers can and do run, at least for a while, without people leadership; however, centers that lack program management quickly close their doors. People leadership and enrichment are at the very heart of a worthwhile early childhood education program. Without it, program quality begins to disintegrate and staff turnover may become a major problem.

Directors can enhance their effectiveness at leading people by developing an understanding of their own interpersonal styles. They also will benefit from studying various approaches to leadership, analyzing their own administrative styles, and determining their strengths and weaknesses in these areas. Most directors have had limited opportunities to acquire this information since they often move into administrative roles because they have been effective as teachers. Fortunately, many seminars, books, videos, and DVDs are available to enable directors to learn about interpersonal styles and management approaches. Many agencies, such as NACCRRA (National Association of Child Care and Resource and Referral Association), offer coaching programs for teachers and directors. Typically, observation of the director or teacher will occur, followed by discussion with the coach. Although many athletic teams have provided this service for their players for years, it is relatively new in early childhood centers.

The professional director understands that the role involves leadership as well as management. Beginning directors usually have to grow into the leadership role, but with motivation and support, they can acquire the characteristics that will help them develop the entire center's organization as a learning system. Their major contribution will be creating and supporting a team whose members work effectively, efficiently, and positively with one another and with clients. For more information on this topic, see the companion volume, *Leaders and Supervisors in Child Care Programs* (Sciarra & Dorsey, 2002).

The center's board of directors may be willing to fund some training opportunities for the director, particularly if board members themselves understand and use this type of information. Possibly, a board member could furnish training or related materials.

Addressing Conflict Resolution

Another option is to provide total staff or joint board-staff coaching in an approach such as conflict resolution. This approach to professional development, if well done, should lead to confirming the director's role as leader, while establishing the responsibility of each staff member for the success of the center's program. The sessions could also emphasize the responsibility of the director to see that staff are involved in decision making and that their ideas are valued and accepted.

However, satisfaction obviously does not mean that everyone's demands will be met. For example, a teacher may be unhappy about working with a particular assistant whom she regards as lazy. When the teacher approaches the assistant with directions about what is to be done, the assistant does not complete the assigned tasks. In such a case, the director can facilitate a discussion between the teacher and assistant. However, had both of them been coached in conflict resolution, it is quite possible they could have solved the problem themselves. This situation certainly does not preclude the director from making a decision about retaining the assistant. However, helping a teaching team learn to work together is often more productive than terminating someone and bringing in a new person. Only when the director is convinced that termination is in the best interest of the children and staff should that decision be made.

Because conflict in any organization is inevitable, preparing people to address it in a straightforward, rational manner can lead to satisfaction. Such an approach also goes a long way to eliminating gossip, dissension, and rumors. Everyone connected with the center—directors, board, staff, families, and children—realizes that their ideas will be respected. They begin to recognize that when disagreements occur, a people-centered approach to a solution is possible. The director does not have to be the judge in most situations. Individuals are empowered to work together to solve problems.

The basic ideas include bringing together the people who are experiencing conflict. This may be two individuals, the staff and director, or any other combination. Once the people who are concerned are together, have them each state what the

problem is. Depending on the situation, it may be helpful to write the results of each step for everyone involved to see. If two teachers want to use the playground at 10 a.m. and there is room for only one group of children at a time, the problem is "How can playground time be scheduled to everyone's satisfaction?" (Notice how similar this is to the problem of two children wanting the same toy at the same time.)

Next, brainstorm solutions. All solutions are presented for consideration. No comments about a potential solution are appropriate at this point.

Examine the suggestions one at a time, eliminating any with which either party disagrees. Continue until a solution that is agreeable to each is reached. Agree to try the solution for a set period of time and to renegotiate at the end of that time if necessary.

In summary, the process is as follows:

1. State the problem.
2. Generate solutions.
3. Select a solution agreeable to all.
4. Implement the planned solution.
5. Check after an agreed-upon time to determine whether the solution is working.
6. If it is not working, return to step 1 and continue the process.

The staff and board members who agree to commit to a conflict resolution type of philosophy use the concept that their customers (children and families) are their first priority as a starting point. By extension, a priority of directors must be staff satisfaction, and a priority of the board must be a successful outcome for the operation of the center. This approach works well when everyone understands it and accepts this basic principle.

Directors who are quite comfortable with an authoritarian role may find it difficult or impossible to relinquish that role, just as teachers who are convinced that a teacher-directed approach is the only appropriate way to work with children may be unable to provide choices for children. Directors who are willing to invest time and effort in learning about management usually will find that they are far more able to lead the staff and clients in ways that are more satisfying to everyone, and that the responsibility for the smooth running of the center will no longer rest primarily with one person.

The staff-oriented director plans time each day to visit each classroom, greet each staff member, and acknowledge their efforts and successes. She coaches and supports them as they develop new understandings and skills and provides honest, sensitive feedback. The staff-oriented director remembers and relates to events and incidents that are significant to staff, children, and families. It may be as simple as commenting to a teacher about how well she managed a frightened child during a thunderstorm by describing specifically the effective approach the teacher used. Perhaps the director stops to greet a child who is proudly bringing his rabbit to school for a visit. Maybe the director telephones a father to thank him for organizing a book fair to benefit the center.

Tending to the personal and professional development of the people associated with a center's program is seminal to the success of the program. The manner in which the director carries out people support tasks is a major contributing factor in program maintenance and vice versa. There is a delicate balance between successfully dealing with the mechanics of efficient program operation and simultaneously creating a caring environment for adults and children.

A director can have the human relations skills, care for others, ask for their ideas and opinions, encourage them to try new methods, and provide positive feedback. But if that same director does not have the skills and knowledge to accomplish the huge amount of work required of an administrator, the program cannot succeed. Similarly, the director who is task-oriented, skilled, and knowledgeable may conduct a center that provides services but never really addresses or satisfies people's needs. Obviously, the director must combine work orientation skills with communication skills. If skills in either area are lacking, precious time will be wasted doing jobs or rebuilding relationships. Meanwhile, the children will not receive the excellent care they deserve.

Throughout this text you will read many more details about both program management and leadership that is required of all directors. You will begin by learning to manage a range of circumstances and tasks. Gradually, as you work at being a manager, if you are committed to developing your abilities and those of the staff, you will find yourself analyzing situations that occur in a child development program. As you reflect on what you do, why you do it, and the outcomes of your decisions, you will be creating new knowledge and understanding for yourself—something that no text or instructor can give you. You will be well on your way to moving from the role of manager to the role of leader.

Realizing that you may be feeling overwhelmed at the magnitude of the director's job, we turn now to a discussion of management tools that you can use to help you manage a challenging role.

MANAGEMENT TOOLS   naeyc

Every director has a limited amount of time in which to do numerous tasks and develop many relationships. This work can be accomplished most effectively if the director is well organized. Then, when the inevitable unexpected event occurs, the director will be in a position that is stable enough to withstand the demands of the crisis. For example, the director whose financial records are in order may not have extra cash available to replace a broken water heater but at least is better prepared to adjust other budget categories to provide the funds. The disorganized director may not even know the income and expenses anticipated within the next few months in order to adjust the budget to meet the financial crisis. An efficient director can comfortably take time to listen to a group of excited children who burst into the office describing all the worms they found on the sidewalk. But a disorganized administrator may be too busy planning menus that are already overdue. It is obvious that administration will not always run smoothly for any director; however, the director who knows about appropriate techniques and uses them is certainly better prepared to cope effectively with the hubbub that often is evident in a child care center.

The use of several management tools can enable directors to administer programs effectively. Key tools for beginning directors include policies and procedures manuals and time-use skills.

Policies and Procedures Manual

A manual containing all the center's policies and procedures facilitates the administrator's job. Generally, when there is a board, the board members make policies and the director develops procedures for implementation. For example, the board may establish a policy to admit any child between the age of 3 and 5 who can profit from the center's program. The director then establishes the procedures necessary to accomplish the child's enrollment such as plans for informing the community, distributing and receiving enrollment forms, and notifying parents that their child has been accepted or that the center is full. The director also designs the necessary forms and includes copies in the manual.

When procedures are overly detailed or cover self-explanatory material, they become burdensome, and even may be neglected or circumvented by staff members. For example, teachers may be required to fill out a lengthy form to request permission to purchase something for which they will be reimbursed; they also might be required to fill out another form after having purchased the item. At this point, some teachers may decide not to bother with purchasing needed items for their classrooms. They can carry their reaction one step further by disregarding the otherwise accepted procedures for using materials from the central storeroom. It is natural to anticipate that some established procedures will be unpopular with the staff, but if directors are open about why the procedures are important, and if they are careful about limiting the number of procedures to be followed, they will find that staff members are willing to comply.

Staff input prior to the establishment of procedures is usual, although the director still may need to make some independent decisions. When directors focus on their own need for power instead of on the establishment of procedures that will ensure the smooth running of an operation, it becomes impossible for the staff to feel respected. Staff members for whom every procedure is spelled out have no freedom. How, then, can they be expected to offer freedom to the children with whom they work?

Other Contents

In addition to policies and procedures, the manual contains the center's bylaws; job descriptions; salary schedules; and information about the center such as philosophy, goals, sponsorship, funding, and perhaps a brief history. Each of these should be dated with the adoptive date. If the manual is large, a table of contents and an index are essential. Placing all materials in a loose-leaf binder enables staff members to add and delete pages as necessary. Each staff and board member receives a manual when first joining the center. It is the holder's responsibility to keep the manual up to date and to return it to the center when vacating the board or staff position.

Using Technology

Taking advantage of current technology can be a major time-saver and organizer. Directors who are not already comfortable using computers will find that the initial learning period may be time consuming. Once users are confident, however, the benefits will accrue.

One question often encountered when applying for financial assistance is "How will your company's financial records be maintained?" Financial record keeping and report generation are essential and time-consuming components of the director's role. Completing these tasks using software saves time and promotes accuracy once data is properly entered. Available software can provide computations for payroll deductions, billing, attendance, inventory, and a range of additional tasks. Most directors have access to a computer and use it for word processing tasks, but many do not use other components. You may choose to contract with a specialty business for payroll, fiscal reporting, and other functions, and yet you may find it reasonable to manage child information on paper. Nonetheless, analyzing staff time in terms of cost plus cost of contracted services compared with software cost and reduced staff time to generate comparable information may be surprising. Admittedly, initial learning time will increase costs. Another consideration is the professional appearance of computer-generated reports.

REFLECTION

Imagine you have planned to spend the evening writing a term paper that is due the following day. A friend telephones. He is terribly upset about his wife's illness. Think about what you might do.

Now imagine that at 3:00 p.m. you, as an early childhood center director, are greeted by a teacher who is leaving for the day and who wants to talk about her husband who has just lost his job. You had planned to spend the rest of the afternoon working on the major equipment order that is needed for a board committee report the following morning. You may choose:

- to listen to the teacher
- to tell the teacher you do not have time to listen because of the report you must prepare
- to schedule time the following afternoon to listen to the teacher
- some other plan

Any of these choices could be appropriate; the director must make the best choice. But the directors who always find themselves too busy to listen and those who always find themselves spending so much time listening that they must work all evening must analyze why their scheduling problems recur. Think about your own reaction to this situation.

To find a software company that fits your center's needs, go to the Internet and do a search for "child care software." Read information provided by various purveyors, contact them, and ask for a demonstration. You can also check professional journals for reviews of child care software. *Child Care Information Exchange* and *Young Children* are potential sources, as are other directors who are experienced users of business software. At regional and national conferences, ask for demonstrations of software packages. Take a list of questions with you and jot down the answers and your impressions.

Consider which features you would like and which are essential. Ask whether you can buy components if you do not want or need a comprehensive package. Many software companies will offer a complimentary trial disc or access to an online trial.

Your staff may also benefit when you add computer technology to your center. Aside from paperwork (child records, assessments, curriculum planning) that they may be able to complete more easily and professionally on a computer, they may also use the computer for continuing education courses. The director can set up a calendar of tasks to be completed, appointments, and so forth. Explore these and other uses and packages thoroughly before buying.

Time-Use Skills

Some directors study time management as a tool to use in allocating available time wisely. The board may provide tuition or released time for a director to attend a time-management course or seminar. Several time-management techniques can be acquired easily and put to immediate use.

Analyzing Use of Time

As a beginning, directors can analyze how they spend their time by writing down in detail everything they do for several days and how much time is spent on each task. The next step is to make a judgment about which of the activities have not been enjoyed, have not been done well, or have not been related either to the personal goals of the director or the goals of the center. When time is frittered away on such activities, less time is available to invest in other, more productive activities. The individual alone can decide which activity should take priority. In some businesses, listening to a client discuss an emotional problem would be considered a waste of the administrator's time. In early childhood education, with its focus on children and families, time that the director spends listening may be the most effective use of the available administrative time.

Voice mail, email, and other computer communication approaches help the director keep in touch while controlling the use of time. However, directors must be careful to avoid communicating with families and staff solely through technology. The sensitive director is alert to the need for a live, human contact and a handwritten note in some situations.

Although some of the director's tasks may not be appealing, they may need to be done. A director can, at least, recognize how much time must be devoted to undesirable tasks; then this amount of time can be put into perspective. The director also may decide to devise ways to make tasks more manageable. Of course, if the majority of tasks seem undesirable, the director may choose to change jobs.

Grouping and Assigning Tasks

The director who needs to economize on time also may decide to make an effort to read and answer all mail, place outgoing telephone calls, and record financial transactions at a specified time each day. Directors who allocate time for these types of chores and establish the policy that they are not to be disturbed during that time will probably have more time for meeting people's needs during the rest of the day.

Directors also should consider which jobs they must do and which jobs they can delegate. For example, could the janitor let the director know on a regular basis what supplies are needed instead of the director checking on supplies? Perhaps the receptionist can be trained to respond to the general calls for information about the center instead of involving the director in a routine conversation about when the center is open and providing the ages of children who are served.

Once the center's operation is reasonably under control, additional staff people can be prepared to fill the director's role in her absence, thereby allowing the director to move into the wider community on occasion. It is not appropriate to insist that other staff people do the director's work, but it is appropriate to begin to coach them to assume the role of director temporarily. In this way, both parties can benefit professionally.

Planning a Time Line

One of the ways a director develops efficiency is through the development of a time line. Jobs that must be done on a regular basis are scheduled, then the director does them according to the schedule.

This simple concept curtails procrastination by helping the director recognize that when a job that is scheduled this week is postponed because it is distasteful, time and energy are going to be spent thinking about it anyway. Since the job must be completed eventually, no time is saved by waiting until next week; nor does the job become easier.

The director checks in daily with teachers and children.

The director insures that the physical plant is well-maintained.

In fact, the director then may be in the uncomfortable position of having to apologize.

Each director must develop a time line based on the personal responsibilities that are unique to the type of program and the clients' needs. No matter which jobs and time frames are included, writing a time line gives the director and others a clear picture of the work to be done. The time line can be flexible when circumstances warrant, but basically, the goal is to adhere to the plan so that regularly scheduled tasks will be completed and time for working with people will be made available.

Throughout this book, you will learn about the importance of the director's interpersonal relationships and that they set the tone for the center. Now, as you prepare to learn more about the director's role, you will see this theme reemphasized. It may seem impossible that a director really could focus on establishing a "we" feeling when most of the chapters present an almost overwhelming set of director responsibilities. Nonetheless, directors who know what is involved in the job, who work to acquire the necessary knowledge and skills, and who use a managerial approach that reflects an understanding of the needs of staff and clients are found in nearly every community.

These competent and successful directors know that being a director is exhausting,
and frequently challenging,
sometimes frightening,
never boring,
sometimes lonely,
many times hectic,
and, yes, even fun.
They also know that being a director—*a really good director*—
a leader,
a manager,
a model,
a coach,
and a supporter
is hard work and time consuming.
And being a director just often enough is
deeply satisfying,
even exhilarating,
and richly rewarding!

SUMMARY

An effective director is a person who combines skills, knowledge, and caring. Although directors fill a variety of roles in countless styles, no effective director can let either the management and operation of the center or the care of and communication with people occupy an inappropriate proportion of time.

For each director in each situation, personal decisions must be made about the style of directing.

Tools that enable the director to blend program management and leading people are the NAEYC Code of Ethical Conduct and Statement of Commitment, the Supplement for Early Childhood

Program Administrators, a policies and procedures manual, and time-use skills. Each director must develop an appropriate balance so that program management—a necessary task—does not override the importance of leading people. Because leadership can readily be overlooked by directors who find themselves in the throes of program management, directors must develop skills that enable them to excel at program management. Only then will they have the time and energy to devote to leading people, which is the very essence of a quality child care program.

TRY IT OUT!

1 Discuss with a classmate the activities on which each of you would like to spend more time. Were there any similarities between the activities you each mentioned? To what did each of you attribute your lack of time for your favorite activities?

2 Discuss with three members of your class the kind of director you would like to be. Review the director's responsibilities as described in the chapter. On which of the director's roles would you like to spend the most time? Put a check mark next to those tasks that you would enjoy doing. Put an X next to those you would not like to do. Compare your ideas with those of your classmates.

3 If you were the director, which of the tasks in the Director's Responsibilities could you assign to someone else? Why?

Director's Resource 1-1

ESSENTIAL DOCUMENT CATEGORIES

–Building–

- Mortgage or lease or rental arrangements and contact person/s
- Insurance for building/contents (theft, fire, storm) and personal injury—agent's name and contact information
- Certificate of Occupancy (CO) from the municipality and related permits
- Fire extinguishers and smoke alarms—record of purchase and schedule for servicing
- Contact information and schedule for carpenter, cleaning contract, garbage collection, glazer, heat/air-conditioning, locksmith, playground maintenance, plumber, snow removal (if needed)
- Paint, tile, carpet, fabric swatches with contact information

–Equipment–

- Keep a full inventory list of equipment by site location, classroom, office, kitchen, playground—include dates of purchase, cost, depreciation if applicable, source of item, and funding
- Prepare a file folder for the equipment in each location: kitchen, office, classroom A, B, C, etc., playground. Keep in each folder the information for each piece of equipment: purchase order or donation source, receipt, warranty, maintenance agreement, and operating instructions

–Program Operations–

- Incorporation papers
- Tax-related papers (tax-exempt letter from IRS, state-exempt certificate, corporate filing papers)
- Charitable organization records (if applicable)
- State and local licenses and accreditations (copies posted in visible location)
- Employment-related payments, tax records, payroll information
- Bank statements and account records—bank branch and contact information
- Investment accounts
- Bylaws, including original and each revision
- Attorney contract or agreement
- Accountant contract or agreement
- Medical personnel contract or agreement
- Insurance policies (copies of relevant policies should be in building and vehicle folders)
- Food documents and permits
- Fire drill procedures and records
- Corporate credit card records
- Funding sources, contracts, reports, etc.
- Journal and periodical subscriptions—payment and renewal schedules

–Vehicles–

- Title or proof of ownership (original in safe-deposit box, copy in files) for each vehicle
- Registration documentation and renewal schedule for each vehicle
- Insurance policies (originals in safe-deposit box, copies in files) for each vehicle
- Automobile club membership
- Authorized drivers, proof of age, copy of license with photo, etc.
- Service and repair arrangements and maintenance schedule for each vehicle
- Gas/oil credit cards (if applicable)
- Parking arrangements in garage or on parking lot

Source: Reprinted with permission from Child Care Information Exchange, P.O. Box 3249, Redmond, WA 98073, (800) 221-2864, http://www.ChildCareExchange.com. Permission conveyed through Copyright Clearance Center, Inc.

 You can download a full-size version of this form on the Education CourseMate website.

REFERENCES

Carter, M., & Curtis, D. (2010). *The visionary director: A handbook for dreaming, organizing, and improvising in your center*. St. Paul, MN: Redleaf Press.

Center for Early Childhood Leadership. (2004, Spring). *Research notes*. Chicago: Center for Early Childhood Leadership, National-Louis University.

Covey, S. (2004). *The 8th habit: From effectiveness to greatness*. Rochester, NY: Free Press.

Lambert, L. (1998). *Building leadership capacity in schools*. Alexandria, VA: Association for Supervision and Curriculum Development.

McCrea, N. (2002). Learning leading for authenticity. *Child Care Information Exchange*, 147, 10–14.

National Association for the Education of Young Children. (2005). *Code of ethical conduct and statement of commitment: Guidelines for responsible behavior in early childhood education*. Washington, DC: Author.

National Association for the Education of Young Children. (2006). *Code of ethical conduct and statement of commitment: Supplement for early childhood program administrators*. Washington, DC: Author.

Sciarra, D. J., & Dorsey, A. G. (2002). *Leaders and supervisors in child care programs*. Clifton Park, NY: Thomson Delmar Learning.

Senge, P. M. (2006). The fifth discipline: The art and practice of the learning organization. New York: Doubleday.

ASSESSING COMMUNITY NEED *and* ESTABLISHING A PROGRAM

Bombeck Family Learning Center

The decision to start a program is best conceived when the voices of multiple stakeholders are heard.

Objectives

After reading this chapter, you should be able to:

- List the factors that influence the need for child care.
- Name the various types of child care used by families.
- Identify information that will help you determine the types of child services needed now and in the future.
- Use your knowledge of data collection methods and resources for assessing the need for child care in your area.
- Compare and contrast mission and values statements.
- Use core values to develop values statements.
- Describe characteristics of different types of centers.

Standards Addressed in this Chapter

naeyc Professional Preparation Standards 2, 3, 6

naeyc Administrator Competencies-Management Knowledge and Skills 2, 6, 7, 9
Early Childhood Knowledge and Skills 1, 6, 10

naeyc Accreditation Standard 8

Creating a new program is an exciting challenge that requires abundant creativity and energy and can be overwhelmingly complex. The process requires the program planners to consider multiple factors in a stream of ever changing priorities. Planners need to be agile decision makers and problem solvers, considering the priority of the day and shifting to the next important decision as needed in order to get a complete picture of both program and community needs. Clearly, there must be a need for the program. And there must be some driving force in the community, whether an individual or a group, that will generate the creative energy to

- examine the need
- develop the program mission and values statements
- decide about the type of program that will fit the need and available resources

These three major activities will be taking place simultaneously, and each will influence the program that is developed.

The driving force for developing the program might be an early childhood educator with a desire to open a center or a group of parents who have an interest in providing child care services for their children. Sometimes community agencies choose to expand their services to include child care. Perhaps there is a need for an expansion of both employer- and public-school–sponsored child care programs. These are a few of the common catalysts for developing a program, and as the need for care continues to increase, it is important to be aware of new forces that impact how a program might be sponsored. The planners, whether an individual, an agency, or a corporation, must be prepared to carry out all preliminary tasks until a director is hired, including dealing with funding issues, undertaking public relations campaigns, and carrying out the needs assessment.

Program sponsors examine what services can be delivered realistically without diluting quality. Usually, it is unrealistic to set up a program that will be responsive to every demand and meet all needs. It is also unrealistic to expect to start a new program and have it fully enrolled immediately.

It can take several years to bring a new program up to full enrollment. It is better to begin on a small scale, carefully weighing the assured need against the services that can be delivered under the existing financial and resource constraints. It is dangerous to overextend by trying to meet everyone's needs or by providing a large-scale operation that overtaxes the resources. Problems also arise when the need is overestimated and a program is set up that is underenrolled. In either case, program quality diminishes and children become the victims of impoverished environments. Then families do not trust the program to deliver the promised services, and it is doomed to failure.

DIRECTOR'S CORNER

"I projected it would take us three years to reach capacity in this new center, which is licensed for 115 children. We are now at the beginning of the third year of operation and we are about two-thirds full—so my prediction was on target."

—Director/owner, franchised center

ASSESSING THE NEED   naeyc

To ensure that the planned program is properly scaled to meet both the size and the nature of the community need, it is important to do a needs assessment during the preliminary planning period. The needs assessment can begin before or after a director is designated or hired, but it must be completed before any financial or program planning begins. The purpose of the needs assessment is to determine the number of families and children that will use a child care service and the type of service desired by those who will use it.

What Must You Know about Need?

The first step in the needs assessment process is to determine what you need to know. Once that has been decided, procedures for collecting the data can be worked out. In some situations, there may be a group of stakeholders, or persons who have an interest in the success of the program and how it is configured. This group can be helpful in informing the fact-gathering process, but they cannot replace more comprehensive data collection.

Number of Families and Children

One way to start the needs assessment is to determine the number of potential families and children that you could serve. It is useless to go beyond the earliest planning stage unless there are families available who will use the service. Simply assessing the *number* of children is not sufficient because number alone does not determine interest or need. If you currently are running a program for preschool children but get many calls for infant/toddler or school-aged child care, you are alerted to a need to expand your program offerings. However, between the time you assemble your waiting lists and accomplish the program expansion, many of those families on your list will have made other child care arrangements. One quick and informal way to decide whether to proceed with a needs assessment is to find out if other centers in the vicinity have waiting lists.

Some planners overestimate the number of families who need child care and fail to consider how many of those families will use or pay for center-based care if it is provided. Although the numbers of preschoolers in child care whose mothers work outside the home has increased sharply over the past five decades, it is difficult to determine who cares for the children of these working families. As of 2008, "more than 60 percent of children under age six and 70 percent of school-age children in 44 states and the District of Columbia have all

TABLE 2-1　Primary early care and education arrangement type the year prior to entering kindergarten[1] 2006–2007 and 2007–2008

	Number of Children (Thousands)	Percent of Population
No nonparental early care and education	653	16.8
In nonparental early care and education	3,240	83.2
• Center-based, non–Head Start	1,949	50.1
• Center-based, Head Start	534	13.7
• Home-based relative	446	11.5
• Home-based, nonrelative	249	6.4
• Multiple arrangement types	63	1.6

[1]Primary early care and education arrangement type the year prior to entering kindergarten is the setting in which the child spent the most hours outside of time with parents. If a child spent an equal amount of time in each of two or more arrangements, he or she is classified as being in multiple arrangement types. Center-based, non–Head Start includes care and education in places such as early learning centers, nursery schools, and preschools. Center-based, Head Start includes care and education in centers identified as Head Start by the parent interview respondent. Home-based, relative includes care provided in either the child's home or in another private home by a relative of the child. Home-based, nonrelative includes care provided in either the child's home or in another private home by a person not related to the child.

Source: http//nces.ed.gov/pubs2010/2010005.pdf

parents in the labor force" (Children's Defense Fund, 2010, p. F-3). However, many of these children are with friends or family members, thus making it difficult to determine how many of these working parents would choose center-based care or family child care homes for their children if it became available to them.

One resource for planners is the Early Childhood Longitudinal Study, Birth Cohort (ECLS-B) sponsored by the U.S. Department of Education's National Center for Education Statistics, a Center of the Institute of Education Sciences (2009). This study collected national data on the early home and educational experiences of children from infancy to kindergarten entry and has been extrapolated to represent the 3.9 million children born in the United States in 2001. Table 2-1 shows a picture of the type of care and education that 4-year-olds use during the year prior to kindergarten in the United States.

Socioeconomic Level of Families

Many families may be interested in child care services but are unable to pay enough to cover the cost of the services they choose or need. For example, "in 36 states and the District of Columbia the annual cost of center-based child care for a 4-year-old is more than the annual in-state tuition at a public four-year college" (Children's Defense Fund, 2010, p. F-6). When families are unable to pay the high cost of quality child care outside the home, operators cannot depend on tuition but must seek outside sources of funding if planned programs are to succeed. It is important to know how many families that express a need for assistance actually qualify

for state or federal subsidy. When families are able to pay, it is important to determine what they are willing to pay for center-based or home-based care. It is reasonable to expect that many families can afford to pay up to ten percent of their total income for child care. However, low-income families could be forced to pay as much as 25 percent of their income for child care.

Ages of Children to Be Served

The ages of participating children affect all the program planning considerations and can make a considerable difference in the cost of delivering the service. Determine the number of families who expect to have infants or toddlers participate in the group care program outside the home. Although early childhood education programs have traditionally served 3- and 4-year-old children, the increase in the number of one-parent families and the number of working mothers has increased the demand for infant/toddler care for before and after school as well as for year-round programs for school-aged children. Therefore, when doing the needs assessment, inquire not only about 3- and 4-year-olds who may need care but also about older children and those under age three.

Type of Service the Families Prefer

In assessing the need for a program, one of the first things you must find out is whether families prefer full-day child care or a half-day program. Working families must have full-day care, and they often will need it for children ranging in age from birth through school age.

While the demand for half-day programs has decreased because of families with all parents in the work force, those families that choose half-day programs may use a program for toddlers and 3- and 4-year-olds (sometimes called preschoolers) but may prefer to keep infants at home. These families might select a five-day program for preschoolers but often prefer a two- or three-day program for toddlers. Parents who wish to become involved in the program may choose to place their children in a cooperative child care program. Other parents may not have the time or the interest in becoming directly involved in the school program.

In some situations, family child care homes may be more suitable than a center-based program because they can serve a broad range of needs, can be available for emergency care, and can provide evening and weekend care. The family child care home involves parents taking their children to someone else's home and paying for child care on an hourly, daily, or weekly basis. These arrangements usually are made individually, although there is often some regulation of the number of children for whom care can be provided in a given home. In a few cases, satellite programs are set up involving the coordination of family child care homes by a child care center staff member or an employer. Parents make arrangements through the child care center or the employer referral service for placement of their children in an affiliated family child care home. They make payments to the center or make use of this employer benefit. The center or employer, in turn, pays the caregiver and provides the parents with some assurance that the home and the caregiver have been evaluated and that placement for the child will be found if the caregiver becomes unable to provide the service due to illness or for other reasons. When the need for care is immediate and critical, it may be useful to locate and organize a few child care homes while the planning and financing of a center-based program is under way.

How Do You Find Out about Need?

Once you have determined the kind of data necessary to substantiate the need for a program, you are ready to decide how to collect the data. Some information for long-range planning can be obtained from census figures, chambers of commerce, or data on births from the health department. However, planners in most communities have access to information from their Child Care Resource and Referral (CCR&R) agency. These agencies are funded through Child Care and Development Block Grants issued to the states through the U.S.

Department of Health and Human Services and were created to support families and providers who are interested in affordable and quality child care. CCR&Rs provide technical assistance for a variety of child care providers including family child care, center-based programs, and after school programs. They support programs that serve infants, toddlers, preschoolers, and school agers. Many CCR&R agencies will generate ZIP code specific program planning reports that can include the number and type of child care slots available as well as the number of children by age in an area. The National Association for Child Care Resource and Referral Agencies (NACCRRA) serves as a professional organization and useful resource for child care, and its website (www.naccrra.org) can be used to locate the Child Care Resource and Referral Agency that supports your area.

Although the CCR&R agency should be the first stop for data collection, other detailed information needed for decision making will likely need to be obtained in order to answer all necessary questions.

Data must be collected, recorded, compiled, and analyzed so that the need for the program can be explained to anyone who is involved in initial planning, including members of a sponsoring group or funding agency. The data collection process might be formal and wide in scope to cover a broad potential population, or it can be informal and confined to a very small group of parents and community representatives. Possible methods of collecting needs assessment data include mailed questionnaires; telephone or online surveys; or informal, small group meetings.

Use of Questionnaires

When a large group of potential clients is sampled, it is wise to develop a questionnaire that can be completed online or that can be returned in an enclosed, addressed, and stamped envelope. Questionnaires provide specific data that can be recorded, compiled, and analyzed. These data are usually quite accurate; however, it is possible that some families will indicate interest in child care and then no longer need it or decide not to use it when it becomes available. In some communities, the use of online survey tools such as Survey Monkey or Kwik Survey might be appropriate. Many online tools are free, easy to use, and can design surveys that collect both open-ended and forced-choice data.

The use of online surveys can reduce the cost and also increase the percentage of returns. The task of developing a good questionnaire or survey can be challenging and getting the survey into the hands

DIRECTOR'S CORNER

At the beginning of our planning process, we worked with our neighborhood elementary school and received permission to sponsor a booth at the school's fall open house. The booth included some information on the importance of quality child care and some enticing trinkets that brought children to the booth with their families in tow. We asked visitors to fill out an interest survey and provided both a pencil-and-paper version and an online version of the survey using a laptop computer. We were somewhat surprised to see how many people preferred to use the computer to complete the survey and many took a card with a link to the survey website with them so that others not at the open house could complete the survey. We were also able to talk with the principal who offered to include a link to our survey and a short article in the school's electronic newsletter which generated a lot of interest and greatly increased the number of completed surveys. When it came time to compile the data, we were able to input our pencil-and-paper data into the online version. The online survey automatically analyzed our results and presented our data in a series of colorful and easy-to-understand charts and graphs which we used as we presented our findings to potential funders.

—Director, Private nonprofit center

imperative to analyze the potential audience first so that items are covered in terms that the audience understands and that it is family friendly; then you must be sure to include inquiries about *all* the information you need while keeping the form brief.

Before planning the location, type, and size of program, and ages of children to be served, it is helpful to ask for the following information:

- number of adults in the household
- number of those adults employed
- number and ages of all children in the household
- number of children cared for outside the home
- number and ages of children with special needs
- estimate of family income
- estimate of how much is or could be spent on child care
- days and hours child care is needed
- preferred location of child care
- whether the family will use the proposed child care center when it becomes available

Use of Telephone Surveys

In the past, the use of telephone surveys was a viable option for collecting data. Today, telemarketing has come under public scrutiny with many households opting out of being called at home by signing up for the federal "do not call" list. While it is unlikely that conducting a needs assessment survey would fall under the "do not call" list guidelines, the public's annoyance with telemarketing calls is clear and many families use caller identification to screen their calls. It is also more common for many families to rely on cell phones versus land lines, which makes acquiring lists of accurate phone numbers challenging. When an existing phone list is available and it is determined that a telephone survey is the option of choice, be prepared for a time-consuming and costly task especially if you expect to include a large number of families. One way to reduce both cost and time is to call a sample of the large potential population to obtain fairly accurate information about the total group without calling each family. If you are involved in an extensive needs assessment program, you should consult a marketing specialist about appropriate sampling techniques. On the other hand, if you have access to a group of volunteers who can do some telephoning and if the population to be contacted is small, calling prospective families may yield accurate data, provided that the questioning is conducted uniformly and that the data collected are what you need to know.

of the right group of people requires some thoughtful consideration. Those who determine that a traditional paper-and-pencil survey is best for their project will need to plan for the cost of mailing the survey with an enclosed addressed and stamped envelope in order to increase the number of returns. They should plan on a lack of response and realize that unreturned questionnaires often create more questions because it isn't clear whether those families are not interested in the service or whether they are interested but have neglected to return the questionnaire.

Whether using a pencil-and-paper or online version, good surveys or questionnaires can be difficult to develop. The questionnaire must be brief and understandable by the recipient, and the items included also must be carefully selected to provide precisely the data that are important to the needs assessment for any given program. Therefore, if you are involved in drafting a questionnaire, it is

To ensure uniformity, telephone surveys also must utilize a questionnaire. The survey caller verbally asks the questions and fills in the questionnaire. The same considerations that apply to mailed or online questionnaires apply to those used in telephone surveys: understandable wording, complete coverage of data, and brevity.

REFLECTION

Think for a moment about being called by someone doing a telephone survey. What was your reaction to the call? Was the call at a convenient time, or did it interrupt your study time or dinner? Did the caller get to the point quickly or waste your time, inquiring about your health or if you were having a good day? What led you to agree to participate in the survey, or decline and hang up? Recalling your reaction to a telephone survey can help you gain insights into how parents might respond to a needs assessment telephone survey.

Now consider an online survey that you have taken. How did this experience compare to the telephone survey? Did you complete the online survey at a time that was convenient to you? During which experience were you more likely to provide complete and accurate information?

Small Group Meetings

Holding informal group discussions with families who express interest in having their children participate in a program is a good way to obtain information about need. It is practical when the potential client population is defined (for example, church members, apartment complex dwellers, employees of a particular company) or when the size of the community or neighborhood limits the number of families who might use the center. Informal meetings have the advantage of establishing a basis of trust and open communication between the providers of the service and the families who will use it. Without the constraints of a specific questionnaire, parents are free to discuss their values and goals for their children, their unique needs and desires in terms of their family situation, and their feelings about different types of programs that might become available. However, this informal data collection process yields information that is often less valid and reliable as well as more difficult to tabulate and analyze than questionnaire data. You may find that it is beneficial to work out a combination of the informal discussion and formal questionnaire procedures by holding a series of small group meetings in which parents fill

out a brief questionnaire at the close of the meeting. Needs assessment data that are collected through both formal and informal channels can provide the basis for the decision about whether or not to have a program, and can furnish information about family values and goals that will enter into formulating the program philosophy. Of course, the values and the educational interests of the program planners and the director also will have a significant impact on the philosophy.

PROGRAM MISSION AND VALUES STATEMENTS   naeyc

The characteristics of an early childhood education program should emerge from the mission and values of the program. Developing the mission and values statements is part of the planners' strategic planning process. These carefully crafted statements guide directors' decisions about hiring new staff and designing appropriate professional development to ensure that all staff members are prepared to implement a program consistent with them.

Decisions about the Mission and Values Statements

Mission statements must reflect the principles of our profession and provide the indicators of quality that define good practice. Decisions about the mission of a program will also emerge from the data that are gathered in the initial planning process. If the data suggest that a full day, 12-month program is needed for preschoolers of middle class professional families who work from 8:00 a.m. to 5:00 p.m. then the mission of the center will reflect this need. A very different mission statement would likely be developed for:

- children of military families who are frequently deployed overseas
- children of school teachers who need nine or ten months of care
- children whose families are in poverty and work split shifts

REFLECTION

Think about the three different groups of children and families described above. How might the mission of each group be crafted to reflect the needs of the children and families to be served?

The cultural, educational, and socioeconomic levels of the child and families are some of many factors that impact how the mission statement is developed. Understanding the construction and purpose of mission and values statements is important for planners engaged in the strategic planning process.

Mission Statements

A mission statement is a brief statement that defines the focus or purpose of the organization. It appears on numerous program documents including personnel policies, the parent handbook, brochures, newsletters, the program website, all promotional and fund-raising materials, as well as stationery and news releases. Having a well-developed mission statement is an indicator of program quality. Sections in both the NAEYC Accreditation Standards and the Program Administration Scale (PAS) require a mission statement. The Program Planning and Evaluation Section of the PAS indicates, under Documents Needed, that programs must have a mission and/or vision statement. Vision and/or mission statements are mentioned in the NAEYC Accreditation Criteria for Leadership and Management Standard.

Developing a Mission Statement

A mission statement should clearly and concisely state the purpose and business of the program in a manner that resonates with the current staff and stakeholders. Radtke (1998) recommends that mission statements be revisited every five years in order to "ensure relevance" and should also answer the following three questions:

1. What are the opportunities or needs that we exist to address? (the *purpose* of the organization)

2. What are we doing to address these needs? (the *business* of the organization)

3. What principles or beliefs guide our work? (the *values* of the organization) (Radtke, 1998. p. 2)

Figure 2-1 shows an example of how one university-affiliated center answered Radtke's three questions to develop a mission statement.

What is the purpose of the organization? To provide high-quality early care and education for young children and professional development for early childhood college students and practicing professionals.

What is the business of the organization? To provide opportunities for a highly qualified staff to work together to learn about, critically reflect on, and collaboratively develop and deliver high-quality and research-supported programs to young children and seek opportunities to share their practice with students and practicing early childhood professionals.

What are our values? The staff and stakeholders value high-quality care and education for young children within a curriculum framework that is child-centered and supports intentional teaching, integration, and inquiry. We value curriculum that:

- is created jointly by children and adults
- is assessment-supported versus assessment-driven

- is emergent at times and negotiated at others so that children investigate important topics in authentic ways
- is intentional so that development and learning are supported throughout the daily routine and environment
- integrates early learning content, developmental domains, and family culture in personally meaningful and socially relevant ways

The mission of this program is to:

- provide high-quality early care and education for young children while demonstrating an assessment-supported, child-centered, emergent, integrated, and science-focused curriculum
- to work together as reflective decision makers who seek to improve the quality of care and education for young children by mentoring early childhood graduate and undergraduate students and sharing research-supported practice with the larger early childhood community

FIGURE 2-1 Developing a Mission Statement
Source: © Cengage Learning, 2013.

REFLECTION

Think about the following mission statements. How well do they answer Radtke's three questions?

- MISSION—To develop and operate model professional early child care programs that meet the diverse needs of the children and families in the communities we serve.

- MISSION—To enhance the cognitive, social, and emotional well-being of the young children in our program and to serve the diverse needs of their families.

Decisions about Core Values and Value Statements

Establishing the core values that will serve as the foundation of the program is a critical step in establishing a meaningful and well-justified program. Core values come from a sound understanding of child development and the best practices in the field. The value statements are important in determining the curriculum and teaching strategies that reflect the program's core values. Let us suppose that a group of program planners identify that one of their core values is that "children learn through inquiry," meaning that children come to understandings about things and people in their world through the process of inventing ideas and developing hypotheses. A value statement that reflects this core value might be developed that identifies children as autonomous investigators. In turn, decisions about how classrooms are set up would support this core value. A classroom guided by this value statement would replace planned activities set up to teach letters or numbers with a print-rich environment that includes many books, charts, and a writing center, and children would enjoy the use of math games, measuring tools, and simple machines such as pulleys and pendulums. Consider Table 2-2 and note how core values are transformed into value statements.

It is important to have a director who fully understands and supports the core values, because he or she will be the educational leader responsible for the implementation of a program that supports these values. When the planners have very specific ideas about either mission or values, or a new director is hired for an ongoing program, the new hire is expected to operate within the program's adopted framework. Frustrations over incompatible values or philosophies can create unworkable teaching situations for dedicated staff who need the support of the new director (Kuykendall, 1990, p. 49). If the core values of a program are based on the philosophical assumption that the child is born a *tabula rasa* (meaning the mind at birth is a "blank tablet" to be written on by experience; the stated goal of education is to fill that tablet with experiences), it is helpful if the program director is committed to that same philosophy. A director with a cognitive-developmental or constructivist point of view who does not accept the *tabula rasa* premise will find it difficult to develop or direct an educational program that would reflect the stated program philosophy. For a discussion of constructivism and a comparison of programs sharing the cognitive-developmental orientation, see DeVries and Kohlberg (1988).

Value statements typically emerge from a philosophical position. The need for a philosophical position as a base for program design seems clear (Decker et al., 2009). Whether it is based on

TABLE 2-2 Sample core values and value statements

Core Values	Values Statement
Children are:	Therefore we provide:
Social beings	Opportunities for children to work and play with each other and with responsive adults.
Independent learners	Environments where children make choices about their learning with adult support when needed.
Problem solvers	Children with a variety of open-ended experiences and authentic materials that prompt a sense of wonder.
Communicators	Opportunities for children to communicate about their wants, needs, and wonderings within a respectful and responsive environment.
Literate learners	A print-rich environment where children see a purpose for letters, words, and numbers and have opportunities to use this emerging knowledge in meaningful ways.

Source: © Cengage Learning, 2013.

developmental theory, social learning theory, the notion of multiple intelligences, or behaviorism, a well-grounded philosophical foundation gives substance and validity to the program. The program philosophy underlies most programmatic decisions. It should reflect the values, beliefs, and training of the director as well as the wishes and interests of the program planners and families who will participate in the program. When administrators attempt to implement programs for which they are unable to state a philosophy nor substantiate their curriculum and accompanying pedagogical strategies in terms of that philosophy, they risk internal confusion, lack of unity, loss of teamwork, and an inability to help parents understand their true purpose.

What Is the Basis for Choosing a Philosophy?

When programs are planned and implemented, the curriculum content and teaching strategies either consciously or unconsciously reflect a philosophy that is based on

- assumptions about how children learn
- values of the program planners and the families involved
- views of the planners regarding basic issues in education

Although the three areas that influence the philosophy of the program can be discussed separately, they interact with one another and, in reality, are almost impossible to identify and delineate.

Assumptions about How Children Learn

In the very broadest sense and in the most simplistic terms, assumptions about how children learn fall into three major categories: environmental, maturational, and interactional. The environmental position assumes that the child's learning is dependent on extrinsic motivators in the form of tokens, compliments, smiles, gold stars, and so forth. What the child is to learn is decided by the adult who then plans lessons designed to teach content and skills. One of the basic assumptions of this position is that anything worth teaching is also observable and measurable. Attempts to relate this particular assumption about learning to some theoretical base usually lead to the mention of people such as Thorndike, Watson, and Skinner.

Goals based on the environmental assumptions about how young children learn might be that in preschool classrooms

- children learn to recite the alphabet through alphabet songs and stories

- children practice rote counting during group time and while at play
- staff help children with letter recognition by using flash cards and word games
- group-time activities include color recognition and color naming exercises

The maturational position assumes that there is an internal driving force that leads to the emergence of cognitive and affective systems, which, in turn, determine the child's readiness for mastery of developmental tasks. Mastery of the task is itself rewarding, so the reinforcement is based on intrinsic satisfactions derived from accomplishment and task mastery. Learning is controlled by an internal growth force and the child selects from various offerings, thereby learning what she is ready to learn. The theorists who are associated with the extreme maturational position are Freud and Gesell.

Goals based on maturational assumptions about how young children learn might be that children in the program:

- show interest and choose to work in various interest areas in the classroom
- choose activities based on their interests and their rhythms
- show evidence of satisfaction after having mastered a task (verbally, with actions, or with body language that communicates pleasure in the accomplishment)

The interactional position assumes that learning results from the dynamic interaction between the emerging cognitive and affective systems and the environment. The interaction with both the material and the human environment is not driven solely by an internal force but also is nurtured, facilitated, and intensified by the timely intervention of significant adults in the environment. The child is intrinsically motivated to select appropriately from the environment, but the adult is responsible for preparing the environment and for timely and appropriate questions and ideas to alert the child to the learning opportunities in each situation. The adult facilitates the development of intellectual competence. The impetus for the interactional approach came from Piaget's work. Additional insights into the interactive theoretical perspective come from Vygotsky's work. He emphasized the important connection between a child's social and psychological worlds for cognitive development (Bodrova & Leong, 2006, p. viii).

Goals based on interactional assumptions about how young children learn might be that in all classrooms:

- play is cherished and play spaces are rich with learning opportunities
- children are encouraged to explore and create
- children enjoy successes that lead to greater self-confidence and independence
- staff members value and are responsive to each child's special abilities, learning style, and developmental pace

REFLECTION

Think about a program that you have taught in or observed. Identify the assumptions about how children learn in this program. Try to formulate an example from that classroom experience that supports the assumption about how children learn. Think about activities you may have planned or behaviors you encourage and try to determine the area of development you most value. What are your assumptions about how children learn?

Values of the Program Planners and the Families

The program philosophy is influenced by the priorities parents and planners set for the children. When questioned, most administrators would state that they value the optimum development of the whole child: the social, emotional, physical, language, aesthetic, and cognitive development of the child. However, when the philosophy or the ongoing program is analyzed, it may become clear that priorities do, indeed, exist. Concern for the development of the whole child is the stated position, but careful analysis reveals that cognitive outcomes are given priority over social and emotional goals, or vice versa.

Views on Basic Issues in Education

A number of basic issues in education are implied, if not directly addressed, in the philosophy and, in turn, the value statements. One of these issues is the content versus process issue, sometimes interpreted as school orientation versus human orientation. Those who subscribe to the content orientation support the notion that the goal of education is to provide children with content that enables them to succeed in school as it exists. Their focus is on preparation for the next step in schooling; achievement is evaluated by relating each child's progress to

norms or to grade level. The goal of education for those who support human orientation, or what might be viewed as the developmental point of view, is the upward movement of the child as an independent learner to higher levels of intellectual competence. The process of learning and the development of problem-solving skills are more important than content mastery. Autonomy, collaboration, and cooperation are valued, and the years in school are considered an integral part of life itself. The major goal is for children to become autonomous problem solvers (Kamii, 1982). Schooling is not viewed as either preparation for later school or preparation for life. Achievement is not dependent on reaching a norm or the next grade level but on the ability to cope with the here and now.

Today, planners and program directors must find a way to be consistent with their philosophical orientation and also develop a program that is both content and process focused. The reality of the school readiness movement, the need to overcome the achievement gap, and accountability pressures from federal, state, and local funders call upon leaders in early care and education to find a way to advocate for childhood as a unique and valuable stage in the human life cycle while providing all children access to rich and challenging experiences that support early learning content. These demands do not need to be mutually exclusive and, with careful planning, it is possible to put in place a framework for curricular decision making that allows teachers to reflect both a grounded philosophy of how children learn and develop with the realities of societal demands for school readiness, content knowledge, and accountability.

At first glance, discussions about program philosophy may seem unrelated to the problems of starting a center or to taking over as director of an ongoing program. However, it is impossible to make program decisions without a commitment to an agreed-upon philosophy. Identifying the elements of this philosophy will be addressed in more depth in Chapter 11.

TYPES OF PROGRAMS   naeyc

A major item to be determined, after the need has been assessed and the mission and values statements are written, is the type of program to be offered. After deciding on the type of program in terms of sponsoring agency and funding, the decision about ages of children to be served must be made before making arrangements for site selection, licensing, budgeting, staffing and equipping the center, and enrolling the children.

Decisions about the type of program will be dependent on the assessed need as well as the development of the mission and values statements. It also depends on the sources of available funds and the source of the impetus for the program. Not-for-profit programs receive financial support through government funding or subsidies from sponsoring agencies, whereas proprietary programs are supported by capital investments of individuals or corporations. Many different terms such as *preschool, nursery school, child care center,* and *early education center* are used when referring to early care and education programs, but there is nothing inherent in these labels that will identify what type of program or philosophy is practiced in the center. A wide range of program philosophies, including Waldorf, Reggio Emilia, and those based on Jean Piaget's or Montessori's teachings, to name a few, can operate under any of the program types discussed in the following section.

Not-for-Profit Programs

There are public and private not-for-profit programs (sometimes called nonprofit) that range in size and scope from the small cooperative preschool to the large, complex, agency-sponsored child care center. Although not-for-profit and nonprofit may be differentiated for legal reasons in some states, in most places the terms are used interchangeably.

Individual Cooperative Programs

Cooperative programs, often called parent co-ops, are owned and operated by a group. Parents are expected to help in the classroom, so the small co-op usually functions with one or two paid staff members, one of whom is usually a teacher/director. Costs are kept at a minimum and tuition is lower than in other centers. Most co-ops are half-day programs because they require parent participation; however, there are co-ops organized as child care centers.

Agency-Sponsored Programs

Many not-for-profit early childhood education programs are sponsored by community agencies such as church groups, labor unions, service agencies, neighborhood houses, and United Way organizations. These programs may be set up as full-day care centers for working families or as half-day enrichment programs. Such programs are found in both rural and urban areas and can serve both low-income and middle-income families depending on how much support is provided by the sponsoring

agency. Agency-sponsored programs sometimes receive partial support from a sponsor such as United Way and obtain the remaining support from tuition, government funds, and/or grants.

Government-Sponsored Programs

Head Start is perhaps the best known of the federal government-sponsored, early childhood education programs and is the nation's leading investment in early childhood care and education. Head Start provides a range of comprehensive education, health, nutrition, parent involvement, and family support services and has primarily served at-risk children and their families since 1965. Head Start actually consists of two programs: Head Start and Early Head Start. Head Start is a comprehensive early childhood development program primarily serving at-risk preschool-age children and their families (National Head Start Association, 2011).

Head Start is administered by the Administration for Children and Families in the U.S. Department of Health and Human Services. Head Start funds are sometimes distributed through and monitored by the local Community Action Agency. Funding for Head Start programs may go to public school systems, universities, and public or private not-for-profit agencies. Larger grantees such as public schools or universities often find creative ways to partner with other agencies to provide opportunities for more families to receive the benefits of this comprehensive government-sponsored child care program. For example, a public school may set up a partnership with a church child care program that serves a number of low-income families. The church, in collaboration with the public school, can offer Head Start income eligible families various health and social service benefits with the help of a Head Start family advocate. The Head Start funding also helps the church cover program expenses for these families. Many unique collaborative arrangements are being worked out between and among various types of child care agencies across the country, all in an effort to better serve children and families.

Head Start programs may be center based or home based and may provide child care on a full-time or half-time basis. Formerly for only preschool children, Early Start, a part of Head Start, is now available to children under age 4. Those who receive funds from Head Start (grantees) are mandated to serve children with disabilities (ten percent of enrollment opportunities) who must be mainstreamed, and receive a total care package through direct services from the grantee or from other resources in the community.

The Department of Defense and the Department of Veterans Affairs also sponsor child care programs in some regions of the country, as do some state governments. Of course, there are many military programs (see the "Military Programs" section).

Public School–Sponsored Programs

Most states are funding some prekindergarten programs, and many of these are in public schools (Neugebauer, 2003). Full-day or half-day public school programs are staffed by people hired through public school personnel offices, and the programs are housed in public school buildings. Local school boards, public school administrators, and teacher unions typically have a voice in making policy as well as in teacher and program evaluation. The building principal is the appointed instructional leader, and at the state level, these programs fall under the jurisdiction of the superintendent of public instruction or the commissioner of education.

Practices in public preschools still tend to focus on academic success, school readiness, and standardized testing, but advocates for developmentally appropriate practice in preschools are challenging this academic readiness position of some public school instructional leaders. With the current trend toward universal prekindergarten, additional government funds are flowing into public schools to support the interest in offering a prekindergarten experience for all children. The aim in some states is to increase the amount of state dollars that come to those systems offering prekindergarten programs.

This could potentially lead to prekindergarten programs that focus on instruction and dilute the caring dimension of the daily interactions between teachers and children. Some states are making an effort to combine public and private funding, which may be a way to have a system that allows for a combination of education plus the caring and emotional support that young children require.

Before- and after-school programs for school-aged children often are housed in public schools. Some are also public school–sponsored, while others are run by community agencies or service groups such as the Salvation Army and YMCA. The public school–sponsored programs may be staffed by teachers in the building or by high school or college students who are free during early morning and late afternoon hours. Often, the person in the school system responsible for the preschool programs also oversees these before- and after-school programs and other wraparound programs, and the building principal is the on-site administrator-in-charge.

Campus Child Care Programs

Laboratory (or demonstration) schools and child care programs for children of students, faculty, and staff are two types of programs found on college campuses. The programs may be sponsored and subsidized by the college or university or by government funds. These programs often provide facilities for research, observation, and teacher training. They may be full-day or half-day and may charge full, or in some cases partial, tuition for those affiliated with

Bombeck Family Learning Center

Many campus-based programs must meet the needs of a broader stakeholders group that includes not only children, families, and staff but also pre-service and in-service teachers.

the university. In some places where student groups as well as the university itself offer support for the care of students' children, the students pay minimum tuition for their children and the program hours are flexible to accommodate the students' course schedules.

Privately Sponsored Not-for-Profit Programs

Many large industries, hospitals, and apartment complexes are including child care centers in their facilities and are offering services for the children of their employees and residents. These not-for-profit centers are set up for the comfort and convenience of the employees and residents. The hours are often flexible, and in some cases, fees are on a sliding scale to encourage full use of the available facilities. In the case of hospital- and industry-operated programs, fees may be part of an employee benefit package implemented through the use of vouchers, direct payment to the caregivers, or a child care allowance to the employee.

Some employers offer a Dependent Care Assistance Program (DCAP) or Dependent Care Reimbursement Program (DCRP) that allows employees to set aside a certain amount of their yearly pretax salary for child care expenses, thereby providing a substantial tax savings to the employee.

Employers are realizing they cannot meet the challenge of fulfilling employees' child care needs on their own and are reaching out to the child care community for help in managing on-site centers. Some contract with centers for a reduced fee or funded slots for employees, whereas others prefer to contract for information and referral services in the area but are not involved in service delivery.

Profit-Making Programs (Proprietary)

Although much is written about not-for-profit programs such as Head Start, United Way centers, and public school programs, a large majority of the early childhood education programs in the United States are proprietary. These programs are set up to provide a service that will make a profit.

Independent Owner

Many full- and half-day child care programs are owned and operated by an individual or a small group (partnerships or small corporations). In the case of the proprietary center, tuition is usually the only source of income, and the operators frequently have budgeting and financial problems, although some proprietary and nonprofits can obtain supplementary funding from other sources, including state funds. The proprietary operators may be able to draw a salary from the tuition that is paid by families using the service, but the operators rarely make a profit over and above that because of the high cost of operating a quality program. Sometimes, proprietors open more than one center in a community or region and begin a small chain operation. Although it is difficult to make a profit from the small chain, quantity buying and shared service costs sometimes can reduce the cost per child and increase the possibility of making a profit over and above operating expenses.

Corporate Systems

Large, for-profit, child care organizations are operated by a parent company that develops a prototype and sets up a number of centers throughout a state or region, or across the nation and into Canada. Some of these corporations have gone public and their stock is traded on the New York Stock Exchange. These national child care chains operate under a central administration that furnishes the financial backing and is usually very powerful in setting the policy and controlling the program. There often is a prototype building and program that are publicized by identifiable slogans, logos, brochures, and advertisements. Some corporate systems operate all centers carrying the chain name, while others work on a franchised basis. In the latter case, an individual purchases a franchise from the parent company for a basic purchase price, then pays the company a percentage of gross intake for the ongoing use of the name and the program. In addition, the parent company supplies guidelines for fees, sample documents, brochures, advertising materials, and the like. Some of these sample documents must be changed by center operators to meet local regulations and/or be in line with local practice. The parent corporation often monitors the franchised centers to maintain the company standard of quality control. Because company policy often controls the program, directors are usually expected to adopt the program as outlined by the corporate body but also can adjust some practices based on their own philosophy.

Employer-Sponsored Programs

There is an increasing demand for employer-sponsored child care. Employers are analyzing the benefits of child care services and seeking creative ways to meet their employees' identified needs. During the early 2000s, the top players among the child care management organizations involved in employer-sponsored care were Bright Horizons Family Solutions and Knowledge Beginnings, now Knowledge Learning Corporation. They accounted for the lion's share of the phenomenal growth in employer-sponsored care in the late 1990s. Much of their growth resulted from contracts to take over centers that employers were previously managing on their own in addition to some acquisitions of other independent child care providers. The concept of employer-sponsored care is not new. In the 1940s during World War II, the Kaiser shipbuilder corporation on the West Coast provided care for the children of women who were called into the workforce to support U.S. troops in the war effort. Companies like Stride Rite and Levi Strauss also were pioneers in the on-site, employer-sponsored child care business. The availability of child care management corporations is relatively recent.

Demand by big industry for services provided by the leading employer child care management organizations leveled off in the first years after the turn of the century for some of the large for-profit child care providers. However, business held and improved slightly for Bright Horizons Family Solutions while it leveled off for others in this group. These companies continue to find that the families who use their centers demand some customized services. Some of these additional services include backup and sick child care; therapy services for children with special needs; crisis intervention; and a number of extracurricular programs, including karate, gymnastics, music, and dance. Other creative ways they serve families are to offer dry cleaning pickup, UPS pickup, gourmet meal pickup, and even haircuts for children. In most cases, parents contract with these special service providers and the center is the appointed location for deliveries and pickups. Centers are not involved in billing or receiving payments.

When unemployment is low, growing numbers of employers begin to view child care as a recruitment and retention tool. For example, hospitals sponsor on-site centers to help with recruitment and retention of nurses and other technical personnel. Employers also look for child care solutions that will work for the employee who telecommutes from home as well as some who work at small satellite offices away from the main campus. Although many employer-sponsored centers are run by the large management organizations, there are employers who seek out public or private groups such as universities or the YMCA to run centers for them. In some cases, the employers provide generous subsidies by building new facilities that are rent free or by offering low-cost leases for ground on which to build. Employers who strive to keep fees down for their employees,

but value quality care and want fully qualified staff as well as low teacher-to-child ratios, subsidize their centers to make up the deficits.

When universities or other nonprofits such as hospitals or YMCAs are called on to manage centers for large for-profit corporations, it is important for the center director to be prepared for many discussions with the corporate partners in order to clarify the mission and goals of the new program. Of course, families and children always will be the focus of those who manage and staff the center. However, it is important to keep in mind that recruitment, retention, employee productivity, and morale are major goals of the corporation that subsidizes and sponsors the center. Directors realize they have many customers, including families, children, and staff, but now directors must realize that one of the most important customers is the sponsoring corporation. When issues and questions arise, the position of corporate customers must be taken into consideration. They may have questions about curriculum or hiring practices, but they are likely to accept the decisions of the early childhood professionals whom they hired to deal with those aspects of the program. For the director, this is no different from handling the usual inquiries and concerns from parents in any type of center. But decisions about hours of operation, changing schedules for children by the week (or even the day), backup care, sick child care, late day or night care, and weekend care are the things a business sponsor may need to make to keep employees who

DIRECTOR'S CORNER

"I have been the director of an on-site center sponsored by a not-for-profit organization for almost 20 years. When that organization contracted with a large for-profit corporation to manage a new center they were ready to build, I was made the director of both centers. The corporation selected us because we had been the recipient of a national award and were well known for the quality program we offered in the on-site center. One of my greatest challenges when I began to work with the point people from the large corporate sponsor was to realize that they were now a customer of my not-for-profit employer. It really forced me to stretch my thinking and rethink what I valued and where I would draw the line on issues and not compromise."

—Director of two large employer-sponsored programs

Programs that serve military families must be prepared to meet the sometimes intense needs related to having a loved one deployed for long periods of time. These programs need to have close connections with the social services offered on the base and also need to be tuned in to the sometimes exceptional emotional needs of the children and families served.

© 2010 Cengage Learning

work different schedules. Corporate sponsors respect the early childhood professional and value the beautiful classrooms and rich programming offered the children. However, to meet the expectations the corporation has for its employees, the center staff may have to reconsider what they view as best for the children and adjust to the interests and schedules of their sponsor without compromising the integrity of their own ethical and professional values.

Military Programs

The Department of Defense (DOD) operates child care programs at military installations across the country. Financed by a combination of government appropriations and sliding scale parent tuition fees, the programs may be full-day, center-based care; part-day preschools; drop-in care; and, in some places, evening and weekend care. Some of this is center based and some is in family child care homes.

Each of the military services (Air Force, Army, Marines, and Navy) operates its own child care service, but all must follow the mandates of the Military Child Care Act of 1989. The act addresses program funding, required training for staff, competitive pay rates for staff, and an internal inspection system. To meet the demand for child care services, the DOD has expanded preschool and school-aged child care options by increasing the number of programs on military installations. It accomplished this by using existing resource and referral programs to help families locate available child care and by contracting with off-installation centers to guarantee spaces for DOD children.

Family Child Care Homes

Family child care is reminiscent of an extended family, with a small group of children being cared for in the home of a child care provider (Gordon & Williams Browne, 2011). Although this type of child care service is most popular for infants and toddlers, these home providers also care for preschool children and offer before- and after-school care. The provider may be an employee of a system but most often operates independently, contracting directly with families who choose home care over center-based care. These providers run their own business. In some states, family child care homes must be licensed, whereas in other places, they are certified or registered by a community agency authorized to pay for children of low-income families who are in the home. Many providers join employer or community agency information and referral registries that take calls from parents seeking child care. Registered family child care homes may or may not be subject to inspection by a responsible community agency. In some places, inspections are made only after a complaint has been filed.

STANDARDS OF PRACTICE

All child care programs of every type listed in the previous section are expected to provide high-quality programs for young children. It is assumed that these programs meet local licensing requirements because without a proper license, programs are not permitted to remain open for business. However, to provide the very best for children and to meet the accepted standards of quality based on expectations of fellow professionals, directors are expected to go beyond meeting minimum standards established by the states and strive for higher standards of quality.

The best-known and most widely accepted standards for quality practice for any and all programs for children, birth through kindergarten, are those developed by the National Association for the Education of Young Children (NAEYC). School-age programs are accredited by the National After-School Association (NAA), while family child care programs are accredited by the National Association for Family Child Care (NAFCC). In some places centers receive accreditation from the National Association of Child Care Professionals (NACCP). (For additional information on accreditation, see Chapter 4.) There is also a quality movement in many states which involves rating early care and education programs based on a series of quality indicators. These systems serve to increase awareness of the importance of quality.

SUMMARY

Starting a center is a challenging and exhausting undertaking. During the early planning stages, a number of concurrent activities interact with one another. The planners that get a center started must assess the need for a program while developing mission and values statements, identifying the program philosophy, and determining the type of program that will meet the expressed need. Many decisions must be made concerning how needs should be assessed, what philosophy will be most representative of the thinking of the planners and the prospective director, what type of program is feasible in terms of financing, and so forth. The people who are interested in starting a center must recognize that a great deal of time and energy must be invested before financial support is available and before a program can begin to deliver service to children and families.

TRY IT OUT!

 1 Review the sample needs assessment questionnaire in Director's Resource 2-1 and adjust it so you could use it for a ten-item online survey.
  a. How would you introduce the survey in an email that encourages potential program users to answer the questions?
  b. What incentive you would offer to encourage participation in the survey?
  c. What follow-up message would you send to those who participated in the survey?

2 Consider a program that you would most like to direct and use Radtke's three questions to develop a mission statement. Be sure to describe the type of population that would be served by this program.

3 Using Working Paper 2-1, discuss and record the thinking of the group about the items listed.

4 Using Working Paper 2-2, write your own program philosophy based on your thinking about the items listed in Class Exercise 1 on Working Paper 2-1.

 The Education CourseMate website for this text offers many helpful resources. Go to CengageBrain.com to access the TeachSource Video Cases and other TeachSource Videos, Expand Your Learning exercises, flashcards, interactive quizzes, the eBook, reflection and enrichment activities, and downloadable forms.

Working Paper 2-1

DISCUSSION FORM

In groups of four, discuss and record the thinking of the group about the items listed below:

1 **What are your assumptions about growth and development?**

2 **How does learning or the development of knowledge come about?**

3 **During the early years of a child's life, what is the adult's role relative to:**

    physical development?

    social development?

    emotional development?

    cognitive development?

    language development?

    moral development?

4 **What goals do you have for the children in your care?**

5 **What is your belief about how families impact development and how they should be served in your center?**

You can download a full-size version of this form on the Education CourseMate website.

Working Paper 2-2

Assume you have been hired as a director of a new center. Based on your own thinking about the items listed on Working Paper 2-1, write a list of core values and corresponding value statements for your new center.

 You can download a full-size version of this form on the Education CourseMate website.

Director's Resource 2-1

SAMPLE NEEDS ASSESSMENT

1 How many adults are there in this household? _____

2 Do all adults in the household work? ❑ Yes ❑ No

If yes, ❑ part time How many? _____ ❑ full time How many? _____

3 What is the total number of children under the age of 16? _____

4 What is the number of children under age 6? _____

Check ages of children under 6:

❑ Under 1   How many? _____

❑ Between 1 and 2   How many? _____

❑ Between 2 and 3   How many? _____

❑ Between 3 and 4   How many? _____

❑ Between 4 and 5   How many? _____

❑ Between 5 and 6   How many? _____

5 Does any child in this family, younger than school age, regularly spend time away from home?
❑ Yes ❑ No

If yes, how many? _____

6 Do any children in the family have special needs? ❑ Yes ❑ No

If yes, how many? _____

If yes, does the condition require attendance at a special school or program? ❑ Yes ❑ No

If yes, describe program(s) needed:

_____

_____

7 Is/are your child(ren) regularly cared for every day in your home by someone who does not live with you? ❑ Yes ❑ No

If yes, is the caregiver a relative? ❑ Yes ❑ No

8 How many children over 5 regularly spend time away from home before or after school? _____ What are their ages? _____

Describe type of program: _____

_____

_____

(continues)

Director's Resource 2-1 *(continued)*

9 For statistical purposes only, please give the total family income in this household:

$0–$15,000 ❑

$15,001–$20,000 ❑

$20,001–$35,000 ❑

$35,001–$50,000 ❑

$50,001–$75,000 ❑

$75,001–$90,000 ❑

over $90,000 ❑

10 Approximately how much do you pay every week for the care of all your children? Give that figure in column A. In column B, mark how much you would be willing to pay for quality care for all of your children. Mark with X.

A	B	
_____	$0–50	❑
_____	$51–75	❑
_____	$76–100	❑
_____	$101–125	❑
_____	$126–150	❑
_____	$151–175	❑
_____	Over $175	❑

11 Parents have a difficult time arranging for the care of their children. Indicate what has been your experience.

❑ Easy time

❑ Not very difficult

❑ Difficult time

❑ Extremely difficult

❑ No opinion

12 If you had a choice of arrangements for the care of your child, what would be your first choice?

❑ Care in child care center for four hours or less

❑ Care in child care center for more than four hours

❑ Care by another mother or someone in her own home

❑ Care by a sitter in your own home

❑ Care in a center before and after school

13 If you could have the type of arrangement you prefer, how many days per week would you want your children to spend there (insert number of days)? _____ Infant _____ Toddler _____ Preschooler _____ After school (Age _____)

14 Where would you prefer to have your child(ren) cared for?

❑ Near where you work

❑ Near where you live

❑ Other location: _____

15 Generally speaking, in selecting an ideal child care arrangement, which is more important to you? (Assume that quality is equal.)

❑ Cost more important

❑ Closeness to home more important

❑ Closeness to work more important

❑ No opinion

16 If a child care center opens across the street from your office (insert home, church, factory, as appropriate), for which age child would you be likely to use it?

❑ Your infant

❑ Your toddler

❑ Your preschooler

❑ Your school-age child(ren)

REFERENCES

Bodrova, E., & Leong, D. J. (2006). *Tools of the mind: The Vygotskian approach to early childhood education* (2nd ed.). Upper Saddle River, NJ: Prentice Hall.

Children's Defense Fund. (2010). *The state of America's children: 2010 Report*. Washington, DC.

Decker, C., Decker, J. R., Freeman, N., & Knopf, H. (2009). *Planning and administering early childhood programs* (9th ed.). Upper Saddle River, NJ: Prentice-Hall Merrill.

Denton Flanagan, K., and McPhee, C. (2009). *The children born in 2001 at kindergarten entry: First findings from the kindergarten data collections of the early childhood longitudinal study, birth cohort (ECLS-B)* (NCES 2010-005). National Center for Education Statistics, Institute of Education Sciences, U.S. Department of Education. Washington, DC.

DeVries, R., & Kohlberg, L. (1988). *Programs of early education: The constructivist view*. NY: Longman.

Gordon, A. M., & Williams Browne, K. (2011). *Beginnings and beyond* (8th ed.). Clifton Park, NY: Delmar Cengage Learning.

Kamii, C. (1982). *Number in preschool and kindergarten: Educational implications for Piaget's theory*. Washington, DC: NAEYC.

Kuykendall, J. (1990, July). Child development directors shouldn't leave home without it. *Young Children*, 49–51.

National Association for the Education of Young Children. (2007). *NAEYC early childhood program standards and accreditation criteria: The mark of quality in early childhood education*. Washington, DC: Author.

National Head Start Association (2011). Basic Head Start facts. Alexandria, VA: Author. (Retrieved 3/30/2011 http://www.nhsa.org/files/static_page_files/48BADE30-1D09-3519-ADED347C39FA16A4/Basic_Head_Start_Facts_rev02212011.pdf)

Neugebauer, R. (2003). Update on child care in public schools. *Child Care Information Exchange: The Director's Magazine*, 150, 66–71.

Radtke, J. M. (1998). *Strategic communications for nonprofit organizations: Seven steps to creating a successful plan*. New York: John Wiley & Sons, Inc.

3

LICENSING *and* CERTIFICATION

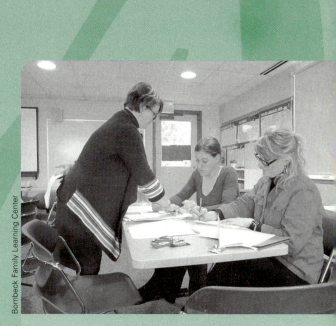

Bombeck Family Learning Center

The primary function of the licensing agent is to ascertain whether a program is in compliance with minimum requirements.

Objectives

After reading this chapter, you should be able to:

- Explain the purpose of licensing.
- Identify the steps in the licensing process.
- Describe various types of licensing regulations and their specific purposes.
- Compare and contrast early childhood program licensing and accreditation.
- Differentiate between early childhood program accreditation and quality rating improvement systems.
- Describe the various levels of individual credentials available for staff in a child care and education center.
- Explain the relationship between director credentialing and career pathways.

Standards Addressed in this Chapter

naeyc Professional Preparation Standard 6

naeyc Administrator Competencies-Management Knowledge and Skills 1, 4
Early Childhood Knowledge and Skills 2, 5, 10

naeyc Accreditation Standards 8, 9, 10

Child care center directors are responsible for understanding licensing, certification, and other regulations pertaining to provision of services for young children. Each type of regulation is developed by a governmental body and each has specific purposes. Directors must understand which regulations apply to their programs and ensure that all requirements are fulfilled in a timely manner. They also must be prepared to pay the requisite fees. In the future, people who assume responsible roles in children's programs probably will have to deal with more and more regulatory functions. This increase in regulation is related to the expanded use of public funds and the broader acceptance of the fact that programs for young children must provide care and protection for children and be educationally sound. Also, educational accountability points to greater focus on the need for certifying or licensing the people responsible for children's programs, while protection of children's health and safety requires licensing of centers. The term *licensing* may cause confusion since it is used to signify that a governing body is giving permission to do something. In this case, what is being permitted is the operation of a child care program. Later in the chapter when we discuss licensing (also known as certifying or credentialing) teachers, what is being permitted is the opportunity to obtain a teaching position.

After programs comply with the minimum standards required for local or state licensing, they can move toward higher standards and gain some form of professional recognition. The National Association for the Education of Young Children (NAEYC) works with child care centers through its National Academy for Early Childhood Program Accreditation "to enhance children's well-being and early learning by improving the quality of early childhood programs serving children birth through kindergarten," which is how NAEYC describes the Academy's mission on its website (http://www.naeyc.org/academy/primary/academy). The National Association of Child Care Professionals (NACCP), the National Early Childhood Program Accreditation Commission (NECPA), the National After School Association, and the American Montessori Association also provide opportunities for accreditation. Additional accrediting organizations can be found on the National

Child Care Information and Technical Assistance Center (NCCIC) website at http://nccic.acf.hhs.gov/poptopics/nationalaccred.html.

On-site directors and boards are responsible for providing the necessary inspiration and leadership to improve the center. They work to move a program from compliance with minimum licensing requirements to meeting quality performance standards. Even beyond these standards lies the goal of dynamic development that continues to produce a quality educational program. Model program directors always are working to refine their programs as they move toward the goal of excellence. The knowledge base in child development and early childhood education is constantly growing, so no program can afford to be complacent about its quality.

▶❚❚ TEACHSOURCE VIDEO VIGNETTE

The Quality of Child Care

This video provides an overview of the importance of quality programming for children's development. Go to the **CourseMate website** and view the video vignette entitled *The Quality of Child Care.* Reflect on the following questions:

1. How does quality care and education support children's development?

2. As a director, what factors should you consider to ensure quality programming for the young children in your care?

LICENSING   naeyc

Licensing of centers is required, but coverage varies from state to state. For example, in some states, only full-day child care programs are required to obtain a license, while in other states, all full-day care, half-day, and home-based programs must be licensed. Depending on the type of program being planned and the geographical location of the center, it is possible that both local and state requirements will need to be met. And when federal funding is involved, there will be additional requirements. In some states, program sponsorship determines program licensing. For example, programs affiliated with public schools may be licensed by the state department of education. Your licensing agent can provide updated licensing information. A directory

of state child care regulatory offices is available from the National Child Care Information Center online at http://nccic.acf.hhs.gov. To view an individual state's child care licensure regulations, go to the National Resource Center for Health and Safety in Child Care at http://nrckids.org/STATES/states.htm. Both of these organizations provide numerous online documents and research results.

The licensing function is a result of legislation, and its thrust is accountability for the health and safety of children and staff. Licensing requirements are usually minimal and enforcement practices in some localities are limited. As a result, program licensure does not guarantee quality of care or protection for children and rarely addresses the educational quality of the program. The licensing function is essential and valuable, but often it is misunderstood. A license gives permission to operate but does not indicate quality.

The 2008 Child Care Licensing Study found there are 329,882 licensed child care facilities in the United States (National Association for Regulatory Administration and the National Child Care Information and Technical Assistance Center, 2010). Approximately 32 percent of these are centers while the remaining 68 percent are licensed family child care homes or other types of facilities.

Family child care homes refer to places in which people care for one or more children in their homes instead of in a center or the child's own home. Some states divide these into categories based on the number of children permitted. In larger child care homes, perhaps 12 children may be cared for. At least two adults are needed, and building regulations should

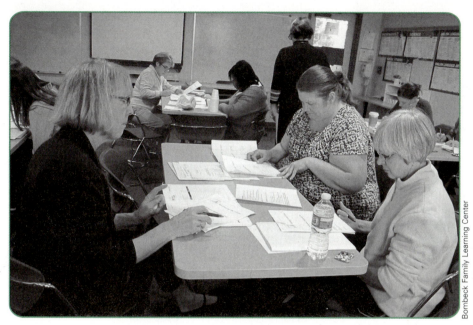

Bombeck Family Learning Center

After programs are in compliance with minimum standards required for local or state licensing, they can work toward higher standards that may lead to accreditation.

be required. Many families prefer this type of care, particularly for infants and toddlers, because of the smaller setting. Although family child care (or family day care as it is sometimes called) has always been a frequently used source of child care, its regulation has been relatively recent.

A recent major increase in the number of states requiring preservice qualifications for family home child care providers was reported by LeMoine, Morgan, and Azer (2003). However, the mandated qualifications related to early childhood training are limited. For example, much of the training may be in first aid, collecting fees, or completing forms for Child Care Food Program reimbursement. Because of the limited hours available for training, information about young children's development and learning is minimal.

Child care center staff preservice training shows a trend toward emphasis on early childhood education. Although not part of the regulatory system for child care centers, the American Association of Colleges of Teacher Education has called for all preschool teachers to have a bachelor's degree. This proposal far exceeds licensing requirements but is consistent with requirements for kindergarten teachers. As a future early childhood teacher or director, you may want to discuss this proposal with your peers or instructors.

In addition to the licensing department, in most localities the building department will review the plans, and the fire, building, and health or sanitation departments will send individual representatives to inspect the proposed space where the services for children will be offered. No matter what system is used in a particular state, an initial inspection and approval is required before the center can begin to operate. Even when the center is moving from one location to another, the inspection and approval must still be done. The regulating departments may be willing to send individual representatives to inspect the proposed space where the services for children will be offered. These inspections can alert the director to major and minor changes that would need to be made. The decision about moving to a particular facility may hinge on the cost and time line for making these changes, as well as on the deadline for exiting the current premises.

The director must play an active role in the licensing process. This may include making frequent phone calls to agencies and walking papers from office to office if necessary. Communication breakdowns can occur and directors must be proactive.

After initial inspection and approval, inspections and license renewals will be required on a regular basis. Directors are responsible for ensuring that their programs are in compliance with regulations and for being familiar with appeal and grievance procedures if conflicts arise regarding compliance with the regulations.

Licensing Regulations

Local and state licensing regulations typically cover building safety and requirements for physical space and establish base teacher-to-child ratios. Although licensing regulations vary greatly from state to state, most licensing regulations include the following points:

❶ *Building safety.* Licensing regulations always include at least the minimum fire, sanitation, and building safety standards that apply to all private and public services. Fire regulations usually cover the type of building construction, ease of evacuation in the event of fire, alarm systems, smoke detectors, sprinkler systems, availability of fire extinguishers, and methods of storing combustible materials. Building codes usually cover wiring, plumbing, and building construction, including building materials. Health department regulations cover conditions in all areas of the building, with particular attention to the bathrooms and food service operations.

When infants and/or children who are nonambulatory are enrolled in the program, the director must be sure to meet licensing requirements for those groups. Typically, these requirements focus on egress in case of emergency. Usually housing these programs on the first (ground) floor is required.

❷ *Physical space.* Licensing regulations usually specify the amount of space necessary for programs for infants, toddlers, and preschool children. The requirement for 3- to 5-year-old children is typically a minimum of 35 square feet per child of indoor space and 60 to 75 square feet of space per child outdoors. Since programs for infants and toddlers require cribs, feeding tables, and diaper-changing areas, such programs require more space per child than do programs for 3- to 5-year-olds. Levels and sources of light, levels of heat, sources of fresh air, fencing of outdoor areas, protection from radiators and low windows, and numbers of toilets also are included in regulations covering physical space. These standards are minimal, and good programs usually exceed them. Providing more than minimal space, particularly for children who will be at the center all day, is likely to make both children and staff more comfortable.

❸ *Teacher-to-child ratios.* Some licensing regulations include minimum teacher-to-child ratios. These state or local ratios vary, but they are in the range of 3 to 8 infants to one adult, 4 to 12 toddlers to one adult, and 6 to 20 preschoolers to one adult. The baseline licensing standards for child-to-staff ratios in child care centers in some states already meet the standards used by NAEYC, but most states are still below these significant ratios. Most regulations require that two

TABLE 3-1   Recommended group size and ratio of children to staff

Child Age	Maximum Group Size	Ratio of Children to Teacher
Infant	6	3:1
Toddler	8	4:1
Three-year-olds	14	7:1
Five-year-olds	16	8:1

Source: © Cengage Learning, 2013.

responsible adults be on the premises at all times. The ratios are established to furnish a baseline standard for protecting the safety of children; however, group size is even more important and also is regulated by some states.

A collaborative report from the American Academy of Pediatrics, American Public Health Association, and the National Resource Center for Health and Safety in Child Care and Early Education (2011, p. 4) recommends the group size and child-to-staff ratios shown in Table 3-1.

Licensing standards seem to be coming closer to these guidelines. Following are the most common child-to-staff ratios required by licensing in 2007 (National Association for Regulatory Administration/National Child Care Information and Technical Assistance Center, 2010):

* for infants, 4:1
* for toddlers, 6:1 (18 months of age) and 8:1 (27 months of age)
* for 4-year-olds, 10:1
* 5-year-olds, 15:1

NAEYC accreditation guidelines provide the rationale for establishing staffing criteria. "Across all the comprehensive research linking structural dimensions of child care to child care quality and to children's optimal outcomes, three dimensions emerge as most predictive: child care providers' compensation, providers' education and specialized training, and the teacher-child ratio" (NAEYC, 2005b, p. 59).

❹ *Staff qualifications.* Teachers' training in child development and their interactions with the children are key factors in creating a quality program. NAEYC's standards continue to uphold the importance of well-prepared staff and appropriate group sizes. These standards also call for teachers who have completed considerable formal education and specialized professional preparation in early childhood. Check the NAEYC website for current information related to teacher and director qualification guidelines.

Although licensing regulations sometimes address staff qualifications, requirements are often minimal. Some states require that caregivers be able to read and write, while others require at least a high school diploma for anyone who is hired as a teacher, teacher assistant, and/or aide. Most states require a director to have at least a high school diploma, while a few states require some college training, which may or may not be in child development or early childhood education. Others, however, require specific training in early childhood education or attainment of the Child Development Associate credential. Professional organizations are working to upgrade the criteria for early childhood staff as one component of the effort to improve staff salaries. As this process evolves, we can expect licensing standards to continue to improve. Psychologists, nurses, doctors on call, and other professionals must meet the appropriate credential requirements of their respective professions.

5 *Transportation.* In centers that provide transportation service, the service usually must meet the state motor vehicle department standards for school bus service. These standards regulate numbers of children, type of vehicle, types of lights on vehicles, proper identification on the vehicle, use of car seats and seat belts, and appropriate licensing and insurance coverage for the vehicle and the driver. Even when it is not required, it is wise to provide drivers with training in child development and management so that time spent on the bus will be positive as well as safe for both children and drivers.

It also is advisable to have a second adult on the bus to assist in an emergency. The driver, of course, should not leave even one child on the bus while seeking help or when walking a child to the door when that child's parent does not come out to meet the bus. Furthermore, some children have a difficult time leaving seat belts on. The driver, who must give full attention to the road, should not have to check constantly to ensure that all children are safely seated. The center also should establish a policy requiring the driver to check the interior of the vehicle thoroughly to be sure no child remains on board. This procedure should be in effect every time the driver leaves the vehicle. This procedure is required by law in some states.

6 *Other standards.* In centers serving infants, licensing usually requires detailed plans for diapering, including the surface on which the baby is placed, a plan for disposing of soiled and wet diapers, and hand washing by staff after each diaper change. Additional requirements for storing food, feeding babies, and washing toys also are included.

As you review this section on licensing regulations, it should become clear that, depending on the size, location, and scope of the program for which you are responsible, you could find yourself working with local, state, and federal regulatory agencies. At times, the regulations from the various bodies are not totally compatible, and they even may be contradictory. It is your task to deal with all these regulatory agents so that your program is in compliance. If your program is not in compliance, you run the risk of having a fine imposed or of being unable to take full advantage of available funds and community resources. There also is the risk of having to delay the opening of a new program or having to close down an ongoing program because of failure to meet minimum licensing requirements. In some cases, noncompliance may jeopardize the well-being of children and staff.

The Licensing Process

Directors who are seeking initial licensing should allow plenty of time for the on-site visits and for conferences with inspectors from all the departments involved because the process is lengthy. It is wise to allow *at least* 90 days to complete the initial licensing process. All departments must provide clearance before the license is issued. On rare occasions, programs are permitted to continue operation when they are out of compliance because licensing specialists are trying to help provide sufficient child care in the community; but the regulatory agencies constantly monitor the work being done to bring the program into compliance with the minimum requirements. The burden is on the operator, who must present data to show that the program qualifies for a license or is working toward that goal within a well-defined, limited time line.

Total compliance with all regulations may be very expensive, so it is important to have a clear understanding about the changes that are essential before a program can operate and those that can be made as money becomes available. For example, the fire inspector may not allow children in the building until all required fire extinguishers are purchased, mounted appropriately, and made accessible. The health department might allow a child care program to begin before a separate sink for hand washing is available in the food preparation area, provided that adequate hand-washing facilities are available elsewhere in the building and that there is a double sink in the kitchen. Monies must be budgeted to move toward compliance in areas that require further work. Therefore, the director and any board members who are involved in budget preparation should be well informed about any aspects of the program and the physical environment that might need modification to be in compliance with licensing standards. The time allowed for total compliance with all the licensing regulations will vary greatly and may be negotiable.

In general, the steps involved in the licensing process are as follows:

❶ Request a copy of licensing requirements from the appropriate regulatory agency.

❷ Ensure that the zoning authorities in the area have approved the land use; that is, does zoning allow child care at the site you have chosen? Because child care may be considered a business instead of an educational program or school, neighbors may be reluctant to allow a zone change. Some may be concerned about setting a precedent that would allow additional businesses to locate in that immediate area. Others may be unhappy about increased traffic and noise, as well as about the compatibility of the building with others in the area. Whether or not a zone change is needed, one of the first jobs of the director is to reach out to neighbors and establish the center as a cooperative part of the neighborhood.

❸ Obtain information from the licensing agent about contacting the sanitation inspector, the fire inspector, the building inspector, and the public health office.

❹ Arrange for conferences with, and on-site visits from, representatives of all necessary departments.

❺ When all inspections have been completed and the inspectors have provided evidence of approval, complete the application for the license and send it, with the required fee, to the appropriate licensing agent. You may be required to submit a detailed plan for operating the center, including number of staff, daily schedule, equipment list, and center policies and procedures. You also may have to show copies of forms you will use for gathering required information such as health and emergency data.

❻ On receipt of the license, post it in a conspicuous place in the child care center so that it is visible to families and visitors.

❼ Check the expiration date and establish a procedure to ensure that the renewal process will be set in motion in time to eliminate the possibility of having to interrupt the provision of services to the children or having to pay a fine.

Some states and localities provide a one-stop licensing process. The idea is that a director can contact one person to set the licensing process in motion. Such a plan eliminates most if not all of the frustration directors may feel they have experienced in the past as they tried to coordinate various departments and agencies. The goal of the various inspectors, as well as of the director, is to ensure that the standards are met.

The director, or in special cases a designated member of the board, is responsible for obtaining a license for the child care center. Renewals, although less time consuming for both the director and the licensing agents, must be taken care of on a regular basis. The cost of a state or local license itself is minimal when considered in light of a total budget, but it is an item that must be included in the budget. Although some states do not charge a fee, others charge varying amounts based on the number of children served. Some states have additional fees for special services such as review of a particular building prior to a decision to obtain that building.

The Licensing Specialist

The primary function of the licensing specialist is to ascertain whether a program is in compliance with the licensing regulations and to issue, or recommend issuing, a license to those programs that meet the minimum requirements. When programs do not meet minimum requirements, the function of the licensing specialist is to provide support and suggest resources that will help bring the programs into compliance rather than close them. The specialist's goal is to improve services for children and families. Licensing specialists are being viewed more and more as people who provide services instead of as people who simply issue licenses or close centers.

Knowledge of the community, combined with a thorough knowledge of the licensing regulations, makes the licensing specialist a valuable resource for directors who are seeking training for staff; looking for educational program consultants; and exploring the best and least expensive ways to meet the fire, health, or building regulations. The licensing specialist also may be available as a consultant when a director is petitioning to have an unusual or unrealistic restriction varied or adjusted. In situations in which licensing regulations are inappropriate for children's programs, licensing specialists are available to support community efforts to have the regulations changed. Often, specialists are not in a position to initiate an action to change a very restrictive regulation. However, they may provide support and information to a group of lay or professional people who organize to bring about changes that will allow quality service to children, and at the same time, free the programs from unrealistic restrictions. If you find yourself confronted with a local or state regulation that seems impractical or unworkable, enlist your licensing specialist's help in making contact with other directors who feel as you do about the regulation, and form a task force to investigate the process necessary to have the regulation changed.

In one locality where all staff people were required to hold first aid certificates, center operators and licensing specialists worked together to adjust the requirement and make it more realistic without jeopardizing the health or safety of the children. Having a first aid license is valuable for everyone, whether at the center or elsewhere. However, when a center experiences high rates of staff turnover, paying for training and providing paid time to complete the training can be a major burden. In some cases, centers require staff to meet this requirement during their own time and at their own expense. The key is ensuring that appropriate numbers of staff are prepared and properly certified to administer first aid at the center, while children are being transported, and on field trips.

An unreasonable or outdated requirement may be included in licensing and may need to be changed, but the regulation may remain until some very pragmatic, energetic director comes along who is willing to organize the forces necessary to create change. You may find yourself interested in doing just that with the help of other directors, related agencies, and your licensing specialist.

DIRECTOR'S CORNER

"I spend a lot of time keeping track of paperwork. I know that I have to have all the staff and child medical records as soon as a new child or staff member comes to the center. That's one of the first things I do. I also make a calendar each year that reminds me when to apply to renew our license, to get our fire inspection, and our kitchen inspection."

—Director, private not-for-profit center

You also may find yourself in a situation in which the licensing requirements offer little effective protection of children. In this case, even though your center exceeds minimum standards, it is your responsibility to advocate for appropriate standards. The NAEYC Code of Ethical Conduct (2005a) discusses, in Section IV, our ethical responsibilities to community and society and points out our obligation "to support policies and laws that promote the well-being of children and families" (p. 7). Often, licensing specialists support the need for more appropriate requirements, yet their authority allows them to enforce only the written rules.

The licensing specialist also can help you work through a grievance process if you encounter a unique problem with licensing. For example, one specialist explained a situation in which the fire inspector was holding to the letter of the law by requiring that an expensive, special type of glass be installed in the windows of a building that was not the required 30 feet from an adjacent building. The regulation requiring 30 feet is appropriate and necessary for adequate fire protection, but in this case, the center windows were 28 feet away from an all-brick, fire-resistant building separated from the center by a grassy area. There was no real hazard to the children in this particular center. The licensing specialist provided special help to the director to expedite the grievance process, and the requirement was waived for the center.

In another situation, a new, all-day program was to begin for a one-year period on an experimental basis. The kitchen facility was totally inappropriate for cooking lunches for children who were to stay all day. The director, with the help of the licensing specialist, was able to obtain a temporary permit to operate the experimental program for one year by having the children bring brown-bag lunches. Bag lunches are strictly forbidden in this particular locality under the center licensing regulations, so this particular experimental program could not have been implemented without the understanding support of the licensing specialists. It was agreed that the conditions in the center's food service area would have to meet minimum standards if the program were to be extended beyond the first experimental year and that the bag lunches would have to be appropriately stored each day during that period. The center provided information to parents about appropriate nutritional content of sack lunches.

Licensing specialists are well acquainted with many directors and teachers in the community, so they can serve as a communication bridge between centers by taking ideas and news from one center to another. For example, sharing the news about how a director in a neighboring community solved a budget or staffing problem (without breaking confidentiality) can be very helpful to the director who is dealing with seemingly unsolvable problems and is isolated from contact with colleagues facing similar problems. The specialist can assist directors who are trying to effect budget adjustments or staffing changes but who are meeting resistance from board members or influential community groups. Occasionally, for economic reasons, some board members will pressure the director to overenroll a group to increase revenue. Overenrolling is a risk because there are days when all the enrollees appear and the classroom becomes overcrowded and understaffed. It may be difficult to convince some board members that overcrowding or understaffing for a few days a month can be demoralizing for staff members and disruptive for children. In some states, overenrolling is illegal.

Although some prefer fewer government regulations, keep in mind that the quality of child care would almost certainly diminish rapidly if state regulations were reduced or eliminated. If child care center licensing were not in place, an individual could assume responsibility for large numbers of children. This is an unsafe condition and one that would jeopardize children's health, safety, and development.

ACCREDITATION

While licensing implies meeting minimum standards, accreditation implies performing at a higher level and meeting additional standards. Directors volunteer to have their center reviewed by an accrediting agency, and those programs that are accredited are deemed worthy of the trust and confidence of both the private and professional communities.

The accreditation process varies depending on the organization conducting the evaluation of the early childhood program. However, the process typically includes an extensive self-study of a center's facilities, staff, and programming followed by validation, which may include a site visit, by professional early childhood educators representing the accrediting body. Programs usually must seek renewal of their accreditation after a specified period in order to maintain their status as an accredited center.

Engaging in the accreditation process is productive for the director, staff, parents, and ultimately for the children. The self-study process may be

revealing to the director because it requires reviewing all facets of the center's operation. The process can also provide opportunities for the director and staff to work together in achieving the quality they desire. Groups such as the American Montessori Society, the Association Montessori Internationale, the Child Welfare League of America, the National Association of Child Care Professionals (NACCP), the National Early Childhood Program Accreditation Commission (NECPA), and the YMCA have various programs to ensure that their centers provide good-quality child care. The NACCP and NECPA also accredit centers. The National Association for Family Child Care offers the only national accreditation system for family child care providers (www.nafcc.net). Additional information regarding accreditation organizations can be found on the National Child Care Information and Technical Assistance Center website (http://nccic.acf.hhs.gov/poptopics/national accred.html).

The most far-reaching effort is that of the National Academy for Early Childhood Program Accreditation, a division of NAEYC. One facet of this professional organization's attempt to improve the quality of life for young children and their families is the accreditation system, based on research and criteria developed over several years with input from a wide range of early childhood educators. While many early childhood professionals and parents recognize the benefits of accreditation, individual states are beginning to recognize the value as well. For example, both Maine and Arkansas offer tax credits to families choosing to enroll their children in NAEYC-accredited programs (State and Local Quality Improvement Support, 2010). Additional information about NAEYC accreditation policies and procedures can be found on their website (http://www.naeyc.org/academy/). The NAEYC accreditation criteria can be found in Appendix D.

DIRECTOR'S CORNER

"We were a little bit leery of going for NAEYC accreditation. It was a lot of work, but the staff and parents really got interested. And when we got the letter saying we were accredited, I felt like we'd accomplished something as a team."

—Director, agency center

QUALITY RATING IMPROVEMENT SYSTEMS (QRIS)

Within the past decade, many states have implemented another approach to increasing the quality of early care and education programming known as quality rating improvement systems (QRIS) or quality rating systems (QRS). The Child Care Bureau defines the quality rating system as a "systemic approach to assess, improve, and communicate the level of quality" of early childhood programs (National Child Care Information Center, 2007). While not an accreditation system, the QRIS process provides a research-based framework of best practices that administrators and staff can use to evaluate and enhance programming. Additionally, quality rating systems provide parents with another indicator they can use to select programs for their children.

QRIS include multiple tiers where each level builds on the previous level. Each tier contains specific standards related to items such as staff-child ratios, administrator and staff education and experience, accreditation, benefits for employees, and implementation and assessment of research-based curriculum.

Most states have adopted a recognizable symbol that programs can use to advertise their center as having successfully completed the QRIS evaluation. For example, stars may be awarded to programs that have met criteria related to a specific tier. In Ohio, early childhood programs can earn up to three stars; in North Carolina, those programs that reach the top tier are awarded five stars.

While completion of a QRIS should not be viewed as a substitute for accreditation, the two systems can work hand in hand to help directors and staff provide the most appropriate program possible for young children. In fact, some states provide support to programs seeking and maintaining accreditation and many have included accreditation as part of their quality improvement rating systems as an indicator of quality (McDonald, 2009).

Additional information about QRIS can be found on the National Child Care Information and Technical Assistance Center website (http://nccic.acf.hhs.gov/topics/quality-improvement-systems).

CREDENTIALING

Individuals who work in a profession may be awarded a credential indicating they have demonstrated the capabilities necessary for successful participation in that profession. While licensing is required for an agency to operate a program, credentials are related to the educational preparation of individual staff members. Credentials may or may not be required by licensing, but they are an indication that the individual has had appropriate preparation for the early childhood profession. There are several types of credentials in the field of early childhood education.

Staff Credentialing

State Teacher's Licensure

Licensing or certification of early childhood personnel has been under discussion in many states for a number of years and more and more states are creating prekindergarten or early childhood teaching licenses. Some people refer to the credential as a certificate, meaning a license to practice the profession of teaching, just as doctors, lawyers, real estate agents, or beauticians may obtain a state license to practice their professions. Although the term *certificate* was more widely used in the past, licensing is now considered to be the base. A certificate may be earned from the National Board for Professional Teaching Standards which indicates that the individual exceeds minimal requirements for teaching. This system is parallel to center licensing and center accreditation. The license usually is issued by the state department of education. In some cases, the state provides enabling legislation; that is, the license is available, but the state does not require that everyone who teaches preschool children be licensed. However, all 50 states and the District of Columbia require that public preschool teachers be licensed. There are many different licensure configurations that include birth to 5 years, birth to 8 years, 3 to 5 years, and so forth.

Individual center policies may require that teachers be licensed, but often directors find that they are unable to find licensed teachers willing to work in child care centers at the salaries offered. Directors who require licensure as a qualification for their teachers must be aware that there are many kinds of teaching certificates. Preparation for elementary or secondary teaching licenses, for example, does not include attention to most of the knowledge, skills, and attitudes necessary for those working with younger children. Therefore, these licenses may not be appropriate criteria for early childhood teaching positions.

National Board Certification

Teachers who desire to demonstrate that they are accomplished in their field may apply to become National Board Certified Teachers through a voluntary program organized by the National Board for Professional Teaching Standards. This nonprofit organization is governed by a board primarily composed of classroom teachers.

Eligibility for the certificate requires the applicant to have

- at least three years' experience working with children ages 3 through 8.
- a baccalaureate degree.
- a valid teacher license or certificate in the applicant's state. In states where a license is not required, the candidate must have taught in programs/schools that are approved to operate by the state.

Applicants prepare a portfolio and a videotape and go to one of the many assessment centers around the country. There they respond in writing to prompts about their specialization, early childhood. Like any worthwhile effort, the process is time consuming and is itself a valuable learning experience for teachers. About 4,000 early childhood educators have obtained this credential. In addition to the recognition the certification carries, a number of states have begun programs to provide compensation to board-certified teachers. For more information, check http://www.nbpts.org, the website for the National Board for Professional Teaching Standards.

Child Development Associate Credential

Another type of credential is the Child Development Associate (CDA) credential. The first CDA credentials were conferred in 1975 under the auspices of the CDA Consortium. Bank Street College administered the program until 1985 when the nonprofit Council for Early Childhood Professional Recognition was established. The Council was established by an agreement between the U.S. Department of Health and Human Services, Administration on Children, Youth and Families and NAEYC to administer the CDA program. To date, more than 200,000 credentials have been awarded to caregivers in three categories:

1. center-based infant/toddler or preschool
2. home visitor
3. family child care

A bilingual endorsement for each of the three types of credentials is also available.

This national credential is included as one of the possible qualifications for directors and/or teachers throughout the United States. Candidates for the credential demonstrate their skill in six competency goal areas, including 13 functional areas such as advancing physical and intellectual competence

(physical, cognitive, communication, creative). A combination of experience and training prepares candidates for assessment based on procedures established by the council. Now, more than 35 years since its inception, the credential is still tied closely to Head Start, the program that led to its creation. The CDA is widely recognized by the entire early childhood community as a valuable addition to professional development.

To be eligible for assessment, candidates must

- be 18 years of age or older
- hold a high school diploma or GED
- have 480 hours of experience working with children within the past five years
- have 120 clock hours of formal education within the past five years

Candidates must be prepared to demonstrate their understanding of the following areas:

- safety
- health
- learning environment
- physical development
- cognitive development
- communication
- creative development
- self (emotional development)
- social development
- guidance
- families
- program management
- professionalism

Although there are fees associated with participating in this credentialing process, scholarships are available, and some agencies pay all or part of the fees. Contact the Council for application materials and a list of fees (see Appendix F).

Certified Childcare Professional Credential

The Certified Childcare Professional (CCP) credential is offered by the National Child Care Association, an organization that addresses the needs of licensed, private childhood care and education programs. The credential authenticates teaching skills and professionalism particularly for those who do not have a college degree or who are entering the field from another discipline. Candidates must have a high school diploma or GED, be 18 years of age or older, and have at least 720 clock hours of recent experience working in a licensed program with children from birth to age 6 years. Moreover, an opportunity exists for candidates to obtain college credit for their work. Additional details and application materials can be obtained from the National Child Care Association (http://www.nccanet.org).

U.S. Department of Labor Registered Apprenticeship for Careers in Child Development

The apprenticeship program for careers in child development is offered by many agencies and organizations throughout the United States. This certificate program, sponsored by the U.S. Department of Labor, targets practitioners and requires both on-the-job training with a mentor and classroom instruction. Increased compensation for participants must be provided as they progress successfully through their apprenticeships. Additional information about the program is available from the U.S. Department of Labor, Office of Apprenticeship (http://www.doleta.gov/oa/) or your state's apprenticeship agency (http://www.doleta.gov/oa/stateoffices.cfm).

Director Credentialing

During the past two decades, a movement toward director credentialing has grown significantly. The idea evolved through the work of advocates in the profession, such as Gwen Wheeler at Wheelock College and Paula Jorde Bloom at the McCormick Center for Early Childhood Leadership, who understood the importance of specific training, education, and recognition of center leaders (Directions in Center Director Training, 2011). Director credentials certify "that an individual has met a defined set of requirements set forth by the grantor of the credential, usually related to skills and knowledge, and may include demonstrations of competence" (National Child Care Information Center, n.d.). The body that awards the credential may or may not be the same organization that delivers the training. A credential may be awarded by a professional association, a state agency, a higher education consortium, or other organization and signifies a consensus by those groups of the validity of the standards set forth.

Many states have established director credentials or are in the process of developing credentialing systems. Because this movement is evolving quickly, check with your licensing specialist to determine the status of your state's progress toward the credential. Additionally, current information can be located on the NCCIC website (http://nccic.acf.hhs.gov/poptopics/pd-credentials.html).

Directors who are working toward a credential can review their understanding of child development by observing in the classroom.

Several organizations offer national director credentials or certificates. For example, the National Administrator Credential (NAC), developed by the National Child Care Association, focuses its efforts on the licensed private child care community (www.nccanet.org). An online child care director's certificate can be earned through the Childcare Education Institute (www.cceionline.com).

The McCormick Center for Early Childhood Leadership at National-Louis University offers an online director credential program that requires completion of nine self-paced modules (http://aim4excellence.nl.edu/). This credential is the first in the nation to be recognized by NAEYC as meeting the *relevant training and credentials* criterion for those directors seeking accreditation of their centers.

When seeking a credential or certificate, you must decide which program meets your needs and the requirements in your state. Typically, credentials are offered through states and reflect a more rigorous process of preparation than do certificates. Programs seeking accreditation from NAEYC must be able to demonstrate that teaching staff and administrators meet specific preparation and education guidelines. The organization does not offer a credential or certificate itself; however, it does provide credit for directors who have earned their NAEYC-approved state administrator credential. Administrator credentials are important because they have the potential to increase the knowledge and skill level of administrators, particularly in the business land management roles they must assume. As a result, the quality of centers is likely to improve, and staff turnover under the leadership of a knowledgeable administrator may be reduced. The director makes the decisions that influence child outcomes while helping to create the culture of the center. Components such as staff-to-child ratios, provision of appropriate resources, and selection of well-qualified teachers lead to high quality. Being credentialed creates value for the role of director and encourages individuals to consider this position as a career. Moreover, credentialing can promote both public and private support as the directorship becomes recognized as a valid professional role. Because much of the early childhood education programming being offered today is of poor quality, the need for well-prepared directors is receiving greater attention.

Career Pathways

Credentials are important indicators of one's developing skill and competency and, as a result, are now being included in many states' early childhood Quality Rating Improvement Systems and career pathways, also known as *ladders* or *lattices*. Career pathways provide clearly defined routes by which professionals can enhance their qualifications, recognize professional possibilities that exist in the workforce, and be

compensated appropriately (LeMoine, 2008). Pathways include a variety of experiences such as completion of in-service trainings or college coursework and attainment of degrees, credentials, or certificates.

One example of a state pathway is the Pennsylvania Keys to Quality Career Lattice (http://www.pakeys.org/pages/get.aspx?page=Career_Requirements). This lattice, part of the statewide professional development system, identifies eight educational levels that need to be achieved in order to fulfill a variety of roles in the field of early childhood education such as assistant teacher, lead teacher, or director. The lattice can be used by individuals to plan professional development experiences that will prepare them for the position they desire. Moreover, the pathway is directly linked to Pennsylvania's QRIS, known as Keystone Stars, and director credentialing. For example, at level three of the state's four-tier QRIS, 100 percent of teachers must have reached Level 5 on the career lattice (attainment of an Associate's degree) and directors must have obtained the Pennsylvania Director Credential. For additional information related to early childhood credentialing and career pathways, visit the National Child Care Information and Technical Assistance Center (http://nccic.acf.hhs.gov/pubs/goodstart/pd_section6.html).

SUMMARY

The director of a child care program is responsible for initiating licensing procedures and carrying through with on-site visits from building, fire, and health inspectors. If program adjustments or building changes are necessary to bring a center into compliance with local, state, or federal regulations, the director must take steps to bring about the changes or risk a delayed opening date or denial of a license renewal. The licensing specialist is a good source of information and advice through the initial licensing process, as well as the renewal process.

Accreditation through a reputable organization is an important approach for improving quality in child care centers and for involving staff in the process. Since licensing is designed to ensure that minimal

standards are met, centers that have participated in the accreditation process demonstrate to families that they are interested in exceeding minimum requirements and that they are attempting to provide high-quality care for their children.

Although licensing of child care programs is mandated in most localities, few states require licensure of prekindergarten teachers, a college degree–based credential. Through special training programs and after specific assessment procedures, some caregivers are qualified to receive the Child Development Associate credential. Directors' credentials also are becoming more prevalent—an added indication of professionalism in the early childhood field.

TRY IT OUT!

1 Invite the licensing specialist from your community to come to a class session to discuss all the services provided by the licensing agency. Prior to the licensing specialist's visit, review the local licensing regulations. After the visit, complete

the following activities in class with a small group:
a. Review the licensing regulations and determine which sections of the code would help you do a more effective job as a center director.

b. Evaluate the regulations and determine which sections (if any) should be revised so that more effective service could be delivered to children.

c. Discuss what you consider to be the most challenging part of the licensing process.

2 Divide the class into small groups to consider the pros and cons of licensure for prekindergarten teachers.

a. Can you think of any individuals or groups that provide services for young children who would be opposed to licensure? Discuss why.

b. Does licensure guarantee quality service to young children? Discuss the reasons for your conclusion.

c. What are the best ways to guarantee quality service to children? Report your conclusions and supporting rationale to the class.

3 You are the director of an early childhood program who is considering working toward NAEYC accreditation for your center. Review and discuss the Four Steps of accreditation (http://www.naeyc.org/academy/) with a small group. Draw a timeline of the process that you can present at your next Board of Directors and parent meetings.

4 With a small group, compare and contrast program accreditation, quality rating systems, teacher/

director credentialing, and career pathways. How are they different? How are they related? How does each contribute to the quality of care and education of young children?

5 Review the career pathway/lattice/ladder for your state or one provided by your instructor. Discuss the following questions with a classmate or small group:

a. How many levels are included in the pathway?

b. What requirements must be completed in order to reach each of the levels?

c. How are the individual levels related to specific positions in early childhood?

d. Given your current experience and educational background, in which level would you be placed in the pathway?

e. Consider your long-term professional goals. Identify those criteria you would need to meet or complete in order to achieve your goal.

6 Working with a small group, review the three sets of standards that appear in Appendices B, C, and D. Identify those standards and competencies that relate to licensing, accreditation, and teacher and administrator qualifications. What are early childhood professionals expected to know and be able to do? Discuss your findings with the class.

REFERENCES

American Academy of Pediatrics, American Public Health Association, and National Resource Center for Health and Safety in Child Care and Early Education (2011). *Caring for our children: National health and safety performance standards: Guidelines for out-of-home child care programs* (3rd ed.). Elk Grove Village, IL: American Academy of Pediatrics, Washington, DC: American Public Health Association, and Aurora, CO: National Resource Center for Health and Safety in Child Care and Early Education.

Directions in center director training: Insights of Paula Jorde Bloom, Yasmina Vinci, Donna Rafanello, and Chip Donohue. (2011). *Exchange, 197*, 18–20.

LeMoine, S. (2008). *Workforce designs: A policy blueprint for state early childhood professional development systems.* Washington, DC: NAEYC.

LeMoine, S., Morgan, G., & Azer, S. (2003, Winter). A snapshot of trends in child care licensing regulations. *Child Care Bulletin, 28.* Retrieved from http://nccic.acf.hhs.gov/ccb/issue28.html#1.

McDonald, D. (2009). *Elevating the field: Using NAEYC early childhood program accreditation to support and reach higher quality in early childhood programs.* Washington, DC: NAEYC.

National Association for the Education of Young Children. (2005a). *Code of ethical conduct and statement of commitment.* Washington, DC: Author.

National Association for the Education of Young Children. (2005b). *Leadership & management: A guide to the early childhood program standard and related accreditation criteria.* Washington, DC: Author.

National Association for Regulatory Administration and the National Child Care Information and Technical Assistance Center. (2010). *The 2008 child care licensing study: Final Report.* Retrieved from http://www.naralicensing.org/displaycommon.cfm?an=1&subarticlenbr=205.

National Child Care Information Center. (n.d.). *Early childhood professional development system toolkit-qualifications, credentials and pathways.* Retrieved from http://nccic.acf.hhs.gov/pubs/goodstart/pd_section6. html.

National Child Care Information Center. (2007 Winter/Spring). *Systemic approaches to improving quality of care: QRS gain ground across the nation.* Retrieved from http://nccic.acf.hhs.gov/files/resources/issue32.pdf.

State and local quality improvement support efforts. (2010). *Young Children, 65*(1), 54–56.

4

ORGANIZING CENTER STRUCTURE *and* WORKING WITH A BOARD

© 2010 Cengage Learning

Board committees do much of the board work and report to the total group for final decisions. (Photo by Keith Klenowski)

Objectives

After reading this chapter, you should be able to:

- Describe four types of business organization.
- Explain the advantages and disadvantages of each.
- Identify circumstances under which a business must have a board.
- List the responsibilities of a center's board.

Standard Addressed in this Chapter

naeyc Professional Preparation Standard 6

When a center is being created, the driving force behind the idea may be one person or a group. The role of this person or group is to make some key decisions. Is this center needed? What is the evidence? Will the center be operated for profit or as a not-for-profit organization (sometimes called a nonprofit)? If the center will be for profit, will it be owned by a sole proprietor, partnership, or corporation? The pros and cons of each type of organization must be weighed before making this decision. Organizers must be sure to explore the legal and tax ramifications of each choice.

If the decision to form a corporation has been made, a board of directors must be put in place. Its members are ultimately responsible for the operation of the organization. The board hires the director of the center, who is then responsible to the board to see that the organization's goals are met. Board members of for-profit corporations are paid, often high salaries. However, board members of nonprofit organizations usually serve as volunteers. Nonetheless, they assume the same types of responsibilities. Although some directors may not realize they are governed by a board, if they work for an agency, a franchise, or a school, they are probably board governed.

ORGANIZATION OF THE CENTER

Anyone who is considering a position as director of an early childhood program must determine how the prospective center is organized and for what purpose before accepting a position. The roles of directors vary widely, based in large part on the organizational structure of the early childhood center or the requirements of the owner. In some cases, a director may also be an owner. "The legal structure … will determine how much paperwork you will have to do, how much personal liability you will incur, how you will be able to raise money, and how your business will be taxed" (Pinson & Jinnett, 2003, p. 59). Let's look at the four main organizational structures.

Sole Proprietorship

Individuals who create centers and maintain ownership are sole proprietors. They can make all the decisions, and they bear all the responsibility. They provide the financing, often through bank loans using their own property as collateral. Some individuals may obtain loans from friends or relatives. This type of operation usually is rather small but may later grow, perhaps then becoming a partnership or a corporation. These business owners, also called *entrepreneurs,* establish new companies to fill unmet need (Greene, 2008).

Being the decision maker has benefits but also can be lonely, particularly when a crisis hits. When the center's furnace must be replaced on the coldest day of the year, or the lead teacher leaves and a replacement can't be found, the proprietor may second-guess the organizational decision. When the waiting list is long and a child gives the owner a hug, the decision seems just right. The owner is at risk, however, in the case of a lawsuit, for example, when a child is injured on the playground. All the owner's assets may be in jeopardy. Carrying liability insurance is essential, even for small proprietary programs.

Creating a sole proprietorship is relatively easy once the financial hurdles have been resolved. Papers must be filed with federal, state, and local governments. Usually a form indicating the name of the business is required. Even if Mary Smith decides to open Smith's Child Care Center, she should file the paperwork stating that she is doing business as (d/b/a) Smith's Child Care Center.

When the percentage of center income required for salaries is considered (see Chapter 5) it would seem almost impossible for an individual owner to make a profit. Nonetheless, over the years, many individual centers grow, with the owners gradually opening more and more centers. Soon regional chains are bought up by larger groups. Today, a corporation may oversee thousands of centers, some of which may have been started originally by individual owners.

One type of child care usually provided by a sole proprietor is home-based care. Many of these providers do not consider themselves to be in business, but in fact they are unless they care only for relatives. They are subject to business requirements such as keeping records of attendance, receipts, expenses, and so forth. They may be eligible for the government food program and, in some communities, may receive visitors who provide information about how children learn, activities and supplies, and answers to the provider's questions. In many communities, home care providers are not licensed and there is no oversight. Serious problems have occurred too often. To protect children and those home providers who are providing appropriate care, every state should have home provider licensing in place, just as every state licenses child care centers.

Partnerships

Sharing responsibility and finances is another possibility. One option is to form a partnership, that is, "an association of two or more persons to carry on as co-owners of a business for profit" (Hatten, 2009). For example, two people might be equal partners, or 60-40, or any other combination. This decision usually impacts the amount of decision making and responsibility each assumes and the amount of financial involvement of each. Being a silent partner also is a possibility. That occurs when one contributes financially but is not involved in decision making. When profits are available, they usually are allocated according to the percentage of investment. In case of a lawsuit, each partner is liable on a percentage basis, and personal assets are at risk. The liability issue is based on the way in which the partnership is legally constituted. A formal contract between or among those entering the agreement is signed to delineate their obligations and responsibilities (Hatten, 2009).

Having one or more partners provides additional capital and a relatively stable business life. Partners can both (or all) contribute to decision making and share responsibilities so that each can have at least some free time (Cohen, 2006).

Because setting up a partnership is somewhat more complicated than setting up a sole proprietorship, employing a lawyer is essential. The paperwork must be prepared with care. Furthermore, even the best of friends or relatives may disagree and decide to end the partnership. Or one or more of the partners may decide that this is no longer the business investment desired. In addition, it must be made clear, in writing, what happens to the partnership in the event of the death of a partner.

Franchise

One way to have your own business using a model that has already been standardized is to invest in a franchise. "A franchise is an agreement that binds a franchisor (a parent company of the product, service, or method) with a franchisee (a small business that pays fees and royalties for exclusive rights to local distribution of the product or service" (Hatten, 2009, p. 125). The owner of the franchise sells the rights to use the logo, program, and company reputation to a buyer and may provide free management training. Buying and using the company supplies and equipment is expected. Because the franchisor sells large amounts to franchisees, the cost may be lower to the individual program. In turn, the buyer will probably be required to follow specific policies and procedures and to complete company paperwork. If the center loses money, the company is unlikely to share in the loss (Hatten, 2009; Pinson & Jinnett, 2003).

Parents can expect that each franchise will be the same as others of the same name with which they may be familiar. The franchisor ensures that the franchisee follows company policies and standards. You may be familiar with this model based on some of the fast-food restaurants you patronize. If you like certain foods prepared a certain way, you expect to find the same product at all franchises of that restaurant. Getting a burger that's not the way you like it isn't a major problem. However, getting involved with any major business opportunity requires careful checking in advance.

Corporation

To form a corporation, articles of incorporation must be filed with the state (usually with the secretary of state). Bylaws, also referred to as regulations or a constitution, must be adopted; and a governing body, usually called a board of trustees, must be formed to set policy and assume overall responsibility for the operation of the corporation.

A corporation is a business owned by one or more shareholders. The shareholders elect directors to manage the affairs of the corporation, and the directors, in turn, elect officers to handle the day-to-day business of the corporation. Both federal and state laws regulate registration of stock issued to shareholders. Stock refers to shares or parts of ownership of a corporation. A stockholder provides an amount of money to a company, often through a broker, thereby becoming part owner of the company. In exchange, stockholders experience the possibility of profit or loss in their own accounts.

Large companies have thousands of shareholders whereas a corporate child care center may be owned by a very small number of friends of the center. Some child care centers, however, become major corporations by creating or acquiring a large number of centers under one corporate name. Examples of large corporate child care programs are Knowledge Learning Corporation and Bright Horizons. These organizations serve thousands of children in hundreds of locations. When you go to their websites, you may see that they are encouraging early childhood program owners to consider selling their program to one of the large companies.

Like large corporate groups, federal, state, and local branches of government are taking on a larger share of the early childhood education role. In some cases, a governmental body will provide funding for child care and education programs. In other cases, a business will be chosen or created to run a tax-funded early childhood program. For example, a school board might hire a corporation that manages a number of children's programs. That corporation would provide staff and equipment, usually at the school, and be paid to run child care for preschoolers and for older children before and after school. Increasingly, public schools are offering their own preschool programs, staffing them, and creating the curriculum. Many parents appreciate this, believing it is easier to have preschoolers in the same building as older siblings and feeling that the young child will not have to transition to a new place for kindergarten. The program may be partially or totally funded by tax dollars. One drawback may be that some programs may operate on the typical school schedule, with no provisions for before- and after-school care or for holidays and vacations. In some cases, the program for young children and for after-school care may be primarily academic rather than focusing on the whole child. Infants and toddlers are rarely included in public school programs. An exception occurs when a school creates a program for the very young children of high school students, in large part to help the teens finish their education.

One aspect of the increased direct involvement in preschool education by public schools is the effect on child care businesses. Because the need for infant and toddler care will still be strong, centers may find that the high cost of care for the youngest children may no longer be balanced by the lower cost of care for 3- to 5-year-olds. As you read more about financing programs for young children in a later chapter, this idea will become more clear.

REFLECTION

Do you think you would like to direct a center in a large chain, or would you rather operate a center independently? Have you thought about working in a child care program managed by an agency such as a hospital or faith-based group? What might be some of the pros and cons of each arrangement? Think about the centers with which you are familiar. How are they organized?

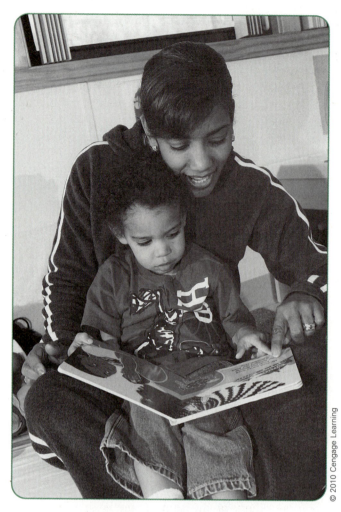

No matter how the center is organized, individual attention to each child is essential.

When a center is to be operated as a corporation, it is a board responsibility to initiate the incorporation process. Because laws vary from state to state, consulting an attorney is essential. The law does not require that child care centers incorporate, but it is desirable.

Although initially setting up a corporation is more complex and more costly than setting up a sole proprietorship or partnership, there are advantages. Corporations may attract funding more easily and may be more stable because they may be less dependent on the involvement of one or a few individuals. Nonetheless, a corporation can be very small and consist of only a few family members.

One advantage that accrues to corporations is the limitation on financial responsibility. Because the liability of the corporation is limited to the assets of the corporation, individuals holding positions in the corporation are generally protected from personal liability for acts or debts of the corporation. A corporation can be sued and lose all of its assets, in effect putting it out of business. However, the personal assets of the director or owners are not included. On the other hand, corporate assets of small child care centers often are obtained by using personal assets as collateral. In that case, individuals' assets are jeopardized.

Profit or Not-for-Profit Corporations

When a center's management plan is to incorporate, the decision to be for profit or not-for-profit must be made. In the case of a not-for-profit corporation, the corporate structure is different. For example, there are no shareholders in a nonprofit corporation.

Instead, there are members who elect trustees to manage the affairs of the corporation. The required number of trustees and officers varies from state to state. Once incorporated, the corporation must function in accordance with the state laws, the articles of incorporation, and the bylaws.

Although it is a common belief that nonprofit entities are organized to provide some sort of charitable, educational, or religious function, the law does not require such a purpose. An organization can provide "almost any kind of good or service on a not-for-profit basis.... Some nonprofits are supported by donations, others depend on income from sales of goods and services, and many receive most or all of their revenues from government" (Herman & Associates, 2005, p. 3). Although nonprofits can receive funds from donors and foundations, only a small percentage of early childhood program funding is from charitable contributions.

Not-for-profit corporation status does not automatically result in tax-exempt status. Based on Internal Revenue Code 501, it is necessary for the corporation to apply to the Internal Revenue Service (IRS) for tax-exempt status and to demonstrate that the organization's purpose is educational or falls under one of the other IRS-exempt categories. A specified Department of the Treasury form must be completed accurately. This form requires a statement of the organization's sources of financial support, fund-raising program, purpose, activities (past, present, and future), relationship to other organizations, and policies (for example, nondiscrimination). This lengthy form also requires a statement of revenue and expenses and a list of governing board members. The process is time consuming and expensive, and may take months and cost thousands of dollars. However, centers that operate on a not-for-profit basis are subject to fewer taxes. For example, with the proper documentation, they usually are exempt from sales tax as well as some federal taxes. Exemption from state and local taxes, including sales tax, is often tied to exemption from federal income tax, but application for exemption must be made to each taxing body.

Because tax law is subject to change, the director and board must keep abreast of new requirements. New directors moving in to existing centers must check to see that the documents are in order and that proper procedures are being followed. Every director must be informed about current tax and reporting requirements of the federal, state, and local governments. Not knowing will not be an excuse.

When donors make contributions to a not-for-profit center, they may be allowed to deduct the amount on their federal income tax subject to applicable tax laws. It is common courtesy to send a written acknowledgement to each contributor, stating the amount of the contribution and any monetary benefit received if any. Furthermore, your letter may enable the contributor to document a tax deduction. In the event that a not-for-profit program ceases operation, its assets must be donated to another not-for-profit organization. Although nonprofits can obtain grants, writing these takes time, effort, and skill. Typically, grants do not cover the capital needed to start a program or cover operating costs.

The profit versus not-for-profit issue is complex. Organizations are advised to consult with attorneys and tax advisers before making this type of decision. When there is a corporate center's board, it will have an important role in this decision making.

DIRECTOR'S CORNER

"I operate a child development center in a low-income neighborhood. Some families aren't eligible for vouchers, so I keep the tuition low enough for them to afford to send their children. It's a problem because the vouchers are worth $170 per child. But since I am charging families without vouchers only $130, the county gives me only $130 per voucher. If I raise tuition to $170, I'll get $170 for each voucher, but some families will have to withdraw their children. I'm losing money, and I'm going to have to make a difficult decision."

—Director, not-for-profit center

THE EARLY CHILDHOOD CENTER BOARD   naeyc

Board membership, board duties, committee structure, and board operations vary, depending on the size and type of center and on the relationship of the center to a sponsoring or funding agency. Despite the inevitable variation in the structure and function of center boards, you will be better equipped to assist in establishing a board or to work with an existing board if you have some basic information about governing boards and how they operate.

The center's director, who is responsible to the board, implements the center's program as mandated by the board. The board's major role is making policy. The director then creates procedures. In practice, board involvement runs the gamut from heavy involvement with the center to deferment of all the work to the director. In the former situation, the board carries out all the functions described in this chapter and then charges the director with full responsibility to act on decisions that the board has reached. In the latter case, the board does not question the rationale or philosophical basis for the recommendations presented by the director for board review and gives carte blanche approval. Ideally, a board should function somewhere between these two extremes by carrying out some functions related to personnel, finance, facility, and program and by keeping in close contact with the director who also is working on fiscal and program matters. Although some proprietary centers operate without the guidance of a governing group, the organizational structure of most agency-sponsored and public-funded programs includes a board of directors.

When the center is an arm of another agency such as a church-sponsored child care program, the agency board may serve as the governing board, sometimes with representation from the center. In other cases, an advisory committee for the center is formed. As the name implies, the role of the advisory committee is much less structured and the committee has less authority than a board. When an early childhood program is part of a public school system, the principal often assumes many of the director's responsibilities and a lead teacher assumes others. The actual board then would be the elected board of education. Because of the great variation among organizations, the center's director may have several administrative levels above her. Primarily, she would report to her immediate supervisor, one level above her position. Decisions may be made at a higher level in some cases.

Board Membership

Most well-planned boards consist of from 10 to 20 members who are either elected or appointed to board positions. A board operates most efficiently when its size is small enough for members to know each other and feel comfortable about speaking out when issues are being discussed, yet large enough for members to cover all the committee assignments that are required to conduct business without overworking any board members. Tenure for board members is specified in the bylaws. Requirements for board membership are based on program philosophy and needs, state laws, and sponsoring agency mandate.

When for-profit corporations involve very large organizations, usually the parent organization manages all the centers by providing regional supervisors (a variety of titles may be used). In this case, since the corporation operates on a major business model and may be traded on a stock exchange, the board also operates commensurate with the rest of the organization. Board members are chosen from a national perspective and usually are paid. Shareholders vote for the board members. Their vote is weighted, based on the number of shares they own. Shareholders are invited to the company's annual meeting, although rarely do small shareholders attend due to lack of knowledge, lack of influence, and inconvenience of travel distance. The boards described in the next sections refer to boards affiliated with individual centers or small groups of centers. A center may also establish a local board when it is part of a very large agency. Such a board usually will not have fiduciary responsibility.

Selection of Board Members

At the outset, boards may be made up entirely of appointed members. After the bylaws are developed and incorporation is accomplished, ensuing boards usually are elected by a regulated process required by law and stated in the bylaws. When a director, a board, or a nominating committee chooses people to be appointed or elected to an early childhood education center's board, the background and personality of the candidates and the current board composition must be considered.

The nominating committee should create a process that will allow it to fill board positions effectively and efficiently. The committee may begin by deciding the types of people who are needed on the board. As the organization's circumstances change, the kinds of board members needed also may change. Although a variety of professionals can be valuable board assets, their expertise should not be exploited. Their perspectives will help guide the board, but when particular professional advice is needed, the board should allocate funds and employ someone not on the board. For example, although it may be advisable to have a physician on the board, that person's role should be one of commitment to the whole program rather than to the health needs only (Bess & Ratekin, 1999). When an organization and a board are small and in a start-up phase, some professionals may be willing to join the board and provide guidance that would not be needed for an established program. They may be serving out of friendship for the director or based on community spirit.

Professionals from the fields of health, education, finance, and law often are asked to serve on child care center boards. These professionals can provide support in decision making in their areas and often volunteer time and expertise to help solve problems. For example, the physician who is a board member may direct the board to accurate information about health practices in the center, or the accountant may help draw up the budget and prepare for an audit. A media specialist or a board member who can write effective proposals and has contacts with various funding sources can be a real asset. A person with knowledge of special education may support the board in its efforts to meet requirements of the Americans with Disabilities Act and may help the center's staff address issues related to inclusion of children with special needs. A computer specialist also may be a valuable asset as a director ponders what types of hardware or software would be best for the center. Some boards reserve a percentage of slots for parents, and a teacher also may be a member, although usually a nonvoting one.

Once the nominating committee has decided on the types of members needed, it may solicit suggestions from existing board members. After creating a master list, the committee begins contacting potential candidates, explaining that it is considering board and committee nominees to determine interest. The committee may send interested persons an information sheet about the organization, including the purpose and philosophy, as well as job descriptions of board and committee members. Each potential candidate may be invited to tour the center. Then, the committee may interview several potential candidates and recommend putting them on the board slate or on a committee until a board opening occurs. No new board member should be surprised when asked to serve on a committee or when asked to contribute and solicit funds for the organization. Board members should be prepared to be active and committed to the organization.

Large agencies usually provide liability coverage for board members, but smaller organizations may be unable to afford this coverage. Nonetheless, board members usually are legally liable for the center's operation. Prospective board members should be informed that they will need to provide their own liability coverage if that is the case. Director liability is controlled by state law. Additional information on this important topic can be obtained from your insurance agent or attorney.

Orienting Board Members

New board members should be expected to participate in an orientation program led by the chair of the nominating committee. Board officers may be asked to participate, both to welcome the new members and to explain their components of the organization. Before this session, each should receive a board book, preferably a loose-leaf binder, containing the following:

- welcome
- board members' names, addresses, and pictures
- mission statement
- bylaws
- strategic plan
- board committees
- minutes from the past year

DIRECTOR'S CORNER

"The board treasurer keeps track of all the tax forms and other reports that are due. Once when we changed treasurers, we forgot to file a particular form and wound up with a big fine even though we hadn't owed any money. The board needed a lawyer on that one!"

—Director, not-for-profit incorporated center

- fiscal statements from past year
- current year budget
- center's information, including philosophy, number of children and ages served, and calendar

At the orientation, new members should learn about the role of the nonprofit agency board and should be alerted to the differences between the roles of board and staff. As a result, new members should be ready for their first meeting with a basic understanding of current and recent issues and decisions. They should enter the meeting knowing a few of the members and should be greeted individually by others. This approach helps new members recognize that they are valued and that the board functions in a businesslike manner with positive interpersonal interactions (Bess & Ratekin, 2000).

Terms for Board Membership

Continuity in board membership is important. Therefore, many boards elect members for a three-year term, allowing for one-third of the members to be new each year. To achieve this ratio, the initial board members draw lots to determine who will hold three-, two-, and one-year terms. This time frame may not be workable for parent members who may not feel comfortable about joining the board until their child has been at the center for a while or who may no longer be interested once their child has left the center.

Although continuity is valuable, stagnation may occur when board members serve for too long. Consequently, bylaws should contain a provision for a limited number of terms of board service. Provision also should be made for replacing members whose attendance is poor. When a board member resigns, an exit interview may provide insight regarding possible changes in board operation. Members who feel overworked or undervalued may choose not to complete a full term.

Board Duties

Board members are required to "act in good faith and in the best interest of the charity, with the same degree of thoughtfulness that a reasonable person would apply to the decision-making process. In traditional legal terms, directors owe the corporation a duty of loyalty and a duty of care" (Silk, 2005, p. 73). Board members must be ready to thoughtfully, yet quickly, adjust the organization's mission and strategies to meet their communities' changing needs and values (Tweeten, 2002). They must also be prepared to find funding that is commensurate with the growing recognition of the importance of providing well-prepared

Board members may be invited when a special activity is planned at the center, and they are always welcome to visit.

© 2010 Cengage Learning

staff. More specifically, the board is responsible for drawing up the bylaws for the center's operation. Subsequently, the board makes policy decisions and provisions for the operation of the center.

Drawing Up Bylaws

Bylaws for operation of the center are written by the board and should contain the following points:

- name and purpose of the organization
- composition of the board of directors, including information about when and by whom its members are elected or appointed officers to be elected, their duties and terms of office, and description of the procedure for elections
- method of replacing a board member or officer when necessary
- frequency of meetings or minimum number of meetings to be held annually
- standing committees and their composition and duties
- relationship of staff to board
- rules governing the conduct of meetings
- provisions for an annual meeting
- procedures for amending the bylaws
- procedures for dissolution of the corporation

Other items may be added to meet the needs of a particular board.

Bylaws should be extensive enough to meet legal requirements and to guide the board. However, when bylaws are too detailed, the board's operation is hampered. Furthermore, changes to bylaws appropriately involve rather detailed procedures that become burdensome if changes must be made frequently. For example, the bylaws should not list the specific month of the annual meeting or the exact number of board members.

Along with the establishment of bylaws, the board works on developing or revising (if needed) the organization's mission statement. The board may also create a vision statement, describing the future to be expected if the mission is carried out according to strategic planning.

Making Policy

After the mission and philosophy have been established, the board sets goals for the program based on

DIRECTOR'S CORNER

"Our staff seemed rather mystified about the board—who they were and what they did. Many board members needed to know more about the center. One of our teachers volunteered to take pictures of the staff and board members and to make a montage of the photos. Afterward, we had an old-fashioned ice cream social, with board members serving the ice cream."

—Director, early childhood center

the philosophy and purpose. If goals have already been established prior to the formation of the board, the board formally adopts them. The board then informs the director and staff about the philosophy and goals that form the basis for establishing the objectives for the daily program. In some cases, a knowledgeable director can take a leadership role in guiding the board's decision making about philosophy and goals that reflect sound theories. In any case, the board establishes policies and the director uses these policies as the basis for formulation of procedures. A *policy* is a course of action that guides future decisions. A *procedure* is a series of steps to be followed, usually in a specific order, to implement policies.

Creation of policies based on the center's philosophy should lead to a cohesive approach to the center's operation. This systemic approach facilitates staff commitment to the overall program because it has been made transparent. Ensuing decisions then will be consistent because they will be based on established policy.

Issues such as required orientation for all new staff should be in policy form, accompanied by procedures such as who will orient staff and what will be included. Regarding personnel, a policy might be, "Written personnel policies will be provided to all employees during their orientation." Procedures for signing in, getting a substitute, or holding parent conferences may be included. Policies regarding board membership and responsibilities should be in place in addition to the statements included in the bylaws. A policy regarding when the bylaws will be reviewed for possible revision should also be included. Since the policies should not be changed without serious consideration, the board should make them general and flexible enough so that the director is able to implement them without disregarding the goals of the center and without being required to request policy changes every time a new circumstance arises. Procedures are more detailed than the policies. Their purpose is to provide an implementation plan that is clear and uniform. Fire drill procedures or procedures for checking out material from the storeroom are good examples. Procedures also may be written for using the building after the children leave, for using equipment in the multipurpose room, or for filling a staff vacancy.

Policy decisions regarding personnel and program are ultimately subject to board approval; in practice, they are often made by the director with official board approval becoming a formality. Occasionally, an involved, knowledgeable board will scrutinize policies presented by a director, often asking for the rationale to support each policy. In some instances, staff and program policies are actually written by board members.

The type of program offered and the population served are both program policies subject to board approval. Decisions about the number and age span of children, the method of selection, and the population served are all board decisions. Examples include decisions about setting up the program schedule to include after-school care or care for children on a part-time basis. Although these policy decisions are usually based on the director's recommendations, the board makes the final determination.

Written policies and procedures are essential, but avoid creating so many that all creativity is eliminated. In fact, in a field such as early childhood education, it is impossible to predict exactly what will happen from day to day.

Operating the Center

The board is responsible for making provisions for the operation of the center. The major decisions in this category are as follows:

1 selecting a director

2 providing for appropriate staff members and for their suitable, in-service training opportunities

3 providing facilities and equipment

4 preparing or approving the budget and overseeing the finances of the center

5 writing proposals and obtaining funding, including setting rates of tuition

6 complying with local, state, and federal laws

7 evaluating the operation of the program and the work of the director and assisting the director in the evaluation of other staff

8 arranging for an annual audit of financial records

9 arbitrating problems between the staff and the director that cannot be resolved by the director

10 replacing the director, as needed, and dismissing the director as the situation warrants

After provisions are made for operating the program, it becomes the director's responsibility to implement the program. At this point, the director becomes accountable to the board for the total program operation.

Board Committees

Board work is usually done by committees. Each standing committee has a charge that is spelled out in the bylaws. When all the standing committees are in place and working, the basic board functions are carried out. As special needs arise, ad hoc board committees are appointed by the board chairperson to perform specific, short-term tasks and report to the board. When the task has been completed, the committee is dissolved.

The board chairperson appoints members to each standing committee based on their interest and expertise and makes an attempt to balance the membership on committees by gender, race, age, point of view, and type of skill. Some boards have special requirements for committee membership. For example, the bylaws may state that each committee must have a parent member or a community representative.

Board committees convene at intervals that correspond to meeting the demands of their workload. When a center is being formed, most committees are extremely active; however, in an ongoing program, some committees have activity peaks. For example, the building committee deals with building maintenance, which is fairly routine. But if a decision is made to remodel, relocate, or build a new facility, the building committee would become very active.

Decisions about the number and types of standing committees needed to carry out the board functions are made when the bylaws are written. Some of the typical standing committees are executive, personnel, finance, building, program, and nominating.

Executive Committee

The executive committee is composed of the board's officers with the center director often serving as an ex-officio member. The executive committee advises the chairperson on actions to be taken, on changes to be made, and on committee assignments. This committee conducts board business between meetings and acts in place of the total board in emergency situations. However, it is critical that the executive committee plan far enough in advance to avoid as

DIRECTOR'S CORNER

"My business partner and I decided to add a second site and to incorporate since our business was growing. At first, the board was just a few relatives. But gradually we realized that we needed people who could really help with the management and oversight of the corporation, particularly when we needed additional investors. Now we have a working board that helps keep us focused on the fact that an early childhood program that is good for children and families must be run as a business."

—Director and president, incorporated for-profit center

many "emergency" situations as possible, lest the way be opened for making important decisions without total board participation. Board members will become disgruntled and fail to contribute time or energy to board business if they find that crucial decisions are being made outside official board meetings. Whenever possible, board decisions should be made by the total board. In some situations, it may be illegal for the executive committee to make decisions.

Personnel Committee

The personnel committee is responsible for hiring a director who will adhere to the philosophy of the center and implement the policies established by the board. To accomplish this task, the committee advertises the position, conducts the interviews, and prepares the director's contract. The personnel committee also is responsible for firing the director if that becomes necessary.

Personnel committee members usually assist the director in writing job descriptions, interviewing job candidates, and discussing the merits of each applicant. After these steps are completed, the hiring recommendations are made to the total board for final approval. Other boards set the basic criteria for staff members and set hiring and terminating employees as the director's responsibility.

In small centers where there is no evaluation committee, personnel committee members may be asked to conduct the evaluation process. In this capacity, the committee determines the method of evaluation, carries out the evaluation of the director, and monitors the director's evaluation of the center staff and program.

Finance Committee

Because they prepare the budget and appropriate the funds, finance committee members must have an understanding of the program's overall operation and the way in which the operation relates to the program philosophy. In situations in which the director prepares the budget and secures the funds, the finance committee approves the budget, monitors the record keeping, and arranges for the annual audit. In some centers, the finance committee sets salary schedules and reviews bids for major purchases. This committee also should teach board members how to read financial statements and what they mean.

Building Committee

The responsibility for finding and maintaining a facility suitable for the type of program being offered

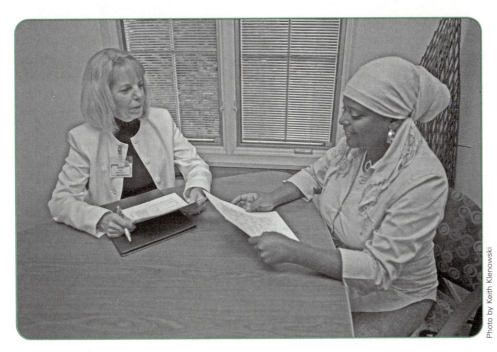

Photo by Keith Kienowski

The director and the board treasurer meet to review the financial report.

rests with the building (or facility) committee. Prior to starting a center or establishing a new facility, the committee spends an extraordinary amount of time making decisions about purchasing, constructing, or leasing a building. The committee is responsible for locating the new facility or the construction site. Building committee members work closely with the architect when the construction or remodeling is in progress and must remember to involve the director who presumably has the most knowledge of what the center needs.

It is the building committee's responsibility to see that the building and grounds are clean, safe, and attractive. Preventive maintenance and emergency repairs also are authorized by this committee. Although directors usually manage the details of applying for a license and arranging for necessary changes at the center to keep the program and facility in compliance with licensing standards, the building committee may be the one designated by the board to monitor licensing.

Many boards also assign the building committee responsibility for the center's equipment. The director must obtain the approval of the committee on major equipment orders, and the committee sanctions orders after considering whether the suggested purchases are suitable, in both type and quantity, and are within the budget. The committee members may also ascertain whether the equipment is properly stored, maintained, and inventoried.

The building committee makes long-range plans by considering questions such as the center's future building needs. It projects the type and amount of space that will be needed and plans for ways to meet those needs. Equipment needs are considered in a similar way. Long-range planning prevents the board from suddenly finding that a major addition or repair is needed when no funds are available. Long-range planning also enables the center to stagger the purchase of equipment so that the quality and quantity are constantly maintained at a high level and so that the budget is not suddenly unbalanced by the need to replace large quantities of worn-out equipment.

Program Committee

The responsibility for all center programs ultimately rests with the program committee; however, in practice, any work on the program is handled completely by the director and the staff. The children's program, the parent program, and the in-service program for staff all may be under the auspices of the program committee. The committee recommends policies to the board focusing on the enrollment and grouping of children; the hours and days of operation; and the offering of ancillary services such as health, nutrition, and social services. Some boards set up separate committees for medical services and social services if these are major components of the center's program. These separate committees are responsible for working with the director to determine what services are needed, where, and at what cost they can be obtained. The committees also may help with transportation arrangements to the medical center if required, and with recruitment of volunteers to assist children and families needing special social or educational services.

Nominating Committee

The nominating committee's function is twofold. Potential members of the board are screened by the committee, which also prepares the slate of board officers for election by the board. The process should be open, and the committee should check with prospective members for permission to nominate them.

A separate committee may be set up for the orientation of new board members, or the nominating committee may serve in this capacity. Continuing the process begun at nomination, the committee ensures that new board members understand their duties and the operating procedures of the board.

Board Communication

From the committee descriptions, it should be obvious that the functions of the committees are interrelated and that communication among committees is essential. For example, the building committee must know what kind of plans the program committee is making in order to provide an appropriate facility. However, the building committee cannot choose a facility without an understanding of how much the finance committee plans to allocate for physical space. To avoid duplication of efforts, each committee's task must be delineated clearly. Sometimes, a board member may be assigned to two closely related committees to facilitate communication between them. Care must be taken to divide the work of the board equitably among its members and to see that every board member is involved in and aware of the operations of the board and of the center.

The board shares responsibility with the director for maintaining open communication within the board itself and maintaining open communication among the board, the sponsoring agency, the staff, and the families who use the center's services. The most successful boards are those whose members communicate effectively with the center's director and with each other. Both the board and the director have responsibilities here, and it may be worthwhile to provide training in interpersonal communication for all concerned. If staff and board members both attend the training sessions, communication skills are improved, staff and board members become better acquainted with each other's values, and the outcome is a greater sense of community among those people who are responsible for the center's operation. An obvious place to start is to make sure that new board members are introduced and that continuing board members also introduce themselves. Perhaps taking new board members on a tour of

the facility and introducing them to the staff also could be planned. When board members and staff members have developed effective communication skills, all will be expected to use the skills. Ideas will be expressed and considered openly; likewise, disagreements will be stated specifically and objectively. Board and staff members lacking these skills may be less willing to address problems directly, with the result that disagreements may not be resolved and factions may develop within the organization.

As with all good communication, that between the board and the staff is two-way. The board informs the director of policies that have been formulated because the director is responsible for seeing that the policies are executed. The board also explains the reasons for its decisions and approaches any necessary changes in a positive way instead of in a dictatorial manner. The director, in turn, communicates to the board any difficulties the staff is having with the existing policies or suggests policy changes, providing reasons for these changes. For example, if the director finds that there are a number of parents asking for a program for their 2-year-olds, the suggestion is presented to the board and is supported with arguments for and/or against the admission of 2-year-olds. Facts concerning the type of services that could be provided, the facilities available, the cost of such a program, and the advisability from an educational standpoint also should be presented to the board. Considering the data and the recommendation of the director, the board makes the final decision about the admission of 2-year-olds.

It is the responsibility of the board to use the director's recommendations and all other pertinent data in formulating policy. Policy decisions must be based on sound data so that they are fiscally responsible, developmentally and educationally sound, and legal. They must also follow good business practice and be realistic. For example, a policy requiring the director to be on duty whenever the center is open may seem sound but will be unrealistic in practice in a child care center that operates for ten hours a day. Similarly, a board policy requiring the director to hire only well-qualified teachers with ECE bachelor's degrees would make the hiring task nearly impossible if available salaries are held at or near the minimum-wage level. Since the director is mandated to carry out board policy, the board ideally gives careful consideration to her recommendations to ensure that final policy is mutually agreeable and feasible.

The board serves as the communications liaison between the center's program and the sponsoring agency. The director keeps the board informed about the center's functioning by sending the board members copies of newsletters, special bulletins, and meeting notices; by reporting at board meetings; and by presenting a written report to the board at least annually. Board members may be invited when a special activity is planned at the center, and they are always welcome to visit. The board, in turn, communicates to the sponsoring agency by reporting regularly to the agency board. This type of communication is two-way in that the board also receives information from the sponsoring agency concerning the expectations of the sponsoring group. For example, a community group may provide partial funding for the center with the stipulation that it be used to provide training for a staff member or parent program, or a church sponsor may expect preferential admissions for members' families. As long as these stipulations and expectations are compatible with the center's philosophy and are legal, they should be fulfilled.

Board Operation

When a new center is starting up, the board must meet frequently—even daily—during very busy planning periods. However, in ensuing years, boards may meet monthly, quarterly, or in some cases annually. When the board is working closely with the director and is intimately involved in policy-making, monthly meetings are essential. On the other hand, the board that assigns most of the decision making to the director may meet only annually to receive the director's report; approve the budget for the ensuing year; and make any adjustments in goals, policies, or procedures that seem necessary.

Notice how unrewarding service on such a board might be.

The board that meets frequently contributes to the operation of the center by working closely with the director and by utilizing fully the skills of all board members. The board that meets less frequently provides the director with maximum freedom to operate on day-to-day matters, although within definite guidelines. Each board must decide which alternative seems to be more appropriate for the type of center being planned, and the director is chosen to fit into the selected method of operation.

Although each board has its own style, board meetings must be conducted according to recognized parliamentary procedures that may be covered in the bylaws. In large, formal organizations, a parliamentarian who is appointed or elected ensures that business meetings are conducted according to the procedures adopted. Although too much formality may be uncomfortable for some board members, total informality leads to loose practices, with disputes arising over decisions that are based on improper voting procedures or other points of order.

The board of an incorporated center is obligated by law to conduct its business in an organized manner and to keep accurate records of all transactions. In situations in which record keeping is not required by law, it is just sensible business practice to operate an agency in an orderly manner. Therefore, minutes of all board meetings, committee reports, and financial records must be kept. Copies of contracts and agreements, job descriptions, and correspondence also should be in the files.

REFLECTION

Consider how you might work most effectively as a director. Would you prefer a board that left the decision making to you and expected an annual report about what you had done? Or would you prefer a situation in which you had to check back with people in authority on a regular basis to get the benefit of their thinking, after which you would follow their lead as you continued your work? You may be able to relate this idea to college classes in which you operated independently and received feedback from your instructor only on the final exam, compared with classes in which you regularly submitted written work throughout the course and subsequently received information from your instructor about your work. It would be wise to give careful consideration to your own needs and administrative style before accepting a directorship.

SUMMARY

Key decisions to be made when new centers are planned include structure (sole proprietorship, partnership, or corporation) and the profit or not-for-profit consideration. A board of directors must be formed as the governing body of an early childhood education center that is incorporated. When members are chosen carefully in terms of the contribution they are capable of and willing to make, the director can receive excellent guidance from them. A well-organized board operates with a group of committees whose functions relate to the major components of the center's operation. Records of ongoing operations keep information about the functioning of the board open to everyone involved, and good communication between the board and the director produces a well-run organization. The board creates policies and the director implements those policies, but it is the ultimate responsibility of the board to see that its plans are brought to fruition.

TRY IT OUT!

1 Find out how many people are on the board of directors of your college or local public school district.

   a. How did they become board members?
   b. What are their duties?
   c. How often do they meet?
   d. Describe a recent decision made by the board.

   If possible, talk with a board member or attend a board meeting. Write your findings on Working Paper 4-1.

2 Arrange to talk to the director of an early childhood education center and ask whether there is a board of trustees.

   a. How are members chosen?
   b. How long is a member's term?
   c. What are the duties of board members?
   d. How often does the board meet?
   e. Are minutes of each meeting kept?
   f. What is the relationship of the director and the board?
   g. Is the director a voting member of the board?
   h. If the center does not have a board, who carries out the responsibilities that would have been met by the board?

   Report your findings on Working Paper 4-2.

3 Obtain a copy of the bylaws of an organization with which you are associated or of any type of community agency. (Consider your YMCA, your church group, PTA, and so forth.) Compare the bylaws of the group you select with the bylaws provided by another student.

   a. How are they similar in structure?
   b. What are the substantive differences?
   c. How do the differences in the documents reflect the differences in the purposes of the organizations?

   Write your answers on Working Paper 4-3.

4 Locate the forms you would need to incorporate a center. You may choose to write to the secretary of state in your state, check the Internet, or use library resources. Your instructor may assign each class member a different state. You may create your own information as you complete the forms, or you may base your responses on a center with which you are familiar.

 The Education CourseMate website for this text offers many helpful resources. Go to CengageBrain.com to access the TeachSource Video Cases and other TeachSource Videos, Expand Your Learning exercises, flashcards, interactive quizzes, the eBook, reflection and enrichment activities, and downloadable forms.

Working Paper 4-1

BOARD MEMBERS FORM

How many people are on the board of directors of your college or local public school district?

How did they become board members?

What are their duties?

How often do they meet?

Describe a recent decision made by the board.

Working Paper 4-2

BOARD OF TRUSTEES FORM

Is there a board of trustees for this center?

How are members chosen?

How long is a member's term?

What are the duties of board members?

How often does the board meet?

Are minutes of each meeting kept?

What is the relationship of the director and the board?

Is the director a voting member of the board?

If the center does not have a board, who carries out the responsibilities that would have been met by the board?

Working Paper 4-3

BYLAWS FORM

1. For which organization did you obtain bylaws?

2. Compare the bylaws you obtained with those provided by another student.

How are they similar in structure?

What are the substantive differences?

How do the differences in the documents reflect the differences in the purposes of the organizations?

Director's Resource 4-1

CHARITABLE LAW SECTION
GUIDE FOR BOARD MEMBERS
FIDUCIARY DUTIES OF TRUSTEES AND DIRECTORS OF CHARITABLE ORGANIZATIONS ATTORNEY GENERAL
STATE OF OHIO
A publication of the state of Ohio
TRUSTEE/DIRECTOR: THEY ARE NOT HONORARY TITLES

Charities depend greatly on volunteers for their governance. Volunteers donate their time for a variety of reasons: Some are interested in the charity's programs, while others may feel that the position brings them some level of prestige. Most often, the motivation is a sense of civic duty and the satisfaction that comes from making a contribution to the community.

Charities often seek prominent members of the community to serve on their boards, perhaps because of that individual's business and management reputation. This could also be a means of honoring that individual and boosting the image and credibility of the charity by having well-known names listed among its trustees. Whatever the motivation of the individual or the charity, joining a board of trustees is a decision not to be taken lightly.

Prospective board members should investigate what such a commitment will entail, and understand the role, function, and responsibilities of a charity's governing body. This guide is intended to assist in that endeavor.

THE LEGAL DUTIES
Trustees and directors of a charitable organization, whether or not the organization is formally incorporated as a nonprofit corporation, have specific legal duties owed to the organization. The primary duties are:
   The duty of care.
   The duty of loyalty.
   The duty to maintain accounts.
   The duty of compliance.

THE DUTY OF CARE
The duty of care requires that a trustee be active in the charity's affairs by attending board meetings and meetings of committees on which the trustee serves. A board member must

You can download a full-size version of these forms on the Education CourseMate website.

Director's Resource 4-1 *(continued)*

keep himself or herself informed to determine if the policies established by the board are being followed and should understand how the charity is functioning.

This duty must be discharged diligently and in good faith. Board members must act with knowledge and after adequate deliberation. They should carefully establish organizational policy and regularly oversee its administration by a competent staff.

Board members who are regularly absent from meetings, are inactive, or who fail to conduct adequate research prior to making decisions are not fulfilling their duties of care. Board members should conduct themselves with the level of care, skill, and diligence exercised by prudent persons in the handling of their own affairs. Generally, a board member who knows the facts, analyzes the probable result of an action, exercises sound judgment, and keeps reasonable records acts prudently and fulfills his or her duty of care. Some ways you can meet your duty of care include:

- Understand the charity's mission by familiarizing yourself with the charity's articles of incorporation, constitution, bylaws, or other governing documents.
- Attend board and committee meetings and be prepared for those meetings by reading and reviewing reports, minutes, and other materials distributed for the meeting.
- Be prepared to ask questions and obtain the information needed for you to make informed decisions in approving and disapproving proposals. Included in your responsibilities is the oversight and review of the performance of the charity's executive director or chief executive officer. You should exercise your independent judgment and not merely acquiesce to the staff's requests.

THE DUTY OF LOYALTY

Many problems can be avoided if board members keep the duty of loyalty foremost in their thoughts. The duty of loyalty requires that the interest of the charity, and, as a consequence, the interest of the public, take precedence over the board member's personal interests. A trustee must, loyally and without self-interest, further the charitable objectives of the organization by acting fairly and in the best interest of the charity.

Trustees may breach the duty of loyalty when they engage, directly or indirectly, in transactions between themselves as trustees and themselves as individuals. They may also violate this duty by being involved in transactions with family members or businesses in which they hold an interest. Board members should not engage in any transaction that is

Director's Resource 4-1 *(continued)*

adverse to the charity, engage in any competing enterprise to the detriment of the charity, divert an organizational opportunity for personal gain, or derive any kind of secret profit or other advantage in dealing with or on behalf of the charity. Caution should be exercised in entering into any business relationship between the organization and a board member. This should be avoided entirely unless the board determines that the transaction is clearly in the charity's best interest. Ways to avoid trouble:

- Ensure that the interest of the charity is always first.
- Establish a written policy for dealing with conflict of interest situations, which should include procedures for written disclosures from board members concerning business dealings with the charity or those seeking to do business with the charity.
- Disclose your financial interest whenever the charity proposes to enter into a business relationship with you, a member of your family, or a business in which you hold an interest. Don't vote on the transaction or participate in any debate or decision on the merits of the transaction.
- Don't divert an opportunity available to the charity for your own gain.
- Avoid transactions involving potential conflicts of interest, appearance of impropriety, and self-dealing situations.

THE DUTY TO MANAGE ACCOUNTS

Board members are responsible for assuring the financial accountability of the charity. Procedures should be established to keep the organization fiscally sound and ensure that it operates in a fiscally responsible manner. Care must be taken for the proper use of any restricted funds. Trustees should oversee the executive director and determine that the charity's purposes are fulfilled without waste. Preparation of a budget is important for providing clear directions for spending and translating program and management goals of the board into financial projections.

The organization should be able to demonstrate the wise use of its funds. Accurate records of all income, expenditures, transactions, and activities must be maintained. Accurate minutes of board meetings should be taken in order to demonstrate board approval of certain expenditures and investments and to show that informed decisions were made with regard to these transactions.

Director's Resource 4-1 *(continued)*

- Keep accurate records of income, investments, expenditures, and transactions, and accurate minutes of board meetings.
- Develop annual budgets that provide clear direction for spending at all levels of activities.
- The budget should be a blueprint of the board's program plans.
- Establish appropriate internal accounting systems, including a system of checks and balances. No one person should retain total control over finances.
- Prudently invest and reinvest assets.
- Assist the organization in acquiring resources for its programs. Develop fund-raising goals and policies. Make certain that fundraising appeals are presented honestly and fairly, and monitor the performance of fund-raising professionals.
- Shop around for the best values in goods and services through comparisons and informed bidding processes. This process should also be applied to contracts entered into with fund-raising professionals.

THE DUTY OF COMPLIANCE

Board members have a duty to be faithful to the organization's purposes and comply with the charity's governing documents. They are also under a duty to be familiar with the laws that apply to the charity and to comply with those state and federal laws that relate to the charity and its business operations.

- Be familiar with and follow the provisions of the charity's articles of incorporation, constitution, bylaws, or other governing documents.
- Familiarize yourself with state and federal laws relating to nonprofit entities, fund-raising, and tax-related issues.
- Comply with state and federal registration and reporting requirements, which may include filings with the Ohio Attorney General, the Ohio Secretary of State, and the Internal Revenue Service.

KEEPING THE BOARD VIGOROUS

To ensure the continuing vitality of the charity and its awareness and responsiveness to community needs, board members should look for ways to continue to breathe new life into the board. Choose board members who have an interest in the charity's mission and

Director's Resource 4-1

represent diverse viewpoints. Actively recruit individuals whose skills and commitment will enhance the charity. Consider term limits and rotation off the board to other assignments as a means of avoiding stagnation, tunnel vision, and the perception that the board is merely an insider's club.

CONSEQUENCES

There can be severe consequences to trustees for breaches of fiduciary duty. Trustees can be held individually responsible to charities for breaches of fiduciary standards. For example, if charitable assets are sold at less than their fair market value, trustees may be held accountable for any shortfalls.

IS IT WORTH IT?

Serving the community and its needs is a worthy act of stewardship. However, a board member who feels that his or her position as trustee is merely honorary is in for a shock. Service on a charity's board requires your acceptance of responsibility for the funds donors have contributed. Donors are placing their trust in you; the public that benefits from the charity's services is depending on you; and regulators are watching you.

These responsibilities need not deter any prospective board member. You need only to be active and involved, use sound judgment, act responsibly and in fairness to the charity, and always have the charity's best interests foremost in all actions. For board members who take their responsibilities seriously, the rewards of voluntary service are immeasurable.

Source: http://www.ohioattorneygeneral.gov

 You can download a full-size version of this form on the Education CourseMate website.

REFERENCES

Bess, G. & Ratekin, C. (1999, May). Recruiting effective board members. *Child Care Information Exchange, 127,* 14–20.

Bess, G. & Ratekin, C. (2000, November). Orienting and evaluating your board of directors. *Child Care Information Exchange, 136,* 82–87.

Cohen, W. A. (2006). *The entrepreneur & small business problem solver* (3rd ed.). Hoboken, NJ: Wiley.

Greene, C. L. (2008). *Entrepreneurship: Ideas in action* (5th ed.). Mason, OH:. South-Western Cengage Learning.

Hatten, T. S. (2009). *Small business management: Entrepreneurship and beyond (*4th ed.). Mason, OH: South-Western Cengage Learning.

Herman, R. D. & Associates. (2005). *The Jossey-Bass handbook of nonprofit leadership & management* (2nd ed.). San Francisco: Jossey-Bass, a Wiley Imprint.

Pinson, L. & Jinnett, J. (2003). *Steps to small business start-up: Everything you need to know to turn your idea into a successful business* (5th ed.). Chicago: Dearborn Trade Publishing.

Silk, T. (2005). The legal framework of the nonprofit sector in the United States. In R. Herman & Associates (Eds.), *The Jossey-Bass handbook of nonprofit leadership & management* (2nd ed., pp. 63–80). San Francisco: Jossey-Bass, a Wiley Imprint.

Tweeten, B. L. (2002). *Transformational boards: A practical guide to engaging your board and embracing change.* San Francisco: Jossey-Bass.

5

Handling FINANCIAL MATTERS

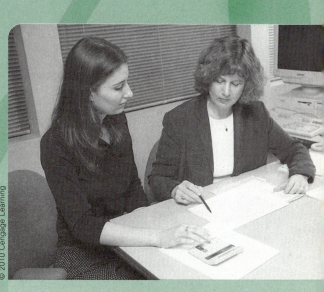

© 2010 Cengage Learning

The director must be involved in financial decision making, even when the board or a financial manager is responsible.

Objectives

After reading this chapter, you should be able to:

- Explain general policies and procedures related to documenting fiscal transactions.
- Describe how and why a budget is created.
- Explain how an approved budget is used.
- List other financial documents and explain why they are needed.

Standard Addressed in this Chapter

naeyc Professional Preparation
Standard 6

The director's role as one who sets the tone for the center has already been established, but the director also must be a pragmatist capable of dealing with all the financial obligations of running a center. As part of the center's overall system, a financial plan must be in place. The two major components of the financial plan are developing a system for managing financial resources and obtaining adequate funding. The latter is discussed in Chapter 6.

Managing financial resources includes creating policies and procedures relative to

- developing and following a plan for using funds
- keeping records, including those mandated by law
- providing required documentation

Every center needs both a long-range financial plan and a plan for the upcoming year. Poor financial planning and management lead to constant lack of funds and continuously hinder personnel as they work to achieve program goals. Although many aspects of a good early childhood education program cannot be purchased at any price, high-quality care for young children is expensive, and funds must be allocated properly to provide a developmentally sound program on which children and parents can depend. No matter how good the intentions of the staff, a program cannot continue to operate for long without a balanced budget and a reserve fund. Therefore, before publicity is in place, before staff are hired, and before detailed plans are made, the board must be sure that sufficient funds for start-up are available, keeping in mind that start-up may continue for many months. (See Chapter 6.)

CREATING A FINANCIAL PLAN

In a new center or one that is reorganizing, a decision must be made regarding who will be responsible for the center's financial management. In a sole proprietorship or partnership, the owner/director may assume these duties. When the owner has hired a director, he may turn the responsibilities over to the director, while requiring regular reporting. In a corporation, the board is responsible. A corporate system may have a regional or national fiscal officer for all of the system's centers. Franchisees manage their own budget within company constraints. For example, fees may be set by the parent company. No matter what the center's organizational structure is, someone must ultimately be responsible for fiscal management. Throughout this chapter, therefore, we will use *director* to include others who may bear responsibility. We will also assume the center could have a fiscal officer. When that is not the case, the director may have to assume all fiscal duties.

Usually, the director has some responsibility for creating an annual budget and for managing it. If a board is involved, the members bear ultimate responsibility. When a center has multiple sites, a financial officer may be part of the staff. This person would be expected to keep day-to-day records, produce financial reports, and consult regularly with the director.

Policies and Procedures

The policies and procedures manual must include a section on fiscal management. Although not all policies and procedures are reviewed annually, reviewing those related to finances helps everyone involved check to ensure that these requisites are being met. Following are some of the policies that must be in place:

- All financial transactions must be checked for accuracy.
- Standard accounting practices will be followed.
- The director will prepare a long-range fiscal plan.
- The annual operating budget will be prepared prior to the start of the fiscal year.
- The budget will be used as a guide throughout the year.

- Every financial transaction must be recorded in a specific location.
- Transactions must be recorded at least weekly, preferably daily.
- A business checking account must be used for all transactions.
- Personal funds and business funds must never be mingled, even if the owner is the director.
- All receipts must be deposited rather than used to pay bills.
- All payroll checks must be available to each employee on the expected date.
- All taxes must be paid by the required date.
- A budget variance report will be prepared at least quarterly.
- Money will be handled by two people, one to receive and record the funds and the second to deposit the funds and record the deposits.
- Amounts, due dates, and payment methods for tuition, as well as consequences of delinquent tuition, must be provided to parents.
- An income and expense statement and a balance sheet must be prepared annually.
- Reports to funders and requests for release of funds will be made on the required schedule.

This list is more detailed than most policy lists. Specific procedures for each of these policies must be written and placed in the policies and procedures manual, available for review by all staff. Spelling out financial requirements in detail can help avoid problems in the future. However, it would be inappropriate for the director to spell out in such detail exactly what each teacher was to do on a daily basis in the classroom.

The director works with staff to prepare policies that are clear and workable. He may spend part of a staff meeting discussing this topic, ask staff to submit suggestions, or prepare the policies and procedures with the fiscal officer and make them available for staff information. Having the entire staff spend time writing fiscal policies would be a poor use of their time. Encouraging them to provide input lets them know that their perspectives are valued and should be taken seriously by both director and staff.

REFLECTION

You have just read a long list of items that must be carried out by the business manager or director. Make a list of the items that are unfamiliar to you. Check the item off as soon as you learn about it. If you cannot find an explanation, ask your professor to provide more information on the topic. Directors must understand the center's finances. Imagine how much easier it will be to learn now rather than when you are a director in the midst of working on many documents.

Establishing a Fiscal Calendar

Because there are so many fiscal tasks and because each of them is important, the director and fiscal officer create a calendar of due dates. Working backward, they schedule dates for reviews of drafts of the proposed budget. Reviews of items such as the budget will be of interest to most staff, so time should be allowed for their input. Preparation of items, such as submission of withheld taxes to government offices, can be done by the fiscal officer as a routine matter but should appear on the calendar.

If your fiscal year begins January 1, the budget for the coming year should be under way in October. The board will be able to review preliminary numbers based on those from the current year, yet modified based on plans for the coming year. For example, a proposed staff raise would be included. By November, with recommendations for changes made, the budget should be resubmitted to the board, it is hoped, for final approval. Since the fiscal records should be closed as of December 31, it is important that the new budget is ready for January 1.

Managing Payroll

A number of dates must be scheduled for payroll items. It is essential that staff receive paychecks on time. But preparing them is complex, even with advanced computer software. Each staff member's name, ID number, address, wage or salary (hourly, weekly, biweekly, or monthly), and local taxing district must be entered into the computer. The fiscal officer must contact federal, state, and local agencies to determine withholding rates, current minimum wage, overtime laws, Family and Medical Leave Act requirements, and any other laws that may affect payroll.

The employer must obtain a federal taxpayer identification number from the IRS because, before an employee is paid, the employer must make appropriate deductions from the amount earned. When submitting these deductions and the company's equal contribution, the company ID and the employee's ID are listed.

The fiscal officer is responsible for withholding from each person's pay the appropriate amount of money for various taxes as well as Social Security and other federal, state, and local payments that are required. The employer pays an amount equal to the percentage withheld from the employee's pay for Social Security and Medicare. The employer must also pay unemployment compensation and workers' compensation. These programs cover payments to the employee for job-related injuries, diseases, and disabilities that occur as a result of working conditions. These amounts must be put aside so they are available for submission to the respective governments on specified dates each quarter. The center may be charged interest and penalties if these payments are not timely or are for incorrect amounts.

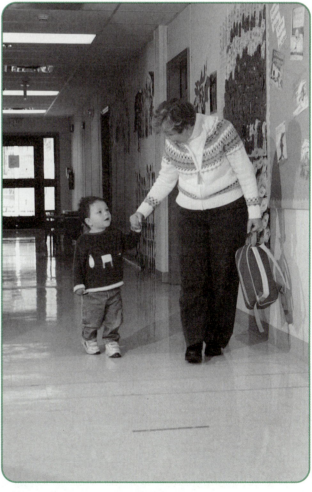

© 2010 Cengage Learning

Despite the need to attend to business matters, directors recognize that the center exists to support children's development.

Your accountant can help you determine the taxes for which you are liable.

Health benefits or partial cost of health insurance may be offered to employees. Retirement plans are also an option in some companies, although many young employees may not be convinced of the benefit of such a plan. Other factors that may influence salaries are public school affiliation, union memberships, and salary standards of the sponsoring agency.

Whenever new employees are hired, the fiscal officer must obtain IRS form W-4 indicating the number of dependents they are claiming. Calculations for the amount of tax to be withheld are made on this basis. Each year, all employees may submit new forms if changes need to be made to the number of dependents. By January 31 annually, a statement of earnings and deductions must be provided to each employee who worked at the center during the year, even if they are no longer employed there.

When all the categories affecting pay are entered into payroll software, the deductions can be readily made. Nonetheless, because preparing the payroll accurately is challenging and time consuming, quite a few centers hire a payroll company to take care of this aspect of their business. Still, the information must be collected and entered by the fiscal officer or by the contracting payroll company. The director is responsible for seeing that these requirements are fulfilled.

REFLECTION

Think about the tuition paid by parents, particularly in regard to its relationship to the salaries paid by a center. Consider a situation in which a teacher's annual salary is $27,000 and the assistant teacher's annual salary is $18,000. With a total of $45,000 a year for salaries, 15 families would each pay $3,000 a year to cover these salaries alone. Unless the center has other sources of income, tuition costs also must cover costs of equipment, supplies, food, facilities, utilities, benefits, taxes, administration, and so forth. The last child will leave the center from 10 to 12 hours after the first child has arrived, so staff members will have to be present on a staggered schedule and additional help will be needed, all of which will increase salary costs. What would tuition have to be to produce a profit for the program sponsors? Think about how much you will probably earn as a teacher in a child care center. If you were to earn minimum wage as a child care center teacher, working eight hours a day, five days a week for a year, what would your total salary be? If you were a parent earning minimum wage, how much could you afford to pay for child care?

Center directors must ensure that they comply with the Fair Labor Standards Act (FLSA). A number of complex issues and conflicting results of court cases make it difficult to determine who is considered a teacher for the purposes of FLSA. This determination can make a difference in whether an employer is required to provide overtime pay and pay for hours spent in in-service training and parent meetings "after hours."

U.S. Department of Labor regulations that went into effect in 2004 consider exempt from FLSA those staff members who are paid a regular salary of at least $23,660 annually, no matter how many hours they work. Their work must relate directly to the management or general business operations of the organization in order to be exempt. For more details, go to www.dol.gov. Keep in mind that professional advice is still important, especially when addressing complex legal matters.

Another major personnel policy relates to hours worked. Will staff be paid for break time, planning time, and required meeting time? Be sure to check labor laws before making this and other policies. Because many child care centers are open for ten or more hours, no teacher is in a classroom for the entire program day. Therefore, many part-time staff members are employed. Will they have paid time to meet with the lead teacher? Will the center provide for an overlap in the schedules of the departing teacher and the arriving teacher so that the children's day is not disrupted?

Planning Reports

Throughout the year, the director and others will need to know how close the center is to meeting budgetary projections. Is your enrollment on target? Is tuition being paid in a timely manner? Do you have enough cash on hand to meet payroll? Then, when the year is over, how did you fare? Was it a good year financially?

Reports that will help you determine the answers to these questions include a cash flow report, which can be prepared monthly; a variance report (monthly, quarterly, or annually); and an end-of-the-year balance sheet. Any of these reports that a center uses can be prescheduled on the annual calendar. We discuss their contents later in this chapter.

PREPARING A BUDGET

A major task of the director or finance committee is the preparation of a budget. A budget is a plan or financial forecast usually set up for a period of one year. One section of the budget contains a list of income categories and dollar amounts; the other section shows a list of categories and dollar amounts for expenditures. The director's goal is to balance income and expenses, and in most cases, to show a profit. Recall that in a for-profit center, the profit may be distributed to shareholders or used for the center. In a nonprofit or not-for-profit center, the profit stays with the center and can be used to build financial reserves or reduce tuition or can be spent on the center in some other way.

Types of Budgets

Budgets are classified in several ways. They may be based on the stage of development of the center, or they may be categorized according to the stage to which the budget itself has been carried. The creation of a new center demands one kind of budget while the ongoing operation of a center requires a budget of a different type.

The director prepares a budget by

- estimating the cost of the program (based in part on the center's goals)
- determining how much income will be available (see Chapter 6)
- seeking more income to equal expenditures, adjusting expenditures to equal income, or doing both

Start-up Budgets

The creation of a new center presents a crucial opportunity for the financial aplomb of the director. When a center is being created, the director prepares *two* budgets: the start-up budget and the operating budget. As discussed in Chapter 6, the *start-up budget* consists of all the expenses incurred in starting the center. These expenses include initial building expenses (down payment on the purchase of the building, the cost of building renovations, or rent deposit), the purchase of major equipment, the cost of publicizing the center, the director's salary for several months prior to the children's arrival, the deposit on telephone service, and the utility charges during the start-up period. Salaries for any additional personnel needed to assist the director of a large center also must be provided. Total start-up costs vary widely. When these costs are incurred, the usual sources of revenue ordinarily have not become available. In these cases, a special grant may be needed or the organizers of the center may arrange for a loan or invest their own funds. When a loan is obtained, the cost of the interest must be recognized as a very real budgetary item.

Occasionally, suppliers will permit purchasers to defer payment for 90 days and the center can schedule purchases so that the first tuition is received before the 90-day period ends. However, the first receipts certainly will not cover all the expenses. If receipts are due from agency or government funds, those first payments usually are made after the services have been provided. In the meantime, suppliers may charge interest on unpaid bills. Therefore, it is important to obtain as much assurance as possible that funds for start-up will be available when needed. Searching for "GSA Child Care Center Startup" on the Web will provide you with a wealth of information, although specific costs are not provided.

Geographic area, projected size of the center, ages of children to be served, in-kind support (such as free or reduced-price space offered by a church), and amount of money to be borrowed all factor into start-up costs for new centers. Therefore, it is difficult to project the cost of a specific center. The Small Business Administration (SBA) recommends that those interested in starting a center create a business plan. Using this approach, prospective owners can determine whether their plan is realistic in terms of potential resources (loans and so forth) and potential success. More information about start-up is available in Chapter 6 and online at www.sba.gov.

Operating Budget

The *operating budget* consists of an income and expense plan for one year and is used when centers enroll children and begin the program, and annually thereafter. The center may operate on a calendar year (from January 1 to December 31) or on a fiscal year, a 12-month period chosen for ease of relating financial matters to other operations of the center. Centers funded by agencies that operate on a fiscal year running from July 1 to June 30 find it easier to work on the same schedule as the funding agency, but many early childhood education centers choose September 1 to August 31 for their fiscal year because those dates relate closely to the start of their school year. Once a center has selected its fiscal year, no change should be made without serious reason. Planning one year's budget from January 1 to December 31 and then changing to a September to August fiscal year in the following year causes confusion and may need to be justified for tax purposes.

Estimating Costs

The financial director's first task is to figure program cost. The task requires an overall understanding of the early childhood education program and its goals and objectives. It also requires reviews of the child care industry spending patterns nationally and locally.

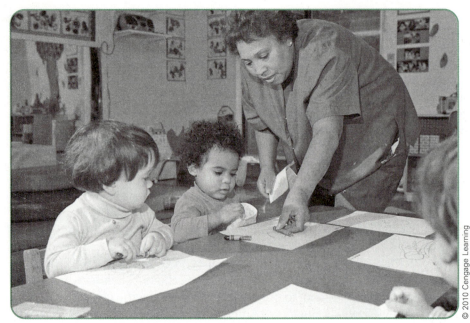

© 2010 Cengage Learning

In planning a budget, directors must be aware of the day-to-day needs of everyone in the center.

At the local level, the director determines what is needed for children in the particular community and program, then analyzes the cost of meeting these needs. These data will be essential in preparing a realistic budget. If other people are preparing the budget, the director works with them in interpreting program needs. Priorities should be established on the basis of the program goals, while the cost and the availability of funds determine the scope of the program. For example, a center may select improving salaries as a primary goal. If new playground equipment is also desirable, the decision about providing equipment in addition to improving salaries will be made based on the availability of funds, as well as on which is the greater need. If the planned primary goal is related to salaries, the center staff may work together to create workable playground enhancements until the desired equipment can be purchased. Nonetheless, in many cases, additional funding will be needed. The director must take a leadership role in implementing a plan for obtaining funding.

Another question that has an impact on both program and finances is: What is the population to be served? For example, does the program serve children from infancy through preschool age and does it provide after-school care? If so, the director will have to recognize that costs for infant programs are considerably higher than costs for preschoolers, based largely on the staff-to-child ratio infants need.

School-age children need fewer adults, and they are usually at the center fewer hours. Consequently, their care is less expensive.

Other questions include: How many teachers will be needed and for what hours? Will it be necessary to have aides? A cook? A janitor? A secretary? A bus driver? Answers to these and dozens of additional questions should be available from the people who are responsible for designing the program and will come primarily from the director. By using this method, the director keeps the goals and philosophy of the center paramount.

Some directors have difficulty with the initial phase of budgeting. Instead of starting with the goals and objectives, they start with the dollars available and attempt to determine what can be done with them. Such a center is truly ruled by the budget (or by the finance director), and maintaining an educationally and financially sound program under these conditions is extremely difficult.

Although program and financial decisions in a corporate system may be made at the national or regional level, the director of each center is responsible for implementing these decisions. The national or regional financial officer provides information about how much money is budgeted for each category; each local director then orders equipment and supplies through the main or regional office and is responsible for generating the required tuition. Some franchisees create their own budget, including fees paid for the right to use the franchised name and logo in the community.

Determining the dollar amount of a budget is a major part of the overall financial plan. This figure is arrived at by listing the items needed to operate the program for a year in categories such as salaries, rent, and equipment. Next, the budget director determines how much each of these categories will cost with as much accuracy as possible. The sum of the costs for each category is the amount of income needed for a year. A sample budget in Director's Resource 5-1 provides an idea of the costs of each category and of the costs of the total program for a hypothetical center. This sample budget is not meant to be utilized in the form presented here but may be used as a guide to budget preparation. In your area, costs may be much higher or lower. More important, the philosophy and goals on which you base your planning may differ widely from those used in this sample. Center directors, and other professional groups and organizations in each community, may provide helpful local information. Companies, such as gas and electric companies, kitchen equipment suppliers, toy suppliers, and business associations, can furnish more specific and relevant cost information for individual centers.

Following are factors that influence the total amount spent by a center and the ways in which that amount is allocated:

* number, ages, and special needs of children enrolled
* teacher-to-child ratio
* staff training
* type and location of building
* amount of equipment already owned or available
* type of program and services provided
* section of the country in which the center is located
* general economic conditions
* amount and type of in-kind contributions
* special considerations, such as free rent

The sum of the costs for each category is the cost of running the center for one year. Dividing this figure by the number of children to be served establishes the cost per child, a figure that can be further examined on a monthly, weekly, daily, or hourly basis. The cost of various program components, such as infant or school-age programs, can be figured this way also. (See description of the break-even point in Chapter 6.)

It is important to consider whether the center is a nonprofit organization or whether one of the goals is to make a profit. This question is sometimes hotly debated among early childhood educators, many of whom feel that early childhood education centers should not be operated for profit because someone then makes money at the expense of the children. Admittedly, early childhood education costs are high and it is difficult to make a profit. Nonetheless, if a person or group can provide a good program, meeting the needs of both children and staff while showing a profit, there is no reason to discourage such a financial plan. It is the director's responsibility to ensure that children are not shortchanged in the interest of making a profit. Nor should teachers receive inadequate pay and benefits. This ethical issue may become even more challenging if the director's salary is tied to the amount of profit.

Adjusting Budget Figures

While it is relatively easy to change the budget figures on paper, the budget must remain balanced. Expenses must not exceed income. Chronic budgetary problems will drain staff energy from the daily operation and will remain unless the center can actually pare costs to the level of income earned. When one budget category amount is increased, obviously another budget category must be decreased.

Each expense must be analyzed with an eye toward its relative importance to the overall program. Can the equipment budget be lowered by substituting some free or inexpensive materials? Can food costs be lowered by cooperative buying? Can the consumable supply budget be reduced without a major effect on program quality? What effect will a particular cut have on the quality of the children's program? How will the cut affect the staff?

At the same time, both new and current funding sources can be approached with clear documentation of the need in relation to goals because expenses must not exceed income. If professional early childhood educators take the approach that it is better to have a poor program than none at all, the problem of adequately funding child care will never be solved. When a center's financial management is poor, the director may continue operating past this point without becoming aware that the inevitable outcome will

DIRECTOR'S CORNER

"Our needs assessment indicated that more than 100 children would use our center. Two major corporations in the neighborhood worked with us, and many of their employees expressed interest in enrolling their children. We were shocked when we spent the whole first year with only nine children enrolled. Luckily, we had strong financial backing, and we have now reached capacity enrollment."

—Director, private not-for-profit center

The director understands that all children need a wide variety of books from which to choose and provides adequate funds to maintain the center's collection.

be a poor-quality program or bankruptcy. If the year begins with a deficit budget (that is, expected expenses exceed expected income), it is highly unlikely that the year will end with a balanced budget. For that reason, deficit budgets should not be approved.

Analyzing Budget Categories

Even when a board fiscal officer assumes major responsibility for preparing the budget, the director is still responsible for understanding and articulating what is needed to operate the program successfully. Many board members have limited knowledge of the actual cost of child care. The director must help them develop this understanding.

Some centers budget by function rather than simply by category; that is, administrative costs and the costs of each aspect of the program are budgeted separately. For example, if 20 percent of the director's time is spent working directly with the children and 80 percent is spent on administration, then 20 percent of the director's salary would be allocated to the children's program salaries category and 80 percent would fall under administration. A complex center may provide and budget several separate functions such as infant program, preschool program, and after-school program. This budgeting method clearly delineates the actual cost of the children's program. And when coupled with a description of the services offered, it provides a mechanism for comparing costs with other programs and for including the value of the services provided in relation to the costs incurred. This method also provides information used in determining tuition (see Working Paper 6-5). However, ever-changing tax laws make it essential for even small centers to have the services of an accountant to guide the director in setting up fiscal systems and to provide information about new governmental requirements. An attorney

also may be needed to help ensure that the center is operating within legal limits. The cost of these services must be included in the budget.

Although requirements at each center vary widely, new directors may be given a general idea of costs if they consider the following rough estimates:

- 70 percent personnel
- 10 percent facility, utilities
- 5 percent equipment
- 3 percent supplies
- 3 percent food
- 9 percent other categories

Attempting to design a budget to fit these percentages would be inappropriate since these figures are provided as general guides.

The following budget categories will provide a rough idea of the costs of early childhood education and the formats used for presenting a budget.

Salaries

In any early childhood education budget, the major component is salaries. A center can expect to spend 70 percent and even up to 80 percent of its operating costs for personnel. This figure includes salaries and wages for full- and part-time staff members (such as director, teachers, cooks, janitor) and for substitutes. It also includes fringe benefits for the full-time staff. In determining the budget for salaries, the personnel policies should be consulted in regard to pay rates and fringe benefits. The salary policies may address issues such as staff members' education level, previous experience, or meritorious service. The director also must comply with the minimum wage laws, tax laws, and laws regarding employer responsibility.

Salaries are considered in budgeting as a cost of doing business. Of course, to the employee, salaries represent livelihood. Employees expect and are entitled to fair pay for the amount and type of work they do. Their job category is usually determined by the preparation and experience they bring to the role. By now, you are well aware that salaries in the demanding field of early childhood education are relatively low. Parents are paying higher and higher tuition. Why, then, aren't staff salaries higher?

The Center for the Child Care Workforce (www.ccw.org) corroborates the salary conundrum. It and many others recognize how low the salaries or pay scales are in relation to the important type of work being done in early childhood centers. This site offers reports and data on the relationships among salary, quality of staff, and quality of program for young children.

The Bureau of Labor Statistics of the U.S. Department of Labor regularly reports wages by occupation. Salaries of preschool teachers and child care workers are separated for analysis and reported by mean (average) and annual dollar amounts. See Table 5-1.

While not all preschool teachers have degrees, the wage assumption is that preschool teachers are more qualified than child care workers. The Bureau of

TABLE 5-1 Comparison of wages by job title, May 2007

Job Title	Hourly Wage	Annual Wage
Preschool Teacher	$14.04	$29,200
Child Day Care Services	$12.27	$25,530
Elementary School Teacher		$52,660

Source: Bureau of Labor Statistics, May 2010, http://www.bls.gov.

Labor Statistics lists teachers, beginning with kindergarten teachers, by annual salary rather than by hourly wage. Kindergarten teachers were listed as earning a mean salary of $51,550. Mean annual salary for preschool teachers was listed as $29,200. The preschool figures appear to be based on a work schedule of 40 hours per week at 52 weeks per year. Since hourly rates are not provided for kindergarten teachers, one can assume that the annual salary is for the school year rather than for 52 weeks at 40 hours each. If preschool teachers, based on this report, worked from September to June, their salaries would be less than the annual $25,800 mean salary (U.S. Department of Labor, Occupational Employment and Wages, May 2010).

An important additional consideration is benefits. Few centers offer fully paid health care to teachers, and few of these cover dependents.

You probably quickly noticed the large disparity between public school teachers, preschool, and child care staff. Consider that in a public school, one teacher is responsible for 25 children for 6 or 7 hours a day. (Most public school teachers also work before or after school and on weekends, planning and preparing for their work.) In child care programs, many more staff are needed for each class of fewer children. When staff work 8 hours a day for 5 days a week, the director still has many "staff hours" to fill. Because many centers are open 10 or more hours a day, many staff are employed on a part-time basis. In the following section, you will learn how directors determine how many staff they need.

Keep in mind that these figures group all teachers in a given category. For example, you may know a beginning public school teacher who is making much less than the $52,660. In that same district, a teacher who has taught for 30 years would be earning much more than $52,660 per year. Also, all the figures mentioned in this section were based on national averages. However, salaries vary widely from state to state and from program to program.

Staffing and Full-Time Equivalents   naeyc

As discussed previously, approximately 70 percent of your operating budget will be spent on staff salaries and benefits. But how does an administrator determine the number of teachers that will be needed and the salaries that can be provided? One strategy you might employ involves computing the full-time equivalents (FTEs) or number of full-time employees that will be needed to meet teacher-child ratios. The following is an example of how you could approach this aspect of the budgeting process.

TABLE 5-2 Overview of center staffing needs

	No. of Children in Each Classroom	Caregiver-Child Ratios	No. of Caregivers Required to Meet Ratio	No. of Caregiver Hours Required Each Day (12-hour day)	No. of Caregiver Hours Required Each Week (5 days per week)	No. of Caregiver Hours Each Year (52 weeks per year)
Infants	6	1:3	2	24	120	6,240
Infants	6	1:3	2	24	120	6,240
Infants	6	1:3	2	24	120	6,240
Toddlers	8	1:4	2	24	120	6,240
Toddlers	8	1:4	2	24	120	6,240
Toddlers	8	1:4	2	24	120	6,240
Toddlers	8	1:4	2	24	120	6,240
Preschoolers	18	1:9	2	24	120	6,240
Preschoolers	18	1:9	2	24	120	6,240
Preschoolers	18	1:9	2	24	120	6,240
Preschoolers	18	1:9	2	24	120	6,240
Preschoolers	18	1:9	2	24	120	6,240
TOTAL	140		24	288	1,440	74,880

Source: Thanks to Dr. Ellen Lynch for contributing this activity and chart.

Assume you are the director of a child care center that serves 140 children, 12 hours a day, five days a week. Your program has an annual operating budget of $1 million. Based on the 70 percent figure, we can presume you will budget approximately $700,000 for salaries and benefits ($1 million × 70%). Let's also assume that your state's teacher-child ratio and group size licensing requirements are less stringent than those found in the NAEYC standards. As a center that will be applying for accreditation, let's assume you have decided to try to meet, and in some cases exceed, the more rigorous guidelines provided by NAEYC.

CAUTION

You may love working with numbers and immediately want to explain Table 5-2 to everyone else—or you may give up as soon as you see so many numbers in one place. In either case, proceed slowly so that you will gradually be able to plan staffing for one classroom, and eventually move to a much more complex setting. Every director must understand this, even if he or she hires someone else to handle it. Showing it to parents, funders, and elected officials should help them appreciate that early childhood centers have complex financial needs.

Table 5-2 presents an overview of your center's staffing needs. You have planned for three groups of infants, four groups of toddlers, and five groups of preschoolers. Based on the caregiver-child ratios you have adopted, *each classroom* will require 24 "caregiver hours" each day (2 teachers × 12-hour day, which equals 24 hours per day). Each classroom will need 120 hours each week (24 teacher-hours per day × 5 days per week). Note that this does *not* mean that teachers work a 12-hour day. This number reflects the number of hours that must be covered by a staff person.

We know that there are 12 classrooms.

Each room needs the equivalent of two teachers for 12 hours a day or 120 hours a week.

12 hours × 5 days × 2 teachers = 120 hours

120 hours a week × 52 weeks a year = 6,240 teacher-hours per room

6,240 teacher-hours per room × 12 classrooms = 74,880 teacher-hours per year

We can see that the total number of caregiver hours required in your center each year is 74,880. If all teachers are full-time employees, then we can assume that they will work a total of 2,080 hours per year.

40 hours per week × 52 weeks = 2,080 hours per year

Therefore, your center would require a total of 36 FTEs.

(FTE = full-time equivalents)

74,880 caregiver hours ÷ 2,080 hours per year = 36 FTEs

That is, to maintain your caregiver-child ratios, you would need to hire the *equivalent* of 36 full-time teachers.

Let's assume you are hiring child care workers at a mean hourly wage of $9.46. Therefore, a full-time teacher would have an annual salary of $19,677 (2,080 hours × $9.46 per hour), and your annual budget for teaching staff would need to be $708,372 ($19,677 × 36 FTEs). Based on your original figure of $700,000 for salaries, it appears that you will not be able to cover your staffing needs. However, you must also consider that fringe benefits, which may add approximately 25 percent onto the salaries, were not budgeted. Moreover, you must consider that this example does not account for administrator and support staff salaries or variations in wages based on the staff member's position (e.g., lead teacher, classroom assistant, aide) or teacher experience.

If, instead of thinking about child care workers' salaries, you wanted to provide *at least* the national average preschool teacher pay of $12.47 per hour, what would your classroom staff cost be? As the program's director, it becomes your responsibility to balance the budget while addressing the needs of your staff and the children and families you serve.

Table 5-2 can be modified to meet your needs. It can be used when you have some full-time and some part-time children. You may not need two teachers in each classroom for the first and the last hour of each day, depending on how many children arrive and leave during those hours, but you must always have a minimum of two staff available at all times.

With this guideline, you can get a starting point in deliberations about the salary requirements for your center. However, you will still need to make your own chart showing each teacher by name, assuming that each teacher's salary is based on qualifications, years of experience at your center, merit, and other potential salary criteria included in your policies and procedures manual. You will also need to make a chart for each room showing what time each staff member arrives and leaves and when they are on break or have planning time. These charts will ensure that you have the desired number of staff in each classroom at all times. Your focus should be on maintaining consistency for the children and avoiding having too many different caregivers in one room over a one week period.

Consultants

A second component of a center budget that is closely related to salaries is contract services or consultant fees. This category covers payments to people who agree to perform specified services for the center or its clients. Most centers have an accountant and an attorney available for consultation on a retainer or an hourly rate. Other possible consultants might be doctors, dentists, social workers, real estate agents, psychologists, nutritionists, and educational consultants. These types of professionals could be employees of a large center or system. However, they usually serve as consultants by agreeing, for example, to give dental examinations to all children enrolled in the center or to provide workshops for teachers one day a month. When the center's staff is not well trained, or when a broad range of services is provided for children, many consultants are needed. Although some centers do not hire consultants and most will hire only a limited number, the overall quality of the program may be increased by the services they provide.

When consultants come from out of town, their transportation, meals, and lodging may be additional costs. Sometimes, consultants are paid a per diem rate to cover meals and lodging. The current per diem rate of the federal government might be used in budgeting. Both the center and the consultant should agree in writing on all financial arrangements and performance expectations in advance of any services rendered. Under no circumstances should the director attempt to classify a staff position as a consultancy to avoid paying taxes and benefits. Serious legal ramifications may be the result.

Plant and Equipment

The largest cost in the physical plant category is rental, lease, or mortgage payments on the facility. The costs for the maintenance of, and the repairs to, the building and grounds also are part of this budget component. When maintenance work is done on a regular basis, the costs usually will be lower in the long run. However, because it is impossible to predict all maintenance and repair needs in advance, a lump sum for this purpose should be allocated each year. A preliminary assessment of the main components of a building (foundation, roof, plumbing, wiring, heating and cooling system, termite damage, and so forth) will provide a rough idea of when major repairs may be expected. Periodic assessments must also be scheduled.

Also included in the physical plant category in the operating budget are utilities (heat, electricity, and water). In some cases, one or more of the utility charges may be covered in the lease, a point that should be fully understood and in writing before an agreement to lease is made. Some centers also may have to pay for garbage removal. When utilities are not included in the lease, an approximate budget figure can be obtained by checking with previous tenants or with the utility companies.

In budgeting for a new center, equipment for the children, the office, and the kitchen is a major part of the start-up budget. For a continuing center, the operating budget includes supplementary pieces, as well as repair and replacement where needed. Leasing and rental charges for equipment are included here. For example, a center may rent a carpet cleaner for a day or two, or lease a copy machine for a year. The continuing equipment budget will be about 10 percent of the start-up equipment budget, so if the start-up equipment budget is $1,000 per child, the continuing equipment budget would be $100 per child per year.

REFLECTION

Think about purchasing a new car. As soon as you drive it away from the dealer's showroom, it becomes a used car and is worth less than you paid for it. Every year, therefore, it is worth less, partly because it is being used and gradually wearing out and partly because newer models with different features are being produced. At some point, it may be worth a lot more to you than to anyone else. You may continue to drive it. But if the cost of repairs becomes very high, you will probably decide that it would be more economical to get a different vehicle.

Think about the building and equipment needed for a center. They too are depreciating.

Depreciation

One of the costs of doing business that may be overlooked is depreciation of major equipment. When a center purchases major playground equipment or furniture such as tables, chairs, and shelves, it would appear that the center had added that amount of dollar value to its assets. However, once an item is purchased and put into use, its value begins to drop or depreciate. Let us assume that the children's furniture will last 15 years, whereas the computer and copy machine will have to be replaced in five years. Dividing the initial cost of the item by the anticipated length of its useful life yields the annual depreciation amount. A $2,000 computer divided by five years results in depreciation of

TABLE 5-3 Five-year depreciation of a $2,000 computer

Year	Worth =	New Value
1	$2,000–$400*	$1,600
2	$1,600–$400*	$1,200
3	$1,200–$400*	$800
4	$800–$400*	$400
5	$400–$400*	$0

*$2,000/5 years = $400 depreciation per year.
Source: © Cengage Learning, 2013.

$400 a year. That is, the computer is worth $400 less each year. Table 5-3 depicts the annual value of the computer. Although the computer may still be functioning adequately, it now has little or no value. When you consider the assets of your child care business, this computer is no longer an asset even though you may continue to use it.

In listing assets, the annual amount of depreciation is deducted so that the value of the equipment is more realistic than if the full cost were listed. At the same time, wise directors build an equipment replacement fund so that when eight infant cribs must be replaced, the center is prepared for that expense.

Supplies

Three types of supplies must be purchased: office and general supplies, classroom supplies, and food supplies. The first category—office and general supplies—includes items such as pencils, stationery, toilet paper, paper towels, cleansers, and brooms. Construction paper, paint, crayons, pet food, and doll clothes are included in classroom supplies. Food supplies encompass all items available for human consumption. Usually, two meals and two snacks per child per day are served in full-day centers, with one snack offered in a half-day program. In any case, sufficient food should be provided so that teachers can eat with the children. Food costs vary depending on the availability of federal food subsidies and on factors in the economy. A nutritionist engaged as a consultant can aid the director in setting up a nutritionally and financially sound food plan. (See Chapter 13 for a discussion of nutrition and the United States Department of Agriculture [USDA].)

Transportation

This category may include the purchase or lease of several buses for transporting children to and from school and on field trips. In such cases, insurance,

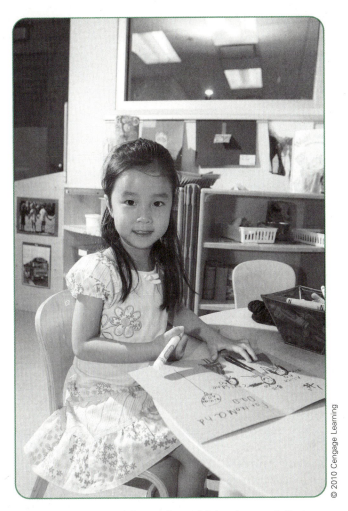

© 2010 Cengage Learning

Supplying art materials to allow children's creativity to develop requires careful budgeting.

gas, maintenance, and license fees must be budgeted. Some centers contract with a company to provide transportation for children, and others may rent a bus for special occasions. Vehicles must be equipped with child safety seats or seat belts, depending on the size and age of the child, and other governmental regulations regarding vehicles must be followed. Based on a ruling by the National Highway Traffic Safety Administration, buses rather than vans are to be used. They must comply with both federal and state laws. Your state may require that you transport children in vehicles meeting special school bus regulations and that drivers have special licenses. The many financial, safety, and liability issues involved frequently lead centers to require parents to provide the child's transportation to and from school.

Costs for staff members to travel to professional meetings, other centers for observation, and homes for home visits are included in the transportation category. The mileage rate for automobile travel reimbursement is usually based on the current federal government mileage rate.

Communication

Telephone costs can be determined by checking with the telephone company. In deciding on the number of telephones to order, consider the center's staffing pattern. For example, if a classroom staffed by one adult is located on another floor away from other classrooms, an extension or cell phone is needed to allow that teacher to get help when necessary. When a teacher is outside or on a field trip, even though at least one other adult is present, it is a good idea to provide a cell phone. In an emergency, the teacher can get help. Licensing requirements in some states specify where a telephone is required. In any case, enough lines should be provided to enable parents and other callers to reach the center without undue delays. Call waiting, often less costly than a second line, improves accessibility for outside callers but can be annoying to some. Although many people now use cell phones, some centers require that they be turned off in the center.

Getting emergency messages through immediately is a priority. Providing staffers with access to a telephone for personal calls during breaks is a benefit that recognizes their needs and helps them feel they are respected members of the organization. In fact, it is a requirement in at least one state.

Many centers rely heavily on email for much of their within-agency communication, as well as contact with families, colleagues, vendors, home offices, and others. The director and other staff also will use various websites for gathering information, contacting legislators in their roles as advocates, and marketing the center. The monthly charge for this access is included under the communication category.

Having a presence on sites such as Facebook and Twitter is a great PR tool for some centers, while others have a policy of not participating and requiring staff to agree that they will not discuss the center online. Such policies must be carefully written.

REFLECTION

Many centers have, or are discussing, rules related to use of social networking online in relation to the center. What are the pros and cons of these regulations? What policies would you suggest that directors create relative to social networking?

Staff Training and Development

Even when a center is fortunate enough to have a staff of well-prepared teachers and assistants whose education was in the early childhood field, continuous in-service programs will be needed. Recognizing that learning is lifelong and that research continues to provide new information about children's development, both directors and staff members need opportunities to participate in conferences, classes, and visits to other programs. When the staff is underprepared, the director must begin their in-service program immediately. State licensing regulations may require a particular number of hours of training annually, usually a minimal level. It is the director's responsibility to determine what is needed and to facilitate the acquisition of that training or education. Some centers provide partial scholarships for classes and may reimburse the staff member on successful completion of a course. Providing current professional journals and books in the staff lounge or supply room will support teachers' growth and development.

Insurance

Insurance agents can quote rates and provide information about appropriate kinds of insurance. A center usually needs at least fire, theft, and liability insurance. If the center provides transportation or owns vehicles, various types of insurance are required. A child accident policy is valuable and relatively inexpensive. If the center has a board of directors, directors and officers insurance is important. Be sure to read each policy carefully and ask questions about any items you do not understand. Find out whether your legal expenses would be covered if, for example, you were sued by a family who claimed you were negligent. What are realistic deductibles for your situation? What exclusions, if any, are written in your policy ("Does Your Insurance Coverage Fit," 2002)?

Postage

Postage covers the cost of mailings to parents, prospective client families, and past and prospective donors. The cost of shipping and other business mailing is included. In some cases, fax or email may be appropriate and less costly, but in all cases, a record of important communication should be maintained.

Billings, especially notices of overdue accounts, usually are mailed. Many families prefer to receive and pay bills online. Some centers establish the policy that payment is due on a particular date each month and no bills are sent. Postage costs can be held down to some extent if information is distributed by sending notes home with the children, but keep in mind that these items may not always reach the parent. If you have a flexible software package, you should be able to accommodate each family's preferences.

Marketing

Marketing includes newspaper and telephone book advertisements, brochures and fliers, and radio or television announcements. Some agencies design a logo and use it on products such as T-shirts, stationery, business cards, and beverage mugs. Also included are promotional items such as open house events, announcements of staff activities (for example, names of teachers who recently attended a national conference), and information about a speaker coming for staff development. In fact, any opportunity to highlight the center without, of course, compromising the privacy of children, families, and staff can be considered *marketing*. (See Chapter 16.)

Licensing

Information about licensing costs can be obtained from the licensing agent; these costs will vary according to the center's location. Other professional fees, such as those for NAEYC accreditation, also belong in this category. (See Chapter 3.)

Audit

Yearly audits are essential. They assure the board and funders that the center's financial matters are being handled properly. You should ask your accountant for a cost estimate and build that into the budget.

Miscellaneous/Other

This category includes funds for small items that do not fall under any of those previously mentioned. However, attributing expenditures to a particular category provides a more accurate picture of the center's financial status and eliminates slippage in expenditures. For example, if postage and advertising were both included under miscellaneous, postage expenditures could skyrocket and not be recognized as a budgetary problem.

In-Kind Contributions

Some budget items are not received in cash and not paid for in cash. These are called *in-kind contributions* and should be shown in the budget so that the true cost of operating the center is known. For example, a center may rent two 600-square-foot rooms in a church building for $200 per month per room. The church may charge the center $4,000 for a ten-month program. If the fair rental cost is at the rate of $10 per square foot (a total of $12,000), then the church is, in effect, contributing $8,000 to the center program. Note that the reverse is also true. Some church schools provide income for their church.

Consultants may volunteer their services, and such services also should be shown as in-kind contributions. For example, assume that a child development specialist conducts a half-day workshop without charging the center. If the specialist's regular fee is $300, her contribution is valued at $300.

Sometimes, directors expect staff to volunteer to work additional hours without pay. This practice is usually inappropriate and may be illegal. Many teachers already spend time at home planning and preparing materials. Furthermore, staff salaries usually are alarmingly low. If staff members are expected to attend meetings and programs outside regular work hours, these conditions should be spelled out in the job descriptions. Some centers include policies relating to staff caring for children who are center clients outside of work hours. At the very least, staff members who are required to work more than 40 hours in a week must be paid overtime rates for the additional hours, unless they are exempt under U.S. Department of Labor regulations.

USING BUDGET SYSTEMS

Once the sources and amounts of income have been determined, these facts must be written down along with the plan for spending discussed earlier in this chapter. This written plan must be prepared in such a way that the people who need to read it will be able to understand it.

Small centers can use a very simple format. Centers that are publicly funded may be required to use whatever system is designated by the funding agency. Many centers use budget codes or account numbers, assigning a code number to each budget category and using separate numbers for each item within that category. For example, if the budget item *equipment* is coded as 110, then the subcategories might be:

111 office equipment
112 classroom equipment
113 kitchen equipment

Similarly, personnel might be coded as 510, with:

511 salaries
512 Social Security
513 workers' compensation

Such a system enables the financial director to record transactions according to appropriate budget categories and to ascertain quickly how much has been spent and how much remains in a given category.

Centers with a large number of classrooms, a range of age groups, or more than one site will certainly use a computer program to manage budgets. These may be modified to meet the center's needs.

An additional consideration in keeping accurate records is the responsibility to maintain ethical and legal practices. Having access to large sums of money is tempting to some people. If safeguards are not in place, the director or an employee who has access to financial records may manipulate them in unethical and illegal ways. A system of checks and balances can deter this behavior. For this reason, board members should be tenacious in insisting on current and thorough financial reports and should not hesitate to question any items they do not understand.

Approving the Budget

Before spending can begin, the budget must be approved by the board and the funding sources. The budget must balance; that is, income and expenses must be equal. When there is a surplus in the income side of the budget, it is categorized as profit or may be put in a reserve fund for large expenses that may occur in a future year. Because not-for-profit businesses obviously do not show a profit, such funds would be added to appropriate budget categories or would be put in a reserve fund. However, if the budget projects a loss, serious attention must be paid to immediate financial trimming. Believing that "something will turn up" is a poor way to conduct business and should not be accepted by a board or funders. At this point, conflict may arise among the board, the funding agency, and the director as each group may have varying interpretations of the center's goals and the means for reaching these goals. Once a consensus has been reached and the budget approved, the budget becomes the working financial plan and the director must see that it is followed.

Budgeting for Subsequent Years

Several months prior to the end of the year, the director and members of the finance committee meet to review the budget prepared for the ensuing year. For the second and subsequent budgets, the previous year's figures can serve as a guide, but the new budget figures, based on experience and on program changes, will usually differ from those of the previous year. Still, income and expenses must balance.

OTHER FINANCIAL RESPONSIBILITIES

The budget is the major tool used by the financial director for management of center finances, but balancing income and expenses is only one aspect of an overall, ongoing financial system. The director has a number of continuing financial responsibilities, all of which relate ultimately to the budget.

Managing Cash Flow

To be sure you will have enough cash on hand to pay staff and order budgeted equipment, you will need to keep track of cash flow. Often, budgets are divided into monthly components with the assumption that each month you will spend approximately one-twelfth of the annual amount. You can assume that income will be received in a similar pattern: one-twelfth of the annual income is expected each month. Realistically some items are paid for annually, semiannually, or quarterly. Similarly, total tuition expected in summer may be lower because some children stay home with older siblings or with parents who work as teachers and are home during the summer. The reverse may occur if you have a school-age program. Children who from September to June come before and after school may spend all day at the center during the summer, thus increasing center income. But suppose your budget includes $1,200 for classroom supplies. Does that mean you can spend $100 a month or can you place a $500 order in March? You need to know whether the cash will be available.

REFLECTION

You have $120 in your checking account. An item of clothing that you have desired for a month has just gone on sale for $100. What factors will you take into account in determining whether to buy it?

Now assume you direct a center. In examining your records for this month, you note that

- income for March 2006 = $20,359.
- expenses for March 2006 = $15,250.

Can you, as the director, therefore, purchase $5,000 of needed equipment for the center? Why or why not? If you have recorded that you had placed an order for $2,000 worth of equipment (even though the bill has not been paid yet), and if you also realize that several other major required expenses are coming up in the next three months, you would know that you had already encumbered (or planned for) $5,000 for equipment that hadn't arrived yet.

To accomplish this, you make a cash flow chart, showing each income and each expense item on a monthly basis. Often, these amounts are shown on a one-twelfth per month basis. At the end of January, you record the amount actually received and disbursed in each category. In another column, you show the difference between what you expected to receive or spend in that category, and what actually happened. Your accountant may refer to these as *accounts receivable* (money that people owe you) and *accounts payable* (money you owe others).

You also may record year-to-date expenses and receipts, as well as year-to-date expectations. Let us assume you listed $100 each month for classroom supplies for an annual total of $1,200. If you spent $0 in January, $50 in February, and $0 in March, you would have a $250 favorable balance in the supplies line. It is not necessary to spend money only as it is available in that line. However, you must be sure you can meet all expenses and not exceed the annual amount allocated without either receiving unexpected, unbudgeted income or decreasing the amount to be spent for the year on another item. Recognize, too, that if you purchase items or services monthly before cash is available to pay for them, you may be faced with high finance charges. Using a good software package to help you keep these records will simplify your task. Director's Resources 5-4 and 5-5 provide examples.

Handling Salaries

Once the budget is approved, the financial director informs the personnel committee of the allocation for salaries. In a new center, the committee then may begin the employment process in accordance with the personnel policies. In continuing centers, pay raises should be considered.

DIRECTOR'S CORNER

"I thought we were in good financial shape. We were showing a solid bank balance and we had full enrollment. What our cash accounting system didn't show was that we had several thousand dollars in bills that the bookkeeper hadn't paid yet. I learned that checking the cash on hand and even looking at how much we had budgeted for a category weren't necessarily appropriate ways to make decisions about what I could spend."

—Director, for-profit proprietary center

The director keeps additional records relating to the budget category *salaries*. Professional staff may be paid monthly, biweekly, or weekly, but their salaries are a fixed expense regardless of the number of hours worked as long as those individuals remain on the payroll. Other staff receive wages based on number of hours worked during the pay period. Employees who are paid hourly must have some way to record the amount of time spent on the job if that is the basis on which they are paid. Some centers have employees record their working time on weekly time cards or by signing in and out on the computer. These records are referred to when paychecks are prepared or may be recorded in one step by the software when the employee checks in and out. The director keeps a record of the sick days and the professional days used for all employees, including those who are salaried.

Payments are made to each individual employee on the basis agreed on in the employment contract. In small centers in which staff have the same schedule daily, time sheets may not be kept. In any event, the director is responsible for keeping track of hours worked, sick leave, and vacation time. Here again, entering this information into a computer database enables the fiscal officer to prepare up-to-date reports and facilitates preparation of the payroll.

Staff members also may be on unpaid leave. Current laws require that certain leaves be available to staff for circumstances such as child rearing. The returning staff member is not guaranteed the exact job but is guaranteed employment when the legal leave concludes. Centers also may create additional opportunities for leave. In any case, accurate records must be kept of leaves requested, granted, and used, and the director or designee is responsible for knowing and following related laws.

Ordering Goods and Services

With an approved budget in hand, the director or purchasing agent (or someone else assigned to this role) can begin to order supplies, equipment, and services. The first step is to consult the person or people who will use the item or services. The janitor may be consulted about a waxing machine, while the teachers should be involved in decisions about tables and chairs for the children. Both janitor and teachers could participate in selecting carpeting for the classrooms. However, when it comes to the actual ordering of the goods and services, as few people as possible—one is preferable—should be involved.

Several methods of ordering goods and services are utilized, depending on the nature of the purchase. Major purchases usually are approved by the director, the board, or a committee. If outside funding has been received, the center's contract may require that bids be submitted for large items or for large quantities of items such as food or paper goods. The purchaser writes out required specifications to suppliers or advertises for bids in the case of a large order. Then, the purchaser examines the bids and contracts that each supplier offers. The lowest bid must be accepted unless the bidder does not meet the specifications. Specifications can refer to a description of the item in question (for example, a commercial dishwasher), to the performance of the item (with water temperature of 180 degrees), or to its delivery date (to be delivered by September 1).

Smaller purchases or those that are routine, such as art supplies, may be ordered from a wholesaler. However, some centers require that price information on such items be obtained and that the item of appropriate quality having the lowest price be purchased. Sometimes, purchases are made with particular outlets because they allow credit, but this choice will be false economy if the quality is not satisfactory.

In some large cities, several centers may band together to purchase large quantities of items at reduced prices in a plan called *cooperative buying*. Each center may contribute to the salary of the person who manages the co-op and must transport items from a central location to its own center.

Making Payments

The director (or someone so designated) is responsible for making all payments. When shipments arrive, they are checked and paid for as soon as possible within the terms of agreement. For example, if the vendor gives 30 days to pay, the center should use the money until the payment is due but should monitor bill payment carefully so that unnecessary interest is not incurred. In cases in which a discount is offered for prompt payment, that may be a wise course to follow. Before paying for any item, it is important to verify that the items received are proper in quantity and quality and that the price on the invoice is correct.

A center should establish a checking account immediately so that payment for goods and services can be made promptly and safely. If the center is small, there may be the temptation to pay expenses directly from cash income. This practice is a major mistake because under such a plan, money can easily be lost or stolen, and errors or misunderstandings are more likely. Furthermore, no audit trail of these items is available. Most centers use checking accounts, and some centers require two signatures on each check, perhaps the signatures of the board treasurer and the director. In small centers or proprietary centers, the director signs all checks. Of even greater importance is the appointment of a person other than the bookkeeper to reconcile the bank balance.

When procedures for money management are in place and followed, fewer errors are likely to occur.

There must be a specific place to store bills and a specific time set aside to pay them. In small co-ops, a parent may work at home recording transactions. In large, complex organizations, all finances may be handled through a central administrative office that may be in another city or state.

Recording Transactions

Whenever a financial transaction occurs, it should be recorded promptly in a specific form and in a specific place. Access to a personal computer and appropriate software makes this task relatively easy and provides clear, readily available reports that show the financial position of the center on a monthly, weekly, or even daily basis.

In fact, many directors who now use computers for record keeping wonder how they managed without these tools. At first, using this technology can be time consuming, particularly if you are completely unfamiliar with the way these machines can work for you. However, once the system is set up, it takes no more time (and probably less time) to enter figures by means of the keyboard as opposed to pencil and paper. The result usually is easier to

read, may be converted readily to chart form on the computer, and can be cross-referenced. For example, you can enter in each child's record the tuition received that month from that family, and without rewriting all the amounts, query the computer for the total amount of tuition received that year to date.

Billing is easy. Once you have enrolled a child, and entered the parent(s) names and addresses, you can direct your computer to print bills to each family, customized with the specific amount owed. You also may want to add a message to each bill such as a reminder about registration for the following autumn or an advance notice of the date of the school picnic. If a family must make tuition payments in cash, provide a numbered and signed receipt and keep a copy. Both checks and cash must be deposited quickly, generally within the week.

Although not directly related to the center's fiscal operation, you may want lists of center children or families by child's birth date, health checkup due date, ZIP code, or by class at the center. You can print out attendance reports (often required by funders), a task that is made even easier if the parent signs the child in and out using a computer. Clip art or your own creative graphics add zest to notices. Just remember that you are directing a professional program and not a "Kutesy Korner."

Getting your payroll out on time can be much simpler with a computer. Once programmed with the hourly or monthly rates, the percentages to be withheld or deducted for various purposes, and other data to be recorded such as sick days used

Bombeck Family Learning Center

Creating a budget spreadsheet makes it easy to modify the budget as it is being planned.

and available, your computer will do the calculations and print the checks. You'll have a record of the transactions, but, as with any other document, you'll make a backup disc or use an external drive and keep it in a secure place.

As you work on budgets, reports to funders, cash flow statements, and any other data, you can use a password that will prevent those who do not need or should not have access to the data from viewing or modifying it. For example, a parent may not want the child's address published on the class list.

Every year, hardware and software manufacturers develop new capabilities for this technology. If you are relatively new to computer usage, finding a knowledgeable board member, volunteer, or consultant to assist you is essential. Choosing computer components requires understanding how you will use your computer. Most centers can't afford to buy a more powerful computer than they will need in the next few years, yet buying strictly on price will probably prove to be false economy. If your computer cannot run the software you need, you may wind up with not much more than an expensive typewriter.

Purchasing software also can be challenging, though not as costly as the hardware. Just as you can add hardware components as you acquire the need and the funds, so, too, can you add software packages. For example, you may add an accounts receivable package. You may also modify or customize existing programs, or you might purchase a basic program and create your own system.

When purchasing software, some of the items you'll want to consider include the following:

- What kind of hardware is needed to run this software?

- Can you try out the software?

- Does it do what you need?

- What kind of support is available and at what cost?

- Are seminars available? Where and when are they held?

- Is there a telephone help line? What are the hours in your time zone?

- Are upgrades provided?

- How long has the company been in business?

Because both computer hardware and software are changing so rapidly, it's a good idea to check with colleagues about what has worked effectively and what they would like to add. Professional journals such as *Child Care Information Exchange* provide regular reviews. Most reputable software companies will permit you to try out the software instead of watching someone else work with it and telling you about it as they go. ProCare Software and Softerware (maker of EZ-CARE2) are two of the most active players in this market. However, you also may find an excellent package developed by individuals who have been or are directors and have worked with computer programmers to design software that meets specific needs. Of course, whether a center uses computerized records or handwritten reports, these will be timely and accurate only when timely, accurate information is recorded.

Summarizing Data

Shortly after a fiscal year ends, the financial director should prepare an income statement for that year. This statement shows all revenue and expenses for the past year and points out the net income or loss. Director's Resource 5-2 provides an example of an income statement.

Sometimes children enjoy and learn by using materials that do not appear in the budget. Nonetheless, the director must carefully plan and monitor the center's financial functions.

To monitor the center's financial position, the financial director lists all assets and all liabilities as well as the equity the owner or owners have in the center. Directors need this total picture to enable them to understand their total financial position.

For example, if the assets are much less than the liabilities, the center is obviously in financial trouble. Notice how important accrued accounting is in creating the statement of financial position. Director's Resource 5-3 provides a sample statement of financial position.

Auditing

In most businesses, including early childhood education centers, an auditor reviews the books annually. The director makes the financial records available to the auditor, whether on computer or in a ledger. Also included are the checkbook, canceled checks, receipts, and invoices. The director or bookkeeper must keep these documents in an organized manner, and they must be regularly updated. Shoe boxes or laundry baskets full of invoices are totally unacceptable and certainly are unprofessional. At the very least, such lack of organization leaves the impression that the financial transactions of the center are not accurately maintained.

Auditors can perform several levels of audit or verification that the financial operation of the center is based on generally accepted procedures. The board will determine which level is needed, but in any event, the auditor will not verify each individual transaction. An annual audit protects the financial personnel of the center by making sure their job is being done according to procedures and protects the entire operation by ensuring that the use of funds is being recorded as planned and that procedures are being followed.

Handling Petty Cash

There are several ways to operate the petty cash fund. Each teacher may receive a specified sum of money to spend for the classroom, or the director may allocate a certain sum per staff member, paying cash when the staff member presents an appropriate receipt. Some centers use petty cash for all unexpected small needs. The director keeps a sum of cash on hand and gives it to staff members who present legitimate requests. For example, if the cook has run out of bread, petty cash may be used to purchase a loaf or two. Petty cash should be used as little as possible to avoid obscuring substantial program expenditures under its heading. If $20 worth of food is purchased weekly with petty cash, then the item *food* in the budget is underrepresented. All expenditures should be recorded (or allocated) to the correct account. This can be accomplished by the bookkeeper when the user presents receipt documentation. Some directors prefer to eliminate petty cash altogether.

... And Finally

If you are not already knowledgeable about financial planning and record keeping, gaining this knowledge is essential, at least at a basic level. Even when a director has no direct responsibility for financial records, inability to understand them is unacceptable. Many books and articles are available to guide you. If you are a real financial beginner, Gail Jack's book *The Business of Child Care: Management and Financial Strategies* will start you off with the basics (Jack, 2005). It contains several sample forms to give you an idea of how they look and what they include. The numbers included are not meant to be used by a center. Rather, you will need to create your own budget and, therefore, your own financial reports.

SUMMARY

To provide a good program for young children, center directors must delegate the responsibility for developing and carrying out a financial plan to a competent financial director or handle this major responsibility themselves. The overall plan must be carried out by a person who has knowledge of basic accounting and budgeting procedures and an understanding of the requirements of a good program for young children.

The plan must be based on the priorities for meeting children's needs and on the available funds. The major tool used by the financial director is the budget, a plan for balancing income and expenses. The director is responsible for all other financial matters, including designing budget systems, ordering goods and services, making payments, recording transactions, and preparing the new budget. An appropriate computer program can save time and money and, if used correctly, can provide timely, accurate data in a readily accessible format.

Perhaps your personal checkbook is seldom balanced. Nonetheless, as a center director or designee, you must record all transactions immediately or see that the person responsible is doing so. Even when another staff member is in charge of financial record keeping, it is the director's responsibility to keep fully apprised of the center's finances on a frequent and regular basis.

TRY IT OUT!

1 Work with a partner. Create a plan for staffing two classrooms for one week. Show what time each staff person will arrive, leave, and be on break. Assume the center is open for ten hours a day. Compare your plan with others created by your classmates. How many full-time staff did you include? How many part-time? How many FTEs did you need?

2 Examine Director's Resource 2: Income Statement, and Director's Resource 3: Statement of Financial Position. What information can you obtain from each of these statements?

 The Education CourseMate website for this text offers many helpful resources. Go to CengageBrain.com to access the TeachSource Video Cases and other TeachSource Videos, Expand Your Learning exercises, flashcards, interactive quizzes, the eBook, reflection and enrichment activities, and downloadable forms.

SAMPLE CHILD CARE CENTER BUDGET

INCOME

TUITION

Infants (8 × $160 × 51)	$65,280	
Toddlers (12 × $150 × 51)	91,800	
Preschoolers (51 × $135 × 51)	351,135	
Total Gross Tuition		508,215

DISCOUNTS

Vacancy (3%)		
Total Discounts		<15,246>

OTHER INCOME

Application Fees (30 × $20)	600	
Interest on account	600	
Fund-raisers	1,000	
Grant award (literacy program)	2,500	
Total Other Income		4,700

TOTAL INCOME		**$497,669**

EXPENSES

PERSONNEL

Director	30,000	
Head Teachers (5)	135,000	
Teachers (5)	100,000	
Assistants (10 part-time)	46,800	
Substitutes	2,000	
Secretary	8,000	
Custodian	7,000	
Cook	8,000	
FICA, Workers' Comp., Unemploy. and Insurance	62,500	
Total Personnel		$399,300

Rent	31,000	
Utilities and Telephone	17,465	
Advertising	1,000	
Food	35,000	
Office Supplies	1,000	
Custodial Supplies	700	
Classroom Equipment & Supplies	5,200	
C.P.A. Fees	1,000	
Insurance	3,500	
Licenses	500	
Staff Development/Training	1,500	
Teachers' Petty Cash	504	
Total Nonpersonnel		98,369
Total		$497,669

You can download a full-size version of this form on the Education CourseMate website.

Director's Resource 5-2

SAMPLE INCOME STATEMENT
FOR THE YEAR ENDED DECEMBER 31, 20XX

Income Statement
For the Year Ended December 31, 20xx

Revenues

Infant Program Income	$70,500	
Toddler Program Income	64,500	
Preschool Program Income	247,120	
Federal Child Care Food Program	41,500	
Donations/Contributions	500	
Parent Fund-raising	1,100	
Other Income	50	
Total Income		**$425,270**

Expenses

Salaries/Wages	267,100	
Health Benefits	19,650	
Employment Taxes and Insurance	21,840	
Management Services Fee	15,000	
Training/Consultant Fees	7,200	
Food/Beverage Supplies	21,300	
Educational Supplies	4,100	
Office & Paper Supplies	3,300	
Rent	16,000	
Payroll Service Fees	1,420	
Cleaning Service Fees	8,920	
Custodial Supplies	950	
Equipment Expense	2,800	
Utilities/Telephone Expense	11,300	
Garbage Removal	650	
Advertising	850	
Travel/Field Trips	1,600	
Bookkeeping/Audit Service Fees	11,500	
Licenses	625	
Maintenance & Repair Expense	5,920	
Insurance Expense	3,200	
Total Expense		425,225
Net Income (Net Loss)		$45

You can download a full-size version of this form on the Education CourseMate website.

Director's Resource 5-3

SAMPLE STATEMENT OF FINANCIAL POSITION
AS OF APRIL 30, 20XX

Assets

Cash–Operating	$7,000
Cash–Payroll	8,000
Accounts Receivable	11,200
Educational Supplies	900
Office Supplies	400
Property, Plant, and Equipment	42,000
Total Assets:	$69,500

Liabilities

Accounts Payable	$11,000	
Wages Payable	5,000	
Mortgage Payable	32,000	
Long-Term Liabilities	11,000	
Depreciation	4,000	
Total Liabilities:		63,000

Equity

Capital	6,500
Total Liabilities and Equity	$69,500

You can download a full-size version of this form on the Education CourseMate website.

HYPOTHETICAL BUDGET BY MONTH CREATED ON SPREADSHEET

Felton Family Preschool
Monthly Budget

	"Reasonable" Budget A3	September	October	November	December	January	February	March	April	May	June	July	August
	(D)	(E)	(F)	(G)	(H)	(I)	(J)	(K)	(L)	(M)	(N)	(O)	(P)
INCOME													
Tuition	344,235	25,000	28,000	30,000	30,000	30,000	30,000	30,000	30,000	30,000	27,078	27,078	27,078
Fund-raising	3,500	292	292	292	292	292	292	292	292	292	292	292	292
County Grant	27,000	2,250	2,250	2,250	2,250	2,250	2,250	2,250	2,250	2,250	2,250	2,250	2,250
Other	2,000	167	167	167	167	167	167	167	167	167	167	167	167
TOTAL INCOME	376,735	27,708	30,708	32,708	32,708	32,708	32,708	32,708	32,708	32,708	29,787	29,787	29,787
EXPENSE													
Payroll Expense													
Salaries-Staff	270,000	22,759	23,793	20,690	23,793	23,793	20,690	21,724	22,759	22,759	21,724	23,793	21,724
Payroll Taxes	24,300	2,048	2,141	1,862	2,141	2,141	1,862	1,955	2,048	2,048	1,955	2,141	1,955
Worker's Comp	13,500	1,138	1,190	1,034	1,190	1,190	1,034	1,086	1,138	1,138	1,086	1,190	1,086
Staff Benefits													
Health Ins.	27,250	2,271	2,271	2,271	2,271	2,271	2,271	2,271	2,271	2,271	2,271	2,271	2,271
Dental Ins.	4,000	333	333	333	333	333	333	333	333	333	333	333	333
Education Allow.	875	73	73	73	73	73	73	73	73	73	73	73	73
Rent	4,800	400	400	400	400	400	400	400	400	400	400	400	400
Janitor	6,000	500	500	500	500	500	500	500	500	500	500	500	500
Insurance													
Liability	2,914	243	243	243	243	243	243	243	243	243	243	243	243
Accident	1,575	131	131	131	131	131	131	131	131	131	131	131	131
Directors Ins.	944	79	79	79	79	79	79	79	79	79	79	79	79
Supplies	15,000	1,250	1,250	1,250	1,250	1,250	1,250	1,250	1,250	1,250	1,250	1,250	1,250
Utilities	2,835	236	236	236	236	236	236	236	236	236	236	236	236
Capital Improvement	2,000	0	0	1,000	0	0	0	1,000	0	0	0	0	0
TOTAL EXPENSES	375,993	31,461	32,640	30,102	32,640	32,640	29,102	31,282	31,461	31,461	30,282	32,640	30,282
SURPLUS (DEFICIT)	742	(3,753)	(1,932)	2,606	68	68	3,606	1,427	1,247	1,247	(495)	(2,854)	(495)

Source: From JACK, The Business of Child Care, 1E. © Cengage Learning.

You can download a full-size version of this form on the Education CourseMate website.

99

REFERENCES

Bureau of Labor Statistics, May, 2007. National Occupational Employment and Wage Data Estimates. Retrieved July 10, 2008, from http://www.bls.gov.

Center for the Child Care Workforce. (2004). Retrieved June 26, 2008, from http://www.ccw.org.

Jack, G. (2005). *The business of child care: Management and financial strategies*. Clifton Park, NY: Thomson Delmar Learning.

National Association of Child Care Resource & Referral Agencies (NACCRA). *Child care patterns and supply*. Retrieved June 25, 2007, from http://www.naccrra.org.

NACCRA. (2007, February). *2006 price of care*. Retrieved June 26, 2007, from http://www.naccrra.org/randd/program.php?Page=1.

6

FUNDING *the* PROGRAM

© 2010 Cengage Learning

When the director is seeking funds, she must be prepared to explain her request to bankers or representatives of a foundation.

Objectives

After reading this chapter, you should be able to:

- Describe the director's role in obtaining funding for a center.
- List several resources potentially available for child care financing.
- Explain how tuition rates may be determined.
- Describe several types of financial reports that funders may require.

Standards Addressed in this Chapter

naeyc Administrator Competencies
naeyc Management Knowledge and Skills 2

All directors, whether previously experienced in business or not, must understand the finances of operating a center. Even the director who does not have day-to-day responsibilities for the financial component of the center's structure must have financial knowledge and understanding. Directors who have moved up from teaching must remember that as teachers they were authoritative, rather than authoritarian. They knew what was appropriate for children and classrooms. Now they must also become authoritative about business.

A major component of the director's responsibility is ensuring sufficient funds to establish and operate the program. Although this assignment is ongoing, responsibilities mount when a new program is created, a new facility is needed, or components are to be added to an existing program. Of course, every director annually addresses the upcoming year's funding, and experienced directors recognize the need for long-range fiscal planning. Certainly, seeking additional funding is important, but shepherding carefully the funds one has is essential. In child care, there are no dollars to waste or lose through carelessness.

GETTING STARTED

Typically in early childhood centers, the director's role is demanding in terms of time, energy, and talent. Throughout this text, you have read about the wide range of expectations placed on the director. When it comes to funding, it often is wise to obtain needed assistance in one of several ways. To begin with, the director must understand that "few organizations are successful in raising funds from their communities without significant and sustained involvement by the board" (Bergman, 2010, p. 19). That is one of the reasons for creating a board with a broad community and business base rather than a collection of outstanding early childhood educators.

Everyone involved with the center should play a fund-raising role, directly or indirectly. For example, the director may assign other staff or enlist the aid of one or more volunteers to assume some additional responsibilities, such as organizing equipment orders or conducting inventory, thereby providing time for the director to engage in fund-raising. A well-trained volunteer may conduct center tours for prospective clients; an enthusiastic parent may do an excellent job of pointing out things parents are especially interested in knowing. A volunteer may answer the telephone one afternoon a week to provide the director with uninterrupted proposal-writing time. Finally, volunteers may participate in the fund-raising process in myriad ways that will be discussed throughout the chapter.

Centers with several sites may be able to afford a full- or part-time funding specialist. Directors of several centers may support each other by creating a joint fund-raising plan. They even may be able to hire a fund-raising consultant to guide their efforts, particularly if they have limited knowledge of the process. In the long run, such an expense may be quite productive.

An example of such cooperative planning and funding occurred when several center directors, together with their local Child Care Resource and Referral Association (CCRRA), were involved in monthly discussions. They were interested in supporting children with social and emotional needs beyond those expected in typical development. As a result, they formed a consortium specifically to work together on funding and implementing the program they all needed. Recently they began writing proposals and receiving grants. A team of specialists was employed and a volunteer teacher coaching program was implemented. Many children, families, teachers, and directors are benefiting from this collaborative approach, yet each center maintains its identity. No matter which approaches to funding you, as director, decide to take, it is essential to recognize that the director alone cannot manage the entire fund-raising process. Every staff member and every family member of the center's children should be involved. "Spreading the word" is one way. Keep everyone aware that you have a high-quality program for young children and that a high-quality program requires a strong financial position.

Funding a New Center

Obviously, starting a new center or expanding an existing center requires a significant amount of planning and money. Before seeking a loan or investing personal assets, remember that you are starting a business. The U.S. Small Business Administration (SBA) and the Service Corps of Retired Executives (SCORE) are good resources (their websites are www.sba.gov and www.score.org, respectively). Some business textbooks provide easy to understand and detailed descriptions of start-up funding (see Greene, 2012 and Hatten, 2009).

A prospective center developer who does not have a strong business background should seek assistance. The SBA recommends that before starting a business you answer the following questions:

- What niche or void will my business fill?
- What services or products will I sell?
- Is my idea practical and will it fill a need?
- Who is my competition?
- What is my business's advantage over existing firms?
- Can I deliver a better-quality service?
- What skills and experience do I bring to the business?
- What will be my legal structure?
- How will my company's business records be maintained?
- What insurance coverage will I need?
- What equipment or supplies will I need?
- How will I compensate myself?
- What are my resources?
- What financing will I need?
- Where will my business be located?
- What will I name my business?

Another possibility is purchasing an existing business. Such a purchase involves real estate, possibly equipment, the name of the center, and the goodwill the center has established (if that is the case). (See Greene, 2012 for what to look for.) Linsmeier (2003) explains how a child care business is valued. As a buyer, you will need to research the value that the seller uses and how that amount was calculated. At the same time, maintaining confidentiality is essential so that the current enrollment is not diminished based on parents' anxiety about changes in ownership. You would not want to buy a center whose status was being compromised by rumors.

In any case, check with your state department of labor about specific policies that will govern your business. (You'll read about other new business requirements in another chapter.) You may need to register your business name and get a business license and sales tax number, and you must definitely open a separate business bank account. You will need to know the federal and state laws governing employees and stay current with business publications in your area. Gather data on whether the market for child care is growing or declining in the area in which you are planning your business. Your local chamber of commerce or CCRRA may be able to help with information and may provide valuable contacts. Even when your business is going well, stay current with your community and its needs.

To obtain money, you must know exactly how much you need, why you need it, when you will need it, and how you will pay it back. You must also commit sufficient capital such as a second mortgage on your home. If you are working as an incorporated company, the corporation will need to demonstrate its sources of funding in addition to the loan being sought. The lender will obtain your credit report; therefore, it is wise to check your own credit report, or that of the corporation, before applying for a loan.

Can you convince key people in your community of the importance of a new child care and education center? Are you and your board confident that your new program is what your community needs so that preschoolers can have the experiences and support they need to learn and develop?

Start-Up Funds

Start-up capital is the money that must be available before the center is opened and for some time thereafter to support the initial program operation until the flow of tuition and other funds is sufficient to support the ongoing program. Once a director is hired, it takes a *minimum* of two to three months (and much more in some cases) to complete the necessary preliminary planning before the program begins. Money for space, equipment, office supplies, and some staff salaries must be available during these early months before the center opens. Programs often are underenrolled during the first few months of operation. Checks from funding sources are sometimes delayed until the program operation is well under way. Therefore, it also is wise to have sufficient capital on hand at the outset to operate the program for at least six months. These operating monies to cover costs for six months of planning and six months of operation are in addition to the capital needed to finance the purchasing or remodeling of a site and to purchase equipment and supplies for the children's program. In other words, it takes a considerable amount of money to start a program, and it is important to make careful calculations to ensure that the start-up money is adequate to cover the costs until regular operating funds become available.

A director who has been a teacher and is now planning to open a center will notice that lenders, suppliers, inspectors, and insurers will not ask about what kind of relationships she plans to establish with children and families, what the curricular objectives are, or what kinds of special activities will be provided. They are interested in *business*. The director will have to have or develop this new focus while continuing to focus on staff, children, and families, and their needs and interests. Although the director may have a close relationship with families since she and they care about their children, she is still the administrator. She must be careful to avoid crossing an invisible line. At some point, the director may have to follow up on a slow tuition payment. A family may decide to dispute the way an injury was handled or to complain about the food being served. The director must maintain an objective and ethical stance. (Please see NAEYC Administrators' Code of Ethics Supplement in the Appendices.)

At the same time, the board and the director must seek out the leaders in their community who can be shown the need to go beyond a bare bones program. Helping them see that young children aren't "just" playing and that the learning that is occurring will be a foundation for continued learning and developing. The process of cultivating individuals and businesses that can help is ongoing. Keeping the program and its importance in the forefront is a major job. The results can be quite rewarding for the center, children, and families.

Most agency-sponsored centers are nonprofit, and many are eligible to receive funding from other community or governmental agencies once there is an established, ongoing program to fund. To get started, however, the agency may need to apply to foundations or other sources for funding. A sample grant application is shown in Director's Resource 6-1.

You may be preparing grants for much larger amounts of money for bigger projects, but this example provides an idea of how a proposal looks. Often agencies conduct campaigns, soliciting first from their own board members, who are expected to contribute. Next, businesses and others who have expressed interest in the work of the agency are approached. Some corporations that operate many centers, or very large centers, obtain funds from investors. Operators of small proprietary centers that are established for profit or that have no sponsoring agency must invest personal capital or arrange for a loan to get started. Foundation money is rarely offered to proprietary centers; it is reserved for serving particular populations chosen by the foundation that meet specific foundation-determined goals.

Community and Governmental Support

When the community expresses great interest in getting a program started, it may be possible to promote a successful fund-raising program. However, only relatively small amounts of money can be obtained through raffles or bake sales. Established philanthropic groups such as Kiwanis, Lions, various community groups, and fraternal organizations sometimes are willing to donate money to cover start-up costs such as equipment or to support a capital improvements fund-raising campaign. They may fund specific activities such as field trips. But like other funders, they seldom provide operating expenses.

A company may provide start-up funding for a center for its employees' children with the understanding that the director will need to secure adequate funding for operating costs from other sources, including tuition. If the company makes something the center could use, such as diapers or packaged food products, it may offer a continuing supply to the center. Other companies may offer a flex plan, a benefit that allows employees to set aside before-tax income to pay for child care. This benefit makes child care more affordable for families. In turn, it provides relatively reliable tuition payments for centers because employees must show a paid receipt from the center or caregiver to collect their own before-tax dollars. If, by the end of the year, the employee has not used all of his child care benefit fund, the money reverts to the employer.

Centers in public schools are usually funded through special government grants, and the central administration may manage the budget. In some cases, public schools offer government-supported programs for children, sometimes specifically for children with special needs. However, families within the community are encouraged to enroll and are expected to pay for children who are typically developing, thus creating a diversified class. In the case of large chains of centers, the corporate office secures investors and then funds the start-up of new centers based on its market research. It may also arrange for franchises, finding individuals who are interested in contracting with the corporation to be a franchisee. (You may be familiar with family restaurants, ice cream stores, or dry cleaners that operate as part of a franchise system. You may also find franchise early childhood programs in your area.)

Centers not connected with other institutions or programs usually need a major source of income beyond tuition. When a center is operated day to day on tuition and small funding campaigns such as raffles or cookie sales, the board and the director will come to realize that a major pool of funds is needed in order to make any real changes, handle an emergency such as water damage from a broken pipe, or cover a sudden drop in enrollment, such as if parents lose jobs and can no longer afford their children's programs. That is one reason for choosing members of the board of directors carefully. When the board has members who have "connections" to people and companies with major resources, they may be able to organize and implement a campaign for a children's program. Such plans must be made well in advance, using a rationale that will appeal to a wide range of contributors. Saying "Our family center needs financial help" won't sell well. But creating a slogan that ignites interest can be quite effective. Programs that start without a sufficient funding base are in fiscal trouble from the outset. It is very difficult to maintain a balanced budget for an early childhood education program. Therefore, it is paramount to keep a balanced budget at the outset by finding enough capital to cover start-up costs as well as to plan for unexpected needs and to enhance the program in a major way when needed.

Break-Even Analysis

In determining the amount of funds needed, a break-even chart is useful. You want to know how many children you need to enroll to break even financially as well as to make a profit or provide some funds for future initiatives. You and your accountant can prepare such a chart by first determining the fixed costs of operating the center, such as rent, utilities, and director's salary. These are costs that will remain at the same level, regardless of enrollment.

Variable costs are calculated. These are the costs for operating the program that change as enrollment increases or decreases. For example, when four or five children are added, the cook probably orders more food, more art materials are needed, and so forth. If you have several years of budget experience available for this program, you can figure the cost of food per child from the previous year by dividing the cost of food by the number of children. In the same manner, you can determine the cost of equipment per child and the cost of teaching staff per child. As prices rise, you will need to increase amounts accordingly.

Although you don't change the line every time an additional child is admitted, it is clear that the more children you enroll, the more expenses you will have. Some figures can be computed per child such as the amount of food or of disposable materials (crayons, paper, soap, etc.). However, when you have a sufficient number of children, you will need additional teachers, furniture, and even an additional classroom, depending on the number of children added.

Let's finish the break-even chart so you can see what the financial effect might be.

At this point the analysis becomes more challenging. Based on licensing requirements and center

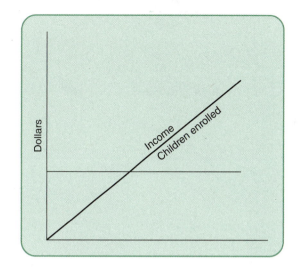

FIGURE 6-2 The diagonal line shows numbers of children enrolled.
Source: © Cenage Learning, 2013.

policies, when a certain enrollment is reached, an additional teacher must be employed. A simple example would be to think of a center with 30 children in which a 1:10 ratio is required. When the 31st child is added, the center must provide an additional teacher, even though the additional tuition generated by one child surely will not pay a teacher's salary. However, if six new children are added, it *may* be feasible financially to have four groups of nine children. Of course, if tuition from ten children is required to pay a teacher's salary expenses, then the director should not add children until she can ensure a class of ten or realize that money will be lost on that class and must be made up by charging higher overall tuition.

The director or accountant can figure a break-even analysis, that is, how many children and what tuition rate will be needed to offset costs. To get an idea of how this works, use the following steps (Hatten, 2010):

❶ Calculate fixed costs. These must be paid no matter how many children are enrolled. These include: rent; phone; utilities; insurance; equipment; and salaries and benefits for director, cook, maintenance staff, secretary, and any other nonclassroom staff.

❷ Determine the number of children you will serve.

❸ Based on the number of children per teacher, calculate the number of teachers and the cost of teacher and assistant salaries and benefits.

❹ Based on the number of children, estimate the cost of food and supplies.

❺ Add the costs to be incurred (items 1, 3, and 4).

❻ Divide the total (from line 5) by the number of children.

FIGURE 6-1 The straight line represents fixed costs.
Source: © Cenage Learning, 2013.

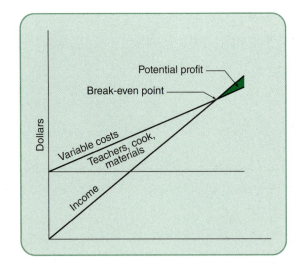

FIGURE 6-3 Chart showing break-even point and profit area.

Source: © Cenage Learning, 2013.

❼ The dollar figure in line 6 represents the amount you will have to receive in tuition to break even.

❽ If at any time you do not have full enrollment, you will lose money.

❾ Therefore, you will want to build into your budget a cushion that will allow for underenrollment. One way to accomplish this is to charge higher tuition than required to break even. However, if any of your tuition comes from government vouchers, you may be limited to the current voucher rate, which will almost certainly be below your tuition costs.

Costs for infants and toddlers are higher than for preschoolers, while costs for school-age care are lower, based primarily on the teacher-to-child ratio. Since infants require a lot more individual care and attention than older children, a teacher can care for only three or four infants at the most. To determine break-even costs when you serve a variety of age groups, do the following:

❶ Divide the fixed costs by the total number of children in all age groups (as described previously). The fixed cost for every child, regardless of age, is the same.

❷ Calculate the variable costs for each age group separately (teaching staff, food, supplies).

❸ Divide each age group's variable costs by the number of children in that age group to find the variable cost per child.

❹ Add the variable cost per child and the fixed cost per child. This amount is the tuition that must be collected from that child to break even.

To carry this further, you may want to investigate how you would figure costs for a center serving eight infants and 36 preschoolers. Notice that although the variable costs for infants will be considerably higher than those for preschoolers, the fixed cost for each child remains the same. Therefore, preschool tuition, although spread over more children in this example, must, in effect, cover part of the cost of caring for infants. (A sample budget in Chapter 5 demonstrates that a center may lose money on infant care but cover that loss with tuition from preschoolers.) Nonetheless, infant care is important for at least two reasons: (1) there is a major need for infant care in many communities, and (2) when children start in a center during

Teachers manage the number of children at an activity. Directors must manage the number of children enrolled to break even.

Individuals who have visited the center may be more likely to contribute to your fiscal campaign.

infancy, the center hopes to retain them throughout their preschool years. If the number of preschool children in a center decreases, the cost of infant care may have to increase or the fees for all children must increase.

By the same premise, school-age care can potentially balance the cost of care for younger children. Centers must carefully plan school-age tuition to be reasonable for families. However, because fewer staff are needed, before- and after-school care is less costly than preschool and may be financially helpful to centers serving preschoolers. The key factor remains retention of high-quality care for all age groups.

Using a break-even chart, the director projects the income based on the enrollment. She then looks for the points at which the total costs meet the income and checks to see at what enrollment levels that occurs (Cohen, 2006; Hatten, 2010).

OPERATING FUNDS FOR NEW AND CONTINUING CENTERS

Operating funds refers to the amount needed to run the center once it is open for business. Operating funds must include all the regular budget items needed in the day to day operation of the center. Once the facility is established and the basic equipment has been purchased using start-up funds, income must be adequate to ensure daily program operation as well as provide an emergency fund. Many centers

have depended heavily on government funds, United Way, and other charitable monies to provide most or all of their operating funds. An analysis of these sources for the twenty-first century indicates that in many cases, it is unlikely they will be sufficient to maintain the quality that centers must provide.

Fund-raising for operating costs must be planned carefully in terms of the benefit to be derived from the contributor's dollars. Imagine a contribution being used to pay for rather mundane, yet certainly essential, categories such as utilities and insurance. Such usage may not encourage the giver. The creative fund-raiser frames requests in terms of projected program accomplishments. One director in an annual fund-raising letter labeled contributions as "your opportunity to nourish the minds and bodies of 62 of our young children." During the preceding weeks, she had sent the local newspapers (with parental permission) pictures of several children engaged in interesting projects such as visiting several local small businesses and discussing with the proprietors how they now use what they had learned in school. Based on this project, the director of their before- and after-school program submitted a proposal for a homework coach. She included quotes from the children who had discussed and written about their community visits. Besides helping with school-assigned homework, the coach was to engage children in games and activities involving logic, problem solving, and creativity. The local businesspeople were invited to join them in these activities. As a result, this successful grant paid for a well-qualified staff member and a wide variety of materials.

Tuition

When the center is largely dependent on tuition for operating funds, it will be necessary to balance the number of children to be enrolled, the amount of tuition their families can reasonably be expected to pay, and the amount of money needed to operate the program. The program will not always be fully enrolled; therefore, the budget should have at least a 3 percent to 8 percent vacancy rate built in. Programs just beginning may have only a few children enrolled for many months, necessitating close management of the initial budget and reduction of variable costs to the lowest possible level. Even some fixed costs can be reduced. For example, a director may employ one or two salaried teachers until the tuition receipts warrant the addition of more staff.

Since the salaries of most preschool teachers are unreasonably low, and since salaries comprise the

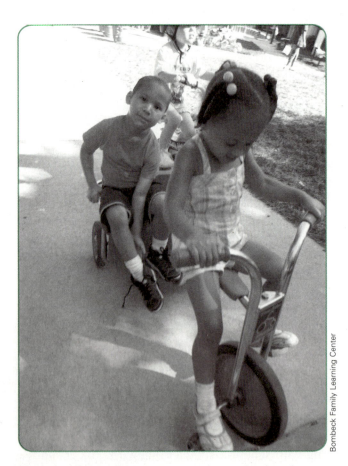

When the center director can convince a funder of the importance of physical and motor development opportunities for children, he may be able to secure funding for outdoor equipment.

Bombeck Family Learning Center

biggest expenditure by far in an education budget, it is sensible to charge an amount that will provide the fairest possible salary to the staff. Therefore, the tuition rate should be based on a number of facts, including

- the amount needed to meet professional commitments to staff.
- the amount that is reasonable in terms of the type of program offered to families.
- the amount charged by comparable centers in the area.

Adjusting Tuition

For many centers, payments by parents are the major source of income. There may be an application fee, which will be applied to the child's tuition when she enrolls. If the child is not enrolled, the center retains the application fee. To assist parents or to attract clients, centers may decide to offer one or more weeks' tuition free for vacation or illness for each child. If you decide to do this, remember to multiply the weekly tuition by 51 instead of 52 weeks or to divide the annual tuition by 51 weeks. Keep in mind that if parents pay 51 times a year, there may be a week when you receive no tuition income. However, if you are following your budget, you will recognize that you should not be spending more than the total amount initially approved. You may specify in your enrollment agreement that the 52nd week of the child's attendance is the week during which no tuition will be due. You may also decide to require two weeks' tuition in advance. If the child will be leaving the center, the parents are expected to give two weeks' notice to the director. They will then not pay for the last two weeks, but the director may have time to find a child to fill the spot.

You may also offer a discount to the second child enrolled from the same family at the same time. But remember, if Jamala's tuition is $5 less per week than that of the other children in her class just because her older brother is also attending the center, you still need to get that $5 per week from some source. If you have ten children who have a sibling at the center, keep in mind this means that each week you are receiving tuition minus $50.

$$\$5 \times 10 \text{ children} = \$50 \text{ less per week,}$$
$$\$50 \times 52 \text{ weeks} = \$2,600 \text{ less income per year.}$$

You then need to reduce the budgeted amount of tuition by $2,600 and reduce (by $2,600) the amount allocated to the expense side of your budget, or find a way to acquire the $2,600 from some other source.

Similar situations arise when parents request that you hold a space for their child. For example, holding a space for a newborn who will be coming to the center in two months can mean that you lose two months of infant tuition. Working parents face the dilemma of finding infant care while center directors face the dilemma of keeping full enrollment.

The director must balance this loss of income against the potential loss of enrollment, but must still make the initial tuition rate high enough to cover such factors. However, since these costs are quite variable depending on how many two-child families are enrolled in the center at a given time, or how many infant spaces become available, they may add to budget instability.

Some centers charge tuition on a sliding scale based on the parents' ability to pay. Often, these centers receive government or agency funds to supplement tuition income. A sliding fee scale formula is prepared that takes into account the amount of income, the number of dependents, and other circumstances such as extraordinary medical bills. However, whenever a family pays less than the actual cost of care, the difference must be covered by making the top of the scale higher than the cost so that some families pay more than the cost of care, or by securing outside funds. A sample sliding fee scale appears in Director's Resource 6-2.

Scholarships

Many center directors encounter situations in which parents would like to enroll their children but are unable to afford the tuition. You may want to plan for some sort of aid for either partial or full tuition. This can be accomplished by establishing a scholarship fund created by charging more tuition than the cost per child and using the excess for scholarships, or by contacting individuals, agencies, and foundations to ask them to support full or partial scholarships.

Think about the purpose of a scholarship. Do you want to assist families that are temporarily unable to afford tuition, families whose income falls between eligibility for government support and the ability to pay tuition, children from other cultures, or children with special needs? In any event, the purpose must be clear. To create a scholarship program, you will need an application process, a review process, and a system for record keeping of funds contributed and disbursed. If the tuition assistance program is large, particularly in a

multiple-site organization, additional staff time may be needed (Vast, 2003).

Assume you need 100 children paying $160 a week ($16,000 tuition per week) to balance your budget.

Think about having ten children on partial scholarship.

Of the $160 weekly preschool tuition, each of the ten families is able to pay $70 per child. The $90 per week that those families do not pay ($160 − $70 = $90) has to come from somewhere:

$90 per week not charged × 10 children = $900
(weekly amount needed to
compensate for scholarships).

If no special scholarship funds are available, the $900 weekly would, in effect, have been divided among the remaining 90 children. (Of course, this would be done before the tuition was announced to the parents.)

100 children total − 10 children at reduced rate means 90 children paying full price.

Calculating the Potential Effect of Scholarships on Tuition

$900 per week (scholarship money) ÷ 90 children = $10 per fee-paying child per week,

$160 per full paying child + $10 per full paying child = $170 per full paying child

Tuition for the year: $170 per week × 90 children = $15,300

$70 per week × 10 children = $700,

$15,300 + $700 = $16,000 per week tuition for the 100 children at the center.

Parents might not be aware that their $170 per week tuition is contributing to scholarships or you may choose to tell them. Such a plan is effective unless the tuition rate becomes higher than nonscholarship families can or will pay.

Tuition Rates

Tuition charges are set by estimating what families are willing and able to pay for services and by considering what rates are charged by competing agencies in the community. Local professional organizations or the local or state universities may have information about the amount of tuition that reasonably can be charged in a particular community. Unless a program offers something very different from that offered by nearby centers (such as NAEYC accreditation or top ranking in state QIRS programs), it may be difficult to convince parents to pay significantly higher tuition for one program over another; therefore, tuition rates must be reasonably competitive. On the other hand, if tuition is lowered to attract clients, it may be difficult to cover costs and compete with other centers in offering teachers appropriate salaries and in hiring competent staff. Directors of quality centers often have to educate members of the community about the differences in program quality and, in particular, about the value of well-prepared and more costly staff.

Although most programs charge tuition, sometimes that charge is even higher than tuition at a college. A typical range for early care and education in a community might be $115 to $215 per child per week. Infant tuition is higher than tuition for preschoolers because of the higher teacher-to-child ratio in infant rooms. Usually parents of children needing child care have had limited opportunities to save for tuition because they are just beginning a career or because they are working in low-paying jobs. College tuition is often supplemented by governmental support, endowments, and grants. Completing college is important for many people, but more and more attention is now being given to the importance of the early childhood years as the foundation for future learning. One factor influencing child care costs is the general cost of living in an area (see **Table 6-1**).

A survey of four early childhood centers in a mid-size Midwestern city showed that infant care ranged from $200 to $230 per week, or $10,400 per year to $11,960 per year. Preschool care in the same centers ranged from $142 to $185 per week, or $7,384 to $9,620 per year. Two of these centers received some support from employers and gave priority to employees' children.

The National Child Care Information and Technical Assistance Center website provides a list of some national organizations and publications with information about employer-supported child care. NCCIC points out that "employers support the child care needs of their employees through a variety of strategies including offering dependent care assistance plans to help employees pay for child care with pretax dollars; providing information to assist employees to find child care in the community; offering child care at or near the worksite; and providing cash vouchers or other subsidies directly to employees to assist in child care costs" (National Child Care Information and Technical Assistance Center, 2005). In 2011 the site, renamed the National Child Care and Information Center (http://nccic.acf.hhs.gov/), provided information state by state on a wide range of data by state. You may want to check this organization's current reports periodical. Items include:

Federal and state expenditures by state

Average monthly number of children served and of families served

Quality assurance program

Financial incentives, etc.

DIRECTOR'S CORNER

"We really couldn't charge more tuition. Parents just couldn't afford it. It means that the board can't pay me for planning time. My contract calls for a 3 percent raise annually, but this summer the board president said to me, 'Jeanine, we're going to have to use your raise to cover the unexpected moving expenses. There's no other way.' I know they tried hard to get other funds."

—Teacher/director, incorporated not-for-profit center

TABLE 6-1 Lowest and highest child care charges for 2007

Lowest price for infant/toddler care	Mississippi	$4,542
Highest price for infant/toddler care	Massachusetts	$14,591
Lowest price for preschool care	Mississippi	$3,380
Highest price for preschool care	Massachusetts	$10,787

Source: From Parents and the High Price of Child Care: 2008 Update. Detail Table 1a. Average Annual Price & Percentage Change of Full-Time Care by State. Retrieved July 8, 2008, from National Association of Child Care Resource & Referral Agencies website: http://www.naccrra.org/docs/reports/ price_report/Price_Report_2008_apdx01.pdf

Community Resources

Many early childhood education programs are subsidized by local charities and church groups. These groups typically do not provide cash to help meet the operating budget. Instead, they provide in-kind contributions such as free rent, janitorial service, coverage of utility bills, volunteer help, and so forth. If the director and the board find themselves with an unbalanced budget at the end of the year because of unforeseen problems with enrollments or unexpected expenditures, some sponsoring agencies will cover the losses. This practice is particularly prevalent when one of the sponsoring agency's goals is to provide child care services to low-income members of the community. However, the director who is not managing her budget well is not likely to be bailed out more than once.

Boards and directors may want to respond to newly identified needs and to creative ideas. To meet these needs, seeking funding is almost inevitable. Occasionally, whoever funds operating costs also may fund special projects. More often, special funding must be sought. Consider the program that served several children—Mindy, Dashawn, and Ronnie—who had developmental delays. The teacher observed that they seemed very interested in caring for classroom plants. She asked the director for gardening supplies and a section of playground so that her whole class could create a garden. Mindy, Dashawn, and Ronnie were to be assigned special responsibilities. Recognizing a creative idea, the director went to a local nursery for help. The owner not only contributed tools and seeds but also volunteered to help the class create the garden and joined them at circle time to discuss her job. Later, the class visited the nursery. Having been so delighted with the children's interest and the positive response from parents, several of whom later made purchases from her, the owner made a follow-up call to the director. She offered to provide a small greenhouse for the school so that the children could start plants earlier the following year. Imagine how much everyone benefited from one idea and one director's efforts to provide funding.

United Way funds, raised through a United Appeal campaign, are available for child care services in some communities. Usually this would be a grant for a specific purpose. Eligibility for these community funds varies depending on the locale, the amount of money available, and the demands placed on that source of funding.

As a director of a program that may need community support money, you should familiarize yourself with eligibility requirements in your community so that you can plan accordingly. Often, a number of preliminary steps must be taken before a program can be presented for funding consideration. Also, some United Way agencies will not give start-up money or operating funds to new programs. Eligibility requirements for funds typically include the following points:

1 The agency must be an incorporated, voluntary, nonprofit, charitable organization possessing tax-exempt status under Section 501(c)(3) from the Internal Revenue Service. The agency must be licensed by the appropriate authority; must provide a needed health, welfare, or social service; and must have a qualified and representative governing body that serves without compensation.

2 The agency must have and must implement a written policy of nondiscrimination and non-segregation on the basis of race, ethnic origin, disabling condition, sex, or religion regarding its governing body, its employees, and the people it serves.

3 The agency must have been established and must have continued to function for a minimum of three years (number varies here) before applying for funds.

4 The agency must be willing to cooperate in the United Way fund-raising campaign and to abide by all the policies of the United Way agency.

Once the minimum eligibility requirements have been met, the necessary steps for funding consideration must be taken by the director of the center or by a designated board member. The director usually is the only person who has all the necessary information for completing application forms and, therefore, is the one ultimately responsible for filing the numerous ongoing attendance and financial records most agencies require. If a board member assumes this responsibility, the director still must provide the necessary data. Therefore, it is important that the director be familiar with the application procedures and clearly understand the ongoing requirements, including reporting requirements for funded programs *before* entering into any agreements with any funder.

The application for funding may seem intimidating to some directors and hinder them from applying for available funds. The process does become easier as the director gains more experience in applying and finds that many applications require similar information. Once the information has been gathered, some of it can be reused in subsequent proposals. Nonetheless, directors must be prepared to spend a great deal of time and energy on routine reporting if they expect to use outside funds. Keep in mind, too, that some funders are targeting certain areas. The area may be a well-baby initiative or ensuring that all school-agers have a safe place to go after school. With national attention currently focused on early childhood education, you may find that an organization in your area will also support that initiative.

Foundations

A *foundation* is a fund administered by trustees and operated under state or federal charter. Foundation funds sometimes are made available to child care centers for major equipment purchases or for a special project. Occasionally, a foundation will provide funds for building or remodeling a facility or for training staff. Foundation support for a program depends on whether the trustees of the foundation have declared education, or more specifically, early childhood education, as an area of interest.

Large philanthropic foundations such as the Ford, Carnegie, and Rockefeller Foundations have broadranging programs with specific interest areas that change periodically. For example, there may be a general interest in funding innovative educational programs, but monies may be going into literacy or single-parent programs during one funding period, only to shift to programs for preschool children with developmental delays or to innovative child care models during the next funding period. Smaller foundations may limit support to programs in a certain geographic area or to a given problem area that may change every few years, while other special-interest foundations limit support efforts to very specific interest areas that do not change.

The Foundation Center is an organization with branches in several major cities. Free classes on various aspects of funding are frequently offered at its sites. In addition, individuals may register to receive regular emails from the center (http://foundationcenter.org). The center publishes research reports, which you can view at its locations or read or purchase online. The reports include *Foundation Giving Trends: Update on Funding Priorities* and *Facts and Figures on Private and Community Foundations*. The website also includes a large section labeled "Foundations Supporting Early Childhood Care and Education." Consider this source when you are looking for funds.

Money from corporate foundations is available in many communities. In smaller cities, it is wise to solicit funds from small, local corporations that often have some funds set aside for use by local agencies. Frequently, the small corporate funds are controlled by corporate managers who are very sensitive to the public relations value of making a gift to local agencies that, in turn, will give due credit and recognition to the funder. The company name may be attached to the contribution, a reasonable expectation. For example, when the XYZ local branch of a department store funds new block areas in all your classrooms, you may install a small plaque "Donated by the XYZ Company." You may submit pictures of a store official handing you a check, building with the children (with parental permission for the photo), or in some other way promoting the company and your center. You, your staff, and the center families may support the store with your business in return.

In an earlier example, a small-business owner recognized a creative and worthwhile idea. She was interested in helping children learn about plants and, therefore, responded to the center's request. Foundations, too, are looking for innovative ideas and approaches to solving problems. You can approach foundations with your opportunity for them to support a good cause (Mitchell, 1996). Mitchell's article, although written a while ago, still offers excellent advice. Your well-prepared and enthusiastic presentation, as well as your strong interpersonal and communication skills, will improve your chances of obtaining funding. Keep in mind, however, that foundations provide only a small portion of the large amounts of money required to provide good child care.

When directors plan to approach a foundation for money, they must know precisely what they expect to do with the money and how they expect to do it. Their appeal for money must be tailor-made to the foundation's interest areas, and all funding requests must move through the proper channels. However, personal contacts with foundation trustees or other people connected with the foundation are considered very helpful. Perhaps a member of the center's parent group or a board member has personal contacts

DIRECTOR'S CORNER

"When I write a proposal, I always try to think of something that will appeal to the proposal reader—a catchy title or an intriguing goal such as introducing preschoolers to good nutrition through 15 microwave cooking projects. In the long run, we not only meet the goal, but we still have the microwave to use for daily food preparation."

—Director, agency-sponsored not-for-profit center

with a foundation or can help find the best channels to use for personal contacts.

Funds tend to flow toward challenging and interesting programs in well-run organizations rather than to needy institutions that are faltering. A few letters of reference from respected sources may increase your chances of receiving funds.

Government Funding

Federal, state, and local governments all have some commitment to the care of the children of working mothers, with the federal government being the forerunner of that movement as far back as the early 1940s. Although state and local government agencies have been involved in licensing and monitoring early childhood care and education programs for some time, the availability of state and local money for child care for working mothers is relatively recent when compared with federal monies available on a somewhat sporadic basis for more than 50 years. Government monies typically are available for programs that serve low-income families or those that serve children with special needs. Currently, the Head Start program and the proliferation of programs for young children with special needs serve as evidence of the federal government's focus on these children's education. California was the first state to establish an extensive network of state-supported child care centers. However, many other states are moving to expand their state-supported systems. In 2006–2007, 38 states provided state-funded preschool at a cost of $3.7 billion. With more than a million children attending these programs, states became the largest source of public preschool (Barnett et al., 2008). Then in 2010 and 2011, with prices rising and unemployment high, many states reduced funding for education at all levels.

Nonetheless, many children, particularly in certain areas, are underserved or receive no services. Others receive no services because their parents do not enroll them for a variety of reasons.

A number of major sources of federal funding were established during the 1960s and continue to provide some basic support for child care and for children with special needs. Although some of these programs have ended, advocates for high-quality early education continue to work to find ways to provide qualified teachers for every child and support for early childhood education and care programs.

Head Start

One of the most well-known federal early childhood initiatives has been Head Start. This large, well-funded program was created in 1965 as part of the "War on Poverty." Designed to serve low-income children and their families, Head Start now focuses on two age groups. The original Head Start program serves low-income preschool children and their families. Early Head Start serves low-income children prenatal to age 3, pregnant women, and their families. Both programs are comprehensive early childhood development programs. Since Head Start's inception, more than 25 million children have been enrolled. Fiscal year 2007

Bombeck Family Learning Center

Some funders may send representatives to observe in classrooms, view center records, and confer with the director.

program statistics show the enrollment as 908,412 children ages 3 to 5 years with an average cost per child for the Head Start program of $7,326. For 2008, $6,877,975,000 was appropriated for the program (U.S. Department of Health & Human Services, 2008). By 2010 (the latest year for which data were available) Congress appropriated $7,234,783,000 for Head Start projects and activities (U.S. Department of Health & Human Services, 2011).

Child Care and Development Block Grants

Another source of federal funding is the Child Care and Development Grant Fund (CCDF). In 1996, to provide eligible low-income families with subsidies to help them afford child care, the welfare reform law consolidated several sources of federal funding to create the Child Care and Development Block Grant (CCDBG). In 2010, this fund provided approximately $5 billion in federal block grants to improve the affordability, supply, and quality of child care in the United States and to enable low-income families to work, attend training, or enroll in education programs. States and territories use some CCDF funds to support child care start-up or expansion grants and loans to providers. A few states established grant programs to help early childhood programs improve their star or quality rating level in the state's Quality Rating System (National Association for the Education of Young Children, n.d.; National Child Care Information and Technical Assistance Center, 2007).

Advocacy

Another approach to meeting the challenge of providing appropriate early childhood education is the initiative referred to as PreK Now, recently funded by the Pew Charitable Trusts and others. The organization's vision is "A nation in which every child enters kindergarten prepared to succeed." To achieve this vision, the group works with the public and with legislators from across the country. Its daily emails highlight current newspaper mentions of early childhood educators and include information about legislators and candidates and their comments on the subject. Individuals are asked to write to legislators about the need for early childhood education for all children (Stone, 2008).

Despite the best effort of early childhood educators nationwide, the issue of funding child care centers presents several dilemmas. First, many parents simply cannot afford to pay the cost of care. Although the government already provides large sums of tax revenue, those amounts have never been enough to provide even basic quality for all the children who need care. Nor has it provided for all the children whose parents want them to participate in preschool education. At the same time, by far the largest part of the child care budget goes to staff salaries. Yet most staff salaries are deplorably low. "We know there is an overall quality problem. And the question is why. Why, when investments in early care and education are soaring, does quality remain low?" (Kagan et al., 2002). Kagan and others have proposed a plan for financing universal early care and compensation. Major ideas include delineating a career lattice that would allow entry-level child care staff to begin work with limited previous training and then participate in professional development at no cost. Staff members with bachelor's degrees would be paid salaries in line with those of public school teachers. All staff would be expected to continue to participate in professional development activities. Directors need to be aware of such initiatives, to contribute ideas, and above all, to work for improved quality in child care and education.

Often, legislation involving child care is controversial. As more women work outside the home and more children grow up in single-parent families, child care has taken on new political importance. Center directors need to keep informed of current and pending legislation and make their views known to state and federal legislators who can provide up-to-date information. Local and national organizations such as National Association of Child Care Resource and Referral Agencies (NACCRRA) and NAEYC are good sources of information on legislation related to young children. Local libraries can help you find the names of your legislators. The Children's Defense Fund provides a newsletter available through email. Regular updates and bulletins on pending legislation are provided. Governmental bodies, individual government officials, and myriad organizations related to funding, education, and similar issues are easy to locate on the Internet. Two recent publications addressing the overall issues of early childhood care and education are *A Vision for Universal Preschool Education* (Zigler, Gilliam, & Jones, 2006) and *Ready or Not: Leadership Choices in Early Care and Education* (Goffin & Washington, 2007).

Center directors are responsible for maintaining current knowledge of how federal, state, and local dollars are being allocated. They should make their opinions known to their legislators and determine whether their programs or the children they serve might be eligible for various types of funding.

SOLICITING FUNDS FROM CORPORATIONS AND INDIVIDUALS

The fund-raising we have addressed so far relates to major government grants and to relatively small amounts raised for a specific immediate purpose such as additional books for classrooms or cooking activities. Most centers require funding that far exceeds tuition paid by parents. Not all centers are eligible for government funding and the owners of home centers prefer to solicit funds from nongovernmental programs.

Since most directors will need to be involved in annual and special fund-raising from corporations and individuals, they must establish policies and procedures regarding this responsibility. These policies and procedures then can be used to create individual funding campaigns.

Step one of a funding campaign is to find the people who will be the fund-raisers. If board members have been selected with this activity in mind, at least some of them will be able to contribute significantly, monetarily or in service, to the fund-raising program. All board members should understand their responsibility to make a contribution to the center, no matter how small. Some board members may have connections with community members or corporations that are prospects for center support. All should be willing to ask for contributions.

Preparing for Fund-Raising

Before beginning any fund-raising program, the board and director must make sure that the center has been formally chartered by the state and has IRS exemption. Forms for the latter can be obtained from the IRS. This status permits individual donors to deduct the amount contributed to the center as a charitable contribution. Specific procedures must be followed depending on the size of the contribution and the value (if any) that the contributor receives in return such as a dinner, book, or ticket to an event. Written reports are required in these cases, and it is the director's responsibility to know and follow the law or to see that the person assigned to this task has complied. Many agencies disseminate this type of information in a special brochure. When the contributor does not receive the proper documentation from the agency, future contributions may be jeopardized.

Whether the center retains an attorney, relies on the volunteer services of an attorney who also is a board member, or keeps abreast of legal requirements in some other manner, the board is responsible for knowing and following the law. Professional

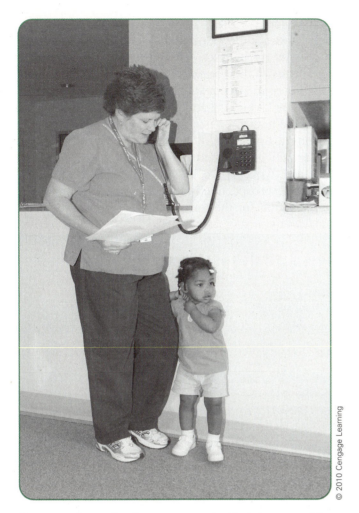

On some days, directors are expected to take care of the needs of homesick children, answer the phone, and, in addition, work on obtaining funds for the program's needs.

© 2010 Cengage Learning

If so, they certainly should give serious consideration to applying for those dollars.

Some programs are funded almost entirely by state or federal government tax dollars. Although one might argue that 3-year-olds are just as entitled to government funds as are 7-year-olds who attend public schools, relying on tax monies to support a program totally can be risky. Funding for some programs or individuals has been eliminated rather abruptly, and there is no guarantee that funds will continue from year to year. Many public elementary and secondary schools engage in additional fund-raising for aspects of the program that are usually considered integral parts of schooling such as music, athletics, field trips, and transportation to school. You must be prepared to participate in the universal preschools debate with information rather than relying solely on your personal opinions.

organizations and journals are helpful in alerting directors to potential changes and to those that have been adopted. But not knowing the law is not accepted as an excuse for not following it.

Once the agency is in a position to seek contributions, the board approves the plan to conduct a fund drive. Next, the director oversees preparation of attractive and informative materials that make the case for the program's current and future operation. The information must be free of jargon and accurate, not overblown or overly dramatic. Important points must stand out with clarity to aid the busy reader who initially may be totally unfamiliar with the center and its mission. Be sure to include the purpose of the request, the total amount being sought, and information on current funding. If the document is based on a request for proposals (RFP) created by a funder, the proposal must state clearly how the funds will be used and relate that information to the funder's goals. RFP guidelines must be followed closely, and meeting the funder's deadline is essential.

A number of reference sources are available to help you plan your fund-raising strategies and to help you target foundations, corporations, and government agencies that are likely contributors to your type of request. *Not Just Small Change* (Bergman, 2010) provides detailed information about working with your organization's board to create and implement a fund-raising program. Your public library is a good resource, as are websites related to foundations. Your board members are usually good sources of contacts, and you may want to engage a professional trainer to help you develop your solicitation plan.

Requesting Contributions

The director is responsible for ensuring that board members are prepared to speak knowledgeably and enthusiastically about the agency and the fund purpose and that they know how to ask comfortably and specifically for funds. Board members (or whoever will request contributions) should determine who will be approached, by whom, and in what time frame. Then the designated person either telephones or writes for an appointment. The latter is usually more successful and may be followed with a brief letter of confirmation. Targeting a specific amount or range for an individual or organization gift is necessary. You may receive a "no" followed by "but I can contribute a lower amount." A request for a vague amount or for a contribution may net you $100 when a specific request for $1,000 may have produced that amount. Many people are uncomfortable discussing money, and even more cringe at the thought of asking someone else for funds. Good fund-raisers focus on the value of the contribution

to the agency's clients and on providing the prospective funder an opportunity to engage in important work. In most cases, the enthusiasm and sincere approach of the requesters go a long way toward eliciting a positive response.

Let us assume that you called on someone for funds. Whether or not the response was favorable, writing a brief thank-you letter will win friends for the agency and is common courtesy. If a contribution is made, your appreciation is certainly warranted, and if the prospective funder chose not to contribute, appreciation for the time spent with you is in order.

REFLECTION

Think about a time when you needed a loan from a bank, your parents, or a friend. Did you plan ahead what you would say and how you would explain your need? Did you mention the amount you needed and the purpose of the loan? How did you decide whom to approach for a loan? A director who writes a proposal must answer similar questions. A fund-raiser seeking contributions must be equally well prepared.

REPORTING TO THE BOARD AND FUNDERS

Whether the funders are organizations providing support to assist needy families, stockholders investing for profit, members of a parent co-op, school board members, or individuals who own and direct the center, every funder needs to know how the business is doing. Accurate, timely, and understandable reports are essential. The director uses the daily transaction records to prepare monthly financial reports available to funders as well as for internal use in making budgetary decisions. (These reports also should be available to those staff members who choose to read them.) The director may present this information at a board meeting or may mail it to board members and other concerned people. Either way, the information should be presented in clear, neat, and concise form. Computer-generated reports can be revised readily so that the most current information is available. The director must be prepared to answer questions regarding the month's operating budget and to justify the figures in the report.

Since the purpose of the report is to inform the reader, it is meaningless to present a highly technical report to a group with no background in reading such reports. On the other hand, large organizations may require that each center follow a particular reporting format. In any event, the information must be presented in such a way that the reader can grasp it easily. Brief comments may clarify various aspects of the report.

The director prepares or oversees the preparation of several types of reports.

Center Enrollment Report

How many children are enrolled and how many are on the waiting list? If the center serves various age groups, the report should be subdivided into the various subgroups such as infants, toddlers, preschoolers, and after-school care. The director also may project the number of children expected to move up to the next age group on a month-by-month basis. For example, if six children will no longer be eligible for the toddler group in March, will there be room for them, based on licensing rules, in the preschool classrooms?

Accounts Receivable

The director should receive a report at least weekly of accounts receivable. In a child care center, this figure will consist primarily of tuition owed. Repeated billing on a specific schedule (usually weekly) is essential.

Budget Comparison Report

This report may also be called the budget variance report. Each month, the director prepares or receives a report from the bookkeeper showing what was spent the preceding month in each category. The report also shows budgeted spending for that month, as well as actual and budgeted spending for the year to date. The director or board then can spot cash flow problems, analyze expenditures, project remaining expenses, and revise the budget if necessary. If a funder requires monthly reports, the budget comparison report may be used.

Statement of Financial Position

On an annual basis, a statement of financial position should be prepared, showing assets (what you own) and liabilities (what you owe). This statement may be helpful as you seek additional funding.

Income Statement

The director or accountant must create an income statement at the end of each year. This statement reflects the total of all revenue earned and all expenses incurred during the fiscal year. The difference between revenue and expense is net income if revenues are greater than expenses, and net loss if expenses are greater than revenues. The income statement is widely considered the most important financial statement because it is a measure of how well a business is doing at the end of the year. The statement shows whether the company has generated a profit or is incurring losses. The income statement represents the actual figures for each of your previously budgeted categories. It can be used as a tool to evaluate monies allocated to specific categories on your budget. For example, if maintenance and repair expense was actually $7,000 for the year according to the income statement but was budgeted at $2,500 on your operating budget, you would want to reevaluate your budgeted figure, provided that the dollars spent for maintenance and repair were not one-time, unusual expenditures. In addition to this latter example, the income statement can be helpful for other kinds of statistical analyses.

Annual Report

At the end of the fiscal year, the director presents a final report showing the amount budgeted in each category and the amount actually spent. Up-to-date cash flow statements make it relatively easy to prepare the annual report. The income statement may be used. In some cases, the report will consist of income and expenses for a particular grant only. The annual report from the center or organization may be distributed to everyone who contributed, to families, to prospective donors, and to local press. The report should be designed to capture the recipients' attention. Information should be succinct, while at the same time conveying the accomplishments of the program. If your organization is large enough, you may want to employ a professional firm to prepare and mail the report.

Purchasing the software you'll need for processing your financial reports is essential. Invest in programs that will make fund-raising presentations more interesting and informative.

SHEPHERDING EXISTING FUNDS

Although obtaining additional funds often requires a significant portion of a director's time and effort, putting into place policies and procedures to manage available resources also is essential. Of course, the director presents these tools in a positive light while making it clear to staff and families that these policies and procedures will be followed. A knowledgeable, skilled director does this without rancor and without antagonizing anyone. The director helps all concerned recognize that lax procedures can lead to reduced resources. From the staff point of view, this can mean reduction in salary, staff, or supplies and equipment. For families, it can mean a lowering of program quality. And for everyone, it can mean eventual closure of the center.

Following are three areas that can lead to unexpected diminishing of funds:

1 collections
2 fraud
3 lawsuits against the center

Collections

It is not uncommon for a family to have difficulty paying bills. Recognizing this, center policies and procedures must be explained clearly and agreed to during the enrollment procedures.

- State verbally and in writing when payment is due and how it can be made (check, credit card, cash, voucher).

- Establish procedures regarding timing, method, and number of overdue reminders and whether a penalty will be charged for late payment.

- Consider a plan for accepting partial payment when a family is hit with a crisis, but keep in mind that the money is needed to meet your budget and that some families will fail to pay when their children leave the center

Your policy may be to inform the parents that the child may not attend the center program until all past due payments have been made and that the child will be readmitted only if the space has not been filled. Because positive relationships have presumably been established with every child and family, this is one of the most difficult tasks a director faces. It should never be turned over to the classroom teacher. In fact, neither the teacher nor any of the other staff need to have this confidential information.

If your policy is to require a week or two of tuition in advance, when a problem occurs, you will have payment for that period of time while you try to replace the child who must leave. This policy also will help when a family decides to move out of the area or finds another child care arrangement.

Fraud

Clear policies and procedures must be in place to protect against fraud. Huge amounts of money are embezzled each year, and a large percentage of that occurs in small businesses. Fraud refers to legally wrong "misrepresentation of a material fact the perpetrator knew was false and made with the intention that the misrepresentation be relied on and the victim did rely on and, as a result incurred a loss" (Lukaszewski, 1997). Some examples of fraud include theft of cash and charging for more hours than actually worked. An employee who has access to the financial records can commit fraud by keeping an employee on the payroll for a period after they leave, writing extra checks to themselves, or charging personal expenses to the business.

Fraud occurs when a person of low integrity is unwittingly given the opportunity to steal. For example, when one person is in charge of receiving, recording, and depositing funds, it may be easy to keep some of that money for personal use. Not accepting cash will limit this opportunity to an extent.

To prevent fraud, the director must be aware of what is happening with the financial records and periodically must cross-check records such as time cards and payroll. The board must review all financial statements carefully. Members must know how to read and understand these reports and must not be afraid to question items that seem out of line to them. However, the most important deterrent is clear, enforceable (and enforced) policies and procedures.

Lawsuits

Directors also should establish and enforce policies that will reduce the likelihood of being sued. For example, training staff and documenting that the training occurred, coupled with adequate ongoing staff supervision, will help prevent accidents. Regularly scheduled checking of equipment, buildings, and grounds, as well as maintenance, is another preventive component. You should document who checked what and on which date. Policies regarding who has access to the premises and who may take children from the center are essential and must be followed strictly. Hand-washing, food storage, and serving procedures should be reviewed regularly, as should all other health and safety policies and procedures. The licensing process may dictate some requirements, such as background checks of center staff. Even if licensing does not require such information, it should be included in your personnel policies.

Maintaining positive relations with all families and keeping them informed on a regular basis and whenever anything out of the ordinary occurs also may lessen the probability of a suit. Certainly, centers should carry insurance that will cover families' expenses in the event of an accident at the center.

The well-prepared director takes a proactive stance in seeking funds for the center and using existing resources wisely. The director also assumes responsibility for coaching the staff to follow the policies and procedures essential to the maintenance of a financially stable organization that provides high-quality care and education.

SUMMARY

Operating a good quality center requires a significant amount of funding, and dependence on tuition and government support is often unlikely to provide sufficient resources. Many programs in early childhood education depend on outside funding for partial or total support. Knowledge of the sources of funding and some skill in writing proposals are important for directors who may be forced to find funds to operate their programs when tuition is not sufficient to support a high-quality program. Some programs receive funds from their sponsoring agencies, while others depend on United Way funds, grants from foundations, or government grants.

When a center operates with a board, the board makes policies about tuition, usually to balance the need to retain enrollment and meet budgetary requirements. Tuition for child care programs is set based on cost of the program, parents' ability to pay, availability of other funds, and the marketplace. Board members also participate in securing funds and in creating the three- to five-year-year financial plan for the center.

The break-even analysis, budget comparison report, statement of financial position, and income statement are important financial management tools for the director and provide a clear, accurate picture for funders.

TRY IT OUT!

❶ Find out who provides money for early childhood education in your community. Are any programs funded by the federal, state, or local governments; United Way; private individuals; chain or franchised centers; universities or colleges; businesses; or proprietors? Is anyone else funding early childhood education in your community? Your professor may assign one student or a group to explore each of these potential resources and provide a written or oral report for the class. Record your finding on Working Paper 6-1.

❷ Contact a rural or inner-city child care center director (not a Head Start center). Inquire about the funding base. Write your answers on Working Paper 6-2.

a. How much tuition do parents pay?

b. How much of the total budget is covered by tuition?

c. What outside funding sources are available to support the program, and how much money is available through those sources?

d. How were outside funds obtained?

Discuss your findings in class. Do the resources seem adequate? What else might the center director do?

❸ Use the figures in Working Paper 6-3 to determine how many children will be in each group for the next six months. If licensing requires one adult for each four infants, one for each eight toddlers, and one for each twelve preschoolers, what effect will the changing enrollment have on your budget?

 The Education CourseMate website for this text offers many helpful resources. Go to CengageBrain.com to access the TeachSource Video Cases and other TeachSource Videos, Expand Your Learning exercises, flashcards, interactive quizzes, the eBook, reflection and enrichment activities, and downloadable forms.

Working Paper 6-1

(for use with Try It Out! 1)

FUNDING FORM

Who provides money for early childhood education in your community?

Federal government?

State government?

Local government?

United Way?

Private individuals?

Chains or franchised centers?

Universities or colleges?

Businesses?

Proprietors?

Other?

What sources of information did you use?

You can download a full-size version of this form on the Education CourseMate website.

Working Paper 6-2

(for use with Try It Out! 2)

FUNDING BASE FORM

1 Name of the center you contacted:

2 Funding base

How much tuition do parents pay?

How much of the total budget is covered by tuition?

What outside funding sources are available to support the program, and how much money is available through those sources?

How were outside funds obtained?

You can download a full-size version of this form on the Education CourseMate website.

Working Paper 6-3

(for use with Try It Out! 3)

ENROLLMENT FIGURES

February

Enrolled

Infants	10
Toddlers	16
Preschool	24

Waiting List

Infants	12
Toddlers	3
Preschool	0

Infants to Toddlers

March	1
April	0
May	2
June	1
July	1
August	0

Toddlers to Preschool

March	0
April	1
May	0
June	2
July	0
August	0

Effect on Budget?

You can download a full-size version of this form on the Education CourseMate website.

Director's Resource 6-1

SAMPLE GRANT APPLICATION*

Doe Learning Center Inc. is a nonprofit corporation that operates four child care centers in the greater metropolitan area. The centers provide quality child care for children ages 3 months through 5 years and also offer school-age care at two of the sites. As a United Way agency, the centers' common goal is to work toward alleviating the current crisis of child care, as outlined in the Long Range Plan for Child Care of the United Way in 2000. This study shows that there is an urgent need for quality programming for children identified as having special needs. Doe Learning Center Inc. has responded to this need by operating four centers whose common goal is the inclusion of all children.

Statement of Agency Commitment

Metropolitan Learning Center (MLC) is located in the central area of the city. The program serves 67 children ages 3 months through 5 years. In the summer we enroll an additional 20 children in our school-age program. Established in 1984, MLC was the first full-day program in this city to be accredited by the National Association for the Education of Young Children.

Largely based on the theories of Piaget and Erikson, the center's philosophy reflects a focus on the development of the whole child and the formation of strong, trusting relationships. The developmental constructivist approach holds the belief that children develop sequentially from one stage of development to another. Because of this we believe that children must be provided with opportunity that will challenge them and aid in their progression from one stage to the next. It is a necessity that learning be based on actual experience and participation. Talking without doing is largely meaningless to young children.

We believe that for children to grow, they must be placed in a setting that meets their basic needs. Therefore, it is our utmost concern that our program provide a nurturing, comfortable environment that is specifically structured to meet the physical, emotional, and cognitive needs of each individual child.

This philosophy was the foundation for the development of the agency. Due to this commitment, the question of inclusion was never discussed, only how to do it well.

In this time of severe staff shortages in the ECE field, MLC feels fortunate to have an outstanding quality of professionals.
• Four preschool head teachers—M.Ed.
• One toddler head teacher—Associate in Early Education

*Names of people and places are fictitious.

Director's Resource 6-1 (continued)

• Two infant teachers—Bachelor Education and two infant teachers—Associate Education
• Dr. John Jones, professor emeritus at the Metropolitan University, has been consulting with our agency for three years. This past year Dr. Jones is working strictly at MLC, coordinating our educational services.

MLC has worked extensively with the Early Childhood Education Department, Metropolitan University. The program has been a training site for the past five years and works with an average of three to four students per quarter.

According to Washington County Child Day Care: The State of Today and Plans for 2010, "Special needs children are still at a great disadvantage. Most child care providers feel ill-equipped to serve children with developmental problems and physical disabilities." MLC has successfully integrated approximately 25 children identified as having special needs. One family called more than 60 child care centers before finding a placement at MLC for their child with cerebral palsy. The center has served many children with a wide variety of special needs, including, but not limited to, pervasive development disorder, fragile X syndrome, autism, mild mental retardation, receptive language disorder, and visual impairments, to name a few.

One of the primary goals of the organization is to meet the needs of the family, parent, and child. MLC has identified its ability to meet these needs as follows:

Needs of the Child
• Placement in a program meeting the standards of developmentally appropriate practice
• Master-level staff capable of identifying and working with high-risk children

Needs of the Family
• Providing high-quality care for their children
• Providing quarterly parent education/training programs
• Providing assistance in identifying (or working with existing) available services (i.e., early intervention) for their children

MLC has been identified in the community as a program that will not only serve children with special needs but also give them access to the services they need or support the work of other service providers as part of the daily program. Metropolitan University acknowledged the endeavors of the center by placing students from the Special Education department

Director's Resource 6-1 (continued)

under the guidance of our experienced staff. We have worked with many agencies to provide more comprehensive services to these children. These agencies include the following:
• Washington County Department of Human Services
• Special Education Regional Resource Center (SERRC)
• Cerebral Palsy Services Center
• Center for Developmental Disorders
• Speech and Hearing
• Speech Pathology
• Child Advocacy Center
• Association for the Blind
• Metropolitan University—Early Childhood/Special Education Department
• Foster Grandparent Program
• The Council on Aging
• The Single Parent Center

Statement of Need
There are currently eight children enrolled in the program who have been identified as having special needs. There are several children that are integrated into the environment and are receiving services from support agencies. MLC feels confident that we can meet their needs without additional services. There are two children that pose challenges to our existing program. One child is currently enrolled in our infant program; he is 20 months old and has cerebral palsy. When we enrolled Ed, we assessed that we could meet his needs in the infant program. Though Ed is nonmobile and nonverbal, he uses smiles, cries, and coos to communicate with his caregiver.

To continue serving Ed,
• we need to be able to meet the challenge of facilitating his growth through experiences with the toddlers.
• we need to acquire the equipment to encourage his further development.
• we need release time for his caregiver to meet with his therapist to learn how to use specialized equipment and participate in his IEP meeting.

Director's Resource 6-1 (continued)

Our second child has been identified with pervasive developmental disorder and mild characteristics of autism. Communication has been the primary barrier in the progression of Ryan's development. This aspect of his disorder carries over into other areas of his growth, including the development of self-control. Ryan has been enrolled in our program for one year and within that period has gone from single-word utterances to communicating in four- to five-word sentences. Because of this increased ability to communicate, the agency believes that a transition to the oldest preschool classroom is the next step. The goal of this move is to place Ryan in an environment of his same-age peers where he might benefit from the modeling of age-appropriate behaviors and participation in activities. Any changes in daily schedule and transition times are extremely difficult for Ryan, and separation from his current classroom teacher will be a tremendous undertaking.

Our belief is that to best aid in this transition, MLC will need the assistance of an additional staff person for the following reasons:
• To meet the needs of Ryan during the period of transition so that classroom staff may continue to meet the needs of his peers
• To act as a facilitator, giving Ryan assistance with social interactions so that he might form relationships with his peers and staff
• To give the classroom staff opportunity to focus on forming trusting relationships with Ryan, without concern that the experiences of his peers are being limited

Purpose of Funding/Budget
The purpose of our funding breaks into three categories: equipment, consulting/training, and additional staff to decrease ratios.

You can download a full-size version of this form on the Education CourseMate website.

Director's Resource 6-1 *(continued)*

Equipment

Type	Purpose	Cost
Outdoor swing	$126.95	
Floor sitter	seat for severely challenged student allows a nonmobile child to interact with peers but have necessary support	$150.00
Button switch toy		$ 42.00
Jelly bean switch toy		$ 42.00
Circus truck		$ 27.00
Bumper car		$ 25.00
Brontosaurus		$ 29.50
Oversized ball	easier to manipulate than typical ball	18" $ 24.35
		34" $ 69.50

Consulting/Training

Topic (we would like to open these to public)	
How to adapt "typical" equipment to meet the needs of physically challenged children	$100.00
How to use switch toys	$ 80.00
How to write an appropriate IEP and how to make the IEP meeting work for the child	$100.00

Consulting

How to arrange the toddler environment to meet the needs of a physically challenged child	$100.00
How to encourage positive peer relationships with typical and atypical children	$ 50.00

Support Staff

Enrolling a physically challenged child into the infant program was within the abilities of our staff. Allowing time for this child to interact with peers of his own age and slowly transitioning him into the toddler room will be a challenge for us. We need time for his caregiver to visit the toddler room with him, and then time for the toddler teacher to have one-on-one time for

Director's Resource 6-1 *(continued)*

him. This cannot be done without additional staff. Any choice we make with the current staff situation will either shortchange Ed or the other children enrolled. We are requesting a part-time assistant for six months.
Cost $ 6,656

Having children that model age-appropriate behaviors has been the most vital ingredient to Ryan's development. To continue his progress, it is imperative that he be surrounded by children exhibiting the behaviors that Ryan is striving for. As mentioned earlier, any transition is very difficult for Ryan. To continue servicing Ryan and meet his needs by transitioning him to be with children of his own age, we will need additional staff.
We are requesting a part-time assistant for six months.

Cost	$ 6,656.00
TOTAL REQUESTED	$14,278.30

Expected Outcome

This grant will enable us to purchase equipment that will
- allow physically challenged children to become more accessible to the other children by being positioned near them on the floor.
- provide stimulation and encourage peer interaction.
- lessen isolation so that relationships with peers will increase.

This grant will enable us to provide sufficient staff to
- allow challenged children to be surrounded with children of their own age providing appropriate models.
- allow staff to meet the requirements of our children with special needs without denying other children the attention they need.
- facilitate smooth transitions that encourage success with meaningful relationships with other children.
- make inclusion a successful experience that will encourage staff to include additional children.

Director's Resource 6-1

This grant will provide technical assistance that will
- give the staff and management the knowledge to include these children and additional children in the future.
- encourage other early childhood programs to attend these training sessions and build support through networking with other teachers participating in inclusion.

We will be asking staff who are working with Ed and Ryan to fill out a short questionnaire before we provide additional services, and again after. We would like to see if these support services change any possible insecurities or feelings of being overwhelmed that had previously occurred.

Director's Resource 6-2

SAMPLE SLIDING FEE SCHEDULE

Parent pays:	20%	30%	40%	50%	60%	70%	80%	90%
Infant	$30/wk	$45	$60	$75	$90	$105	$120	$135
Toddler	$25	$37.50	$50	$62.50	$75	$ 87.50	$100	$112.50
Preschooler	$20	$30	$40	$50	$60	$ 70	$ 80	$ 90

You can download a full-size version of these forms on the Education CourseMate website.

REFERENCES

Barnett, W. S.; Hustedt, J. T.; Friedman, A. H.; Stevenson, J.; & Ainsworth, P. (2008) *The state of preschool 2007*. New Brunswick, NJ: National Institute for Early Education Research, Rutgers, The State University of New Jersey.

Bergman, R. L. (2010). *Not just small change: Fund development for early childhood programs*. Redmond, WA: Exchange Press.

Cohen, W. A. (2006). *The entrepreneur & small business problem solver* (3rd ed.). Hoboken, NJ: John Wiley.

Goffin, S., & Washington, V. (2007). *Ready or not: Leadership choices in early care and education*. New York: Teachers College Press.

Greene, C. L. (2012). *Entrepreneurship: Ideas in action* (5th ed.). South-Western, Cengage Learning.

Hatten T. S. (2009). *Small business management entrepreneurship and beyond*. South-Western, Cengage Learning.

Kagan, S. L.; Brandon, R. N.; Ripple, C. H.; Maher, E. J.; & Joesch, J. M. (2002, May). Supporting quality early childhood care and education: Addressing compensation and infrastructure. *Young Children, 57*(3), 58–65.

Linsmeier, D. (2003, May). Valuing your child care business. *Child Care Information Exchange, 151*, 56–59.

Lukaszewski, T. (1997). Who can you trust? *Child Care Information Exchange, 116*, 20–24.

Mitchell, A. (1996). Fishing for dollars in philanthropic waters. *Child Care Information Exchange, 111*, 7–10.

Morgan, G. & Emanuel, B. (2010). *The bottom line for children's programs: What you need to know to manage the money* (5th ed.). Watertown, MA: Steam Press.

National Association for the Education of Young Children. (n.d.). *Child care and development block grant*. Retrieved July 16, 2008, from http://www.naeyc.org/policy/federal/ccdbg.asp.

National Child Care Information and Technical Assistance Center. (2005, January). *Employer-supported child care*. Retrieved July 16, 2008, from http://nccic.acf.hhs.gov/poptopics/employersupportedcc.html.

National Child Care Information and Technical Assistance Center. (2007). Retrieved July 15, 2008, from http://stateplan2006-2007/executivesummary.

Stone, D. (2008). *Funding the future: States' approaches to pre-K finance, 2008 update* (rev. ed.). Washington, DC: Pre-K Now, 2008.

U.S. Department of Health & Human Services, Administration for Children & Families. (2008). *Head Start program fact sheet*. Retrieved July 13, 2008, from http://www.acf.hhs.gov/programs/ohs/about/fy2008.html.

Vast, T. (2003, July). Establishing and managing a tuition aid program: Guidelines for helping families with financial difficulties. *Child Care Information Exchange, 152*, 27–32.

Zigler, E.; Gilliam, W.; & Jones, S. (2006). *A vision for universal preschool education*. New York: Cambridge University Press.

DEVELOPING *a* CENTER FACILITY

© 2010 Cengage Learning

Directors work with architects and contractors before and during the building or renovation process.

An early childhood education program should be housed in a spacious, attractive facility that has been created or redesigned for children and that also meets the needs of staff members and parents. The director is responsible for ensuring that appropriate space is available; therefore, space needs are analyzed carefully for both ongoing and new programs. The director may assume full responsibility for analysis of space needs or this job may be done in cooperation with the board building committee or with staff members. Corporate systems often have a prototypical design for all centers in the system, and they usually designate an employee to provide and manage the physical facilities for the system's centers. Similarly, preschool facilities in public schools may be planned by central administration, although the principal may have a major decision-making role. In any case, the facilities must be well maintained. The director is responsible for the development of a maintenance system and for seeing that it is implemented.

As we work to meet all the standards and requirements imposed for good reason, let us also reflect on the words of beloved early childhood educator and author, Jim Greenman: "An environment is a living, changing system. More than the physical space, it includes the way time is structured and the roles we are expected to play. It conditions how we feel, think, and behave; and it dramatically affects the quality of our lives" (Greenman, 2007, p. 1).

Objectives

After reading this chapter, you should be able to:

* Describe an early childhood facility that meets the needs of children, staff members, and families.
* Explain the director's role related to facilities management.
* Identify the individual consultants involved in planning an early childhood facility.
* Explain the director's role in creating a new facility.
* Describe the tasks involved in moving a program to an existing facility.

Standard Addressed in this Chapter

naeyc Accreditation Standard 9

ANALYZING SPACE REQUIREMENTS

In providing a suitable facility, the first task is to analyze the space needs. When a program is already in operation, this analysis is made periodically to ensure the availability of proper facilities for both present and future needs. If the center's program or enrollment changes, it may be necessary to modify, add, or eliminate space in the existing center. In some cases, a different location may be needed. Under any of these circumstances, the director may have to assume major responsibility for ensuring that appropriate facilities are provided. A thorough space analysis should be made before any renovation, relocation, or initial facilities choices are made.

REFLECTION

Think about a place to which you often go. Maybe it's a library, a store, or a college building. What kind of experience do you have as you approach the building? Is it easy to find the entrance? Is it accessible? Do you feel comfortable entering, or are you a little bit intimidated? Once you enter, can you find the area you need? If not, is help available (a receptionist, signs, a computer information kiosk)? How do you feel when everything seems quite unfamiliar and no one seems to care that you have arrived?

How might a 3-year-old feel on his first day in preschool?

Users of an early childhood education facility fall into three groups: children, staff, and families. An analysis of space requirements must be based on the needs of each of these users. Space needs are based on consideration for the users, program requirements, and governmental regulations. Therefore, the director must have up-to-date information in all these areas. One option for creating a space analysis is to chart the hours that the center is used by one or more people. How many people will use each space, at what times, and for what types of activities? Of course, the desired number of children to be enrolled will be of major importance. Very small centers may be more costly (per child) to operate while those that serve hundreds of children may overwhelm the child. Large centers must be very carefully designed so that children have private spaces. What the child encounters on a daily basis, in terms of both facilities and people, must be manageable for each child.

DIRECTOR'S CORNER

"When we received funds to move out of a church basement, we designed our new center in two pods. Each pod has rooms for infants, toddlers, and preschoolers. Each pod has playground spaces, one for infants and toddlers and one for preschoolers. The large motor activity area, office, staff space, and area for visitors serve both pods. A few years later, when our enrollment continued to grow, we added a third pod. We find that the children, families, and staff identify the pod as 'their' school, while the teachers and families feel part of a school community as well as of a specific pod.

—Director of an employer-sponsored child care center

Basic Requirements

NAEYC describes the standard for physical environment as "a safe and healthful environment that provides appropriate and well-maintained indoor and outdoor physical environments" (NAEYC, 2008). Lella Gandini, official liaison in the United States for the Administration of Early Childhood Education of the Municipality of Reggio Emilia, Italy, emphasizes the importance of recognizing the "special qualities of local life." She also points out, "One of the greatest challenges in designing institutions is to transform a physical plant into a human environment. One part of the transformation has to do with discovering ways to allow impersonal rooms and hallways to reflect the lives of the children and adults who spend so many active hours in that space" (Gandini, 1994).

Both children and adults are bombarded with stimulation. Using decorations judiciously can minimize environmental "noise." For example, limit what is on walls and windows. Children's art and photographs, documentation of projects, and information for parents and staff are all legitimate items to be posted. When space surrounds each posting, it is more likely that someone will notice the item. When displays are changed frequently, the newness draws children and adults alike to inspect them.

Since a child care center is planned primarily to meet the needs of children, all child care facilities should be comfortable and convenient, both in terms of children's sizes, their developmental levels and needs, and their interests. Preschool children need space for active and quiet play; for having breakfast, lunch, and snacks; and for taking naps.

Very young infants need a play area that is safe from crawlers. And crawlers need plenty of space to move around and explore their environment without being stepped on by children who have just begun to walk.

Each child needs an individual space to keep outdoor clothing and for a change of clothes. Infants and toddlers need separate storage areas for diapers and other personal items that are provided by parents. Preschoolers need a place to store special items they bring to show others but not to share with them.

Programs for school-age child care before and after school require space for older children and must take into account the need for active play as well as relaxing, studying, and preparing and eating snacks. Children who spend six or seven hours in a school classroom need a change of pace and should not feel they are in a schoolroom before and after school.

The building also must be comfortable and convenient for adult users. To work effectively with the children, staff need a place designed for breaks and

The design of a diaper-changing station must take into account the child's needs as well as staff convenience and back health. Maintaining safe and sanitary procedures is essential.

planning time. To feel comfortable in the center, families need a welcoming entry experience and a place to meet with other families and with staff.

The primary needs that planners must consider for each of these users are

- health and safety
- accessibility of facilities
- controlled traffic flow
- personal space
- opportunities for independence and growth
- aesthetic character of all spaces

Meeting the needs of each group of users has a cumulative and reciprocal effect because when the needs of one group are met, a step is taken toward meeting the needs of the other two groups. The dynamics of a human environment involve the impact of each group on the others. In a well-run center, the three groups interact effectively because each is involved in the joint, sensitive process of child development.

Health and Safety

Center planners must be aware of the safety aspects above and beyond those stipulated in licensing regulations. A hazard-free building meets the needs of staff and parents, as well as children. Directors must keep abreast of environmental issues. For example, asbestos and lead paint, once considered appropriate building materials, now are not used in child care centers. Some sealed buildings in which air is recirculated may be simply redistributing poor-quality air. Recently, several schools have extensively renovated sections of buildings in which mold had developed, usually from a leaking pipe. Although not ordinarily visible on the surface, mold may cause children and teachers to become ill. The solution is to close off the area while qualified personnel remove contamination. In some cases, the director may be required to close the center while the work is done.

Governmental regulations usually will determine the type of building and decorative materials (such as carpeting) to be used, the number and type of exits (including panic hardware and lighted exit signs), the number and location of fire extinguishers, smoke detectors, and fire alarm systems, and the location of furnaces and water heaters relative to the children's play area. All these regulations protect children and staff from dangers associated with fire. Choosing environmentally friendly materials whenever possible will ultimately enhance the environment and the health of everyone.

Children also must be protected from such hazards as tap water that is too hot, slippery floor surfaces, unsafe or unprotected electrical outlets and wiring, and poorly lighted spaces. Because of the hazards to both children and adults, smoking must not be permitted in the building or on the grounds. Covered convenience outlets or specially designed safety outlets are needed throughout the classroom for audio-visual equipment, computers, aquaria, and so forth. The director must ensure that the flooring is even; that there are no protrusions to cause falls; that stairs are provided with sturdy, low rails; and that protective screening is installed on all windows. Although the director is primarily responsible for establishing and maintaining a basic safety plan for the center, every staff member must remain alert to potential hazards and must teach children simple safety procedures such as reshelving toys and mopping up spilled water.

In public schools where older children use the hallways, plans for entering and exiting the building and moving about must be made so that young children experience minimal encounters with large groups of grade-schoolers. Although older children can move about the building independently, additional staff may be required so that young children will have escorts when they go to the library, the office, or the restroom. Ideally, each classroom for young children will have its own adjoining bathroom.

In any building, many safety practices revolve around the enforcement of center safety rules, such as prohibiting children from climbing on window sills, but it is preferable to adapt the building itself so that it is a safe place for children. Placing locks on the furnace room door is less disturbing to everyone and far safer for children than telling them they must not enter the furnace area. Be sure, however, that security devices such as locks or gates do not block an emergency exit. Guidelines for fire safety can be obtained by consulting the fire inspector. All staff must understand and follow written procedure for everyone's safety. Situations that may require calm and immediate use of these procedures include fire, tornadoes, hurricanes, presence of an intruder, a building lock-down because of a situation in the area, and so forth.

For safety reasons, programs for children usually are housed on the ground-floor level of the building, even when licensing regulations do not require this. Stairways are dangerous obstacles to quick and safe building evacuation. In the event of a fire or other emergency that requires building evacuation, preschool children may become confused or frightened and will need individual guidance to reach safety.

In such situations, staff members caring for infants, toddlers, and nonambulatory preschoolers will be able to remove only the one or two children they can carry. Some centers place several babies in a crib and roll the crib to safety. If children are on an upper floor, remember that it is unsafe to use elevators in an emergency.

Over and above promoting the ease of evacuation, other safety considerations make ground-level facilities immediately adjacent to fenced outdoor space very advantageous. When children can go directly from their classrooms to a fenced outdoor area, the teaching staff can supervise both those children who choose outdoor play and those who remain indoors. One teacher would be outside with children there and another teacher would be inside with those children. An adult must be able to see every child at all times and to reach each of them quickly and easily. The outdoor space is viewed as an extension of the indoor space. Fenced-in play areas prevent children from leaving the play space and prevent others from entering and damaging equipment, interfering with children's play, or leaving dangerous materials such as broken glass around the area. A covered outdoor space provides an additional advantage because it can be used on rainy days or on very hot, sunny days.

All exits from the building and the outdoor playground should be in locations where supervision of who comes and goes can be maintained readily. While the center may welcome community visitors, strangers should not be permitted to wander through the building. Similarly, children should not be able to leave unnoticed, either alone or accompanied by anyone other than authorized personnel. Panic hardware must be provided on all exit doors, but they should be locked so that visitors cannot enter without being admitted. Parents and staff probably will have to be reminded that holding the door open for an arriving visitor is unwise since that person's presence in the center may go unnoticed.

Accessibility of Facility

All users must have easy access to the building. Many parents do not want to subject their children to long daily trips to and from the center, and they prefer a center close to home. Others will look for a center close to the workplace so that they can visit the child during the day. Location near public transportation also is desirable for staff and parents.

Access to the center is increased when people feel comfortable about entering the building; therefore, the scale of the building is another consideration. As children approach the center, they should feel that it fits them. Even a large building should have some features that indicate to each child that the building is theirs. Entranceways and the areas surrounding them can be scaled to the children's requirements so that the children are not overwhelmed by a huge, heavy door or a stairway wide enough for a regiment.

Because parents and visitors often form opinions about a program on the basis of external appearances, the grounds must be well maintained, and the building itself must be inviting. A building welcomes people through its scale, color, texture, and design. When the building is compatible with other buildings in the neighborhood, the center can begin to establish itself as a positive force in the community and be considered as an integral part of the total community. Understandably, an ultra contemporary building might not be welcome in a traditional residential neighborhood.

The parking area should be located near the center's entrance and should be large enough to accommodate the cars of staff, parents, and visitors. A safe walkway from parking to entry is essential because many parents will arrive with several children, diaper bags, and favorite toys. Some children are so excited about arriving at their center that they may run quickly, but not safely, to the door.

Building Entry

When a child care center is housed in a building shared by other users, the center should have a separate entrance that is clearly marked so that families and visitors can find it. Entrances used by older students, agency clients, or other tenants may mean heavy traffic that can intimidate children and may make supervision of their arrival and departure more difficult. Many centers now have entry systems requiring visitors to ring a bell, while designated family members enter a code that unlocks the door. The code may be changed periodically for security.

Inside the building, there should be clear indications of where to proceed. Signs, supergraphics, or pathways incorporated in the flooring (such as tile arrows) can lead visitors to the proper place, even if no receptionist or secretary is available. A pleasant greeting from a receptionist is ideal, especially when the child and parent are called by name, but many centers are unable to afford a staff member to fill that role.

When the receptionist's or secretary's office has a large glass window overlooking the entry, visual contact can be made with people as they arrive, and parents or visitors will feel more comfortable about asking for assistance. In the office adjacent to the entry, the center staff can greet people and

receive forms and payments from families. If parents or visitors find no one with whom to communicate when they enter the building, they may become disgruntled and leave, feeling that no one cares about their needs. Or a visitor may search out the classrooms and begin a conversation with a busy teacher, disturbing activities there and probably inviting a cursory response that is detrimental to good public relations. The entry also should be accessible to the director's office so that he is highly visible and readily available. Furthermore, it is imperative that all visitors be screened to ensure that everyone who enters has a legitimate purpose.

Many centers require an access code to open the door of the center. As technological development continues, an even wider variety of options, such as voice and fingerprint recognition, may be readily available to programs. Although some centers have already installed surveillance cameras at exterior doors and in hallways, these may become more commonly used by centers. Some programs have these cameras in classrooms so that parents can access views of their children's activities from their places of employment. A simple safety feature, such as

A pleasant greeting from a receptionist makes everyone feel welcome.

Often staff and visitors are required to wear identification badges. Another important identifier of you and your staff is the warm greeting you give one another each day.

well-lighted exterior doors, makes it easier and safer for staff and parents arriving and leaving the center during early morning and evening hours.

In many centers, staff wear identification badges. Visitors are given a temporary visitor badge. In other centers, parents sign their children in and out via computer, connected to the center's software package. More elaborate screening devices are used in very large centers, requiring visitors to insert their driver's license into a machine that records the data with the exact date and time of arrival. To exit, the process is repeated.

In any case, the entry itself should say "welcome." The colors used in the entry should indicate that this is a place for growth and vitality; grayness and drabness do not belong here. Lighting is as important here as it is in the classrooms. The area should be bright but not harsh. Avoid glare, perhaps by using sheer window covers, awnings or shades. Sunshine is ideal, but when that is not available, an artificially, brightly illuminated area with softer lighting in cozy areas sets the tone for the real warmth that children and families can expect to experience throughout the center. Entry surfaces also are important and must be designed to withstand muddy shoes or boots and dripping umbrellas. Although the entry should be large enough to accommodate several people without being crowded, it should not be too large since such space has minimum use but still costs about as much per square foot as areas that are heavily used. Furthermore, large entranceways may overwhelm a child or

intimidate an unsure parent. Some children will interpret large open spaces as an invitation to run.

The required minimum number of entrances and exits is determined by fire laws, but to determine the best locations for these doors, the planners should take into consideration the traffic patterns of people who come to the building. Teachers like to greet parents as they arrive with their children; therefore, locating the arrival point close to the classrooms helps parents and children as well as teachers. Similarly, when the children leave, teachers can see the parents briefly.

Just as children should be able to reach their classrooms without walking through long, uninteresting, and perhaps frightening hallways, adults should be able to get to their areas conveniently and without disturbing children's play. For example, deliveries to the kitchen or other service areas should be easy to make without having to negotiate stairs or move through the children's space.

Accessibility carries an additional importance for those who have special needs. The Americans with Disabilities Act (ADA) requires that facilities be designed so that all services can be used by all clients and employees. Entrances and exits, traffic flow patterns, and facilities throughout the building and grounds should be designed for ease of use by people who have disabilities. People (children included) in wheelchairs or on crutches should be able to move about comfortably; to use bathrooms, drinking fountains, and telephones; and to participate in all aspects of the center's program. Seemingly small items such as the type of faucet on sinks or the handles on cabinets can be designed to facilitate use by people who otherwise would have to ask for assistance. The ADA requires these accommodations for most centers that meet certain conditions, but even in situations where the accommodations are optional, concern for the comfort of all individuals necessitates that efforts be made to modify buildings.

Control of Traffic Flow

Planners should consider the children's daily traffic patterns between indoor and outdoor spaces, as well as within those spaces. For example, children will move from classroom to multipurpose room and back, and from classroom to outdoor area and back. They may leave from the outdoor area if they are playing there when their parents arrive. A good floor plan takes into account the fact that young children should be able to go directly outdoors, preferably from their own classroom, or at least with minimal walking in hallways or in areas used for other purposes.

Coat storage should be near the door where the children enter. When coats are stored in the classroom, shelving may be used to create a coat area separate from the play space.

Well-planned children's areas are designed so that teachers can supervise all areas from almost any vantage point without excessive walking and certainly without screaming at children. A teacher in a room with an alcove may have to walk over to that area repeatedly to know what is happening there. An L-shaped outside area may be spacious, but such an area becomes very difficult to supervise without extra staff because as soon as children turn the corner, they are out of sight and beyond the reach of their teacher.

Food Service

Serving meals to children further complicates the traffic flow in the center. Because preschool children usually eat in their classrooms, there is no need for a separate cafeteria. In fact, in a public school, the noise and confusion of a cafeteria is inappropriate for preschoolers and the furniture is too large to accommodate them comfortably. Preschool classrooms, therefore, must be large enough to contain tables and chairs for all the children and teachers without crowding the play space. The kitchen should be nearby. Steps or doorways between the kitchen and the classrooms make moving food carts or carrying trays difficult, and long distances between the kitchen and classrooms may mean long walks for teachers and long waits for children when something extra is needed during mealtime.

When teachers sit at the table with children and eat the food that is served to the children, they model good eating habits and appropriate manners without lecturing children on how to behave and what foods are good for them. The center budget should include enough food for teachers since this is part of their job. Some teachers will prefer to provide their own lunch to be eaten during their break time. Nonetheless, those teachers should still have lunch with the children and eat at least small amounts of the food served.

The kitchen must function primarily in relation to the classrooms and secondarily in relation to adult areas. The amount of kitchen space required varies according to the activities to be conducted. The center that uses a catering service for lunches may need very little space, while the center in which hot lunches are prepared will require additional equipment and space. In very large centers, a kitchenette may be provided for staff use and for preparation of refreshments for various meetings.

REFLECTION

Think about how the traffic pattern of a building you use frequently affects you. When you arrive at this building, which room do you go to first? Where is that room in relation to the door you use to enter the building? Think about the directions in which you move through the building during the day. Are there any places that could be rearranged to save you steps? Classrooms can be arranged for variety and ease of traffic flow if areas within the room are clearly demarcated and exits are located so that traffic does not cross through a number of areas. Shelves for blocks are excellent room dividers that can be used to separate the block area from the housekeeping area and from the heavy traffic area, thereby providing a special space for undisturbed block building. Reading and writing areas can be separated from noisy carpentry or music areas by shelves or dividers; then children can find quiet, secluded spaces for solitude and concentration. Children can work comfortably without being disturbed when traffic patterns in the classroom are taken into consideration. One of your roles as director will be to help teachers recognize the value of planned traffic flow.

Bathroom Locations

Licensing laws regulate the number of toilets and sinks required, but the location of the bathroom is equally important. Children need bathrooms immediately adjacent to their classrooms, multipurpose room, and outdoor play areas so that they can get to them quickly. Each of these areas may not need a separate bathroom, but planning can include location of one bathroom to serve two areas. Prekindergarten boys and girls are comfortable sharing the same bathroom. However, the philosophy of some programs and the requirements of some governmental bodies now necessitate separate toilet facilities for boys and girls. Certainly these are needed for school-age children. As with all other areas, restrooms require adequate adult supervision.

Location of adult bathroom facilities is often determined by designing a plumbing core around which the bathrooms and kitchen are built. Although a plumbing core design is economical, it may not be practical in terms of the traffic pattern and the program needs because adult bathrooms must be placed appropriately to serve the people in classrooms, offices, meeting rooms, and the kitchen.

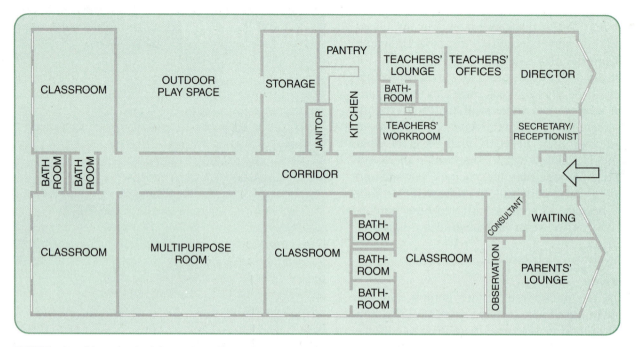

FIGURE 7-1 Hypothetical floor plan showing relation of staff space to child space.
Source: © Cengage Learning, 2013.

Arrival Area

Figure 7-1 shows an example of a plan for a child care center, but because each center should be designed to meet the needs of its clients and staff, it is not meant as a model. Several of this plan's characteristics are worth imitating, however. Note that as families arrive, the receptionist (or director) can greet them and then they can go directly to the classrooms. (The arrow to the right on Figure 7-1 indicates the entrance.) An observation booth is shown overlooking one classroom. When space is available, this feature may be desired for all of the children's spaces. Parents and visitors can observe without being seen by the children. Observation booths enable future teachers to learn about children's development and related good teaching practices. Note, too, that each classroom has an adjoining restroom for children and that a multipurpose room is available for large-muscle activities.

Staff Area

In planning for traffic flow, the staff's daily traffic patterns also must be considered with attention focused on which areas they use in what sequence on a typical day. Figure 7-1 shows the relationship of staff members' spaces to children's spaces in one center. Teachers need a conveniently located general storage room to enable them to set up the day's activities efficiently. They must be able to move comfortably and quickly from the storage areas to the classroom, the outdoor area, or the multipurpose room, depending on where the equipment or the

supplies are needed. Teachers each need a locked cabinet or drawer in which to store personal belongings of value. In or near the classroom, they need a place to hang coats, gloves, etc. needed when they go outside with the children.

Bathroom facilities for teachers should be separate from those used by the children, and there should be a lounge area in which to have refreshments during break times. Work space includes places in which they work with children, places in which they prepare materials for classrooms, and places in which they do paperwork or hold conferences. Work space that meets the staff members' needs assists them in performing their duties well. Some personnel have specialized work spaces (maintenance staff; the cook; and specialists such as a nurse, speech and language therapist, psychologist, or other consultants). Each workplace must be of a size suitable for the activity in question. For example, full-time office staff each need approximately 100 square feet of office space. This space should be arranged to provide for some privacy and sound control so that work can be accomplished with minimal interruption. Sometimes, with proper written documentation from parents and the child's physician, a teacher will be asked to administer medication at school. Therefore, a locked cabinet is necessary in each classroom. In or next to the cabinet, one should find a clipboard or notebook on which to document the administration of the medication. This responsibility is very important; making a mistake could be quite damaging to the child. Paying attention to licensing guidelines as well as center policies and procedures related to these issues is essential.

Office space sometimes is placed close to the classrooms so that immediate additional supervision can be provided in an emergency situation; however, planners may decide to place the offices farther away from the classrooms to eliminate distractions for the director, off-duty teachers, or other staff members. An intercom system can be installed to facilitate communication in emergency situations and to eliminate disturbances. The intercom or a telephone may be a necessity if a classroom or any other area used by children is isolated from direct contact with the rest of the center. For example, all classrooms may be located on the ground floor while the multipurpose room is a level above them. A teacher using the multipurpose room needs a telephone to reach additional help if a crisis occurs. In any case, policies regarding the use of the intercom and telephone should be in place, largely to eliminate unnecessary noise and disturbance in the classrooms.

Figure 7-2 shows additional ideas for arranging center facilities. If you have ever browsed through magazines showing floor plans of various homes, you may have found yourself saying, "There's a feature I like" or "I'd never want to have a room like that." Consider these floor plans in the same way. Examine them to see what you would like and why. Keep in mind that the ages and numbers of children to be served will have a major effect on the plan for the building and grounds. Geography and topography also will play important roles. For example, on a sloping lot, both the front and the back of a building may be at least partially at ground level. This condition is an important planning issue.

Spaces for Children

A comfortable and convenient classroom for young children includes enough space for each child to work and play without being disturbed by other activities. Thirty-five square feet per child is considered minimum, so a classroom for ten 3-year-olds must have at least 350 square feet, measuring about 18 feet by 20 feet. Fifty square feet per child is more realistic, and more space should be provided whenever possible. However, extremely large classrooms

FIGURE 7-2 Hypothetical floor plan.
Source: © Cengage Learning, 2013.

are difficult to supervise and may feel overwhelming to children. When determining classroom square footage, do not include permanent fixtures such as a sink in the classroom or immovable cabinets. Also keep in mind that when children's storage cubbies are in the classroom, the space immediately in front of the cubbies is rarely usable for classroom activities (except getting outdoor clothing on and off). Space in front of doors is also not usable for activities (entrance door, bathroom door, and door to outside play area).

Rooms for infants require more space because of their cribs. Infants need a quiet area so that they can sleep on their own schedules. Infants able to play on the floor need space to practice moving from place to place by scooting, creeping, and crawling, while others are trying to roll from side to side, to work on sitting up, and to try to reach a toy that is just slightly out of reach. Meanwhile one of the caregivers may be rocking and soothing an uncomfortable child, feeding a hungry baby, or changing a diaper. Therefore, groups of infants are kept quite small with a 1:3 or 1:4 adult-child ratio and two adults at all times.

Toddlers are becoming a little more independent, more mobile, and more interested in exploring *everything* in the environment. They still need the support of and access to an adult frequently during their waking hours. Toddler rooms should also be a little larger per child than are rooms for preschoolers.

In all classrooms where diapers are changed, a special area is needed with a changing table, access to supplies needed such as gloves for the adult, cleansing supplies, clean diapers, and a place to deposit used diapers—all within the reach of the adult who is at the side of the child being changed to prevent falls. A sink immediately adjacent to the changing table is needed for adult hand washing. Keep in mind that, while diaper changing is occupying one adult, the other adult must be alert to the needs of the remaining five to seven babies. One can see why infants and toddlers are placed in small groups!

All children need cozy places where they can relax while they look at books, examine interesting objects, or just daydream. These spaces should be small enough to promote a sense of privacy and intimacy, yet large enough to be shared with a friend or two. For preschoolers, a loft can meet this need. It must be quite sturdy and have some kind of siding to prevent objects from falling to the floor and hitting anyone below. The space under the loft can be used for storage or small group activities. The teacher must be able to supervise the area. Furthermore, a loft and all other spaces designed for children's use should be accessible to each child.

The classroom also must include a meeting area that is large enough for a number of children to gather for a story or special activity. Furniture can be moved for these occasions: movable shelving and furniture facilitate such rearranging. These movable pieces also will be valued when teachers are placing cots for children's naps. Too much furniture moving detracts from the teacher's real role, but most centers do not have a separate nap room and must consider how to place cots so that children will not be too close to one another (a requirement of many licensing rules). When cots are too close together, children may find it difficult to rest. Space also must be available for cot storage.

Some centers also offer care to children from kindergarten through third or fourth grade or older. These children come to the center for before- and after-school care and may even be transported between sites by a center bus. School age children will treasure some personal space. Imagine spending ten hours a day in a relatively small space with 30 people, primarily following someone else's directions. Although many adults do spend eight hours in a work environment crowded with equipment and people, they have the opportunity to go out for lunch or take a short break. Children in schools usually are required to stay with their class for the entire day. After school, having some private space provides a welcome respite.

Before and after school, elementary grade children also need spaces for organizing clubs and playing games, for informal sports, and for creating and carrying out their own wonderful ideas. They need adult

In after-school care, many children enjoy working on projects.

supervision, but at the same time, they need much more independence in organizing and reorganizing the space, perhaps decorating it so it is theirs. Because these needs are quite different from those of younger children, it is clear they need separate spaces.

Family Space

Parents and visitors need a comfortable lounge area in which to wait for their children or to talk with each other. Parents also need a space that is large enough for group meetings and space that is small enough for individual conferences with a teacher or the director. Even if a whole room is not available, centers can at least provide some seating in another area. Fire laws may preclude having furniture in hallways. Facilities for observing the classrooms, while going unnoticed by the children, represent both a convenience and a learning experience for parents and visitors.

Often, employer-sponsored child care is provided near the work site. Parents will appreciate an area in the classroom where they can spend quiet time with their own children, sharing a book or puzzle. In infant centers, a private space for nursing offers a relaxing time for mother and baby.

Opportunities for Independence and Growth

The facility should be planned to promote the independence of both children and staff. An environment for children fosters independence and growth when it is arranged so they can make decisions and solve many of their own problems. Such a setting has child-size appointments, including sinks, toilets, and drinking fountains, doorknobs that children can reach and operate (where that is desirable), and wall decorations that are placed at the children's eye level. Planners must keep in mind that independence is equally important for children with special needs.

A setting that encourages independence also has classroom storage that is directly accessible to children, enabling them to find and reach all the materials and equipment they use. When such shelving is adequate, each piece of equipment is displayed so that the children can see it easily, remove it from the shelf without moving other items stacked on top of it, and return it to its proper place. Clearly marked storage space for children's personal belongings, located so that children can get to it, also will promote independence. In addition, however, storage space that is out of children's reach also is needed in each classroom so that teachers can store materials and supplies they do not want the children to obtain, such as gallon jugs of glue.

Single-purpose buildings allow programming to be based on users' needs (especially those of children) rather than requiring that the program be planned based on the needs of a range of occupants. A center allows teachers to feel independent when the design of the facility enables them to plan programs for their children without constantly checking with other teachers. For example, teacher independence is curtailed when a preschool class is housed in a public elementary school where the young children must use the bathroom, lunchroom, or outdoor play space for specific time blocks because older children use these facilities at other times. Even if the children's needs suggest a deviation from this schedule, the teacher may be required to follow it. Some teachers in centers that move children from room to room for various activities find that they are not able to plan as independently if they have to direct children from the art room to the music room and then to the playroom on a daily basis at a predetermined, scheduled time rather than having the children move at their own pace. Children may feel frustrated at having to move to another area just as they are getting interested in writing a message or serving dinner in their "restaurant." Obviously, balance is needed. Children and teachers usually have to stop at a particular time for lunch. And when it's time to go home, a parent may be able to spend a few minutes while her child finishes an art project, but then it's really time to leave.

The environment that fosters independence and growth is one in which variety is apparent, offering children an *appropriate* number of choices. They are not overwhelmed with choices or bored with repetitive sameness in design of space. Variety in color, texture, floor level, and building materials, if not overdone, can give children a sense of vitality that can be stimulating. Noise level is another area in which variety can be appropriate. Some spaces may be set aside for noisy play while others are retained for quieter activities. Although acoustical ceilings, carpeted floors, and curtains all absorb sound and contribute to the auditory comfort of everyone in the center, children still can learn to use appropriate sound levels in each space and to choose their activities accordingly. The environment leads to cooperation as well as to independence. When staff members find themselves working in a well-designed, appropriate space, they are happier, which leads to a better program for children (Sussman, 1998).

Aesthetic Character

An environment for children should be aesthetically pleasing to them. The factors relating to other users' needs and to program requirements can be designed

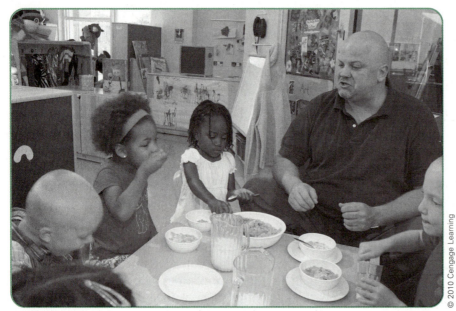

Children develop independence and friendships when they enjoy meals together. Teachers always sit with the children and share the meal.

© 2010 Cengage Learning

so that they appeal to the children's sense of beauty. For example, it is just as easy to have an interesting painting in the classroom as it is to put up a fake window with curtains over the play sink. Both are intended to make the room more attractive. Children can enjoy a wide range of art, but the value of a fake window is limited, at best.

Provide as much natural light as possible while avoiding glare. Artificial lighting should be bright enough for children's activities but also adjustable. Lamps that cannot be tipped over, ceiling lighting that can be controlled with dimmer switches, and area lighting all contribute to a feeling of physical and emotional well-being and help foster productivity, relaxation, and comfort. Incandescent lighting and full-spectrum lighting seem more appropriate than fluorescent. Consider purchasing energy-efficient light bulbs, which, though initially more expensive, are longer lasting and environmentally friendly.

Wall surfaces can provide texture and color that contribute to the room's vitality. Garish decorations or "cute" wall coverings, emblems, or cutouts contribute little to children's appreciation of beauty. Carpets replete with numbers and letters add "busyness" to the environment and provide neither aesthetic nor intellectual stimulation. Children and staff probably will be more inclined to take care of an attractive environment. It is easy to develop messy habits when the surroundings are poorly designed with inadequate facilities and unappealing spaces. It is equally easy and more satisfying for everyone to develop good habits and an appreciation of beauty when the facilities are well designed. Note

that the touches a teacher adds may be inexpensive or free: a single flower from her garden, attractively mounted pictures of the children at play, or a crystal hanging in the window to catch the light and project interesting colors and patterns throughout the room.

Having analyzed the facility requirements for a high-quality early childhood education program, and the information provided by a specific needs assessment, the director can determine the center's current facility needs and project the building and grounds needs of the center for several years. This long-range planning is useful in enabling a center to coordinate program, facility, and financial decision making. Whether the director is analyzing need in terms of possibly rearranging or remodeling the existing center's facilities, or of leasing or constructing a new center, the users' needs are kept in the forefront when working toward a decision.

DIRECTOR'S CORNER

"Our entire staff spent hours discussing what our ideal center would look like. We listed all the criteria for each space, including details such as height and depth of classroom sinks, number of feet of shelving in the toy storage room, and types of doorknobs. We couldn't have everything we wanted because of the cost, but we all felt like we had helped design our new center."

—Director, agency-sponsored center

Programmatic Requirements

The director and building committee members must be thoroughly familiar with the early childhood education program before they attempt to evaluate an existing or proposed facility. They must understand the types of activities planned, the program goals, and the enrollment projections. For example, in contrast to a half-day program, a full-day program must provide a place for resting and for eating meals. Many children who spend the entire day at a center also need room in which to seclude themselves from the group for short periods of time, a quiet place supervised by the teacher but free from the intrusion of other children.

The center's philosophy influences the type and arrangement of space. If the philosophy places heavy emphasis on parent involvement, space will be needed for meeting rooms and a lounge, and additional parking will have to be provided. The prevailing climate also affects the type of building. If children are able to be outdoors most days on a year-round basis, they will need more outdoor space and slightly less indoor space. On the other hand, a center located in a region with temperature extremes will put emphasis on indoor areas and will give major consideration to effective heating, ventilating, and air-conditioning systems. Floor-level temperature in the children's areas is critical since children frequently play on the floor.

Planning for carpeting and tiling sections of the classroom floor should be done with activities in mind. Cleaning is facilitated when art and food activities take place on hard surfaces, and teachers will be able to focus on the children's needs instead of

protecting the carpeting. A sink in the classroom is a much-used and much-desired convenience and also should be on the tiled area.

Keep in mind the importance of the outdoor environment. Just as children need to test ideas in the classroom, so, too, do they need to test ideas outdoors. They also need opportunities to test what they can do physically as they explore an environment created to challenge and stimulate them. Similarly, children need time to try new ways of doing things—new ways of interacting with water, mud, plants, and people. As more and more information becomes available on the problems caused by childhood obesity, directors must plan for spaces and opportunities for children to engage in significant periods of large motor activity.

Children need extensive opportunities to interact with the green environment. Digging in the soil, planting, caring for, and enjoying what they helped produce provide important science learning. Walking and running on paths surrounding green spaces provides much more interest than running on a concrete surface surrounded by more concrete, metal, and wood equipment. When the outdoor environment is aesthetically pleasing for children and adults, well maintained, and designed with lots of movement in mind, it beckons them to come out and be involved.

Governmental Regulations

In communities that have zoning laws, an early childhood education center that is operated for profit may be limited to locating in a business or less restrictive zone, while a nonprofit educational facility generally may be located in any zone. Local

Trees and grassy areas enhance the children's playground.

© 2010 Cengage Learning

rulings may also limit nonprofit use of certain areas. Prior to signing a lease or contract to purchase property, the director must check with the local zoning board to see if usage of the particular piece of property is in compliance with the zoning code. In some cases, a zoning variance may be allowed; that is, the director may petition to use the location for a center if it can be shown that the presence of the center will not have a negative effect on neighboring sites. Zoning ordinances also may include parking requirements, and off-street parking provisions may have to be made for center staff and visitors, including those who have special needs.

When a new facility is built or an existing building renovated or put to a new use, current codes usually apply. For example, a building being used as a public school would be inspected based on the codes in existence when that building was put into use. However, if a child development center leases the space, the owner will be required to meet the *current* regulations. When a building is renovated or a new facility is constructed, the Americans with Disabilities Act (ADA) must be followed. Some requirements include access by means of ramps instead of, or in addition to, stairs; accessible restroom facilities; doors that can be opened by a person in a wheelchair; and low drinking fountains.

Other governmental regulations pertain to licensing. These are discussed in an earlier chapter and include number of square feet of space for children's use both indoors and outdoors, fencing, exits, building materials, and toilet and hand-washing facilities. Before you purchase, lease, or renovate a building, ask your licensing agent to ensure that the facility is in compliance with governmental regulations or can be renovated appropriately and at an affordable price. There may be a charge for this consultation. Also make sure that your lease and all conditions make it worthwhile for you to pay for the required changes to the building.

Sometimes, a church, community service organization, or school will permit or invite an early childhood education center to use its facilities at little or no charge. Available rooms also may be found in school buildings. This contribution is a major cost benefit to the program. Before agreeing to this use of the building, however, both the contributor and the center's board should have a clear, written understanding of the rights and responsibilities of each party. For example, both will need to know how liability and property insurance will be handled and exactly what is covered.

Get written answers to your questions.

- Will the center be able to operate if the agency or school is closed for vacation or for a holiday, such as Presidents' Day, when many parents must still go to work?
- What maintenance responsibilities will the early childhood center have?
- How will the rest of the property be maintained?
- Will the agency or school be responsible for all grass cutting, snow removal, utilities, garbage collection, and recycling?
- Will the center area be wired for phones, computers, and other technology?
- How many parking spaces will be reserved for staff and parents?
- With whom can the director communicate if a problem occurs, such as a leaking roof?

Check details carefully. You don't want to be in a situation in which the agency's behavior leads to serious problems for the center. For example, suppose the agency neglected to pay the utility bills as agreed, leaving the center without heat or water.

Cost and Quality

Cost is a factor in every aspect of facility development and maintenance. Using low-quality materials to save money often proves to be expensive in the long run. For example, inexpensive carpeting may be difficult to keep clean and may have to be replaced frequently. Many "cute" or unusual details put in place to attract parents may do that in some cases, but may add nothing to the quality of the children's experience. Examples include elaborate entryways, themes related to TV or film characters as part of the permanent decor, and so forth. Center directors have many opportunities to choose environmentally conscious materials, such as electrical appliances that use reduced amounts of energy. Ensuring that a building is well insulated can save many dollars on heating and cooling bills.

Planning a New Center

In planning for a new center, the sole proprietor, the partners, or the corporate board will be the final decision maker(s). As discussed in an earlier chapter, the director may also be an owner. In any case, it is the owners who must decide or agree that a new center is needed. They must also raise the necessary funds and employ appropriate contributors (realtor, architect, attorney, banker, contractor). If the director is an employee, the owner may charge him with the responsibility to do a preliminary property search, to provide a list of criteria for the building, and, in some cases, to take on the major responsibility of planning and implementing the entire construction process. To avoid conflict, wasted energy, and probable cost overruns, roles and responsibilities must be clearly delineated early in the planning stage. The decision may be to construct a building; to buy, rent, or lease an existing building; to renovate an existing facility extensively; or to locate space that would be donated by the owner on a temporary or permanent basis.

Planning for a new center involves the same analysis of space requirements that is done when an ongoing program facility is assessed. The one item that usually stands out as being important in decisions about planning a new center is cost. Although cost is a major factor, the key concept is the value of the setting to children, staff, and families.

Let us assume that a new center is being created. The owners already have several centers in other cities. They are not early childhood educators and they do not want to spend time on the details. Therefore, they have hired a director and given him the major responsibility of planning the center. He is to report to the designated owner on a weekly basis. The owners will make the final decision on all major issues.

The director starts facilities planning with a needs assessment in the community (recall that needs assessment was discussed in Chapter 2). The director must also obtain applicable information about zoning and licensing. These data, combined with the availability of a particular amount of money, are applied as criteria in the search for appropriate facilities. Some centers assess needs, locate facilities, and then mount a fund drive, anticipating that sufficient money will be obtained. The director or building committee must assess realistically the amount of money that will be *available* for establishing and maintaining the center facility and the amount of money that will be *required* to meet the assessed need.

The building committee works closely with the budget committee to determine the amount of money needed and available for constructing, purchasing, renovating, or leasing a building. Costs of real estate and construction vary widely depending on geographical location, and within a given city they vary from the inner city to the suburbs. Costs must be checked for each locale. Careful planning is essential because once construction starts, changes are costly.

Considering New Construction

Both land and building costs must be considered. The lot must be large enough for a building of the required size; for a playground of at least 75 square feet per child (groups of children may use this area at different times); and for parking for staff, parents, and visitors. The cost of the building will depend on the size of the building, on the quality and elaborateness of the materials used, and on the intricacy of the design. A major advantage of new construction is that the building can be created to meet the specific needs of children. Furthermore, it can be designed to look like a place for children. And if it is well designed, it will be a place in which the program can be delivered efficiently, effectively, and with a high level of comfort for all users. Talk with your architect about "going green," that is, using environmentally friendly materials and design, as well as taking advantage of the natural setting. Often a company that owns many centers will have a standard building plan that will be used no matter where the building is located.

Using Existing Buildings

Costs involved with the use of an existing building are purchase price, lease or rent, and renovation. A center may incur none, one, or two of these costs, depending on the owner and on the condition of the building.

If funds are available, a down payment on the purchase of a lot or a building, or plans for extensive remodeling, may be made. The board must be certain that funds for monthly payments, including interest as well as principal, will be available. A bank or savings and loan company can provide information on interest rates, length of mortgage, and payment procedures. It also can explain penalties, foreclosures, and insurance requirements.

Renting or Leasing

Because purchasing a building involves high initial costs, many centers rent or lease all or part of a building. Both renting and leasing involve periodic payments. Under a lease, the lessor and the lessee agree that the space will be available and paid for during a specified length of time, usually at least a year. A longer lease is preferable because moving can be expensive and clients may be lost if the center changes locations. Relocation costs include staff time spent in the following activities:

- fund-raising
- attending additional board committee meetings
- locating a new site
- negotiating the lease

- arranging a loan for additional costs
- communicating with staff and families about the move
- arranging for required and desired renovations
- planning logistics of the move
- working with a licensing specialist
- arranging for reaccreditation as needed
- managing the unexpected

Following are direct costs of relocation:

- attorney fees
- architect and contractor fees
- materials needed for renovation
- cleaning prior to the move
- movers
- changing address or other information on stationery, brochures, website
- reaccreditation fee
- paying staff overtime to prepare the new site just before the center opens

One of the most challenging aspects of moving a center is making the move so that service to children and families will be interrupted as little as possible. Another challenge is the possible loss of families if the new location is not as convenient for them. The director is then faced with recruiting new families quickly while managing the settling-in period in the new center. When a space is rented, the renter may have to pay only for the period during which the space is actually used. For a nine-month preschool program, this savings could be important and significant. Such a situation occurs primarily when renting from a church. The school's equipment may have to be moved out during the summer months or may be used by other groups as part of the rental agreement. If you are renting space, try to negotiate limitations on rent increases.

A lease should spell out these conditions and include items such as:

- the beginning and ending dates of the lease
- whether or not the lease is renewable
- if renewable, what limits, if any, will be set on a fee increase
- whether or not the lease can be terminated early
- if terminated, what penalties apply
- whether or not you can sublet
- who is responsible for maintenance and repairs; what is included; who pays for it; who provides

materials, supplies, and tools; when maintenance and repairs will be done
- who is responsible for compliance with the building code
- who pays for utilities

For example, if the board of health requires the addition of a hand-washing sink (a permanent fixture), will the center or the landlord pay for the sink and its installation? The center cannot operate a program without the sink because a license will not be granted; but if the center should move, the landlord will still have the sink.

If the landlord is responsible for maintenance, can an agreement be reached that the grass is not cut during children's regular playground hours? Think about securing a written agreement about spraying for insects and rodent control. Insist that it be done when children are not present and that no residue harmful to children will remain.

If the facility is shared because the landlord uses part of it or rents part of it to someone else or because the center owns a building and rents or leases part of it to someone else, all the preceding items must be considered. In addition, the building committee or director will settle the matter of who has access to the building and when they may have access. For example, if a teenage group uses the building in the evenings, will they be allowed to use the playground during the late afternoon before all the children have left? Other points to be considered include the following:

- Who may have master keys?
- Who may use what equipment and supplies?
- Who is responsible for ordering and paying for shared equipment and supplies?
- Who pays the telephone bill? Internet service?

Other questions involve use of the center's space by other organizations or individuals when the children are not present, such as during the evenings or on weekends. The use of the facilities (their own and that of others) by center staff members and the parent group during evening, weekend, and holiday hours also must be considered.

It is easier to reach agreement on these issues before the building committee signs a lease and takes occupancy. If a lease has been signed, the center usually cannot be moved without financial penalty, which could mean that an uncomfortable situation exists for a number of months. When the lease clearly details the rights and responsibilities of each party, most questions can be settled amicably.

DIRECTOR'S CORNER

"When the renovation was initially being planned and the architects were working up the drawings, the chairperson of the committee and I went in and talked about what we would like to see happen. It seemed to break down after the initial meetings, and there were some outcomes that we were not that pleased with. Everything was ordered and halfway done before I realized what was happening. There wasn't any way that we could go back and ask for changes."

—Director, preschool in a church facility

Renovating

Renovation costs also vary widely depending on the location of the building and the type of work to be done. Complex changes such as relocating plumbing; rewiring electrical circuits; or installing exits, stairways, and fire-resistant surfaces are costly. The type and amount of renovation to be done will be based on the particular licensing requirements, including fire and building codes, and on the requirements of the planned program. If the center owns the building, renovation usually is a worthwhile investment.

WORKING WITH OTHER PROFESSIONALS

A variety of professionals outside the field of early childhood education can be helpful in planning a space for young children. Usually, the cost of their services is relatively high on an hourly rate, but in the long run, the expertise they contribute to the center's development is worth far more than the actual expenditure. However, checking references and credentials before you sign an agreement with the individual or company is critical. Written agreements with each service provider also are essential.

Licensing Agent

Because most programs must be licensed, the first professional that the building committee contacts is the licensing agent. This specialist often provides free services and is funded through state or local taxes. Through this agent, the committee works with other professionals in the building, sanitation, and fire departments. Community planners also may be involved, either at the governmental level or through community councils. Even though these professionals are not paid by the center, the licensing and inspection fees must be paid as required.

Realtor

Whether you are looking for an existing building or land for a new building, a realtor may be able to save you a lot of time. Many realtors specialize in certain areas and may know of property that will be available but has not been advertised. They can also look for the type of property you need, keeping your price range in mind. The realtor can assist you in determining the zoning requirements in the area you select and may be able to help you determine whether a zone change or exception can be obtained. Once you are settled into your new center, your realtor will be well aware of your program when home buyers ask about programs for young children in the area.

Architect

During the very early planning stage, retaining an architect can produce positive results. An architect can evaluate a site in terms of a center's needs or can examine an existing building and make recommendations about the renovations that are necessary for safety, efficiency, and aesthetics. And of course, an architect can design a new building to fit your needs.

Ongoing architectural services can be contracted at an hourly rate, flat fee, or on a percentage (of building or renovation cost) basis. The contract should include the fee for services and the payment due dates. In addition, the architect should spell out clearly in the contract the services that are to be provided—such as survey, site selection, design, working drawings from which a building can be built or remodeled, building permit clearance, contractor selection, construction supervision, and/or final inspection.

Your architect also will assist you in selecting materials if that is part of your contract. For instance, gypsum wallboard (which is inexpensive) is readily dented, gouged, and subject to corner damage. It is usually not the best choice in areas used by children. If you are not familiar with building materials, the architect's recommendation of an alternate material could save you money and repeated repairs in the long run.

When selecting an architect, choose someone with whom you feel comfortable. Some architects are unfamiliar with child care center needs, and you will want to choose one who is willing to listen to your concept and incorporate your ideas. Keep in mind, however, that architects have knowledge about design and construction that can help you attain a more attractive, more functional building within your budget. A few architects will want to put a great deal of emphasis on the exterior of the building, using such a large portion of the budget there that little money remains for finishing and furnishing. Listen to your architect with an open mind, but be willing to insist on components essential to your program.

Also be sure to let your architect know what kind of budget you are working with. You may have dreams of an elaborate center with all kinds of wonderful enhancements, but your budget may dictate that you have a much more straightforward approach. A good architect can help you get the most for your money. Figure 7-1 shows a very simple, relatively inexpensive design. Only the essential spaces are included for this hypothetical half-day program. A rectangular building is often the least expensive to build.

When the plans are complete, asking a colleague to review them with you may help uncover details you hadn't considered. Changes made at this stage are relatively easy; changes made once construction begins may be impossible. At the very least, they usually are quite expensive.

Generally, the architect will oversee the job, but the general contractor is responsible for scheduling subcontractors, ordering materials, and so forth. Some architects also serve as construction managers, and some contractors offer building design services.

Contractor

A contractor may plan the construction or remodeling of the center's building and carry the work through to completion. Parts of the job, such as the electrical or plumbing work, may be subcontracted, but the contractor retains responsibility for the satisfactory and timely completion of that work. Nonetheless, the director must pay attention to the job as it moves along. Balancing frequent site visits with allowing the contractors to do their work is necessary, but asking questions is essential when you aren't sure about an aspect of the construction or when the work is not completed as promised. Sometimes, directors feel intimidated because they don't understand the drawings and specifications for the work. Part of the contractor's job is ensuring that the work is done to the client's specifications as determined by the written contract.

Accountant

The building committee works with an accountant to determine the amount of money that can be invested responsibly in construction, purchase, or rental. The accountant also may help locate a lending agent and may help the building committee find the best interest rate. Information about depreciation and taxes also may be provided. An accountant may charge an hourly rate or a flat fee for a particular piece of work. Some centers pay an accountant a monthly retainer in exchange for whatever services are needed, including preparation for the annual audit.

Attorney

When the building committee decides to enter into a contract or sign a lease, its attorney reviews the document to ensure that the center's needs are being met and that all legal aspects have been covered. The attorney also participates in settling disputes in relation to payment, failure to perform work satisfactorily, and so forth. In a few cases, these disputes may be taken to court. In those special situations, the attorney would represent the center in court. The attorney may be on retainer or paid an hourly fee.

SUMMARY

Whether it is a brand new building or one that was constructed years ago for another purpose, the ideal early childhood education center environment is created to meet the needs of the children, the staff members, the parents, and the visitors while satisfying all licensing requirements. Health and safety, accessibility of facilities, traffic patterns, personal space, opportunities for independence, and aesthetic character are the guidelines for determining the design. Professional services from the architects and contractors who work with building committee members, staff members, parents, children, and other professionals provide these aspects within the framework of the budget to create a center that is best suited for carrying out the program for which it has been designed.

TRY IT OUT!

1 Work with a classmate to design a floor plan for a child care center for 44 children (six infants, eight toddlers, 14 3-year-olds, and 16 4-year-olds). Also show the spaces that are used by adults. Be prepared to explain your design to the class.

2 Work with a classmate to design a building plan for a half-day preschool for 14 3-year-olds and 16 4-year-olds. Make your drawing approximately to scale.

3 Compare the drawings in Try it Out! 1 and 2. Are any of the differences attributable to full-day versus half-day child care?

4 Assume that you and your classmates are board members of a child care and education center for 60 preschool children located in a community center building. They had asked you to set up the program four years ago. Now the community center director feels he needs your space for additional adult activities during the day. You need to move out of the building in 30 days. What will you do? Consider all the options. Then make a plan.

a. Consider children, families, and staff as you make your decision.

b. If you decide to move, consider what you will do to avoid this type of occurrence in the future.

REFERENCES

Gandini, L. (1994, March). Not just anywhere: Making child care centers into particular places. *Child Care Information Exchange*, 48–50.

Greenman, J. (2007). *Caring spaces, learning places: Children's environments that work*. Redmond: Washington: Exchange Press.

Kielar, J. (1999). An antidote to the noisy nineties. *Young Children, 54*(5), 28–29.

Sussman, C. (1998). Out of the basement: Discovering the value of child care facilities. *Young Children, 53*(1), 10–15.

8

EQUIPPING *the* CENTER

© 2010 Cengage Learning

Supplying appropriate equipment contributes significantly to the success of early childhood programs.

Objectives

After reading this chapter, you should be able to:

- Identify the necessary equipment that will meet child, adult, and service area needs.
- List criteria for choosing equipment and vendors.
- Describe a system for ordering equipment.
- Describe a system for managing equipment.

Standard Addressed in this Chapter

naeyc Administrator Competencies
Early Childhood Knowledge and Skills 9

It is both challenging and rewarding to equip a child development center. Your personality will be reflected in the physical environment you create as you strive to meet the needs of the children and their families, and as you select components that enable the entire staff to maintain congruence with your program philosophy. Although many programs are being implemented with inadequate, unsuitable materials, supplying equipment that is appropriate contributes significantly to successful program implementation. Creating rich learning environments that are replete with abundant opportunities for children to be actively involved with age-appropriate and individually appropriate materials requires thoughtful, careful selection of classroom equipment and supplies. Furthermore, staff members are able to do their assigned jobs more efficiently and comfortably when they work in adequately equipped environments.

One component of your organization's systems approach (described in Chapter 1) will center on equipment. Establishing a center-wide value to the role of equipment and supplies in carrying out your mission will support staff decision making as they develop curriculum, arrange their classroom environments, and support children's learning on a day-to-day basis. Whole staff discussions on the role of equipment in support of children's learning and development helps teachers create a more cohesive, meaningful philosophy. As new teachers enter the staff, they can observe the similarities across classrooms as well as the individual differences in equipment selection, arrangement, and use.

Establishing clear and pared-down policies and procedures for selecting, ordering, storing, and maintaining equipment and supplies will streamline this element of your system. Within the system and the philosophy it supports, staff members will be free to create classrooms they and their children find to be joyful and productive.

ESTABLISHING NEEDS

There are three major areas to equip in a child care center. The director, with input from the staff, must determine the type and amount of equipment needed for each one. When the center is already operating, teachers will join in this decision making. Areas to be equipped are

1 children's spaces, both indoors and outdoors.

2 adult spaces, including offices, waiting rooms, conference rooms, and lounge areas.

3 service areas.

Equipment refers not only to furniture but also to appliances, computers, and other durable goods. Included in this budget are supplies, consisting of items that have a relatively short useful life or that are disposable. Examples are paper for the printer, finger paint, food, and paper towels. The equipment and supplies budgets should provide for initial purchases as well as for long- and short-term replacement of both basic furnishings and consumable supplies.

Directors entering an ongoing program begin by taking inventory of what is on hand, setting up a priority system for securing new equipment, replacing worn-out items, and replenishing supplies of consumable materials. Directors of new centers are confronted with the somewhat overwhelming task of equipping an entire center. Some companies will provide lists of equipment you will need and suggest room arrangement.

One detailed equipment list, *Selecting Educational Equipment and Materials for School and Home*, addresses both methods and materials for classrooms for infants through elementary school. Each section has been authored by a well-known early childhood specialist. Another valuable source is *Community Playthings*, which produces sturdy blocks, wood trucks, and other accessories and furniture for children. This company can provide you with drawings of sample room arrangements and a description of materials needed for your classroom. They also offer free floor plans and room arrangement information for students who are preparing to be teachers.

Children's Spaces

Program philosophy and the needs of children dictate what will be ordered for the children's spaces in the center. Let's assume that every child comes with a parent or "comfortable-to-him" adult to visit the classroom before school starts or at a time when no other children are present. Think about what the room says to a child opening the door. Some children may be overwhelmed with delight as they quickly visually take in a world of interesting walls, shelves, areas, and a new-to-him adult. Other children may be frightened by the magnitude of the space, the overwhelming variety of objects to see, and the sounds that they can't yet decode. Some children may take days, even weeks, to feel comfortable. Others can't wait to move right in.

Too much in a room can overwhelm a child and even his parents, even after they have been enrolled for months. Having everything in bold, bright colors can make a room seem "loud." Well-designed classrooms with uncluttered shelves, walls, floors, and tables help children find their way. Organizing space so that areas are somewhat separate helps children decide on a place to start. Everything needed for a particular type of activity should be available in that area.

When a building has a common storage area for classroom materials, teachers can share toys, tools, or objects to be used by children. When children's interests change or teachers want to present new materials to support children's learning, they can choose what they need from the shared storage area. Later some of the same objects may be returned to the classroom as children are ready to use them in different ways. The director's role is to see how this system is working and to encourage teachers to establish policies and procedures for using shared equipment and supplies.

Most early childhood programs provide basic interest areas in each classroom. These usually include areas for art, music, blocks, books, science, manipulative activities, and pretend play as well as spaces for math games and writing materials. All of these curricular areas require special furnishings and materials. Provisions also must be made for water and sand play, carpentry, cooking, building, and large-muscle activities. Note that an interest area often addresses more than one content area. For example, puzzles in the manipulative area may depict characters from a book that the teacher has read to the children. In the science center, children may be recording observations of an animal; in the block area, you may find a child working on developing symmetry; and in the music area, a child may be listening to a song sung in Chinese or Spanish. You'll read more about the director's role in curriculum in a later chapter.

Furniture for working, resting, and eating is needed, including such accessories as clocks, planters, wastebaskets, and curtains. Most preschool groups gather together daily and need a space large enough so that everyone is comfortable. Children need spaces to work alone or in small groups. Low dividers can define spaces, but shelving is often used for the same purpose. Often a few rolling shelves are moved back to make the gathering space available. When quickly and easily locked by the teacher, the shelves won't roll.

Children of all ages need outdoor play time. Almost every activity that can be done indoors can be moved outdoors as well. Infants can enjoy the swaying and rustling of leaves. Toddlers can feel powerful climbing a low grass-covered hill and running or rolling down it. Outdoor play also offers essential opportunities for gross motor activities and skill development such as climbing, swinging from rung to rung, running, jumping, and so forth. Some large equipment may be provided to encourage some of these motor activities, but plenty of space, along with cushioning material, must surround each piece of large equipment. Such equipment must be installed with firm, deep anchors that are below ground level and should be checked regularly for protrusions, splinters, or any other potential hazard.

Although this type of equipment is found on many playgrounds, explorations of nature also appeal to children and help them begin to understand its importance in our lives. Running around curving paths and "hiding" in bushy alcoves easily supervised by a teacher are exciting and fun for children. Planting and caring for their own gardens also interest and teach children. Even digging in soil and finding "treasures" such as a stone, a root, or an insect can fascinate children, especially those who live in areas where there are no yards. Walking in a summer rain, making and throwing snowballs, and crunching fallen leaves all go beyond going up and down a slide (although that is fun too).

If the director is not familiar with early childhood curriculum and the associated equipment, room

Experiences with nature allow children to enjoy and learn about their world.

arrangement, and scheduling, the center definitely will need an education coordinator who has this knowledge and who is an experienced early childhood teacher. She must also be familiar with programs for infants, toddlers, and school-age children if those groups are to be served. Taking courses in early childhood education curriculum and child development will also enable the director to develop a better understanding of why some materials are important and why others are not supportive of program goals and children's needs. Curriculum courses also provide information on how and why to integrate curriculum. Suggested books on curriculum and child development are included in the Director's Library in Appendix D.

Adult Spaces

Adults, working together to meet the common goal of providing rich, fulfilling experiences for children, need space to meet together, to think and plan together, and, at least briefly, to relax together. They need space to write reports and to converse with parents in private. Teachers need access to a telephone for parent contacts and for personal calls when they are on break. The location of the telephone should allow for quiet talks and for privacy. Staff also need a few comfortable chairs for lounging during breaks, a refrigerator and microwave for snacks, and any other amenities that the center can provide. A bowl of grapes, cherries, or even, once in a while, mini chocolate bars would be welcomed by most teachers, especially after a week of staying inside due to very bad weather.

Even a very small center requires some office space with a locked file cabinet for records at the very minimum. Since adult desks are not used in classrooms for young children, some desk space for teachers is essential. A resource library and a work-table with a paper cutter, laminator, and storage for supplies such as poster board, scissors, and markers support teachers in their work.

Almost every professional child care center director now relies on a computer for record keeping, billing, correspondence, writing reports, information gathering, and emailing. Many teachers also use computers to maintain professional currency through the use of the Internet. Therefore, purchasing appropriate hardware and software becomes a significant contribution to the smooth running of a center. If your knowledge of computers is limited, recognize that everyone has experienced this beginning stage, and avoid saying you understand if that is not the case. Other staff members can assist you or you may find free courses at your library or online. Purveyors of software want you to like and use their material. Although it is not uncommon to find glitches in computer software, you still should expect the vendor to provide needed support in rectifying the problem. Protecting against computer viruses with special software is essential.

Directors of large centers find that a copy machine is a worthwhile investment in terms of the time and money saved in duplicating such items as newsletters, menus, forms, and interesting articles to share. Although these machines are initially expensive, they pay for themselves over time by saving staff time and enabling the center to produce materials of professional quality. At the same time, consider ways to avoid overcopying by using other ways to communicate whenever possible.

When the families who are affiliated with your center have access to the Internet, you may want to send information via email. This process may be used for communicating with the entire center's population, with

families from a particular classroom, or with an individual parent. Setting up a listserv with the email addresses of those families who choose to be included makes communication easy and quick. However, other ways of reaching those who are not using this technology must be provided. Remember, too, that personal, face-to-face communication is still highly desirable whenever possible. Look for ways to communicate in the language most familiar to the recipient. Parent or community volunteers may be available to facilitate translation, including through the use of sign language. You may also want to communicate with members of the broader community by creating and maintaining a website. In some areas, this approach can be developed into a successful marketing tool.

In addition to communications tools, the staff needs a place for meetings. When staff meetings

Some centers provide a small lounge for parents and visitors.

© 2010 Cengage Learning

are held after children leave, the classrooms can be used. However, it certainly is more comfortable for the adults attending meetings to have a space furnished with adult-size chairs and tables. Comfortable furniture should be provided for use by parents who come to the center for conferences and by consultants who come to meet with staff members. Bulletin boards and coat racks are convenient accessories for adult spaces. Consider the seating and other furnishings and equipment in terms of adults who may have special needs.

Some centers provide a separate lounge for parents and visitors. This area should have comfortable seating, lamps, tables, a bookshelf for pertinent reading materials, and perhaps facilities for coffee or other refreshments. Wall hangings or pictures, plants, a rug or carpet, and curtains all enhance the appearance of the space. A shelf of toys and books for visiting children indicates that the center is sensitive to children's needs. The goal is to let families know that they are valued and welcomed.

Service Areas

Basic equipment in the bathrooms, kitchen, laundry room, and janitor's closet is usually built in and,

(A)

(B)

Equipment and supplies for maintaining cleanliness must be child and environment friendly. Keep in mind also that some children or staff members may have allergies or asthma.

therefore, is not purchased from the equipment and supplies budget. In a new facility, some appliances may be included in the equipment line. Consumables for service areas must be furnished, and, of course, appliances must be replaced over time. Dishes, cutlery, cooking utensils, and serving carts must be provided in centers where lunch is served. In large centers, special appliances such as commercial dishwashers, rug shampooers, heavy-duty automatic washers and dryers, and large refrigerators and freezers are needed. The local board of health may have very specific requirements about the type of kitchen equipment that must be provided. The fire department will usually require alarm systems and may also require a fire suppression system. A battery-operated radio with weather channel is an important tool to help the center prepare for weather emergencies. Flashlights in every classroom are also helpful. However, these items are useful only if you replace batteries regularly.

First aid supplies must be available in all classrooms, in the office, and in vehicles used to transport children. You may want to install an alarm system that would notify the police in the event of an emergency or a break-in when the center is closed.

If you have decided to provide child transportation, you will find many companies offering small buses equipped with seat belts and outfitted to accommodate car seats. Since the driver needs to focus on safe driving, a second adult should ride with the children to see that they remain in their car seats and that they are delivered directly to the pre-agreed upon adult.

When ordering cleaning supplies for your center, keep "child friendly" and "environmentally friendly" items in mind. Keep in mind also that some children or staff members may have allergies or asthma. Some states now require schools to use environmentally sensitive cleaning products. This requirement reduces exposure of children and staff to dangerous chemicals. Early attempts to regulate emission of formaldehyde used in producing some furniture may become law in some states. Find out from vendors of furniture, toys, and other equipment what kind of glue and paint are used (White Hutchinson Leisure & Learning Group, 2007). Also check periodically with the U.S. Consumer Product Safety Commission to determine whether various products have been recalled.

Choose recycled paper and encourage everyone in the center, including children, to recycle. In addition to paper, glass, and plastic, ink cartridges can be recycled. Everyone in the center can learn to conserve water, and the director can ensure that leaky faucets are repaired quickly (Stoecklin, 2005).

USING SELECTION CRITERIA

Selection of all equipment should be based on a set of pre-established criteria that you have created as part of your system. The primary consideration is usefulness; that is, will a specific piece of equipment meet the needs of this center? Other criteria are versatility, safety, suitability, durability, ease of maintenance, attractiveness, and user preference. Some equipment for children should encourage and even necessitate cooperative play. All equipment should work the way it is supposed to and should be durable and economical. Although these criteria apply to all equipment purchases, this chapter primarily covers information about equipment that children will use. Refer to Director's Resources 8-2 and 8-3 for further information.

The goals and objectives of a particular center will dictate purchases. That means that the director and all staff members must focus on the goals and objectives that have evolved from the center's mission. The recent emphasis in the media on preparing children for kindergarten has led some centers to focus heavily on academic content and may lead some directors to order materials suitable for older children as an approach to preschool learning. As director, you must assume responsibility for keeping current on developments within the early childhood field as well as within the broader population. Helping staff maintain familiarity with these issues enables them to speak knowledgeably with parents and community members and to offer a curriculum that meets the needs of children. For example, many elementary schools are reducing or eliminating recess so that children will have more time to develop literacy skills. You can help staff understand how to explain the value of play, particularly outdoor play. One would hope that most staff could respond comfortably and professionally.

As director, you may feel pressure from parents and from observing how some early childhood centers operate, and you may begin to question your system's goals. Would it be better to use funds for pre-K workbooks? To find the answer, you must return to your understanding of how children learn. Is your program providing opportunities for children's development in all areas, including literacy? Consider the children's small motor development, understanding of recording a correct answer rather than choosing an interesting picture to circle, and ability to work in silence in a group, all of which are often necessary for completing required worksheets. Many people would agree that children entering kindergarten should be prepared and that the kindergarten system should be prepared for the children. When you are a director, your role is to determine how best to prepare children for kindergarten as well as for their lives in the here and now. You must base this on knowledge of how children develop, how learning occurs, and the needs and interests of each child in your class rather than on more narrowly focused goals such as readiness for kindergarten in a particular content area. Most kindergarten teachers value children's age-appropriate social and emotional development as more important to them at the beginning of kindergarten than whether children are well versed in letter-sound relationships.

REFLECTION

As a student, you are required to spend a certain number of hours observing and assisting in a preschool classroom before student teaching. The teacher starts the day with a drill on the sounds that letters make. (You wonder when was the last time she ever heard a letter make a sound. Oh well, it's her classroom.) Then they practice counting from one to 30. You are surprised because yesterday you asked two children who were playing a game, "Which is more—seven or nine?" Neither of them had any idea. You begin to wonder whether you will teach this way or will you do something different.

After you finish reading this, ask yourself what you plan to do in your own classroom. Why?

Today's standards-driven educational approaches require that administrators and staff become familiar with standards set forth by state departments of education and national professional organizations. In some cases, working to ensure that all children meet these standards will be mandated. For example, in some states, preschool centers that receive state funds are expected to be guided by the standards and to demonstrate how standards are met in each "lesson" or activity. More and more, children entering kindergarten are being tested to determine what they know, particularly related to specific literacy skills. Directors who have a good grasp of developmentally appropriate curriculum will be able to help teachers work toward the standards within the context of routines, schedules, and plans that meet each child's needs while supporting children's progress toward meeting the content standards. Eliminating play and the related materials and equipment is not an option.

How will such knowledge relate to purchasing equipment and supplies? You must think about how equipment will be used and how it will support children's interest in learning in all areas. For example, early childhood educators understand that providing blocks and offering long periods of time and space to explore ways to use them can help children learn in all the content areas (math, science, social studies, literacy) and in the arts (Dodge, Colker, & Heroman, 2002; Hirsch, 1995). Knowledgeable directors realize that during block play children also develop skills in planning, balance, organizing, cooperating, and persistence toward a goal. The other interest centers in an early childhood classroom lead to similar development with the guidance of a well-prepared teacher.

Elsewhere in this book you can read about the important role of the director in selecting and orienting teachers who will support children's development. You'll also consider how the director supports teachers as they develop more competent ways of enhancing children's growth and change in all areas. It is the director's responsibility to use a systematic approach, blending facility, equipment, staff, families, and finances to accomplish the mission related to children's care, growth, and development. Equipping a center is costly, and when mistakes are made, replacements are doubly costly. Therefore, plan your purchases carefully by first assessing your needs, then developing criteria for equipment selection, and finally relating needed and desired items to your budget.

Many equipment suppliers will be happy to provide sample equipment and supplies lists. Even more valuable is the Association for Childhood Education International (ACEI) publication listing suggested purchases for various age groups from infants through school age (Moyer, 1995). These comprehensive lists are not intended as mandatory purchases but as guides to be adjusted and supplemented based on the needs of particular children, staff, and families. As new materials become available, they can be considered based on their appropriateness for the children who will use them. For example, although vinyl records and audiotapes were widely available in preschools some years ago, today centers are more likely to purchase CDs, DVDs, or digital music files.

Suitability of specific curricular materials is not discussed here since a number of texts include this information in the context of program development. Please see Appendix G for related books.

REFLECTION

Think of yourself as a director who is responsible for equipment purchases. Did you realize that you would pore over websites and catalogs for classroom equipment and materials and would find yourself searching through office equipment and restaurant supply catalogs, websites, and ads? Your duties now have expanded from educator and administrator to purchasing agent. This responsibility probably seems overwhelming at the moment because many of you have been responsible for purchasing only personal items and, in some cases, basic household equipment. You are, no doubt, beginning to realize that the role of the director has many facets and requires a wide variety of special skills.

understand that everything in their classroom has its own place, and they usually learn quickly to return things to their specified location. Many creative preschoolers find new uses for classroom items. For example, a child may take yarn from the art area to use as spaghetti in the house play area. Whether or not this creative use is encouraged depends on the philosophy of the program.

Preschool children need equipment and materials in all of the interest areas. Some of these materials will be specifically designed for children, while many others will be of interest to both children and teachers such as items from nature; maps; and books and posters depicting and identifying birds, flowers, cars, or dinosaurs. Adult musical instruments often appeal to children, especially if the children are permitted to both listen and try their hand at bowing or strumming. Opportunities to prepare and eat most kinds of food provide chances to learn about

Developmental Needs

The developmental levels, capabilities, and the age range of the children enrolled influence what will be purchased. A center serving 2-year-olds will need some pull toys and small climbers that would not be needed if the youngest child were 3. Infants require special furnishings such as cribs and changing tables. Although younger infants are always held during feeding, infants who are able to sit independently are also ready to help feed themselves and should be encouraged to do that. High chairs had been standard equipment for this purpose, but because of the danger of the child's falling from the chair, they are usually replaced by low feeding tables, similar to high chairs but with shorter legs. A teacher sits in a low chair opposite the children and helps when help is needed. Infants also require washable and chewable toys, bibs, sheets, blankets, and disposable diapers. Parents may be asked to furnish some of those necessary items and to take responsibility for their infant's laundry.

When center bathrooms have adult-size toilets and sinks, children will need step stools to be able to use the equipment independently. Preferably, the center will have installed child-size toilets and sinks at the appropriate height. Toddlers also need toys that provide opportunities for filling and dumping, big toys that can be carried during early walking stages, and lots of duplicates so that sharing will not be necessary. Toddler rooms are arranged in interest centers, but since many toddlers like to practice walking and carrying items in each hand, materials are often found in a variety of places. Preschoolers can

© 2010 Cengage Learning

The director who understands child development and ways of learning is prepared to equip classrooms appropriately.

nutrition, food from other cultures, heat and cold, textures, comparisons, contrasts, the safe use of tools and appliances, math, literacy, social studies, science, arts, turn taking, preferences, and sharing good times with friends.

School-age children in after-school care programs need games and crafts that are far too complex and frustrating for younger children. They also need well-lighted working areas for homework; larger furniture in which they can sit and work comfortably; and equipment for active, semiorganized sports and games. A place to store and eat snacks and an area to relax away from the group provide some feeling of being independent.

Programs for school-age children should enable them to participate as fully as possible in activities that other children their age enjoy. When the center is well equipped to meet these needs, it will provide not only activities that the children could have been doing at home after school but also enriching group activities that encourage children to develop new interests and hobbies.

Children with special needs may require modified equipment or equipment designed to meet a particular need. A director with contacts at agencies serving people with disabilities can seek their assistance in providing modifications or special equipment. The equipment should allow the child to function as independently as possible. If the director is new in the area and does not have needed contacts, one of her priorities should be to become familiar with the community and its resources.

Usefulness

The usefulness of a piece of children's equipment is measured first by how well it meets the developmental needs of the children in the program and second by whether the equipment can be put to multiple uses by those children. When a piece of equipment meets both these criteria, a director may be able to convince a potential funder to support a request for funding. For example, a set of large, sturdy, wooden boxes can serve as cozy places to hide, houses for pretend play, and places to climb on and jump from; a wooden board added to the area can function as a stage, slide, or tent. Of course, all the wood needs to be well sanded and protected from weathering.

Versatility

A piece of equipment that can be used in several ways is a bonus, both financially and in terms of enriching the learning environment for children. Such a piece saves space and money and gives children the opportunity to use their imaginations in creating different functions for one object. For example, the large, hollow blocks that can be used to make a puppet stage or a grocery store can serve as individual work spaces for children's small projects. A bookshelf can be a room divider and a storage facility. Two-year-olds may find the water table to be a relaxing place for splashing, while 4-year-olds may be more interested in using this equipment for constructing a water maze. Many pieces of equipment may be shared by two or more classes for the same

© 2010 Cengage Learning

Providing safe equipment is an important first step to planning for playground safety. Positioning it with safety in mind is the next step, followed by regular evaluation of the condition of the equipment and vigilant supervision by the staff.

or different purposes, eliminating the purchase of duplicate materials and freeing up money for other purchases.

Some equipment can be used both indoors and outdoors, a practice that is economical and provides a wider variety of learning experiences for children. Easels, water tables, and a workbench are a few items that may be moved outside if the building and play area have been planned to facilitate such indoor-outdoor movement. When that planning has not occurred, teachers will not be able to leave the children in order to make several trips to carry equipment, and the children will not have access to those items. Perhaps a janitor, or older children in elementary settings, may be able to help set up outdoor equipment. In some situations, equipment must be put away and locked up when children are not in the outdoor area.

Safety

No matter how versatile, attractive, durable, economical, and suitable a piece of equipment may be, it must be rejected if it is not safe. A climber with protruding bolts, blocks of soft wood that splinter, and tricycles that tip over easily must not be used in the center. A kitchen appliance that requires a long extension cord is a hazard to the cook and should be avoided. All equipment used by the children must be of nontoxic material and must not have sharp or pointed edges. Safety is maintained by staff members who make a point of being constantly alert to the condition and the arrangement of the equipment that is placed in the learning environment (Wortham & Frost, 1997).

No one but a curious toddler seems able to spot a small button that has fallen from another child's clothing. Nonetheless, every classroom should be checked for safety hazards daily and throughout the day. Items used in infant/toddler rooms must not have small pieces that could be dislodged, such as the eyes of stuffed animals or small beads on a wire in a board counting book. Even some 3-year-olds are still mouthing small items.

However, a safety issue may be inadvertently overlooked. Three areas to which staff must give special attention are fall zones, entrapment, and protrusions (Wardle, 1999). Fall areas occur under climbers and swings. Entrapment refers to the possibility of a child getting a body part trapped in a piece of equipment (for example, when fence slats are close together, but not close enough, a child may get an arm or a leg caught). Look carefully at elaborate climbing towers with tunnels. It is possible for a child to become frightened while in the tunnel, yet the tunnel may be too long or narrow for the adult to reach the child. Protrusions also may pose safety issues. Sharp corners on furniture or screw heads extended from a flat surface may injure a child.

The U.S. Consumer Product Safety Commission provides voluntary standards for children's playgrounds as well as up-to-date safety alerts at its website (www.cpsc.gov). Its March 2007 update reported that the majority of falls requiring hospital treatment resulted from climbers and stated that climber-related falls resulting in injuries have increased since 1998. This does not mean that climbers should be banned. Rather, they should be surrounded by appropriate and adequate cushioning material and should be located away from other activities to avoid having children run or ride through the climbing area. Other playground injuries result from hot surfaces, entanglement of clothing in the equipment, head entrapment in openings, and entanglement in ropes. Selection of appropriate equipment and close supervision on the playground are major factors in preventing injuries. Nonetheless, the active play, motor skill development, confidence building, and enjoyment that children experience on the playground should not be denied.

Some furniture may tip over and is particularly dangerous if a heavy object such as a computer monitor or aquarium has been placed on top. A child may try to pull or climb on the furniture, causing it to tip over.

A U.S. Consumer Product Safety Commission study (1999) found that two-thirds of the child care centers participating had at least one potential safety hazard. These included the use of clothing with drawstrings at the neck (38 percent of settings), lack of safe playground surfacing (24 percent), and cribs with soft bedding (19 percent). If you go online to the U.S. Consumer Product Safety Commission you will find a very lengthy list of toys that have been recalled due to lead paint use, swallowing hazard, etc. Although as center director you may be sure to purchase safe toys and equipment, a child may bring his own favorite toy to school. Some centers have policies encouraging children to show their toys at group time but to put them in their cubby immediately afterwards.

Most directors know that lead paint has been banned for consumer use for many years, but they may not be aware of the lead hazard lurking in playground equipment. Commercial users still coat products with paint containing lead. Products from other countries, especially toys, should be checked for lead paint. Children need consume only small quantities on a regular basis to create a harmful lead level. In 2007, news media reported that millions of toys in homes and schools contained lead, small magnets, and other components harmful to children, leading to a massive recall. Be aware that even the surface under playground equipment may contain lead. Having a trained inspector check a playground periodically for lead and other hazards is a wise investment (Aronson, 1997). Paying attention to recalls is essential.

Suitability

Some equipment must be provided in several sizes to meet the needs of each user. For example, the secretary must have a standard adult-size chair, preferably ergonomically designed. Chairs for children are usually 10, 12, and 14 inches high, depending on the child's age and height. Chairs that are so tall that seated children cannot put their feet on the floor are not suitable for them. Children's chairs also should have a wide base so they will not tip.

For meals, school cafeteria tables and chairs are not at all suitable for toddlers and preschoolers. If these children are to use a school cafeteria, they must have low tables and chairs. Eating in their own classroom is often a better option. When older children are also present, the noise and activity levels may be distracting for preschoolers and toddlers. Children in before- and after-school programs should never be expected to use preschool-size chairs and tables. They need furniture, space, and equipment designed to fit their needs.

Stereotypes

Equipment must be chosen with the understanding that it may be used equally by all children. Staff members who plan curricula in a stereotyped way will need special guidance on this point so that boys are not relegated to playing with blocks and trucks and girls are not always expected to dress dolls and play quiet table games. People with special needs should be depicted in books, puzzles, and classroom displays, and they should be shown participating in a variety of activities. Classroom materials should reflect many cultures and depict a variety of roles being chosen by members of various cultures and of both genders. For example, dolls of many races should be available. The play figures that are used as block accessories might include a female postal worker and a black doctor rather than

depicting all white males. Books, music, food, and posters should be carefully selected to avoid any stereotyping and to depict the culturally pluralistic society in which the children live. This principle applies even when the center serves children from only one racial or ethnic group, a situation that may occur when students all come from a segregated neighborhood.

Special Needs

Educators today focus on planning a curriculum and environment that allows all children to participate. Using a concept referred to as *universal design,* teachers work to include everyone as they plan. This idea does not mean that everyone does the same thing the same way at the same time, but that each child can participate in a meaningful way in understanding the activity, in implementing it, and in demonstrating what he is learning. Often, consulting a special educator facilitates this type of planning.

In determining the suitability of equipment, you must consider children with special needs. A child who cannot walk, for example, may need easels and water tables that can be used while the child sits in a chair or a wheelchair. Sometimes, such equipment is very low to enable children who are sitting on the floor to use it. In selecting the equipment, you should consider the height of the chair or wheelchair that is used and the length of the child's arms. In this way, you can determine the optimum height of the working space for a particular child. Consider purchasing tables with adjustable heights. If children are crawling in body casts or leg braces, they need comfortable floor surfaces. Wheeled equipment such as a sturdy wagon or a special buggy with seat belts will make it possible for *all* children to enjoy tours around the center's neighborhood.

REFLECTION

Think about your previous experiences with individuals with disabilities. Have you had enough experience to be aware of their special needs? If you have a friend or relative with a lifelong disability, imagine what his or her special needs might have been during the preschool years. Now consider yourself responsible for equipping an environment that is suitable for that child along with a group of typically developing children. What special provisions would have to be made for your friend or relative with special needs to provide a suitable learning environment?

Some children may need an augmentative communication system so they can interact with staff and other children. Children with hearing loss may need ample visual cues such as pictures attached to storage areas so they can tell where equipment belongs, even though they cannot hear the teacher's directions. Children with visual impairments may need some toys that vary in terms of weight, texture, and sound. Balls with a bell inside and storage containers covered with different materials (for example, velvet on a container of beads or corduroy on a box holding small blocks) are especially appropriate for these children. When children who do not have disabilities use these same materials, they may develop greater insights into the experience of children with disabilities.

In purchasing equipment for a center, the director will need to know, in general, what the lifestyles of the families are and what the learning styles and interests of individual children are. Children must be provided with enough ordinary, simple equipment so that they need not be bombarded nine hours a day with novelty. A balance of the familiar with the novel creates a learning environment that is neither overstimulating nor boring; the proper balance may be different in full-day child care centers than it is in half-day programs.

Some directors purchase packaged kits or curricula for their centers, particularly when the staff members have had little early childhood educational background. In such cases, it is essential that the materials be appropriate since they may be used with the belief that because they were included in a curriculum package, they must be good. The director has a major responsibility for ensuring that the components meet the needs of children and teachers. (Often, similar materials can be purchased separately at lower cost.) The director must also provide training to ensure that teachers are using a curriculum plan to meet the needs of children rather than following a page-by-page or random plan. Not every component must be implemented. Such a preplanned curriculum can be viewed as a framework rather than a mandate. It is the director's responsibility to determine who prepared the curriculum and what premises about teaching and learning are supported through its use. Keep in mind that it is unlikely that someone who does not know the children in your center could develop a day-to-day curriculum that would meet the needs and interests of your children.

Ease of Maintenance

Ease of maintenance also should be a consideration in choosing equipment. Sinks, toilets, and drinking fountains that must be cleaned daily and tabletops that must be washed several times each day should be extremely simple to clean. The surfaces should be smooth and all areas easy to reach. Small pieces that are hard to clean around may cause problems and harbor dirt and germs. Equipment parts that are cleaned separately, such as feeding table trays, should be easy to remove and replace. Some plastic chairs have surfaces that are slightly roughened or ridged. And although the surface feels relatively smooth to the hand, there are actually shallow indentations that attract and hold dirt. It is almost impossible to wipe or even scrub these chairs so that they look clean. This type of furniture may be slightly less expensive than other furniture, but maintenance problems outweigh the possible savings. A clean, well-maintained environment is important for all children and staff, but it may be critical for children and staff who have allergies or asthma. In those cases, it may be helpful to have curtains, drapes, and carpeting cleaned frequently or they may have to be eliminated.

Outdoor equipment that must be repainted frequently should be designed so that it can be sanded and painted easily. Places that are difficult to reach are a nuisance, and surfaces that catch and hold rain increase the need for maintenance. Equipment that will rust or rot easily should not be purchased for outdoor use.

Aesthetics

Child care center equipment should be well designed and aesthetically attractive. Most parents and teachers would like their children to appreciate beauty, and one of the best ways to help children acquire this appreciation is to surround them with beauty. An attractive environment also carries the subtle message that children, families, and staff who enter the setting are much appreciated and that great care is taken to make their environment beautiful. A material that is aesthetically appealing need not be expensive. In fact, it often is the ability of the director or teacher to find beauty in nature that provides the most attractive places for children. For example, a colorful tablecloth on the housekeeping area table with a small vase of wildflowers in the center makes that classroom area attractive and inviting. A large square of interesting gift-wrapping paper, neatly trimmed, or a square yard of fabric serves as an attractive and inexpensive wall hanging and can be changed or cleaned often.

Be aware of the wide variety of art forms and styles developed by each culture. Displaying these introduces children and families to beauty they may not have had the opportunity to experience and provides an interesting and appropriate way to begin discussions and explorations of other cultures.

REFLECTION

What does beauty mean to you? Think about the art that appeals to you. Where did you find it? Do you know who created it? Is there a story behind it? Can you remember how you developed your ideas about art and its value? What ideas do you have for bringing art to young children?

When equipment is made for the classroom, it should be prepared with special attention to its visual appeal. A math game, for example, can be made using well-designed stickers or beautiful pictures cut from duplicate copies of magazines instead of cartoonlike gimmicky stickers or drawings. The cardboard should be cut evenly and laminated or covered with a plastic coating instead of being presented to children with rough, crooked edges. Preparing beautiful materials takes a little longer and may require initial costs that are somewhat higher, but the product is worth the investment. One of the director's roles is to help staff and children value quality rather than quantity and to appreciate and care for the beauty in the objects around them.

User Preference

The classroom is a place in which the teacher can express her personality. By including some items that represent her interests, she communicates to children and families that she has preferences just as they do. It's reasonable to expect that sometimes teacher preference determines the type of equipment ordered. One teacher may choose to buy many books while another depends heavily on the library, or one sees an autoharp as a necessity while another finds this instrument encumbering. One teacher may choose a guinea pig as the ideal classroom pet, another prefers fish, and still another considers all pets to require an inordinate amount of the teacher's time. As long as these teacher preferences are not contrary to appropriate classroom practice, they are legitimate and should be honored if at all possible. When budgeting constraints or other equipment needs make it impossible to fill all teachers' requests, the director must notify teachers that their preferences are under consideration and that plans are being made to fill all requests as soon as possible. The teacher who wants an autoharp may have to wait

DIRECTOR'S CORNER

"Our board is meeting today to discuss how to spend the $1,000 board members earned by selling coupon books. The board members asked each teacher to keep a wish list on hand. When the order comes in, we have a celebration, with the board and staff gathering to open the cartons."

—Director, agency-sponsored child care center

until next year's budget provides it, but meanwhile, the director can support that teacher by informing the staff of planned equipment purchases. Each teacher's preference deserves careful consideration because each teacher will ultimately set the stage for learning through the use of the center's equipment. Of course, the director will have to intervene if a teacher chooses to order inappropriate items such as toys and games with very small pieces for toddlers or flash cards for preschoolers.

WORKING WITHIN A BUDGET

As you bring together information about purchases to be made, notice how various components of your program's systems come into play. You are addressing finances, staff, and equipment simultaneously, and you will follow the policies and procedures established around the center's equipment. With that perspective in mind, you will be ready to relate the choices that you and the staff have made, the needs of the children, and a component of the budget.

Major considerations when working with an equipment budget are durability and economy. Often, they go hand in hand. The climbing apparatus that costs three times as much as a competitor's product is worth the original investment if it lasts three times as long or is safer and sturdier. When more durable items are purchased, the center is not faced with the problem of replacement so often, and considerable shipping costs are saved, particularly with large pieces of equipment. Price and durability are not always perfectly correlated, but it is safe to say that inexpensive tricycles, which may be appropriate for home use, are inappropriate for group use. When used at a center, the standard equipment that is used at home will be in the repair shop far sooner and more frequently than will the sturdier, more expensive equipment that is designed for school use. Keep this fact in mind when well-meaning board members want to donate items their children

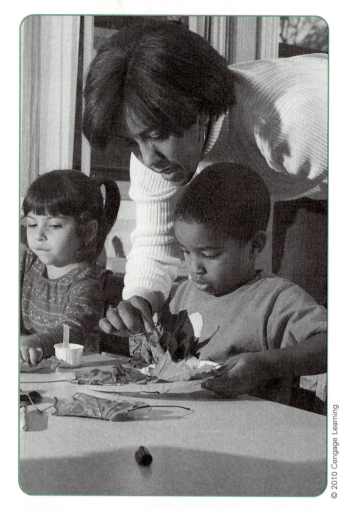

Children enjoy working with some found materials such as leaves found on the playground.

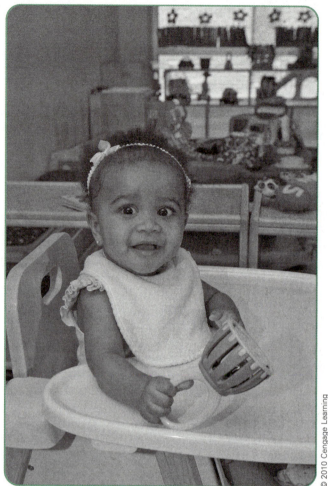

(A)

Order furniture based on the children's age, size, and ability.

have outgrown instead of including sufficient dollars in the equipment budget.

In child care center kitchens, many adults (and occasionally children) use the equipment. This heavy usage (and perhaps misuse), coupled with lack of care, may lead to the need for earlier replacement. Refrigerator and freezer doors are opened frequently and often are left standing open while children, accompanied by a teacher, of course, take out ice cubes or put in trays of sloshing Jell-O™. Dishwashers may be improperly loaded or overloaded, and sinks are sometimes scoured with rough scouring pads or abrasive powders. It is important to provide heavy-duty kitchen equipment because equipment made for home use will require costly service calls when it is subjected to the hard use it inevitably will get in a center. A prepaid maintenance agreement may be a cost-effective way to manage equipment repairs. Checking the total cost of the maintenance agreement against the record of repairs typically needed over time for a particular

type of equipment is a smart practice. Two possible sources of such information are consumer guides, usually available at libraries, and discussion with other directors. Furthermore, instructions on how to use equipment may be posted on each item, and a short in-service session may be helpful.

In setting up a new center, the director can expect to spend $10,000 to $30,000 per classroom on equipment. The variance is due to the number of children in each classroom and the quality of the items purchased. A typical budget for manipulatives (puzzles, table toys, and small blocks) for a center of about 75 children is about $4,000, assuming that the items are centrally stored so that teachers can share them. Morgan and Emanuel (2010) suggest allocating $60 per child for classroom supplies and $60 per child for kitchen and office supplies as part of the start-up budget. They also suggest you will need $700 to $1000 per child for all equipment including kitchen and office, with $50,000 to $98,000 for playground equipment. They offer many

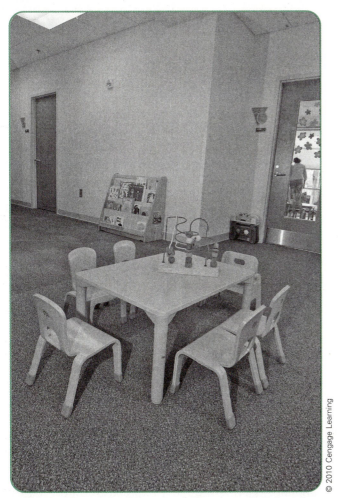

© 2010 Cengage Learning

(B)

Preschoolers and their teachers lunch together using child sized tables and chairs.

examples to help you with all aspects of managing your center's money. Directors often search for free materials and supplies to reduce these costs. However, the director then may have to pick up the items or enlist a volunteer for this service. Recognize that free items are not necessarily worthwhile and expensive items are not always better.

ORDERING EQUIPMENT

Decisions about what, when, and where to buy equipment are usually left to the director. In any case, directors are consulted and they have considerable control over what is bought with the money that is budgeted for equipment and supplies.

Equipment Requisition

Directors usually develop an equipment request procedure. Staff members notify the director, in writing, of the type of equipment needed or desired, providing additional information such as the rationale to support the need, a possible vendor, and an estimated purchase price. All of these data are helpful when final purchase decisions are made. Some centers use purchase order or requisition forms, which are nothing more than request forms that can be sent to vendors with a duplicate retained for center records (see Working Paper 8-1). Even though this request procedure is formal and perhaps cumbersome, it puts the purchase of equipment on a businesslike basis and gives each staff member an equal opportunity to bid for the equipment dollars in the budget.

In corporate systems, requisitions are processed through a central purchasing agent and shipments are made directly to the center from the manufacturer. The central office handles all the orders and saves money through collective, quantity buying and careful selection of suppliers. This approach cuts costs but limits the options for those staff members selecting equipment. Public school programs usually have specific purchasing procedures to follow, with supplies requisitioned through the principal or through a supervisor responsible for the preschool or after-school programs. However, if a nonschool organization is implementing the program within a school building, that group may have wisely negotiated an agreement that will allow them to provide and own their own equipment. The program director will then be able to maintain the philosophy that the center espouses. If the school system no longer has room for the center or prefers to run its own program, the organization maintains its equipment.

DIRECTOR'S CORNER

When I think about ordering equipment for our center, I recall a five-generation Community Playthings block family. About 40 years ago, a great-grandmother and her daughter ordered blocks for a little boy on several occasions, providing him with quite a collection which he used daily. This year, the boy's mother ordered more blocks to be added to his collection and given to his two sons. The boys are still too young to understand that this tradition of block giving was started years ago by their great-great grandmother, but they (and their father) are maintaining the tradition of playing with their blocks daily.

In centers where directors are fully responsible for receiving staff requests and placing orders, they check requests against the established selection criteria and the budget allowance before completing order forms. All order forms should include quantity, price, catalog order number (if available), and name or description of each item. When making final decisions on purchases, make certain that careful consideration is given to possible savings through bulk buying. For example, newsprint for painting can be bought from some vendors for much less per ream when bought in 48-ream packages. Economies realized through bulk buying are practical only if adequate storage space is available for the unused materials.

Equipment costs also can be reduced in nonprofit centers by applying for tax-exempt status. When orders are sent to suppliers, the center will not be charged sales tax if the order includes the center's tax-exempt number. Some centers have provisions for teachers to purchase specified dollar amounts without permission and within a given time period. For example, a teacher may receive $200 to spend for the classroom each year (in addition to the center-wide purchases that the director makes). In most cases, the purchase is made, and the teacher is reimbursed on presentation of the receipts to the director or fiscal manager. Giving teachers some freedom to provide for special program needs helps them meet children's interests without having to wait for more formal procedures.

REFLECTION

Assume that your classroom, which is stocked with basic equipment for your 15 4-year-old children, has been allocated $200 from petty cash. Think about how you might spend it.

Purchase Time Line

Equipment purchasing occurs in three different time frames:

1 start-up
2 supplementary
3 replacement

First, there must be a major start-up equipment purchase when a center is opened so that all the basic aspects of the program can function with appropriate equipment. This phase obviously is the most expensive of the three, but extensive purchases at this point are absolutely essential because it is unfair to children and staff to operate a program without basic equipment. To save money, some secondhand, borrowed, or homemade equipment can be used, keeping in mind the criteria described earlier. There is no formula that can tell a director exactly what must be provided, but the staff will need equipment of the type, quantity, and quality that will allow them to focus on the children and their needs instead of on the equipment or the lack thereof. Children in a classroom with inappropriate or inadequate equipment will be quite likely to engage in inappropriate behavior as they seek to create something interesting to do.

Providing enough appropriate storage is also essential. In the classroom, teachers need storage for supplies that they will use later in the day or week. Major classroom storage space should be available to the children so they can independently choose and put away materials. Crowded shelves and cluttered spaces make it difficult for children to find the materials they want to use. Children are also more likely to leave materials strewn about the classroom when it is not clear where they belong.

The second phase of equipment purchasing is the supplementary phase that provides for additional equipment purchases throughout each year. When supplementary equipment purchases are spaced throughout a program year, both children and staff members enjoy greater variety and a change of pace. Furthermore, teachers can adjust equipment requests to meet the needs of particular children such as a child with special needs who enrolls midyear and requires a chair with particular supports, a prone

When ordering cots, consider where and how they will be stored, as well as ease of setting them up daily and keeping them clean.

board, or a walker. Although outside funding may be available for some of these larger items for an individual child's use, teachers still need to consider books with large print, puzzles with large knobs, or writing tools that have been adapted for easier handling.

Lastly, the replacement phase helps maintain a constant supply of equipment that is in good repair and allows for adjustments in available equipment and materials as program needs change or as new items come on the market. For example, a few years ago, all African-American dolls had Caucasian hairstyles and facial features, but newer dolls have features that more closely match the ethnic group being represented. Nontoxic, washable markers have replaced the old odorous markers. Similarly, film-strips have been replaced by videos and DVDs. At the same time, much-loved children's books such as *Goodnight Moon* (Brown, 1947) remind us that new isn't always better.

The budget also should include enough money for emergency replacements. Although careful usage, combined with a fund for maintenance, minimizes the need for emergency replacements, unexpected breakage or loss is sure to occur. When a copier repair is too costly, it is sometimes more economical to buy or lease a new model than to repair the old one. As for buying a maintenance plan, consider what the warranty covers and for how long before paying for a plan.

Sources of Equipment

Much of the equipment for early childhood education centers is purchased from catalogs. If the dealers are reliable, this arrangement is satisfactory. It is wise to check with other directors, professional organizations, or the Better Business Bureau to determine the suitability of making purchases from a particular company. Among the advantages of purchasing by catalog are the wide variety of merchandise that is available and lowering of costs with bypassing the retailer. On the other hand, shipping costs may be charged and return of unsatisfactory merchandise may be cumbersome. It is helpful to have a supply of catalogs offering good quality merchandise available to the staff. Catalogs from companies that sell easily breakable toys, items that are always in only very bright colors, cars and trucks with faces, etc. should be discarded. Most companies will be pleased to put your center on their mailing list. Refer to the list in Appendix E.

When you are placing a large order, request a discount. Another opportunity for price reduction is prompt payment. Vendors who establish a relationship with your center are more likely to inform you of upcoming special prices. Then it is up to you to purchase items because the center needs them instead of because they are on sale. Many companies charge about 30 percent of the cost of items that have been returned, unless, of course, they arrived damaged. In addition, the center pays the return shipping. Impulse buying is irresponsible when you are in charge of purchasing equipment.

Equipment purchased from local retail outlets can be seen and tried out, which has obvious advantages. But most retail outlets cater to home users and carry a limited stock of classroom equipment. If a local outlet has access to a manufacturer of school equipment, it may be possible to order from a catalog through a local retailer. A buying co-op is another equipment source worth investigating because group buying can be very economical. In this system, the co-op group buys in quantity at a wholesale price and sells items to co-op members at just enough above cost to pay the co-op's operating expenses.

Exhibit areas at state or national early childhood conferences provide great opportunities to view a huge range of products for early childhood classrooms and to talk with the vendors. Keep in mind that their goal is to sell their products, but a careful shopper can garner a wealth of information and sometimes a special price. Particularly at the end of the exhibit hours, vendors would just as soon give you a discount as ship materials back to their home base. Remember also that conference sponsors rarely endorse products being displayed. Conferees are responsible for using their own good judgment since what is available is not always appropriate for early childhood education.

Toy libraries are popular equipment sources in some areas. A center director or teacher may borrow anything from a puzzle to a complete set of housekeeping equipment, just as one borrows library books. Sometimes, a group of center directors finds it worthwhile to help establish a toy library for their mutual benefit, and it is especially helpful to have toy-lending programs that furnish materials for special-needs children. Occasionally, toy-lending or toy-sharing systems are set up by community organizations to make equipment available to centers and parents.

Secondhand shops, discount stores, antique shops, and garage or yard sales frequently are excellent sources of equipment or raw materials for pieces needed by the center. The buyer may discover a garlic press that can provide an interesting physical knowledge experience for children when they are working with Play-Doh. Using imagination and

All children need access to a wide range of books, some of which may come from the public library.

© 2010 Cengage Learning

effort, directors can turn large ice cream cans into storage places for musical instruments or some other equipment that demands a number of relatively small, easily accessible spaces. Perhaps a used desk or file cabinet for the center office can be located. When such discoveries need to be put into finished, usable, and attractive form, it sometimes is possible to enlist the help of the parent group, a high school vocational class, or a senior citizens' organization whose members enjoy repairing and painting. In some regions, high school woodworking or metal-working classes or Junior Achievement groups make new equipment and sell it to centers at reasonable prices.

Another way to obtain equipment is to solicit the help of parents, teachers, board members, or residents of the community in equipment-making parties. This activity enhances the feeling of community in the center's program. Child care center staff members often take advantage of the children's nap time to make classroom materials. Encouraging staff members to make some materials is important because few centers have unlimited resources, and commercial equipment cannot always be suitably adapted to meet individual children's needs.

Gifts of equipment are usually welcome, but their suitability must be measured against the same criteria employed for equipment purchases. A gift such as a toy gun in a center where pretend gunplay is discouraged or the gift of an animal that induces allergic reactions in some children must be refused graciously.

MANAGING EQUIPMENT

Even before equipment is delivered to the center, the director must consider how it will be managed. All equipment must be checked and inventoried on delivery, and before it is stored or put into use, a maintenance plan should be set up to minimize repair and replacement needs.

Checking and Inventorying Equipment

When equipment is received, it must be checked against the order to ascertain that it corresponds with the order in terms of quantity, size, color, and so forth. It also is important to make certain that only the items actually received are listed on both the order and the packing slip and that prices are correct. If discrepancies are found, the vendor must be notified immediately. It is wise to keep original packing materials in case any equipment needs to be returned.

Most center directors keep a record of at least the major items purchased, and some directors keep a running account of all small items and consumables as well. An inventory of purchases can be recorded as items are unpacked by listing each item on the computer or a file card, noting the description, supplier, price, date of purchase, and location in which the item is to be used. Some directors mark equipment with the name of the center, with an inventory number, or with an identifying number so that if a center owns four identical computers, each is

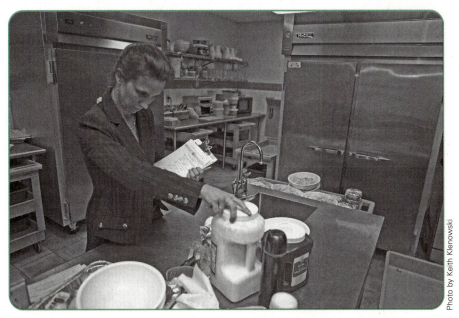

Photo by Keith Klenowski

Most center directors keep a record of at least the major items purchased, and some directors keep a running account of all small items and consumables as well.

individually identifiable. In public schools, the usual practice is to put the room number on each piece of equipment. The labeling practice is helpful when pieces are sent out for repair, when school buildings are cleaned during vacation periods, or when items are stolen. Of course, valuable equipment should be insured. When equipment is added or removed from the center, the inventory must be updated.

An accurate record of equipment will always be available when the inventory is updated regularly. Working Paper 8-2 shows a suggested inventory form. A backup disc of the inventory should be kept in a safe place—a fire-resistant file cabinet or other storage unit if possible—so that losses can be reported accurately in the event of fire or theft. Furthermore, an ongoing, updated inventory minimizes the work of taking an annual inventory (usually necessary for insurance purposes) for annual reporting to the board or the sponsoring or funding agency or for reporting to a corporate central office that must have an accurate annual inventory to determine the assets of the corporation. Updated inventories also give directors a clear picture of what is available in the center and help pinpoint areas or types of equipment that are incurring heavy damage. This information is useful in determining how much and when to reorder and in making decisions about changing vendors or brands of equipment ordered. Information about persistent damage in certain areas should lead to a careful examination of the storage and maintenance system.

After the equipment is checked in and inventoried, the director must notify the staff that the new equipment is available for use. No doubt, everyone will know when a new climbing tower arrives or when a new microwave oven is available, but if a dozen new puzzles are placed on the shelves or a fresh supply of felt markers is stored, it could be weeks before all teachers in a large center discover the new materials.

Maintaining and Storing Equipment

As soon as equipment is placed in the center, the job of maintenance begins. In the very act of placing equipment, maintenance decisions are made. For example, an untreated wooden climber that is placed outdoors in a rainy area is doomed to rot. It will need immediate treatment, followed by periodic coatings of a penetrating, nontoxic stain if it is to withstand weathering. Large tempera paint containers that are left open will dry out quickly, as will clay that is not properly stored.

Equipment used by the children must be checked daily and removed if it is in need of repair, even if immediate replacement is impossible. Children need attractive, usable equipment and should not be subjected to the frustration of trying to make sense out of broken or incomplete classroom materials. Puzzles with missing pieces, tricycles with broken pedals, or books with torn or defaced pages should not be left in the classroom.

Storage of equipment also is directly related to its maintenance. It is easy to return equipment after it has been used when each piece has a specific, clearly delineated storage space. The space, whether in a storage room or on a classroom shelf, must be large enough so that the object does not have to be jammed into place and perhaps damaged. The space must be accessible to staff members (and in many cases, to children) to ensure that it will be used for storage purposes. When storage is far from a classroom or the teachers have to go through another area such as the director's office to get to the storage room, it is more likely that the equipment and materials will be shoved out of the way in the classroom rather than returned to the storage room. Each center must work out a method for storing certain equipment and supplies that are used daily and must remain in the classroom. Other supplies should be designated for return to a central area. Storage also must be provided for items such as tricycles that are used daily but must be protected from weather and theft. Additional storage is needed for items that are purchased in quantity for long-range use such as paper towels and paint.

When a large number of people have access to the central supply storage areas, there is some tendency for each person to assume that someone else will maintain order and cleanliness in the area. Therefore, many of the users feel little or no responsibility for maintaining the area. When this happens, some users return materials in a haphazard way, fail to place them on the correct shelves, or return them in poor condition. Other staff members become irritated when they try to find what they need and have to cope with a messy storage area. These frustrations lead to conflict and a breakdown in positive staff relationships. Sometimes, this problem can be avoided by assigning each teacher the responsibility for maintaining a specific storage area, such as the area for art materials, outdoor equipment, or books and records, for a given length of time. In other centers, periodic work sessions are scheduled to involve the entire staff in cleaning and straightening central

Date	Item	Teacher	Date Returned
10/7/11	Large Legos	Denice	10/28/11
10/7/11	Magnetic Letters	Sam	
10/10/11	CD: Ella Jenkins CD: Elgar violin	Maria	10/31/11

FIGURE 8-1 Sample checkout sheet for equipment and materials.
Source: © Cengage Learning, 2013.

storage areas. Some centers institute a system for checking equipment in and out of the storage room that is similar to how libraries operate; an example is shown in Figure 8-1. In a large center, putting the checkout list on a computer may be helpful, but in most centers, posting a clipboard with a checkout sheet is more likely to be convenient for teachers. A few centers keep all the equipment in classrooms on shelves available to the children or in closed cabinets available to the teacher, but this practice is expensive because it requires so much duplication.

In whatever way equipment is stored, its placement should be neat and easy to find so that children and teachers alike will be encouraged to maintain some degree of order in their attractive environment. The director's job is to establish and follow routines that lead to the easy accessibility of all equipment to everyone. These routines make putting things away far less burdensome for both teachers and children. Orderliness does not have to be an obsession; rather, it is an appropriate way to manage a large variety of equipment that is used in a number of ways by a wide range of people.

Summary

Appropriate equipment allows the staff to focus on the essentials of their work as they provide an excellent early childhood program. Initial purchases are made when a center opens, and additional items for children's and adults' spaces and for service areas are purchased to supplement and replace this equipment. Most centers acquire equipment from a variety of sources, but all equipment should be considered in terms of its usefulness, durability, economy, ease of maintenance, attractiveness, teacher preference, and safety. Once equipment is made available, it must be properly maintained and stored. A plan for use and care of equipment must be developed for both children and staff as a component of the center's program.

TRY IT OUT!

1 Work with fellow students on the following role-playing situations. Have several students role-play, using different approaches to each problem. Discuss the strengths and weaknesses of each group's approach.

a. You are a preschool director. Mrs. Jane Jones has just given you 24 coloring books with an advertising message for her husband's business on the cover. You never use coloring books at the center because you believe they are not developmentally appropriate and would not meet NAEYC guidelines. How might you handle this?

b. Suppose that the same situation in problem (a) occurred but that the donor is Mrs. Thomas Vanderbilt. Last year, she gave your center $10,000 for equipment. What might you say to Mrs. Vanderbilt?

2 Your preschool class is in the planning stage and will be held in a public school building. Discuss with your principal your 4-year-olds' needs and ways in which their equipment will be different from that of older children. Use a role-play format, working in pairs, or perhaps volunteering to role-play for the class.

Working Paper 8-1

PURCHASE ORDER FORM

REQUISITION/PURCHASE ORDER

THE CHILDREN'S CENTER

To: _____

_____

_____

Catalog No.	Description	Quantity	Price	Total

Ship to: The Children's Center 1099 Main Street Centerville, CA 00000–0000

Account charged: _____

Approved by: _____

Date ordered: _____

Date received: _____

Source: © Cengage Learning, 2013.

Working Paper 8-2

SAMPLE INVENTORY FORM

INVENTORY FORM					
Date Purchased	Description	Identifying Number	Source	Price	Location in Center

Source: © Cengage Learning, 2013.

You can download a full-size version of these forms on the Education CourseMate website.

REFERENCES

Aronson, S. (1997, January). Lead paint poisoning from playground equipment. *Child Care Information Exchange*, 79–81.

Brown, M. W. (1947). *Goodnight Moon*. New York: Harper.

Dodge, D.; Colker, L.; & Heroman, C. (2002). *The creative curriculum for preschool* (4th ed.). Washington, DC: Teaching Strategies.

Hirsch, E. (Ed.). (1995). *The block book*. Washington, DC: National Association for the Education of Young Children.

Morgan, G. & Emanuel, B. (2010). *The Bottom line for children's programs: What you need to know to manage the money.* (5th ed.) Watertown, MA: Steam Press.

Moyer, J. (Ed.). (1995). *Selecting educational equipment and materials for school and home.* Wheaton: Association for Childhood Education International.

Stoecklin, V. (2005, July). Creating environments that sustain children, staff, and our planet. *Child Care Information Exchange, 164*, 39–48.

U.S. Consumer Product Safety Commission. (1999). Washington, DC: U.S. Government Printing Office.

Wardle, F. (1999). The story of a playground. *Child Care Information Exchange, 128*, 28–30.

White Hutchinson Leisure & Learning Group. (2007, May–August). Illinois becomes second state to require green cleaning, reducing chemical exposure for children. *Children's Learning Environments eNewsletter, VI*(2), 1.

Wortham, S. C., & Frost, J. L. (Eds.). (1997). *Playgrounds for young children: American survey and perspectives.* Reston, VA: American Alliance for Health, Physical Education, Recreation and Dance.

9

STAFFING *the* CENTER

The center director sets the emotional tone for the program.

This chapter focuses on the importance of developing good leadership skills, then using these skills—with good communication skills—to be an effective administrator of a child care program. Obviously, the person in charge must have knowledge of how to develop and oversee a budget, write policy and job descriptions, and determine the program's facility and equipment needs. However, writing policy, hiring staff, developing budgets, and ordering equipment all will be wasted efforts unless the manager has the interpersonal and communication skills necessary to hire and motivate the staff. Once the policies have been established, the staff are hired and the children enrolled, the function of the director becomes catalytic or facilitative.

Objectives

After reading this chapter, you should be able to:

- Discuss ways to create a positive climate through:
  - modeling
  - community building
  - communicating
- List ways to motivate staff through:
  - encouragement
  - job enrichment
- Describe the major sections of an employment policy.
- Write a job description for each position in a child care center.
- Understand the interview and hiring process.
- Develop an orientation process for new employees.

Standards Addressed in This Chapter

naeyc Professional Preparation Standard
naeyc Administrator Competencies
    Management Knowledge and Skills 1, 2, 3, 9
    Early Childhood Knowledge and Skills
naeyc Accreditation Standards 10

DEVELOPING INTERPERSONAL RELATIONSHIPS naeyc

Clearly, the interpersonal issues and the time it takes to resolve them are at the very core of being an effective administrator. Much of what is discussed in this text deals with budgets, boards, licensing, and record keeping, but the real task of the director as a manager is to work effectively with, and provide support to, those who will implement the program. The terms *manager, director, administrator*, and *leader* used throughout this book all refer to the person in charge of, and responsible for, the program. The manager must relate to the staff and motivate them to do the tasks delegated to them. Members of the staff implement the program, but the director, acting in the capacity of leader and motivator, orchestrates so that all the components work together.

Creating a Positive Climate

As a leader, the director has the major responsibility for creating a climate of care, trust, and respect. This climate can be achieved best by demonstrating caring behavior, by taking steps to build a feeling of community or partnership, and by creating a climate for good communication among and between all members of the center community. The goal is to optimize the developmental potential of children, families, and staff in an environment that respects diversity. The director not only sets the emotional tone of a center but also works with staff to develop structures that empower, organize, and build a sense of community.

Modeling

The director creates a climate of warmth, caring, and acceptance by relating to staff members, parents, and children with honesty and openness. Mutual trust will grow in an environment in which respect is earned, and the best way to earn respect is to show respect for others. When respect for difference is modeled, the tone is set for the entire center.

Maturity and self-awareness are the basic characteristics of a leader who can maintain professional interaction in even the most intense situation. Self-awareness is being able to identify one's own emotions and the ability to link those emotions to one's actions. Leaders who are self-aware and attuned to their emotions and actions are better equipped to understand the emotions of others (Bloom, 2007). These leadership attributes create a climate that, in turn, motivates others to be understanding, accepting, and warm. Most of you have read about and observed "modeling" in young children. One child who is perceived as the leader displays a pattern of behavior, and others imitate it. One child might say, "Yuck! Spinach!" and soon everyone at the table is saying "Yuck, spinach!" However, if the child were to say, "Yummm, spinach!" then other children are more likely to respond positively to the vegetable being served. Although this example is clearly an oversimplification of what typically happens in a group, behavior *is* contagious, and there is evidence that a leader who serves as the model does, indeed, drive the behavioral climate of the setting.

Modeling begins with the very first encounter the director has with new staff members as they come into the center for interviews or when a newly hired director is introduced to the staff for the first time. The trust and mutual respect that are communicated during these initial meetings are the building blocks for the relationships that will develop over time. During the first meeting of a new year, at a new center, or with a new director, there is a unique opportunity to establish procedures and practices that will set the stage for future respectful interactions. Additionally, the director who shows intellectual curiosity and is always seeking more information to do a better job can inspire others to do the same. A leader who does not serve as a model of professional commitment and enthusiasm for learning more about children, families, human relationships, and trends and issues in early childhood

---

DIRECTOR'S CORNER

"In most cases, to be successful as a director of a child care center, you have to be a people person. You have to realize that this job goes far beyond administrative policy and doing paperwork—that being the boss here is not really being a boss in the traditional sense. Being the boss here has to do with forming trusting relationships with your staff, respecting their individuality, being firm when you need to be firm and being gentle when they need a gentle hand. It's important to remember that you won't get respect if you don't show respect. Also, remember that others can do the paperwork, but you are the one who must build the relationships with your staff. Of course, you are also responsible for building and maintaining relationships with parents and the community."

—Director of a community nonprofit child care center

cannot expect staff members to invest energy in these areas. The leader's responsibility is to show interest and enthusiasm for what is going on in the program and in the profession and to serve as a resource for staff members and parents.

Community Building

The director is responsible for developing and maintaining a sense of community among staff, parents, and children. Morale will be higher and the environment more conducive to growth for all involved if there is a "we" feeling of belonging. As the feeling of belonging increases, feelings of anxiety, self-doubt, hostility, and rejection decrease.

Staff members who feel a sense of ownership about the program will be more self-assured and enthusiastic about assuming responsibility. They will not only perform the tasks they were hired to perform but will be more likely to invest energy into learning more so they can extend their area of responsibility. The total task of serving children and families becomes *our* task, and *we* provide the richest and best service we can.

The "we" feeling radiates beyond staff to families and children. It becomes "our" center or "our" program, and children begin to talk about "my" school. The feeling of community permeates the entire environment; all who participate in the many aspects of the center program feel they play an

important part in the total program. All participants feel that they *own* a piece of the program and contribute to its success or failure. Parents and children alike recognize that they, and their cultures and languages, are valued, that diversity is at the very core of the program, and that their contribution to the program is important. They come to understand that they are the very reason for the center's existence. There would be no reason for the center to continue if there were no families and children to serve.

REFLECTION

Take a moment to reflect on your own practicum experiences. Think about whether there was a sense of community in the center in which you gained experience. Consider whether you were made to feel that you were an important member of the community. If you recall feeling positive about the experience, who was most instrumental in creating that accepting environment for you? Did you sense the children also felt this was *their* place? Who was responsible for creating the "we" feeling in the classroom?

DIRECTOR'S CORNER

"I often think back on my own experiences in the classroom when I was there eight hours a day. I remember that I was expected to be nurturing and giving of myself *all* day long—it helps me remember how much I, in turn, needed to be nurtured. That's why I have an 'open door' policy for my staff—I take time to actively listen, to problem-solve with them, to encourage them. I often have to put my paperwork aside because I know that a staff person sometimes needs to talk *right now!* This job goes beyond, 'I'm the boss and you're the staff person' relationship. The other side of this is knowing when and where to set the boundaries. When and how do I set limits on my availability to staff members or family members so that I can focus on what will be best for others and for me, as well as what is best for the program?"

—Director, for-profit corporate center

Communication

Every director will engage in a certain amount of written communication. When there is a need to communicate in writing, the first question to ask is, "Who needs to know?" Interpersonal relationships are often damaged inadvertently because some members of the group do not receive information that they feel should have been relayed to them. For example, although a change in next week's menu may, on the surface, affect only the cook in a child care center, a teacher who has planned a special science activity around one of the foods to be served on a given day may be very annoyed to learn about the change in menu *after* implementing the special lesson. The message itself, including the exact wording, can be more easily drafted once the audience for the message has been determined. Therefore, the audience receiving the message will determine both the content and the wording.

Although some communication will be in writing, much of it will be face-to-face verbal or nonverbal. To be an effective leader, the director must be a competent communicator and must take responsibility for helping the entire staff develop communication skills.

Verbal communication skills can be learned. The director can learn to send effective messages, to become a good listener, and to engage in effective problem solving. It is possible to define specific behaviors, both verbal and nonverbal, that block communication. It is possible to improve communication skills and, as a result, enhance interpersonal relationships. Note that we have said this is *possible,* but it is not easy. Unless directors believe wholeheartedly in the importance of open communication for good interpersonal relationships, they are unlikely to invest the energy necessary to develop the skills and to practice them until they become totally integrated into a personal communication style. However, once this integration has come about, the director's communication style inevitably will serve as a model for others. The model will set the pattern for all the other people in the center and will create an atmosphere more conducive to open communication.

It is important that verbal and nonverbal messages be congruent. Sensitive leaders will take care to convey the *real* message with both their words and body postures. Words that convey approval or acceptance but are accompanied by a frown and a closed body posture conveying rejection and hostility send a mixed message that is confusing to the receiver. Supportive, positive words and actions will help build trusting relationships among the people in the center. In a trusting relationship, criticism or negative reactions can be handled without destroying the relationship, provided they are given discreetly and are carefully timed. For the director to criticize a teacher in front of the receptionist when the teacher is on the way to the classroom to help a crying child is the epitome of poor communication skills and will have a negative impact on future attempts at open communication. Other, more subtle blocks to communication that will set the stage for a defensive response, hostility, or feelings of inadequacy include

- demanding and controlling messages
- put-downs
- use of sarcasm or threats
- flip, humorous responses to serious concerns

It is important to consider what needs to be said, how to say it, and when to say it, always being aware of the cultural nuances of language.

A sensitive leader is well advised to consider carefully whether a situation calls for *telling* or *listening.* Telling often comes more easily than listening but must always be done with full awareness of the cultural nuance of language. However, in many situations, listening is a better vehicle for maintaining open communication and strengthening a relationship. Dealing with the personal problems of families or professional issues of staff members often requires listening instead of telling. The benefit of listening is not only to gain information, it is also to validate the message of the sender. Such communication can be energy draining and time consuming but when done well has a powerful and positive influence on the network of interpersonal relationships. It is time and energy well spent.

Despite all the care and planning that go into creating a supportive atmosphere, conflict will arise. This is human nature and does not necessarily mean poor management, nor does it imply weakness in the network. It does, however, require attention. There are communication skills that can be learned by the director and the staff to facilitate conflict resolution. Recognizing that conflict will exist is the first step in developing a system for dealing with it. Because many find conflict to be uncomfortable, it is common for people to try to avoid it. Effective leaders overcome the natural tendency to overreact or to avoid, blame, or punish those who are involved in the conflict. They maintain a calm, rational style of interaction. Being proactive is an effective tool to deal with conflict as it arises. It includes developing a conflict resolution policy and communicating it to both teachers and families as part of the orientation process. Addressing expectations for dealing with conflict before the emotions of an actual tense situation arise is an important strategy to implement. Consider the conflict resolution policy shown in Figure 9-1.

Motivating the Staff

The director does the orchestrating, but programs are implemented through the efforts of staff. The staff of a center must be motivated to plan and implement the total program. Just as communication skills can be learned, the skills for guiding mental and physical energies toward defined goals can also be learned. Without training in how to guide and to motivate human energy toward shared goals, the director will follow some rules of thumb that may leave the role of director-as-motivator to chance. This practice may be compared to designing a program for young

DIRECTOR'S CORNER

"As a director, I want my staff to know that it is good to have different opinions about any number of things, and when I hear about these differences, I want to provide an opportunity for discussion rather than have concerns turn into bad feelings, unproductive activity, and gossip."

—Director, church-based not-for-profit program

Conflict Resolution Policy

We provide a safe, secure environment where children learn to respectfully resolve conflicts that naturally occur in a child care setting:

- Adults help children develop vocabulary that expresses not only their wants and needs, but other's feelings as well as their own.
- Adults model respectful interactions with others, using their own words and actions to develop an understanding of how to deal with conflict.
- Adults affirm everyone's right to be safe emotionally as well as physically by setting standards for behavior and implementing caring, consistent consequences aligned with developmentally appropriate expectations according to the children's age levels.
- Adults facilitate resolution between preschool children by asking guided questions, but resist solving the children's problems for them, thus providing children the opportunity to make decisions and practice self-regulation of socially responsible behavior.

Conflict between Adults

While every effort is made to meet the needs of children, parents, and staff, we realize that from time to time a conflict may occur between parents, staff, and administrators. The following process is followed should a conflict occur:

- Step One – A respectful discussion is held between the persons directly involved at a time and place that assures privacy and sufficient time for a thorough resolution to take place.
- Step Two – If resolution is not found at the first meeting, a second meeting is held with the Director for the purpose of creating a plan for resolution and a timeline for expected success.
- Step Three – If the conflict is not resolved according to the timeline, adjustments may be made to the plan, and an additional timeline be established, or:
- Step Four – If at any time the Director determines that resolution is not possible s/he will consider one of the following for immediate action:
  - Removal of the child from the classroom
  - Withdrawal of services from the center
  - Suspension of the staff member until disciplinary steps can be taken
  - Involvement of the Assistant Dean of the School of Education and Allied Professions

Grounds for determining that a resolution is not possible include but are not exclusive of the following:

1. any person involved displays inappropriate behavior such as shouting, accusing, name-calling, swearing, or physical assault
2. any person involved refuses to follow the prescribed process
3. any person involved jeopardizes the process by spreading information concerning the conflict to those outside the immediate conflict or those involved in the resolution of the process.

FIGURE 9-1 Sample conflict resolution policy.

Source: Reprinted with permission from the Bombeck Family Learning Center of the University of Dayton.

children based on knowledge gained from having been a child, having parented a child, or having been through a public school system. Although these experiences may be useful, they cannot substitute for theoretical knowledge and a sound educational background in the field.

As directors begin to think about ways to motivate employees, they usually think about salary increases, a better building, new equipment, more help in the center, and a number of other items that are related to money and budget. Certainly, low salaries and poor working conditions can lead to dissatisfaction, but

the promise of more money—or the threat of less—probably will not have far-reaching or long-lasting effects on individual or group performance levels. However, if a leader is using dollars to control and motivate performance, it becomes increasingly more difficult to find the necessary supply to meet the demand. In addition, extrinsic incentives motivate employees to get the rewards but rarely alter the emotional or intellectual commitments that underlie behaviors.

What, then, is a director to do? There are a number of useful strategies for motivating people to commit themselves to a task and to actualize their potential. Two of the strategies that seem particularly applicable to the early childhood setting are use of encouragement and provision of job enrichment.

Use of Encouragement

Rewards or reinforcements may motivate the staff, but as with teaching, they tend to increase dependency on the one who controls the source of the rewards. They also heighten competition, thereby defeating the overarching goal of developing a sense of a cooperative community. Encouragement, on the other hand, tends to build self-confidence and a sense of intrinsic job satisfaction.

Just as the classroom teacher makes sure that encouragement is specific, focused on process, usually given in private, and neither judgmental nor evaluative, the director also keeps these same principles in mind when working with staff. To encourage a teacher who has just helped a screaming toddler, you might say, "I noticed how calm you managed to be with Tommy while he was having such a hard time in the bathroom. It worked out well." These words of encouragement are more specific and process oriented than, "I like the way you work with toddlers." Telling the teacher of 4-year-olds, "You must have done some detailed planning for the science experience you did today to make it go so smoothly. It's surely fun for you to watch how engaged the children were in inflating their model lungs" is more specific and less evaluative than, "That was a nice science activity."

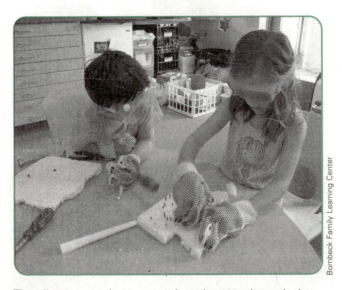

The director needs to recognize when teachers design quality experiences and communicate that recognition regularly.

DIRECTOR'S CORNER

"Encouraging staff is *so* important. The little words of praise, 'good job' or 'how nice' do not mean the same as when you take ten minutes of conversation with a staff person to say, 'Look at the changes in your room! What happened that made you think about changing the dramatic play area to a doctor's office? The design of the area and the detailed thought you've given to the choice of props are surely a delight for the children.' "

—Director, independent not-for-profit center

Job Enrichment

Carter and Curtis (2010) encourage leaders to view teachers as competent thinkers and learners.

How you (the director) see teachers and the scope of their work is critical to your success in helping them develop. If you view your staff as people with problems, only noticing their lack of skills and knowledge to manage behavior or plan lessons for learning, you will most likely approach your coaching with quick fixes, one-size-fits-all techniques, and impatience rather than engage them in the dynamics of the teaching and learning process. In contrast, if you acknowledge the complexities of working with children and regard your teachers as competent human beings with rich life experiences, important perspectives and the potential to rise to their best selves, you will invest the time, resources, and enthusiasm to engage with them in their work (p. 131).

Job enrichment is a management strategy that enhances job satisfaction and honors the strengths of staff by presenting more challenges and increasing responsibility, which, in turn, produce a sense of personal achievement and on-the-job satisfaction. It is possible to design a job enrichment program for a child care center so that staff members are motivated to higher levels of commitment. As a result, they will experience greater intrinsic rewards. The job enrichment principles particularly applicable to child care centers are listed below:

1 Give new and added responsibilities to staff members so they are constantly challenged and empowered to control aspects of their work setting.

2 Provide opportunities for ongoing training and college-based education that will contribute to quality of performance and to personal and professional growth.

3 Give staff members special assignments by occasionally delegating coworkers' or supervisors' jobs to broaden each person's understanding of the total operation of the organization. This is recognition but has no monetary reward. This procedure can bring more recognition from other staff members and open up greater opportunities for advancement.

Obviously, there is some overlap among the three stated principles, both in terms of the method used and the outcome expected. There also are other ways to enrich staff members' jobs that will broaden their experience and bring them both intrinsic and extrinsic rewards. The many possibilities are limited solely by the creativity and imagination of the person in charge.

At first glance, it may seem that added responsibility will lead to dissatisfaction and demands for more money or other material rewards. However, there is evidence to suggest that, more often than not, the person who is challenged and who "stretches" to assume more responsibility will feel a sense of pride and achievement. For example, the classroom aide who, at midyear, is given the added responsibility of meeting and greeting parents and children at arrival time probably will find that job intrinsically satisfying. The aide will develop better skills for helping children make that first daily break from a trusted caregiver and acquire new skills for accomplishing the added responsibility. Assigning added duties can be accomplished best in an atmosphere of mutual trust, and it must be done through the use of positive communication skills.

The training needed to develop the skills necessary for managing a new task effectively often can be offered informally by other members of the staff and by exposure to resources such as books, pamphlets, videos, PowerPoint presentations, or opportunities to observe. Ongoing training can be expanded to include more formalized in-service sessions on curriculum, child abuse, communication skills, working with children with special needs and their families, or other topics selected to serve a specific need within the center program. Use of release time or financial support for workshops and seminars, online resources, and additional course work are still other ways to provide job enrichment opportunities for the personal and professional growth of staff members.

Delegating special assignments to staff members usually evokes a sense of achievement and recognition, even though it means extra work. A cook who is consulted about menu planning and buying, and who is later asked to help evaluate the total food service program when the center is undergoing a self-study for accreditation, not only gains an understanding of what is involved in the total food planning and preparation program but also develops a greater potential for advancement, whether in the current job or in another work setting.

Designing Employment Policies

Directors of new centers are faced with the daunting task of developing new employment policies while directors of existing centers must deal with the recurring task of reviewing and revising these policies. Employment Policies are required documents for NAEYC accreditation in the Leadership and Management Standard. The Program Administration Scale (PAS) has Employment Policies as part of the Human Resources Development System. When writing or revising employment policies, it is important to consider the purpose served by the policies, the best interests of all parties covered and affected by the policies, and what is to be included in the policies.

Purpose

The need of personnel for security and confidence in job performance should be balanced with the center's need to function effectively in the establishment of carefully conceived employment policies. When staff members are unsure of their rights and their responsibilities, some of them may tend to probe and test to determine where the limits lie. The dissension among staff members that ensues drains energy from child care. Staff members who know what is expected can recognize how their assigned roles fit into the overall organization and can function more comfortably in those roles. Administrators also can function more effectively when there is little doubt about policies.

Inclusive employment policies tailored to a specific child care operation, whether staffed by a few or by many, serve two purposes.

1 They reduce procedural errors and free administrators from unnecessary involvement in resolution.

2 They reduce anxiety by helping each staff member to understand expectations and move, independently and as part of the team, toward efficient operation of the program.

A written statement of the employment policies and procedures should be given to each employee at the beginning of the term of employment. These policies set the parameters within which the staff will function. Of course, the administrator should periodically check with employees to ascertain whether the policies are understood. Although these policies must be tailored to the needs of each program, the samples in Director's Resource 9-1 can serve as a guideline for their preparation.

Source

The task of writing employment policies is complex and the sphere of their influence is extensive. They must not only be precise, well written, and inclusive but also take into consideration the best interests of staff, children, and families. The interest of the sponsoring group, whether it be to make a profit or not, deserves consideration as well. Those who are responsible for writing the policies must have both an understanding of the scope of the program and insight into the vested interests of all involved.

Employment policies might be prepared by such persons as the hired director of a community-sponsored center, an owner of a proprietary center, a human resources department for a center sponsored by a corporation or institution, or the human resources director of a national child care chain. Existing public school employment policies for teachers or, in some cases, for civil service employees often will be applicable in programs sponsored by public schools or on military bases. When the center staff is part of a labor union, the union contract will likely impact how policies and procedures are written to reflect agreements that were made during the contract negotiations.

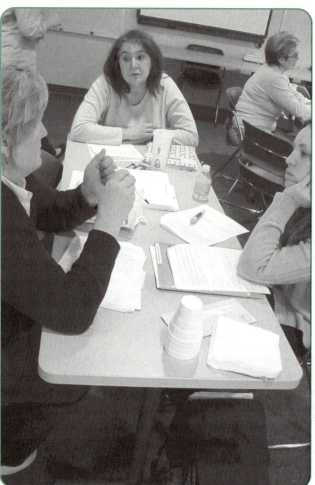

Good employment policies need to be revisited with staff in order to be fair and current.

Bombeck Family Learning Center

It is somewhat common practice for child care settings to have policies drawn up by a subcommittee or a standing human resources committee of the policymaking board. The bylaws, as drawn up by the policy board, should contain the mechanism for creating a human resources committee and should detail the manner in which the membership of that committee will be selected. The center director serves on the committee and represents the staff's interest. Other members of the committee might be parents, people from the community, and representatives of licensing and/or certifying groups who would, in each case, represent the interests and diversity of special-interest groups.

Inclusions

Employment policies cover all matters relating to employment and include job responsibilities, organizational charts, schedules of reimbursement for services, evaluation and grievance procedures,

---

DIRECTOR'S CORNER

"During my new staff orientation program, I sit down with each new employee and read through the employment policies, leaving time for questions and discussion. I give special attention to the section on holidays, sick days, personal days, and vacation time. It helps me feel comfortable that this new staff person has at least looked at the employment policies once and not just put the document in a file or on her night table to read later when she has more time."

—Director, private not-for-profit center

and description of the steps necessary to change the policies themselves. They must conform to union requirements, where applicable, and to all regulations that apply to employment practices. For example, as of July 1994, employers with 15 employees or more must comply with the Americans with Disabilities Act (ADA), which covers nondiscrimination practices related to recruitment, advertising, tenure, layoffs, leave, fringe benefits, and all other employment-related activities (Americans with Disabilities Act, 1991; see Director's Resource 9-2). Since many of these elements are included in the employment policies, it is important to understand the implications of the ADA for you and your staff to ensure compliance with these regulations, as well as to protect your program. Employment policies specifically spell out the rights of employees and what they may expect from the employer and they should include the following items:

Job Descriptions

The job description is a detailed outline of what is expected from the person who fills a specific position.

Career Lattice

Developing a career lattice or opportunity for progression is a challenge to the director and/or the board. Each center must develop a career lattice after reviewing the roles and responsibilities of each staff position, budget limitations, and the professional goals of the center. The career lattice clearly defines education, experience, and corresponding salaries and benefits for every step in the hierarchy (Bloom, Sheerer, & Britz, 2005).

Contract

The contract usually is a bilateral agreement signed by both parties that mutually binds the employee and the employer to agree upon certain rights from each other. In this case, the employee agrees to provide a service (as defined by the appropriate job description) and the employer agrees to reimburse the employee for the service at a given rate for a specific length of time. Of course, those employers who have an at-will policy do not use employment contracts.

Salary Ranges

Salary ranges for each position on the career lattice should be indicated clearly. Salary ranges should be based on the training, experience, and years of service required for each position. If salary increases are performance based, the plan for those increases is stated in the employment policies.

Each state may have its own laws regulating minimum wage and overtime pay, but all state regulations must be compatible with the federal Fair Labor Standards Act (FLSA). In that act, employees classified as "exempt" from FLSA are professional, salaried staff, while those who earn an hourly wage and are entitled to overtime pay are considered "nonexempt" and are covered by the FLSA. (The federal government has instituted new rules that clarify employee rights and employer obligations relative to overtime pay.) Because these definitions and rules are scrutinized and revised regularly, it is important to consult an attorney with expertise in labor law when making decisions concerning questions related to compliance with government regulations. The Child Care Law Center can provide information on the current status of the issues involving how the FLSA affects child care employees in different states

Staff and Fringe Benefits

Fringe benefits available to employees must be stated clearly in the employment policies. Retirement plans, health insurance, educational opportunities, and other policies that impact the lives of employees should be reviewed in detail during orientation and should also be available for reference when questions arise. Changes in benefits must be communicated with staff in writing and updates must be maintained in benefits documents.

Employment at Will

"Employment at will" is common in most states and refers to an employment status in which the employee does not have an annual or ongoing contract and can be terminated without reason. "Even in states which allow for 'at will' employment (as opposed to states which require 'good cause' for termination), an employer may still be found liable if the employer violates its own employment policies" (Cohen, 1998, p. 86). The sample employment policies in Director's Resource 9-1 provide exact wording for those who choose to use the employment at will provision. But that being the case, it is important to use caution in wording the staff handbook to avoid wording that can be viewed by the court as a contract. Employment law is changing all over the country and regulations vary state by state; therefore it is wise to consult an attorney on employment-related questions or issues.

Health and Safety Measures

A health examination for all staff members is required upon hire in most states. In many localities, the law requires the health examination of center administrators who are viewed as being ultimately responsible for the health and safety of the children in the center. Those who work with children should be free of any infectious disease, whether or not there is a local certifying or licensing group responsible for monitoring health regulations. In addition, all staff are required in most states to have universal precautions (blood-borne pathogens) and hazardous materials training. It also is recommended that child care staff be advised to update their immunizations, because close contact with children puts them at risk for contracting a variety of infectious diseases. Furthermore, since the work is often physically demanding, the examination protects members of the staff by exploring their health limitations and by reminding them to follow basic practices such as getting adequate rest and proper nutrition.

Child abuse and other child safety issues are a major concern among child care professionals. Therefore, there is an increasing trend to seek ways to certify that employees do not use drugs and have no criminal records. Some states and government-funded programs require that prospective staff be screened for one or more of these. Employers with more than 15 employees must comply with the ADA when dealing with employment issues. The problem of AIDS is causing concern as well. Congress intended that the ADA protect people infected with AIDS and HIV. Therefore, employers may not ask candidates, AIDS and HIV status on applications or during the prehiring process (Director's Resource 9-2.)

Most states require that applicants for positions working with children complete a form declaring that they have not been convicted of a crime involving children. It is also common to require background checks. Many states have required forms for this important information which can be used to glean information that is not permitted to be asked directly in an interview. The sample form in Figure 9-2 that covers the criminal record issue will serve as a guide for a way of obtaining information from staff members as well as job candidates about some sensitive areas of inquiry. If there are questions about the legality of making inquiries of this nature, contact the Equal Employment Opportunity Commission (EEOC) or seek legal counsel.

Employment policies should state clearly that professional staff must submit certified copies of credentials and that personal and professional references furnished by all new employees will be contacted before job offers are made.

Daily Hours and Employment Period

Careful scheduling of personnel is critical for effective and efficient operation of all centers. This schedule should be stated in the employment policies and should be reiterated in each contract or letter of employment if these are used. Daily hours will not be the same for each staff member. Some staff members must arrive before children to prepare the learning environment. A large child care center will need extra staff to cover peak hours. For example, if school-age children come to the center before and after school, or for lunch, the staffing needs will be increased during those hours. A key staff member must be present late in the day to chat with people who pick up the children near closing time. When all children have gone, the center must be in order for the early arrivals the following day; therefore, some of the staff must stay beyond the time that all children leave.

The complexity of the staffing schedule and the format used to lay out the schedule in an understandable way will vary. It should be set up to provide sufficient coverage to meet the licensing requirements, where applicable, and to guarantee safety of children and adequate staff to maintain high standards of quality throughout each day. In planning the staffing patterns, directors should keep in mind the concerns about child abuse in child care centers and take preventive measures. Schedule at least two caregivers to be present at all times, particularly early and late in the day and during nap and toileting routines. This will help protect children and staff if one is unjustly accused of abuse (Cohen, 1998). The sample staffing plans in Director's Resources 9-3 and 9-4 will serve as guidelines for setting up staffing schedules. Use of graphing, listing by staff member, listing by room, or listing by program are a few of the ways to record a staffing schedule so it is clear to those who are interested in it, including staff, board members, licensing agents, and especially parents.

Relief Periods

A planned system of daily relief periods or breaks should be stated. The policy on rest periods may be very flexible or carefully scheduled. In either case, the policy should clearly state and include the designated space where staff may take breaks. In half-day programs, it is rare to find a set policy on rest periods due to the short time span of concentrated effort required by staff members. On the other hand, in child care programs in which a teacher may work an eight- or nine-hour day that includes having lunch with children, it is essential to provide time to rest and be away from the children. Some centers prefer

Staffing the Center   181

Ohio Department of Job and Family Services
STATEMENT OF NONCONVICTION
FOR CHILD CARE CENTERS AND TYPE A HOMES

This statement must be signed by every individual owner, administrator and employee of a child care center, Type A Home and all persons eighteen years of age and older who reside in a Type A Home. This statement must be kept on file at the center or Type A Home. Please note that owners and administrators must also attach the JFS 01314 which is a supplement to this form.

Employee Name (please print or type)

☐ I hereby attest that I have never been convicted of or pleaded guilty to child abuse or other crimes of violence set forth in section 5104.09 of the Revised Code and that no child has been removed from my home as described in section 2151.353 of the Revised Code.

Employee Signature	Date

Street Address

City	State	Zip Code	Telephone Number

☐ I am unable to sign the statement above because I have been convicted of a crime included in section 5104.09 of the Revised Code. However, after reviewing the rehabilitation requirements of rule 5101:2-13-26 or 5101:2-12-26 of the Administrative Code with the administrator, it has been determined I meet the rehabilitation requirements. Please see attached verifications that the requirements for rehabilitation have been met.

Note: Anyone who withholds information from, or falsifies information on this statement is guilty of falsification, a misdemeanor of the first degree. If the offender is an owner of a center or a licensee of a Type A Home, the conviction constitutes grounds for denial, revocation, or refusal to renew a child day care license application. If the offender is an employee of a center or Type A Home, or is a person eighteen years of age or older who reside in a Type A Home, and if the owner or licensee had knowledge of, and acquiesced in the commission of the offense, the conviction constitutes grounds for denial, revocation, or refusal to renew a child day care license application.

Please note: effective June 1, 2006 all civilian background checks must be submitted electronically through use of WebCheck or other approved methods. More information can be accessed at: www.webcheck.ag.state.oh.us.

The administrator is required to sign and date below verifying that fingerprints have been electronically submitted to the Ohio Bureau of Criminal Identification and Investigation (BCII), or mailed if electronic processing exemption criteria are met.

A criminal records check for the above named individual was requested on (date) _____

☐ Ohio records check   ☐ FBI records check (please check)

Signature of Administrator	Date

TYPE A HOMES ONLY

In addition to the above, the licensee of a Type A Home must sign the following statement.
I hereby attest that no one who resides in my home and who is under eighteen years of age has been adjudicated a delinquent child for committing a violation of any offense listed in section 5104.09 of the Ohio Revised Code.

Signature	Date

This is a prescribed form which must be used to meet the requirements of section 5104.09 of the Revised Code. Failure to complete the form shall preclude issuance of the child care license or certificate.
JFS 01313 (Rev. 9/2006)   Page 1 of 2

FIGURE 9-2 Sample statement of nonconviction form for prospective employees.

Source: Ohio Department of Job and Family Services. http://www.odjfs.state.oh.us/forms/file.asp?id=262&type=application/pdf

Section 5104.09 Prohibitions Against Employment

Homicide
1. R.C. 2903.01 – Aggravated murder
2. R.C. 2903.02 – Murder
3. R.C. 2903.03 – Voluntary manslaughter
4. R.C. 2903.04 – Involuntary manslaughter

Assault
5. R.C. 2903.11 – Felonious assault
6. R.C. 2903.12 – Aggravated assault
7. R.C. 2903.13 – Assault
8. R.C. 2903.16 – Failing to provide for a functionally impaired person

Menacing
9. R.C. 2903.21 – Aggravated menacing
10. R.C. 2903.22 - Menacing

Patient abuse and neglect
11. R.C. 2903.34 – Patient abuse, neglect

Kidnapping and related issues
12. R.C. 2905.01 – Kidnapping
13. R.C. 2905.02 – Abduction
14. R.C. 2905.04 – Child stealing (as this law existed prior to July 1, 1996)
15. R.C. 2905.05 – Criminal child enticement

Sex offenses
16. R.C. 2907.02 - Rape
17. R.C. 2907.03 – Sexual battery
18. R.C. 2907.04 – Corruption of a minor
19. R.C. 2907.05 – Gross sexual imposition
20. R.C. 2907.06 – Sexual imposition
21. R.C. 2907.07 – Importuning
22. R.C. 2907.08 – Voyeurism
23. R.C. 2907.09 – Public indecency
24. R.C. 2907.12 - Felonious sexual penetration (as this former section of law existed)
25. R.C. 2907.21 – Compelling prostitution
26. R.C. 2907.22 – Promoting prostitution
27. R.C. 2907.23 – Procuring
28. R.C. 2907.25 – Prostitution
29. R.C. 2907.31 – Disseminating matter harmful to juveniles
30. R.C. 2907.32 – Pandering obscenity
31. R.C. 2907.321 – Pandering obscenity involving a minor
32. R.C. 2907.322 – Pandering sexually oriented matter involving a minor
33. R.C. 2907.323 – Illegal use of a minor in nudity-oriented material or performance

Arson

34. R.C. 2909.02 - Aggravated arson
35. R.C. 2909.03 - Arson

Robbery and Burglary
36. R.C. 2911.01 – Aggravated robbery
37. R.C. 2911.02 – Robbery
38. R.C. 2911.11 – Aggravated burglary
39. R.C. 2911.12 – Burglary

Offenses against the family
40. R.C. 2919.12 – Unlawful abortion
41. R.C. 2919.22 – Endangering children
42. R.C. 2919.24 – Contributing to unruliness or delinquency of a child
43. R.C. 2919.25 – Domestic violence

Weapons control
44. R.C. 2923.12 – Carrying a concealed weapon
45. R.C. 2923.13 – Having a weapon while under disability
46. R.C. 2923.161 – Improperly discharging a firearm at or into a habitation or school

Drug offenses
47. R.C. 2925.02 – Corrupting another with drugs
48. R.C. 2925.03 – Trafficking in drugs
49. R.C. 2925.04 – Illegal manufacture of drugs or cultivation of marijuana
50. R.C. 2925.05 – Funding of drug or marijuana trafficking
51. R.C. 2925.06 – Illegal administration or distribution of anabolic steroids
52. R.C. 2925.11 – Possession of drugs or marijuana that is not a minor drug possession offense in section R.C. 2925.01

Other
53. R.C. 2905.11 - Extortion
54. R.C. 3716.11 – Placing harmful objects in food or confection
55. R.C. 2909.04 - Disrupting public services
56. R.C. 2909.05 - Vandalism
57. R.C. 2917.01 - Inciting to violence
58. R.C. 2917.02 - Aggravated riot
59. R.C. 2917.03 - Riot
60. R.C. 2917.31 - Inducing panic
61. R.C. 2921.03 - Intimidation
62. R.C. 2921.34 - Escape
63. R.C. 2921.35 - Aiding escape or resistance to authority
64. Or an existing or former offense of any municipal corporation, this state, any other state, or the United States that is substantially equivalent to any of these offenses.

FIGURE 9-2 *(continued)*

to have some staff members work a split shift to provide time for rest, shopping, or study at midday. This serves to reduce costs at a time of low need.

Vacations, Holidays, and Sick Leave

A statement on vacations and holidays should appear in the employment policies. Specific details about lead time for vacation applications and the length and timing of vacations is advisable for larger, year-round centers, but smaller centers in session only during the typical school year may not require the same specificity in their policy. However, both large and small centers observe certain holidays. These holidays will vary depending on the religious and ethnic orientation of the staff and/or the children served, the agency with which the school is affiliated (church or public school,), and the community standards. All employees should know exactly which holidays will be observed by the center.

Sick days, personal days, maternity leave, newborn parental leave for either parent, and special leave days for jury duty should be included in the employment policies. Directors can check the Family and Medical Leave Act (FMLA) regulations when dealing with these requests. It also is wise to cover details like use of unused leave days, the necessity for documenting illness, and policies about closings due to bad weather. The center's plan for hiring substitutes for each staff position during vacation periods, for special holidays, and for sick days must be spelled out clearly. The policy should state that all health, safety, and training qualifications for staff also apply to substitutes. Maintaining a substitute file that includes the necessary employment information and payroll paperwork on available people will make it easier to find substitutes on short notice. A plan for hiring substitutes prevents confusion when emergencies occur and also facilitates budget planning for these special needs.

Probationary Periods

Many programs include probationary periods after initial employment to allow an adjustment period for both adults and children in the program. A director may be appointed on an "acting" basis for as long as a year. The time period must be long enough for the new employee to demonstrate competency in a given position but not so long that valuable aspects of the program can be undermined by an incompetent individual.

Teacher competency can be validated in a three- to six-month probationary period by an experienced director who operates under a clearly defined philosophy of education and evaluates with an experienced eye. Since the teacher works directly with the children and any incompetence could have direct detrimental effects on them, the probationary period for teachers should be delineated carefully and understood clearly at the time of employment. This practice not only protects the welfare of the children but also is more equitable for the teachers in the long run because they come into a new role with a clear understanding of the time allowed for initial review and evaluation. Precise and thorough evaluation and documentation throughout the probationary period is essential because there is the possibility that this trial period could lead to termination of the employee.

Staff Evaluation and Grievance Procedures

Performance evaluations should be scheduled on a regular basis. Evaluation and grievance procedures are included in the employment policies (Figure 9-3). These procedures should be made available to all center personnel. Ideally, they will include details about the following:

- who evaluates whom
- when the periodic evaluation will take place
- what techniques or instruments will be used in the evaluation
- who makes the decision on whether or not the criteria are met
- what the consequences are of not meeting the stated criteria

Not meeting stated criteria could mean no recommendation for a raise, no opportunity for advancing to a higher-level position, or termination. When there are other actions that could cause dismissal, such as use of corporal punishment, these should be in writing. In some situations, there may be no recourse once a decision to deny a raise or to terminate an employee has been made. Although that may seem unfair, it is better to state it at the outset than to deal with all the negative feelings generated by the decision when an employee is unaware that there is no way to appeal it.

Performance Evaluations

Staff members are entitled to know evaluation procedures as well as evaluation criteria. Therefore, performance evaluations for all staff positions should be part of employment policies and/or the orientation materials and discussed during staff orientation. Teaching staff is usually evaluated by the director who, in turn, may be evaluated by the human

Evaluation and Grievance Procedures

1 Frequency of Evaluation

Performance evaluations will be made twice during the probationary period for every new staff member—at the midpoint and the end of the probationary period—and annually thereafter. It is the responsibility of the Personnel Committee to evaluate the work of the Director and the responsibility of the Director to evaluate all members of the staff. All evaluations will be shared with the employee and then become part of the employee's file.

2 Purpose of Evaluation

The primary purpose of the annual evaluation is to create a mutual understanding between the Director and each member of the staff of what is expected and how they both view the best way to move toward fulfilling those expectations.

Annual evaluations will be used as a basis for continued employment, horizontal or vertical movement on the career ladder, salary increments in cases where the job description allows for merit raises, and demotion or dismissal.

3 Basis for the Evaluation

Staff members will be evaluated on knowledge of the job as described in the job description, quality of skill demonstrated in fulfilling the job, interest and initiative, dependability, personal and professional growth, attendance and punctuality, and ability to work effectively in cooperation with other staff members.

Evaluation forms for each staff position in the center are included in these personnel policies.

4 Evaluation Procedure

Each staff member will be notified as to when his/her evaluation will take place. The evaluation will be discussed with the staff member, at which time the staff member will be given the opportunity to express his/her disagreement or agreement with the evaluation. The outcome of this discussion will become part of the staff member's record.

5 Review of Grievances

The staff member who wishes to present a grievance must present it first to the Director. Failing to reach settlement with the Director, the staff member may submit to the Chairperson of the Personnel Committee a written statement of the situation, requesting that the grievance be reviewed by the Personnel Committee. The Personnel Committee will review the grievance and report with recommendations to the Board of Directors for action.

FIGURE 9-3 Townville child development center (a United Way agency) evaluation and grievance procedures.
Source: © Cengage Learning, 2013.

resources committee of the board or by the human resources director in cases where centers are part of a larger organization. Other support staff may be reviewed and evaluated by the director or by other designated staff. The sample Annual Performance Evaluations (Director's Resource 9-5) paired with a Lead Teacher Job Description (Director's Resource 9-6) might be used as a prototype for performance evaluation tools. Although there may be some overlap in areas covered by the evaluation forms, such as physical and mental health, ability to work well with other adults, and personal attributes such as enthusiasm or sense of humor, some are unique to a given position. For example, the cook must be able to manage time well in order to have meals ready for serving at a given hour, whereas a

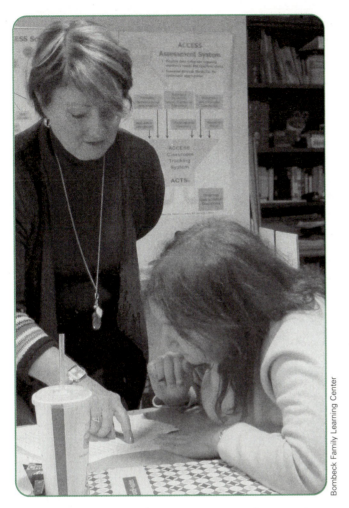

Staff are entitled to know evaluation procedures and criteria.

Bombeck Family Learning Center

teacher must adjust the daily schedule based on the changing needs of children. Performance evaluation forms usually are based on job descriptions. Knowledge of evaluation criteria helps build a sense of trust and partnership between staff to be evaluated and the evaluator, who is either the director or another staff member.

Organizational Chart

An organizational chart that is sometimes part of the employment policies and is made available to all members of the staff can clarify lines of communication and responsibility for everyone in the center. For a newcomer, even a very simple organizational pattern may be difficult to see unless it is presented in a diagram or flowchart (Figure 9-4). An organizational chart enables an employee to determine how each position meshes with other positions in the center. This information, coupled with complete job descriptions, performance evaluation procedures and forms,

and open staff communication, leaves little doubt about expectations, areas of responsibility, and who will be the evaluator for each position. It, in a sense, defines reporting relationships as well as limits of authority.

Amending and Changing the Policies

The employment policies should contain a section that details the procedure for amending the policies. The amending procedure presumably parallels the one that was used initially for developing the policies and that is stated in the bylaws, but the policy-making body now may be expanded to include staff members or parents who were not available during the initial stages of development. As the center undergoes its regular evaluation period, the employment policies also should be checked to determine whether changes are needed. Then the board or the policymaking staff can follow the amendment procedures when it becomes necessary to make changes. Once a change has been adopted, it is important to inform all personnel of the changes, and the director is charged with implementing the new policy.

Clearly, small private centers will not use all the preceding items in their employment policies. However, large, complex organizations undoubtedly will include all of these and more. Policies are drawn and shaped to the unique needs of each center and are constantly evaluated and modified to meet the ever-changing and growing needs of the program for which they are written.

STAFFING THE CENTER

The basic tools used in developing plans and procedures for hiring the child care center staff are written employment policies and job descriptions. On the surface, these documents and procedures appear to be easily drawn and delineated; at a more subtle level, they reflect the philosophy of the overall program as it focuses on individuals and their worth as human beings. As policies and procedures are adjusted and changed, they will reflect the ability of responsible administrators in the organization to make optimum use of available human resources.

An analysis of each center's purposes and manner of operating will determine the broad policy areas to be covered in the employment policies. The center that employs large numbers of professional and ancillary staff may have policies with separate sections for each category of employee and other employment, including substitutes, resource teachers,

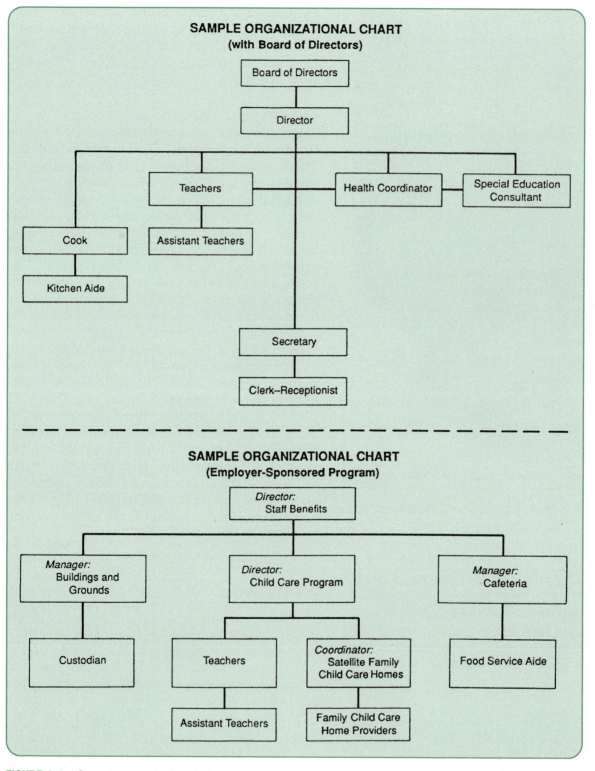

FIGURE 9-4 Sample organizational charts.
Source: © Cengage Learning, 2013.

and other support staff. In all cases, every policy statement should contain an affirmative action section that verifies the center's intent to adhere strictly to acceptance of all personnel regardless of race, age, sex, creed, national origin, sexual preference, or disability. (For information regarding employment discrimination and affirmative action issues, contact the U.S. Equal Employment Opportunity Commission, 800-669-3362, www.eeoc.gov, or call 800-669-4000 to be connected to your state EEOC office.)

Staffing the Center **187**

Developing Job Descriptions

One mechanism for reducing conflict and uncertainty for staff members is to provide a clear definition of the role of each member on staff. Each role requires a thorough description so that no matter who fills the role, the same basic job will be done. The description can be written to clarify expectations yet retain the personal freedom of all staff members to follow through in the performance of their roles according to their own unique style. Well-written job descriptions provide a framework within which an individual can function creatively while performing the tasks required for the program. Detailed descriptions of required knowledge, skills, and physical abilities are important because subsequent performance evaluations are based on the job description. For teaching staff job descriptions, include the idea that staff will be able to supervise children within sight and sound and have the ability to physically attend to the children. For infant and toddler teachers, also add that the staff person will have the ability to lift at least 40 pounds regularly during an eight-hour period. The applicants then are asked if they can perform the duties as described in the job description.

A sample job description (Director's Resource 9-5) provides a prototype for writing descriptions for various staff positions, including full-time and part-time professional and support staff for both agency-sponsored and proprietary child care centers, as well as public school preschools. Job descriptions may cover some of the following plus other items as needed:

- job title
- person to whom responsible
- people for whom responsible
- qualifications (education, experience, personal health, physical abilities, and so forth)
- duties and responsibilities
- salary schedule and work schedule

Job descriptions should be reviewed on a regular basis to determine whether changes are necessary. Such periodic review is useful because the director or governing body can deal with changing rules or regulations governing practices, adjust the policies as role expectations at different levels shift, and change job descriptions when new personnel bring changing talents and skills to a staff. For example, menu planning and shopping may be part of a director's job description, but a new cook who has been trained to plan meals may take over that function. Job descriptions for both the director and the cook can be adjusted accordingly, allowing staff members to perform at their highest creative level.

Think about yourself as a practicum student or a new teacher, and remember the uncertainty and accompanying anxiety you felt when you did not have a clear understanding of what was expected of you. How did you feel when you were unsure about who was to set up the snack or who was to straighten up the storage room? How did you manage when you were not sure about who to call when you knew you would be late because you had missed the bus? How did you react to criticism when you did not put all the blocks on the shelf while another adult had the children outside, and you had not been informed that you should do that? Can you remember how energy draining these experiences were and how they interfered with your creative work with children? A carefully written job description for your position might have helped you have a clearer understanding of your role.

Initial writing of job descriptions is only the first step in an ongoing process. This process requires expertise in using information from the program evaluation and an ability to adjust to changing and growing strengths of personnel to make efficient use of available talent for a more effective program.

Recruiting

Once the job descriptions have been written, the major hiring procedure begins. In fact, in many large centers or in programs with a board, the first task assigned to a new director is to initiate staff-recruitment procedures. Each center establishes and follows some general procedures regarding advertising, interviewing, and selecting employees to use during initial hiring in a new center and in filling vacant staff positions for an ongoing program.

Advertising for new staff is usually the director's responsibility. However, in some public schools and in corporate settings, the human resources office may set up school district or company advertisements that cover available positions throughout the organization. If the center program is ongoing, the director first should notify current staff members, board members, and parents about job openings as they become available. People in the organization may choose to apply for the new job, or they may know qualified individuals who would like to apply. For employees to learn of openings in their own center from an outside source is disconcerting, and it exemplifies poor communication within the center.

Sample Classified Advertisement for the
Waynesburg Chronicle

Teacher Assistant in a Child Care Center. Responsibilities include assisting the classroom teacher in the planning and implementation of the daily program for children, assisting in the family involvement aspect of the program, and taking responsibility for some designated record keeping. Must have an Associate Degree in Early Childhood Education or equivalent. Experience preferred. Job available immediately. Send written resume to P. O. Box 320, Waynesburg, Iowa 36103, or e-mail wayneecce@aol.com. Our employees know about this opening. We are an Equal Opportunity Employer.

Sample Classified Advertisement for the
Local Association for the Education of Young Children Newsletter

Director wanted for the Community Head Start Center. Responsibilities include hiring and supervision of entire staff for a program serving 75 children, record keeping, proposal writing, working with Center staff, Community Action agency, parents, and other community agencies. Applicant must have a Master's Degree in Early Childhood Education with some training in at least one of the following: social work, special education, administration. Three years' administration experience required—Head Start teaching experience preferred. Send resume to

Community Head Start Center, 352 Ninth St., Sioux City, Iowa. Deadline for applications, July 1. We are an Equal Opportunity Employer.

Sample Classified Advertisement for
The New York Times

Preschool teacher wanted for suburban church-affiliated preschool. Responsibilities include planning and implementing an age-appropriate developmental type early education program for a group of 15 3- and 4-year-old children. Bachelor's Degree required—early childhood education teacher experience preferred. Write for application to Ms. D. L. Jones, Director, Upper Plains Christian Church, 130 Meadows Place, Upper Plains, New York 11112, or call (713) 431-6037 Monday through Thursday from 1:00 to 3:00 p.m., or e-mail upperplains@hotmail.com. We are an Equal Opportunity Employer.

Sample Classified Advertisement for the
Parkville Times

Cook wanted for child care center at outskirts of town. Responsibilities include preparing snacks and lunch for 65 preschool children, cleaning kitchen appliances and cupboards, and making weekly shopping list. Experience preferred. Please send resume to P. O. Box 932, Parkville, VA 23221. Equal Opportunity Employer.

FIGURE 9-5   Sample advertisements.
Source: © Cengage Learning, 2013.

Affirmative action statements must be included when advertising for center personnel. These statements are always included in advertising for staff, not only because that has been the usual practice, but, more important, because it is essential that centers strive to maintain and enhance staff diversity. It is helpful to have advertising appear in a range of publications to make the information available to diverse segments of the population. Figure 9-5 shows examples of some advertisements. Local professional organizations that publish classified ads in their newsletters are good places to advertise for classroom staff, as are high schools, colleges, or universities that have child care training programs. Ads also may be placed in national professional journals or put on their websites if there is sufficient time to meet publication deadlines. Some colleges and vocational high schools maintain placement services, and some

hold placement conferences so that employers can interview applicants. Notices of job openings also can be posted on community bulletin boards and in community papers that reach special segments of the population, such as the African-American or Native American community and non-English-speaking groups, and on various appropriate websites.

The classified section of newspapers is frequently used for advertising, but the result may be large numbers of unqualified applicants who then must be screened before interviewing can begin. Nonetheless, when a position must be filled quickly, advertising in both small community weekly newspapers and large city daily newspapers is helpful because information is quickly disseminated to large numbers of people.

Personnel ads should include enough information to minimize the number of applications from completely unqualified people but should not be so narrowly written that qualified people fail to apply. If you are expected to write the advertising copy, you must be completely familiar with all the qualifications that are essential for performance of the job. Careful review of the job description is a good way to become familiar with the desired qualifications for potential candidates. Each advertisement should include the following:

- job title
- brief job description
- essential qualifications
- method of applying (telephone, letter, application form)
- name of the person to contact with a telephone number, street address, or email address

Starting date, working hours, starting pay, fringe benefits, and goals of the organization also may be included.

Advertisements that clearly state all nonnegotiable items will eliminate practically all unqualified applicants. On the other hand, negotiable items stated equivocally tend to attract a more diverse pool of candidates from which to choose. For example, "experience necessary" is much more restrictive than "experience preferred." If experience is a nonnegotiable qualification, then say, "experience necessary." However, if the position could be filled by a person with good training and a variety of life experiences that may or may not have been with children, then say "experience preferred." The latter phrase appeals to a broader population and will not only increase the number of applicants but will also have appeal to a more diverse group.

The director should be cautious about luring people into the field by presenting a glowing picture of life in a child care center. Hiring staff members under false pretenses can lead to job dissatisfaction quickly. Rapid staff turnover disrupts program continuity and is very hard on the families and children who must constantly establish new relationships. During the past decade, the staffing crisis in the early childhood field has increased the challenge for directors who prefer to wait until they find qualified candidates to fill vacancies but are unable to meet required teacher-to-child ratios because of staff shortages. Many well-qualified early childhood teachers are choosing to move into public school or Head Start programs where pay and benefits often are better than those in other child care settings. The availability of qualified staff is limited and the competition for their services is keen. But dealing with the consequences of hiring staff who are unable or unwilling to do a good job inevitably leads to more turnover that is hard on other staff, families,

and children. Therefore, a job opening notice that lists the required job qualifications in specific and realistic terms and careful hiring increase the probability of getting the best match between applicants and available positions and reduces turnover.

Careful consideration must be given to the best method for receiving applications. If the need is urgent and immediate, it may be necessary to accept applications by telephone. This option means that a new employee can be found quickly because an interview can be scheduled moments after a notice is seen. But it also means that current staff members may have to spend hours on the telephone, which detracts from their work with the children and puts them in the position of answering questions from people who are not seriously interested in the job.

Listing a post office box number in an ad places fewer demands on the director and the staff because potential candidates do not know the identity of the center and are unable to call. On the other hand, qualified people may decide not to apply if they are unsure of the source of the ad. Others may feel that they could be applying to the center in which they work, another reason for notifying all employees of every opening. In fact, occasionally ads read, "Our employees know about this advertisement."

Allowing applicants to apply in person can be very inconvenient and is inappropriate for some positions. Unless the center has its own human resources director or is affiliated with a sponsoring agency such as a public school, having applicants appear at the door during the hours in which children are present is awkward. However, this problem can be handled by setting specific hours during which interviews may be scheduled. In neighborhoods where many people do not have telephones and where writing letters is difficult for some adults, it may be appropriate to have people apply in person. If the job does not entail making written reports, such as in the case of a cook or a housekeeper, then the ability to communicate effectively in writing may not be a criterion for selection, and there is no need to see a resume or written application. On the other hand, in the case of a teacher, teacher assistant, or special education resource teacher, writing skills are important. For these positions, a written response offers helpful data for initial screening of applicants and should be mandatory before an interview is scheduled.

The advertiser also will have to decide whether to have the candidates request an application form or send a resume. If a secretary is available to answer requests for application blanks, the process can be speeded up. If the director will be distracted from work by recording the name and address of

Sample Application Form
(Suggested for use when no resume is on file)

Application for Employment

Jewish Community Child Care Center—Fairmount, Pennsylvania

Name of Applicant _____

                   Last   First   Middle or Maiden

Address _____

State _____ ZIP _____

Telephone _____ Social Security No. _____

Citizenship: USA _____   Other _____

Record of Education

School	Name and Address of School	Check Last Year Completed	List Diploma or Degree
High		1 2 3 4	
College		1 2 3 4	
Other (Specify)		1 2 3 4	

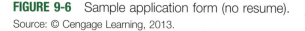

FIGURE 9-6   Sample application form (no resume).
Source: © Cengage Learning, 2013.

applicants and mailing out applications, it is wiser to have candidates mail in resumes and fill in a formal application when they are interviewed. Sample application forms (Figures 9-6 and 9-7) show how applications are adjusted depending on availability of a resume from the applicant.

When all the applications have been collected, they must be screened to eliminate obviously unsuitable candidates. If no suitable candidates have applied and attempts to recruit staff from other centers have failed, the advertising and application process is reopened. The director or the chairperson of the human resources committee usually screens the applications

for those that meet the job requirements, particularly in the areas of education, health, or experience. Then interviews can be arranged. Interviewers should not be burdened with candidates who have no qualifications for the job. Therefore, the careful writing of the job opening notices to interested qualified candidates and the initial screening process to eliminate totally unqualified candidates are both important steps in the recruiting process.

Applications that are received from people who are not subsequently called for an interview should be retained so that affirmative action procedures can be completed where that is a requirement. A record

List below all present and past employment, beginning with your most recent

Name and Address of Employer	From Mo./ Yr.	To Mo./ Yr.	Describe in detail the work you did	Weekly Starting Salary	Weekly Last Salary	Reason for Leaving	Name of Supervisor

List all professional and community organizations with which you are affiliated. *(Indicate if you hold office in the organization.)*

Write your educational philosophy.

What do you feel most qualifies you for this position?

What are your professional goals?

List names and addresses of three references.

_____

_____

_____

I give permission to contact references _____
                                                                    (signature)

FIGURE 9-6 *(continued)*

must be kept listing the reasons why any applicant was not interviewed, and they should receive written notification that they will *not* be interviewed. Applicants who are called for an interview should be advised to bring identification to prove citizenship. A candidate who is not a U.S. citizen will be required to prove eligibility to work in this country. To be in compliance with the Immigration Reform and Control Act of 1986, every person hired must complete Form I-9, available from the Immigration and Naturalization Service (INS).

Interviewing

Interviewing is essential and should not be eliminated no matter how urgent the need for obtaining a staff member may seem. Even though a candidate can make an excellent impression during an interview and then turn out to be an ineffective staff member, interviewing will provide insights that cannot be gleaned from written applications or resumes and will facilitate judicious hiring decisions in the majority of cases. The relative amount of time spent interviewing can be extremely profitable when compared with the amount of time that might otherwise be spent solving personnel problems and higher staff turnover because a poor candidate was hastily selected. "Although not a magic solution to cure all turnover woes, effective interviewing is a step in the right direction" (Hamrick, 2000). The person or group responsible for staffing the center must decide

Sample Application Form
(Suggested for use when a resume is on file)

Application for Position

University Day Care Center—Ogden University, Ogden City, Michigan

Name of Applicant _____
                  Last   First   Middle or Maiden

Address _____

State _____ ZIP _____

Telephone _____

Title of position for which you are applying. _____

What do you feel best qualifies you for this position? _____

_____

_____

Would you be willing to continue your education by taking college courses or in-service training if
recommended to do that? _____

_____

_____

What satisfaction do you expect to receive from this position? _____

_____

_____

List three references (preferably one former employer, one former teacher, and one community person).

    1. _____

    2. _____

    3. _____

I give permission to contact references _____
                                                  (signature)

FIGURE 9-7 Sample application form (resume on file).
Source: © Cengage Learning, 2013.

who will review applications and interview the candidates and must develop the plan for the interview.

Reviewing Applications

Reviewing applications is the first step in the total interviewing process. The director or group in charge of staffing the center first must make sure that the job description for the position being filled is up to date. It also is helpful to think about what type of person will best fit the position. Consider not only what the job description defines as required for the position but also the center's culture, the match with other staff, and the comfort level for working with the center's families. These considerations will keep the focus on finding a good match with the existing center "family" as well as enhance and support the center's interest in diversity. Using a systematic approach for application screening makes the job easier and will cover you later if anyone questions your hiring decision.

Begin the application review process by developing a form that covers the required qualifications for the job, including education, experience, and specialized training. Add qualifications that may not be required for the position but are preferred and could contribute to the candidate's ability to do the job. For example, experience working with diverse populations may be a requirement, but special experience on a Native American reservation or student-teaching in Latin America could be a plus, depending on the location of your program and the population served. Include items on the form that would cover those special experiences by having a place to check whether or not the candidate has had experience with diverse groups and a place to note which ethnic, cultural, and socioeconomic groups were part of that experience. The changing demographic profile in our society calls attention to the importance of adjusting staff hiring practices so they will be responsive to the diversity among families, children, and program staff. The screening form should include all the items that are on the application and also cover the job description.

Develop a rating scale for the items on the screening form so each reviewer can arrive at a total score for each applicant (Hamrick, 2000). A three-point scale can be used for this purpose. It is helpful to provide reviewers with some definitions for the three levels on the scale. If the candidate does not meet the requirement at all, the score on that item would be 0. Ratings might be defined as follows:

1 = barely meets requirement
2 = meets requirement
3 = exceeds requirement

Definitions of ratings will vary, depending on exactly how the requirements or criteria for the job are stated. In any case, a rating scale gives those who screen the applications a way to evaluate the qualifications of the candidates and provides a score for each one. There should be places on the screening form for comments and recommendations of reviewers and a place where they can note that the candidate does not have the qualifications to fill the position that is open. All applications are kept on file should there be any question about the hiring procedures.

When the reviewers meet to discuss the next step in this process, they can eliminate those candidates who do not have the qualifications for the job as described in the job description and use their scores on the screening forms to rank the remaining candidates. The next steps are to decide who will be interviewed and who will do the interviewing.

Interviewers

While applications are being collected and screened, decisions are made about who will interview the viable candidates. In a very small program, the director may take full responsibility for all interviewing or may do it with the help of one or more of the following:

- staff person
- member of the board
- community person
- other professional (social worker, special educator, physician, school principal)
- person responsible to the new employee
- parent representative

In some programs, the interviews are conducted by committees, often by the human resources committee.

The composition of the interview committee may be established by the board beforehand, as in the case of the human resources committee; the committee can also be set up by the director to pertain specifically to the job being filled. For example, when there is an opening for a teacher, the committee might include the director, a teacher, and a parent. The expertise of a teacher on the interviewing team is very valuable. Including teachers also makes them feel valued and appreciated. Community people could be included as well as people from other professions, such as community health or special education. There might be more than one person from a given category, but if the committee is too large, its effectiveness will diminish. It can be difficult for large numbers of people to interview a given candidate at one time and the procedure can be very threatening for the candidate. Nonetheless, it is best if the committee is diverse and is representative of the center staff with whom the person will work, of the families who use the center, and of the people who represent the sponsoring agency.

Although the committee makeup may vary depending on the type of center and on the position to be filled, both the committee members and the candidates must be aware that the organizational structure of the center takes precedence in making hiring decisions. For example, if a janitor is being hired, it may be appropriate to have the teachers express a preference for the candidate who would be most able to meet their needs for classroom maintenance. However, if the person who becomes janitor is going to be responsible to the center director, then the director's opinion must weigh heavily in the final hiring decision.

A major exception to this hiring and interviewing procedure is in programs sponsored by public schools in which hiring is based on established school district policies. Public school union contracts often dictate hiring policies and procedures. Sometimes, the human resources office will handle advertising, interviewing, and hiring. Involving teachers or parents in the process is unlikely. This could result in a team that will have to spend time building a partnership and working through possible philosophical differences.

Preparation for the Interview

Just as candidates should come to the interview prepared to express their strengths, weaknesses, goals, expectations, and past experiences, so the interviewers should be prepared for each interview. Their questions should reflect a thorough knowledge of the center, its program, its staff, and the clients served by the program. Interviewers should be familiar with the information in the candidate's resume, application form, and reference letters, and they should look for evidence of warmth, good-natured calmness, and ease of relating to others. As Greenberg notes, it is important to select caregivers who have "the right stuff" to start with because "you can teach people to conform to certain schedules, perform specific acts, use assorted tips and techniques—but you cannot develop an entirely different character, personality, and self-esteem in a staff person" (1993). An interview is conducted most productively when all parties are well prepared and when the environment has been set up for a meaningful dialogue between interviewers and interviewee.

Interviewer Information

Each interviewer should be totally familiar with the job description for the vacant position and should have copies of the candidate's application and references. When contacting references, it is important to have a consistent process so that references will provide comparable data for all candidates. It has become more common for responses to be collected using electronic questionnaires that are sent via email. The most popular method of collecting feedback from references is by phone. Figure 9-8 shows a sample questionnaire that is administered by phone.

Interview Plan

Interviewers plan the type of interview they will conduct. Sometimes, a predetermined list of questions is developed so that all candidates will respond to the same questions. This procedure provides uniform data but is somewhat inflexible and may not elicit the most useful data from each candidate. Sometimes, questions are developed as the interview progresses. This spontaneous procedure is more likely to give rise to potentially constructive data but requires more skill on the part of the interviewers.

The person who develops the questions should keep in mind the parameters of the job description and should understand the requirements of Title VII of the 1964 Civil Rights Act, the EEOC, and the ADA. There must be a "business necessity" for all questions asked during the interview. Consider the

---

University of Dayton Telephone Reference Check List

This list includes suggested questions for telephone reference checks. Please select questions you wish to uniformly and consistently use for each candidate. If you wish to ask other questions, please contact the Office of Human Resources Staffing Department at 229-2722 on guidance whether questions are legally permissible.

My name is (_____) and I work at the (name of center/program). We are filling a position within our department and would like to verify employment information on (applicant's name), who was employed by you from (beginning date) until (ending date).

❶ What was the nature of his/her job?

❷ What did you think of his/her work?

❸ What are his/her strong points?

❹ What are his/her weak points?

❺ How did he/she get along with other coworkers?

❻ Would you comment on his/her:

- Attendance:
- Dependability:
- Ability to take on responsibility:
- Ability to follow instructions:
- Degree of supervision needed:
- Overall attitude:
- Quality of work:

❼ Why did he/she leave the position? Would you rehire the person? Yes or No? If No, why not?

❽ Is there anything else you would like to comment on regarding (applicant's name) employment or job performance?

FIGURE 9-8 Telephone reference check list.

Source: Reprinted with permission from the University of Dayton, Office of Human Resources.

list shown in Figure 9-9 when determining what questions to ask and avoid during an interview.

The first question of the interview should be open ended and require more than a simple yes or no answer. Furthermore, it should focus on previous jobs, education, hobbies, or any other subject matter with which the candidate is very familiar. This technique puts the candidate at ease and creates an environment for more focused probing later in the interview. For example, the interviewer might say, "I see in your resume that you have worked for Head Start in California and that the committee was made up of Mexican and Asian parents. What were the aspects of that job that you liked best?" or "I see you studied at Wheelock in Boston. Tell us about that program." From these questions, it is possible to cull out material that can be examined at greater depth. "You said you enjoyed working with the Parent Policy Committee in California. What did you do with that group that you think is applicable to this job?"

Interviewers can learn a great deal about the ways in which a teacher candidate would fit into their center's program by posing hypothetical situations and asking questions such as, "What would you do if a child kicked you?" or "How would you work with a toddler who is not yet talking?" This type of question can produce ideas about curriculum, classroom management, parent involvement, staff relations, and understanding of the development of young children. Of course, the questions should relate to the job for which the person is applying. For example, a prospective cook might be asked, "What would you do if sandwiches were on today's menu and the bread delivery had not been made by 10:00 a.m.?" A list of sample questions in Director's Resource 9-7 can give you some ideas for questioning both degreed and nondegreed job candidates.

Interview Setting

Before the interview, give careful thought to the setting:

- Will the candidate be as comfortable as possible?
- Will everyone be able to see and hear everyone else?
- Is the seating arrangement comfortable and planned so that desks or large tables do not separate the candidate from the interviewers?
- Is the interviewing room free from distractions?
- Has the time of the interview been chosen appropriately so that everyone can focus on the interview instead of on the next appointment, and are all cell phones turned off?

- Is adequate time available for developing rapport and exploring details of the answers to the questions?
- Has provision been made to offer water or some refreshments to the candidate?

When the goal is to make applicants feel welcome and at ease, the interview setting becomes a matter of central concern. The interviewers are revealing to the candidate a major part of the center's culture and philosophy as they create an accepting environment for an interview and are more likely to obtain an accurate picture when the candidate is at ease.

REFLECTION

Can you recall your first job interview? If so, you may be able to remember some of your reactions during that interview. Were you put at ease when you entered the room? Were you introduced to everyone before the questioning began? Did you feel the interviewers had prepared for the session by reviewing your resume and credentials? Were you given time to ask questions? How did they close the interview? As you think about being interviewed and recall the stress you experienced, you will increase your sensitivity to an applicant's feelings.

The director sets the nonverbal tone for the interview by being relaxed and friendly. It is important to sit back, smile, and maintain an open posture with arms down in the lap and body facing the candidate.

The Interview

At the beginning, candidates should be given some idea about the length of the interview and informed that there will be a time at the end of the interview to ask questions. Interviewers should be prepared to present information about the program's philosophy, the job, and the center and should clearly and honestly answer the applicant's questions. The interviewers should maintain eye contact and let the applicant do most of the talking. They can refer to the employment policies and clarify thoroughly the expectations regarding performance standards for the position.

The interviewers will look for an applicant who plans to stay with the center for a number of years, because staff stability provides continuity for children and nurtures a sense of community at the center. Nonetheless, caution should be used about requesting any information in sensitive areas mentioned earlier. It is recommended that employment records be limited to that information relevant to employment decisions and disclosures of that

Subject	Questions Permissible to Ask in an Interview	Question to Avoid in an Interview
Name	Inquiry whether an applicant's work records are under another name, for purposes of access to these records: "Have you worked for the University under a different name?"	A. Inquiry into any title which indicates race, color, religion, sex, national origin, handicap, age, or ancestry. B. To ask if a woman is a Miss, Mrs., or Ms.
National Origin/Citizenship	A. To indicate that the institution is an equal opportunity employer B. "What languages do you read, speak, or write fluently?" (This question is fine, as long as this ability is relevant to performance of the job)	A. If native-born or naturalized. B. Proof of citizenship before hiring. C. Whether parents or spouse are native-born or naturalized.
Age	Any inquiry limited to establishing that applicant meets any minimum age requirement that may be established by law.	A. Requiring birth certificate or baptismal record before hiring. B. Any inquiry which may reveal the date of high school graduation. C. Any other inquiry which may reveal whether applicant is at least 40 years of age.
Sex/Gender/Sexual Orientation	None.	A. Any inquiry which would indicate sex. B. Any inquiry made of members of one sex, but not the other.
Marital/Parental/Family Status	A. Whether an applicant can meet specified work schedules or has activities, commitments and responsibilities that may hinder the meeting or work attendance requirements. "This job requires overtime occasionally; would you be able and willing to work overtime as necessary?" (This question is fine as long as *all* applicants for the job are asked consistently). B. "Would you be willing to relocate as necessary?"	A. Before hiring: to ask marital status: "What's your marital status (married, single, divorced, engaged)?" B. To ask the number and/or age of children, who cares for them, and of applicant's plans to have more children? C. "Whom do you live with?" D. "Do you plan to have a family? When?" E. "How many kids do you have?" F. "What are your child care arrangements?"
Education	A. Inquiry into nature and extent of academic, professional or vocational training. B. Inquiry into language skills, such as reading and writing of foreign languages, if job related.	A. To ask the racial or religious affiliation of schools attended. B. Inquiry as to what mother tongue is or how foreign language ability was acquired.
Work Schedule	Inquiry into willingness or ability to work required work schedule	Any inquiry into willingness or ability to work any religious holidays.

Category		
Religion/Creed	Questions pertaining to the applicant's familiarity and/or their interest in coming to work for a Catholic/Marianist Institution.	A. Any inquiry which would indicate or identify religious denomination or custom of the applicant. B. Request pastor's recommendation or reference.
Organizations/Affiliations	Inquiry into membership in professional organizations and offices held, excluding any organization, the name or character of which indicates the race, color, religion, sex, national origin, handicap, age, or ancestry of its members.	Inquiry into every club and organization where membership is held.
Personal/Physical Data	Inquiries as to ability to perform actual job requirements.	Being a certain height or weight will not be considered to be a job requirement unless the employer can show that no employee with the ineligible height or weight could do the work.
Disabilities	To ask whether the applicant is capable of performing the essential functions of the job with reasonable accommodation. Note: This question may be asked after the interviewer thoroughly described the job and if all applicants are going to be asked in a consistent manner whether they are able to carry out all the necessary job assignments and perform them in a safe way.	A. Before hiring: to initiate questions regarding the specific accommodation needed. B. Inquire if job applicant is handicapped or ask about nature and severity of handicap: "Do you have any disability." C. "Have you had any operation or recent/past illnesses?"
Criminal Record	Inquiries into conviction of specific crimes related to qualifications for the job applied for.	Any inquiry relating to arrests if not substantially related to functions and responsibilities of the particular job in question. "Have you ever been arrested?"
Military Service	A. Inquiry into service in U.S. Armed Forces when such service is a qualification for the job. B. Require military discharge certificate after being hired.	A. Inquiry about the type of discharge. B. To request military service records. C. To ask about military service in armed service of another country.
References	To request general and work references not relating to race, color, religion, sex, or national or ethnic origin, age, disability, or marital status.	To request references specifically from clergy or any other person who might reflect race, color, religion, sex, or national origin, age, disability, or marital status.

FIGURE 9-9 What not to ask when interviewing candidates.

Source: Reprinted with permission from the University of Dayton, Office of Human Resources.

Observing the candidate in a classroom setting provides the committee with data on rapport with children and classroom presence.

Bombeck Family Learning Center

information to third parties be strictly limited when not authorized by the candidate or employee. It is advisable that child care centers develop written policies and procedures concerning this issue. Also, because federal law provides only a portion of the employment discrimination picture and many states have their own discrimination laws, it is wise to consult an attorney regarding applicable state laws for your center and to clear up uncertainties about the content of interview questions.

Interviewers should obtain as much information as possible during the interview, but note taking or discussing the candidate's qualifications should be done after the interview. Some discussion about the candidate is useful, and reaching a group consensus serves a worthwhile purpose. Discussion provides the opportunity for interviewers to share their impression of the candidate as they draw on each other's perceptions. Confidentiality is a critical issue, and all committee members must understand that information on candidates and any committee discussion must be kept confidential.

Teaching Interview

Observing a teacher or assistant teacher candidate in a classroom setting provides the committee with additional data on classroom presence and skills with children. Some candidates are able to give interviewers all they want to hear in an interview, but when observed in a classroom, it becomes obvious they are not comfortable with children. It is unfair to have the regular classroom teacher leave a new person alone in the classroom because of the anxiety that would be produced in both the candidate and

the children, but a great deal can be learned by observing a prospective teacher read a story to a few children or join a small group for snacks. Asking to see sample lesson plans, resource files, or picture files also provides useful information to the interview committee. Some centers select candidates from the substitute list or from among a pool of student teachers whom they know. In this case, the center staff will have worked with the candidate before the interview.

Second Interview

A second interview for prospective candidates after the teaching interview can be helpful when there are several candidates with comparable training and credentials or when more information is needed prior to making the final hiring decision. Having a second interview also offers opportunities to discuss the teaching interview and to answer questions the candidate may have at this point in the interview–hiring procedure. Additional questions that focus on the candidate's opinions and personal style also can be discussed at a second interview. Director's Resource 9-7 gives sample interview questions for first and second interviews.

Selecting the Employee

When interviewing is completed, the person or committee responsible for selecting the employee uses material such as the employment policies and the job description, combined with all the information from the interview and the observation, to reach a final decision. All data are weighed and balanced

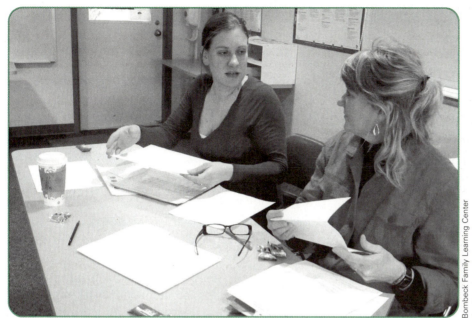

Bombeck Family Learning Center

A mentoring system assists the director with orientation of new staff.

until the best match among job description, current staff composition, and candidate qualifications is obtained. It also is important to review the nondiscrimination prohibitions in this decision-making process, especially if you have an applicant who is disabled. An employer is not required to give preference to a qualified applicant with a disability over other applicants; however, the employer may not consider the candidate with disabilities unqualified if that person can perform the essential functions of the job. It may be helpful to have a second interview with selected candidates from the pool who seem best qualified for the position in order to further narrow down the choice. The procedure for making a decision should be clear to all interviewers. Will the director ultimately choose the employee? Will the director present two or three names to the board, and have the board make the decision? If there is a board, will that group make the decision, or will the committee rule by majority vote? Generally, the director will make the decision, taking into account the recommendations of the interviewing committee. Final approval from the board sometimes is part of the hiring policy.

The selected candidate should be notified of the job offer by the director or the chairperson of the committee. On acceptance, the new employee may be asked to sign a contract stating the salary and the length of time covered by the contract, provided the employment policies do not state that all employees are employees at will. Immediately after the new employee has been informed of the job and has accepted it, all other interviewees are informed of the selection, thanked for their interest, and told that their resumes will be kept on file in case another vacancy occurs.

Orienting the Employee

The director is responsible for introducing the new employee to the work environment. The new person will need to know where to find work space, what storage facilities and materials are available, and what schedule is to be followed. A tour of the building and introductions to all other staff members, either during the tour or at a staff meeting shortly thereafter, are essential to the orientation procedure. The person who conducts the tour and makes the introductions sets the tone for the employee's future interpersonal relationships with the other staff members. Each staff member has an obligation to become involved with making the new employee's transition to the staff position as smooth and satisfying as possible. For an in-depth discussion of staff orientation, see Sciarra and Dorsey (2002).

The new employee also should be introduced to parents at the earliest possible time. Some directors notify parents of staff additions or changes by mail; others use their bulletin boards, email, website, or newsletters; and still others introduce the new member informally as the occasion arises or at a regularly scheduled meeting.

During the initial weeks of employment, it is important for the director to check with the new staff member to answer any questions and make a conscious effort to build a positive relationship. At

DIRECTOR'S CORNER

"We do a five-day orientation for each new staff person before we finalize the hiring process. The prospective employee is paid for those hours of classroom participation, meetings with me, joint reading of dos and don'ts in the classroom, etc. It's well worth the time and money and has helped us make good hiring decisions. Always mindful of possible legal issues, we protect ourselves by carefully documenting the details of this process in the event we should decide to terminate this prospective employee."

—Director, private not-for-profit center

the same time, the director can continue to reiterate expectations and expand on ways to follow and implement the program philosophy. A carefully planned staff orientation program can promote better staff relationships and reduce staff turnover. A written Staff Orientation Plan is a document that is required as part of the Human Resource Development system for the Program Administration Scale (PAS).

Sometimes, it is difficult for the director to be available to the new teacher often enough. It can be helpful to establish a mentor program or assign a staff member to watch over the new staff person. Mentors can help new staff with basic orientation questions, like where to find and file various forms, and introduce them to all staff and support people such as the van driver and custodian. Mentors also can provide new staff with information about special talents of other teachers, such as planning effective group times, planning and carrying out smooth transitions, or making challenging math games. A mentoring system assists the director with orientation of new staff and enriches and enhances the self-esteem of the mentor (Carter, 1998).

It also helps for the director to leave a note in the teacher's box asking questions like, "What went well today?" or "What did I miss today in your room that you would like to share with me?" The director also might leave a message about being available the next day at nap time or a plan to stop in before lunch to see how things are going. These steps help make the new teacher feel that the director really is available to give support and help.

Some centers have handbooks for each employee. In corporate centers, the parent firm may prepare a handbook for use in all centers, whether franchised or run by the corporation. Guidelines in this handbook may detail how many children should be permitted in blocks or dramatic play at any given time, or exactly how the daily cleaning is to be done by the classroom teachers. However, handbooks are rarely that detailed and usually do not include expectations for teachers to clean the premises. More often, they include items such as the following:

- philosophy of the center
- bylaws of the board (if applicable)
- employment policies
- policies and procedures for the children's program
- copies of forms used by the center
- information about the community the center serves
- information about the staff (job titles, home addresses, telephone numbers, and so forth)
- NAEYC Code of Ethical Conduct (see Appendix A)

A handbook is useful because it gives everyone a common reference point and provides new employees with materials that familiarize them with the center.

REFLECTION

Perhaps you can recall your first day as a new student or employee in a child care center. How did you feel on that first day? What else do you wish you had known about the center or the program? Do you recall what it was like not to know where the extra paper towels were kept or how awkward it was when you could not find the easel paper? As you recall those feelings, consider what you would tell a new teacher in your center if you were responsible for orienting the new employees.

Handling Turnover

Each year approximately 30 percent of the early childhood workforce changes jobs or leaves the field altogether. Such instability in the child care workforce has a negative impact on quality (Gable, Rothrauff, Thornburg, and Mauzy, 2007). It is estimated that staff turnover can cost, at a minimum, $3,000 for each lost employee. Centers cannot afford the high cost of staff turnover, especially when turnover results not only in financial costs but also damage to employee morale, customer satisfaction, and center image (Hamrick, 2000). Although some would say low wages and poor benefits are the major causes, it is important to recognize that there are many different ways to think about turnover. As Hamrick (2000) points out, poor hiring decisions are a major factor along with compensation concerns.

In making hiring decisions, take time to reflect on what type of person would best fit the position. What are you looking for in this person in terms of the fit with

- the center culture?
- the parent group?
- the support staff?
- the teaching staff?
- the administrative staff?

The first step in reducing turnover is to hire the right people. Collins (2005) emphasizes how important it is to "get the right people on the bus." He goes on to point out that it is often difficult to "get the wrong people *off* the bus," thus making it doubly important to get the right ones on in the first place.

Although compensation and careful hiring have an impact on turnover, they are not the only factors affecting staff stability. There is evidence that highly trained teachers are more likely to remain at their jobs. It follows that these teachers are usually compensated at a higher level and work with other highly trained staff who are also inclined to stay with a job. These qualified staff people are also more often in accredited centers, and there is also evidence that accredited centers have a more stable workforce and less turnover.

Finding dollars to offer the kind of wages and benefits to keep qualified staff is difficult. Although some staff turnover is inevitable, and some may even allow for positive changes, clearly, much of the time, loss of a staff member is disappointing and traumatic for the families, children, and staff who remain.

The director's task is to try to reduce staff turnover by attending to variables that can be adjusted and changed. There are a few inexpensive perks that may compensate staff and help them feel good about their job. Consider the following:

- flex time
- treats in the staff lounge for break times
- occasional personal use of the office copier (limits are necessary here)
- token gifts for birthdays and other special days
- opportunities to attend conferences as well as take additional education courses

This last item does involve some cost to the center, but there may be tax breaks for this benefit (check with your tax adviser or attorney).

Striving to give staff higher wages and more benefits is worthy, but stabilizing the workforce by refining hiring practices, improving the work environment, and making sure there is a thorough orientation plan in place for all new hires can all be done without great cost. Because there are no magic solutions to solving the problem of staff retention, directors are almost always involved, at some level, in looking for and hiring new staff.

Work Environment

Work environment is an inclusive term covering the physical space and, more important for our purposes, the interpersonal climate—that is, relationships with coworkers. An involved director constantly evaluates the quality of the work environment and makes adjustments when possible. (See Chapter 15 for more discussion on evaluating work environment.) Sometimes, alterations in the physical environment are costly and can happen only if the budget allows. However, adjustments can be made to alter other aspects of the work environment with little or no added expense. For example, it is very important for every staff member to feel respected and valued. Offering staff opportunities to write for the newsletter, help with the design and equipment choices for the new playground, join an advocacy group, or serve on the committee to plan the center's tenth anniversary celebration are but a few ways staff can feel a sense of ownership in the center's total program. There is pride, commitment, and collegiality among those who share ownership in a successful enterprise.

"In child care we tend to spend very little time on adult development. We are often more democratic and participatory in spirit with children than we are among ourselves" (Whitebrook & Bellm, 1999). Although classroom teachers are encouraged to help children solve problems, resolve conflicts, and make decisions, in some programs major decisions are made by administrators with minimal input from staff who are very much affected by those decisions. Adults who are accustomed to top-down management may initially need a lot of support and encouragement from the director who really wants active participation in writing articles, planning center events, leading staff meetings, or joining focus groups. When staff are invited to help plan meeting agendas and submit their questions and concerns for group meetings, they feel they are valued and important to the organization. When directors seek staff participation in decision making and help teachers feel valued, they are nurturing loyalty and commitment in the work environment.

Issues of race, class, and culture are aspects of the work environment that impact interpersonal relationships and can affect staff turnover. Directors like to describe their programs as color blind, but on careful analysis of the reasons for turnover, they may find that issues of class, color, or culture contributed to friction that led to resignations. Constant attention to open communication with a focus on understanding and acceptance of diversity is essential, because diversity can never be taken for granted.

Exit Interview Questionnaire

It is important for the director to try to understand the cause of turnover. One approach to collect this information is the exit survey or interview. Some turnover situations result in strained relationships in which the exiting staff member is unlikely to participate in an open and sincere exit interview or complete and return a survey. However, many exiting staff leave the center on good terms and are willing to provide feedback about the factors that led to their decision. It is important to try to get information

from both disgruntled former employees and those who left the center on good terms. Whether using an exit interview or survey, careful thought needs to be given to the types of questions to be asked. Directors' Resource 9-9 shows a sample Exit Interview Questionnaire. This sample is extensive but provides a variety of questions to select from and add to in order to develop a questionnaire that meets the needs of the center. Once results are collected, they should be analyzed and strategies developed to minimize future turnover when possible.

REFLECTION

Think about the best and the worst job you ever had. What made you stay with the best one? What made it appealing? What was bad about the worst job? How much were your feelings about the best and worst jobs affected by the relationships you had with other adults in the setting?

SUMMARY

The importance of good interpersonal relationships and trust within a center cannot be overstated. Only through a feeling of community and a spirit of cooperation can a director create a supportive environment in which both adults and children can grow to their fullest potential. There must be a strong element of acceptance and positive regard in the surrounding climate to establish a mutually helping relationship for staff, families, and children. It is the responsibility of the director as a leader to serve as a model of caring and respect for others in order to build a strong sense of community among all the diverse people involved in the center program. Effective interpersonal communication among the staff members, children, and families also is an important basic element in creating a supportive, comfortable environment at a center, and it is up to the director to be the model of good communication in order to create an atmosphere of openness, warmth, and acceptance.

The director uses encouragement and job enrichment to motivate staff members. Neither of these motivational means requires money; however, both require

special interpersonal skills a director can acquire. Effective use of these support tools will not only facilitate personal growth and feelings of self-worth but also will help move the center program forward.

The staffing process in a child care center is based on the employment policies and job descriptions that define the staffing requirement to operate the center's program. Decisions about the content of recruitment advertising, interview questions and procedures, and final hiring should be based on specific job requirements that are detailed in the job descriptions. Interviewing may be done by one person or by a group and should be a time for two-way communication between the candidates and the representatives of all aspects of the center's programs. Questioning should focus on the requirements of the position and the candidate's potential for fulfilling those requirements. The purpose of the entire process is to provide the employer with the information necessary for selecting the best available person for each staff position. Directors can minimize costly and disruptive staff turnover by improving the work environment.

TRY IT OUT!

1 In small groups with other class members, discuss the motivating factors that you as a director can control or change.

   a. List five effective motivating factors directors can control.

   b. Compare the lists produced by the small groups, and develop a final list of strategies (that do not cost money) to encourage staff and enrich jobs.

2 Think about yourself as the director of a center where you have observed or taught. Using Working Paper 9-1, write appropriately phrased acknowledgments and create the job enrichment strategies requested.

3 Review the job description for the cook in Working Paper 9-2 and develop a list of questions that would be appropriate to ask candidates applying for the job.

   a. Select three class members to serve as interviewers of applicants for the cook. Select one class member as a candidate for the position.

   b. After the three interviewers review the candidate's application for the position, have them role-play an interview with the candidate using the questions that the team developed.

   c. After the interview, have all class members participate in summarizing the candidate's qualifications for the job. Use Working Paper 9-3 to complete this exercise.

Working Paper 9-1

(for use with Try It Out! 2)

JOB ENRICHMENT STRATEGIES

1 Based on your understanding of the use of encouragement as a motivator, write an appropriately phrased positive acknowledgment for:

the secretary

the cook

the custodian

a volunteer

2 Describe a way you could use the job enrichment strategy with:

the assistant infant teacher

the van/bus driver

a student teacher

a lead teacher

You can download a full-size version of this form on the Education CourseMate website.

Working Paper 9-2

(for use with Try It Out! 3)

JOB DESCRIPTION

Cook

Schedule: Monday through Friday—7:30 a.m. to 3:30 p.m.

Reports to the Head Start director.

Responsible for the following:

1. safely preparing all food (breakfast, lunch, and snacks)
2. requisitioning appropriate amounts of foodstuffs based on designated menus
3. checking food deliveries against orders
4. storing foods appropriately, before preparation, in refrigerator, freezer, bins, cupboards, and the like
5. preparing all foods using methods that maintain food value and freshness
6. following menus, recipes, or other directives furnished by Head Start nutrition consultant
7. recording amounts of food used daily and maintaining an inventory of staples on hand
8. washing and sterilizing dishes and all utensils according to sanitarian's directions
9. cleaning appliances and storage areas according to a designated schedule
10. supervising assistant cook

Qualifications:

Advertisement for cook:

Working Paper 9-3

(for use with Try It Out! 3)

INTERVIEW SUMMARY

Candidate Qualifications for Preschool Teacher

Education:

Experience with children:

Other relevant experience:

Ability to express ideas verbally:

Congruence of philosophy to that of the center:

General appearance:

Evidence of ability to work as part of the teaching team:

Other comments:

 You can download a full-size version of this form on the Education CourseMate website.

Director's Resource 9-1

(example 1)

Sample Child Care Program (SCCP)
Human Resource Policies And Practices

TABLE OF CONTENTS

Director's Resource 9-1 *(continued)*

Director's Resource 9-1 *(continued)*

INTRODUCTION AND PURPOSE

Responsibility

The Executive Director of the Sample Child Care Program, (SCCP) has responsibility for administering written personnel policies, which have been approved by the Board of Directors. To handle situations not covered by written policies, the Executive Director may take problem solving action without Board approval, keeping the Board informed of any significant outcome which may indicate need for future development of formal policies.

Each employee with supervisory responsibility is expected to be familiar with these personnel policies and should consult with the Executive Director or Associate Executive Director on questions of interpretation before decisions are made or actions are taken. All employees will receive a copy of these personnel policies.

Notice of Employment

This Summary of Policies, including other matters addressed in it, is presented only as a matter of general information. This is not a contract of employment. Your employment with the Sample Child Care Program (SCCP) is an employment-at-will relationship. Any individual may voluntarily leave employment or may be terminated by SCCP at any time for any reason or without reason. Any oral or written statement or promises to the contrary are hereby expressly disavowed and should not be relied upon by any prospective or existing employee. Statements in this handbook, specifically including but not limited to those concerning discipline or reasons for discharge are only general guidelines used by SCCP. SCCP may take disciplinary action other than that outlined in a particular case and may discipline or discharge an employee for reasons not listed in this handbook.

In addition, certain employee benefit plans are defined in legal documents such as insurance certificates or plan documents. Such legal documents are controlling. Should there be any conflict between this handbook and the certificate, plan, or other legal document, the legal document governs and not the descriptions contained in this handbook or in any other description or notice provided by SCCP. This handbook and/or any policy or provision/

Director's Resource 9-1 *(continued)*

contained herein may be revised, modified, altered, or revoked by SCCP at any time with or without notice.

GENERAL RULES

Confidentiality

Records of all children are confidential and only staff and referral agencies may have access. A file may not leave the director's office without approval. An employee may be dismissed for discussing children outside of the school, staff, or referral agencies.

Open Door Policy

An open door philosophy is an essential part of maintaining strong communication and a positive work environment. We are interested in knowing our employees' ideas, questions, suggestions, problems, or concerns.

In most instances, your immediate supervisor is the person best qualified to solve a problem or answer a question. Therefore, we urge you to initially contact your supervisor and discuss anything that is on your mind. Give your supervisor the first opportunity to resolve any questions or conflicts you may have before taking it to the next level of supervision.

However, there may be times when you wish to discuss a concern or problem with someone other than your immediate supervisor. You are encouraged to bring these matters to another member of the management. *Where feasible, you should still advise your immediate supervisor that you wish to meet with another member of management.*

Reference Inquiries

All reference inquiries about current or past employees must be forwarded to the Executive Director. This is the only person authorized to share employee reference information with anyone outside the company. A current or ex-employee must provide a signed release for reference information to be shared with another party.

No Solicitation

In order to avoid interruption of your work and to protect you from unnecessary annoyance, solicitation and/or distribution of literature on SCCP premises is limited to the following rules:

Non-employees of SCCP have no right to distribute materials or solicit our associates on SCCP property at any time.

 You can download a full-size version of this form on the Education CourseMate website.

Director's Resource 9-1 (continued)

Employee to employee solicitation, distribution or acceptance of literature by employees during work hours and in work areas is prohibited. Work time does not include time before or after employees scheduled work hours, meal periods, or paid break periods.

This policy includes solicitation and distribution of literature for all purposes, such as lotteries, raffles, charitable or political organizations and the like. The Executive Director of SCCP must make any exceptions to this policy.

Resignation

If you choose to resign your employment, it is requested that you submit a written two-week notice.

EMPLOYMENT

Nondiscrimination

Sample Child Care Program recognizes our employees as one of our greatest assets. We are committed to provide equal employment opportunity to all qualified persons, consistent with applicable federal, state, and local equal employment opportunity laws prohibiting discrimination based on race, gender, age, handicap and/or disability, religion, ancestry, sexual orientation, marital status, color, or national origin.

These opportunities include, but are not limited to, recruitment, hiring, training, promotion, compensation, benefits, and all other terms and conditions of employment.

Harassment

It is SCCP's policy to maintain a working and learning environment free from all forms of harassment or intimidation including but not limited to, race, gender, or religion. This policy pertains to employees, supervisors, students, parents, suppliers, and other non-employees. Unwelcome sexual advances, request for sexual favors, and other verbal or physical conduct of a sexual nature are serious violations of our policy and will not be condoned or permitted. Not only is sexual harassment a violation of our policy, but it may violate Title VII of the Civil Rights Act and other federal and state laws.

If you are subjected to sexual harassment or intimidation, you should contact your supervisor, any other supervisor, or any member of management with whom you feel comfortable, for immediate help. All complaints of sexual harassment will be promptly and confidentially investigated and appropriate action will be taken against anyone found to have violated this policy. No employee who reports unlawful harassment or who assists in any

Director's Resource 9-1 (continued)

investigation by SCCP will be subjected to retaliation of any sort, and such retaliation will not be tolerated and is itself a violation of SCCP policy. Submission to such unwanted conduct will never constitute a condition of employment. Any employee violating this policy will be subject to disciplinary action up to and including termination; sexual harassment of SCCP employees by parents may result in the child being dismissed from the center, harassment by suppliers or other outside parties may result in termination of business relationships with SCCP and will also be addressed in accordance with applicable state and federal laws.

Employee Classifications

Every employee is classified appropriately for the purpose of determining uniform standards for benefits, conditions of employment, and compliance with applicable wage and hour laws.

Non-exempt (hourly) positions are paid on the basis of "pay for work performed". Non-exempt employees are entitled to overtime pay under specific provisions of federal and state laws.

Exempt positions are paid on a salary basis due to the nature of their position. Such employees are excluded from specific provisions of federal and state wage and hour laws and are not eligible for overtime pay.

Full-time employees are those who are regularly scheduled to work 35 hours or more a week and are considered to be eligible for full employee benefits.

Part-time employees are those who are regularly scheduled to work between 10 and 34 hours per week on a regular basis and will be eligible only for reduced vacation benefits and holidays.

There may be times, or even periods of time when SCCP permits a part-time employee to work more than part-time hours during a workweek. This does not change an employee's part-time status or their eligibility for certain benefits. An employee keeps their part-time status until SCCP specifically notifies the employee in writing that it has changed.

Unclassified employees are those regularly scheduled to work less than 10 hours per week or workers hired as interim replacements to temporarily supplement the work force, to assist in the completion of a specific project, or in a seasonal position. Employment assignments in this category may be of a limited duration. Unclassified employees are paid under the company's normal payroll system and must adhere to the company rules and policies. Unclassified employees are not eligible for benefits.

Director's Resource 9-1 (continued)

Probationary Period

Your first ninety (90) days of employment are considered a probationary period. During your first ninety (90) days, your director/supervisor will provide information regarding your job duties and responsibilities. You will also receive feedback on your job performance throughout this period. If any performance problems develop during the probationary period, you may be counseled. If at any time during the probationary period it becomes obvious to either the employee or SCCP that the employment relationship is unsatisfactory, separation from employment will occur, without regard to reason.

Licensing Requirements

All employees must meet current Ohio Department of Jobs & Family Services child care licensing requirements for their positions. For example: current medical exam every three years.

Personnel Records

Your personnel record contains information pertinent to your employment. Generally, your file contains such things as your application, resume, tax forms, and performance appraisals/development plans. The file is confidential and is the property of the organization. If you would like to see your file, contact the center director/department head. Medicals, trainings, and certificates are available on request.

Termination of Employment

Certain circumstances, depending on the seriousness of the offense, may result in a final written warning, suspension, or a termination without any prior notice or corrective counseling.

Certain types of conduct are offensive to our employees and children and cannot be permitted. The following examples illustrate some (but not all) types of conduct that may result in immediate dismissal without warning:

- Direct refusal to comply with legitimate request from a supervisor.
- Flagrant discourtesy to a child, parent, or employee. This includes, but is not limited to, fighting, or inciting a fight, using obscene or abusive language, or threatening an employee, parent, or child.
- Immoral, indecent, or illegal conduct reflecting negatively on the company or violating the rights of the employees or children.

Director's Resource 9-1 (continued)

- Reckless conduct resulting in injury or harm.
- Falsification of any company records, such as employee records, timekeeping records, activity reports, etc.
- Misuse or unauthorized removal of company, employee, or children's records, or confidential information of any nature.
- Unauthorized use, blatant misuse, destruction, removal, or embezzlement of property or money belonging to SCCP, its employees, or the children.
- Possession, sale, distribution, or use of alcohol or illegal drugs while on work time or company property.
- Possession or storing of firearms, weapons, ammunition, or explosives on company property.
- Violation of the company harassment policy.

OPERATION OF OUR FACILITIES

Working Hours

Teaching Staff—Employee's hours will be set upon hiring. Schedules will change according to enrollment and all teachers are required to sign in and out each day. If an employee should be late for any reason, he/she must call the center to notify staff as early as possible. Employees are required to attend all staff meetings and are expected to attend parent meetings when scheduled, along with any activities to improve parent-teacher relationships. When staff meetings are scheduled after shift hours, non-exempt employees will be compensated for this time in accordance with applicable wage/hour laws. All employees are required to have time sheets signed and approved by their supervisor or Center Director.

Administrative/Management Staff—SCCP currently maintains a regular scheduled workweek of 35 hours or more for full-time employees. Employee's hours will be set upon hiring. Individuals may adjust their scheduled daily hours only by prior agreement with their supervisor.

Meal and Rest Breaks

If you are a non-exempt employee and you work four hours but less than seven hours, you are entitled to a paid 15-minute rest break. When you work at least seven hours, you will receive a paid 30-minute break. Break time is to include meals and/or rest. Break time is calculated from the time you stop performing assigned tasks until the time you resume them.

 You can download a full-size version of this form on the Education CourseMate website.

Director's Resource 9-1 (continued)

Children and Closing
It is the closing employee's responsibility to confirm that all children have been picked up before leaving the building. Two employees must always be present when a child is in the center. In the event that a child is not picked up at the closing of the center, the remaining employees will follow these guidelines:

If attempts to reach parent at work and home are unsuccessful, call emergency contact number.

If attempts to contact emergency contacts are unsuccessful, contact the director immediately. YOU ARE A PROFESSIONAL: AT NO TIME MAY YOU TRANSPORT A CHILD OR LEAVE A CHILD UNATTENDED.

Dress Code
All employees are encouraged to wear comfortable clothing. A professional appearance must be maintained at all times. An employee reporting to work in inappropriate clothing may be asked to go home and change before returning to work.

Attendance and Punctuality
SCCP employees are expected to be on the job, on time, on a regular basis. Our work schedules are based upon the understanding that all employees will be at work and at their workstations on time. We recognize that on occasion, it may be necessary for an employee to be tardy or absent from work due to illness or personal problems; however, absence or tardiness can hamper or prevent others from performing their jobs properly. Repeated or chronic tardiness will subject an employee to discipline (up to and including discharge) at the discretion of SCCP.

If you are unable to come to work on a scheduled or regular work day, you must give notice to your supervisor or director as soon as you are aware that you will be absent. If your absence is due to illness, injury, or other personal reasons, you must call in as soon as possible. If you know that you will be absent for more than one day, you must advise your supervisor or director of that fact and the expected duration of your absence. Otherwise, you must call each day of your absence.

Subject to the provisions of the Family/Medical Leave Act, the Americans with Disabilities Act, or other applicable laws, any employee who is absent more than 15 days in a calendar year, whether for reasons of illness, injury, personal reasons or otherwise, will be subject to discharge. In the case of serious illness or injury, unpaid leave may be granted at the

Director's Resource 9-1 (continued)

discretion of the Director; however, no such leave will exceed 30 days and any employee who is absent for more than 30 days for any reason shall be subject to discharge.

Outside Employment
While employed at SCCP you may decide to seek employment outside of your regular working hours at your center. SCCP has no objections to this type of work, provided it does not interfere with your assignments and responsibilities at SCCP. Furthermore, you cannot be employed by a competitor of SCCP that would create a conflict of interest in your employment.

At times the families enrolled in the program request teachers to provide child care in their homes after program hours. This is not encouraged or endorsed by SCCP. Each parent and teacher is asked to sign a disclaimer releasing SCCP of any liability if they enter into an arrangement.

COMPENSATION

General Compensation Policy
Our goal is to attract, retain, and reward competent employees. To accomplish this we will provide you with a series of potential rewards, including competitive pay and competitive benefits. The SCCP compensation program is competitive within the early childhood education profession and the local markets within which we conduct business. Increases to compensation will be based on the individual employee's performance and the overall performance of the company.

Overtime
Exempt Salaried Employees are paid the same pre-determined amount for each period that they perform any work. The salary is paid for the work done, not for the number of hours worked. Therefore, these employees are exempt for overtime pay.

Non-Exempt Hourly Employees, who work in excess of the normal workweek, which has been previously assigned or approved by their supervisor, will be compensated accordingly. Any work in excess of 40 hours will be compensated at 1-1/2 times the hourly rate. Sick leave, personal days, vacation, or other non-worked time off are not to be used in calculating hours worked per week.

Compensatory time can be authorized under special circumstances for work which cannot be done within the usual working hours. Non-exempt hourly employees must first have approval by their supervisor. Final approval shall be with the Executive Director. Accrued

Director's Resource 9-1 (continued)

compensatory time may not exceed 40 hours, unless approved by the Executive Director for extraordinary circumstances. At time of termination, there is no cash reimbursement for unused compensatory time.

Pay for overtime is included in the semi-monthly payroll. Overtime must be authorized in advance by the supervisor.

Split Shift
Split shift is a schedule where an employee agrees to work a minimum of eight (8) hours and where those hours are divided with at least a two (2) hour break.
(Example: 7 a.m.–1 p.m. and 3 p.m.–5 p.m.) Employees will earn an extra two dollars ($2.00) per hour for working a split shift when it is not a standard or regular work schedule.

Wage Reviews
Wages are reviewed at least annually and will be based on individual and/or team performance and external market conditions. Your individual supervisor can provide more information on wage reviews.

Payday
Employees are paid on a semimonthly basis, on the 15th of the month and the last day of the month. Payment on the 15th of the month will cover the period from the 1st to the 15th of the month for salaried exempt employees and for the period from the 16th to the last day of the previous month for hourly employees. Payment on the last day of the month will cover the period from the 16th to the last day of the month for salaried exempt employees and for the period from the 1st to the 15th of the month for hourly employees. *If the 15th or last day of the month falls on a holiday or weekend day, pay will be issued on the last workday before the holiday or weekend.*

For your protection, your paycheck or direct deposit stub will be released only to you unless you provide advance written authorization. The person picking up your check will be required to present photo identification proving his/her identity.

Your paycheck is confidential; you should never show it to, or discuss it with, another employee. To do so will be considered a violation of confidentiality. Questions or concerns should be discussed with your supervisor. You should inform your supervisor of any possible errors in your paycheck. SCCP reserves the right to adjust subsequent checks if an error is discovered.

Director's Resource 9-1 (continued)

Payroll Deductions
Federal and state laws require that certain deductions be withheld from the pay of all employees. Among these are Social Security and Medicare taxes, federal income tax, and state and local taxes, where applicable. Should your wages be legally garnished or other court ordered deductions be required, the payroll function will reduce your pay as required.

When eligible, you may authorize the following deductions:
- Benefits (e.g., medical, dental, life insurance, etc.)
- Charity (e.g., United Way, etc.)
- Savings (maximum $150 direct deposit)

EMPLOYEE BENEFITS

Protection For Your Future
At SCCP, we strive to offer you a comprehensive and competitive benefits package. The company offers plans that are available to *assist you in preparing for your future*. You can join the plans after satisfying the eligibility requirements designated for each plan.

Section 125 Flexible Benefits Plan
SCCP offers a Section 125 flexible Benefits Plan. This plan allows employees to have payroll deducted health, dental, and other insurance premiums deducted from their paychecks on a pre-tax basis. This allows employees to have their taxable income reduced by the amount of these deductions.

Health Insurance
Employees who regularly work 35 or more hours per week as a permanent schedule are eligible for paid health insurance. SCCP offers quality health care plans to eligible employees to ease the burden of costs associated with illness. *New employees will become effective on the first billing date after becoming eligible with completion of 30 days of employment.* Should an employee choose other than standard coverage or to include other family members, all costs above the employee's basic cost will be the obligation of the employee through payroll deduction. (Single standard plan costs are paid by SCCP.)

You can download a full-size version of this form on the Education CourseMate website.

Director's Resource 9-1 *(continued)*

The design of our health care plans is guided by:

- A commitment to make cost-efficient health care possible
- An expectation that employees are responsible for personal health as a function of life style, prevention, dietary habits, and self-care, taking responsible precautions to ensure good health
- A cooperative effort to work toward influencing external factors to control health care costs
- A review of health care plans on a continual basis to satisfy the needs of SCCP and its employees

Life Insurance

Employees who regularly work 35 or more hours per week as a permanent schedule are eligible for paid life insurance and accidental death & dismemberment benefit coverage. SCCP provides eligible employees with financial protection through term life insurance for their families in case of the employee's death or amputation or loss of a body part (dismemberment).

New employees will become effective on the first billing date after becoming eligible with completion of 30 days of employment. The plan provides each employee with coverage of $50,000. Plan coverage is provided at no cost to the employee.

Retirement Savings Plan

The company participates in a 403(b) Retirement Savings Plan. All employees are immediately eligible to participate in the plan on a voluntary basis. You may contribute on a pre-tax basis between 1–20% of your gross salary each calendar year up to an annual maximum set by the federal government. Your taxable income is reduced by the amount you save through your pre-tax deferral.

Vacation/Sick Days

Each employee may take vacation/sick days with full salary at such time is mutually agreed upon by his or her supervisor. The eligibility for paid vacation/sick days is based on the status of employment and length of continuous service.

Full-time staff employees After thirty (30) days of employment they will receive three (3) vacation/sick days to be used in his/her first year of employment. After six (6) months of employment, they will receive four (4) additional vacation/sick days to be used in his/her first

Director's Resource 9-1 *(continued)*

year of employment. After one year of employment, vacation/sick day entitlement is as follows:

Upon 1st year anniversary	10 days
Upon 2nd year anniversary & forward	12 days

Part-time staff employees After thirty (30) days of employment they will receive two (2) vacation/sick days to be used in his/her first year of employment. (*Part-time employees are to be paid only the number of hours they would regularly be scheduled to work. For example; a part-time employee regularly scheduled to work four (4) hours would be paid four (4) hours for the vacation/sick day.*)

Upon 1st year anniversary & forward	5 days

Full-time management employees After thirty (30) days of employment they will receive six (6) vacation/sick days to be used in his/her first year of employment. After three (3) months of employment, they will receive six (6) additional vacation/sick days to be used in his/her first year of employment. After six (6) months of employment, they will receive fifteen (15) additional vacation/sick days to be used in his/ her first year of employment. After one year of employment, vacation/sick day entitlement is as follows:

Upon 1st year anniversary & forward	27 days

An employee may accumulate up to a maximum of ten (10) vacation/sick days that may be carried based on their service anniversary to be used to cover planned medical reasons (maximum ten days). Proper physician authorization is required. Unused accumulated vacation/sick days will be paid out upon termination of employment.

Personal Days

After thirty (30) days of employment each full-time staff employee (excluding full-time management employees) will receive one personal day each month. The director or scheduler will schedule these days no more than three (3) months before, and no less than one (1) month before. The center reserves the right under special circumstances to reschedule personal days. An employee may save up to three (3) personal days per year to be used as paid time off. They must be used within the same year. *These days are not accrued vacation and no paid compensation will be due to staff that resign or are terminated.* If, due to a staffing shortage, an employee elects to forfeit a personal day within twenty-four (24) hours of their scheduled day off, and they come in to work, they will be paid time and a half for the hours worked.

Director's Resource 9-1 *(continued)*

Holidays

Eligible full-time and part-time employees are paid for the following recognized holidays where it is a regularly scheduled work day for them: New Years Day, Martin Luther King Day, Memorial Day, July 4th, Labor Day, Thanksgiving Day, and Christmas Day. Part-time employees are to be paid only the number of hours they would regularly be scheduled to work. For example; a part-time employee regularly scheduled to work four (4) hours would be paid four (4) hours for the eligible holiday.

Child Care Tuition Reduction

Center employees may be granted a reduced tuition rate for childcare as follows:

All-full time employees: 20% tuition reduction.

Reduced tuition slots are limited based upon available accommodations and management's discretion. Tuition under this policy must be paid with employee payroll withholding.

Jury Duty

Jury duty is considered a civic duty; therefore no deduction from salary will be made for time actually served, subject to the procedures as indicated following. As a full-time employee and once you have completed your 90-day introductory period, you will receive your regular pay for each regularly scheduled work day you are on jury duty. You must show the court summons to your supervisor before commencing jury duty leave. Any income received for jury duty will be returned to the agency. You will be required to furnish a court prepared work statement or similar documentation from the court to authorize your request to receive your regular pay. Upon completion of jury duty for the day or after being excused from any service for the day, the employee must call their supervisor to determine whether they must report for work for the remaining period of the day. Should an employee not call to allow their supervisor to make such determination and it is found that they did not complete a full day of jury duty; they will no longer be eligible to receive regular pay for each regularly scheduled work day they are on jury duty.

COBRA

SCCP reserves the right to treat any leave as a triggering event as defined under the Comprehensive Omnibus Budget Reconciliation Act ("Cobra") and to notify the employee of his/her right to continue any group health insurance coverage at the employee's cost for the duration of such leave.

Director's Resource 9-1 *(continued)*

Subject to the provisions of the Americans With Disabilities Act, the Family and Medical Leave Act, or other applicable state or federal laws, time spent on leave of absence shall not be counted as actual service time for purposes of calculating such items as vacation or sick time accrual, or any other fringe benefits. Further, an employee on leave of absence may not engage in any form of gainful employment or occupation without prior written approval from the Director. Violation of this policy will result in cancellation of the leave and termination of employment.

LEAVES OF ABSENCE

Medical Leave

For absences due to serious personal illness or injury that exceed five days in length, an employee may be eligible for medical leave of absence. Any employee, full- or part-time, who has completed 90 days of service, is eligible. To initiate a medical leave, the employee must submit a doctor's note that indicates the nature of the situation and the expected dates of leave to their supervisor. The supervisor will notify the Executive Director as soon as possible. The Executive Director is responsible for final approval of medical leave requests.

Generally, a medical leave may not exceed 13 weeks, including any portion that would be covered by vacation pay, sick pay, personal days, or unpaid leave. Should the employee reach an unpaid status during the leave, the employee must submit payments for insurance premiums that would normally be deducted from pay in order to keep the coverage intact.

Every effort will be made to hold the employee's position open during the leave. Should business conditions require that the position be filled, every effort will be made to restore the employee to a position of similar pay and status upon return to work. In no event shall the employee be replaced without first being notified. A doctor's note releasing the employee to return to work may be required for any illness of five days or more. Failure to return from scheduled leave will be considered a voluntary resignation.

Family and Medical Leave Act (FMLA)

Pursuant to the Family and Medical Leave Act of 1997, employees may be entitled to up to twelve (12) weeks of unpaid leave per year under certain circumstances as set forth in the Act. During leave taken under the terms of the Act, medical insurance and certain other benefits in which the affected employee is a participant will be maintained on the same basis as for active employees. While the employee does not continue in "active service" for purposes of accruing vacation, retirement or other benefits related to length of service, leave

You can download a full-size version of this form on the Education CourseMate website.

Director's Resource 9-1 *(continued)*

taken pursuant to the Family and Medical Leave Act does not constitute a "break in service" for such purposes. At the completion of leave taken pursuant to the Act, the employee will be restored to his or her former position or, if necessary and appropriate in light of the needs of SCCP and at SCCP's sole discretion, to a position substantially similar in terms of pay, benefits, and conditions of employment.

Under the Family/Medical Leave Act, employees who have been employed by SCCP for at least twelve (12) months and who have been credited with 1250 hours of active service during the year immediately preceding the requested leave period are eligible for this leave.

The Act provides that eligible employees may take up to twelve (12) work weeks of leave during any twelve (12) month period for one or more of the following: (1) birth of a child of the employee, in order to care for such child; (2) placement of a child with the employee, either through adoption or foster care; (3) to care for the employee's spouse, child, or parent with a serious health condition; (4) a serious health condition of the employee that makes it impossible for the employee to perform the functions of his or her employment.

Leave taken pursuant to the Act will be offset by paid or unpaid leave otherwise available to the employee, i.e., accrued vacation, personal, medical, and/or sick leave must be used as the first part of the twelve (12) week maximum leave period.

In the event of the birth or placement of child, the employee's entitlement to leave to care for such child expires twelve (12) months after such birth or placement. Further, if a husband and wife are both employed by SCCP the maximum leave for both spouses combined will be twelve (12) weeks in any given year for the birth or placement of a child or the care of a parent with a serious health condition. Under the Act, any employee requesting leave must give SCCP thirty (30) days advance notice if the need for the leave is foreseeable. Otherwise, notice is required as soon as practicable. An expected date of return shall be determined prior to the commencement of any leave, and may be extended for good cause but in no event past the maximum leave period allowed by the Act. If the leave is requested because of serious health condition, certification signed by a bona fide health care provider shall be provided and a request for a second opinion may be required at SCCP expense. SCCP may also require re-certification on a reasonable periodic basis. During any such leave, the employee shall be required to check in with his or her supervisor on Monday of each week to determine the employee's status and to discuss possible changes in the employee's expected date of return.

While the employee is on leave under the Act, SCCP will continue group health coverage on the same basis as though the employee continued to be in active service. If the employee fails to return to work after the leave period has expired for reason other than a continuing serious health condition or other circumstances beyond the employee's control, SCCP will be entitled to recover from the employee the cost of any health coverage provided during the leave period. Employee co-payments or contribution for such coverage will be required to keep coverage in force during leave under the Act.

Consult with your supervisor or the Director for more details about the terms and procedures applicable to leaves under the Family and Medical Leave Act.

Personal Leave

An employee may be eligible to take a leave without pay for personal reasons, other than those covered by medical leave or the Family and Medical Leave Act. Any employee who has completed 90 days of service is eligible. The employee must submit a written request to the supervisor stating the reason for the request and the proposed dates of leave. The supervisor will notify the Executive Director as soon as possible. The Executive Director is responsible for final approval of personal leave requests. A personal leave may be approved for up to 13 weeks. Every effort will be made to hold the position open during the leave. In no event shall the employee be replaced without first being notified. Eligible accrued time off available to the employee, i.e., accrued vacation, personal, medical, and/or sick leave must be used first as part of the requested leave period. When taken in conjunction with a medical leave, vacation, or other paid time off, the total time away from work may not exceed 13 weeks. When the employee is on unpaid status, he/she must submit payments for the employee's portion of insurance that would normally be deducted from pay in order to keep coverage intact.

EMPLOYEE DEVELOPMENT

Performance Development Requirements Regardless of their previous education or experience, employees will be expected to continue studies of and training in early childhood education practices in order to keep abreast of new developments in the field. This continued study and training may take place on the employees, own time outside of regular working hours, and as recommended by the director. Methods employed may include, but are not limited to, in-service training classes at the center, attendance at a recommended professional conference or meeting, membership in a professional organization and attendance at its monthly meetings, and/or enrollment in pertinent courses offered by local colleges and universities.

Director's Resource 9-1 *(continued)*

Child Development Training

Each employee must meet the training and professional development requirements established by our funders and quality initiatives. These requirements will be reviewed during orientation.

In certain circumstances, management may require employees to take other courses or training that broaden their knowledge and help them further contribute to the goals of the corporation.

In-Service Training

Two (2) days each year, typically on Good Friday and the Friday after Thanksgiving, the center will be closed for in-service training. The in-service days will consist of training and individual time for planning, goal setting, etc. Every employee must attend. If someone misses due to illness they must make this time up on a Saturday and replacement training will be at their own expense. This in-service must be made up within thirty (30) days of it being offered/scheduled.

Corrective Counseling

SCCP recognizes that on occasion it may be necessary to discuss specific areas of an employee's performance or conduct that are below the expected standards. These discussions are designed to help the employee correct whatever problem may exist. The corrective counseling may range from a verbal discussion to written warnings or termination.

Recruitment

Applications are always to be accepted and filed. The center works with local universities and vocational schools to provide placements for students in teacher training programs. When a position becomes available within the corporation, employees are notified and can be considered for the position if qualified.

Performance Appraisal

Employees are evaluated on an annual basis. Details regarding these procedures are included in the Orientation Manual.

Position Descriptions

Job descriptions are reviewed with the employee at the time of hire and a copy of their job description will be maintained in their personnel file. Job descriptions can be revised by the Director/Supervisor with the approval of the Executive Director.

Director's Resource 9-1 *(continued)*

Promotions and Transfers

Upon notification from an employee of his/her interest in another position or transfer to another location, the Director/Supervisor over the position or location will determine the eligibility for promotion and/or transfer. The employee must meet the following criteria to be eligible:

Minimum of six (6) months in current position.
Current job performance is satisfactory, meeting expectations or above.
No pending corrective counseling or disciplinary warnings in effect.
Recommended for the position by their current Director/Supervisor.

Once the above criteria are met, the employee can be interviewed for the open position or transfer opportunity. The receiving Director/Supervisor will make final determination on the promotion and/or transfer.

STANDARDS OF CONDUCT

Arrest, Indictment, or Conviction

If you are arrested, indicted, or convicted, you must notify your supervisor as soon as possible and we will consider all available facts before taking action.
You may be:

A. Allowed to continue employment until conviction. If you are convicted, your employment status will be reviewed by management at that time.
B. Suspended because your presence at work could cause substantial disruption to the workplace.
C. Terminated from employment.

The termination decision will be made on an individual basis and may be based on the following:

A. You are unable to return to work due to incarceration.
B. Your presence at work could cause substantial disruption.
C. The crime for which you are accused is of such a grave nature that it adversely affects our legitimate business interests.
D. The nature of the crime is such that allowing you to continue to work results in a "good faith" probability of future harm to your co-workers, our customers, visitors, or business interests.

You can download a full-size version of this form on the Education CourseMate website.

Director's Resource 9-1 *(continued)*

If you are exonerated, consideration may be given to reinstatement.

If you have information of a co-worker's arrest, indictment, or conviction, you should immediately inform an appropriate supervisor.

It is SCCP's policy that all employees obey local, state, and federal laws.

Confidentiality

All business information, practices, and records, including any that pertain to customers and employees, are considered confidential. The release of confidential information to unauthorized persons could result in disciplinary action and possible termination from employment. If someone asks you for information and you are unsure whether to give it or not, ask your supervisor first.

Smoking

In keeping with our intent to provide you and our children with a safe and healthful work environment, smoking by employees, visitors, or any parties is prohibited within our facilities.

Substance Abuse Control

We are committed to providing a healthful and safe workplace for everyone. Consistent with that commitment, we have established a policy which promotes a drug- and alcohol-free work environment. We understand that some problems related to drugs and alcohol are more than one person can handle. Therefore, we encourage you to talk with your supervisor should you need help.

We expect you to report to work in the mental and physical condition necessary to perform your job in a satisfactory manner. The legal use of prescribed drugs is permitted on the job only if it does not impair your ability to perform the essential functions of the job effectively and safely.

The use, possession, sale, or transfer of illegal drugs or alcohol are prohibited on company premises, while using company vehicles, or while you are taking part in any company business.

Under the Drug-Free Workplace Act, you must notify the company within five days of any criminal conviction for drug-related activity occurring in the workplace.

If any supervisor has reason to suspect that you may be:

1. under the influence of alcohol or drugs while at work or your job performance is being adversely affected by the possible abuse of drugs or alcohol, or

Director's Resource 9-1 *(continued)*

2. keeping drugs or alcohol on your person, in your desk, locker, or other personal belonging or company area

We may ask you to:

1. open the area for inspection
2. consent to be tested
3. leave the premises

If you are found to be in possession of illegal drugs or alcohol, refuse to consent to testing, or leave the premises if requested, or test positive, you may be disciplined up to and including termination of employment. Pre-employment and post-employment drug test may also be conducted.

Use of Company Property

Use company property for business only. Do not use company property for personal reasons. Also, office supplies and other company property must never be taken from the facility (unless authorized to do so). This shall include all business and computer related files and/or records.

CONFLICT RESOLUTION PROCEDURE

Employee Questions, Concerns, or Complaints SCCP, Inc. acknowledges that circumstances may arise about which an employee may desire to seek formal assistance in resolving questions or concerns about employment. SCCP wishes to provide all employees with considerate supervision and fair treatment. To that end, the following conflict resolution procedure has been adopted to resolve such questions or concerns.

1. Every employee question or complaint should first be discussed with the director within three (3) days of the occurrence of the cause of the complaint. (If the director is the cause of the complaint, the employee may begin at Step 2.) It is hoped that a satisfactory resolution of the complaint can promptly be reached between the employee and the director. In any event, what the director proposes shall be given in writing to the employee with a copy sent to the Executive Director and the Associate Executive Director.
2. If the employee is not satisfied with the resolution of the complaint proposed by the director, the employee may appeal his or her complaint in writing to the Executive Director and the Associate Executive Director. They will jointly render a written decision within ten (10) working days after the filing of the appeal.

Director's Resource 9-1 *(continued)*

3. The decision of the Executive Director and the Associate Executive Director shall be final and binding on all parties and not subject to any further appeal. They shall keep the President of the Board informed of personnel concerns involving such formal complaints.
4. In the case of a complaint either against or by a management employee, including the Associate Executive Director, the Executive Director shall hear and review evidence presented by the complaint. In the case of a complaint either against or by the Executive Director, the President of the Board shall hear and review evidence presented by the complaint; if deemed necessary by the President of the Board, he/she shall appoint a committee of the Board to hear the complaint. If this committee fails to satisfy the parties involved; an appeal may be made in writing to the President for a hearing before the entire Board. Decision by the Board will be final.

The Associate Executive Director and the Executive Director shall maintain an "open door policy," in which any employee may, in private, present a complaint or other agency concern.

Director's Resource 9-1

EMPLOYEE'S ACKNOWLEDGMENT

I have received and read the *"Cincinnati Early Learning Centers Inc. Human Resources Policies and Practices."* I expect to be guided by the policies contained therein. I further understand and agree that my employment with Cincinnati Early Learning Centers Inc. (CELC) is at will and may be terminated by me or CELC at any time for any reason or without reason. I understand that nothing in the Human Resources Policies and Practices or in any oral statement or representation by any employee or representative of CELC shall be deemed to create a contract of employment or any other modification of the at-will employment relationship. I also understand that any or all of the provisions contained in the Human Resources Policies and Practices may be modified, amended, or eliminated by CELC at any time with or without notice.

_____
Print Name

_____
Signature

_____
Date

_____
Employee SSN

_____
Director/Supervisor Signature

_____
Employment Location

_____
Date

Reprinted with permission of the rights holder.

Source: Reprinted by permission of the copyright holder.

You can download a full-size version of this form on the Education CourseMate website.

Director's Resource 9-2

STAFFING SCHEDULES

The sample staffing schedule offered here can be used to staff a small program or an infant unit in a larger program. Guidelines follow (on p. 73) for its use in programs with varying numbers of children. This schedule assumes a 1:3 adult-child ratio for 12 infants. It is not recommended that group size be larger than eight so 12 infants and four caregivers, despite being the correct ratio, ideally would not be all in one room.

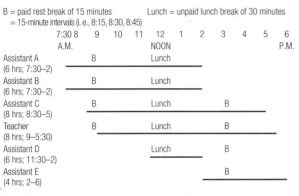

B = paid rest break of 15 minutes   Lunch = unpaid lunch break of 30 minutes
= 15-minute intervals (i. e., 8:15, 8:30, 8:45)

```
         7:30 8   9   10  11  12  1   2   3   4   5   6
         A.M.                 NOON                    P.M.
Assistant A        B           Lunch
(6 hrs; 7:30–2)
Assistant B    B        Lunch
(6 hrs; 7:30–2)
Assistant C        B        Lunch          B
(8 hrs; 8:30–5)
Teacher            B        Lunch          B
(8 hrs; 9–5:30)
Assistant D                  Lunch      B
(6 hrs; 11:30–2)
Assistant E                             B
(4 hrs; 2–6)
```

*These eight teacher hours may be covered by more than one qualified teacher.
Note: This schedule shows child care staff only. Hours for administration and house-keeping or other mainte-nance personnel are not included.

Reprinted with permission from the National Association for the Education of Young Children.

Source: Reprinted from A. Godwin and L. Schrag, Setting Up for Infant/ Toddler Care: Guidelines for Centers and Family Child Care Homes, Rev. ed, (Washington, DC: NAEYC, 1996), 9. Reprinted with permission from the National Association fro the Education of Young Children (NAEYC).

Director's Resource 9-3

SAMPLE STAFFING PLAN—MULTIPLE PROGRAM B

Staff Plan by Staff Member

Title	How Many	Schedule	Recommended Salary	Total Yearly
Director/Administrator	1	MWF 7:30 a.m.– TTH 12:00 p.m.	$ 11.00/hr $22,880/yr	$ 22,880
Head Teachers	5	7:30–3:00 p.m. 30-min. break between 12:00–1:30 p.m.	$ 8.50/hr $17,680/yr	$ 88,400
Teachers	5	11:00–7:00 p.m. 30-min. break between 1:00–2:30 p.m.	$ 7.00/hr $14,560/yr	$ 72,800
Morning Assistants	5	7:30–12:30 p.m. 15-min. break between 11:00–12:00 p.m.	$ 5.00/hr $ 6,500/yr	$ 32,500
Afternoon Assistants	5	12:30–7:00 p.m. 15-min. break between 2:30–3:00 p.m.	$ 5.00/hr $ 8,450/yr	$ 42,250
Secretary/Bookkeeper	1	9:00–5:30 p.m. 1-hr. lunch	$ 6.00/hr $10,400/yr	$ 12,480
Custodian	1	5:00–10:00 p.m. Mon.–Thur. 5 hrs. on Sat. 15-min. break	$ 5.00/hr $ 6,500/yr	$ 6,500
Cook	1	7:30–3:00 p.m. 30-min. lunch	$ 5.00/hr $10,400/yr	$ 10,400
Total Yearly Salaries:				**$288,210**

Director's Resource 9-3 *(continued)*

STAFF PLAN BY CLASSROOM

Classroom	No. of Children	Staff/Child Ratio
Infants Rm: 101	8	required: 5:1 maximum: 8:3 minimum: 8:2
Toddlers Rm: 201	11	required: 7:1 maximum: 11:3 minimum: 11:2
3-year-olds Rm: 202	17	required: 12:1 maximum: 17:3 minimum: 17:2
3- and 4-year-olds Rm: 203	17	required: 12:1 maximum: 17:3 minimum: 17:2
4-year-olds Rm: 204	17	required: 14:1 maximum: 14:3 minimum: 14:2

Each classroom will be staffed as follows:

1 Head Teacher	7:30 a.m.–3:00 p.m.
1 Teacher	11:00 a.m.–7:00 p.m.
1 Assistant	7:30 a.m.–12:30 p.m.
1 Assistant	12:30–7:00 p.m.

This flexible schedule allows ample time for classroom planning in the morning and evening when the ratios will be low because most children arrive at the center between 8:00–9:00 a.m. and leave between 5:00–6:00 p.m. Nap time is when team planning and communication takes place.

Director's Resource 9-3

ADDITIONAL COMMENTS ABOUT STAFFING

- Breaks must maintain staff-to-child ratio at all times.
- Flexibility in scheduling breaks is necessary to meet the immediate needs of the classrooms.
- Short restroom breaks or emergency phone calls could be arranged as needed, as long as ratio is maintained.
- Staff schedules are designed for enhancing staff communications and for meeting the needs of the children.
- Swing scheduling for directors is designed to encourage and maintain communication with all staff members, family members, board, and community contacts.
- It is the teacher's responsibility to take care of housekeeping emergencies during the day.
- The cook is solely responsible for cleaning the kitchen, other than the cleanup after the afternoon snack, which is the teacher's responsibility.
- One morning snack, one afternoon snack, and one full meal will be provided each day.
- Encourage male applicants for all positions to balance male–female models.
- Parent(s)/surrogate(s) provide transportation.
- Tuition is $95/week for infants and $85/week for all others.
- Eighty percent of tuition income goes for salaries.

Source: © Cengage Learning, 2013.

You can download a full-size version of these forms on the Education CourseMate website.

Director's Resource 9-4

PERFORMANCE APPRAISAL—LEAD TEACHER

Name: ___ Date: ___

To establish and maintain a safe and healthy learning environment	seldom	some-times	frequently	always	Comments
1. Establishes and maintains an environment for children which is clean, safe, stimulating, and appropriate for each child's developmental level.					
2. Responsible for the appearance, décor, and learning environment of the classroom.					
3. Assumes an equal share of the joint housekeeping responsibilities.					
4. Promotes healthy eating practices.					
To advance physical and intellectual competence					
1. Supports emerging literacy and language development in response to each child's interests through whole language experiences.					
2. Implements a curriculum that fosters the construction of mathematical knowledge through hands-on activities.					
3. Provides an integrated curriculum that meets the needs of individual children.					
4. Uses equipment and materials for indoor and outdoor play that promotes children's fine and gross motor development.					
5. Designs and implements activities that foster the development of physical knowledge.					

Director's Resource 9-4 *(continued)*

To support social and emotional development and provide positive guidance	seldom	some-times	frequently	always	Comments
1. Gears program to the needs of the individual child and pace of learning.					
2. Considers the individual child in relationship to his/her culture and socio-economic background.					
3. Treats each child, co-worker, and parent with dignity and respect.					
4. Helps each child to become aware of his/her role as an integral member of the group.					
5. Plans and implements a curriculum that reflects the cultural diversity of the group.					
6. Provides an environment that fosters the development of self-esteem.					
To establish positive and productive relationships with families					
1. Views parent-teacher relationship as a partnership, focusing on each family's individual strengths and abilities.					
2. Plans and implements hands-on activities that develop self-esteem.					
3. Uses and promotes positive guidance techniques and a variety of creative and expressive activities.					
4. Coordinates with the Associate and Assistant Teacher.					
5. Gathers information from team members for feedback to families.					

Director's Resource 9-4 *(continued)*

	seldom	some-times	frequently	always	Comments
6. Parent concerns are directed and handled by the Lead Teacher.					
To ensure a well-run, purposeful program responsive to participants' needs					
1. Plans, supervises, and implements the curriculum in accordance with the policies and philosophy of the program.					
2. Uses support services and resources relating to the individual needs of the families and children.					
3. Maintains daily, weekly, and monthly written plans that reflect the individual interests and abilities of the children.					
4. Observations and documentation of individual progress through anecdotal notes, development checklist, portfolio assessments, and other designated screenings.					
5. Documentation is completed with agency guidelines and time limits.					
6. Paperwork for local, state, and federal agencies completed.					
7. Effectively supervises the Associate, Assistant Teachers, and volunteers in the classroom.					
8. Effectively assists the director in evaluating classroom staff.					

Director's Resource 9-4

	seldom	some-times	frequently	always	Comments
9. Facilitates weekly staff meetings to address children's development and makes necessary adaptations to the environment.					
10. Punctual in meeting daily work schedule.					
11. Follows attendance and punctuality policy of the center as stated in the employee handbook.					
12. Maintains professional appearance at all times as stated in the employee handbook.					
Additional Comments:					

Name of Supervisor ____

Reprinted with permission from the rights holder

Source: Reprinted by permission of the copyright holder.

You can download a full-size version of this form on the Education CourseMate website.

Director's Resource 9-5

JOB DESCRIPTION—LEAD TEACHER

Description:
The Lead Teacher is responsible for the care and education of a group of children as part of a teaching team, and functions as a team leader, or co-leader. The teacher plans and implements the curriculum, and with active participation of other members of the teaching team, works with parents and assesses the needs of individual children.

Accountability:
The Lead Teacher reports to the Director.

Minimum Qualifications:
Must have thorough knowledge of and be able to implement a developmental constructivist approach. Must be at least 18 years of age, a high school graduate, and have an Associate or Bachelor's degree in Early Childhood Education, be professionally prepared as a teacher of young children. In addition, he/she must be able to meet the requirements of the city and state licensing agencies.

Responsibilities:
To establish and maintain a safe and healthy environment
1. Establish and maintain an environment for children, which is clean, safe, stimulating, and which is appropriate for each child's developmental level.
2. Be responsible for the appearance, décor, and learning environment of the classroom.
3. Assume an equal share of the joint housekeeping responsibilities of the staff.
4. Design appropriate room arrangement to support the goals of the classroom.
5. Promote healthy eating practices.

To advance motor and intellectual competence
1. Supporting, emerging literacy and language development in response to each individual child's interest through whole language experience.
2. Implement a curriculum that fosters the construction of mathematical knowledge through hands-on activities.
3. Design and implement activities that foster the development of physical knowledge.
4. Provide an integrated curriculum that meets the needs of individual children.

Director's Resource 9-5 *(continued)*

5. Use equipment and material for indoor and outdoor play that promotes children's fine and gross motor development.

To support social and emotional development and provide positive guidance
1. Gear the program to the needs of the individual child and pace of learning.
2. Consider the individual child in relationship to his/her culture and socio-economic background.
3. Treat each child, co-worker, and parent with dignity and respect.
4. Help each child to become aware of his/her role as an integral member of a group.
5. Plan and implement a curriculum that reflects the culture diversity of the group.
6. Provide and environment that provides development of self-esteem.

To establish positive and productive relationships with families
1. View parent-teacher relationship as a partnership, focusing on each child's individual strengths and abilities.
2. Plan and implement hands-on activities that develop self-esteem.
3. Use and promote positive guidance techniques and a variety of creative and expressive activities.
4. Responsible for coordinating with the Associate and Assistant Teacher.
5. Gather information from team members for feedback to families.
6. Parent concerns should be directed and handled by the Lead Teacher.

To ensure a well-run, purposeful program responsive to participant needs
1. Planning, supervising, and implementing the curriculum in accordance with the policies and philosophy of the program.
2. Access support services and resources relating to the individual needs of the families and children.
3. Maintain daily, weekly, and monthly written plans that reflect the individual interests and abilities of the children.
4. Observation and documentation of individual progress through anecdotal notes, development checklist, portfolio assessments, and other designated screenings.
5. All documentation must be completed within agency guidelines and time limits.

Director's Resource 9-5

6. Complete paperwork required for local, state, and federal agencies.
7. Responsible for supervising the Associate and Assistant Teacher, and volunteers in their classroom.
8. Assist the director in evaluating classroom staff.
9. Facilitate weekly staff meetings to address children development and needed adaptations to the environment.

To maintain a commitment to professionalism
1. Attend all staff meetings, parent meetings, and other mandatory or required in-services.
2. Promote agency's code of ethics.
3. Maintain flexibility and consistency with all staff.
4. Maintain confidentiality regarding staff, families, and children at all times.
5. Relate to families in a positive and respectful manner.

From Blueprint for Action: Achieving Center-Based Change Through Staff Development *developed by P. J. Bloom, 2005. Lake Forest, IL: New Horizons. Reprinted with permission of the author.*

Director's Resource 9-6

INTERVIEW QUESTIONS

(In the interest of time and to ensure fairness, consider choosing four or five questions that are particularly applicable to your program to ask of all candidates. Ask additional questions as time allows.)

Degreed Candidate

1. Tell us about your past experiences in this field—both your previous work experience and/or your practicum placements.
2. Of all the theories and ideas you studied in school, what had the greatest impact on you regarding discipline in the classroom?
3. How do you think children learn? Give an example of how you would set up an experience for learning about a simple machine like an inclined plane or a pulley.
4. What would you do when an irate parent approaches you about an incident (such as biting in the classroom)? How would you handle that?
5. How would you handle problem solving in the classroom? For example, if two children are arguing over a basket of Lego® blocks, each saying she had it first, what would you do?
6. Choose an area of the curriculum (e.g., science, math, music, etc.). Tell us how you would set it up.
7. How do you view your role as a preschool teacher?
8. What would you strive for in a parent/caregiver relationship?
9. What do you see as strong points in our program? Weak points?
10. How do you feel about themes when planning a curriculum?
11. How do you feel separation issues should be handled? For example, a child comes in with a special toy from home, and he is very reluctant to have Mom leave him. How might you handle that situation?
12. What are your long-term professional goals?
13. Since consistency is important in every program, how do you feel about committing to one year here?

Source: From Blueprint for Action: Achieving Center-Based Change Through Staff Development developed by P. J. Bloom, 2005. Lake Forest, IL: New Horizons. Reprinted with permission of the author.

You can download a full-size version of these forms on the Education CourseMate website.

Director's Resource 9-6 (continued)

Nondegreed Candidate

1. Tell us about your experience in the field of early childhood education, as well as any other work experience you have had.
2. What do you see as your particular strengths that would apply to a position like this?
3. What are your professional goals? Would you be willing to attend some training sessions in the fall?
4. How would you handle an irate parent who approaches you at the end of the day when the teacher has gone?
5. If two children are arguing over Legos, each saying she had them first, what would you do?
6. What do you see as your role in the classroom?
7. What do you think the purpose of child care should be?
8. How would you handle a situation in which a child has just knocked down another child's block building?
9. How do you think discipline is different from punishment?
10. What did you see during your tour of our center that you particularly liked? What were some of your questions as you toured the classroom?
11. What special skills and abilities do you feel you can bring to our program?

• Adapted and used with permission from the rights holder.

Second Interview Select three or four questions that seem appropriate for the candidate being interviewed.

1. What was the parenting style of the person who cared for you (mother, father, other)?
2. Do you think babies can be spoiled? How?
3. How can you help a child (baby, toddler, preschooler) who cries when his parent leaves in the morning?
4. How would you handle a situation in which two children (toddlers, preschoolers) are holding the same toy and both are shouting, "mine"?
5. What is your favourite book to read to children?
6. What was the last book you read for your own information or pleasure?

Director's Resource 9-6

7. What did you like best (least) about the last job you had?
8. What are some things you might talk about when a parent comes to pick up a child at the end of the day and asks, "How was my child's day?"

Source: Reprinted by permission of the copyright holder.

You can download a full-size version of this form on the Education CourseMate website.

REFERENCES

Americans with Disabilities Act: Questions and answers. (1991, July). Washington, DC: U.S. Equal Opportunity Commission.

Bloom, P. J. (2007). *From the inside out: The power of reflection and self-awareness*. Lake Forest, IL: New Horizons.

Bloom, P. J., Sheerer, M., & Britz, J. (2005). *Blueprint for action: Achieving center-based change through staff development*. Lake Forest, IL: New Horizon.

Carter, M. (1998). Principles and strategies for coaching and mentoring. In R. Neugebauer & B. Neugebauer (Eds.), *The art of leadership: Managing early childhood organizations*. Redmond, WA: CCIE.

Carter, M. & Curtis, D. (2010). *The visionary director* (2nd ed.). St. Paul, MN: Redleaf Press.

Cohen, A. J. (1998). Bettering your odds of not getting sued. In R. Neugebauer & B. Neugebauer (Eds.), *The art of leadership: Managing early childhood organizations*. Redmond, WA: CCIE.

Collins, J. (2005). *Good to great and the social sectors*. New York: Harper Collins.

Gable, S., Rothrauff, T. C., Thornburg, K. R., & Mauzy, D. (2007). Cash incentives and turnover in center-based child care staff. *Early Childhood Research Quarterly, 22,* 363–378.

Greenberg, P. (1993). *Character development: Encouraging self-esteem and self-discipline in infants, toddlers, and two-year olds*. Washington, DC: NAEYC.

Hamrick, J. (2000). Reduce staff turnover through effective interviewing. *Child Care Information Exchange, 134,* 26–28.

Sciarra, D. J., & Dorsey, A. G. (2002). *Leaders and supervisors in child care programs*. Clifton Park, NY: Thomson Delmar Learning.

Whitebrook, M., & Bellm, D. (1999). *Taking on turnover: An action plan for child care teachers and directors*. Washington, DC: Center for Child Care Workforce.

10

Recruiting CHILDREN

Bombeck Family Learning Center

Families are more likely to choose a program where they feel they belong.

Objectives

After reading this chapter, you should be able to:

- Identify how family needs can be addressed in early care and education.
- Use mandates from federal laws to design policies and practices that support children with disabilities in early care and education settings.
- Make informed decisions about grouping children in centers.
- List steps in the intake process.

Standards Addressed in This Chapter

naeyc Professional Preparation
        Standards 2, 6

naeyc Administrator Competencies
        Management Knowledge and
        Skills 2, 4, 6
        Early Childhood Knowledge
        and Skills 1, 5, 10

naeyc Accreditation Standards 4, 6

Effective directors are informed decision makers who consider multiple and sometimes competing factors before coming to conclusions. Decisions related to enrolling and grouping children are complex as many factors related to the needs of children and families as well as the quality of the program must be considered. Of course, there are pressures to admit all applicants when enrollment is not full. However, it is important for the director to exercise good professional judgment and base admission decisions on what is in the best interests of children and families.

Ultimately, the director is responsible for the decisions about how children will be admitted to the program and how they will be grouped. The teachers may be called on to assist in these decisions and sometimes a standing committee authorized by the board is asked to make policy or give advice. An admissions and recruitment committee might be charged with policy-making decisions about the population the program is designed to serve as well as the procedures to be followed when enrolling children. There are also decisions to be made about how children will be grouped and about how the program can support children with disabilities.

MEETING THE NEEDS OF CHILDREN AND FAMILIES naeyc

Quality programs are inclusive and strive to meet the needs of all of the children and families admitted to the program. This means that directors must have a realistic understanding of the strengths and limitations of the program and the unique needs of the children and families to be served. Developing this understanding requires that the director and staff engage in ongoing program evaluation to understand what the center can do, where improvement or support is needed, and what the realistic limits are to the types of services a program can offer.

For example, a program may wish to increase enrollment by serving a larger number of subsidized children, but an economic downturn at the state level has led to severe cuts in the reimbursement rates. The center must now look elsewhere to increase enrollment or end up with a budget shortfall. Additionally, many of the families that are eligible for a county subsidy are also eligible for Head Start, where children have access to additional program options such as dental and medical evaluations and, in some instances, mental health services. Directors need to make an honest assessment of what their program can provide for children and families and if services can be enhanced by partnering with other agencies.

A center director may understand the need to include children with special learning or developmental needs. Noting an increase in the number of children with autism spectrum disorders, a director might recognize a limitation in the expertise of his or her staff and determine that special training is needed so that teachers understand and can implement strategies that support children with autism. The director might also note that many children with autism require early intervention services to best meet their needs. Directors need to maintain an ethical balance between striving to be inclusive, working with families to find services to best meet the needs of children, and recognizing the strengths and limitations of their program.

Professionals at the center must decide if the available staff and the particular program offerings at the center can provide the most enriching experience for a particular child. In other words, can *this* program provide what *this* child needs to develop to his or her fullest potential? If there is any doubt in the minds of either the members of the family or the director, careful consideration should be given to a number of questions.

- Can the program be adjusted to accommodate this child?

- Is there another program with a different focus that would provide a better match for this child and family?

- Are there programs to partner with that would enhance what can be offered in order to meet the needs of children and families?

Partnering with the local school district or the county early intervention program can provide access to itinerant special educators who will work with children with special needs in child care and home settings. Likewise, many Head Start grantees have developed partnerships with child care programs, allowing children and families to reap the benefits of Head Start services in a child care setting.

An inclusive directors see that their program can be one option on a continuum of program options for children and families. Progressive directors need to be realistic while also understanding the need to grow and change to meet the needs of children and families facing the demands of the twenty-first century. One particular challenge is to understand the myriad of federal laws, mandates, and procedures that govern how children with special needs are to be served in inclusive settings.

Admission of Children with Disabilities

A federal law that directors must be familiar with is the Americans with Disabilities Act (ADA), which was enacted in 1990 and amended in 2008. Knowledge of the ADA is important as directors review requests for admission of children with disabilities. Centers are prohibited from denying admission to a child simply because of a disability *unless* such admission would "fundamentally alter the nature of the program" (ADA Amendments Act, 2008). Likewise, children who pose a *direct threat* or "a substantial risk of serious harm to the health and safety of others" do not have to be admitted into a program. The determination that "a child poses a direct threat may not be based on generalizations or stereotypes about the effects of a particular disability; it must be based on an *individualized assessment* that considers the particular activity and the actual abilities and disabilities of the individual" (U.S. Department of Justice, n.d.).

Directors in early childhood education programs must be prepared to address the challenge of providing quality inclusive environments for increasing numbers of young children with disabilities. They are obligated to understand that a child may not be excluded simply because he or she has a disability. It is important for them to know how the law applies to

Directors attend to the importance of inclusion.

© 2010 Cengage Learning

infants, toddlers, and preschoolers and to understand how early childhood programs are likely to fit into the scheme of services for children with disabilities. They also should know what role they and their staff can play as part of the interdisciplinary, interagency team effort to give these children the benefit of quality early childhood education experiences. The well-being of the child is best served when families are a part of the team.

Another important law that was enacted by Congress is Public Law 99-457, which amended the Education of Handicapped Act (EHA, PL 94-142). This 1986 amendment mandated services for children 3 to 5 years of age. The reauthorization of both PL 94-142 and PL 99-457 came in 1990 with the passage of PL 101-476, Individuals with Disabilities Education Act (IDEA). It was further amended in 1997 as PL 105-17. The law requires that states provide a free, *appropriate* public education to everyone with a disability between the ages of 3 and 21. In the past, IDEA was specific to public school–based programs for preschoolers and older children with special needs. However, states are now applying the early childhood itinerant model, which brings early intervention services to community-based early childhood programs (Dinnebeil et al., 2001). This means that children with disabilities can now receive inclusive intervention services in child care and other community-based programs, opening a wide variety of options for families.

Provisions of the IDEA

IDEA, as amended by PL 105-17, the Individuals with Disabilities Act Amendments of 1997, extends all rights and due process protection to children with disabilities ages 3 to 5. Therefore, preschool children with disabilities are ensured free public education in a least restrictive environment based on an individualized education plan (IEP) developed by a team that includes the child's parents. The programs are to be administered through state or local education agencies (LEAs), which may contract with other service providers to offer a range of service models. The designated state agency ultimately is responsible for monitoring overall services and use of the federal funds. Other sources of funding such as Medicaid or Maternal and Child Health also must be utilized when the children are eligible, and the new funds are to supplement, not supplant, these existing sources. Therefore, the new funds may be used *in addition to* but not *instead of* existing sources of funding.

According to Allen & Cowdery (2011), IDEA also establishes a state grant program to provide financial assistance to states to maintain and implement a comprehensive, multidisciplinary system of services for infants and toddlers with disabilities. Part C of IDEA, known as *discretionary legislation,* says that states may serve this age group but are not required to do so. The exception is for those states that serve nondisabled infants and toddlers: they must serve those children who are disabled in that age group. The governor of each state designates a lead agency in the state to administer the program. That agency develops eligibility criteria, and the law allows but does not require extension of services to those babies viewed as "at risk" for developmental delay based on medical or environmental factors, in addition to identified infants with disabilities. A case manager, sometimes called a service coordinator, must be designated for each child. That person, who is the liaison between agencies and services needed, also is responsible for the development of the individualized family service plan (IFSP), which must have evidence of multidisciplinary input and include information about the child's level of development, the family's strengths and needs as these relate to the child, the specific intervention services planned, and the projected outcomes for the child and the family. Therefore, the IFSP is somewhat comparable to the IEP required for the age 3-to-5 population and brings the focus to the importance of the family in each young child's life.

Role of Child Care Centers

IDEA allows for variation in length of day, as well as range and variety of programs. This means that services to be utilized may be part-time or full-time, home-based or center-based. This is likely to lead to more inclusion models as state and local agencies contract with half-day and full-day child care programs to expand the continuum of services to include more center-based care in integrated settings. Now that the values of early childhood education programs are sufficiently high and demand public notice, state education agencies that have discretion to choose program models see that these programs offer viable alternatives to the current typical public school categorical model. In addition to integrated child care options that are now available through itinerant services, Head Start is an option for many low income families, as 10 percent of Head Start's classroom slots must be reserved for children with disabilities.

The vast majority of unserved children with disabilities who come into programs under the new law are identified as needing mild to moderate intervention. Most children who require intensive intervention already receive services and may or may not be included in preschools or child care centers depending on how well their needs would be met in an inclusion environment. However, based on ADA, each applicant must be considered on a case-by-case basis and may not be excluded merely because a disabling condition. If the program can include the child by making reasonable accommodations in the environment, then it is expected to do so (U.S. Department of Justice, n.d.).

IDEA requires that children with disabilities have access to the "least restrictive environment" (LRE). Legally, this means that every effort must be made to integrate children with their peers in a regular educational setting. In practice, the least restrictive environment is one that facilitates opportunities to function and grow optimally in all areas of development. Directors of centers are responsible for

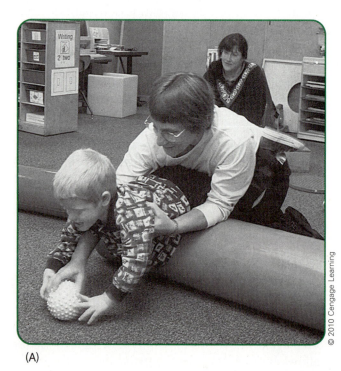

(A)

© 2010 Cengage Learning

(B)

© 2010 Cengage Learning

The needs of applicants with disabilities must be carefully assessed to ensure that this is the best possible program for them.

providing such an environment for children with disabilities, who must share the pedagogical and social environment; teachers are expected to be specifically trained to facilitate interaction among and between typically developing children and those who have special needs. They should also have an understanding of the implications of developmental differences and be able to adapt the learning environment to enhance the development of children with diverse abilities.

Although there is evidence that significant benefits accrue to children with special needs who participate in groups with typical peers, these benefits are not the result of merely being in the same classroom. The factors that determine how well children with special needs do in an inclusion environment depends on the quality of the program and the presence of a teacher who has developed specific intervention plans to support interaction between and among the children with disabilities and their typically developing peers (Allen & Cowdery, 2011).

When available staff struggle to find sufficient time or lack the background to provide the special support for children with special needs in the classroom, it may be possible to reach out into the community for additional help. In addition to reaching out to school districts and early intervention providers, volunteers from parent groups, senior citizens, service organizations, or students from university early childhood or special education programs can help in the classroom. Special training for the volunteers and the staff can be arranged through special educators at the local school or university, or from other community agencies (Allen & Cowdery, 2011).

Including children who have been identified with special needs can be both inspiring and challenging for the teaching staff and the director. However, because so many resources are available to children with special needs and their families, inclusion can work out to benefit everyone involved. The more vexing challenges are those faced when a new child enters the program and, soon after admission, begins to manifest social and/or emotional problems through disruptive emotional outbursts in the classroom. In these cases, neither the director nor the teaching staff has had a chance to prepare themselves or the children for this new student. It becomes stressful and time consuming to work with this new family and to provide the necessary support for the troubled child and the classroom teacher. In these situations, directors are pulled in many directions, sometimes struggling with a screaming, angry child; sometimes talking with hostile, defensive, or bewildered parents; sometimes taking time after hours to give support to an exhausted teacher.

These are the times when directors must call on all their professional skills to help the child, the family, and the teacher cope and eventually move forward toward resolution.

In the past decade, the challenge of working with troubled, angry children has created a great deal of interest among early childhood educators as they consider preventive measures as well as explanations for the phenomena and any remedies that might help children, their families, and their teachers. One sample of such a remedy focuses on refining and adjusting classroom practice to promote the emotional well-being and resilience of all children in the classroom, not just of those who are seen as "troublesome." This type of refined and modified approach to children and families requires training and coaching for all staff, including administrators, with a director who participates and serves as a model for other staff. It is essential that everyone who sees, greets, or talks with children and families reflects the same focus of respect and caring. Everyone must engage in what the center views as *best practice*. The adjusted attitude and practice focuses on strengths of children and families and provides very predictable, safe, and supportive experiences throughout the center. The classroom is a place where children come to know and trust that they are respected, protected, and heard by trusted adults. When this modified approach is implemented throughout a program, it seems to minimize the need for the more traditional identification/referral/intervention procedure for troubled children. That

DIRECTOR'S CORNER

"When a child with a disability becomes part of a classroom in our center, the teachers meet with me to identify the resources that the teaching team has to offer this child and family and to identify areas where the team might need assistance. I see my role as facilitating the conversation and also as helping teachers see how their areas of strength can support the child. I also realize that my role is to act as a sounding board when needed and to identify community resources available to the teaching team so that they can better meet the needs of the child. I know I need to provide opportunities for the team to talk. There are times when teachers need to vent and there are times when teachers are asking for help. My job is to know the difference."

—Director, university-affiliated child care center

Response to Intervention: The Three-Tier Model in a Preschool Environment

This video provides an overview of how the "Response to Intervention" (RTI) process might be used to meet the needs of young children with special needs in a preschool setting. Visit Chapter 10 of the **CourseMate website** and view the video vignette entitled, *Response to Intervention: The Three-Tier Model in a Preschool Environment.* Reflect on the following questions:

1. How do you think that the RTI process might impact the child-centered and play-based practice that is valued in many early childhood settings?

2. As a director, how might you support teachers who are exploring how to use RTI in their classrooms?

traditional routine is reserved for those children and families who require specialized support in addition to the support provided by the uniquely trained and qualified staff that understands the importance of the emotional well-being of children, families, and colleagues.

Role of the Director in an Interdisciplinary/Interagency Effort

Cooperation among education agencies, social service agencies, medical groups, and early childhood education providers is essential if young children with special needs and their families are to be well served. Directors conversant in the law and its implications for child care programs will be able to respond more knowledgeably to professionals from related agencies who make inquiries about placements for children with special needs. These directors may be called on to make decisions about whether their programs can meet the needs of the selected special needs children; to serve on interdisciplinary teams where IEPs are developed and referral decisions are made; and to support their teachers who will be working with special educators, therapists, and the children's families. If the children are to benefit from what early childhood educators have to offer, "turf guarding" must be set aside; yet directors must assertively advocate developmentally appropriate practice, which is the area of expertise they bring to the interdisciplinary and interagency team.

To facilitate communication between and among members of interdisciplinary teams and to support

their work, directors must understand how and why inclusion works and what prevents it from working. That often means directors must learn more about children with special needs through additional training and reading to prepare themselves for coaching classroom staff and for working with an interdisciplinary team. When members of the interdisciplinary team view each other as colleagues, all of whom bring special skills and training to the situation, and when they keep in mind that their common goal is to provide the best environment for the children and their families, they can work together to that end.

GROUPING THE CHILDREN   naeyc

As part of the process of meeting the diverse needs of children and families, directors need to make informed decisions about how the structures of the center impact a variety of stakeholders, including children, families, and staff. Decisions about how children are grouped create structures that affect how staff are called upon to work together, how children and families interact at the center, and how much such care costs. Decisions about grouping also reflect a program's philosophy of education and the approach that the program has adopted. These decisions need to be carefully considered as they are more than logistical but will have a long term impact on the children, families, staff, and budget of the program

Decisions about grouping the children—group size, ages of children, and composition of the groups—must be reached before making the group assignments and pursuing all the subsequent steps in the enrollment procedure. Once assignments have been made, teachers can contact families and initiate the enrollment process. Although the degree of flexibility around grouping in ongoing early childhood education programs is sometimes more limited than in half-day programs, even there the cyclical nature of demand usually follows the public school year, thereby giving rise to numerous grouping decisions for newcomers in the fall.

A number of factors are considered in dealing with the complex question of how children should be grouped appropriately. The size of groups is determined by a variety of factors, including the physical space available, the licensing requirements, the number of staff members, and the program philosophy. Appropriate group size has a positive influence on both children and teachers (Decker & Decker, 2008). Other factors that relate to grouping of children are the needs and skills of the staff, the needs of the children, the question of chronological age grouping versus vertical (sometimes called family or multiage grouping), the number of children with special needs to be enrolled, and the nature of their disabilities.

Total Number of Children

To a large extent, the number of children available and the size of the physical space determine the total number of children in a center. If it is a new program, once the needs assessment in the community has been completed (Chapter 2) and the facility has been selected (Chapter 7), the final decision about the total number of children in the center must be made. Often, this decision is simply to take all available children. However, when the requests for service are overwhelming or when the available space cannot accommodate large numbers of children, the director and/or the board may want to limit the enrollment. Accreditation standards and many state licensing regulations limit total group size as well as adult-to-child ratios, both of which affect program quality. (See Chapter 3 for further details.)

Centers for young children must radiate a feeling of intimacy and warmth. Little children often feel frightened and uncomfortable about entering a large, forbidding building. The noise, the inevitable confusion, and the motion created by many people concentrated in one area can provoke anxiety in young children. It is difficult to maintain an inviting, comfortable atmosphere for small children when buildings are very large and when children are moved through crowded play yards, hallways, or receiving areas before they reach *their* room and *their* teacher.

Because the atmosphere in large public school buildings can be overwhelming for very young children, it is important for early childhood professionals and public school educators to give special attention to the selection of the classroom and play yard space for the preschool children. Partnerships between early childhood educators and public school personnel can result in site selection for public-school-sponsored programs that may be in a separate wing of the building or in a facility completely separate from the school building. Some of the advantages of funneling preschool and full-day child care services into public school sponsorship include greater stability, insulation from political attack, and protection from sudden economic shifts.

Space and Group Size

Group size varies according to the licensing regulations and how the available space is organized. Licensing regulations often limit the number of

DIRECTOR'S CORNER

"Children had to go down the hall and upstairs when the teachers wanted to take them to the gym for large-muscle activities. I always asked my teachers to try to avoid having the preschoolers in the halls of the school building when the older children were moving in and out of the auditorium or the lunchroom. It was very confusing for the younger children to be taken through the long lines of older children—especially if remarks were made like 'make room for the baby group' by the children or the elementary teachers."

—Director, Head Start program in a public school building

children in a room and usually dictate the adult-to-child ratio for children of different ages. Since space requirements and adult-to-child ratio standards in the licensing regulations are not always based on the knowledge of experienced professionals, it is wise to follow a standard of small groups with low teacher-to-child ratios, meeting NAEYC standards or achieving even lower ratios under special circumstances (National Association for the Education of Young Children, 2007).

The organization or plan of the available space affects the size of the groups that can be accommodated. When bathrooms are two floors down or outside areas are not directly adjacent to the classroom, groups must be smaller to be manageable during the transition periods when children move from one place to another. If fenced-in play areas outside can be reached directly from the classroom, the total space can be supervised more easily and a larger group could be assigned to the space.

REFLECTION

Can you recall how you felt as a first-year high school student when you initially entered your big high school building? Were you afraid and anxious? How did it feel to be the youngest or the smallest in the whole school? Did you feel that you might not be able to find your room or your locker? Did you ever have nightmares about forgetting your schedule or losing your most important notebook? If you can recall any of those feelings, perhaps you can begin to relate to the young child who leaves a familiar home environment and enters a large, strange, crowded building.

When space is adequate to accommodate large numbers of young children, some directors and teachers find creative ways to use dividers, draperies, or movable partitions to break the space into smaller units. Even where available space would accommodate larger groups, smaller groups are viewed as optimal.

Skills of Staff and Group Size

In deciding on the size of groups, the director considers the skill level of the staff and factors that into the decision about how many children should be assigned to each classroom. The staff for each group must be available to provide frequent personal contact; promote age-appropriate, meaningful learning experiences; create a nurturing environment using effective classroom management strategies; and respond immediately to all emergencies.

Needs of Children and Group Size

It is beyond the scope of this book to discuss the policy of making group size or placement decisions on the basis of differing individual family and child needs or ages of children, even though every director must consider such needs carefully. However, some basic considerations apply to all children, whether infant, toddler, preschool, or school age.

The needs of children will vary depending on their experiences, their level of development in all areas, and their ages. However, it is generally agreed that very young children in their first group experience find it most satisfying to relate to a constant adult.

After the initial shift in attachment from the primary caregiver (usually the mother) to a constant adult at the center, the child begins to branch out and relate to other adults and other children in the group. This developmental progression suggests that the child's first experience should be in a small, intimate group with a consistent adult. The children in this group may be the same chronological age, or they may range over a year or two in age. Volunteers, student teachers, or parent helpers may rotate through the classroom, but the one primary constant caregiver becomes the trusted adult figure to whom children can turn when they need caring and attention. Continuity of care is especially important for infants and toddlers, who should have an assigned primary caregiver who works closely with the parents. When change is carefully planned and minimized, infants and toddlers begin to be able to predict what will happen, thus feeling less powerless or uneasy and more secure (Gonzalez-Mena & Widmeyer Eyer, 2008).

For young children spending the full day in a center, it is wise to consider small, intimate grouping patterns. Because children in full-day programs spend practically all of their waking hours in the center, it becomes a surrogate home for them. Young children who are dealing with all the stimulation and interpersonal relationships of a large group for an extended period of time may be exhausted by the end of their long day. Small groups in a carefully planned space provide both time and space for the child to be alone, to establish close relationships with just one or two children, or to spend time alone with just one adult. Quiet and intimacy in a comfortable

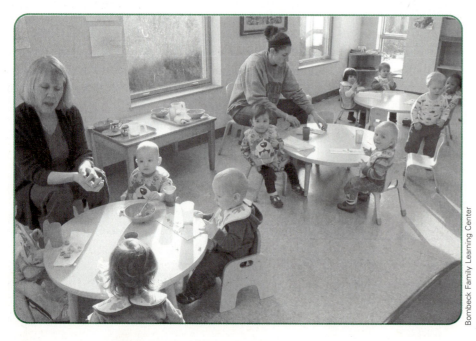

Bombeck Family Learning Center

The younger the child, the more important it is that experiences should be in a small, intimate group with a consistent and responsive adult.

setting with a few people more closely resembles the home environment and can soften the institutional atmosphere that prevails in many large centers.

Careful planning and adequate staffing enable directors to maintain consistency in caregivers and to avoid having to regroup children to maintain required staff/child ratios throughout each day. In fact, some programs take significant steps to maintain continuity of care by grouping children in broader age ranges such as 3 months to 3 years or by implementing a practice called "looping," in which teachers follow a group of children from infancy through preschool. Both of these grouping practices offer the children the benefits of consistency throughout these formative years. Moving children to different spaces for the critical and sometimes fragile times of separation and reunion creates tension for everyone involved. If at all possible, directors should plan staffing so that children stay in the same familiar space with their caregivers from the time they see that special parent disappear behind that closed door in the morning to the time they see that familiar face reappear for pickup at day's end. It is recommended that children of all ages have an assigned primary caregiver.

REFLECTION

Think about your first practicum experience in a classroom. Think about how many children you were able to manage at one time. Could you comfortably work with five children? If you were asked to work with ten children without a second person to help, did you still feel that you could practice effective management skills? What adult-to-child ratio and total group size is most comfortable for you, keeping in mind your philosophy of early childhood education?

Chronological versus Vertical Age Grouping

There is no consensus on the best grouping practice. Although there has been some movement toward greater homogeneity in classrooms for young children, which usually results from chronological age grouping, there is a resurgence of interest in multiage or vertical grouping (Decker & Decker, 2008). Program philosophy may dictate the preferred approach to grouping the children. However, unless licensing regulates how children should be grouped, the way classrooms are organized within the program is left to the discretion of the director and the professional staff.

Directors are faced with the challenge of maintaining full enrollment while keeping groups balanced and exercising caution when decisions are made about moving children among established center groupings. When infant-toddler groups are at capacity but there are openings in the preschool, it is tempting to move some of the older toddlers to the preschool to make space for families on the waiting list. It is important to balance the need for full enrollment to meet budget requirements against the social-emotional readiness of these very young children and their ability to manage a more complex environment with older children and new adults.

Too often, children are moved based solely on their chronological age or in response to pressure to make room for new children, rather than on a careful analysis of the readiness of the children involved in the move. The first step is to give careful consideration to a child's readiness to thrive and grow with the older children. Then take note of the challenges to the family and teachers involved in supporting the child through this critical adjustment to many unknowns, such as different spaces with new adults and few familiar faces. The transition process for any child to a new group in the center can be eased by setting up a transition plan that parallels the phasing-in process described in the "Intake Procedures" section of this chapter (page 232). The family and the teachers from both rooms will be involved in the transition process, just as a parent and the teacher are involved when a new child enters the program.

Parents may need a special conference with the director to clarify the importance of the parent role in the transition process, not only when the child enters the program but also for all subsequent transitions from one group to another and the final one when the child leaves the center. Meeting with the child's parents as these transition times approach offers the director the opportunity to help them understand how their presence in the new room can help reduce stress for their child as both are adjusting to the families and staff. It is helpful to parents if they understand that taking time for their child during potentially stressful changes will contribute to the emotional well-being of their child.

Chronological Grouping

Grouping by age traditionally has been a more common practice in early childhood programs than vertical grouping. It involves grouping based solely on the basis of age: 3- and 4-years-olds are in different groups and toddlers are separated from infants. When children are grouped chronologically, there is

▶❚❚ **TEACHSOURCE VIDEO VIGNETTE**

Preschool: IEP and Transition Planning for a Young Child with Special Needs

Visit Chapter 10 of the **CourseMate website** and view the video vignette entitled, *Preschool: IEP and Transition Planning for a Young Child with Special Needs.*

Transitions meetings are common when children move from public school preschool programs to kindergartens that are part of the same school system. Child care providers who work with children and families but who are not part of the school system are often not included in the transition planning meeting. As director, how might you facilitate avenues to support children and families to be more of a part of this transition process?

little discussion about which group a given child will join. The director's task is simplified because in accepting the center program, parents understand that their 3-year-old will be in Group 1 and their 4-year-old will be in Group 2. Of course, there will be ranges of ability and behavior within an age group due to individual differences, but the child's exposure to differences is inevitably lessened when chronological grouping is used. Therefore, the child's opportunity to develop a broad appreciation for diversity is diminished. On the other hand, there are advantages to age grouping, such as simplifying the planning of the learning environment and making classroom management less troublesome. The less experienced teacher may find this type of grouping more comfortable.

Chronological age grouping is based on the assumption that children of the same age are within the same range in ability and level of development. Because children of the same age are not homogeneous, many programs go to multiage grouping where children advance at their own rate through individualized or differentiated programming. Multiage grouping allows for children's uneven development and provides an environment in which younger children engage in more interactive and complex types of play with older children, who are easily accessible. There is also compelling evidence that children will do well when they are in a mixed-age group where children not only differ in age but also in ethnic and socioeconomic backgrounds. With the guidance of a well-trained teacher, children will engage in projects that match their interests and move toward more cooperative play (Katz & Chard, 2000).

More on Multiage Grouping

Multiage grouping, or vertical grouping as it is sometimes called, involves placing children of different ages in the same group; the children in any one group may range in age as much as 2 to 3 years. This multiage grouping more closely resembles one that would occur in a family, and is sometimes referred to as *family grouping*. Depending on licensing requirements, infants and sometimes even toddlers must be kept in separate groups. When vertical grouping is the pattern, decisions about the size and the composition of each group, as well as the number of adults needed for each one, become more complex. The broad age range also complicates managing the children and planning their learning environment.

Sometimes, parents object to having their 2-year-old with older children who may be viewed by the toddler's parents as being loud and rough. These parents often are concerned about the safety of their toddler and sometimes fear that their young child will be unable to cope in a group covering a wide age range. However, many of these parents can be helped to see that a young child in a multiage group has more opportunity to learn from older children in the group and that every child has a chance to teach the other group members. Peer teaching and learning have intrinsic value because they not only enhance a child's sense of mastery and worth but also facilitate cooperation and appreciation of others. For example, 2-year-olds may not be as efficient as 5-year-olds about putting equipment back on the shelf, but the total concentration they give to an activity like water play and the curiosity they show in exploring this material may help their more controlled 3- or 5-year-old counterparts to try splashing in the water. Parents who are familiar with programs that have chronological age grouping are usually aware of differences in tuition as children move up from infant to toddler to preschool in these programs. Costs are lower because of more generous ratios in classrooms for older children, and that is a financial benefit for families as children move up from one level to the next. This cost differential and its inevitable result are a reality that program sponsors and directors must deal with when they choose to do vertical age grouping. Fees per child in vertical grouping are usually the same, regardless of the child's age.

The director must cope with the skeptical parents and with the teachers who are reaching out for support as they work with a broad age range. However, sometimes the advantages of multiage grouping, such as peer modeling and peer tutoring, are outweighed by the challenges of planning for the age span and equipping and managing the classroom. Helping families understand that it is typical for the development of 3- to 5-year-olds to vary across developmental domains comes from teachers who also understand this concept and can communicate it in clear and consistent ways. Consider using graphics that show how the profiles of individual children might intersect with the skill levels of older and/or younger children. As children mature into the primary grades, this variation in developmental rate tends to even out. However, typical 3- to 5-year-olds are very sporadic in their rate of development and many children have peaks and valleys which make the opportunities to connect with older and younger children in a multiage group configuration very appropriate (see Figure 10-1).

REFLECTION

How might you, as a director, use Figure 10-1 to equip your staff so they can convey a clear explanation of multiage grouping to families?

Directors become coaches and sources of support for staff as they try to meet challenges. Teachers who are able to individualize planning for a multiage group also will be better qualified to create culturally responsive programs for children from diverse backgrounds and inclusive programs for children with special needs. These teachers develop a keen awareness of the fact that "one size does not fit all." Directors can help teachers both develop these skills and also become proficient in communicating what they do and why to families.

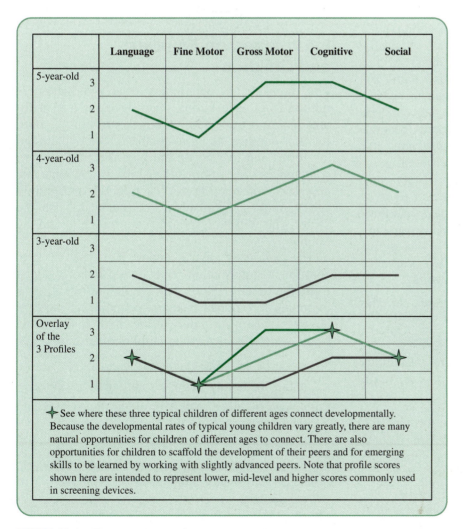

⭑ See where these three typical children of different ages connect developmentally. Because the developmental rates of typical young children vary greatly, there are many natural opportunities for children of different ages to connect. There are also opportunities for children to scaffold the development of their peers and for emerging skills to be learned by working with slightly advanced peers. Note that profile scores shown here are intended to represent lower, mid-level and higher scores commonly used in screening devices.

FIGURE 10-1   The development of young children varies in rate so that typical children of different ages are often working on the same developmental skills.

Source: © Cengage Learning, 2013.

Impact of Children with Exceptionalities on Group Size

When children with exceptionalities are included in the group, the size and composition of the group may need to be adjusted accordingly to ensure that enough adults will be available to respond to the children's needs. Consider which group can best meet the needs of the child with the disability, as well as how that child can offer something to the group. Unless the child is truly integrated into the group, which will likely require scaffolding from the teachers, there is a risk that the child with the disability will be ignored and not reap the benefits of being included with typical peers. The least restrictive ruling is not necessarily a mandate to enroll all children with a disability into regular programs; however, the advantages of inclusion for both nondisabled children and children with developmental disabilities are numerous and well documented (Allen & Cowdery, 2011). Social competence and the ability to maintain higher levels of play are enhanced for children with exceptionalities who have the opportunity to interact with typically developing peers in inclusive classrooms. At the same time, their language and cognitive gains are comparable to their peers in self-contained special education classrooms. On the other hand, children without disabilities in inclusive classrooms become more accepting of others who are different and become more comfortable with those differences.

There is no ideal exceptional-to-normal ratio, and recommendations range from at least two or more to an even balance (50–50), to more disabled than non-disabled, sometimes called "reverse mainstreaming" where nondisabled make up one-quarter to one-half of the enrollment (Allen & Cowdery, 2011). Variables that must be considered include the following:

- severity of the disabling conditions of the children with special needs
- characteristics of the nondisabled children
- how to explain and understand peers' disabilities
- expertise of the available adults who are to work with the inclusive group (Taylor, 2002)

Multiage groups are advantageous for children with special needs because they provide peer models who have a broad range of skills and abilities. The atypical child is exposed to the peer model who has higher-level skills or abilities and also will have a chance to develop friendships with younger children who may be more compatible developmentally.

Decisions about group size or group patterns will affect program planning, child and teacher behaviors, group atmosphere, and ultimately the experiences of both teacher and child in the learning environment. An inclusive program must consider the uniqueness of every child and family in the classroom and how each child's strengths and needs will be addressed (Allen & Cowdery, 2011). Therefore, grouping the children is a complex issue that has far-reaching results.

ENROLLING THE CHILDREN

Filling out forms, interviewing parents, and visiting back and forth between home and school are the major components of the enrollment procedure. The director is responsible for developing forms that will provide the center staff members with the information they need about the families and the children. The director also manages the planning and timing of this procedure; however, these plans must be discussed with staff members and parents who will be required to carry them out.

Information on Families and Children

The director first determines what information is needed from each family, then develops a plan for obtaining it. Forms and interviews can both be used for this purpose. It is up to the director to design the forms and to develop the plan for interviews or conferences. The ultimate goal is to assemble the necessary information for each child and family and to make it available to selected adults at the center who will be responsible for the child and the family.

The following list includes the type of pre-enrollment information that is typically obtained from the family. Note that all the information is important to efficient business operation of the center, to the health and safety of the children, and to the better understanding of the child and the family.

- name of the child (including nickname)
- names of family members and ages of siblings
- names of other members of the household and their relationship to the child
- home address and telephone number
- name, address, telephone number (home, work, cell), and email addresses of employer(s) of parent(s)
- arrangement for payment of fees
- transportation plans for the child (including how the child will be transported and by whom)

- medical history and record of a recent physical examination of the child by a physician
- social-emotional history of the child
- name, address, and telephone number of the child's physician or clinic
- emergency medical treatment authorization
- name, address, and telephone number of a person (outside the family) to contact in an emergency if a member of the family cannot be reached
- permission to participate in the total school program (field trips, photos, videotaping, research, and so on)

To ensure that you have all the information and signed releases required to satisfy licensing and to cover liability questions, contact your local licensing agent and consult an attorney.

Forms

A number of sample forms included in the Director's Resources on the CourseMate website demonstrate various ways in which the information just listed can be recorded. These are only sample forms and cannot be used in the exact format presented, but they can provide a basis for developing appropriate forms to meet the specific needs of each center. For example, the director of a small cooperative preschool does not need all the data on family income that is required by Head Start or publicly funded programs, but needs details on family schedules to plan for parent participation.

Programs sponsored by public schools may or may not require family income information but will require a Medicaid number for those children entitled to the benefits of that program and also may need a birth certificate to validate the age of the child.

Because there is so much variation among programs about information required on children and families, directors must develop forms that meet the specific needs of the program.

In the case of early childhood education centers and preschools, applications for admission are often included on the center's webpage, which allows families to print out the forms that are relevant to them. In some instances the forms are automated so they can be submitted to the center electronically. If selection and grouping of the children require more subjective data than can be gleaned from the application form or any other written information that has been collected prior to admission, the director can arrange to talk with the parent(s).

After most of the children have been admitted and assigned to groups, those who have not yet been placed are held for deferred enrollment, or in the case of ongoing programs, put on a waiting list. If a child is rejected for reasons other than full enrollment, the reasons should be discussed with the family to avoid any misunderstandings that quickly could undermine the public relations efforts of the center staff and impair communication between the staff and potential clients from the community.

Confidentiality

Information on families and children that is recorded on forms or obtained by staff members during interviews or home visits is confidential and *must not be released* to unauthorized people without parental consent. Furthermore, the Family Educational Rights and Privacy Act of 1974 (FERPA) provides that any public or private educational institution that is the recipient of federal funds made available under any federal program administered by the U.S. Department of Education must give parents access to their children's educational records. Since all information in the files must remain available to parents, it is important that staff members use discretion when recording information to be placed in a child's permanent record. Parents should be informed of what information will be kept confidential and what will be available to teaching staff, office staff, and other support staff. Parents decide how much detail they are willing to release. They realize that emergency telephone numbers and names of people authorized to pick up the child will be needed by all teaching and office staff. However, they may choose to have medical histories and income information available only to the director and the lead teacher (Taylor, 2002).

Records and other confidential information should not be disclosed to anyone other than center personnel without written consent of the parent or guardian, unless its disclosure is necessary to protect the health or safety of the child. Written parental consent is required in order to pass information on to the public school by any preschool or Head Start program. As a general rule, parental consent should be obtained except in emergency cases or when it appears that the parent is a threat to the child (Family Educational Rights and Privacy Act, 1974). Centers that receive funds from government sources should be familiar with any regulations or guidelines on confidentiality and privacy that are tied to the funding source.

Center directors in collaboration with staff, parents, and board members can develop written policies for the protection of confidentiality and the disclosure of children's records. These policies should be made available to all program personnel and families (Feeney & Freeman, n.d.). The trust that develops between staff and families will be damaged if there is a breach of confidentiality. Setting aside one staff meeting each year to review the confidentiality policies is one way to encourage the staff to reaffirm their pledge to maintain confidentiality.

Intake Procedures

The director decides which staff members will be involved in each step of the intake procedure, but it is imperative that the child's teacher actively be involved throughout. The adult who will work directly with the child must interact with the child and family to begin to establish feelings of mutual trust among the child, the family, and the teacher.

Parents often feel apprehensive about placing children in an early childhood program. A carefully planned intake process that provides frequent opportunities to talk with the teacher, the director, and the social services staff (if available) can help parents cope with their feelings. At the same time, young children are often upset when they first are separated from their parents and family. Children worry about who will take care of them or how they will get home. Some children display regressive behaviors. Both teachers and parents need help to understand that children are uneasy about this new experience and must have special attention and care during this initial transition. Because children feel frightened and lonely, their transition to a new physical and social environment is done gradually and must be accompanied by continuous support from family members. For the mental health of both the parents and children, the sequences followed in the intake process should be arranged so that everyone involved will be able to cope successfully with the separation experience. Four steps are commonly employed in introducing the family and the child to the center program and to the teacher. They are discussed here because it is the director's responsibility to ensure that this careful intake procedure is implemented.

Initial Interview with Parents

The purpose of an initial interview is to get acquainted with the parent(s), answer their questions about the center program, communicate what will be expected of them, take them on a tour of the center, and familiarize them with the forms that must be filled out before their child can be admitted. It may be useful to go over the family information, the

child's social history, the medical history, the emergency information record, and the various release and permission forms during the interview to answer questions about any confusing items. The sample forms in the Director's Resources give some idea of the way these forms may look. The informality and friendliness of this first personal contact will set the tone for all future contacts. This is precisely the time to establish the foundation for mutual trust among director, teacher, parent, and child, so it is important that these interviews be conducted in a nonthreatening manner.

Scheduling the interview is usually done at the convenience of the family. Even though the teacher or the office staff may do the interview scheduling, it is essential that the director monitor it to ensure that families are not unduly inconvenienced. Careful consideration of family needs indicates that the center staff is sensitive to individual lifestyles and family preferences. When parents work, evenings or weekends may be best for interviews. Center staff members also must consider the transportation problems for some families, the availability of babysitters, and the schedules of other children in the family.

Home Visit with the Family

A home visit may be the next step in the intake procedure. The director first describes the purpose of home visits to the staff and goes over a home visit report with them before family appointments are made (see Working Paper 10-2). The purpose is

DIRECTOR'S CORNER

"We make it clear at the outset and are fairly firm with parents about spending some time here with their child because we know, from experience, that even a child who comes in with apparent ease may have a problem two months hence, which harks back to skipping the gradual transition into the group. Even if a parent can spend only 15 minutes in the morning with a child for a week or two, we accept that and make it clear we expect it. My staff is sold on the importance of gradual separation and will even come in 15 or 30 minutes early—before we open—to give a new child time in the classroom with both the parent and the teacher present."

—Director, corporate-sponsored center

not to evaluate the home, but rather to gather information that will enable the staff to have a better understanding of the child. Trust between the parent(s) and the staff will be destroyed and communication impaired if the family interprets the purpose of these home visits as evaluative. Observing a family at home will help the teacher understand the family lifestyle and the family attitudes toward the child.

Initial Visit to the Center

The scheduling of the initial visits to the center is arranged by the director and the staff before home visits begin so that information about visiting the center can be given to parents during the home visit.

This initial visit to the classroom is planned to help the child make that first big step from home and the trusted caregiver to the center and a new caring adult. For preschool children, the visit can last from 30 to 45 minutes and should terminate before the child is tired or bored. This entire orientation process is longer and more complex for infants and toddlers. Although the teacher is clearly responsible for working with the child and the accompanying adult during preliminary visits, it is important for the director to be available to greet the newcomers and answer any questions that might arise. It provides a perfect opportunity for the director and the parent(s) to get to know each other better and is a good time to give them a copy of the parent handbook (see the CourseMate website for a sample of a parent handbook).

Phasing in the Children

The first three intake steps for preschool children described here can be implemented in all types of center-based programs. The scheduling of each step should be adjusted to individual family needs and obviously is much more difficult for working parents. In fact, the scheduling of these steps may seem to be somewhat unrealistic for full-day child care programs but can be done through very creative planning. Implementing the intake procedures for all ages of children in child care programs could involve evenings, early mornings, or weekends. The director, therefore, must work out the scheduling with the staff and may give comp time to professional staff or overtime for hourly employees.

The phasing in (or "staggered entrance"), which is the fourth and last step in the intake procedure, will, of necessity, be very different in ongoing child care programs than in programs that are just starting or in those based on the typical school calendar. Arranging for the staggered entrance of a group of 12 to 15 preschool children at the beginning of the year poses a complex scheduling problem, but it is an essential step in the orientation process. Because scheduling is very involved, it is important for the director and staff to consult with parents about convenient times for them to come and stay with their child. Successful implementation of the plan depends on staff and family commitment to it. Extended intake procedures for younger children can require special planning.

In public school–sponsored programs, which usually have no precedent for gradual intake of new children, early childhood staff will have to meet with administrators and building principals to explain the importance of this procedure for the well-being of children and families. Because some early childhood programs in public schools are considered part of the elementary school and are accredited with the elementary school in the local school district, they usually are expected to provide a given number of instructional days to maximize the amount of state funds they receive. Developmentally appropriate practices like phasing in children often is one of the first issues that creates conflict between developmental early childhood educators and the more academic-school, readiness-focused elementary educators.

In full-day child care programs, the major problem is to find a trusted adult to stay with the child until all people involved feel comfortable about the child being at the center every day for the full day. When a family needs full-day care for a child, both parents usually are working, or the child may be a member of a one-parent family or in foster care. In these special cases, a grandparent or other member of the extended family may be the best person to provide the emotional support necessary for the child during the phasing-in period.

If there is any question among staff members about the importance of the gradual orientation program for the child, the family, and the success of the total program, it is up to the director to help everyone understand that this process represents the next logical step in developing mutual trust within the teacher-child-family unit. Orienting children is usually exciting and productive for the teacher, but it is also time consuming and energy draining. The process can be successful only if the entire staff understands its relevance to the total program and recognizes it as being consistent with developmentally appropriate practice.

SUMMARY

Most of the decisions about grouping children appropriately are made by the director, who must consider the unique needs of the children, available space, and licensing regulations about ratios and group size. Policy decisions about chronological or multiage grouping must be made before children are assigned to groups. Skills and experience of staff, ages of children, and the numbers and types of children with special needs selected for admission are all factors that will affect where children will be assigned.

Enrolling children involves filling out forms, interviewing parents, making home visits, and gradually phasing in the children. Although the staggered-enrollment procedure is complex and time consuming, it is a critical step in the process of building trust among the school, the child, and the family.

TRY IT OUT!

❶ Using Working Paper 10-1, work out a staggered enrollment schedule for 12 children, then reflect on your personal reactions to the information in this chapter under the heading "Intake Procedures" (page 232).

  • Did you think about how parents might feel about the procedures described in the various steps of the intake procedures?
  • Were you having any particular negative (or positive) feelings about the intake procedures?
  • Did you identify with this material as a
    • student?
    • classroom teacher?
    • prospective parent?
    • director?
    • other?

❷ Working with another student, role-play an initial interview with a young mother who is sending an only child who is 3 years old to your program. The Sample Personal History (Director's Resource 10-1) and the Policy Summary Form (Director's Resource 10-2) are to be explained during this interview. At the close of the interview, discuss reactions to this role-play with the entire group.

❸ In groups of four, role-play a home visit with a mother, father, and their 3-year-old daughter. When you arrive, you see no evidence of toys in the home, and you find the child dressed and sitting in a chair with her hands folded, apparently having been told to "be good and sit quietly while we talk to your teacher." The purpose of the visit is to explain the initial visit to the center and the staggered enrollment plan for the child.

❹ After the role-play, stay in groups of four and evaluate your reaction to the child and to the family. Evaluate your reactions as you played teacher, mother, father, or child. Consider how successful the teacher was at developing a relationship with the child. Fill in the Home Visit Report (Working Paper 10-2) in sufficient detail so the director will have a clear picture of what transpired during the visit.

Working Paper 10-1

(for use with Try It Out! 1)

DEVELOP A STAGGERED ENROLLMENT PLAN

- Enroll 12 children over a period of eight days.

- The plan is for a half-day preschool that meets from 9:00 a.m. to 11:30 a.m. daily.

- Remember to have children come for shorter hours, in small groups, and gradually move toward having all children together for the full 2 1/2 hours on the ninth day of school.

- Fill in the time slots with the child's number—1, 2, 3, …, 12.

- Time slots can be adjusted to suit your plan.

Week 1	Monday—1	Tuesday—2	Wednesday—3	Thursday—4		Friday—5	
9:00							
9:30							
10:00							
10:30							
11:00							
11:30							
Week 2	Monday—6	Tuesday—7	Wednesday—8	Thursday—9		Friday—10	
9:00				Children 1–12		Children 1–12	
9:30							
10:00							
10:30							
11:00							
11:30				↓		↓	

Working Paper 10-2

(for use with Try It Out! 4)

SAMPLE HOME VISIT/PARENT CONTACT REPORT

Center _____

Type of Program _____

1 Name of visitor _____ Title _____

2 Child's name _____

3 Parent or guardian _____

4 Address _____

5 Date and time of visit or meeting _____

6 Purpose of visit or meeting _____

_____

_____

7 Specific action taken as result of visit or meeting _____

_____

_____

_____

_____

_____

_____

_____

8 Observations and comments _____

_____

_____

_____

_____

_____

_____

_____

_____

You can download a full-size version of this form on the Education CourseMate website.

Director's Resource 10-1

(for use with Try It Out! 2)

SAMPLE PERSONAL HISTORY—YOUR CHILD'S DEVELOPMENT

Date _____

Child's Name _____ Nickname _____

Address _____ ZIP _____ Phone _____

Date of Birth _____ Place of birth _____ Sex _____

I. The Child's Family

   Parents or Guardians

   A. Name _____ Birth Date _____

      Education (include highest grade completed or degrees) _____

      _____

      Occupation _____ Usual working hours _____

      Work phone _____

   B. Name _____ Birth Date _____

      Education (include highest grade completed or degrees) _____

      Occupation _____ Usual working hours _____

      Work phone _____

   Status of Parents (Check)   Living together _____   Living apart _____

   Child lives with _____

   If parents work or are students, who keeps the child in their absence?

   Circle one   Grandparent   Other Relative   Friend   Paid Sitter   Other

   Other children in the family (list in order of birth)

Name	Sex	Birth Date	What grade if in school

Additional members of household (give number)

Friends _____   Others _____

Boarders _____   Relatives _____

(Indicate relationships)

(continues)

Director's Resource 10-1 *(continued)*

What part do these other persons have in the care of your child? _____
_____

Has your child been separated from his/her parents for long periods of time, and if so, why?
_____

Have you moved frequently? _____

What language is usually spoken at home? _____

(If more than one, what other language(s) are spoken?) _____

C. Income _____ (per month) _____ (per year) _____

D. Medical card number _____ (parent)

   Child's number _____

II. Development in Early Childhood

Comment on the health of the mother during pregnancy _____

Comment on the health of your child during delivery and infancy _____
_____

When did you child walk? _____ When did your child talk? _____

Is your child adopted? _____ Does he/she know it? _____

Does your child have bladder control? _____ Child's terminology _____

Does your child have bowel control? _____ Child's terminology _____

Does your child need help when going to the bathroom? _____

Does your child need reminding about going to the bathroom? _____

Does your child usually take a nap? _____ At what time? _____

Describe any special needs, handicaps, or health problems. _____
_____

Does your child have any difficulty saying what he/she wants or do you have any trouble understanding his/her speech? _____

III. Eating Habits

What is your child's general attitude toward eating? _____

What foods does your child especially like? _____

For which meal is your child most hungry? _____

Does the child feed himself/herself entirely? _____

Does your child dislike any food in particular? _____

Is your child on a special diet? _____

Does your child take a bottle? _____

(continues)

Director's Resource 10-1 *(continued)*

Does your child eat or chew things that are not food? Explain. _____

Do you have any concerns about your child's eating habits? Explain. _____

Is there any food your child should not eat for medical, religious, or personal reasons? _____
_____

IV. Play and Social Experiences

Has your child participated in any group experiences?_____

Where?_____

Did your child enjoy it?_____

Do other playmates visit the child?_____

Does your child visit other playmates in their homes?_____

How does your child relate to other children?_____

Does your child prefer to play alone? _____ With other children?_____

Does your child worry a lot or is he/she very afraid of anything?_____

What causes worry or fear?_____

Does your child have any imaginary playmates? _____ Explain _____
_____

Does your child have any pets?_____

What are your child's favorite toys and/or activities?_____
_____

What is your child's favorite TV program?_____

How long does your child watch TV each day?_____

What are your child's favorite books?_____

How many times a week is your child read to?_____

Is there anything else about your child's play or playmates which the school should know?_____
_____

V. Discipline

In most circumstances, do you consider your child easily managed, fairly easy to manage, or difficult to manage?_____

What concerns do you presently have about your child?_____
_____

How are these concerns dealt with?_____
_____

(continues)

Director's Resource 10-1 *(continued)*

VI. Parent's Impression and Attitudes

From your point of view, what were the events which seemed to have had the greatest impact on your child (moving, births, deaths, severe illness of family members, divorce)? _____

_____

_____

How would you describe your child at the present time? What changes have you seen in your child during the past year? _____

_____

Does your child have any behavior characteristics which you hope will change? Please describe. _____

_____

In what ways would you like to see your child develop during the school year?

_____

_____

_____

_____

_____

_____

_____

_____
Signature(s) of person(s) filling out this questionnaire

You can download a full-size version of this form on the Education CourseMate website.

Director's Resource 10-2

SAMPLE SUMMARY OF POLICIES FORM

(for use with Try It Out! 2)

BOMBECK FAMILY LEARNING CENTER SUMMARY OF POLICIES

PLEASE SIGN AND RETURN THAT YOU HAVE RECEIVED AND READ THIS NOTICE. THANK YOU!!!!

_____

I have received and read the summary of Bombeck Family Learning Center polices.

Child(ren)'s name: _____

Parent Signature: _____

Date: _____

The following is a summary of some of the policies that impact daily life at the center. Complete information can be found in the Parent Handbook which we encourage you to read and keep on hand for reference. Please address questions or concerned to the director.

Attendance

A parent should *notify the Center by 9:00 a.m.* when a child will not be attending on a scheduled day. This procedure also applies to those children who attend half-day kindergarten.

Drop Off–Pick Up

Children must be brought to and picked up inside the child's classroom. A Child Release Form must be on file in the office for anyone other than a parent or guardian to pick up a child. Picture ID is required. Children may be dropped off at any time during the day except lunch and naptime.

Illness/Sick Policy

As a Center licensed by the State of Ohio, we are required to strictly follow procedures concerning communicable diseases to protect the children and staff at the Center. *The parent will be expected to pick up the child immediately if a child exhibits the following symptoms:*

Temperature of at least 100 degrees Fahrenheit – or less if accompanied by another symptom of illness

Two or more bouts of diarrhea

Severe coughing

Difficult or rapid breathing

Yellowish skin or eyes

Redness, discharge, burning, itching of the eye

Infected skin patches, spots or rashes

Dark urine or gray or white stool

(continues)

Director's Resource 10-2 *(continued)*

Stiff neck with elevated temperature

Lice, scabies or other parasitic infestation

Vomiting one or more times, or if accompanied by another symptom of illness

The child or staff member will not be readmitted to the center until s/he is symptom free for a period of 24 hours, or until a physician's written permission verifies that there is no risk of contagion.

Medications

"Administration of Medication by the Center Personnel" form must accompany any medication, prescription or over-the-counter drugs to be administered to a child. The child's name and specific times and dosage must be written on the form provided in the classroom each day. "As needed" is insufficient information.

Administration of medication by a person other than a center staff member and other than the parent, requires written permission signed by the parent. Name of the person, date, time and dosage should be included.

Payment of Tuition

Tuition payments are to be paid one full week in advance. If payment is not received on time a *$25.00 late charge will be added to the balance.*

Tuition payments and late charges not paid by the following week are cause for withdrawal of service by the center

Late Pick Up Fees

A late fee will be charged for children left at the Center after 6:00 p.m. Late fees are charged as follows: (center clock used as basis). Calls ahead do not negate late charges.

6:01–6:30 – one dollar per minute 6:31 – on is five dollars per minute

Back Up Plan

Please have a back-up plan in place for medical exclusions or emergency closings.

Parent Participation, Visitors and Custody

Any custodial parent, custodian, or guardian of a child enrolled at the Center is welcome to visit at any time.

Visitors to the center are required to sign in and out of the building at the front desk.

When custody rights or visitation of a child has been determined by a court or other legal entity, a copy of the order must be provided to the Center.

Medical Emergencies

The center's staff is trained in First Aid procedures. If a serious medical emergency should arise, a call to the University Public Safety Department would summon an emergency vehicle staffed with EMTs who would evaluate the situation and transport to an area hospital if necessary. Parents will be notified immediately and a staff member will stay with the child until parents arrive. The child's emergency transport, health and medical records will accompany them. A child safety seat is available if needed.

(continues)

Director's Resource 10-2 *(continued)*

Accidents

In case of accidents, a staff member will complete an incident report that is given to the parent on the day of the occurrence, which must be signed and returned to the teacher.

Child Abuse

If any abuse or neglect is seen or suspected involving a child enrolled at the Bombeck Center, the situation must be reported to the Children's Services Board in the county in which the child resides.

Discipline

Discipline is not punishment. If conflicts occur, staff members strive to help children find alternative modes of behavior and explain why inappropriate behavior is not acceptable. The Center strictly adheres to the discipline guidelines set forth by the Ohio child care Licensing Code.

Emergency Closings

The Bombeck Center will make every effort to remain open in the event of inclement weather. However, if weather conditions warrant closing, the center will follow the University's directions for the closure. Please check your local television broadcast of school closing. Closing will also be posted on the Bombeck Center Facebook page.

Vacations

Families are entitled to five vacation days annually. One week advance notice is requested. Vacation request forms may be picked up at the front desk

Grievance Procedures

In the event that a problem or complain should arise, the following are suggested procedures for resolution:

It is strongly encouraged the issue be resolved with the staff member involved. If the issue is not resolved at that level, the issue should be brought to the attention of the director, who will counsel with all individuals involved in order to resolve the issue in a positive way.

Use of Videotapes and Photographs

The parent of every child enrolled at the Center must sign a "Permission to Videotape and Photograph Form". University students may be required to periodically videotape or photograph the children as they participate in classroom activities. The university photographer also takes photographs at the Bombeck Center.

Source: Reprinted by permission of the Bombeck Family Learning Center of the University of Dayton.

You can download a full-size version of this form on the Education CourseMate website.

Director's Resource 10-3

SAMPLE PERMISSION FORM

While your child is enrolled in this program, he/she will be involved in a number of special activities for which we need your permission. Please read the following information carefully. You are encouraged to ask questions about anything that is unclear to you. You, of course, have the option of withdrawing permission at any time.

_____
(Child's Name)

(Please circle your choice)

A. I DO DO NOT give my permission for my child to go on walks with the classroom teacher and class in the nearby neighborhood.

B. I DO DO NOT give my permission for my child to be screened for speech and language.

C. I DO DO NOT give my permission for my child to be screened for hearing.

D. I DO DO NOT give my permission for my child to be screened for specific educational needs.

E. From time to time photographs of our preschool program will be made for educational and publicity purposes. These pictures will be representative of the enriching experiences offered your child during the year.

I DO DO NOT give my permission for my child to be photographed for use in educational, nonprofit publications/presentations intended to further the cause of public education. This permission is applicable for current as well as future project use.

As part of this program, your child's records may be included in research that evaluates the value of the program. In all cases, the confidentiality of individual children's records is maintained.

_____
Parent's Signature

_____
Date

Director's Resource 10-4

SAMPLE CHILD CARE APPLICATION (requesting income information)

For office use only

District Status: _____

Income Status: _____

Priority Status: _____

Date Application Received: _____

Date Eligible for Entrance: _____

Enrollment Age: _____

Child's Name: _____ Date of Birth: _____ Sex: _____

Race, Nationality, or Ethnic Group: _____

Address: _____ Phone: _____

Mother's Name: _____ Date of Birth: _____ SS # _____

Father's Name: _____ Date of Birth: _____ SS # _____

Child lives with _____

Children attend the center-based program four (4) half days per week; they eat lunch and snack at the center. Transportation is provided for handicapped or special needs children.

Do you wish to apply for center-based program? Yes ___ No

Session preferred A.M. ____ 8:45–11:45

P.M. ____ 12:45–3:45

Children and families in the home-based program are visited once per week in the home and are transported to the center on Friday for a group experience. The home-based teacher will assist parents in creating a home environment to promote children's growth and development. This program is in the morning only.

Director's Resource 10-4

Do you wish to apply for home-based program? Yes ____ No ____

* *

Family Size: _____

Family Income:

$ _____ per week $ _____ per month $ _____ per year

Source of Reimbursement or Services (Circle "Yes" or "No" for each source)

YES	NO	EPSDT/Medicaid (Latest certification #):	___
YES	NO	Federal, State or Local Agency:	___
YES	NO	In-kind Provider:	___
YES	NO	Insurance:	___
		I.D. #:	___
YES	NO	WIC	
YES	NO	Food Stamps	

Does this child or any of your family members have a disability or special need?

Describe: _____

How well does your child speak and understand English? _____

How did you obtain information about this program? _____

Director's Resource 10-5

SAMPLE APPLICATION (no income information requested)

Walnut Corner Children's Center Preregistration Form

CHILD'S FAMILY INFORMATION

Child's Name _____ Name Used _____

Date of Birth, or Expected Date of Birth _____

Child's Address _____

Father/Guardian Name _____ Mother/Guardian Name _____

Home Address _____ Home Address _____

Employer _____ Employer _____

Address _____ Address _____

Business Phone _____ Business Phone _____

REQUESTED DAYS OF ATTENDANCE

Days: M   T   W   TH   F   Hours: _____ AM _____ PM

Requested Start Date: _____

HOW DID YOU LEARN ABOUT WALNUT CORNER CHILDREN'S CENTER?

Personal Referral/If so, who? _____

Newspaper _____ Radio _____ Website _____ Other _____

Thank you for this information

PLEASE INCLUDE THE NONREFUNDABLE $25 REGISTRATION FEE WITH THIS FORM.

THIS FEE WILL SECURE YOUR CHILD'S NAME ON OUR WAITING LIST.

 You can download a full-size version of these forms on the Education CourseMate website.

Director's Resource 10-6

SAMPLE STUDENT ENROLLMENT FORM

(Public School-Sponsored Program) STUDENT ENROLLMENT FORM

(MUST BE RETAINED IN STUDENT'S CUMULATIVE RECORD)

Assigned to: Gr _____ Hr _____
SDF sent to Census _____
Type a new CR _____
CR in office file _____
CR requested _____
Health Record Yes _____ No _____
Rec'd. 4-part SDF _____

Name of school student is entering _____ Grade Enter _____ Special Ed _____
Name _____
Student's Legal Name (as listed on birth certificate)

Circle   Circle
Sex: Male Female   Race: Black White Other
Address _____ Apt. No. _____ ZIP Code _____ Phone No. _____
Place of birth _____ Date of birth _____
          City   State   Country   Mo   Day   Yr
Check one of the birth verifications listed below:
❑ Birth Certificate No. _____   ❑ Baptismal Certificate _____
❑ Physician's Record   ❑ Passport

	DPT	Polio	Measles	Rubella	Mumps
IMMUNIZATION DATA					

Director's Resource 10-6 *(continued)*

	Name	Place of birth State	Country	Deceased (Date)
Father:				
Mother:				
Step-Parent:				
Guardian:				

SOCIAL RECORD

	Occupation	Place of Employment	Business Phone No.
Father's occupation			
Mother's occupation			

If family is supported by another source indicate: _____

Name of Brothers and Sisters:	Still in School:	
School Attendance	School of Preschool	

Circle one:
Family Status: Married   Single   Divorced   Separated
                   Remarried
Of parent: Student is living with_____ Relationship_____
LANGUAGE OTHER THAN ENGLISH SPOKEN IN HOME: _____
Did student attend this school last year?
❑ Yes
❑ No Name of school _____ Address _____

Director's Resource 10-6

❑ Yes – Privacy Requested: If this box is checked, no information pertaining to this student will be released to any person or institution (including colleges or universities) without your written approval.

❑ No – Privacy is not requested Parent/Guardian's Signature _____ Date: _____
In case of emergency, call _____
          Name   Relationship   Phone No

Director's Resource 10-7A

Bombeck Family Learning Center

Demonstration School for the School of Education and Allied Professions
941 Alberta St.
Dayton, Ohio 45409
(937) 2292158
http://www.udayton.edu/education/bombeckcenter

PRE-ENROLLMENT FORM OF CHILD DEVELOPMENT LEVELS

Child's Name: _____ Today's Date: _____
Child's Date of Birth: _____ Current Age: ____ yrs. ____ mos.
Parent/Guardian filling out form: _____

Birth to 9 months: Security Stage

Sensory Preferences: My child enjoys learning about his/her world **most** by :
____seeing ____hearing ____tasting ____smelling ____touching
Relationships:
    My child responds to others by:
____gazing ____making faces ____smiling ____making sounds ____other:
    My child gets my attention by:
____crying ____gesturing ____holding on tight ____squealing ____other:
Language: My child's language development is shown by:
____smiling/gurgling when spoken to
____using different cries/sounds for different needs
____imitating sounds, rhythms, tones of adult talk
____playing games like peekaboo, pat-a-cake, etc.
Movement: My child's physical development is evidenced by:
____moving his/her arms, legs, and other body parts
____enjoying touching and being touched
____rolling over ____holding up his/her head ____scooting/crawling ____other:
Emotions: My child is generally
____calm ____agitated ____fussy ____sensitive ____alert ____happy ____demanding
Health: My child has ___no health issues ____colds ____allergies ____fevers ____other:

Developed by Diana Smith, Director of Program Development, University of Dayton, Bombeck Family Learning Center   1 1/4/11

You can download a full-size version of these forms on the Education CourseMate website.

Director's Resource 10-7B

Bombeck
Family Learning Center

Demonstration School for
the School of Education
and Allied Professions
941 Alberta St.
Dayton, Ohio 45409
(937) 2292158
http://www.udayton.edu/education/bombeckcenter

PRE-ENROLLMENT FORM OF CHILD DEVELOPMENT LEVELS

Child's Name: _____ Today's Date: _____

Child's Date of Birth: _____ Current Age: ____yrs. ____mos.

Parent/Guardian filling out form: _____

8-18 months: Exploration Stage

<u>Sensory Preferences:</u> My child enjoys learning about his/her world **most** by:

_____seeing _____hearing _____tasting _____smelling _____touching

<u>Relationships:</u> My child responds to others by:

____making sounds ____physically approaching /touching ___ watching ____imitating _____other:

My child gets attention by:

___ squealing/crying ____touching /hitting_____ pinching /biting____ watching/waiting_____ other:

<u>Language:</u> My child's language development is demonstrated by:

_____responding to their name, to directions, or to questions

_____expressing emotions through verbalizing

_____demonstrating an awareness of concepts of cause/effect, more/less

_____adding words to their vocabulary, imitating the tone and rhythm of adult speech

_____recognizing people and objects by name

_____demonstrating an interest in books and pictures

<u>Movement:</u> My child's physical development is evidenced by:

becoming mobile by ___scooting ___bouncing ___crawling ___cruising ___walking___other:

___standing or sitting _____ going up or down ramps/steps _____ bending over without falling

___ holding objects ____ pushing toys ____ opening/closing items ____using tools ____gesturing

<u>Emotions:</u> My child displays his/her emotion by:

____smiling/laughing ____cuddling _____crying ____ tensing/screaming when angry ____other:

<u>Health:</u> My child generally has:

___no health issues____colds____ear aches ___ allergies ___breathing problems ____fevers____other:

Developed by Diana Smith, Director of Program Development, University of Dayton, Bombeck Family Learning Center   1 1/4/11

Director's Resource 10-7C

Bombeck
Family Learning Center

Demonstration School for
the School of Education
and Allied Professions
941 Alberta St.
Dayton, Ohio 45409
(937) 2292158
http://www.udayton.edu/education/bombeckcenter

PRE-ENROLLMENT FORM OF CHILD DEVELOPMENT LEVELS

Child's Name: _____ Today's Date: _____

Child's Date of Birth: _____ Current Age: ____yrs. ____mos.

Parent/Guardian filling out form: _____

16 to 36 months: Toddlers – Independent Stage

<u>Sensory Preferences:</u> My child enjoys learning about his/her world **most** by:

_____seeing _____hearing _____tasting _____smelling _____touching

<u>Relationships:</u> My child responds to others by:

____communicating wants/needs ____asserting themselves _____ displaying empathy _____other:

My child gets attention by:

_____asking questions ____demanding _____cooperating _____physical interaction _____other:

<u>Language:</u> My child's language development is demonstrated by:

_____initiating conversations, back and forth discourse, conflict over "mine" or "no"

_____ repeating after others or re-enacting series of events or daily adult tasks

_____ saying single words ____phrases ____sentences ____

_____following directions, asking questions, naming objects, people, places

_____demonstrate understanding of concepts of shape, size, color, type, other cognitive skills

_____ "telling" stories through play - with or without words

<u>Movement:</u> My child's physical development is evidenced by:

_____ walking _____running _____climbing _____jumping _____stepping "over" _____ up and down stairs

_____using small objects _____using writing and art materials _____pouring/serving food ____other:

<u>Emotions:</u> My child displays emotional responses such as:

_____empathy ____pride in accomplishment _____ generosity _____comforting ____demanding ____other:

<u>Health:</u> My child generally has

_____no health issues____cold/flu____earaches ___allergies ____asthma ____fevers____other:

Developed by Diana Smith, Director of Program Development, University of Dayton, Bombeck Family Learning Center   1 1/4/11

Director's Resource 10-7D

Bombeck
Family Learning Center

Demonstration School for
the School of Education
and Allied Professions
941 Alberta St.
Dayton, Ohio 45409
(937) 2292158
http://www.udayton.edu/education/bombeckcenter

PRE-ENROLLMENT FORM OF CHILD DEVELOPMENT LEVELS

Child's Name: _____ Today's Date: _____

Child's Date of Birth: _____ Current Age: ____yrs. ____mos.

Parent/Guardian filling out form: _____

3-5 years – Preschooler

<u>Physical Development:</u> My child's physical activity includes:

___running ___jumping ___climbing ___ skipping ___galloping ___ creative movement such as dancing

___ coordinated movements ____small muscle control ____large muscle control ____other:

<u>Social/Emotional Development:</u> My child displays the following behaviors:

___ enjoys learning ____develops friends _____ follows directions/rules ____ relates well to adults/peers

___ emotional awareness ___shares easily ____takes turns ____resolve conflicts without aggression

___ develops conscience ____copes with stress ____shows resilience to adversity ___exhibits self-control

<u>Cognitive Development:</u> My child has the ability to :

_____ think about past/present/future

_____re-enact storylines accurately following sequence of events

_____coordinate and assume roles during dramatic play

_____organize thoughts into explanations, questions, and other categories

_____ uses symbols such to represent reality – ie pictures, words, numbers

_____ understands "pretend" and the difference between imaginary and real in most instances

_____ able to predict what will happen next with some accuracy

_____solves problems through thoughtful reasoning with guidance

_____ expresses thoughts and feeling several ways (verbalizes, draws, sings, moves creatively)

<u>Health:</u> My child generally has:

___no health issues____cold/flu ___ earaches ____ allergies ____ asthma/breathing difficulty __ fever

_____within normal range of physical growth ____has regular check-ups ____ has received immunizations

Developed by Diana Smith, Director of Program Development, University of Dayton, Bombeck Family Learning Center   1 1/4/11

Director's Resource 10-8

SAMPLE CHILD'S MEDICAL STATEMENT

Enrollment Date _____

Day Care Center/Preschool Certificate of Medical Examination To be Completed by Family Physician or Clinic

This is to certify that _____

Child's Name _____   Birth Date _____

Mother _____ Address _____ Phone _____

Father _____ Address _____ Phone _____

was examined by me on _____, and based on his/her medical history

Date of Examination _____ and physical condition at the time of this examination, is free from apparent communicable disease, and is in suitable condition for enrollment in a child day care facility; and has had the immunizations required by Section 3313.671 of the Revised Code for admission to school, or has had the immunizations required by the State Department of Health for infants and toddlers, or is to be exempted from these requirements for medical reasons.

Tuberculin Test (within last year for new enrollee) Date _____

Type of test _____ Results _____

DPT Series and booster dates 1st _____ 2nd _____ 3rd _____ 4th _____ 5th _____

Oral Polio

Series dates 1st _____ 2nd _____ 3rd _____ 4th _____

The 5th DPT and 4th polio are normally administered just prior to kindergarten.

Source: Reprinted by permission of the Bombeck Family Learning Center of the University of Dayton.

 You can download a full-size version of these forms on the Education CourseMate website.

Director's Resource 10-8

Measles (Rubella, 10-day)	Date _____	
Rubella (3-day)	Date _____	
Mumps	Date _____	
Haemophilus b Polysaccharide (HIB)	Date _____	(HIB vaccine is required for children ages 2 years through 4 years)

Is able to participate in all regular activities except _____

Remarks _____

Physician's Signature _____ Date _____

Clinic Name _____ Phone _____

Office Location _____

City, State, ZIP _____

Parent should retain this sheet when child withdraws from center

Director's Resource 10-9

SAMPLE EMERGENCY INFORMATION RECORD

Child's Name _____

Home Address _____

_____

Father's name/Husband   Place of Employment _____   Bus. Phone _____
(or guardian) _____

Mother's name/Wife   Place of Employment _____   Bus. Phone _____
(or guardian) _____

Please fill in information below so that the school may act more effectively in event of illness or injury to the child.

EMERGENCY: Person to be called if parent (husband or wife) cannot be reached

Name _____ Address _____ Phone _____

Date _____ Parent's Signature (or guardian) _____

Director's Resource 10-10

CHILD RELEASE FORM

To maintain the safety and protection of your child, please provide us with a complete list of persons who may pick up your child or children from the center. Anyone other than the parent should sign in at the front desk. The staff will ask for picture identification before releasing the child(ren).

Child's name: _____   Classroom: _____
Child's name: _____   Classroom: _____
Child's name: _____   Classroom: _____
Child's name: _____   Classroom: _____

The following individuals have my permission to pick up the child(ren) listed above from the Bombeck Family Learning Center:

Name: _____   Relationship: _____
Name: _____   Relationship: _____
Name: _____   Relationship: _____
Name: _____   Relationship: _____

I have instructed these individuals to sign in at the front desk and be prepared to present picture identification when requesting release of the child(ren). Questions or concerns should be directed to me at the following phone numbers:

Work: _____   Home: _____   Cell: _____

If efforts to reach me should fail, please call the following person to verify permission to pick up my child(ren):

Name: _____   Relationship: _____

Parent Signature: _____   Date: _____

Source: Reprinted by permission of the Bombeck Family Learning Center of the University of Dayton.

You can download a full-size version of these forms on the Education CourseMate website.

REFERENCES

Allen, K. E. & Cowdery, G. E. (2011). *The exceptional child: Inclusion in early childhood education* (6th ed.). Clifton Park, NY: Thomson Delmar Learning.

ADA Amendments Act of 2008, Public Law 110–325, 122 Stat. 3553 (2008).

Decker, C. A. & Decker, J. R. (2008). *Planning and administering early childhood programs* (9th ed.). Upper Saddle River, NJ: Prentice Hall.

Dinnebeil, L., McInerney, W., Roth, J. & Ramaswamy, V. (2001). Itinerant early childhood special education services: Service delivery in one state. *Journal of Early Intervention, 24,* 35–44.

The Family Educational Rights and Privacy Act (Buckley Amendment). (1974). The 1974 Education Amendments, 20 U.S.C.A. Sec 1232g. (Supp. 1975).

Feeney, S. & Freeman, N. (n.d.). *Ethics and the early childhood educator: Using the NAEYC Code of Ethics, Section ll.* Washington, DC: NAEYC.

Gonzalez-Mena, J. & Widmeyer Eyer, D. (2008). *Infants, toddlers and caregivers: A curriculum of respectful care and education* (8th ed.). New York: McGraw-Hill.

Katz, L. G. & Chard, S. C. (2000). *Engaging children's minds: The project approach* (2nd ed.). Stamford, CN: Ablex.

National Association for the Education of Young Children. (2007). *NAEYC early childhood program standards and accreditation criteria: The mark of quality in early childhood education.* Washington, DC: Author.

Read, K., Gardner, P. & Mahler, B. (1993). *Early childhood programs: Early childhood relationships and learning* (9th ed.). Orlando, FL: Harcourt.

Taylor, B. (2002). *Early childhood program management: People and procedures.* Columbus OH: Merrill.

U.S. Department of Justice (n.d.). Commonly asked questions about child care centers and the Americans with Disabilities Act. (Retrieved from http://www.ada.gov/childq%26a.htm.)

11

Supporting QUALITY CURRICULUM

Bombeck Family Learning Center

Program administrators support curriculum so that enriching experiences are woven throughout every child's day.

For the director and educational leader of an early childhood program, decisions about curriculum are among the most difficult to make. The increasing national focus on the importance of the early years for brain development, school readiness, and sound emotional development provides both opportunities for the field and pressure to make informed decisions for the director and staff (Denton Flanagan & McPhee, 2009; Dickinson & Porche, 2011; Education Commission of the States, 2009; Kagan & Kauerz, 2007; Klein & Knitzer, 2006). Public awareness of the importance of quality early care and education is growing. Understanding the many factors that constitute quality and which impact today's curriculum decisions is a monumental task for the director, who must understand developmentally appropriate practices, early learning content standards, accountability, appropriate assessment, school readiness, achievement gaps, and teaching children in poverty, children with disabilities, and children who are English-language learners. Not only do young children require an experience-rich environment in the early years, but it is now apparent that children who lack key experiences are more likely to start kindergarten without the fundamental knowledge and skills necessary for school success (Preschool Curriculum Evaluation Research Consortium, 2008). With this in mind, the director must be the "curriculum mentor" who embraces the challenge of leading a program that meets the needs of the whole child while also sorting through societal pressures that challenge the traditional notions of early childhood curriculum. (In some larger programs, the director may share the role of curriculum mentor with a curriculum specialist.)

Objectives

After reading this chapter, you should be able to:

- Describe the role of the director as educational leader and curriculum mentor.
- Explain the need for a comprehensive definition of curriculum.
- Apply the principles of developmentally appropriate curriculum when mentoring teachers.
- Describe how the director can encourage practices that support intentional teaching.
- Identify the components of a developmentally appropriate assessment system and explain how to coach teachers to develop assessment practices that work in their classroom.
- Explain effective strategies for helping teachers to address content standards and developmental skills within a developmentally appropriate curriculum.
- Identify the strategies that support a seamless birth to age 3 early childhood system.

Standards Addressed in This Chapter

naeyc Professional Preparation Standard 1, 3, 4, 5, 6

naeyc Administrator Competencies
Management Knowledge and Skills 4, 8
Early Childhood Knowledge and Skills 2, 3, 4, 9

naeyc Accreditation Standards 2, 3, 4, 9

As the educational leader of an early childhood program, the director needs to be aware of curriculum requirements that constitute a quality program and that support the center's mission. The director must monitor the richness and appropriateness of the curriculum and serve as a curriculum mentor for teachers who need a forum for critical reflection and feedback as well as support and resources. The director is responsible for ensuring that all teachers in the center know that everyone is accountable for offering a high-quality program each and every day. The curriculum should be part of the center's culture, which means that it reflects the culture of the children and families who use the center and its programs and is also informed by the culture of the professionals who design and implement it. By being part of the center's culture, high-quality curriculum should be apparent to all who enter the center and see children's work samples and documentation on the walls. Evidence of the importance placed on curriculum should be apparent when teachers talk in the break room, during staff meetings, and most definitely during dedicated planning time. Parents should see evidence of curriculum in the parent handbook and should hear about it informally during drop-off and pick-up transition times and more formally during the centers' open house events and parent conferences. The importance placed on curriculum should also be evident on the center's website and Facebook page, where parents and other stakeholders can get daily updates including the curriculum in action.

By meeting regularly with teaching teams to discuss the curriculum that is evolving in each classroom, the director and the curriculum specialist, if applicable, clearly articulate the importance placed on curriculum quality. These meetings help to establish a climate in which staff reflect critically

DIRECTOR'S CORNER

"We are an NAEYC Accredited center and have earned the highest level on our state's quality rating system. Of all of the indicators of quality that parents and visitors see when they enter our building, our curriculum which reflects our mission is what they comment on most. Part of our mission is to demonstrate high-quality science and inquiry experiences with young children. This emphasis on science transforms our environment and is obvious to all who enter the building."

—Director of a university-affiliated demonstration school

TEACHSOURCE VIDEO VIGNETTE

The Quality of Child Care

In this video Ellen Galinsky, from the Families and Work Institute, describes the findings of three research studies related to early care and education. She discusses the characteristics of high-quality child care and warning signs parents should look out for.

Visit Chapter 11 of the **CourseMate website** and view the video vignette entitled *The Quality of Child Care*. Reflect on the following questions:

1. As a director, what factors should you consider to ensure quality programming for the young children in your care?

2. How might you use this information to communicate the benefits of a quality program for the children?

In its *Summary of Essential Findings*, the Center for the Developing Child at Harvard University found:

- Early experiences determine whether a child's developing brain architecture provides a strong or weak foundation for all future learning, behavior, and health.
- Young children who grow up in homes with high incomes and high parent education levels have more than twice the expressive vocabulary at age three compared to children raised in homes characterized by low socioeconomic status.
- The basic principles of neuroscience tell us that providing the right conditions for healthy development in early childhood is likely to be more effective than treating problems at a later age.
- It is possible to improve a wide range of outcomes for vulnerable children well into the adult years, as well as generate benefits to society far in excess of program costs (National Forum on Early Childhood Program Evaluation & National Scientific Council on the Developing Child, 2007).

on their practice and center leaders come to understand the decisions that teachers make and the resources and support that they need. As a curriculum mentor, the director works with staff to establish curricular expectations and to ensure that teachers feel valued for their quality curriculum contributions. The director also needs to be aware of areas of weakness or lack of follow-through so that teaching teams in need of curriculum intervention are given the support and oversight needed to improve.

DEFINING CURRICULUM IN EARLY CHILDHOOD naeyc

In order to establish a culture that embraces high-quality curriculum, communicates curriculum to others, and participates in curriculum reflection and mentoring, there must be a common understanding of what is meant by *curriculum*. Kostelnik, Soderman and Whiren, (2010) define curriculum as "all the organized educational experiences provided for children by the early childhood program [that] take place inside the classroom or beyond, involving educators, family members and other people in the community" (p. 226). Others go beyond experiences for children and include program content as well as training and supervision of staff so that they can implement high-quality programs, and also include evaluations that assess program effectiveness (Epstein, Schweinhart & McAdoo, 1996). While the field uses a variety of definitions of curriculum, a literature review conducted by Grisham-Brown, Hemmeter, and Pretti-Frontczak (2005) revealed that "many consider a curriculum to be a comprehensive guide for instruction that is composed of several elements including assessment, content, and teaching methods" (p. 19). For the context of this book, a comprehensive definition of curriculum will be used and will include:

- well-informed understanding of what to teach as defined by children's interests, developmental skill expectations, and early learning content standards/guidelines

- the incorporation of developmentally appropriate methods that support learning and development

- the utilization of effective assessment strategies that inform instruction, document child progress, and provide data for continuous program improvement

- careful staging of the environment (in the classroom, in the building, and on the grounds) which, when carefully planned, inspires children to learn and provides opportunities for development

- thoughtful selection of authentic materials that make learning meaningful and that facilitate development

- the implementation of professional development that enhances the teachers' ability to work with children and families to construct high-quality curriculum

- opportunities for curriculum mentoring that support critical reflection, quality curriculum, and intentional teaching

The importance of a quality and developmentally appropriate curriculum is evident; however, the reality is that for many, the term *curriculum* refers to a commercially produced book that is adopted by the program in order to satisfy a regulation or mandate. Moving the curriculum from a book on the shelf to an integral and visible component of the program's culture requires staff buy-in and strong educational leadership.

DEVELOPMENTALLY APPROPRIATE CURRICULUM naeyc

In order for a program to maintain a developmentally appropriate curriculum, the director needs to be aware of, understand, and be able to articulate the positions established by early childhood professional organizations. Keeping up-to-date with position statements and standards provides evidence of a commitment to the profession. One important document related to early childhood curriculum is the joint position statement on *Early Childhood Curriculum, Assessment, and Program Evaluation* developed by NAEYC and the National Association of Early Childhood Specialists in State Departments of Education (NAECS/SDE) (2003). The guidelines presented in this statement are considered to be necessary components of an early childhood program that provides developmentally appropriate and long-lasting benefits to the children attending the program. NAEYC and NAECS/SDE present developmentally appropriate and effective curriculum as a *shared responsibility* between policy makers, early childhood professionals, and others who share in the care and enrichment of the lives of young children. Key components of this position statement include a comprehensive system of curriculum, assessment, and program evaluation based on sound early childhood practices, effective early learning standards, and a core belief in values, ethical behavior, and support for children and families. Curriculum is to be "thoughtfully planned,

NAEYC Program Standards and Accreditation Criteria
Standard 2: Curriculum

Program Standard: The program implements a curriculum that is consistent with its goals for children and promotes learning and development in each of the following areas: social, emotional, physical, language, and cognitive.

Rationale: A curriculum that draws on research assists teachers in identifying important concepts and skills as well as effective methods for fostering children's learning and development. When informed by teachers' knowledge of individual children, a well-articulated curriculum guides teachers so they can provide children with experiences that foster growth across a broad range of developmental and content areas. A curriculum also helps ensure that the teacher is intentional in planning a daily schedule that (a) maximizes children's learning through effective use of time, materials used for play, self-initiated learning, and creative expression as well as (b) offers opportunities for children to learn individually and in groups according to their developmental needs and interests. (NAEYC, 2008, p. 1).

Source: Excerpted and reprinted from NAEYC, NAEYC Early Childhood Program Standard and Accreditation Criteria: The Mark of Quality in Early Childhood Education, (Washington, DC: NAEYC, 2008), 9. Reprinted with permission from the National Association for the Education of Young Children (NAEYC).

challenging, engaging, developmentally appropriate, culturally and linguistically responsive, comprehensive, and likely to promote positive outcomes for all young children" (2003, p. 1). Indicators of an effective curriculum include evidence that:

- curriculum is comprehensive
- children are active and engaged
- goals are clear and shared by all
- curriculum is evidence-based
- valued content is learned through investigation, play, and focused, intentional teaching
- curriculum builds on prior learning and experience
- professional standards validate the curriculum's subject-matter content
- curriculum is likely to benefit children (NAEYC, 2003, p. 2)

Another important document that the informed early childhood director should be well versed in is the NAEYC Program Standards and Accreditation Criteria (2008). This set of standards demonstrates the evolving priority that the field places on curriculum and is the standard that directors should strive to achieve.

This standard is effective in negating the "either/or" perspectives on curriculum that many in the field have practiced as the call for more accountability has become more prominent. The standard moves the conversation from, "Should curriculum for young children be child-centered and play-based *or* should it focus on content standards?" to "How can

children be exposed to early learning content standards within the context of a child-centered and play-based curriculum?" This standard encourages a "both/and" dialog such as, "It is possible to be intentional in our planning and also rely on an emergent curriculum that follows the child's lead." The role of the director is to facilitate ongoing "both/and" conversation about how this standard can be implemented in each and every classroom. Each classroom will demonstrate this standard in its own unique way as the curriculum must reflect the individual children in the room, the culture of their families, and the personalities and teaching styles of the teaching staff. This means that the director must provide opportunities for discussion of and reflection on classroom curriculum.

CLUES TO QUALITY: OPPORTUNITIES FOR FEEDBACK, SUPPORT, AND INTERVENTION   naeyc

As the educational leader of an early childhood program, the director must be able to provide valuable and informed feedback that reflects an understanding of what developmentally appropriate and quality practice for young children looks like. Some directors rely on formal tools such as the Early Child Environment Rating Scale-Revised (ECERS-R) and the Infant/Toddler Environment Rating Scale, Revised Updated Edition (ITERS-R), which can evaluate the quality of such aspects of the classroom as space and furnishings, personal care routines, support for language and reasoning, as well as the quality of activities, interactions, and more (Harms, Clifford & Cryer, 2006). Another tool that is well regarded for assessing high-quality teacher-child interaction is the Classroom Assessment Scoring System (CLASS) (Pianta, La Paro & Hamre, 2008). The CLASS assesses emotional support, classroom organization, and instructional support, and offers insight into important but sometimes difficult to measure qualities of teaching such as active and engaged learning and concept development. Results from both the ECERS-R/ ITERS-R and the CLASS can serve as impartial data that can inform teaching goals. In addition to relying on formal tools, directors also need to consider the following as clues to quality as they are observing their staff and providing feedback.

Is the Classroom Curriculum Child-centered?

"Child-centered practice" has been synonymous with quality for many early childhood professionals. However, the meaning of the phrase is not conclusive, as over 40 definitions have appeared in the literature, starting with Froebel in 1778 (Chung and Walsh, 2000; Tzuo, 2007). The term, in one of its simplest interpretations, encourages a curriculum that focuses on the child's interests. It is often contrasted with teacher-directed approaches that give the control for content and selection of materials and activities to the teacher. In reality, the notion of child-centeredness is complex but should "attempt to balance the requirements of building a secure, socially responsive environment in which all individual and group interests are respected, and attention to progress in the acquisition of academic skills" (Tzuo, 2007, p. 34.).

In a child-centered classroom, the director should note the classroom emotional climate, as children whose needs are not being met often become disengaged, emotionally distraught, and/or disruptive. A child-centered classroom can include some large group and even teacher-directed activities, but it also needs to include opportunities for children to make choices, play and learn in small groups or individually, and be active in experiences that support developmental skills across all domains (motor, social, emotional, cognitive, language, and aesthetic) and academic content. When mentoring a teacher, it is important for the director to look for evidence that all of the developmental domains are being addressed. The children must be given opportunities for large motor activity every day, preferably

Bombeck Family Learning Center

This child-centered classroom is investigating how bridges are built. While all of the children are investigating the topic, they are encouraged to explore an aspect of the topic that most interests them. This child is interested in how much load different types of supports can hold and is stacking blocks on a variety of columns. The children in the background have chosen to work together to explore different types of bridge-building materials.

outdoors whenever weather permits, and for artistic expression as part of a comprehensive program that supports all developmental domains and academic content areas.

What Is the Role of the Adult in This Classroom?

If a child-centered approach is favored in your curriculum, the director's approach may be to encourage teachers to let children solve their own problems and be responsible for their own achievements. However, Honig (2010) suggests there are times when a bit of teacher intervention may be just the right thing to do:

> Children can accomplish some tasks on their own after trying hard. Others are too easy or too difficult. Children get restless and bored when toys or tasks are too easy. They feel frustrated when tasks are too challenging. The Russian child-development theorist Vygotsky taught that teachers are priceless in supporting child learning and accomplishment when a task is just a bit too difficult at the child's present level of development. Then a teaching adult provides just that bit of help that will result in further child learning and satisfaction. Vygotsky used the term" zone of

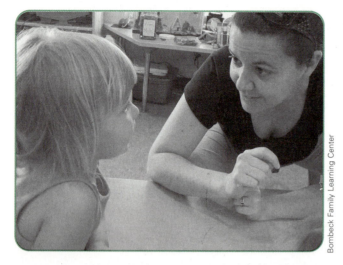

Taking the time to listen to children is the basis for high-quality teacher-child interaction. Children can read the listener's face to see if they are being heard.

proximal development" for the difference between what a child can do on his or her own compared with what the child can do with adult help. With the assistance of an adult, a child will be able to succeed at a cognitive or social learning task beyond what he or she could have accomplished alone.

How Does the Teacher Communicate the Use of Play to Support Learning and Development?

Early childhood educators typically understand the importance of play as a vehicle for learning in young children. People outside the field, including many parents, often miss the connection between play and learning and, unless its importance is explained proactively and consistently, may question

Bombeck Family Learning Center

▶❚❚   **TEACHSOURCE VIDEO VIGNETTE**

Young Children's Stages of Play: An Illustrated Guide

This video provides a description of play as the medium through which young children learn. An overview of the stages of play is presented with examples of real children engaging in play at each stage.

Visit Chapter 11 of the **CourseMate website** and view the video vignette entitled *Young Children's Stages of Play: An Illustrated Guide.* Reflect on the following questions:

1. As director, what will you look for in a toddler classroom that suggests that play is being adequately supported? What kinds of materials and equipment should be available? How should the adults in the room be supporting play?

2. Now consider an observation of a preschool classroom. What will you look for in a toddler classroom that suggests that play is being adequately supported? What kinds of materials and equipment should be available? How should the adults in the room be supporting play?

its value. One role of the director can be to help teachers be proactive and explain and document what children are learning. Directors should find ways to help teachers articulate their practice so that the information flow becomes an automatic part of what teachers do, allowing others to understand the learning that is occurring in their classroom.

One reason that some teachers have difficulty explaining what children learn during play is that many use free play as a time to do other things; many are not involved in children's play. While

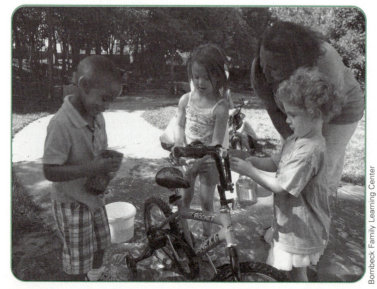

Bombeck Family Learning Center

The children in this picture are engaged in dramatic play around a bike-washing service on the center's playground. They are developing oral communication skills while also learning the purpose of money when providing their service to other children who brought their bikes to school for the day. The teacher is enhancing their play by asking them how they might attract more customers. She will chart each child's response in order to document their ability to answer questions and solve problems.

play is an ideal time for children to practice evolving skills that can be enhanced with the support of an adult, many teachers use free choice or play time to attend to housekeeping, paperwork, or other classroom organization duties. Additionally, some teachers are not accomplished in supporting play and do not understand how to augment play without dominating it. Directors can help teachers to understand how to become participant observers who support language, concept development, and social development through play. They can also learn to use play as a vehicle for assessing and documenting learning and development.

Is the Curriculum Emergent?

Emergent curriculum has been considered a hallmark of quality in early childhood programs. It is, for many teachers, a difficult concept to understand, and it frequently challenges the teacher who is inclined to plan well in advance in order to meet

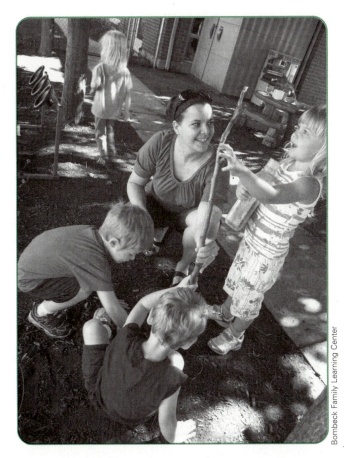

This teacher is taking advantage of a teachable moment in which children showed an interest in the difference between a stick, a branch, and a tree. Because this teacher has collected data on what the children know and are able to do related to content standards, she knows that she can easily incorporate the standards into an extended investigation of trees.

Bombeck Family Learning Center

his or her need for control. To facilitate instruction that follows the children's lead and incorporates their interests, the director can ask teachers how the children and their interests were included in instructional decisions. Some teachers cite the need to focus on content standards as a reason not to use an emergent curriculum framework. The director needs to facilitate a "both/and" paradigm shift and point out that it is possible to create a child-directed and emergent curriculum that addresses content standards. Specifics about how this can be done are explained in more detail in the following section.

How Does the Teacher Plan and Integrate Curriculum?

While the NAEYC identifies an integrated curriculum as a preferred practice, many early childhood professionals struggle with how to plan connected and meaningful experiences for young children. The new NAEYC Position Statement (2009) identifies as good practice that "[t]eachers make meaningful connections a priority in the learning experiences they provide children, to reflect that all learners, and certainly young children, learn best when the concepts, language, and skills they encounter are related to something they know and care about, and when the new learnings are themselves interconnected in meaningful, coherent ways." This standard includes the following element: "Teachers plan curriculum experiences that integrate children's learning *within* and *across* the domains (physical, social, emotional, cognitive) and the disciplines (including language, literacy, mathematics, social studies, science, art, music, physical education, and health)" (NAEYC, 2009, p. 21). It is clear that an integrated curriculum is identified as good practice, but how can the director support teachers who are uncomfortable with this process?

The director can be instrumental in supporting teachers in the planning process by establishing expectations for connected curriculum and by working with teachers to develop a planning system that supports integration. One easy strategy that can have a huge impact on the types of curriculum created is the lesson planning form that is adopted by a program. Consider the form that is currently used: Does it support the notion of interconnected and meaningful curriculum? Or does it represent a perceived need to keep children busy? Consider the lesson planning format shown in Figure 11-1.

This form represents the type of planning that is very common in many early childhood classrooms. Directors will very often collect such lesson plans

	Monday	Tuesday	Wednesday	Thursday	Friday
Morning Meeting/Circle Time					
Free Play/Center Time — Art					
Blocks					
Housekeeping/Dramatic Play					
Science					
Math/Manipulatives					
Writing					
Computer					
Snack					
Gross Motor/Play Ground					
Closing					

FIGURE 11-1   Fill the Week Lesson Planning Format—Blank
Source: © Cengage Learning, 2013.

weekly and review them. For some teachers, the lesson-planning process is perfunctory, with the goal being to fill the boxes communicating that the children in their classroom will be busy and, perhaps, even engaged. The director often tends to review these plans at a cursory level, looking to see that all of the boxes are filled. Now take a closer look at the types of experiences that a child might encounter in a given day by examining Figure 11-2. Note that the items with an asterisk are strategies or programs listed on the USDE *What Works Clearinghouse* list of programs that have been shown to improve reading or math skills in young children (IES What Works Clearinghouse, n.d.). Imagine that you are a child in this program and consider your experience for each of the days as planned. Even though you, as the child, are able to experience

these research-based strategies, what are your thoughts on the continuity of the day? Do you see any connection between one activity and the next? Do you understand why you are engaged in the activity? Are you asked to engage in inquiry or study a topic in depth?

As director, it is imperative that you understand the complexity of planning curriculum for young children. Your role is to push planning beyond the surface level—a mere clerical activity. Effective directors guide teachers into reflective and intentional planning that connects learning in deep and meaningful ways. As our society continues to be invested in research-based, research-supported, and evidence-based practice, it is important to understand the curriculum as a whole and maintain your vision for the complete program.

		Monday	Tuesday	Wednesday	Thursday	Friday
Morning Meeting/ Circle Time		Dialogic picture book reading*	Dialogic picture book reading*	Dialogic picture book reading*	Dialogic picture book reading*	Dialogic picture book reading*
Free Play/Center Time	Art	Finger painting	Found object collage	Watercolor markers	Pudding painting	Tempera at the easel
	Blocks	Add farm animals to the blocks this week				
	Housekeeping/ Dramatic Play	Kitchen with pretend food this week				
	Science	Aquarium observations	Sensory table	Plant seeds	Water the seeds	Water the seeds
	Math/ Manipulatives	SRA real math activity*	Geoshapes	SRA real math activity*	Puzzles	SRA real math activity*
	Writing	Phonemic awareness* the letter g	Phonemic awareness* the letter h	Phonemic awareness* the letter i	Phonemic awareness* the letter j	Phonemic awareness* the letter k
	Computer	Headsprout early reading*	SRA real math*	Headsprout early reading*	SRA real math*	Headsprout early reading*
Snack		Goldfish and juice or milk	Apple chunks and juice or milk	Pretzel sticks and juice or milk	Mini muffins and juice or milk	Cheese chunks and juice or milk
Gross Motor/ Play Ground		Outside play or obstacle course in the gym	Outside play or trikes in the gym	Outside play or balls in the gym	Outside play or parachute in the gym	Outside play or trikes in the gym
Closing		Sing goodbye song	Sing goodbye song	Sing goodbye song	Sing goodbye song	Sing goodbye song

*Included in the USDE *What Works Clearinghouse* list of programs that have been show to improve reading or math skills.

FIGURE 11-2   Fill the Week Lesson Planning Format—Completed

Source: © Cengage Learning, 2013.

REFLECTION

Think about yourself as a director and curriculum mentor to the teacher who created the plans in Figure 11-2. How would you support this teacher to create more connected and inquiry-based experiences for young children?

Planning webs are a way to assist teachers in integrated planning. It has become common for teachers to identify a curriculum goal as the basis for integration. In Figure 11-3 note how the curriculum goal "To become familiar with shapes" has been used to connect the experiences throughout the day. This planning strategy places great value on having children learn a discrete skill. The children experiencing this plan are likely to have a more cohesive and meaningful day and, depending on the quality of the experiences, are likely to learn the skill.

Another planning process shifts away from "skill-centered" planning and toward planning focused around "in-depth investigations of various topics—ideally, topics worthy of the children's time and energy" (Katz and Chard, 1998, p. 1). Eliason and Jenkins (2008) describe a variety of planning webs that focus on themes, units, concepts, projects, or

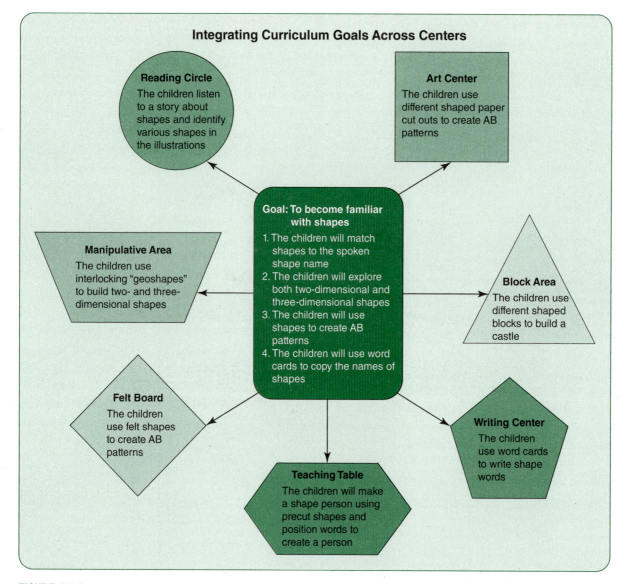

FIGURE 11-3   Integrating Curriculum Goals across Learning Centers
Source: © Cengage Learning, 2013.

extended investigations and identify the following as helpful steps for web-based planning:

1. Identify a theme and related subtopics
2. Brainstorm
3. Identify desired learning outcomes
4. Prepare for teaching
   (Eliason and Jenkins, 2008, p. 82.)

Extended investigations are the basis of such early childhood approaches as the Reggio Emilia Approach developed by Loris Malaguzzi and the Project Approach created by Lilian Katz and Sylvia Chard. Inspired by the work of Malaguzzi, Katz, and Chard, the *ACCESS to Science Concept Planner* (Figure 11-4) was developed to facilitate in-depth concept development through the investigations of science topics (Adams, Baldwin,

Comingore & Kelly, 2011; Baldwin, Adams & Kelly, 2009). In contrast to many web-based planning strategies that focus on a theme, unit, or topic and culminate in a topic-related literacy lesson, a math lesson, an art activity, or another discipline-specific lesson, the *ACCESS to Science Concept Planner* generates experiences that lead to deep understanding of concepts related to the science topic. Content-area skills are incorporated into the experiences in authentic ways that give the skills a purposeful context. When children see how discrete skills can help them understand or document an investigation, they tend to be more motivated to learn new skills.

To complete the planning process using the *ACCESS to Science Concept Planner*, teachers identify a science topic that is worthy of study and that reflects the children's interests. The quality of the

▶❚❚ TEACHSOURCE VIDEO VIGNETTE

Exploring Math Concepts through Creative Activities: Integrated Curriculum in Early Childhood

This video shows how a series of lessons that were integrated around the curriculum goal, "The children will become familiar with shapes." The lessons included whole group direct instruction and center-based, small-group experiences designed to teach discrete skills related to shapes. Visit Chapter 11 of the **CourseMate website** and view the video vignette entitled, *Exploring Math Concepts through Creative Activities: Integrated Curriculum in Early Childhood*. Reflect on the following questions:

1. The teacher tells us that there is a language of spatial relations that children learn best "if there is a visual attached to the word." This teacher is very intentional in her planning and can articulate her purpose well. As a curriculum mentor, what processes can you put into place so that other teachers can be intentional planners who can explain why they do what they do?

2. How well did the lessons that this teacher planned teach the curriculum goal and lesson objectives? Explain why.

3. How well did the lessons make the material connected and meaningful? Explain your answer.

4. How well did the lessons support inquiry?

▶❚❚ TEACHSOURCE VIDEO VIGNETTE

The Reggio Emilia Approach

This video describes the Italian approach to early childhood known as Reggio Emilia, which focuses on the organization of the physical environment, child-directed activities, opportunities for creative thinking, and collaborative problem solving. Visit Chapter 11 of the **CourseMate website** and view the video vignette entitled, *The Reggio Emilia Approach*

Reflect on the following questions:

1. How does the Reggio Emilia Approach facilitate integrated curriculum and inquiry?

2. What is the role of the physical environment in the Reggio Emilia Approach?

3. How well does this approach translate to programs outside of Italy?

investigation is dependent, in part, on the teacher's content knowledge related to the investigation. This is not to say that teachers should only teach what they know; rather, teachers need to be lifelong learners who seek out new information about the topics to be investigated. One goal of the *ACCESS to Science Concept Planner* is for teachers to develop in-depth understanding of science content related to

the topic of study so they can plan experiences that lead to a deeper understanding by the children. In contrast to the planning web in Figure 11-3, in which the activities are focused on a discrete skill, the *ACCESS to Science Concept Planner* provides opportunities for inquiry, depth of understanding, and a context for the discrete skills that children are learning. Connected and meaningful learning are also a goal of the planning method, which illustrates for teachers how it is possible to:

- focus on interesting topics
- identify the important concepts needed to understand the science topic
- design experiences that allow children to explore, investigate, and understand the concepts deeply
- identify how those experiences support developmental skills, and address early learning content standards (indicators) and IEP goals in meaningful and connected ways.

Several children were engaged in an investigation of race cars and the physics that makes them go faster or farther down an inclined plane. The teacher provided the children with ramp-making materials, small toy race cars, and a variety of measuring tools. Up until this point, the children had shown little interest in learning about measurement using blocks, cubes, and other nonstandard units of measurement considered to be appropriate for preschoolers. After racing their cars down the ramps for awhile, the children decided that they wanted to keep track of the distance that the cars traveled. They constructed a long measuring tool and sought out a pencil and paper so that they could record the distances after each race. This experience provided a context and purpose for measurement and a reason to learn to write numbers.

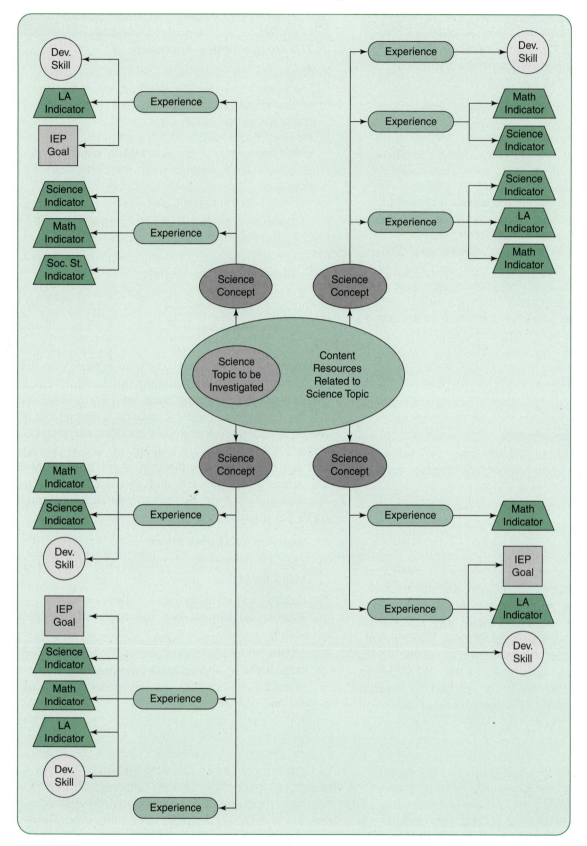

FIGURE 11-4   ACCESS to Science Concept Planner

Source: Reprinted with permission from Adams, S. M., Baldwin, J. L., Comingore, J. L. & Kelly, M. K., 2011.

Integration that is centered around an important topic can bring meaning to content areas while supporting developmental domains. This investigation of ants inspires children to count, problem-solve, and recreate the ants' habitat. This group of children asked the teacher to include ant-related words in the habitat so that they could write them when they recorded their observations in their science journals.

Examine the planning progression in Figure 11-4 from the central science topic outward to the concepts, then the experiences. Notice how the experiences are designed to support the science concepts but also support meaningful and connected integration, as math and science indicators might be emphasized in one experience while art, science, and language arts might be included in another. Now consider Figure 11-5, in which the central unifying science topic is obscured; with the *Fill the Week* planning method, it is possible to address academic content standards, developmental skills, and IEP goals without a unifying topic of study. The result is a series of unrelated or disconnected experiences in which children are left to determine the relevance of what they are learning. Directors may find these figures to be useful training tools as they guide their staff toward deeper and more meaningful curriculum development.

How Are Early Learning Content Standards Implemented?

As of 2010, all states have developed or are in the process of developing early learning content standards (also known as early learning guidelines) for preschool children, and 30 have adopted guidelines for infants and toddlers (National Child Care Information and Technical Assistance Center, 2011). Early learning content standards are new to some early childhood educators, and may appear to contradict the child-centered practice and emergent curriculum model that has been preferred practice in the field. Many early childhood teachers struggle with the notion of how to blend systematic instruction of content with NAEYC's 12 Principles of Learning and Teaching (NAEYC, 2009).

One common concern about content standards for young children is the potential for academic content to be taught inappropriately. Working together to address this concern and clarify the purpose of content standards for young children, the NAEYC and the NAECE/SDE developed a joint position statement that states that early learning content standards must align with K–12 standards in a very "careful" manner. This means that early learning standards are to be developed in an age-appropriate manner, giving emphasis to all domains of early development and learning. Likewise, content standards are to be "meaningful and important to children's current well-being and later learning" (NAEYC & NAECS/SDE, 2002, p. 2).

The role of the director in addressing content standards in the curriculum is to work with teachers to establish a planning process that includes standards but does not allow standards to be taught as a series of disconnected activities. Content standards should not drive the curriculum, but they must be addressed in connected, accurate, and meaningful ways. It is also important for teachers to have an understanding of the content represented in content standards. Directors need to provide opportunities for the staff to gain current professional knowledge in literacy, mathematics, science, and social studies in addition to development and appropriate teaching strategies. It is no longer acceptable for children to learn inaccurate content because teachers only know the myths associated with Thanksgiving or they still think Pluto is a planet because they haven't had any exposure to science content since high school.

Directors need to have a big picture view of curriculum and understand that developmentally appropriate content standards can be taught within the context of a wide variety of projects, units, or themes. This reality allows for emergent curriculum. It is also important to note that within an emergent curriculum model, it is common for teachers to gravitate to projects, units, or themes that interest them. Because of this, some project topics, units, or themes are very overused. For example, many teachers include the study of butterflies, dinosaurs, apples, leaves, and pumpkins in their curriculum. It is quite possible for young children to study these topics every year from the age of 2 through the primary grades. Teachers are less likely to focus on topics

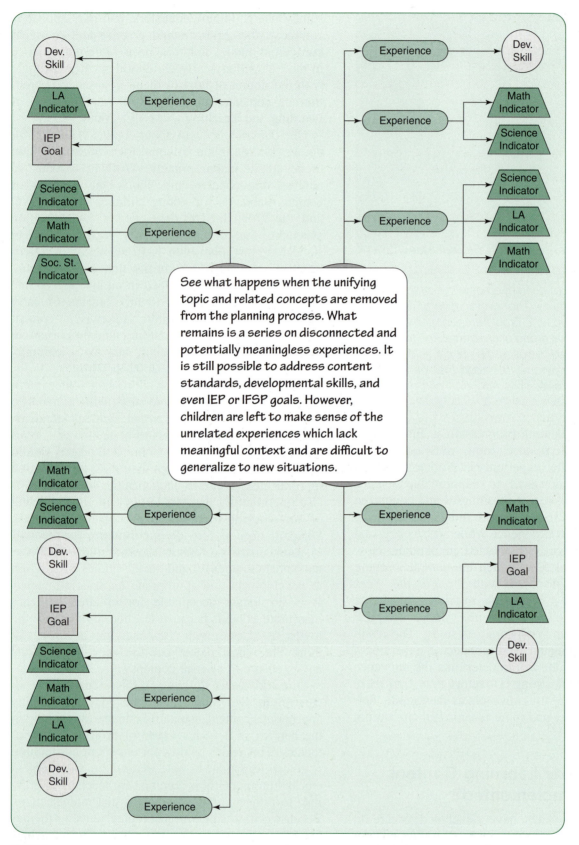

The text within the diagram's central callout box reads:

See what happens when the unifying topic and related concepts are removed from the planning process. What remains is a series on disconnected and potentially meaningless experiences. It is still possible to address content standards, developmental skills, and even IEP or IFSP goals. However, children are left to make sense of the unrelated experiences which lack meaningful context and are difficult to generalize to new situations.

FIGURE 11-5 ACCESS to Science Concept Planner with Topic Covered

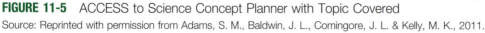

Source: Reprinted with permission from Adams, S. M., Baldwin, J. L., Comingore, J. L. & Kelly, M. K., 2011.

related to earth or physical science, in part, because they are unfamiliar with or intimidated by the content. The director needs to encourage a more comprehensive curriculum that pushes teachers to learn new content so that they can provide enriching experiences for children.

How Does the Program Facilitate the Development of Language and Emergent Literacy Skills?

The role of the early childhood program as a vehicle to reform education in the United States has altered the way that language development and emergent literacy is viewed for children from birth through age 5. Research-based literacy instruction has been identified as a means of reducing the achievement gap between children from the middle and upper socioeconomic classes and those who are raised in poverty. Once the National Early Literacy Panel (NELP) reported that "conventional reading and writing skills that are developed in the years from birth to age 5 have a clear and consistently strong relationship with later conventional literacy skills" (2008, p. vii), national reform dialog focused in on literacy instruction for young children. What does this mean for the director who must advocate for appropriate practice for young children, address the concerns of worried parents, and deal with the forces from outside the field who are pushing for more accountability related to systematic literacy instruction? Today's director must address the needs of multiple stakeholders while still keeping the needs of the children front and center. The research review

conducted by the National Early Literacy Panel has impacted what is considered to be best practice for young children, and teachers must be aware of the panel's findings. Directors should ensure that teachers are aware of the research on emergent literacy and also provide their staff with a forum to discuss how best to infuse research-supported practice into a developmentally appropriate curriculum.

The National Early Literacy Panel has identified several core competencies as having a consistently strong relationship with later conventional literacy skills: Many early childhood professionals who are well grounded in developmentally appropriate, child-centered, and play-based curriculum may review these competencies with intense reservation. There is a very real possibility that inappropriate and potentially harmful practice could be developed to address these skills. Children face long-term harm when they lack experiences that support the development of these skills. The role of the director is to make sure the staff is well grounded in both the early literacy research and developmentally appropriate practice so that curriculum can be developed that infuses these skills in age-appropriate, meaningful, and connected ways. Directors should also be watchful for teachers who see these skills as typical for older children and who might thus be inclined to use instructional strategies that are common in the primary grades. Set the expectation that curriculum in the program will honor the age of the child and support a system that encourages critical reflection and problem solving so that the skills identified above are included in the curriculum in developmentally appropriate ways.

Early Literacy Skills with a Strong Relationship to Later Literacy Skills

- alphabet knowledge (AK): knowledge of the names and sounds associated with printed letters
- phonological awareness (PA): the ability to detect, manipulate, or analyze the auditory aspects of spoken language (including the ability to distinguish or segment words, syllables, or phonemes), independent of meaning
- rapid automatic naming (RAN) of letters or digits: the ability to rapidly name a sequence of random letters or digits
- RAN of objects or colors: the ability to rapidly name a sequence of repeating random sets of pictures of objects (e.g., "car," "tree," "house," "man") or colors
- writing or writing name: the ability to write letters in isolation on request or to write one's own name
- phonological memory: the ability to remember spoken information for a short period of time.

(National Early Literacy Panel, 2008, p. vii)

Early Literacy Skills with a Moderately Strong Relationship to Later Literacy

- concepts about print: knowledge of print conventions (e.g., left–right, front–back) and concepts (book cover, author, text)
- print knowledge: a combination of elements of AK, concepts about print, and early decoding
- reading readiness: usually a combination of AK, concepts of print, vocabulary, memory, and PA
- oral language: the ability to produce or comprehend spoken language, including vocabulary and grammar
- visual processing: the ability to match or discriminate visually presented symbols.

(National Early Literacy Panel, 2008, p. viii)

The NELP's list of competencies that have a moderate relationship to long-term literacy acquisition includes skills that may be more comfortable for teachers of young children. These broader skills are common in print-rich early childhood environments which tend to emphasize oral language, including vocabulary development, matching, and book handling skills. A comprehensive language and emergent literacy component of a complete early childhood curriculum establishes a purpose for literacy. When observing in a classroom, the director can note how print is used. For example, is there a purpose for print where the teacher has decided to label and name everything in the room? Children begin to understand that there is a purpose for print when they use a picture label on a shelf to decide where to put a toy. When everything in the room is labeled (i.e., door, table, chair), however, it communicates that the purpose of print is to label. Are the environment and experiences set up so that children understand how writing can help them to record, remember, track, and communicate? The teaching staff needs to be aware of the literacy research, but also needs feedback and support so that they have a purposeful print-rich environment in which literacy has a context and meaning.

How Do Teachers Support Math, Science, and Inquiry in the Classroom?

STEM (Science, Technology, Engineering, and Math) has emerged as an important acronym in the educational reform movement. While STEM may be relatively new, theorists such as Jean Piaget and Constance Kamii have a long history of exploring mathematical concepts with young children. The

importance and appropriateness of mathematics for young children was further validated in the National Math Panel (NMP) report which found that "most children acquire considerable knowledge of numbers

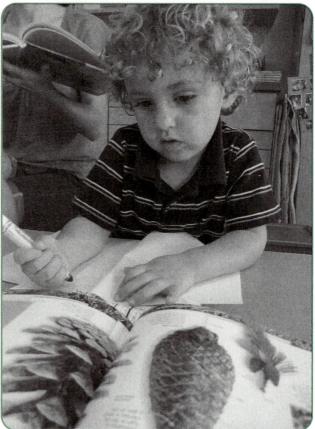

Bombeck Family Learning Center

Children are more likely to choose to write when the purpose is clear. This child is fascinated by the investigation of seeds in which his class is engaged. Using attractive nonfiction books has inspired him to keep track of his own seed collection by locating the seed and "writing" its name in his science journal.

and other aspects of mathematics before they enter kindergarten. This is important, because the mathematical knowledge that kindergartners bring to school is related to their mathematics learning for years thereafter—in elementary school, middle school, and even high school. Unfortunately, most children from low-income backgrounds enter school with far less knowledge than peers from middle-income backgrounds, and the achievement gap in mathematical knowledge progressively widens throughout their PreK–12 years" (2008, p. 18). Like the NELP report, the NMP report highlights the importance of experience with academic competencies as an important factor in later learning and in reducing the achievement gap.

The release of national reports like the NMP report has impacted policy recommendations for both math and science. The National Institute for Early Education Research (NIEER) Preschool Policy Brief on Math and Science made the following policy recommendations:

- Mathematics and science should be treated as essential components of a comprehensive, high-quality preschool program, not as extras.

- Policymakers must be certain that curricula, learning standards, and teaching expectations for early mathematics and science are research based and must outline expectations that are attainable and appropriate for preschool learners.

- Early education policies should define mathematics as more than counting and numbers, and science should be treated as more than learning lists of facts.

- Pre-service and in-service educators need improved preparation to understand math and science content and to provide experiences integrating this content into their teaching practice.

- Appropriate accountability systems that focus on the classroom, the teacher, and the child must be built to support high-quality early mathematics and science education.

- Mathematics and science learning should be integrated with each other and with other content domains.

(Brenneman, Stevenson-Boyd & Frede, 2009, p. 1)

This policy statement emphasizes the need for the director to oversee the quality of science and math experiences but also encourages the meaningful integration of science and math. It is important for teachers to be aware of these policy recommendations, which should be considered as part of the program's professional development plan.

What Is the Role of Technology in This Classroom?

"The push to integrate technology into early childhood settings can lead to inappropriate use of technology" (Cruikshank, 2010). While there are appropriate ways to include the use of technology in developmentally appropriate programs for young children, there has been a reluctance on the part of many who fear that the passive use of technology will replace active play and high-quality, play-based interactions between children and/or adults. "Educators who are grounded in child development theory and developmentally appropriate practices, and are technologically and media literate have the knowledge, skills, and experience to select and use technology and digital media that are appropriate for the ages and developmental levels of the children in their care, and they know when and how to integrate technology into the program effectively. Educators who lack technological and media literacy are at risk of making inappropriate choices and using technology with young children in inappropriate ways that can negatively impact children's learning and development" (NAEYC, 2011). Because of the impact of what is being called the "digital divide" on children in poverty, it is no longer an option for early childhood professionals to be uninformed about the use of developmentally appropriate technology with young children. Children who have access to technology tools and the Internet at home are more likely to have highly developed technology skills at an early age. Children who lack these experiences, commonly because of limited financial resources, start school behind their peers (Becker, 2000; Burdette & Whitaker, 2005; Calvert & Rideout, 2005). Directors should remind teachers about the important role they play in ensuring equity by providing access to developmentally appropriate technology for all children (Judge, Puckett & Cabok, 2004). The director also needs to find opportunities for teachers to develop technology skills and reflect on how technology might be incorporated in meaningful ways.

SUPPORTING INTENTIONAL TEACHING   naeyc

The director can be informed by the policies, position statements, and research reports that have been highlighted thus far in this chapter, but creating an environment where teachers use this information to inform their practice requires structures that support intentional teaching. "Intentional teaching

Technology Recommendations for Classroom Practice

Infants and Toddlers

During the earliest years, infants and toddlers need interactions primarily with human beings. They need to freely explore, manipulate, and test everything in the environment. Increasingly in today's world, this includes the exploration of digital technology and interactive media. Children of this age are drawn to buttons and cause-effect toys. Technology tools that infants and toddlers might use must be safe, sturdy, and not easily damaged. Just as toddlers tend to chew on their books, children under 2 are very likely to chew on technology tools.

- Allow children to explore digital materials in the context of human interactions, with an adult as mediator and coplayer. As with shared book reading, use shared technology time as an opportunity to talk with children, use new vocabulary, and model appropriate use.
- Avoid passive screen time. Although many parents claim that baby videos calm an otherwise fussy child, there is little research to suggest that infants and toddlers learn from watching videos. If they are distressed, they need the comfort of a caring adult, not an electronic toy.
- Provide children with toy representations of digital objects to encourage toddlers to begin pretending about the ways in which others use technology: cell phones, cameras, laptops, CD players, etc.

Preschool and Kindergarten

During the preschool years, young children are developing a sense of initiative and creativity. They are curious about the world around them and curious about learning. They are exploring their ability to create and communicate using a variety of media (crayons, felt-tipped markers, paints and other art materials, blocks, dramatic play materials, miniature life figures) and through creative movement, singing, dancing, and using their bodies to represent ideas and experiences. Digital technologies provide one more outlet for demonstrating their creativity and learning.

- Freely explore touch screens loaded with a wide variety of developmentally appropriate interactive media experiences that are well designed and enhance feelings of success.
- Begin to explore and feel comfortable using "traditional" mouse and keyboard computers for using Flash-based websites or looking up answers with a search engine.
- Capture photos of block buildings or art work that children have created; videotape dramatic play and replay for children to view.
- Celebrate children's accomplishments with digital media displayed on a digital projector or on a classroom website.
- Record children's stories about their drawings or their play; make digital audio files for documentation of progress.

Source: Excerpted and reprinted from NAEYC, "Technology in Early Childhood Programs Serving Children from Birth Through Age 8." DRAFT position statement. Washington, DC: NAEYC. Reprinted with permission from the National Association for the Education of Young Children (NAEYC). Copyright © 2011 by NAEYC. Full text of all NAEYC position statements is available at www.naeyc.org/positionstatements.

means teachers act with specific outcomes or goals in mind for children's development and learning. Teachers must know when to use a given strategy to accommodate the different ways that individual children learn and the specific content they are learning" (Epstein, 2007, p. 1). Intentional teaching requires that teaching teams have time for reflection and planning and that assessment is an integral part of instructional decision making. Directors can establish ground rules that support a climate where it is safe to express opinions in respectful ways. They will need to be creative in how they develop a center schedule so time exists for teachers to plan as a team. The program should have an established

While the time at a computer should be limited and the software carefully selected, the computer can support focused collaboration and inquiry.

assessment system with the expectation that documentation will be collected, recorded, and used to make instructional decisions, track the progress of individual children, and inform program evaluation.

Time for Planning and Critical Reflection

> ▶❚❚ **TEACHSOURCE VIDEO VIGNETTE**
>
> ### Curriculum Planning: Implementing Developmentally Appropriate Practice in an Early Childhood Setting
>
> The video case reveals how excellent curriculum planning must be based on developmentally appropriate practice (DAP); be inclusive and integrated; highlight play; and take cues from the children. You'll see all these principles implemented in an early child center, as Ke Nguyen and her colleagues plan activities and interact with the children. You'll also see the children engage in teacher-initiated and child-initiated activities, and learn together in small and large groups.
>
> Visit Chapter 11 of the **CourseMate website** and view the video vignette entitled, *Curriculum Planning: Implementing Developmentally Appropriate Practice in an Early Childhood Setting*
>
> Reflect on the following questions:
>
> 1. How does the center director define DAP?
> 2. Ke, the lead teacher, tells us that her teaching team meets regularly to discuss DAP and related curriculum development. Describe the dialogue that takes place during Ke's team meeting that suggests the team is responding to the developmental needs of at least one child.

Peer observation is a valuable practice for both the teacher being observed and the peers who are observing. Ideas can be shared between classrooms and teachers have an opportunity to articulate their practice.

Intentional Teaching in the Daily Routine

Planning is an important component of intentional teaching. Teachers are often much more enthusiastic about planning big projects and special celebrations than they are with establishing daily routines that constitute a significant portion of the program.

Daily routines can serve as excellent vehicles for teaching with a purpose. Consider something as ordinary and mundane as the daily sign-in procedure. One teaching team noted that persistent upheaval occurred each morning when parents were trying to sign in with children clinging to their legs. Several children expressed an interest in being able to "sign-in" on the same chart as the parents. The teachers met to reflect on this situation. They referred to the early learning content standards and related assessment data and determined that, while the children were at various stages on the emergent writing continuum, most, if not all, of the children could benefit from a station where they could "sign in" while their parents signed in. Not only did this practice ease transition time strife but it also provided a purposeful opportunity for children to write their name at least once every day. Periodically, teachers collected and documented work samples, which showed the progression of skills that started with mark-making and advanced over time until all children were able to print their name using uppercase and lowercase letters. As director, be on the lookout for examples such as the one described above and find a place to showcase examples that demonstrate intentional teaching.

Time for Planning, Sharing, and Critical Reflection

Consider a profession in which teams of adults are expected to work together to implement a complex and coordinated program with a very unpredictable client group whose education, health, and safety is dependent on the team's ability to know what each other is thinking from across the room. Now

This preschool teacher worked with her team to plan naturally occurring and meaningful ways for children to recognize their name and the names of the other children in the class. After a while, the placemats will be moved, motivating children to identify who they get to sit next to at the next meal.

consider that the team has little or no time to plan together in order to develop a common understanding of the goals of a lesson or educational philosophy for the classroom. This scenario is all too common in early childhood classrooms, where the budget is so tight that paying two or three teachers to plan is incredibly difficult to manage. An early childhood teaching team without planning time is like an orchestra without practice time. It does not matter how talented the musicians are: Notes will be missed, the timing will be off, and the audience will be left unimpressed. Teams who plan together are able to brainstorm and plan in a way that allows

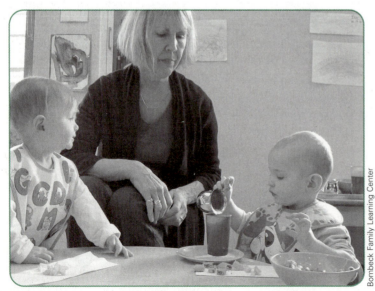

Meals and snacks can be planned with intentionality. This teacher knows that toddlers need opportunities to develop independence. The teacher has provided a small pitcher partially filled with milk and a much larger cup in order to increase the child's ability to pour his own milk with success. Staging the environment in this manner involves reflective, insightful, and intentional planning as well as a sound understanding of what the child is able to do.

Team planning time is essential for teachers to brainstorm ideas, develop a planning web, share resources, and establish a common understanding of the children and the curriculum.

the talents of the individuals to emerge. Classroom tasks can be chosen by team members who have the skill and enjoy the task in contrast to being assigned based on some institutional hierarchy. Directors must find and support team planning time and, in order to encourage the best use of this time, must help teams establish models for respectful interaction and critical reflection as well as a team decision-making process that encourages open communication.

Assessment Supported versus Assessment Driven

Assessment data is an important tool for teachers who are engaged in intentional teaching and is considered to be an essential component of a quality curriculum. While the NAEYC and NAECS/SDE recommendations state that quality curriculum is dependent on appropriate assessment to support instructional decisions, assessment of content and development in early childhood settings is an emerging practice for the field (Meisels, 2004; Meisels et al., 2002). Assessment techniques that are used with older students are not valid or reliable for preschoolers. Additionally, many experienced early childhood educators are unfamiliar with assessment strategies that are appropriate for young children. An important role of the director is to help teachers make sense of

assessment and how it can be used and managed in their classroom. It is not enough to require that teachers collect assessment data and documentation for their children; there must be a system in place that helps teachers collect meaningful data and organize it in way that that is useful and that informs instruction. Many teachers are committed to data collection and have found ways to observe children and note their progress. The challenge becomes what to do with all of the work samples, anecdotal records, post-it notes, and portfolios that accumulate in piles around the classroom. Many teachers struggle with how to pull data together in a way that allows them to make instructional decisions for a class or track the progress of an individual child.

Methods for collecting data often represent a combination of program requirements and teacher preference. If teachers are given the freedom to design a method of collecting data that works for them, then they are more likely to follow through and make the system work. The director needs to make teachers aware of the required components of the program's assessment system while also communicating where teachers have freedom to design their own strategies. The director also needs to make sure that intentional planning informed by ongoing assessment is part of the curriculum culture of the center. The expectation for data collection needs to be clear and teachers need to know that their assessment efforts will be discussed during curriculum mentoring sessions.

Figure 11-6 represents the assessment system developed by the Bombeck Family Learning Center of the University of Dayton. The teachers and leadership at this center worked with early childhood faculty to develop a tracking system that allows teachers to record the data collected through a variety of teacher-determined assessment strategies. The curriculum mentor works with teachers to ensure that they have an understanding of appropriate and unbiased ways of documenting what children know and are able to do. Once the teachers understand sound assessment practices and are aware of a wide array of tools and strategies that they can use to collect data, they are allowed to develop an assessment plan that works for their teaching team. The teachers determine who will collect data, when the data will be collected, and what tools will be used, realizing that a variety of tools will be necessary. Each teaching team shares its assessment plan and is held accountable for follow-through. It is important for the director to understand how teachers have chosen to assess children so that he or she can ensure that assessment is completed in an ongoing and sufficient fashion. By expecting teachers to compile their

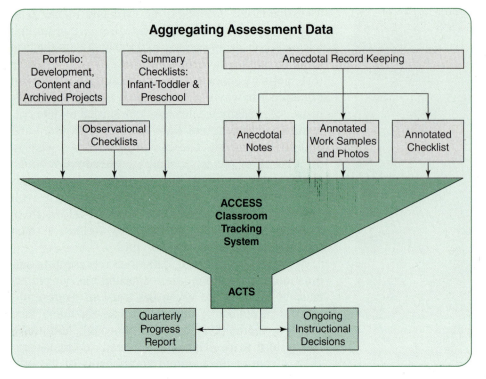

FIGURE 11-6   ACCESS Assessment Funnel

Source: Reprinted with permission from Adams, S. M., Baldwin, J. L., Comingore, J. L. & Kelly, M. K., 2011.

assessment data onto the ACCESS Classroom Tracking Sheet (ACTS) and bring an up-to-date ACTS to all curriculum planning sessions, teachers are held accountable for implementing their assessment system and for using data to make instructional decisions. While there is a program-wide assessment system in place, teachers determine the data collection methods that work best for them.

Developing an Assessment System

One of the director's responsibilities is to work with staff to develop and oversee an assessment system that provides strategies to support teachers as they make decisions about children's learning in order to meet their current developmental needs and, in turn, to lay the foundation for their success in K-12 schools while maintaining developmentally appropriate classrooms that rely on play and other child-directed instructional techniques (Meisels et al., 2001). Additionally, assessment is to be an integral component of the curriculum, with results used to guide teaching, identify concerns for individual children, and provide information to improve and guide interventions. Assessment methods to be used are those that are "developmentally appropriate, culturally and linguistically responsive, tied to children's daily activities, supported by professional

development, and inclusive of families" (NAEYC, 2003, p. 2). Indicators of effectiveness for assessment systems include:

- Ethical principles guide assessment practices.
- Assessment instruments are used for their intended purposes.
- Assessments are appropriate for ages and other characteristics of children being assessed.
- Assessment instruments are in compliance with professional criteria for quality.
- What is assessed is developmentally and educationally significant.
- Assessments use multiple sources of evidence gathered over time.
- Use of individually administered, norm-referenced tests is limited.
- Assessment evidence is used to understand and improve learning.
- Assessment evidence is gathered from realistic settings and situations that reflect children's actual performance.
- Screening is always linked to follow-up.
- Staff and families are knowledgeable about assessment.

▶❚❚ TEACHSOURCE VIDEO VIGNETTE

Progress Monitoring: Using Transitional Time in an Early Childhood Classroom

The teacher in this video demonstrates how, through intentional planning, she can collect data to document the progress of the children in her class. Visit Chapter 11 on the **CourseMate website** and view the video vignette entitled *Progress Monitoring: Using Transitional Time in an Early Childhood Classroom*

Watch how the teacher engages the children as they prepare to transition to the next experience in the day and reflect on the following questions:

1. Click on the "artifacts" button and examine the "Progress Monitoring Form." List the three curriculum goals on which the teacher is gathering data. How many children met their goals and how many did not? How might the data that she has collected inform her instructional decisions?

2. Note that this teacher is using the form a little differently than how it was intended. How was the form supposed to be used, and how did the teacher adapt it? Was this appropriate? Why or why not?

ADVOCATING FOR A SEAMLESS BIRTH THROUGH AGE 8 SYSTEM   naeyc

Early childhood educators agree that an emergent, play-based, child-directed, and constructivist approach is preferred practice (Copple & Bredecamp, 2009; National Association for the Education of Young Children & National Association for Early Childhood Specialists at State Departments of Education, 2002). However, the recent results of a multistate study of prekindergarten classrooms make it clear that 48 percent of children experience moderate to serious problems in making a successful transition into kindergarten (National Center for Early Development & Learning, 2005; Clifford et al., 2005; Pianta et al., 2008). There is often a poor fit between the skills of incoming kindergarteners and the expectations of their teachers. Additionally, there has been no common definition of kindergarten readiness, meaning that preschool teachers are often preparing children to meet standards that vary greatly from school district to school district, from school to school and, in some instances, from teacher to teacher. In the past, it was common for early care and education to exist in a separate silo from K-12 schooling. This separation leads to misperceptions and a lack of understanding of what programs for younger children accomplish and what kindergarten and primary grades programs expect.

Pianta & Kraft-Sayre (2003) note the importance of effective kindergarten transition practices which are enhanced by a seamless system of early childhood for children ages birth through third grade. Directors of programs for young children need to understand their role in this system and act accordingly. Looking for opportunities to reach out to the kindergarten teachers and principals of the schools that receive your children is important. One effort that can provide for this process is the 2009 *Linking Ready Kids to Ready Schools* policy brief that represents the commitment of the governors of five states. Funded by the W. K. Kellogg Foundation and the Education Commission of the States, this effort calls for a mind shift toward a seamless birth to third grade system and also provides supports for center directors and K-12 principals and teachers who wish to establish these connections.

DIRECTOR'S CORNER

"Like many other communities, our county's children and families are subject to a void of communication between preschool and kindergarten. There is no common definition of kindergarten readiness and the methods used to screen readiness are varied and inconsistent. My teachers dreaded the time of year when local school districts start screening children for kindergarten entry because parents want answers to the ongoing question, "Is my child ready for kindergarten?" We believe that the readiness process starts before birth and is enhanced through rich and engaging experiences that grow the brain. We also hold firm to the idea that all children are ready to start school when they are chronologically eligible and that it is the responsibility of the kindergarten teacher and receiving school to meet the needs of all of the children who come to them. What we believe, however, can be irrelevant when a family has their child screened by three different schools only to have one school report that the child is ready, a second identify the child as advanced, and a third say that child should be held out for a year because he has a summer birthday and cannot write his name. No wonder parents are confused and doubt our stance on readiness even though it is supported by NAEYC."

—Director of a university-affiliated child care center

SUMMARY

In this chapter the importance of the role of the director as the educational leader and curriculum mentor in the program was described.. One important component of this role includes a sound knowledge of the research that informs quality curriculum.

The chapter was organized around a series of considerations that directors can consider when preparing staff feedback. It also describes how directors can support intentional teaching and enhance a seamless system for children ages birth through grade three.

TRY IT OUT!

Work in a team to integrate curriculum using the ACCESS to Science Concept Planner shown in Working Paper 11-1. Assign one member of the team to be the curriculum mentor and the others to be members of the teaching team.

Background Information: The teachers determined that ants would be a worthy topic of investigation after the preschoolers found an anthill on the playground. The children became fascinated in watching the ants enter and exit the nest and were amazed at the strength of three ants who were able to carry a potato chip across the sidewalk. The teachers followed the children's interest but were also aware that there was a need to address an area of life science sometime during the year.

1 The curriculum mentor should begin by facilitating a brainstorming session to generate the concepts about ants that children can learn more about. Avoid introducing activities at this stage and redirect team members who start with activities, materials, or experiences. Focus on the science concepts that support an understanding of ants. Use Working Paper 11-1 to record your concepts. Note that several concepts have

been done for you. If the Internet is available, look up ants to add to the team's content knowledge; if not, take time after class to do some research. What new information did you learn that would have made your concept planner more complete?

2 Now that you know what is possible for children to know about an interesting topic, consider the experiences that you facilitate so that children can investigate the topic. How will the teachers find out about what questions the children have about ants? What authentic materials would support their inquiry?

3 Once the team has completed the concepts and experiences, consider language arts, math, science, social studies, art, music, and/or movement goals that children can learn through the experience. Try to identify two main goals from two different content areas. Include developmental skills that can also be supported through the experience.

4 How did this planning process support inquiry and connected learning? What were the pros and cons with planning in this manner?

The Education CourseMate website for this text offers many helpful resources. Go to CengageBrain.com to access the TeachSource Video Cases and other TeachSource Videos, Expand Your Learning exercises, flashcards, interactive quizzes, the eBook, reflection and enrichment activities, and downloadable forms.

Working Paper 11-1

ACCESS TO SCIENCE CONCEPT PLANNER: A STUDY OF ANTS

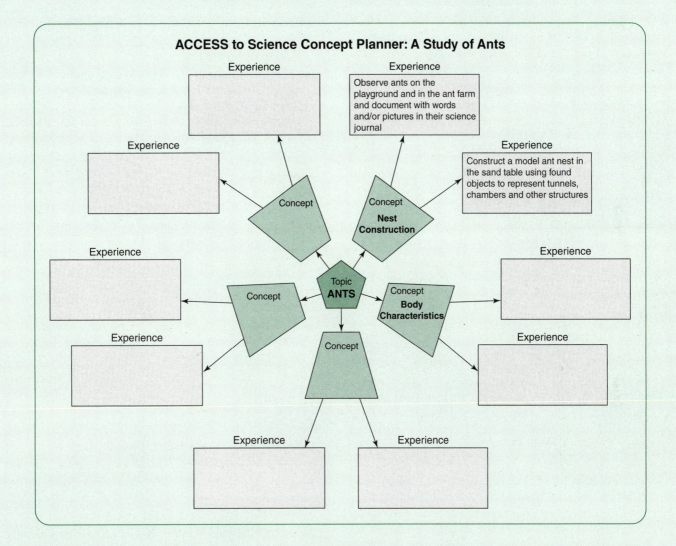

ACCESS to Science Concept Planner: A Study of Ants

Topic **ANTS**

Concept **Nest Construction**
- Experience: Observe ants on the playground and in the ant farm and document with words and/or pictures in their science journal
- Experience: Construct a model ant nest in the sand table using found objects to represent tunnels, chambers and other structures

Concept **Body Characteristics**

You can download a full-size version of this form on the Education CourseMate website.

REFERENCES

Adams, S. M., Baldwin, J. L., Comingore, J. L. & Kelly, M. K. (2011) ACCESS: A framework for intentionality, integration and inquiry in early childhood. Dayton, Ohio: University of Dayton.

Baldwin, J. L., Adams, S. M. & Kelly, M. K. (2009). Science at the center: An emergent, standards-based, child-centered framework for early learners. *Early Childhood Education Journal 37*, 71–77. DOI 10.1007/s10643-009-0318-z

Becker, H. J. 2000. "Who's Wired and Who's Not: Children's Access to and Use of Computer Technology." *The Future of Children (Children and Computer Technology)* 10 (2).

Burdette, H. L., & R. C. Whitaker. 2005. "A National Study of Neighborhood Safety, Outdoor Play, Television Viewing, and Obesity in Preschool Children." *Pediatrics* 116 (3): 657–662.

Calvert, S. L., V. J. Rideout, J. L. Woolard, R. F. Barr, & G. A. Strouse. 2005. "Age, Ethnicity and Socioeconomic Patterns in Early Computer Use: A National Survey." *American Behavioral Scientist* 48 (5): 590–607.

Chung, S. & Walsh, D. J. 2000. Unpacking child-centeredness: A history of meanings. *Curriculum Studies, 32*(2), 215–234.

Clifford, R. M., Barbarin, O., Chang, F., Early, D., Bryant, D., Howes, C., et al. (2005). What is prekindergarten? Characteristics of public prekindergarten programs. *Applied Developmental Science, 9*(3), 126–143.

Copple, E. & Bredekamp, S. (2009). *Developmentally appropriate practices in early childhood programs.* Washington DC: NAEYC

Cruickshank, A. (2010) Empowering images: Using photography as a medium to develop visual literacy. *Exchange for Early Childhood Leaders.* (Sept./Oct.). Retrieved July 17, 2011 from https://secure.ccie.com/resources/view_article. php?article_id=5019553&action=view.

Denton Flanagan, K. & McPhee, C. (2009). *The children born in 2001 at kindergarten entry: First findings from the kindergarten data collections of the early childhood longitudinal study, birth cohort (ECLS-B)* (NCES 2010–005). National Center for Education Statistics, Institute of Education Sciences, U.S. Department of Education. Washington, DC.

Dickinson, D. K. & Porche, M. V. (2011). Relation between language experiences in preschool classrooms and children's kindergarten and fourth-grade language and reading abilities. *Child Development, 82*(3), 870–886.

Education Commission of the States. (2009). *Linking ready kids to ready schools: A report on policy insights from the governors' forum series.* Denver, CO: author and Battle Creek, Michigan: W. K. Kellogg Foundation. Retrieved July 11, 2011, from http://www.ecs.org/docs/4208_COMC_report_forweb.pdf.

Eliason, C. & Jenkins, L. (2008). *A practical guide to early childhood curriculum* (8th ed.). Columbus, OH: Merrill/Prentice Hall.

Epstein, A. S. (2007). *The intentional teacher: Choosing the best strategies for young children's learning.* Washington, DC: National Association for the Education of Young Children.

Epstein, A. S., Schweinhart, L. J. & McAdoo, L. (1996). *Models of early childhood education.* Ypsilanti, MI: High/Scope Press.

Frede, E. & Ackerman, D. (2007, March). Preschool curriculum decision-making: Dimensions to consider. *NIEER policy brief* (Issue 12). New Brunswick, NJ: National Institute for Early Education Research. Retrieved July 11, 2011, from http://nieer.org/resources/policybriefs/12.pdf.

Ginsburg, H. P., Lee, J. S. & Boyd, J. S. 2008. Mathematics education for young children: What it is and how to promote it. *Social Policy Report, 22*(1), 3–11, 14–22.

Goodson, B., Layzer, C. Simon, P. & Dwyer, C. (2009). *Learning to talk and listen: An oral language resource for early childhood caregivers.* Washington DC: National Institute for Literacy. Retrieved July 11, 2011, from http://lincs.ed.gov/publications/pdf/LearningtoTalkandListen.pdf.

Grisham-Brown, J., Hemmeter, M. L. & Pretti-Frontczak, K. (2005). *Blended practices for teaching young children in inclusive settings.* Baltimore: Brookes.

Harms, T., Clifford, R. M. & Cryer, D. (2006). Early Childhood Environment Rating Scale-Revised. New York: Teachers College Press.

Harms, T., Cryer, D. & Clifford, R. M. (2006). Infant/Toddler Environment Rating Scale-Revised. New York: Teachers College Press.

Honig, A. S. (2010). *Little kids, big worries: Stress-busting tips for early childhood classrooms.* Baltimore, MD: Brookes.

Institute of Education Sciences, National Center for Education Evaluation and Regional Assistance, U.S. Department of Education. (2003). *Identifying and implementing educational practices supported by rigorous evidence: A user friendly guide.* Retrieved July 11, 2011, from http://ies.ed.gov/ncee/pubs/evidence_based/evidence_based.asp.

IES What Works Clearinghouse. (n.d.). *Early childhood education abstract.* Retrieved July 11, 2011, from http://ies.ed.gov/ncee/wwc/reports/early_ed/abstract.asp.

IRA (International Reading Association) & NAEYC. (1998). *Learning to read and write: Developmentally appropriate practices for young children.* Joint position statement. Retrieved July 11, 2011, from http://www.naeyc.org/dap.

Judge, S., Puckett, K. & Cabuk. B. (2004). Digital equity: New findings from the early childhood longitudinal study. *Journal of Research on Technology in Education*, *36*(4), 383–396.

Kagan, S. L. & Kauerz, K. (2007). Reaching for the whole: Integration and alignment in early education policy. In R. C. Pianta, M. J. Cox, & K. L. Snow (eds.), *School readiness and the transition to kindergarten in the era of accountability*, 11–30. Baltimore, MD: Paul H. Brookes.

Katz, L. & Chard, S. (1998). Issues in selecting topics for projects. *ERIC Digest*, *8*, 1–2.

Kaufman Education Exchange. (2002). *Set for success: Building a strong foundation for school readiness based on the social-emotional development of young children*. The Ewing Marion Kauffman Foundation: Kansas City, MO. Retrieved on July 11, 2011, from http://sites.kauffman.org/pdf/eex_summary.pdf.

Klein, L. & Knitzer, J. (2006). Effective preschool curricula and teaching strategies. *Pathways to early school success* (Issue Brief 2). New York: National Center for Children in Poverty. Retrieved on July 21, 2011, from http://www.nccp.org/publications/pdf/download_100.pdf.

Kostelnik, M. J., Soderman, A. K. & Whiren, A. P. (2010). Developmentally appropriate curriculum: Best Practices in early childhood education (5th ed.). Upper Saddle River, NJ and Columbus, OH: Pearson Prentice Hall Merrill.

Meisels, S. J. (2004). Should we test 4-year-olds? *Pediatrics*, *113*, 1401–1402.

Meisels, S. J., Harrington, H. L., McMahon, P., Dichtelmiller, M. D. & Jablon, J. R. (2002). *Thinking like a teacher: Using observational assessment to improve teaching and learning*. Boston: Allyn & Bacon.

Meisels, S. J., Bickel, D. D., Nicholson, J., Xue, Y. & Atkins-Burnett, S. (2001). Trusting teachers' judgments: A validity study of a curriculum-embedded performance assessment in Kindergarten–Grade 3. *American Educational Research Journal*, *38*(1), 73–95.

National Association for the Education of Young Children. (2009). *Developmentally appropriate practice in early childhood programs serving children from birth through age 8*. Washington, DC: Author.

National Association for the Education of Young Children. (2008). Overview of the NAEYC early childhood program standards. Washington DC: Author.

National Association for the Education of Young Children. (2007). *NAEYC early childhood program standards and accreditation criteria: The mark of quality in early childhood education*. Washington, DC: Author.

National Association for the Education of Young Children. (2003). *Position statement with expanded resources: Early childhood curriculum, assessment, and program evaluation: Building an effective, accountable system in programs for children birth through age eight*. Washington, D.C.: Author.

National Association for the Education of Young Children & National Association of Early Childhood Specialists in State Departments of Education. (2003). *Early childhood curriculum, assessment, and program evaluation: Building an effective, accountable system in programs for children birth through age 8*. Joint position statement. Retrieved on July 21, 2011, from http://www.naseyc.org/dap.

National Association for the Education of Young Children & National Association of Early Childhood Specialists in State Departments of Education. (2002). *Early learning content standards: Creating conditions for success* [Joint position statement]. Washington, DC: National Association for the Education of Young Children.

National Association for the Education of Young Children & National Council of Teachers of Mathematics. (2004). *Early childhood mathematics: Promoting good beginnings*. Joint position statement. Retrieved on July 21, 2011, from http://www.naeyc.org/dap.

National Center for Early Development & Learning. (2005). *Multi-state study of prekindergarten*. Chapel Hill, NC: University of North Carolina.

National Child Care Information and Technical Assistance Center. (2011). State early learning guidelines. Washington DC: U.S. Department of Health and Human Services. Retrieved July 21, 2011 from http://nccic.acf.hhs.gov/resource/state-early-learning-guidelines.

National Early Literacy Panel. (2008). *Developing early literacy: Report of the national early literacy panel*. Jessup, MD: National Institute for Literacy at ED Pubs. Retrieved July 11, 2011, from http://lincs.ed.gov/publications/pdf/NELPReport09.pdf.

National Forum on Early Childhood Program Evaluation & National Scientific Council on the Developing Child. (2007). *A science-based framework for early childhood Policy: Using evidence to improve outcomes in learning, behavior and health for vulnerable children*. Cambridge, MA: Center on the Developing Child at Harvard University.

National Mathematics Advisory Panel. (2008) *Foundations for Success: The Final Report of the National Mathematics Advisory Panel*, Washington, DC: U.S. Department of Education.

Pianta, R., Howes, C., Burchinal, M., Bryant, D., Clifford, R. M., Early, D., et al. (2005). Features of pre-kindergarten programs, classrooms, and teachers: Do they predict observed classroom quality and child-teacher interactions? *Applied Developmental Science*, *9*(3), 144–159.

Pianta, R., La Paro, K. & Hamre, B. (2008). Classroom assessment scoring system. Baltimore, MD: Brookes.

Pianta, R. & Kraft-Sayre, M. (2003). Successful kindergarten transition: Your guide to connecting children, families, & schools. Baltimore: Paul H. Brookes.

Pre-K Now. (2008). Pre-K Now-Pre-K Teachers Resource Center. Research-based Curricula. Retrieved July 11, 2011 from http://www.preknow.org/educators/resource/curricula.cfm.

Preschool Curriculum Evaluation Research Consortium. (2008). *Effects of preschool curriculum programs on school readiness* (NCER 2008-2009). Washington, DC: National Center for Education Research, Institute of Education Sciences, U.S. Department of Education. Washington, DC: U.S. Government Printing Office. Retrieved July 11, 2011, from http://ies.ed.gov/ncer/pubs/20082009/index.asp.

Samara, J. & Clements, D. (2004). Building blocks for early childhood mathematics. *Early Childhood Research Quarterly*, *19*, 181–189.

Tzuo. P. W. (2007). The tension between teacher control and children's freedom in a child-centered classroom: Resolving the practical dilemma through a closer look at the related theories. *Early Childhood Education Journal*, *35*(1), 33–39.

U.S. Department of Education, Office of Elementary and Secondary Education. 2007. Title I—Improving the academic achievement of the disadvantaged; Individuals with Disabilities Education Act (IDEA): Final rule. *Federal Register*, *72*(67): 17747–17781. Retrieved July 11, 2011 from http://www.ed.gov/legislation/FedRegister/finrule/2007-2/040907a.html.

U.S. Department of Education. (2002). No Child Left Behind Act of 2001. Washington, DC: Department of Education. Retrieved July 11, 2011 from http://www.ed.gov./policy/elsec/leg/esea02/index.html

12

MANAGING *the* FOOD AND THE HEALTH AND SAFETY PROGRAMS

© 2010 Cengage Learning

Health and safety information should be posted where both parents and teachers can see it.

The director ultimately is responsible for the center's food service and health and safety programs, despite the fact that the components of these programs may be the immediate responsibility of assigned staff members. In large programs, a nutritionist and/or food service coordinator and a cook may have full responsibility for the center's food service, but the director should be knowledgeable about the program and is accountable to the board, the funding agencies, and the center's families. Similarly, a social service or health coordinator may plan and implement the health and safety program, but again, accountability for the program remains with the director. Directors of small programs often have full responsibility for both planning and implementing the food service and health and safety programs. Because you, as a director, will be expected to supervise and monitor these programs, or in small centers to fully implement them, you must be informed about the elements of the food service and the health and safety programs and about the importance of these programs to the children and families in your center.

Objectives

After reading this chapter, you should be able to:

- Describe the components of a complete food service program.
- Explain the procedures for caring for injured or sick children.
- Describe the need for staff training and reporting in the area of child abuse and neglect.
- Formulate plans for various emergencies including natural or national disasters.

Standards Addressed in This Chapter

naeyc Professional Preparation Standards 1, 3, 6

naeyc Administrator Competencies
Management Knowledge and Skills 2, 5
Early Childhood Knowledge and Skills 5, 7

naeyc Accreditation Standards 5, 9, 10

FOOD SERVICE PROGRAMS

The total food service program, whether it is limited to a midmorning snack or consists of a two- or even a three-meal-a-day program, is important, not only because nutrition affects the mental functioning and the physical well-being of the child but also because nutritional habits and attitudes toward eating are established during the early years. Establishing an appropriate emotional atmosphere and providing variety in food choices and the style of serving the food are foremost considerations, whether the children's meals and snacks are catered, served from frozen prepackaged microwave dinners, come from public school or company cafeterias, or are prepared completely from start to finish in the center's kitchen.

In some programs, children bring brown-bag lunches, a practice that can be a boon to your budget and provide an opportunity to help parents learn more about good nutrition. All brown-bag lunches must be dated and properly labeled. They must be refrigerated, and all leftover foods must be discarded and not sent home in the child's lunch box. It is also important to make certain that children do not trade food with their friends. Nutritious foods should be offered daily, using variations in serving styles such as self-help and group snacks, family-style and cafeteria-style meals, picnics, bag lunches, and more casual food service for special occasions.

It should be understood that the adults in the classroom sit down with the children when food is served, that the adults eat the same food that is served to the children, and that the adults take charge of creating pleasant conversation among the entire group during snack time or mealtime. Conversation can focus on food, on what children have been doing or expect to do later in the day, or on any topic that is of interest to most children. An accepting adult who avoids having children wait to be served, who encourages but doesn't demand tasting new foods, who uses utensils appropriately and suggests that children try to manipulate their own small forks or spoons, and who avoids associating unpleasantness or punishment with food is demonstrating healthy habits and attitudes toward eating.

For the young infant, a caring, familiar adult who is unrushed is important during feeding time. Infants should be held while taking a bottle but encouraged to begin to hold it for self-feeding as voluntary control progresses. Staff must be reminded *not* to prop bottles for infants because of dangers of choking and of falling asleep with milk or juice in the mouth, which is detrimental to healthy gums and teeth and could lead to a possible increase in ear infections. In addition, for their emotional and social well-being, it is critical that babies be held and cuddled while being fed.

Older infants benefit from sitting in adapted chairs near the table with older toddlers and preschoolers, whenever that is possible. They often can enjoy finger foods with the toddlers and participate in the pleasant atmosphere of eating time. Choking may be a problem for babies who are beginning to feed

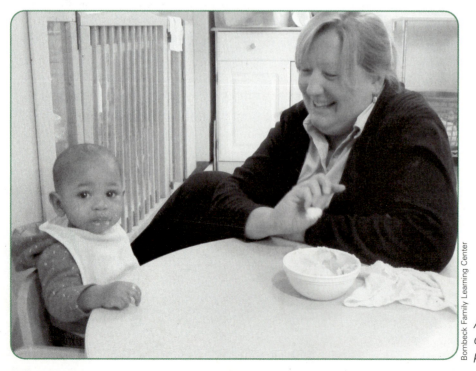

Bombeck Family Learning Center

Adults should sit with children during meals and encourage pleasant interaction.

themselves, so a caregiver must be close by at all times. Foods should be cut in bite-size pieces, be of proper consistency, and at the very beginning, be offered one piece at a time. Make sure the cook and the caregivers in the program know that there are high-risk foods that are likely to cause choking in young children. Ninety percent of all fatal chokings occur in children under age 4. Additionally, the Committee on Injury, Violence and Poison Prevention of the American Academy of Pediatrics (2010) reports that approximately one child dies every five days in the United States due to choking on food.

Foods that may cause choking include the following (AAP et al., 2011):

- hot dogs
- nuts and seeds
- popcorn
- raw carrots
- chunks of meat
- marshmallows
- chips
- peanut butter (spoonfuls)
- pretzels
- whole grapes
- hard candy
- raw peas
- rice cakes

It also is essential for children to sit down and to be supervised while eating or drinking to further avoid the dangers of choking.

Directors are responsible for all aspects of the food service program, so they must monitor and supervise the atmosphere, health, and safety features of mealtimes. They also must oversee the planning, buying, and preparation of food and provide opportunities for in-service training to the food service staff members and other adults who work with the children during snack and mealtime.

Menu Planning

The proportion of the total daily food requirement provided by the center depends on the total number of hours the child spends in the center. Licensing regulations vary, but general guidelines state that

- children in care eight hours or less should be offered at least one meal and two snacks, or two meals and one snack.
- children in care for more than eight hours should be offered at least two meals and two snacks, or one meal and three snacks.

FIGURE 12-1 The USDA's MyPlate logo is designed to remind individuals to eat healthfully.

Source: http://choosemyplate.gov. U.S. Department of Agriculture.

- a nutritious midmorning and midafternoon snack should be offered to all children.
- children should be offered food at intervals of not less than two hours and not more than three hours apart unless the child is asleep (AAP et al., 2011).

Of course, infants in group care have very different needs and require individualized eating schedules with carefully prepared formulas and special diets.

The MyPlate food guidance system (Figure 12-1) has been developed by the USDA to provide guidelines for daily food intake. Portion sizes and food selections for young children are presented in the *Dietary Guidelines for Americans, 2010* publication available from the USDA (http://www.cnpp.usda.gov/DietaryGuidelines.htm).

REFLECTION

Think about your earliest recollections of eating with the family or with a teacher. Do you recall being pressured about table manners, finishing your main course before dessert, and tasting new foods that you disliked? Can you recall how you felt at those times? What emotions did you feel? How did you feel about the adults who made demands on you? How did you feel about eating and mealtime when you were put under pressure to eat too much or eat foods you disliked? What are your current attitudes about eating and about unfamiliar foods? Can you relate these current attitudes to your earlier experiences with eating and sampling new foods?

Nutritious meals and snacks can be selected from among the following food groups:

- bread, rice, cereal, and pasta
- vegetable
- fruit
- milk, yogurt, and cheese
- meat, poultry, fish, dry beans, eggs, and nuts
- fats, oils, and sweets

Careful planning involves including ample choices of fruits and vegetables along with dairy products; some meat, fish, and poultry; and some selected items from the bread and pasta group. It is important to check local licensing standards for additional details on nutrition requirements. For centers involved in the USDA Child and Adult Care Food Program (CACFP), nutritional standards for meal and snack serving sizes for children birth through age 12 can be found on the USDA website (http://www.fns.usda.gov/cnd/care/ProgramBasics/Meals/Meal_Patterns.htm).

Every precaution must be taken to ensure that children with food allergies or other conditions requiring a special diet, such as cultural or religious customs or family food practices (e.g., vegetarianism), are served only those foods on their prescribed diet. Both the cook and all classroom staff must be alerted to these special dietary requirements, and both the director and the staff must know the emergency procedures to follow in the event a particular child has an allergic reaction. The most common foods that cause allergies are milk, eggs, fish, shellfish, wheat, soy, peanuts, and tree nuts such as walnuts and pecans (Graville, 2008). With the increasing incidences of peanut allergies among young children, some programs choose to eliminate all peanut products, including peanut butter, from their menus. For some special diet cases, parents may choose to send food for the child. It is important that these packed lunches be properly refrigerated until served and *not* be shared with other children. Any food from home must be labeled, showing the child's name and date.

Nutritional considerations in meal planning for young children are necessary but not sufficient to guarantee that children will be adequately nourished. Children's appetites and food preferences also must be taken into consideration when meals are planned. Three- and four-year-old children tend to have small, unpredictable appetites, and they are prone to food sprees. Their foods must be neither too hot nor too cold, not too spicy or gluey, and it is best if they are cut into bite-size and manageable portions. Variation in texture, color, and flavor also are important considerations in planning children's meals. Every effort should be made to limit use of salt and sugar as well as foods high in fat. Serving certain ethnic foods will provide wider variation for all the children and make available familiar foods to the children from specific ethnic groups represented in the classroom. It is always a good idea to introduce a new food along with old familiar favorites.

Further considerations that affect menu planning are the availability of equipment and utensils and the preparation time for each menu item when all foods are prepared in the center kitchen. It is virtually impossible to prepare hot breads, an oven-cooked main dish, and a baked dessert for one meal if only one oven is available. Also, the number and sizes of pots and pans must be checked when menus are planned to ensure that there is an adequate supply

Children often want to know, "What's for lunch?" So post the weekly menu where they can find the answer to that question.

of equipment of an appropriate size to prepare the foods for a particular meal. Preparation time is another factor that influences meal planning. Meals that require too much last-minute preparation create problems for the cook, which, in turn, could delay the serving time. Hungry children who are forced to wait for their food become impatient and restless, and teachers then must find ways to help them cope with these unnecessary delays.

Meal and menu planning can be systematized and simplified by using meal planning guides, standardized recipes, and sample menus. A number of government booklets and other menu planning guides are useful in planning four to six weeks of basic menus. Menu changes based on the availability of seasonal or plentiful foods can be made on a weekly basis. But beyond those minor changes, basic menu patterns can be repeated every four to six weeks.

Teachers and parents often have helpful suggestions about changes in the basic menu patterns, so a process for collecting feedback should be established. Some lunches include too many items that are difficult for children to manage or too time-consuming to serve. For example, a menu of soup, banana sections that have to be peeled, and packaged crackers that have to be opened is both difficult to serve and a problem for children to manage.

To demonstrate respect and support for diversity, programs will want to consider families' cultural and religious needs during menu planning. Additionally, some parents may be interested in organically or locally grown foods.

Inviting the cook to lunch with the children provides an opportunity for the cook to hear comments from the children about the food and to observe how well they manage the foods served. A "cook's mailbox" not only invites children to write requests for favorite foods and send thank-you notes to the cook, but also serves as an excellent meaningful literacy experience as well. The mailbox and the lunch with the children also give the cook a chance to feel more a part of the total center program, rather than one who spends all day in the kitchen and away from the children.

Parents often are interested in what children have been served for snacks and/or for breakfast and lunch, so it is helpful to post weekly menus or publish them regularly in the parent newsletter. Posting menus not only helps the parents plan for a child's meals at home but also serves as a model for parents who may be inexperienced with planning balanced family meals.

An interesting feature to add to the menu-posting area is a pictorial menu for the children. The cook, another staff member, or an interested parent may be

willing to collect food pictures and post each day's snack and lunch on an eye-level bulletin board for children to "read." It creates interest among the children, who can look forward to a dish they especially enjoy, and it becomes part of the center's nutrition program.

Food Buying

Careful menu planning reduces cost and waste and provides a clear-cut basis for setting up shopping lists for daily, weekly, and monthly food buying. Whether meals are catered, partially prepared from prepackaged meals especially designed for children, or fully prepared in the center kitchen, the food budget will affect both meal planning and food purchasing. Quantity buying and cooperative buying arrangements among a group of centers sometimes results in lower prices but also might limit choices, increase the pressure to purchase foods of lesser quality, and create storage problems when quantity purchases exceed the available storage space. Therefore, although price is an important consideration, quality, available storage space, and, of course, food preferences of the children must be taken into consideration when food-purchasing decisions are made.

Catered meal services require practically no shopping time, no storage space, and very little time selecting foods and developing the shopping lists. They also eliminate the need for a complete meal preparation space and a full-time cook, but the services may be more expensive than meals prepared at the center. In addition, the food could turn out to be less satisfying to the children and the number of food choices available may be limited.

The prepackaged frozen meals that are prepared in convection or microwave ovens are a very expensive convenience. This type of food service requires large freezers and special ovens, yet requires neither a full-time cook nor complete meal preparation space. The director must select carefully so the choices are appropriate for young children and there is variety in the menu. Fresh foods and beverages must be bought daily or weekly as needed to supplement prepackaged meals.

Using company or public school cafeterias requires planning with the cafeteria manager and staff. Foods brought from cafeterias serving adults or older children are sometimes served in containers or in portions difficult for young children to manage. A whole hamburger, a large strip of dill pickle, catsup in a sealed foil container, and milk in a sealed carton are all difficult for young children to handle. But since that is standard public school cafeteria fare, you may find no other choices for your children. Also, cafeteria service customarily means self-help and carrying trays. That is out of the question for young children. It is important to develop clear-cut guidelines for portion sizes, family-style service, and alternative menus so you can work with the cafeteria food service staff to find ways to make appropriate adjustments for young children.

Meals prepared at the center mean that the center must have a complete meal preparation space that meets all licensing requirements and must employ a full-time cook if it is a full-day child care program. Preferably, the cook will have planning and buying skills. If not, a staff person (sometimes the director) plans and purchases the foods in consultation with the cook. Planning purchases, doing the shopping, and checking deliveries are all time consuming; however, total meal preparation at the center allows for greater variation in foods served and more involvement of the children in shopping, preparation, and serving. It also guarantees that items on the

menu will be prepared and served with young children in mind.

USDA Child and Adult Care Food Program

Some centers serve children who are eligible for free or reduced-price meals from the USDA Child and Adult Care Food Program. While CACFP is federally funded, individual states are responsible for management of the program. Determination of a family's eligibility is based on income, and child care centers (not-for-profit or for profit), home-based programs, and after-school care programs may participate. The Child Nutrition and WIC Reauthorization Act of 2004 permits for-profit centers to participate when 25 percent of the center's enrollment or licensed capacity receives either Title XX assistance or is eligible for free or reduced meals. For those providers who may not qualify under the Title XX criteria, they may meet other qualification expectations. The National Child Care Association (NCCA) is a helpful resource for for-profit programs. Although some programs may have a designated staff person or cook do some of the paperwork to receive the USDA reimbursement, in most cases the director does the necessary paperwork or at least is responsible for making sure it is done correctly.

Eligibility of children for free or reduced-price meals is based on family income. Income levels for family eligibility and reimbursement rates for providers are adjusted annually effective July 1 of each year. To obtain the most recent information regarding eligibility and management of the food program, visit the Child & Adult Care Food Program at http://www.fns.usda.gov/cnd/care/CACFP/aboutcacfp.htm. Other helpful sources of information include your state licensing agent or your state agency that administers the CACFP (http://www.fns.usda.gov/cnd/care/default.htm).

A Meal Benefit Form must be on file for every child who receives meals under the USDA food program (http://www.fns.usda.gov/cnd/care/Management.htm). These forms must be kept on file for at least three years to ensure they will be available at the time your agency undergoes monitoring reviews. It is essential that the information on the forms be complete and accurate to avoid the possibility of penalties if errors are discovered at the time of periodic reviews. USDA forms vary from state to state, so the federal form may not match those required by your state. Also, new forms are issued yearly with updated income guidelines.

To obtain forms from your state, contact your state agency that administers the CACFP

DIRECTOR'S CORNER

"One of the things I learned quickly when I started to work with this program in the public school was to become friendly with the cafeteria manager. Now she cuts the hamburgers in quarters, sends pickle slices instead of those huge strips of dill pickles, and includes a sharp knife for my use when there are apples to be cored and sliced or oranges to be quartered."

—Director, public school Head Start program

(http://www.fns.usda.gov/cnd/care/Default.htm). The state agency will provide not only updated application forms but also worksheets that can be used to determine eligibility of your clients and worksheets for record keeping and for applying for reimbursement. Most states require centers to submit the final information and request for reimbursement online.

Providers who fit into one of the following categories may receive USDA reimbursement for eligible children enrolled:

- nonresidential public or private not-for-profit child care and ADC centers (some forms or documents replace ADC with Temporary Assistance for Needy Families [TANF])
- profit-making child care centers that receive Title XX compensation for at least 25 percent of the children attending
- Head Start programs
- settlement houses and recreation programs
- family child care homes (only if they participate in the CACFP under a sponsoring organization that has tax-exempt status)

All participating agencies must serve foods that follow the USDA Child and Adult Care Food Program meal patterns (http://www.fns.usda.gov/cnd/care/ProgramBasics/Meals/Meal_Patterns.htm). These patterns provide information about the types and portions of foods that must be served to each child for meals and snacks in order for programs to receive reimbursement. Following USDA guidelines ensures well-balanced meals; however, some recommended serving sizes may be overwhelming for young children if put on the plate all at one time.

Directors of centers enrolled in the USDA food program must complete extensive paperwork on a regular basis. Reimbursement claims and financial reports must be filed monthly, reporting data on:

- attendance
- number of meals served
- cost of food, which is calculated on the basis of information obtained from a monthly food inventory
- labor and purchased service costs
- income from reduced lunch fees and other sources

To complete these claim forms, you must have accurate attendance records, invoices or cash tapes and receipts for all food and some nonfood purchases, canceled checks, and financial records on all cash received from those families who pay full or reduced lunch costs. The reimbursement form helps with record keeping. Some states provide worksheets to assist with record keeping. Directors may also develop their own worksheets.

Even when there is an extra person on staff to do the USDA paperwork, data collection for the reports and preparation for reviews involve the director, the cook, and the teaching staff. Some states require regular training for all staff involved in the food program. Items such as point-of-service meal counts, safe and sanitary food handling, record keeping procedures, and size of servings are appropriate topics for these mandatory staff training sessions. Although the sessions are time consuming and costly, it is important that all staff understand details of the requirements to qualify for reimbursement from the CACFP because it is the center's primary source of revenue to finance the food program for eligible families. Federal regulations require that programs taking part in CACFP must be reviewed periodically. The purpose of these reviews is to ensure that all CACFP regulations are being addressed. Documents that will be examined during reviews include:

- income eligibility forms
- attendance records
- enrollment forms (to confirm that children listed as eligible for reimbursement are enrolled)

In addition to reviewing records on children, the food program official will examine administrative records such as:

- record of meal counts
- menus
- monthly food inventories
- documentation of food and supply costs
- documentation of labor costs
- documentation of Title XX enrollments if it is a proprietary center

As a director, it is essential that you understand the USDA program so you can do the paperwork if it is part of your job description, or delegate the responsibility and then coach those who are doing the detailed record keeping and reporting.

Food Storage

Food storage requires careful planning so that sufficient quantities of food items are conveniently accessible to the preparation area and storage areas and containers are sanitary and chilled. The available shelf space and containers must be appropriate to accommodate the packaged size of the food items as they are delivered from the supplier. All food items should be stored separately from nonfood items, and food storage rooms should be dry, relatively cool (60°F to 70°F), and free from insect or rodent infestation. Commodities should be stored in tightly covered, labeled metal or heavy plastic containers that are at least six inches above the floor level to permit air circulation and to protect them from dirt. Dating containers ensures food supplies will be used in the order received.

Perishable foods must be stored at temperatures that prevent spoilage. Refrigerator temperatures must be 41°F or lower; freezer temperatures should be 0°F or lower (AAP et al., 2011). Shelf space must allow for air circulation around the refrigerated foods, and thermometers in the warmest sections of refrigerators and freezers should be checked daily.

Food Preparation

Cooks must be instructed to follow recipes in meal preparation and are expected to adhere to directions about cooking times and temperatures, proper techniques, temperatures for holding prepared foods, and proper methods for storing and using leftovers. Sanitation in the food preparation area is of utmost importance. The food service staff must follow sanitary food-handling practices and maintain good personal hygiene while handling foods and cleaning food preparation equipment and utensils. Even though there may be a nutritionist or other staff member responsible for the total food service program in the center, it is advisable for you, as director, to make periodic checks on the food preparation techniques and the sanitation practices of the cook as food is prepared and served to the children. It often becomes the director's responsibility to coach the cook when correct preparation procedures are not being followed.

Sanitation guidelines are available from your local health department or your state or local licensing agent. The licensing regulations at all levels include clearly stated sanitation requirements related to food preparation in child care centers. A local health department staff member or your center licensing agent is an excellent resource for helping interpret and implement the sanitation regulations applicable in your area.

Resources

Every state has a child nutrition agency (http://www.fns.usda.gov/cnd/contacts/statedirectory.htm). These agencies can supply copies of laws, regulations, and guidelines in response to questions about nutrition and health. The following list includes

© 2010 Cengage Learning

It is advisable for you, as the director, to make periodic checks on food preparation and service.

additional places to go for printed material and for consultation on the center's nutrition component:

- public health nutritionists in your state or local health department, or the county extension agency
- nutritionists in local dairy councils or comprehensive health centers
- USDA extension home economists
- dietitians in nearby high schools or universities
- dietitians in local hospitals

HEALTH AND SAFETY PROGRAM   **naeyc**

The center's staff members are responsible for the health and safety of the children while they are at the center; therefore, directors must be knowledgeable about health and safety regulations as stipulated in the licensing regulations, about staff liability in cases of accidents at school, and about procedures for protection from and reporting of communicable disease and child abuse and neglect. Although some large centers may have a health consultant on staff, in most places the director is the designated individual responsible for the health program.

The health services provided through the child care center may range from no service at all to comprehensive service, including regular physicals, dental checkups and treatment, vision screening, hearing screening, and mental health services. The scope of the health services program depends on the program's health policies set by the funding agent, the socioeconomic status of the families, the family expectations, and the licensing regulations. All centers should maintain up-to-date health and immunization records on the children, whether or not direct health services are provided.

Health Records for Children and Staff

Children's health records cover information up to the time of registration and any new health or medical information received while the child is in the program. Formats for these records vary and may be set by local health departments. The information provided (in addition to the basic demographics such as name, birth date, parents' names, and the like) should include medical and developmental information and must be completed and signed by the child's health care provider. The medical report on the child should include the following:

- results from the child's most recent well care visit with physician's signature

- health history including records of the child's immunizations

- description of any disability or special need and a care plan for how these needs will be accommodated

- assessment of the child's growth based on height, weight, and head circumference (percentile for these if the child is younger than 24 months)

- results of developmental screenings as well as those for vision, hearing, dental health, nutrition, tuberculosis, hemoglobin, urine, lead, etc.

- dates of significant communicable diseases

- prescribed medications, including information on recognizing and reporting potential side effects

- description of current acute or chronic health problems under or needing treatment

---

▶❚❚ **TEACHSOURCE VIDEO VIGNETTE**

Communicating with Parents about Health Issues

Informing parents about the health-related policies and procedures of an early childhood program is an important responsibility of administrators and teachers. Go to the **CourseMate website** and view the video vignette entitled, *Communicating with Parents about Health in Early Childhood: A Parent-Teacher Meeting*. Reflect on the following questions:

1. What types of information should be shared with parents about health-related issues?

2. What are the benefits of meeting face-to-face with parents to discuss health policies and procedures?

3. What advice is given to parents regarding a child's return to the classroom following an illness?

- description of serious injuries sustained by the child in the past

- special instructions for the caregiver

- emergency medical/dental care authorization form (AAP et al., 2011).

It is preferable to have the child's medical report on file prior to or on admission, but it is imperative that it be completed within six weeks after admission or as required by licensing laws. These records should be updated every six months for children under 2 years and every year for children ages 2 to 6.

A dental screening should be included in the medical report. An authorized health care provider often does the dental screening on children under age 3, at which time the child should visit a dentist. If the earlier dental screenings reveal special oral or dental problems, the child should see a dentist immediately.

Staff medical records that follow the licensing requirements must be on file at the center. Even when not required by licensing, there should be a medical record on every adult who has regular contact with the children, including substitutes, volunteers, practicum students, cooks, and van drivers. The staff records should include not only a physical assessment but also an evaluation of the emotional fitness of those who are to care for the children. The staff health appraisal should include the following:

- health history

- physical and dental exams

- vision and hearing screening
- tuberculosis (TB) screening with the Tuberculin Skin Test (TST) or the interferon gamma release assay (IGSA)
- review of immunizations (measles, mumps, rubella, diphtheria, tetanus, polio)
- review of occupational health concerns
- assessment of need for immunizations against influenza, pneumococcus, and hepatitis B (and those required by individual states)
- assessment of any other condition that may impair a staff member's ability to perform the job (AAP et al., 2011).

Unless licensing regulations require more frequent updating of staff health records, it is recommended this be done every two years. After many years of decreasing numbers of cases, tuberculosis seems to be on the rise again, so it is wise to consult your local health authorities to determine the frequency of repeat TB testing.

Currently, there are no screening or self-appraisal tools to identify specific health conditions that may seriously impair a caregiver's ability to provide safe and healthy experiences for children. However, there are some obvious things that a director can assess. These include the ability or willingness to

- move quickly to supervise and assist the children
- lift children, equipment, and supplies
- sit on the floor and on child-size chairs
- respond quickly in case of an emergency
- practice frequent hand washing
- eat the same food served to the children
- hear and see at a distance for playground supervision
- not be absent from work due to illness more frequently than the typical adult, in order to provide continuity of care for young children (AAP et al., 2011)

Communicable Disease

Cases of communicable diseases at the child care center must be reported to all center families and to the local health authorities. The usual children's diseases, as well as cases of meningitis, scarlet fever, infectious hepatitis, and head lice, must be reported so that necessary precautions can be taken immediately. It is important that pregnant staff

---

▶❙❙ TEACHSOURCE VIDEO VIGNETTE

The Daily Health Check

The daily evaluation of a child's health status takes very little time, but can yield numerous benefits. Go to the **CourseMate website** and view the video vignette entitled, *Infants & Toddlers: Daily Health Checks.* Reflect on the following questions:

1. You are the director of an early childhood program who has just hired a new toddler teacher. What information would you provide to this new employee regarding the benefits of the daily health check in your center?

2. What information should be included in a form that teachers might use as they conduct daily health checks?

---

members consult their physician about precautions related to exposure to communicable diseases at the workplace.

Directors and some of the teaching staff should have training in communicable diseases to enable them to recognize symptoms and make decisions about exclusion of children from the group. Communicable disease training is available in most communities through the Red Cross or the local health department. Licensing usually requires updated communicable disease training for classroom staff. Every center should provide easy access to a communicable disease chart to help staff recognize symptoms and make exclusion decisions. Many states require that teachers conduct a daily health check as each child arrives to identify potential health issues.

The most important measure in preventing the spread of disease in child care centers is hand washing, not only after toileting or diapering, but also after nose blowing or helping a child with a runny nose or cough, and before handling dishes or serving food (Figure 12-2). There are other occasions when hand washing should be considered. For example, some states mandate hand washing following outdoor play. You may also wish to encourage the practice before and after water play or following the handling of class pets. Sanitizing surfaces after diapering or on tables before using for eating also will help cut down on the spread of disease. Cleanliness is the major contributing factor to effective disease control in child care environments.

Staff members responsible for giving first aid to children and those likely to come in contact with

1. Have paper towel ready.

2. Wet hands and wrists under warm, running water.

3. Apply soap and lather hands to loosen dirt and bacteria.

4. Rub hands together vigorously for at least 30 seconds, washing carefully between fingers and under nails.

5. Rinse thoroughly under running water.

6. Before turning off the water, dry hands carefully.

7. Use the paper towel to turn off the faucet.

FIGURE 12-2 Correct hand-washing technique.

Source: From MAROTZ. Health, Safety, and Nutrition for the Young Child, 8e. © 2012 Wadsworth, a part of Cengage Learning, Inc. Reproduced by permission. www.cengage.com/permissions

blood or body fluids should have special training in dealing with blood-borne pathogens such as HIV or hepatitis B. Child care programs are required to offer free hepatitis B immunizations to employees when hired or within 24 hours following exposure to blood or body fluids containing blood (Marotz, 2012).

The spread of disease also is minimized through precautionary measures for handling situations when children become ill during the day and when children are ill on arrival. A written policy regarding management of sick children must be conveyed to parents when children are enrolled. Very few centers have facilities to care for a sick child who must be separated from the other children, so the usual practice is to call the parent or a designated adult to come for the child. In the meantime, the child usually is removed from the classroom and rests or plays quietly under adult supervision. Often, the director is the only staff person who has a schedule flexible enough to allow for time to stay with the sick child. An extra cot and a few toys for use while children are waiting to be picked up by a parent is standard equipment in many directors' offices.

Exclusion Policy

Exclusion policies must be made clear to parents and to the child care staff. If the purpose of excluding an ill child is to prevent the spread of infection to others in the group, it is important to specify which types of illnesses require exclusion and under what circumstances children will be sent home. This list may include conditions such as:

- diarrhea
- vomiting three or more times within the 24-hour period prior to attending the center
- fever above 101°F (oral), 102°F (rectal), or 100°F (axillary) with changes in behavior or other symptoms such as lethargy, sore throat,

Bombeck Family Learning Center

Sick children should be removed from the classroom and be made comfortable under adult supervision.

vomiting, or rash. Note that a rise in body temperature is common in young children and may or may not be a symptom of a contagious or serious illness. Nonetheless, most centers have strict policies about exclusion of children with a fever. Infants younger than 4 months should be evaluated by medical personnel if they have an unexplained temperature above 100°F (axillary) or 101°F (rectal).

- abdominal discomfort present for more than two hours or intermittent pain accompanied by other symptoms such as fever
- rash accompanied by fever or behavior changes
- mouth sores accompanied by drooling
- chickenpox (until lesions have crusted)
- head lice (until after the first treatment has been received)
- scabies (until after first treatment has been received)
- impetigo (until 24 hours after treatment has begun)
- strep throat (until 24 hours after treatment has begun)
- rubella, pertussis, mumps, measles, hepatitis A (each has a specific exclusion period and criteria for exclusion) (Aronson & Shope, 2009)

In many cases, the child's physician will provide information relative to the child's readiness to return to the center.

When the exclusion policy is clear, it helps both parents and staff make decisions about when to exclude children from the group and can reduce stress for all concerned (Button, 2008). Programs that have staffed facilities to care for mildly ill children can have more liberal exclusion policies than those without staff or space for these children to receive the extra rest and supervision they require. For working parents, finding alternative care arrangements for sick children is often a real problem. If parents don't have family leave time to use, it is helpful to provide resources for finding alternate care for an ill or recuperating child. Referring them to community agencies such as "sitters on call" or nanny services may be an answer for some families. If you locate alternative services in your community, they could be posted on the center website or published in a newsletter as a way of letting parents know that you will try to help as much as possible when their sick child is temporarily excluded from the classroom.

Although there is an ever-increasing amount of information on the risks posed by children infected with HIV (a viral infection that can lead to AIDS) attending child care programs, evidence is inconclusive at this time. Since new information about HIV and AIDS is being generated constantly, stay in touch with local health authorities or the Centers for Disease Control and Prevention (CDC) for updated information and guidance. If a child infected with HIV applies for admission, the public health department and the child's physician can help determine if it is safe for the child to be in a group situation. They also will provide help in determining whether the presence of this child exposes other children and adults to undue risk. It should be noted that it is illegal to ask about a child's HIV/AIDS status at admission.

The number of children in group care infected with HIV may increase because newer medications and treatments are making it possible for infected children to live longer. These HIV-positive children are protected under the Americans with Disabilities Act and, therefore, cannot be denied access to educational programs. The overwhelming majority of children who are infected acquired the HIV virus from their mother during pregnancy, labor and delivery, or breastfeeding (UNAIDS, 2010). A major risk of admitting children with HIV/AIDS is that these children run a greater risk of contracting illnesses and infections from the other children because their immune systems are not functioning properly (CDC et al., 2009), and these infections can pose a serious threat to the child's life. The current information regarding HIV and the hepatitis B virus (similar to HIV but more infectious) is that neither is easily transmitted in school or child care environments, nor through casual contact such as touching, hugging, eating together, or sharing bathrooms. However, many centers are choosing to have a written policy on HIV and hepatitis B to protect the rights of an infected child and the other children in the center.

It is recommended that children with HIV be excluded from the group *only* if they have open sores or bleeding that would put other children at risk from exposure to the infected child's body fluids (Marotz, 2012). Whether or not there are known cases of HIV/AIDS among enrolled children, it is essential that staff follow standard precautions to prevent transmission of disease through bodily fluids such as blood, saliva, vomit, nasal/eye discharges, and human waste (urine, feces). Specific recommendations include:

- Use single-use disposable gloves when handling or cleaning up bodily fluids and human waste and when staff members have cuts or breaks in the skin. Utility gloves can be used, but must be sanitized with soap and water and then dipped in a disinfectant solution up to the wrist and air dried. Disposable gloves should be discarded without being handled.

- Sanitize diaper-changing surfaces, toys, floors, walls, bathrooms, tables, and other surfaces that come into contact with bodily fluids, including human milk and human waste.

- Wash hands after coming into contact with infected surfaces/materials even if gloves are worn.

- Place contaminated materials in a plastic bag that is then securely tied and disposed of away from the children (AAP et al., 2011).

To obtain updated information on this question or others involving infectious diseases, contact your local health department or the Centers for Disease Control and Prevention.

Sick Child Care

As more children under 5 require some type of care outside the home, there is the consequent increase in the need for sick child care. The first alternative is to have the child at home with a caring parent whose employer allows time off for that purpose. Being at home may be the best alternative, but it is not always the most realistic. That means child care professionals, with the help of health professionals, are beginning to develop alternative sick child care models. For example, sick children might be accommodated in:

- a sick bay at the center (a "Get Well" room)
- a center in a separate building that might be the cooperative venture of several child care programs
- a center in a wing of a hospital or on hospital grounds that is available to the general public
- a "satellite" system of family child care homes linked to a child care center
- the child's own home under the supervision of a trained person sent from the center or local health agency

Because children with AIDS are extremely vulnerable to infection from other children, it may be unwise to have them in a sick child care facility where they would be exposed to other sick children.

Disaster Planning

Although licensing regulations may not always require disaster plans, it is important to plan for building evacuation in the event of fire and to detail additional measures to be taken during tornadoes,

earthquakes, smog alerts, floods, sudden loss of heat or air conditioning, or any other major emergency or national disaster. The director must instruct all staff members on the best ways to evacuate the premises and the safe places to shelter children in weather or other emergencies. It is important to practice all emergency procedures with staff so they are conditioned to respond and less likely to panic. An evacuation plan should be posted in every classroom (Figure 12-3). Fire emergency plans show alternative exit routes, and evacuation drills should be held regularly so children become familiar with this routine. Parents must be informed in advance about alternative shelters so they know the whereabouts of their children during emergencies.

Daily attendance records and information needed to reach parents must be maintained in a convenient location and removed from the building by the designated adults as part of the evacuation procedure. The "chain of command" regarding who will call for emergency fire or police help, who will secure the building and make a final check that everyone is out, how the building will be secured, and who will contact the parents all must be arranged in advance and communicated to staff by the director. Fire alarms, fire extinguishers, and emergency exit lights should be checked regularly to ensure they are in working order.

Supplies stored in emergency evacuation areas and to be taken to the alternative shelter include the following:

- first aid kit
- blankets
- food and water
- battery-operated radio
- flashlight
- children's books, crayons, paper, etc.

ARLITT CHILD DEVELOPMENT CENTER

117 116 115 114 113 112 111 110 107 108 109 105 106 103 104 101 102

LEGEND:
—— PRIMARY EXIT ROUTE
-- -- SECONDARY EXIT ROUTE

EVACUATION PLAN:
(1) Sound the alarm.
(2) Evacuate the building using the PRIMARY EXIT ROUTE.
(3) If PRIMARY EXIT ROUTE is impassable, proceed to SECONDARY EXIT ROUTE.
(4) Proceed and gather on sidewalk along parking lot fence line parallel to Dennis St.
(5) Call 911. Give name and address of center.
(6) Take attendance and match to classroom attendance form; account for all children and adults.
(7) Do not re-enter building until cleared by Fire Department.

DENNIS STREET

PARKING LOT

FIGURE 12-3 Sample evacuation plan.

Source: © Cengage Learning, 2013.

Fire, earthquake, tornado, and national emergency plans and drills are important, but keep in mind that there are many other disasters that can impact the child care center in addition to those that require building evacuation. Rehearsals for building evacuation are a necessity, but how will the staff respond when a sleeping child stops breathing, when an angry noncustodial parent appears with a gun, or when an inebriated person harasses departing parents and children? How will the staff deal with a warning of a terrorist threat? There are resources in most communities to call on for help as you develop emergency plans for a vast array of possible emergencies and as you train the staff to deal with unexpected events. Invite local law enforcement personnel, health professionals, Red Cross, legal aid, and social service people to assist you with developing procedures and doing staff training. Additionally, the National Association of Child Care Resource and Referral Agencies provides several resources to assist early childhood programs in preparing for disasters (http://www.naccrra.org/disaster/) as does the National Child Care Information and Technical Assistance Center (http://nccic.acf.hhs.gov/emergency/topic_emprep.cfm).

Directors' responsibilities do not end with plan development, training and rehearsing staff on procedures, and carrying out the plan when a real disaster strikes. They also must handle the follow-up for parents and children and deal with the press. After a crisis such as a fire, a shooting, the death of a child at the center, an allegation of child abuse or neglect, or a national disaster, it is critical that accurate information be presented to families and to the public through the press. Although this responsibility usually falls to the director, it is wise to consider who else might serve as a spokesperson. A carefully selected, knowledgeable spokesperson who is savvy about handling the press can help protect the center and its families when serious emergencies or damaging allegations arise. Choices for spokesperson may be

- the center's lawyer
- the director of public relations or human resources if it is an employer-sponsored center
- a priest, rabbi, or minister if a center has a religious affiliation
- a board member or other volunteer who has a vested interest in the center, is respected in the community, and is trained in public relations (Copeland, 1996)

All staff must be trained to deflect media questions to the spokesperson or director and to answer informal questions from parents and others by quoting center written policy or by referring these inquiries to the director.

To obtain more information on the best methods to provide protection in particular areas, directors can contact local health and fire department and national security officials, building inspectors, the Environmental Protection Agency, or the Occupational Safety and Health Administration. Also, make sure *all foreseeable issues* are covered by various insurance policies.

Emergency Safety, Health, and Accident Planning

The twenty-first century presents those who care for children with new challenges relative to planning not only for children's health, injury and accidents, and natural disasters but also for the possibility of terrorist attacks. All of these plans are usually developed by the director with input from parents, staff, the board, and community groups responsible for homeland security.

Some centers may have disaster plans that are in place in case of hurricanes, tornadoes, or other weather-related events. In some cases, they will suffice for possible national security alerts as well. However, these plans need to be reviewed to make sure they are broad enough to cover bomb threats, exposure to hazardous material, and various potentially violent situations. Many states and licensing agencies prescribe forms that must be used for emergency plans (Figure 12-4).

An emergency health plan is also developed by the director. It includes the step-by-step procedures to be followed when a child is injured at the center. The purpose of this plan is to provide the center staff with a detailed set of instructions to follow when giving an injured or sick child the best and quickest treatment, notifying the family, and filling out the necessary papers for maximum liability and insurance protection for both staff and family. Many states require that centers have a medical treatment consent or authorization form on file for every child in the program (Figure 12-5). This form, when properly completed, will give the center the authority to obtain medical treatment in an emergency situation. It usually contains specific information related to the child, such as the child's name, date of birth, address, known allergies, the child's physician, and medical insurance information. Often, there is a requirement to have this form notarized. A good resource for information on what is required for this form is your child care licensing agency.

Ohio Department of Job and Family Services
MEDICAL, DENTAL AND GENERAL EMERGENCY PLAN
For Type A Homes and Child Care Centers

Center Name	Center Address
Campus Children's Learning Center	555 Any Street
Center Telephone Number	
(XXX)XXX-XXXX	

EMERGENCY TELEPHONE NUMBERS
Including 7-digit back up number as well as area code if area code must be dialed to complete the call.

Emergency Squad	Hospital
911 or (XXX)XXX-XXXX	911 or (XXX)XXX-XXXX
Police Department	**Fire Department**
911 or (XXX)XXX-XXXX	911 or (XXX)XXX-XXXX
Poison Control	**Public Childrens' Service Agency**
(XXX)XXX-XXXX)	(XXX)XXX-XXXX

LOCATION OF:

First Aid Kit(s)
Each classroom, gyms, and closet located in main hallway

Fire Extinguishers
Each classroom and hallways

Fire Alarm System/Main Panel
Mechanical room west wing

Fire Alarm Pull Stations
Located throughout the building.

Electrical Circuit Box
Hallway next to kitchen and mechanical rooms

Children's Records
Front office

Child Safety Seat (Or a statement that the center will use the emergency squad for emergency transportation of children.)
Storage closet/teacher's work room

In case of a **Dental Emergency**, stay with the child and summon help. When an additional staff member is present to assume responsibility for the rest of the group, consult the Dental First Aid Chart which should be posted in each room. Follow instructions indicated, notify the parents, and write an incident report. Remember if blood is involved, use vinyl or non latex gloves and sanitize afterwards following standard precautions.

Names of staff with current training in First Aid/Communicable Disease:
Identify staff members by name.

Names of staff with current training in CPR:
Identify staff members by name.

In case of an environmental emergency such as fire or tornado/weather alert, consult the posted evacuation plan/diagram or route to your classroom's "safe place". (Your local fire department or Emergency Management service should be able to help you determine this "safe" location ahead of time.)
Fire: Take attendance roster, secure the classroom, and exit the building with the children to the designated meeting place, which is Southwest corner of PS Playground/West side of Parking Lot. Account for all children and notify administrator or staff in charge whether all children are present or if any are missing. Do not return to classroom until the all clear is sounded. The administrator or designee should be responsible

FIGURE 12-4 Medical, dental, and general emergency plan for a child care center.

Source: Ohio Department of Job and Family Services.

for contacting the fire department or 911 if system is not automatic.

Weather Alert: Take attendance roster, secure the classroom, and lead children to the designated "safe place," which is classroom bathrooms and coat rooms. Account for all children and have them assume the safe position, covering head and neck. If blankets or protective covering are available, cover children. Notify administrator or staff in charge if all children are present or if any are missing. Stay in designated "safe place" until the all clear is sounded.

Emergency Evacuation (bomb threat, gas leak, etc.): Take attendance roster, first aid kit, and emergency contact information for children. Account for all children and exit building to the primary evacuation spot, which is southwest corner of PS playground/west side of parking lot. Account for all children with a name to face check off. Follow instructions from emergency personnel as to whether to stay in that spot or to proceed to your secondary evacuation location (which should be further away from your center in case the area around your facility also must be evacuated). The secondary location is Frericks Center on Campus. Always follow instructions of the emergency personnel on site. Parents should be notified as soon as possible. Continue to complete name to face attendance check offs on a regular basis to assure children are not lost. Complete an incident report and provide to the parents as soon as possible. ODJFS must be notified within 24 hours.

Threat of Violence: Secure children in the safest location in the building or outside. Take attendance roster and contact 911/Police. Follow instructions from authorities, account for all children with name to face attendance, notify parents as soon as possible, and complete an incident report for parents.

Loss of Power, Water, Heat: Contact utilities company to notify of outage and assess expected time of outage. Evaluate factors, including safety, temperature, daylight, refrigeration requirements, and ability to follow sanitary hygiene practices. Administrator or designee will make the determination whether the center needs to be closed or not. If in doubt contact your licensing specialist or your local health department for assistance in determining whether you can continue to provide child care services and meet rule requirements.

In the event of a **Serious Injury or Illness:** Stay with injured/ill child at all times and summon additional help if needed to supervise rest of children. Quickly complete an assessment: <u>Appearance</u>, <u>Breathing</u>, <u>Circulation</u>. Summon a staff member trained in First Aid/Communicable Disease if you are not trained, and determine whether EMS needs to be contacted. Check child's health information to determine if a Medical/Physical Health Care Plan has been completed for the child and contact parents. Provide basic first aid until EMS or parent arrives. Complete an incident report for parents. If child is ill, isolate away from other children; reference the ODH Communicable Disease Chart and follow instructions. Determine whether illness needs to be reported to ODH. Post exposure sign or written notice for parents. Complete an incident report for child's parent and sanitize cot/blanket if used. If blood or bodily fluids are involved, remember to wear vinyl or non-latex gloves and follow standard precautions for cleanup.

If situation requires medical attention, ODJFS must be notified within 24 hours of the incident and report submitted within three days.

Supervision: Children must be supervised at all times. Children in the group must be kept within sight and hearing until additional staff are available to take control of children. Staff shall stay with children until the parent arrives.

This plan should be posted in every room used by children and by every telephone. Every room should also have posted: written instructions for fire and weather alert, diagrams showing evacuation route and "safe place", and a Dental First Aid Chart.

Additional instructions for this facility:

FIGURE 12-4 (continued)

Emergency Contact Information

Child's Name _____   Date of Birth _____

Address _____   Home Phone _____

Mother's Name _____   Business Phone _____

Father's Name _____   Business Phone _____

Name of other person to be contacted in case of an emergency:

1. _____   Address _____

Relationship (sitter, relative, friend, etc.) _____   Phone _____

2. _____   Address _____

Relationship (sitter, relative, friend, etc.) _____   Phone _____

Authorization is hereby given for the Child Development Center Staff to release the above named child to the following persons, provided proper identification is first established (list all names of authorized persons, including immediate family):

1. _____   Relation: _____
2. _____   Relation: _____
3. _____   Relation: _____

Physician to be called in an emergency:

1. _____   Phone _____ or _____
2. _____   Phone _____ or _____

I, the undersigned, authorize the staff of the Child Development Center to take whatever emergency medical measures are deemed necessary for the care and protection of my child enrolled in the Child Development Center program.

_____
(Signature of Parent or Guardian/date)

Signature witnessed by:
(Notary)

_____
(Signature of Parent or Guardian/date)

The above statement sworn before me on:

_____

_____

FIGURE 12-5   Sample emergency contact information form.

Source: From MAROTZ. Health, Safety, and Nutrition for the Young Child, 8e. © 2012 Wadsworth, a part of Cengage Learning, Inc. Reproduced by permission. www.cengage.com/permissions

If the child must be taken away from the center for emergency care, the caregiver must stay with that child until the parent arrives or accompanies the child to the hospital. A signed consent form from parents that gives detailed information on where the child should be taken for emergency treatment and permission to transport the child for emergency treatment should be in each child's folder (Figure 12-5). Because the parent cannot give informed consent in advance for emergency treatment (the nature of the injury being unknown), it is essential that parents understand that the center must know their whereabouts or that of another responsible adult at all times. It is suggested that the telephone numbers on the child's emergency record, including those for the child's usual source of health care, be updated several times a year.

The director, as well as some members of the teaching staff, must be trained in administering first aid, including cardiopulmonary resuscitation (CPR), so preliminary emergency treatment can begin before professional help arrives and so minor injuries will be handled correctly. An injury report must be filled out any time a child is hurt, and it should be filed in a central location with a copy in the child's

Injury Report Form

Name of Child _____   Birth Date _____

Parent Name _____

Address _____   Phone Number _____

Usual Source of Health Care _____

Date of Injury _____ Time _____ Age _____ Sex _____

Type of Injury (circle) Bite Broken Bone Bruise Burn Choking Cut Eye Injury Foreign
                     Body Head Injury Poisoning Scrape Sliver Sprain Sting
                     Other _____

Location Where Injury Occurred _____
                  e.g., child care room, bathroom, hall, playground, large-muscle
                  room, bus, car, walk

Type of Equipment Involved _____

How Injury Happened (details of who, what, when, how): _____

_____

_____

_____

_____

Type of Treatment Required _____
                  e.g., first aid only in day care, visit to doctor's office or clinic,
                  emergency room, hospitalized, sutures, cast, bandage, medication
                  given

Signature of Person Filling Out the Report _____

Signatures of Witnesses _____

Name of Medical Professional Consulted _____

Date _____Time _____ Advice _____

FIGURE 12-6 Sample injury report form.
Source: © Cengage Learning, 2013.

file (Figure 12-6). It is essential to follow the accident plans, have staff properly trained to deal with injuries, and fill out injury reports, both for the safety and well-being of children and for the protection of staff. Directors and board members must understand that taking all these precautions may not protect the staff from liability completely. Therefore, the center should carry accident insurance on the children and have liability coverage for the staff as additional precautionary measures. It is wise to consult an attorney and an insurance agent about what constitutes adequate coverage.

Child Abuse and Neglect

Directors must be vigilant and take steps to prevent the possibility of abuse on the premises, recognize signs of abuse on children who come to the program, and make certain that suspected cases of abuse are properly reported.

Prevention on the Premises
Precautions must be taken to prevent both physical and sexual abuse on the premises. Physical abuse occurs most often when adults are stressed; further, the abusive act is unplanned and explosive and usually occurs when other adults are not around. Sexual abuse, on the other hand, is frequently planned ahead (although it also occurs when other adults are not around). Pedophiles may seek employment in child care centers to gain access to children. In the latter case, careful preemployment screening and use of criminal record checks and fingerprinting may provide helpful information.

Since abuse of all types usually occurs when other adults are not around, the preventive measures mentioned in connection with staffing patterns (Chapter 9) and developing the facility (Chapter 7) and making it clear to everyone that parents may visit at any time should help eliminate the possibility of abuse occurring in your center.

Recognizing and Reporting Abuse and Neglect

All directors and members of the teaching staff in child care programs should have some training in recognizing the physical and behavioral signs of abuse and neglect, whether or not licensing requires it. In most states, professionals involved with children are required to report suspected cases of abuse. When mandated to report suspicion of abuse or neglect, those reporting are not required to prove their allegations. Nonetheless, reports should be made carefully because much harm can come to children and families when the accusations are unfounded. The director should be notified of all suspected cases of abuse and review the case with the staff member who has found evidence of abuse before the case is reported to the authorities. In most states, information is given to law enforcement agencies or child protective agencies. Familiarity with state laws and local rules for reporting is essential for all child care directors.

Legal Issues: Health and Safety

Lawsuits by parents resulting from injury to a child in playground accidents, exposure to serious illnesses such as HIV or AIDS, injuries inflicted by other children, or alleged child abuse are a major concern of almost all center staff, administrators, and board members. Lawsuits are to be avoided, not only for reasons of wanting children in our care to be kept safe and healthy but also because the suits can be won by plaintiffs even when the center staff is right. These unfortunate results can occur as a consequence of the sympathies engendered in the courts and in the press. Centers risk losing insurance coverage and suffer irreparable damage to their reputations.

The possibility of being sued for any reason, whether for an accident, a suspicion of child abuse, or alleged wrongful exclusion of a child, can be minimized by building preventive steps into your day-to-day practices.

1. Promote open, trusting communication with parents from the time they walk in the door. When parents trust center staff, they are less likely to sue when things go wrong. The positive regard they hold for the staff encourages them to talk it through and make more rational decisions before calling in their lawyers.

2. Maintain a well-trained staff in adequate numbers to ensure proper supervision and appropriate health and safety procedures throughout each day. Make sure that staff are aware of adults who are approved to pick up children from the center. Train staff to inspect all toys and equipment for safety hazards, report all problems in writing, and carefully fill out detailed accident reports.

3. Purchase adequate liability insurance and accident insurance on all the children, even when parents have health insurance. It promotes good will and means some parents will not have to cover a deductible or co-pay requirement. You will also want to work closely with insurance agents to promote principles of risk management at the center.

4. Check all applicants' references carefully and question any gaps in their employment history. Document that references have been checked under the applicant's current name as well as all previous names.

5. Keep records of all board meetings, staff meetings, licensing monitoring reports, and staff training sessions. A plaintiff's attorney can subpoena copies of any or all of these documents, in addition to other related materials such as personnel files, memos, and appointment books.

6. Have your lawyer review all promotional and marketing materials for information that might be viewed as "deceptive" under your state's consumer protection legislation.

7. Choose an attorney who is very familiar with both liability and child care laws in your state, and periodically check with your legal advisers. Make sure you discuss the idea of "due diligence" with your attorney regarding the health and safety of children and adults in your program. It is also essential to ensure that all members of your staff understand the behaviors that constitute due diligence and that they are expected to practice those behaviors.

Keep in mind that individual staff are rarely held personally responsible for claims against the center. It is the employer who is held responsible, provided the act in question occurred within the scope of employment. Staff members may be held individually responsible only when they cause harm outside their legitimate scope of authority.

Centers are especially vulnerable to legal actions over issues of playground equipment safety and supervision and of performance of specialized health procedures to children with special needs. Recently, centers have become vulnerable over transportation issues based on changes by the National Highway Traffic Safety Administration regulating bus and van safety, as well as other changes in state regulations. (Material in this section is taken from Cohen, 1998, and Strickland & Lenbarg, 1998.)

SUMMARY

Directors are responsible for overseeing the food service and the health and safety programs in the child care center. Although a designated staff person and the center cook may plan menus, order food, and prepare meals, the director is accountable to both the center families and the sponsoring or funding agency for the quality of the food service program.

Monitoring the health program and implementing plans to care for children in the event of a national or natural disaster or for those who are injured or sick also is part of the director's responsibility. It is important to have written policies and reporting procedures for all emergencies and to rehearse for various emergency procedures. Plans for caring for sick children with specific exclusion guidelines are helpful. It also is important to take preventive precautions regarding child abuse in the center and to make certain that suspected cases of abuse are detected and reported. Consult with your attorney on a regular basis and take the necessary precautions to avoid legal action against your agency.

TRY IT OUT!

1 Before class, obtain the current reimbursement rates for both free and reduced-rate meals for eligible children on the USDA Child and Adult Food Program website (http://www.fns.usda. gov/cnd/care/Management.htm). In class,
   a. Using Working Paper 12-1, record reimbursement allowances in the spaces provided.
   b. Using information from Working Paper 12-1 and the information given in the chart "Number of Meals Served" (Working Paper 12-2), complete Working Paper 12-2 by calculating the amount to be reimbursed for meals served during the month.
   c. Share your results with a classmate. If your results differ, review your calculations together. If you are unable to resolve the discrepancy, share your results with another student pair.
   d. Discuss the potential administrative challenges in maintaining accurate records related to the food program.

2 Work with another student and role-play a conference between a director and a cook, assuming the two roles as follows:

Director: As a director, you are responsible for monitoring food preparation and serving methods. You have read numerous government publications on the best way to prepare vegetables to retain nutrients. You know that cooking time should be short, that the amount of water used should be small, and that the vegetables should be prepared only minutes before eating. Furthermore, you know that children's foods should be cut in bite-size portions, that is, stew meat in half-inch cubes, bread slices in quarters, fish sticks halved, and so forth. Your cook prepares all vegetables early in the day and keeps them over low heat until serving time. Even though the recipes indicate that meat should be served in bite-size pieces and portions should be small, the meat comes from the kitchen in the same sizes in which it was delivered from the meat market.

Cook: You were hired for this job in the child care center after being an assistant cook in a restaurant for five years. You have looked forward to having your own kitchen, and you are proud of your previous experience and what you know about preparation of food in quantity.

As director, you must call the conference and deal with the problem. Keep in mind that you are committed to maintaining open communication and to promoting the personal and professional growth of your staff.

3 As a group, discuss the evacuation plan for the room in which you are now having class. Do you see exit signs or evacuation directions in this room or in the adjacent hallways?

a. If you were responsible for this building, what steps would you take to develop a building evacuation plan and inform the staff about it?

b. If you had to use this room for a children's classroom, how would you evacuate the children and how would you prepare the children for an emergency evacuation procedure without creating anxiety and fear?

c. What issues would you need to consider in order to evacuate children or staff with medical or mobility concerns?

4 Your local chapter of the NAEYC has asked you to give a presentation to their New Director Discussion Group regarding the development of an emergency preparedness plan. Discuss what needs to be included in such a plan and develop an outline for your presentation. What resources would you share with the group?

5 Working with two classmates, review the three sets of standards that you will find in Appendices B, C, and D at the end of the textbook. Identify those standards and competencies that relate to the health, safety, and nutrition of young children. What are early childhood professionals expected to know and be able to do related to these three areas? Discuss your findings with the class.

The Education CourseMate website for this text offers many helpful resources. Go to CengageBrain.com to access the TeachSource Video Cases and other TeachSource Videos, Expand Your Learning exercises, flashcards, interactive quizzes, the eBook, reflection and enrichment activities, and downloadable forms.

Working Paper 12-1

(for use with Try It Out! 1a)

FOOD REIMBURSEMENT ALLOWANCES

	Free	*Reduced*
Breakfast	_____ per child	_____ per child
Lunch/dinner	_____ per child	_____ per child
Snack (supplements)	_____ per child	_____ per child

Fill in the above chart with information from the USDA Child and Adult Food Program website (http://www.fns.usda.gov/cnd/care/Management.htm). Use this information to complete the assignment on Working Paper 12-2.

You can download a full-size version of this form on the Education CourseMate website.

Working Paper 12-2

(for use with Try It Out! 1b)

NUMBER OF MEALS SERVED

Date	Breakfast		Lunch/Dinner		Snack	
	Free	Reduced	Free	Reduced	Free	Reduced
3	12	2	21	3	21	3
4	13	2	20	3	20	3
5	11	1	18	2	19	2
6	15	1	18	2	19	2
7	15	2	18	1	18	1
10	12	1	17	1	18	1
11	14	2	21	1	20	1
12	15	1	20	2	20	2
13	15	2	18	3	18	3
14	13	2	18	3	18	3
17	12	2	19	2	19	2
18	11	2	19	1	19	2
19	13	1	18	3	19	3
20	13	1	17	3	19	3
21	14	2	19	3	18	3
24	13	2	19	2	19	2
25	14	1	18	3	18	3
26	15	1	18	2	18	2
27	16	0	19	3	19	3
28	14	2	18	3	18	3
31	14	2	20	3	20	2
TOTAL						

Using the information from Working Paper 12-1 on reimbursement amounts for free and reduced-rate meals and the information from the chart "Number of Meals Served," fill in the following table:

Breakfast	Number of free meals × Free rate =	_____
	Number of reduced meals × Reduced rate =	_____
Lunch/dinner	Number of free meals × Free rate =	_____
	Number of reduced meals × Reduced rate =	_____
Snack	Number of free meals × Free rate =	_____
(supplement)	Number of reduced meals × Reduced rate =	_____
	Total claim for reimbursement	_____

You can download a full-size version of this form on the Education CourseMate website.

Managing the Food and the Health and Safety Programs **301**

REFERENCES

American Academy of Pediatrics, American Public Health Association, and National Resource Center for Health and Safety in Child Care and Early Education. (2011). *Caring for our children: National health and safety performance standards: Guidelines for out-of-home child care programs* (3rd ed.). Elk Grove Village, IL: American Academy of Pediatrics, Washington, DC: American Public Health Association, and Aurora, CO: National Resource Center for Health and Safety in Child Care and Early Education.

Aronson, S. & Shope, T. (2009). *Managing infectious diseases in child care and schools: A quick reference guide* (2nd ed.). Elk Grove Village, IL: American Academy of Pediatrics.

Button, L. (2008). When is a child too sick? Devising a "sick child" policy for your center. *Child Care Information Exchange, 183*, 88–91.

Centers for Disease Control and Prevention, National Institutes of Health, HIV Medicine Association of the Infectious Diseases Society of America, Pediatric Infectious Diseases Society & American Academy of Pediatrics. (2009). *Guidelines for the prevention and treatment of opportunistic infections among HIV-exposed and HIV-infected children*. Retrieved from http://www.aidsinfo.nih/gov/Guidelines/GuidelineDetail.aspx?MenuItem=Guidelines&Search=Off&GuidelineID=211&ClassID=4.

Cohen, A. J. (1998). Bettering the odds of not getting sued. In R. Neugebauer and B. Neugebauer (Eds.), *The art of leadership: Managing early childhood organizations*. Redmond, WA: CCIE.

Committee on Injury, Violence and Poison Prevention, American Academy of Pediatrics. (2010). Policy statement—prevention of choking among children. *Pediatrics, 125*(3), 601–607.

Copeland, M. L. (1996). Code blue! Establishing a child care emergency plan. *Child Care Information Exchange, 107*, 17–21.

Graville, I. (2008). Food allergies: Being aware and planning for care. *Child Care Information Exchange, 192*, 42–44. Redmond, WA: CCIE.

Marotz, L. R. (2012). *Health, safety, and nutrition for the young child* (8th ed.). Belmont, CA: Wadsworth Cengage Learning.

Strickland, J. & Lenbarg, M. (1998). Teacher aides and other dangerous instruments: Lessons in self-defense. In R. Neugebauer & B. Neugebauer (Eds.), *The art of leadership: Managing early childhood organizations*. Redmond, WA: CCIE.

UNAIDS. (2010). *UNAIDS report on the global AIDS epidemic 2010*. Retrieved from http://www.unaids.org/globalreport/Global_report.htm.

U.S. Department of Agriculture. (n.d.). *Choking hazards*. Retrieved February 15, 2011, from http://www.mypyramid.gov/Preschoolers/FoodSafety/chokinghazards.html.

WORKING *with* FAMILIES, VOLUNTEERS, AND THE COMMUNITY

Bombeck Family Learning Center

Family and community partnerships can enrich the curriculum, making learning more meaningful for children.

In her classic 1984 article, Ellen Galinsky states, "The job of the child care center director is one that calls for enormous skill, particularly in working with parents. It is being a professional who simultaneously creates a friendly atmosphere yet retains an appropriate distance; an expert who builds competence in others, who is understanding, empathetic, yet at times firm. Most important is the role of the model—whose words or way of handling a sad, tired, or exuberant child are inspiring to parents" (p. 4). Developing a first-class program for children is the goal of the child care center administrator and having a high-quality program cannot happen without involving families and tending to their needs. Working with volunteers and community organizations or agencies also is an integral part of the total center program that falls within the director's purview. Creating a positive climate based on good communication and demonstrating cross-cultural competence is essential for the success of this part of the program.

Objectives

After reading this chapter, you should be able to:

- Identify strategies for establishing reciprocal relationships with families.
- List items to be included in a handbook for families.
- Discuss contents and the value of center newsletters.
- Understand the process of recruiting and adding volunteers and becoming active in the community in which services are provided.

Standards Addressed in this Chapter

naeyc Professional Preparation
Standards 2, 3

naeyc Administrator Competencies
Management Knowledge
and Skills 6, 7, 8, 9
Early Childhood Knowledge
and Skills 6

naeyc Accreditation Standards 7, 8

SUPPORTING AND INVOLVING FAMILIES   naeyc

Center directors have a unique role in helping to establish a program that is respectful of families while also meeting the needs of children and staff. Sometimes conflicting needs of these stakeholder groups arise and the director needs to be intentional about creating a system of policies and procedures as well as opportunities for relationship building that promote a positive outcome for all. While classroom staff members or someone designated as a family coordinator may assume some responsibility for family involvement strategies, directors are ultimately responsible for monitoring these efforts, providing an effective role model, and serving as a resource for both staff and families.

With the recent revision of the NAEYC Position Statement on Developmentally Appropriate Practices (2009), expectations regarding family support and involvement have increased and are clearly stated in the fifth guideline, shown in Figure 13-1.

Developmentally appropriate practices derive from deep knowledge of child development principles and of the program's children in particular, as well as the context within which each of them is living. The younger the child, the more necessary it is for practitioners to acquire this particular knowledge through relationships with children's families. Practice is not developmentally appropriate if the program limits "parent involvement" to scheduled events (valuable though these may be) or if the program/family relationship has a strong "parent education" orientation. Parents do not feel like partners in the relationship when staff members see themselves as having all the knowledge and insight about children and view parents as lacking such knowledge.

Such approaches do not adequately convey the complexity of the partnership between teachers and families that is a fundamental element of good practice. The following describe the kind of relationships that are developmentally appropriate for children (from birth through the primary grades), in which family members and practitioners work together as members of the learning community.

1 In reciprocal relationships between practitioners and families, there is mutual respect, cooperation, shared responsibility, and negotiation of conflicts toward achievement of shared goals. (Also see guideline 1, "Creating a Caring Community of Learners.")

2 Practitioners work in collaborative partnerships with families, establishing and maintaining regular, frequent two-way communication with them. (With families who do not speak English, teachers should use the language of the home if they are able or try to enlist the help of bilingual volunteers.)

3 Family members are welcome in the setting, and there are multiple opportunities for family participation. Families participate in program decisions about their children's care and education.

4 Teachers acknowledge a family's choices and goals for the child and respond with sensitivity and respect to those preferences and concerns, but without abdicating the responsibility that early childhood practitioners have to support children's learning and development through developmentally appropriate practices.

5 Teachers and the family share with each other their knowledge of the particular child and understanding of child development and learning as part of day-to-day communication and in planned conferences. Teachers support families in ways that maximally promote family decision-making capabilities and competence.

6 Practitioners involve families as a source of information about the child (before program entry and on an ongoing basis) and engage them in the planning for their child.

7 The program links families with a range of services, based on identified resources, priorities, and concerns.

FIGURE 13-1 Establishing reciprocal relationships with families.
Source: © Cengage Learning, 2013.

▶❚❚ TEACHSOURCE VIDEO VIGNETTE

Infants and Toddlers: Family Interactions, School, and Community

Visit Chapter 13 of the **CourseMate website** and view the video vignette entitled *Infants and Toddlers: Family Interactions, School, and Community.*

As part of the newly revised guidelines for developmentally appropriate practice, the NAEYC explains the importance of "establishing reciprocal relationships with families" (NAEYC, 2009, p. 23). Read the excerpt from the position statement above and consider how well the teachers in this video met this guideline. How did the teachers in this video strive to involve families as partners in the care and education of the toddlers?

▶❚❚ TEACHSOURCE VIDEO VIGNETTE

English Language Learners: Partnering with Parents to Promote Oral Language and Early Literacy

Visit Chapter 13 of the **CourseMate website** and view the video vignette entitled, *English Language Learners: Partnering with Parents to Promote Oral Language and Early Literacy.*

Home language is highly valued in this video, with parents being encouraged to use the family's native language at home. What strategies can teachers use in their classrooms that show that they value home language while helping children learn to speak English at school?

Reciprocal Relationships with Families from Diverse Backgrounds

The director must demonstrate a positive attitude toward families and what they can contribute to the center program. As is stated in the NAEYC Position Statement, the success of these efforts is dependent on a reciprocal relationship with families which is based on mutual respect. Establishing and maintaining this kind of relationship with families is challenging because of the different cultures that make up today's society and the resulting diverse views on parenting and education. The recent U.S. census reports that 20 percent of families use a language other than English at home (U.S. Census Bureau, 2009). This diversification of the U.S. population is impacted not only by language differences but also by varied values, beliefs, traditions, and customs related to childrearing, parenting, education, health, and a myriad of other topics that can lead to miscommunication, mistrust, and discord. It is important to recognize that differing opinions will exist, conflicts will arise, and there is a need for an open exchange of ideas, goals, and needs between families, staff, and the director.

Interactions between center staff and families must be respectful; staff must demonstrate intercultural competence. With the significant alterations in the American family, the changing complexion of center families requires a multicultural mindset that values diversity (Gordon & Browne, 2010). As U.S. society becomes more heterogeneous, intercultural competence is an essential skill set for all service providers who work with young children and their families. The need to be interculturally competent is critical for all who work with young children and their families (Hanson, 2011).

Challenges to Communicating with Parents

In addition to language and cultural differences, there are a number of reasons why parents may be hesitant about communicating with the center director or staff. Parenting is a challenging endeavor in even the most optimal of circumstances. Parents who are successful in other areas of their lives may have great difficulty dealing with the unpredictability of or lack of control associated with having young children. Many parents are amazed by the skill that early childhood practitioners demonstrate in getting young children to cooperate. These same parents often report feeling incompetent when they struggle to transition their crying or uncooperative children into the classroom. Add in additional factors such as poverty or a lack of school success, and many parents feel inhibited in their ability to communicate their needs to center staff (Decker & Decker, 2008). Feeling fully included in the center's community may also be difficult for parents who face challenges such as being a single parent, having a child with a disability, being a victim of domestic violence, having limited competence in English, or struggling with literacy.

Teachers tend to interface most easily with families who are most like their family of origin. "Teachers are unlikely to find another family that exactly duplicates the families with which they are most familiar, in which they grew up. Families are created by the ideas, emotions and experiences of unique individuals. Their living places, their foods and family traditions, and their styles of communicating and living together are familiar and comfortable to those within the family and to no one else" (Gestwicki, 2010, p. 4).

The actions of staff and the atmosphere at the center must communicate to family members that each is valued as an individual and that each is highly regarded as the child's first teachers and as those who know a great deal about the child. All parents should be aware that they are welcome to come as frequently (or as infrequently) as they wish.

Any number of things can communicate a feeling of acceptance and trust to family members, although some are more tangible than others. A parent-receiving area is the place where parents establish their first impressions of the center. Take time to look at this transition space from the perspective of a rushed parent who is late for work or a tired grandmother or uncle who enters the building to drop off or pick up a child. Is it welcoming and aesthetically pleasing, softly lit, freshly painted, carpeted, and clean? It can be made to feel "homey" and more pleasant if there is comfy adult seating with a collection of items for children to handle and explore. A fish tank or collection of musical instruments can draw both parents and children into the center, helping to facilitate more calm and pleasant transitions.

Parent information folders in this space sometimes contain information about the center, highlight interesting articles, and display a calendar of coming events. Pamphlets and journals on parenting, child development, toy selection, nutrition, and other resources for families can be made available in the parent-receiving area. A parent and child book lending library or toy lending library might be located nearby. Sometimes, interested family members are asked to manage the entire lending program.

Some centers choose to offer additional family-friendly supports such as take-out meals or dry cleaning pickup. When James Hymes originally presented this idea, he was responding to a need during World War II when mothers worked seven days a week, and many did not drive or had a limited gasoline supply if they did drive. Although few present-day parents work day or night shifts seven days a week, many find themselves using time-saving, affordable measures that help them meet their family's needs. These offerings can help ease some of the nagging stresses on young families. If you choose to offer these "extras" to your families, you must consider the space and staffing requirements, as well as costs to you and your staff in time and energy. All related expenses then should be factored into your cost per child.

The less tangible things that make family members feel welcome include the manner in which their calls are handled by the staff member who answers the telephone or the greeting they receive from the van driver who picks up their child each day. Parents' feelings about the center program and staff also are substantially influenced by their first contacts with their child's teacher or the center director. It is very difficult to perceive what is having the most significant impact on the parents' reactions to a center program, so directors have to be alert to any number of subtle factors that may be influencing parental attitudes and feelings.

The building of reciprocal relationships with families depends on the feelings of trust that are established among the center staff, the children, and the families who use the center. Such trust begins to develop at the first contact and will continue to grow as it is nurtured by center staff.

The family program can be divided into three major categories:

1. family interactions
2. family support
3. family involvement

Clearly, these three aspects of the program overlap; however, they are separated here for the purpose of discussion.

Family Interactions

Family interactions range from the most informal arrival or departure greetings, phone calls, email, and Facebook postings to formal interviews, regularly scheduled conferences, and special conferences when problems are encountered. Whatever the occasion, interactions with family members can be the basis for establishing trusting relationships. It is through these contacts that the center staff members communicate to parents that they have important information to share with one another and that they have a very special mutual concern for a child whom they both value. Information that is not shared during enrollment or orientation will often be shared when trust has been established, so it is important to provide ongoing opportunities to talk. Viewing parents as partners rather than as "we" versus "they" enhances the family/center staff relationship. Chapter 10 discusses details of initial interviews and intake procedures. When staff members are not fully prepared to handle initial contacts with families, in-service training time should be devoted to discussion or role-play of parent interviews and intake procedures. (See Chapter 14 for the discussion of in-service training.)

Contacts with families range from the daily drop-off and separation in the early morning and occasional phone calls and exchange of information during the day, to the late day reunion that can be emotional and rushed. In addition to these daily casual contacts, have a system in place for daily written communication to parents through a report form or a parent journaling plan so teachers can share something special each day about each child. All of these occasions provide opportunities to greet, welcome, and exchange information with parents but are inappropriate times to address a child's progress or to bring up more substantial problems or issues that require focused attention and discussion. It is best for teachers, families, and, ultimately, the child if these discussions are left for a planned phone conference or a scheduled parent conference.

Regularly scheduled parent conferences provide an opportunity for parents and teachers to meet at a mutually agreed-upon time and place to discuss the child. It may take several scheduled conferences and unscheduled calls or casual contacts before a teacher is successful in creating a totally relaxed environment in which both parent and teacher can discuss the child comfortably. When a good relationship

DIRECTOR'S CORNER

"I make it clear at my very first meeting with a prospective family that we are open to parents visiting at any time. Our parents understand that even before admission to the program, they can come by to observe in our classrooms as they are weighing the pros and cons of sending their child to this center. It's the first step on the road to building a trusting relationship between the staff at the center and the families that we serve."

—Director and owner, for-profit center

exists, the scheduled conference is a time when parents and teachers can discuss the child's progress, present their concerns and their satisfaction about the child's progress, and develop a plan to follow both at home and at school that will help the child grow to full potential. In the interval between scheduled conferences, casual telephone calls and informal contacts at the center are both ways to quickly comment and update how the plan for the child and the family is working.

Preconference planning sheets can be a useful tool in planning some parent conferences. Depending on the parent population being served, you, as a director, may have both the parents and the teachers complete a preconference planning sheet (Figure 13-2). Those parents who may have limited writing or reading skills may feel uncomfortable filling out a form with open-ended questions like those in the sample. In cases like this, teachers can call or chat with the parents when children

Bombeck Family Learning Center

Transition times can provide a unique opportunity for informal but important conversations.

Child's Name: _____

Parent(s) Name: _____

Date and Time of Conference: _____

Above is the date and time of your parent/teacher conference. Please call the office and reschedule if the assigned time is not convenient.

   I look forward to talking with you about your child. Some of the things I have planned to share with you are:

   I am specifically interested in finding out about the areas of interest or concern that you would like to discuss with me. Please use the space below to tell me what those things are.

Please return this to my box in the office at least a week before the scheduled conference.

Thank you very much.

FIGURE 13-2   Sample preconference planning sheet.
Source: © Cengage Learning, 2013.

are brought to the classroom. When dates and times are set in these casual conversations, it probably is wise for the teacher to remind families when their scheduled conference time draws near. Experienced teachers can plan the conference based on information from their notes and observations of the child, the information supplied by the family, and their knowledge of the characteristics of an effective parent conference. The director can model and provide some coaching for inexperienced staff before they conference with parents. Role-playing works well when coaching teachers.

After the preconference planning sheet has been developed, it can be used as a basis for outlining the conference itself. Items on the conference outline might include the following:

- greeting and stating the plan for this conference
- sharing a positive experience the child had within the past couple of days
- asking parents how things are at home and actively listening to their responses
- showing work samples from the child's portfolio and discussing developmental expectations in various areas represented in the samples (e.g., art, writing, and the like)
- sharing anecdotes that will focus discussion on the child's strengths as well as on those areas for potential growth (e.g., math concepts, social interactions, self-help and independence, self-control, and so forth)

- asking the parents to share what they would like to see happening for their child in the classroom during the ensuing months
- developing a plan that will facilitate the child's progress toward the agreed-upon goals and expectations discussed during this conference
- closing with consensus on when the next conference should be held, while making sure the door is left open for ongoing dialogue

It is important that parent conferences start and end on a positive note and that incidents or samples of work be used to make specific points about the child's progress. Parents must be given time to express concerns while teachers practice their best listening skills. During the conference, attention to differences in communication skills, beliefs, values, and child-rearing practices, all of which reflect growing up in a particular region or culture, will shape the tone and direction of the conversation. Just as early childhood professionals build trust with children by listening to concerns and reflecting those feelings, so they build trust with parents by practicing those same listening skills. Putting parents at ease and avoiding arousing anxiety enhances the quality of the relationship during the conference and carries over to the daily interactions with parents as well.

Special conferences sometimes are necessary when either parents or teachers have a need to discuss particular concerns about a child or the center program. The special conferences are likely to produce anxiety for everyone because they are called most often when a problem arises. Sometimes, the director is asked to sit in on a special conference to give support to both teacher and the family and to help clarify what is being said and heard. The teacher may have a conference with the director prior to a particularly difficult parent conference so that they both have a clear understanding of the problem to be discussed. The teacher also may ask the director to recommend the best way to present a problem and to offer some suggestions on how to handle the parents' questions and reactions during the conference. Sometimes, these special conferences include other specialists or consultants from other agencies, such as a mental health specialist or a speech and hearing professional. Both the teacher and the director should be well prepared for special conferences because they will be expected to make a knowledgeable contribution to the discussion about the child. In some cases, when outside specialists are called in, they will have to provide support for the parent, who may feel tense and threatened.

Uninterrupted time and a comfortable space are essential for successful parent conferences. Timing is important; the time of day or evening that is chosen must suit both the staff members and the family so that no one feels pressured or rushed. The time allotted must be long enough to discuss matters thoroughly, but not so long that the discussion becomes tedious. Consider allowing at least 30 minutes of uninterrupted conversation time for a conference. Usually both parents are encouraged to attend conferences, but in cases of divorce or separation, teachers may be expected to arrange a conference with each parent. Both teacher and family members leave a successful conference feeling they have accomplished their goals. In addition, parents should go away with an awareness that their child is valued and appreciated. Finally, it is *critical* that parents have complete confidence that confidentiality will be maintained. The parent-teacher trust relationship will be seriously damaged if a parent learns from some outside source that shared information about the family or the child was not kept confidential.

A postconference review will help teachers evaluate the quality of their participation. It is especially important for the director to meet with inexperienced teachers after they have had a conference with a center family, even if the director participated in the conference planning or the conference itself. It is an excellent way to support new teachers and provides a time to encourage them to reflect on how they are feeling about the conference as well as

what may help them in their subsequent interactions with the family. The following checklist will help them focus on their responses during the conference. Directors may want to review the following questions with their teachers after their encounters with parents:

- Did you give the parents plenty of time to talk about their concerns?
- Did you remain an accepting listener?
- Were you able to restrain yourself from giving advice? Did you ask rather than tell?
- Did you remember that suggestions usually are nothing more than advice under a different guise?
- Did the parents do most of the talking?
- Were you able to restate to the parent the feelings just expressed, always using your best active listening skills?
- Are you comfortable that the parent left feeling that you really cared?

Family Support

In recent years the field has moved away from the parent education model that tends to focus on deficits and toward a family support approach designed to build on their strengths and foster resiliency. One such effort is the *Strengthening Families* program developed by the Center for the Study of Social Policy. This free and open access program is research-based and incorporates an approach to build five protective factors in families. Originally the program was designed to "reduce the incidence of child abuse and neglect by providing parents with what they need to parent effectively, even under stress" (Center for Social Policy, n.d.). It is noted, however, that many of the strategies in this program have been useful for families who have not been identified as at risk. *Strengthening Families* has been adopted by many states as the framework for state-sponsored family support programs for child care and other programs for young children and families.

One popular strategy from the *Strengthening Families* program is the "Parent Cafe," an approach that has been used in many programs for young children nationally. The "Parent Cafe" concept brings families together to discuss topics that they feel are important. This program capitalizes on the skills and strengths of families through a series of informal but structured small group conversations that are facilitated by trained parent leaders. The goal is to directly engage parents in building the protective factors needed to prevent maltreatment and promote healthy outcomes for their children.

The Center for the Study of Social Policy has learned that this approach is especially effective in engaging parents because:

- The intimacy of the conversation and parent leadership help to create a level of candor that might not be achieved in a standard focus group or other feedback or input process.

- The careful structuring of the questions helps synthesize knowledge across a range of individual experience.

- Parents trained as cafe hosts feel that they have an area of expertise and skill base for other leadership roles (Center for the Study of Social Policy, n.d.).

Directors who seek to strengthen families look for opportunities to meet needs that are specific to the population that they serve. For example, a center that serves many immigrant families may consider offering a program for English language learners. Some centers provide vocational education programs or special remedial classes to help parents complete high school or take the General Education Development test (GED). (A successful score on the GED leads to a high school equivalency certificate.) One center that served many busy professional families offered parent support resources online and chose to moderate an ongoing blog in which parents could ask questions and participate in conversations from their home or office computer. Regardless of the format and content of the parent support program, they must be built on mutual trust and strive to foster a reciprocal relationship with families.

DIRECTOR'S CORNER

"A group of parents came to me with a request for a workshop on parenting skills. We had held workshops like this in the past that were not very well attended and one that ended with several parents arguing about an approach that was recommended by one of our staff members. I have to say I was a little gun shy about offering a workshop. We then learned about the 'Parent Cafe' through our local child care resource and referral agency. Because the 'Parent Cafe' was sponsored and facilitated by families it was well attended. Parents talked about topics important to them and a support network was created."

—Director, suburban for-profit center

Planning parent support programs is the responsibility of the director, but the planning group should include parent and staff representatives. Format and content must reflect the needs and interests of the parents and be adjusted to the level of education and previous training of the parent population. Centers that serve families from diverse educational, cultural, and socioeconomic backgrounds should present a wide variety of choices from which the parents can select programs that are best suited to their needs.

Activities in the parent support program may be as informal as casual classroom observations followed by one-to-one or small-group discussions with a staff member or as formal as a planned lecture, workshop, panel discussion, or seminar. The planned activities should meet the parents' needs in terms of timing, content, and presentation strategy. Casual classroom observations are particularly helpful to parents who are curious about how their child's behavior compares with that of peers. For example, a mother who feels great concern about the explosive yelling and unacceptable language of her preschool son may feel reassured when she observes other 4-year-olds who also are noisy and explosive. It is then helpful for that mother to discuss these erratic outbursts with the director or a staff member who can interpret the behavior in terms of expected behaviors at this developmental stage. Group discussions, lectures, films, videotapes, DVDs, or workshops that are offered by center staff members or by outside consultants can be useful tools for providing parents with information on parenting, child development, or topics related to parental problems and concerns. Including a social time along with information sharing creates a nonthreatening, relaxed, learning atmosphere.

Topics of interest and concern to parents range from specific questions like, "What do I do about my child who awakens at 4:30 a.m. every day and wants to get up?" to broader issues facing employed parents who struggle with the stresses of job, home, and family. Programs should build on family strengths that increase parents' sense of expertise. In planning parent support programs, consider emphasis on empowering parents to explore ways to cope with their concerns and issues around parenting.

Directors are responsible for ensuring that parent support programs and parent meetings are both timely and responsive to the parents' interests and concerns. A designated parent educator may select some of the topics for parent meetings, but when parents are involved in planning parent meetings, the topics are more likely to be relevant to parents' interests (Hildebrand & Hearron, 2010).

Parent meetings usually are considered part of the total parent support program. The frequency of scheduled parent meetings varies widely from program to program. Some programs offer monthly meetings, while others have as few as one or two meetings a year. The first meeting of the year for a preschool on the typical public school calendar often is devoted to introducing the staff and taking parents through a typical day at school by using slides, videos, DVDs, or classroom visitation. The format for all parent meetings should include time for questions and for informal socialization. Regular parent meetings are a good way to create a parent support group that can be mobilized to act as a strong political force when threats to child care programs arise in your community.

Low parent turnout is a chronic issue and often very discouraging for center directors and staff who plan for parent visits to the classroom, prepare refreshments, and look forward to meeting and sharing with parents. It requires creative planning, taking time to determine the best timing for meetings, and exploring what might interest this particular population of parents. Maybe they want to learn about using the Internet or have a tasting party of Thai foods. Shifting from an exclusive focus on parenting sometimes can encourage more families to attend center functions. As center gatherings become popular, parents may begin to ask for more meetings that focus on parenting issues or child development.

Parent Involvement

Parent conferences and parent support programs are, indeed, parent involvement, but the parent involvement concept implies a more extensive parental commitment than participation in parent conferences or in selected parts of the parent education program. Although parents should be encouraged to become involved, they also should have the option to remain uninvolved. It is an imposition on the parents' right to choose if they are made to feel that they must become involved in the center program. Of course, if the program is a co-op, then by definition it requires full parent participation.

The NAEYC has incorporated family and community culture as an important influence in designing quality developmentally appropriate practice for young children (2009). One purpose of parent involvement is to get parents active in planning, implementing, and evaluating the total program. In some comprehensive child care programs such as Head Start, parents may serve on advisory and policy boards, participate in all aspects of program planning and classroom activity, take part in the evaluation of staff and program, participate in budget and personnel decisions, and come to understand their role as advocates for their children.

Parents sometimes enjoy working regularly in the classroom or helping with children's parties or field trips, and some center programs depend on the help that parents can provide. Before parents participate in any aspect of the children's program, they should know something about classroom ground rules, routines, and what to expect of the children. The mother who comes to read to the children may need some help on how to include children other than her own in a small, informal, shared reading experience. The father who takes a morning off to come and read to the children may be disappointed when only three or four children are interested enough to stay for more than one book. He must be helped to understand that children have choices and that they are free to choose not to participate. It also is helpful if he knows the ground rules about deciding who chooses books to be read and techniques for helping children wait to have their choice read. Parents who work in the classroom on a regular basis should be expected to participate in a more extensive orientation program before being assigned specific tasks when they come to the center. Both parents and volunteers can attend the same orientation sessions.

There are innumerable ways for parents to be involved in the center program other than direct classroom participation. They can do clerical work, repair or make equipment, take responsibility for the lending library, babysit during conference periods or

Parent volunteers can inspire children to look at an existing activity as new and novel.

Bombeck Family Learning Center

committee meetings, drive carpools, and participate in advocacy endeavors with help from staff. If they have special talents or interests in fund-raising, they can serve as a resource for the center board or the director. If they have special language skills, they can provide priceless service in bilingual programs. There also are many opportunities for parents to serve in a variety of ways on the board, on advisory committees, or on any number of standing or ad hoc committees. (See Chapter 4 for the discussion of the composition of the center board and of the committee structure.)

Clearly, when the director is committed to parent involvement and that attitude prevails throughout the center, it is possible to find a special place for every parent to participate, provided the parent has the time and interest to become involved. However, it is important for the director to be sensitive to individual family situations. Employed parents who are unable to be involved with center activities must be reassured that they are free to choose not to participate. Successful parent involvement does require some management; therefore, the center staff must make a commitment to that program to give it the time and attention it requires.

Working with Demanding Parents

The best centers work to empower parents. Administrators and teachers develop partnerships over time with parents who gradually come to feel they are a valued participant in their child's care at the center. There always will be angry parents and some "high maintenance" parents who will challenge the staff. Staff members will have to remember and practice their best communication, conflict resolution, and problem-solving skills when faced with these parents.

There are situations in which staff feelings and perceptions work against forming partnerships with parents. Parents can become "they" when these staff members get together for staff meetings. "They don't tell us what is happening at home." "They don't follow through at home." "They don't set any limits at home." Or "They are too restrictive at home." Staff might comment, "They don't care" when referring to a parent who seems to have no interest in discussing child-related issues. On the other side of that coin, a staff member may comment, "She will not leave me alone—she questions me about everything he did or said while he was here at school and wants to know exactly what I did in response to his actions." Helping staff value diversity in family lifestyles and attitudes, as well

as how various parents choose to communicate or not communicate with staff about their concerns, is something directors can plan to discuss at staff meetings and staff retreats and can model in their interactions with families (adapted from Greenman, 2003). It is helpful if staff can manage to view parents as partners and find ways to see situations from the parents' point of view.

Every program, sooner or later, will have to deal with angry and/or "high maintenance," demanding parents. Directors can encourage all staff to make encounters and exchanges with these, as well as all, parents as customer friendly as possible. Child care staff may not view families and children as customers, but a review of what customers are may clarify for all that the center clients are its customers. Customers are

- people who buy products or services from you
- not dependent on you; you are dependent on them
- not interruptions to your work; they are the purpose of your work
- not people you argue with; they are people you value and serve (adapted from Phipps, 2003)

Directors and all center staff are obliged to work on building positive relationships with children and center families (customers). When confronted with the angry parent's tirade or the needy "high maintenance" parent's demands on their time, it is an opportunity for center staff to make effective conflict-resolution part of their customer service plan strategies (see Figure 13-3). Customer interests and needs must be dealt with in a helpful and respectful manner, even when they are extreme and unrealistic in terms of center policy or developmentally best practices or violate privacy and confidentiality rights of the director, teachers, or families.

Responses to parent demands will depend upon the nature of the concern and availability of resources to meet those demands. Many of them will be best served by talking with them; inviting them to observe; or encouraging them to attend parent meetings that focus on topics such as child development, early childhood practice, or center policies regarding transitions, fees and admissions, referrals, and so forth. Parents who demand that toddler teachers use whatever procedures necessary to toilet train their child or insist the "biter" in the classroom be removed from the program may respond to reading materials about toddler development or a discussion group with other toddler families, after discussing the issue with the director. Preschool

Conflict Resolution Policy: Conflict between Adults

While every effort is made to meet the needs of children, parents, and staff, we realize that from time to time a conflict may occur between parents, staff, and administrators. The following process is followed should a conflict occur:

- Step One – A respectful discussion is held between the persons directly involved at a time and place that assures privacy and sufficient time for a thorough resolution to take place.
- Step Two – If resolution is not found at the first meeting, a second meeting is held with the director for the purpose of creating a plan for resolution and a timeline for expected success.
- Step Three – If the conflict is not resolved according to the timeline, adjustments may be made to the plan, and an additional timeline be established, or:
- Step Four – If at any time the director determines that resolution is not possible, s/he will consider one of the following for immediate action:

- Removal of the child from the classroom
- Withdrawal of services from the center
- Suspension of the staff member until disciplinary steps can be taken
- Involvement of the Assistant Dean of the School of Education and Allied Professions
- Grounds for determining that a resolution is not possible include but are not exclusive of the following:

1. any person involved displays inappropriate behavior such as shouting, accusing, name-calling, swearing, or physical assault
2. any person involved refuses to follow the prescribed process
3. any person involved jeopardizes the process by spreading information concerning the conflict to those outside the immediate conflict or those involved in the resolution of the process.

FIGURE 13-3 Sample conflict resolution policy in a parent handbook.
Source: Reprinted with permission from the Bombeck Family Learning Center of the University of Dayton.

parents who insist that their child be taught the alphabet through drill and practice or finish all the food on the plate before leaving the table may need to better understand center curriculum and be willing to look over a copy of the center's Curriculum Framework and discuss it with the director, or attend a meeting with other preschool parents to hear the staff talk about best practices for this age group. When there are issues regarding meals, a parent might be interested in observing mealtime in one of the preschool classrooms followed by a conversation with the director and the teacher about developmental expectations that relate to eating and appetite for this age group. Working with demanding parents is time consuming and difficult but essential for center morale, center community building, and letting families know that their needs and concerns are taken seriously and will be heard.

Parent Feedback

Parents' viewpoints and suggestions can be solicited with rating scales or questionnaires. Some method of gathering evidence about family satisfaction with the parent program or parent involvement opportunities

should be done annually. The information gathered is then summarized and evaluated so adjustments can be made to best meet parents' needs. Much information can also be gleaned from parent-teacher conferences, when teachers can make family-specific inquiries such as "Are your needs for information on Alley's daily experiences and interests being met?" or "How would you prefer we communicate during your maternity leave about how Ben is handling the arrival of the new baby?" However, written evaluations or rating scales that draw attention to particular features of the total parent program, like the daily reports that are prepared for parents or the specialists brought in to discuss issues relevant to kindergarten readiness or infant "tummy time," offer respondents time to ponder and reflect on the attention given to the program. As families have time to consider what is offered, they will not only realize the breadth and depth of the parent program but also may choose to communicate ideas about how it might be improved. Directors must try to continue to let parents know that they are eager to hear from them and to partner with them to provide the best possible experiences for all members of the center community.

DIRECTOR'S CORNER

"I realize now that I really have to keep in touch with what parents are thinking about our program and how they see us. Last year we had two or three families leave our program, and I wasn't really sure why they were making a move. When I contacted several of them, I realized they were feeling that the quality of our program was not what they had come to expect from us. Of course, I acted on that immediately, but I also developed a rating scale for parents to complete so they could let us know how we're doing."

—Director, suburban for-profit center

WRITTEN COMMUNICATION MATERIALS FOR FAMILIES   naeyc

A handbook for families is a convenient way to communicate basic program information and should be distributed to all families at some point in the enrollment procedure. The contents may change from year to year and vary from program to program, so directors will have to use some general guidelines for developing a handbook, then adapt those to their specific program. Some items, like program philosophy or grouping children, may or may not be part of the marketing brochure but could be repeated in the handbook. As a director, you will have to decide what information parents need to know and the best way to convey it to them. If a handbook seems too overwhelming for the particular parent population in your program, consider putting an item or two on colorful single sheets to be handed out over a period of several weeks after admission to the program.

The suggested list of items that follows is not exhaustive but provides broad guidelines for developing a parent handbook (see sample handbook for families in Director's Resource 13-1). Directors often choose to avoid including items likely to change, such as names of staff and fees. One option is to have a pocket in the back cover where single pages can be added and removed as updates are needed.

- brief statement of the program philosophy
- outline of the daily program and an explanation of how it fits into the program philosophy

- fees and arrangements for payment, including details about reimbursement possibilities and credit for absences
- car pool and/or transportation arrangements; if transportation is not provided, indicate that fact and state what information you need to have about the family's transportation arrangements for the child
- expected arrival and pickup times and procedures
- center policy on health and safety precautions to be taken by the family and the center staff to ensure the health and safety of children; state your policy about bringing medication to the center and children coming to the center when symptoms of illness are apparent, and cover the procedures used by the center staff when a child becomes ill at school and so on
- explanation of liability and medical insurance carried by and/or available through the center
- sample menus for snacks and/or meals and any expectations the staff may have about eating
- services the center staff will offer to children and families, such as opportunities for having conferences, special medical or psychological services or referrals, discussion groups, group meetings, and so on
- center discipline policy
- requests for help from parents such as for time spent in the classroom, help on field trips, clerical help, making materials for the classroom, and so on
- summary of scheduled events at the center and what families may do at the center to celebrate holidays and birthdays; make the policies in this regard reflect the program philosophy by including what to send, what to expect the child to bring home, which holidays will be celebrated, and so on
- expectations about the child's use of transition objects while getting adjusted to the center and policies about bringing other items or food from home, making clear how these policies are developed to meet the needs of children and to reflect the program philosophy
- description of the legal obligations of center staff to report any evidence of child abuse

This list provides guidelines for developing a handbook that ultimately must be fashioned to fit your program and your parent population. In writing material for a handbook, it is important to consider content, format, length, and, most important, style of writing. Should the style be scholarly or chatty, formal or informal, general or detailed? Answers to these questions can be found by giving careful consideration to the families being served by the program.

The family handbook is a useful tool to acquaint parents with the center program initially and to help them understand what to expect. However, it must be supplemented with other written and verbal communications to keep them abreast of center events and the progress of their children. Other details concerning your program can be listed on your website. In some communities, it will be necessary to publish not only the handbook but all written materials in another language in addition to English.

Some directors send parents a newsletter describing special events that are being planned for children or families. It is important for parents to know that one family brought their new baby to visit the classroom or that a musician from a symphony orchestra came to show the children a slide trombone. Such information will help parents understand a child's questions and any ideas that are expressed at home. Newsletters can keep parents informed about the center's progress, program philosophy, special programs, and future plans. It can include a monthly calendar, information about fund-raisers, updates of staff changes, and activities. Including a profile of a staff person, another parent, or a center volunteer is a sure way to generate readership and enthusiasm about your newsletter. News items from each classroom are always welcome, especially if children's names are mentioned. Parents will search the pages to find a mention of their child or their child's teacher. Best of all, parents are eager to read the "Director's Message," which is a must for each issue. Remember, the director sets the "feeling tone" for the center, and the tone of a "Director's Message" communicates that to parents (Jones, 1996).

Other ways to communicate with families include meetings, regularly scheduled parent conferences, use of email, a center website, and telephone calls to tell parents about happy experiences their children had at school. Center staff must take advantage of every opportunity to communicate with the family to learn more about them and their child, to share ideas about the child, and to strengthen the basic trust in the relationship.

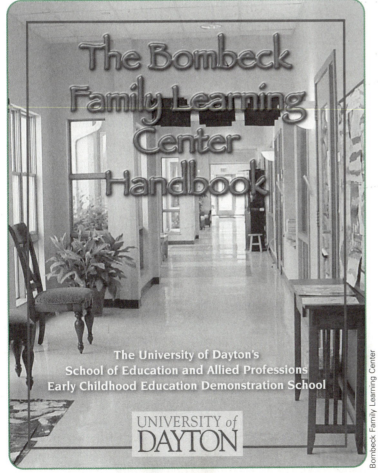

Bombeck Family Learning Center

Parent handbooks can be made available as a hard-copy booklet or online as part of the program's website.

VOLUNTEER PROGRAM   naeyc

Volunteers are welcomed in most early childhood education centers, and the volunteer program usually is managed by the center director. Occasionally, a member of the center staff other than the director or a volunteer who is willing to undertake the coordinating responsibilities manages the volunteer activities. The coordinating function includes recruiting, orienting, and scheduling the volunteers. Other aspects of the volunteer program, such as planning activities for the volunteers and handling the supervision and record-keeping responsibilities connected with a volunteer program, either must be delegated or performed by the director. Volunteers are often interested in ways to advocate for children.

Volunteer Recruitment

Recruiting volunteers is time consuming, but there are individuals in every community who are potential volunteers. Finding those people who have both the time and the interest in serving a child care center may present a problem at the outset; however, a program that provides both challenge and appropriate incentives soon will build up a roster of available volunteers who come regularly.

Available sources for recruiting volunteers will vary, depending on the size of the community and the demands of other agencies in the community. Larger cities have organized volunteer bureaus, Junior Leagues, universities with student volunteer programs, child advocacy groups, and any number of philanthropic groups that can supply volunteers. Church groups, high schools, senior citizen groups, and business groups are other sources that can be found and approached in both large urban communities or small rural areas. The volunteers must feel that they are welcome and needed; in addition, they must feel a sense of personal regard for their efforts.

Once volunteers are recruited, screening them is essential to the success of the program. Meeting with each one personally will enable the director or volunteer coordinator to find a good fit between the volunteer's interests and abilities and program needs. Volunteers must understand that they will be supervised by the volunteer coordinator, who will apply essentially the same principles of supervision that are used for regular staff.

Volunteer Orientation

Participation in the volunteer orientation program should be a requirement for every person who chooses to give time to the center program. Although it may seem presumptuous to insist that volunteers participate in an orientation, it is essential that they become completely familiar with the operation of the center and that they have a clear understanding of how their services fit into the total service offered by the center program. Furthermore, the volunteers usually recognize that a center staff person who will take the time to plan and carry through a meaningful and helpful orientation program for them also will value their involvement in the center program.

Orientation meetings should provide volunteers with a staff directory and introduction to as many staff members as possible. The director should talk about the organizational structure of the agency, the goals and objectives of the center program, and the importance of volunteer help in meeting those goals and objectives. Further, licensing standards and health requirements for volunteers must be explained. That will clarify what is expected of them regarding immunizations, health examination, and classroom health and safety procedures and help them understand the rationale for restrictions on their participation. For example, in most places, a volunteer may not be alone at any time with a group of children because of licensing and insurance requirements. When the rationale for that ruling is understood, volunteers are less likely to be offended when told they may not take the children on a walk or drive them the few blocks to the park.

Confidentiality is an issue for everyone at the center, including the volunteers. It is wonderful to have volunteers who become ambassadors for the program in the community, but it is essential that they adhere to a strict policy of absolute confidentiality. Volunteers who share their general enthusiasm about working with the children or doing other work for the center can be a great asset, but talking about specific children, families, or teachers can be very damaging to your program.

Other details that should be covered at the orientation meeting include sign-in and sign-out procedures for volunteers, and where they should call if they expect to be absent. Record keeping is necessary because many publicly funded centers must report volunteer hours, and some private agencies often choose to keep records and reward volunteers based on their hours of service. Evidence of a strong commitment to a program by volunteers is useful when applying for grant money.

Volunteer Activities

Volunteers can do most things that family members do in a center program, and they often have more free time than working parents or parents with

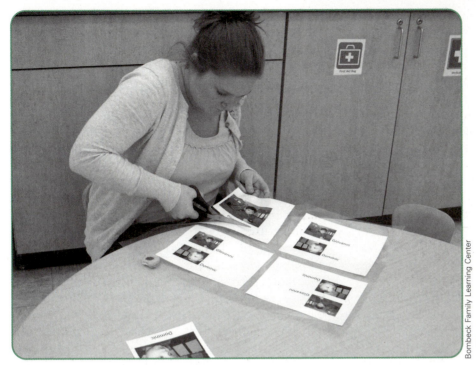

Bombeck Family Learning Center

Volunteers are sometimes asked to participate in setting up classroom activities.

young families. Volunteers, like parents, must be made to feel welcome, and like parents they must leave with a sense of satisfaction and a feeling that their services are needed and appreciated. Since they do not have the reward of seeing the joy their own children experience by having them participate in the program, it is doubly important for the center staff to make them feel welcome, to define their task for them, and to let them know how highly their service is regarded. Volunteers will continue to serve only in situations in which they feel needed.

REFLECTION

Think about your own volunteer activities. Perhaps you tutor younger students or work in a program for children with disabilities. What motivates you to be there at the scheduled time? Do you look for excuses not to go? If not, why not? How do you feel about yourself after you spend time volunteering? What rewards do you receive?

ORGANIZATIONS AND AGENCIES

In addition to working with parents and volunteers, the director is responsible for involvement with professional organizations, referral agencies, and the community in which the center is located. In each

case, the amount of time and degree of involvement vary according to the type of center and the director's individual style. Involvement in professional organizations and community outreach are both addressed in NAEYC Accreditation Standards and the Program Assessment Scale (PAS).

Professional Organizations

Directors frequently join one or more local, regional, and national professional organizations. Sometimes, the board encourages and assists them by paying their dues (a list of professional organizations is presented in Appendix F). Through these memberships, directors can accomplish several goals.

First, directors can obtain information and make contacts that may be personally and professionally helpful. Therefore, they may select organizations that focus on development of administrative skills, presentation of research data, and provision of information about legislation and funding. Through contacts at group meetings, the director may meet potential staff members, although "pirating" staff from other centers certainly should be avoided. Directors also may see professional organizations as providing a forum for their ideas, a place where they can speak before a group and discuss their concerns with other professionals. They may volunteer to hold meetings at their centers, thereby providing opportunities for others in the field to see different early childhood education facilities.

When directors join a professional organization, the organization is enhanced since the directors have had a number of years of education and experience and carry some influence in the community. As a result of their having belonged to these organizations or similar groups for a time, they have expertise that can help move the group forward, and they can give guidance to newer, less experienced members.

Directors may join professional organizations to become part of a group that effects change. The professional groups offer many advocacy opportunities. Legislators who will not listen to an individual's recommendations on teacher-to-child ratios or low-wage issues may be persuaded by an organization's stand, and directors can have input through their membership in the organization.

In some communities, directors form support groups because they need a forum to discuss problems unique to their particular position. They can share information and ideas and work out cooperative plans for staff training. With the increased, widespread focus on child care, national support groups are forming to provide hotlines, websites, consultation services, and management retreats.

When they join organizations, directors serve as models for staff members. In some cases, the staff profits more directly from the organization than the director, but staff members put off joining or may even be hesitant about attending meetings if they do not know other members. Directors can provide an incentive by offering to accompany teachers to the first meeting and by notifying staff members of upcoming meetings. Directors may work out a plan for released time from center duties that staff members can use to participate in the work of professional organizations. They also may provide staff meeting time for members who have attended sessions to share their information.

For similar reasons, directors should attend (and facilitate staff members' attending) lectures, courses, and conferences that are related to early childhood education. Directors also have the responsibility for reading current books, periodicals, and resources on the Internet and passing relevant materials on to staff members. Most staff members will respond positively to an article from the director that is marked to indicate a personal application such as, "This article addresses an interest of yours, new ways of teaching math concepts." Or, "Have you seen the reviews of these new multicultural books? Which ones should we order?" This personal touch encourages the staff member to read the article and perhaps discuss it

further with the director. When the director has provided a model of this behavior, staff members may begin to circulate articles or books that they have found to be worthwhile.

Referral Agencies

Directors contact referral agencies and advise staff members to use special services when that is appropriate. Directors also help staff members delineate the boundaries of their own professional expertise and recognize those circumstances under which an opinion obtained from another type of professional could be useful.

The job of relating to referral agencies begins with the collection of a list of services that are available in the surrounding community. In some areas, a booklet is published that contains the names of all the social service agencies, their addresses, telephone numbers, fax numbers, websites, hours, charges, what services are provided and to whom, and whether a referral from a physician or case worker is required. Some communities add other kinds of information, such as lists of recreation centers, churches, schools, and government agencies and officials. If this type of directory is not available, a center director can develop a referral list. Writing the data on file cards or putting the information into a computer file provides a convenient reference that can be updated easily.

After determining which agencies provide services related to the clients' needs, directors should attempt to make personal contact with as many of these agencies as possible. This contact can be accomplished by visiting the agency, attending programs sponsored by the agency, and meeting its staff members at professional meetings. Later, when the need arises for services from such an organization, it will be easier for the director to make contacts with the people whom he already knows. The director also is in a good position to explain the nature of the services provided by these agencies to the center staff and to parents when that is necessary.

In addition to working with the staff in referring children and families for care and treatment, directors make use of agencies in other ways. For example, agencies usually have personnel and material resources available for in-service training or parent meetings. Some agencies in the community, such as Community Coordinated Child Care (4Cs) or Child Care Resource and Referral agencies, provide consultation and technical assistance. A range of services may be available from other types of

DIRECTOR'S CORNER

"When I first became a director, one of the things I had trouble finding out about was the whole referral network, and I realize that takes time and comes with experience. You have to know the agencies, how they work, and the particular people to contact before you can help your teachers or your families with referrals. I always feel better when I can call a specific person whom I have already met. In addition to growing my network over time, I started with two key resources available in most counties—our referral hotline that could direct me to services across a variety of needs and our Child Care Resource and Referral agency, which was a one-stop shop for information related to young children, families, and child care services."

—Director, YMCA-sponsored center

agencies such as the public library, which usually offers storytellers, films, and teachers' collections of books.

If the center's program includes the provision of medical, dental, and mental health services to children, the director may be able to provide these services at low cost and with convenience in scheduling through agency contacts. For example, arrangements can be made for a physician to come to the center to do routine physical checkups so that children do not have to endure long trips; boring waiting rooms; and strange, frightening buildings. The director, who is well acquainted with physicians, psychologists, speech therapists, and social workers, is able to depend on their services but is sensitive to the needs and limitations under which they operate. It is important that directors establish reciprocal relationships with these professionals by being open to accepting children referred to the center by them and their agencies.

WORK WITH THE COMMUNITY

The director explains the center to the community and, in turn, explains the community to the staff. This function requires familiarity with the community in which the center is located. If some or all of the children who attend the center live in other communities, the director should become informed about those areas as well.

In marketing and publicizing the center to the community, the director uses public relations and communications techniques that were covered in Chapter 10. These include news releases, open houses, and tours of the center. The effective use of the interpersonal skills that were discussed in Chapter 9 is particularly appropriate when working with the community. The appearance and maintenance of the center's building and grounds also can have an influence on the relationship with the community.

Sometimes, individual members of the community become interested in the center and its work through the director's efforts. For example, the owner of a lumber yard may agree to provide scrap lumber for the children's woodworking projects, or a printer will offer to save all the paper ends from print jobs for the children's use. If the director and staff have met the local grocer and other shopkeepers, these businesspeople may be far more responsive to the children when they visit on field trips or when they walk by as they explore the area with classmates. A university in the area may be interested in sending architecture or product design students or may come to do research. In addition, there are child advocacy groups in the community that will offer information and support to center staff and families.

Directors help their staff members understand the community by encouraging involvement in community activity and by providing information about life in the community. Having knowledge of the historical background of the area and the cultural or ethnic groups that live there will increase staff awareness of the needs of families who come to the center. The director is responsible for making center staff members sensitive to the customs, language, and values of the people they serve. Frequently, staff members live in other communities and represent different cultural or ethnic groups. It is impossible for staff members to work effectively with children and parents from a culture about which they have no knowledge.

When the director has done a good job of understanding the community, and when all the pertinent information is conveyed to the staff, everyone at the center gains a greater appreciation of the community, and a strong working relationship can emerge. The center's team of staff, parents, and children working together can be expanded to incorporate community members as well.

Summary

The director works with or is accountable for establishing a reciprocal relationship with families. A major aspect of this role is helping staff members establish effective relationships with parents. Attention needs to be paid to family interaction, family support, and family involvement. The director needs to emphasize the participation of individual parents to the degree that is appropriate and comfortable for them. Directors also are involved in recruiting and orienting volunteers and in providing recognition for their services. In addition, they work closely with professional organizations, referral agencies, and members of the community. Part of their role involves setting an example of an appropriate amount of professional involvement for staff members and training them in the techniques of working with a variety of resources. Directors also provide information to staff members and give them opportunities to make use of the services that professional organizations, referral agencies, and the community have to offer.

Try It Out!

1 Using Working Paper 13-1, develop a list of specific tasks a volunteer could do in the specified classroom areas.

2 Divide into groups of three for the purpose of role-playing a parent conference. The situation is one in which a young mother has requested a conference about her 3-year-old son who spends a great deal of time in the housekeeping area in the classroom. He also plays with dolls, washes dishes, and dresses up in a skirt and high heels at home. The father is very upset and annoyed by this behavior and has pressured the mother into calling for a conference. The father is unable to attend the conference. The roles are as follows:

- male teacher
- mother
- female director

Using the checklist in Working Paper 13-2, discuss each item listed. If you were the director or the mother in the role-play, give your perception of how well the teacher handled the questions asked.

Working Paper 13-1

(for use with Try It Out! 1)

VOLUNTEER TASKS FORM

List specific tasks a volunteer could be assigned to do in each of the classroom areas or activities listed below. Think beyond supervising children. Consider care and development of materials, enriching the area, or making it more aesthetically pleasing.

Dramatic play (expand beyond house-type play)

Carpentry

Literature/library area

Writing center

Lunchtime

Nap time

 You can download a full-size version of this form on the Education CourseMate website.

Working Paper 13-2

(for use with Try It Out! 2)

ROLE-PLAY CHECKLIST

After the role-play in Try It Out! 2 is completed, discuss the items in this checklist. If your role was that of director or parent, respond to the questions in terms of your perception of how well the teacher handled the conference. You are expected to give more than yes or no answers. Document your answers with examples from the conference.

Did you give the parent time to talk about her concerns?

Were you a receptive listener?

When you made comments, did you talk in terms of the parent's feelings?

Were you able to restrain yourself from giving advice?

Did the parent do most of the talking?

What was accomplished during the conference?

You can download a full-size version of this form on the Education CourseMate website.

REFERENCES

Center for the Study of Social Policy. (n.d.). *Strengthening families: A protection factors framework*. New York: Author. Retrieved June 22, 2011 from http://www.cssp.org/reform/strengthening-families.

Decker, C. A. & Decker, J. R. (2008). *Planning and administering early childhood programs* (9th ed.). Upper Saddle River, NJ: Prentice Hall.

Galinsky, E. (1984, July). How to work with working parents. *Child Care Information Exchange*.

Gestwicki, C. (2010). *Home, school & community relations* (7th ed.). Belmont, CA: Cengage Wadsworth.

Gordon, A. M. & Browne, K. W. (2010). *Beginnings and beyond: Foundations in early education* (6th ed.). Clifton Park, NY: Thomson Delmar Learning.

Greenman, J. (2003). Places for childhoods includes parents, too. In R. Neugebauer & B. Neugebauer (Eds.), *The art of leadership: Managing early childhood organizations* (rev. ed.). Redmond, WA: Child Care Information Exchange.

Hanson, M. J. (2011). Diversity in service settings. In E. W. Lynch & M. J. Hanson (Eds.) *Developing cross-cultural competence: A guide for working with children and their families*. (4th ed.). Baltimore, MD: Brookes.

Hildebrand, V. & Hearron, P. F. (2010). *Management of child development centers* (5th ed.). Columbus, OH: Merrill.

Jones, R. (1996). Producing a school newsletter parents will read. *Child Care Information Exchanges*, 91–93.

Phipps, P. A. (2003). Working with angry parents: Taking the customer service approach. In R. Neugebauer & B. Neugebauer (Eds.), *The art of leadership: Managing early childhood organizations* (rev. ed.). Redmond, WA: Child Care Information Exchange.

U.S. Census Bureau. (2009). *American FactFinder*. Author: Washington, DC. Retrieved on June 11, 2011 from http://factfinder.census.gov/servlet/NPTable?_bm=y&-qr_name=ACS_2009_1YR_G00_NP01&-geo_id=01000US&-ds_name=ACS_2009_1YR_G00_&-_lang=en.

14

PROVIDING *for* PERSONAL AND PROFESSIONAL STAFF DEVELOPMENT

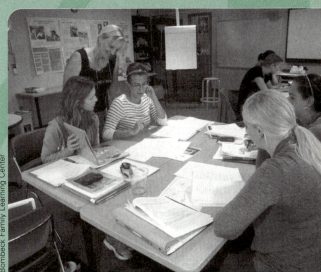

Bombeck Family Learning Center

Professional development is most effective when it is job-embedded, interactive and follow-through is expected.

Objectives

After reading this chapter, you should be able to:

- Describe the process of scheduling and planning for staff meetings and professional development.
- Discuss the elements of an effective staff development system.
- Identify characteristics of teachers at all levels of the career lattice and plan professional development to meet their needs.
- List the four principles of supervision.

Standards Addressed in this Chapter

naeyc Professional Preparation Standard 6

naeyc Administrator Competencies Management Knowledge and Skills 1, 3, 8, & 9 Early Childhood Knowledge and Skills 10

naeyc Accreditation Standards 10

The center director is responsible for the personal and professional development of the staff. In very large centers or in corporate systems, the business and fiscal maintenance functions may be separated from the educational program maintenance, in which case the education director is accountable for the educational program and the accompanying staff development programs. However, in most centers, one person is responsible for both the business and educational program components.

The basic assumptions underlying staff development programs are that learning is a lifelong process and that adults have the capacity to change and grow. This capacity is, in a sense, analogous to that manifested by children in their growth processes. The director's responsibility as it relates to the center staff parallels that of the classroom teacher: to create a favorable environment for optimum growth and development of all the people in the environment. When the director serves as a model of professionalism in handling staff meetings, staff training or coaching programs, and staff supervision and in assessing staff problems, the personal and professional development of the center staff is facilitated and enhanced.

The core of the staff development system is staff training and professional development, both of which are supported and promoted through staff supervision and coaching. The specific content or the specific strategy employed in any aspect of the staff development program depends on group composition. In the same way that classroom teachers assess the needs of children in planning appropriate learning environments, directors evaluate staff needs and plan staff development programs accordingly. In teaching young children, the responsible adult offers many opportunities to make decisions, but there are times when children are expected to follow certain rules and expectations; likewise, the director establishes expectations for teachers that represent the bottom line and that are expected to be followed (Jones, 1993).

THE EARLY CHILDHOOD CAREER LATTICE naeyc

In place of the "career ladder" common to many professions, the field of early care and education has adopted the metaphor of the "career lattice." It represents the multiple entry points for and the expertise of those in our field who have years of experience and job-embedded professional development but may be pursuing a degree by stacking credentials and degrees incrementally. Others in our field may have relatively new degrees in early childhood but lack the experience of the veteran teacher. To meet the needs of both groups of teachers, the field must provide multiple opportunities for growth and development. Early childhood professionals often need to advance the career lattice horizontally, vertically, or even diagonally to meet their goals. (See Figure 14-1.)

STAFF MEETINGS naeyc

One vehicle for providing ongoing and job-embedded professional development is the staff meeting. The director is responsible for planning and conducting meaningful and relevant staff meetings. Bloom states that meetings are very important. In fact, she says meetings are "the glue that holds the organization together" (Bloom, 2002, p. 1). Although conducting a staff meeting may seem to be a routine and relatively easy task, holding meetings that are satisfying and worthwhile for both the director and the staff requires careful planning and

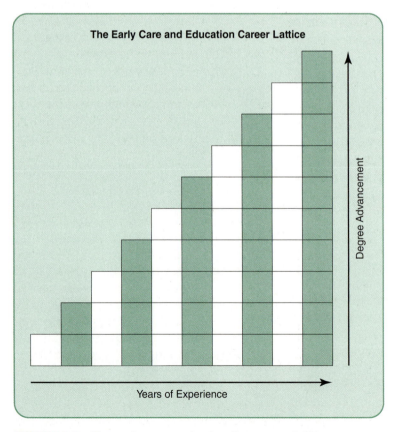

The Early Care and Education Career Lattice

Degree Advancement

Years of Experience

FIGURE 14-1 The early care and education career lattice.
Source: © Cengage Learning, 2013.

preparation. Effective implementation of the planned agenda is dependent, largely, on the director's ability to maintain open communication among those attending the meeting.

Purpose of Staff Meetings

Communication is the main purpose of staff meetings. Although much can be communicated through email, newsletters, posting bulletin board notices, and exchanging information on a casual one-to-one basis, many issues and problems are resolved most effectively in a meeting. Communication should be two-way, with opportunities for staff to solve problems, share ideas, engage in team discussion, and complete important tasks.

Two-way communication in a meeting permits an interchange of ideas and feelings and provides a forum for thoughtful discussion and clarification of problems and issues. The final outcome for each individual should be a better understanding of problems and issues and of self and others. When staff members are involved in discussing program issues or problems, when their opinions have been heard, and when they have had some voice in decision making, they feel a greater sense of self-worth and consider themselves to be a more integral part of the total center community. To be comfortable for everyone, staff meetings must provide a safe environment where staff members can ask questions, challenge others by presenting alternative ideas, and share feelings with the group.

To prevent the meeting from deteriorating into a "gripe session," the director can take an active role in channeling the complaints and concerns toward improvement strategies. Open communication during staff meetings is one way to develop cooperation and harmony and to encourage the "we" feeling among staff members. This is further advanced when staff members are encouraged to suggest staff meeting agenda items. A sense of community is fundamental for the creation of a favorable environment for the personal growth of staff members, children, and families who participate in the center program.

When the director becomes aware that there is an undercurrent of discontent among the staff, a staff meeting discussion focused on concerns and issues may be useful, but only after talking informally with several staff to see if the problem can be remedied, thereby leaving staff meeting time for other agenda items. If, however, staff unrest persists, it may be necessary to assess staff morale through the use of a *climate survey*. A well-designed survey tool that includes items related to motivation, commitment, satisfaction-dissatisfaction, and other concerns can yield useful information that directors then can use to provide a framework for a staff meeting discussion. The climate survey becomes a means to an end because it helps staff focus on their most urgent issues, and it helps the director bring the staff meeting discussion toward problem resolution. Bloom, Sheerer & Britz (2005) suggests that the climate of the organization is akin to the personality of the center. Both the director and staff can have input into the design of the survey tool, which can be developed easily through such online tools as Survey Monkey, a platform for surveys that can be completed anonymously and which also compiles the data into easy-to-read charts. It may be appropriate to share the results of the survey at the next staff meeting, presenting new action items as appropriate.

Staff meeting discussions may involve specific questions, such as which piece of outdoor equipment to buy, or whether to buy tricycles or books with the equipment money available at the end of the year. Sometimes, discussions focus on the use of available

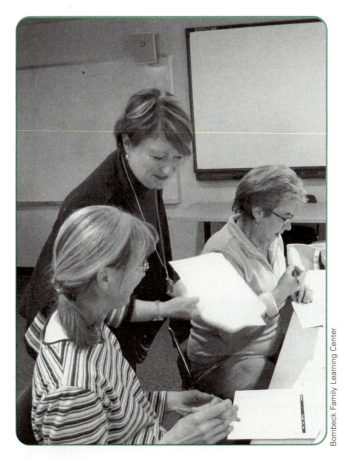

Staff meetings can be good times for training if the amount of time needed is short and the task at hand would benefit from peer or director support.

Bombeck Family Learning Center

building or outdoor space, or on the appropriateness of timing the meal service or the monthly fire drill. The director may decide to use staff meeting time to discuss more general philosophical or educational program issues such as, "What changes should we consider in our program planning in order to focus more attention on emerging literacy?" A question that logically follows is, "How do we, as a staff, learn more about the application of a balanced and interactive early literacy approach?" Discussions about both educational program and general program philosophies often lead to group decisions about the focus and content of future in-service training sessions. If the group makes decisions about the training needs of the teaching staff, there undoubtedly will be a greater commitment to the training program than if the director makes those decisions without group input.

Nonetheless, when staff meeting discussions are not of particular relevance to those in attendance, boredom and restlessness become apparent, and members feel that the time is wasted. To maintain interest and open communication, try to select agenda items that are of concern to most of the staff members who are expected to attend the regular staff meetings. Remember to use icebreakers and various problem-solving strategies that will help maintain interest and keep staff focused. Make certain that the purpose of the meeting, whatever it may be, is clearly stated and understood by everyone at the meeting (Bloom, 2002). The agenda items that pertain only to the work of a few can be reserved for special meetings or assigned to small committees for discussion and subsequent decision making.

Timing of Staff Meetings

The frequency and timing of staff meetings vary, depending on the amount of business typically transacted and the amount of time devoted to each meeting. Weekly or biweekly meetings that are well planned and brief may be more productive than long sessions that are held less frequently. Although staff members usually prefer daytime meetings because they need evenings and weekends to rest and take care of personal matters, evenings may be the only time everyone can meet together.

In half-day programs, staff meetings can be scheduled after the children leave at noon, or in centers with double sessions, either early in the morning or late in the afternoon. However, full-day programs present special problems because the centers are open from early morning until very late afternoon, and the center staff usually works a staggered schedule. Nap time is often the time set aside for meetings because most staff members are present in the middle of the day; however, sleeping children must be supervised. Use of volunteers or parents for nap time supervision is an alternative but one that licensing disallows in some places. In smaller centers, hiring substitutes to cover nap rooms may be a better solution.

The center staff and the director decide which staff members, in addition to classroom staff, should be encouraged to attend staff meetings. It may be beneficial to have the bus driver, the cook, or the receptionist at staff meetings because the kind of contact these staff members have with the children and families enables them to make a unique contribution to staff meeting discussions. Directors also may find it useful to ask the consulting psychologist, the special education resource teacher, or other professionals who are involved in the program to attend staff meetings. Anyone who can profit from, or contribute to, the discussions should be encouraged to come to the meetings.

Preparation for Staff Meetings

Both the director and the staff members must prepare for a staff meeting so that the meeting will be productive for everyone. The director is responsible for obtaining staff input on agenda items, preparing and posting the agenda, and distributing any material that should be read by the staff before the meeting. Even though the director holds final responsibility for planning the agenda, all staff members should be invited to suggest agenda items either before or after the agenda is posted. The posted agenda might include a brief description of each item and the action to be taken. (See Figure 14-2.)

For example, if the agenda item about the use of outdoor space is to cover the timing for its use, the responsibility for setting up and cleaning up, and the equipment needs, then all these subjects for discussion would be listed. The agenda also should state clearly which items are open for discussion *and* group decision and which items are open only

for discussion. In the latter case, the director hears the discussion, considers the ideas and feelings of the staff, and subsequently makes the decision. In the case of the outdoor space questions, the classroom staff probably should decide about the timing for the use of outdoor space; the total staff, including the janitor or housekeeper, should be involved in the discussion and decision about setting up and cleaning up the space; and the final decision about equipment purchase is made by the director after hearing the preferences of the entire staff. When all these expectations are spelled out clearly on the posted agenda, there is little room for confusion or misunderstanding about what will occur during the meeting.

Each item on the posted agenda includes the name of the person responsible for presenting the item and

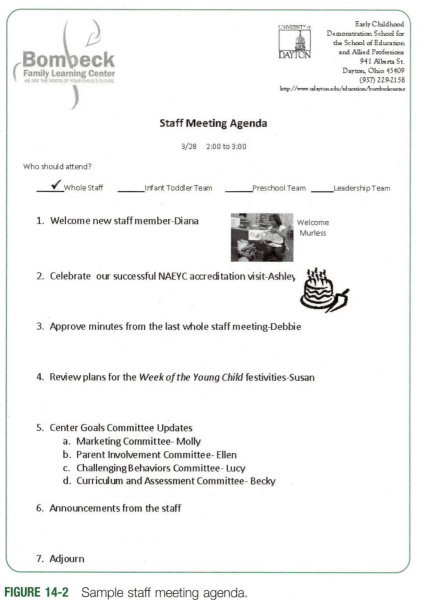

FIGURE 14-2 Sample staff meeting agenda.

leading the discussion and a rough time estimate for adequate coverage of the item (see Figure 14-2). This procedure notifies staff members about their responsibility during the meeting and ensures coverage of the entire agenda within a specified meeting time. Giving staff members responsibility for selected agenda items is an excellent way to encourage interest in center operations. Reserving part of each meeting to have a staff member present on a topic of interest also contributes to the feeling of collegiality.

The director should distribute copies of readings, minutes from previous staff or board meetings, and any other information that will provide a common basis for discussion to enhance the quality of the dialogue during the meeting. For example, if there is to be a discussion about curriculum planning as it relates to authentic assessment, research studies and program ideas on this topic could be duplicated and given to staff members several days before the meeting. Individual staff members can also be encouraged to search out additional information on the topic so the time spent during the meeting is productive and informative for everyone. Occasionally, a specialist from the community can be invited to a staff meeting to contribute to a discussion that requires particular expertise, such as services provided by the local children's protective agency or new information on infectious diseases in child care centers. When the director prepares the agenda carefully, and both the director and the staff members come well informed, the outcome is more likely to be satisfying for everyone.

Staff Meeting Procedure

The director usually serves as the convener and assumes the responsibility for moving the group through the agenda by facilitating but not dominating the discussion and helping the group maintain a balance between dealing with tasks and dealing with interpersonal processes.

At the outset, it is important that the meeting begin at the stated time and end on schedule. When the convener does not call the meeting to order on time and moves immediately to the first agenda item, group members are inclined to come late because they assume the meeting will not start on time. When the discussion of an agenda item extends beyond the time assigned, the convener should call attention to that fact and have the group decide whether more time should be spent on that item.

Time management is important. Time is finite, and you and your staff must develop good time management skills to accomplish as much as you can

within a specified time frame. The staff meeting is an excellent place for you, as a director, to demonstrate good time management.

Clearly, conducting an effective staff meeting takes careful planning and requires special skills on the part of the director. However, when meetings are satisfying and productive for the staff, they serve as a vehicle for communication and promote cooperation and good feeling among staff. Furthermore, staff meetings give the director a chance to model interpersonal communication skills that serve as the basis for all interactions with children, parents, and other staff members.

REFLECTION

Think about your class and study schedule and your other responsibilities. When a class is scheduled to convene at 4:00 p.m. and end at 5:30 p.m., you feel very frustrated if you rush to arrive on time only to find that the instructor is 15 minutes late. Furthermore, you may have to get home to family or prepare dinner, and you become restless and inattentive if the class goes beyond 5:30 p.m. The only way you are able to manage your time well is to have others with whom you must interact regularly maintain their time commitments to you. The same is true for you and your colleagues at the workplace.

STAFF TRAINING/PROFESSIONAL DEVELOPMENT

The staff training and professional development program begins with the orientation of new staff members and includes all aspects of in-service training. Planning the total staff professional development program depends on the composition of the center staff. Just as the classroom teacher individualizes approaches to children, the director recognizes the developmental level of each teacher and plans training accordingly. The staff professional development must be adjusted to the experience level and career stage, as well as to the specific concerns, capabilities, and perspectives of each person and should focus on long-term growth and change in individuals' thinking skills (Bloom, Sheerer & Britz, 2005).

It is the director's job to work with staff to construct a professional development program that meets the needs of the staff in a manner consistent with the center's mission. Comprehensive, job-embedded professional development is required for teachers to advance through what Tanner and Tanner (2007) describe as the three levels of teacher competency. In a field where many teachers have limited training, it is common to find early childhood programs with teachers who are at Tanner and Tanner's "first level," in which teachers rely on materials made by others (e.g., kits, worksheets, and prepackaged curricula) and do not engage in critical evaluation of materials or instructional activities. Frequently teachers at this level implement a series of disconnected activities that fill the day but lack the capacity to reflect on what children know and are able to do in order to design curriculum that incorporates the children's interest and meets the children's individual needs. Teachers in this stage require professional development that recognizes where the teachers are and supports their progress to the next level.

As teachers receive higher levels of professional development and support, they develop competencies at Tanner and Tanner's "second level," which requires them to recognize that instruction should reflect the emerging issues of the classroom and should also integrate content areas and developmental skills. A teacher at this level may understand that effective classrooms respond to individual needs but may be unsuccessful in knowing how to put their understanding into action. For example, Tanner and Tanner (1995) describe one Level II teacher who tried to focus on a letter of the week and connect it with each new theme because she knew that good programs support emergent literacy and connected learning. Her lack of understanding of how to implement this understanding led to simplistic connections, such as choosing the letter "d" for the farm unit and singing BINGO (because it was about a dog) and also signing the "Farmer in the Dell" (because dell begins with "d") (p. 10). Level II teachers may be more aware of what young children should know and be able to do, but lack the skills to design instructional environments that fully integrate curriculum content into learning experiences that challenge and inspire young children. Directors who have a lot of teachers at Level II will need to be very intentional in providing professional development that moves the staff from where they are to Level III.

Teachers at Level III are able to exercise independent judgment and adapt curriculum to meet children's individual needs (Tanner & Tanner, 2007). Tanner and Tanner describe a Level III teacher's ability to make curricular decisions in an example where the teacher had planned to teach a theme about living things and began the theme with a class visit to a pet store. Although the teacher had planned to focus on pets in general, she adapted her curriculum when she saw the children's excitement about the snake that was fed a live mouse, which led to a more specific focus on snakes and their prey (1995). In this example, the teacher had a sound understanding of what children should know and be able to do and had sufficient understanding of related content knowledge. The teacher also demonstrated a sense of efficacy in that she had confidence in her skill to design a learning environment that capitalized on the interest of the children and facilitated an extended investigation of a topic worthy of study.

According to Tanner and Tanner (2007), no matter what a teacher's background, he or she cannot implement a curriculum well without initial training and ongoing professional development. To be effective, such training should be provided by individuals who are familiar not only with adult learning principles, but also with the realities of teachers' classrooms. Tanner and Tanner (2007) advocate for the use of comprehensive professional development plans.

Professional Development Plans

Professional development plans should be comprehensive in terms of the staff's professional level and in terms of the length of time that the staff member has been at the center. Fully trained and qualified classroom teaching staff members should have basic child development information and should be able to plan curriculum and classroom management strategies with minimal additional training. However, they may be ready for some help on working with the special education resource teacher who comes to consult with them about the children with disabilities in the center. Because special classroom strategies must be employed to truly include children with disabilities into a noncategorical classroom, training in techniques and strategies to accomplish that integration also will be helpful to the experienced teacher. The interdisciplinary classroom team of early childhood and special educators must work together to provide quality programming for all children in an inclusive environment. An interdisciplinary team-building and staff development approach for both the special educators and the early childhood staff is to provide mutual training so these professionals together develop their own professional skills, as well as come to appreciate more fully the knowledge and skills of other members of the team. As team members come to accept and extend the skills and knowledge of fellow professionals, mutual respect and camaraderie are reinforced.

Teachers at Tanner and Tanner's (2007) first level, assistants, aides, and other paraprofessional classroom staff may need coaching in preparing classroom materials, in understanding growth and development, or in developing basic management skills. It is the classroom teacher's responsibility to ensure that all adults working or volunteering in their classroom understand the program's philosophy as well as the curriculum being implemented. It is common for those who work in the field of early care and education to be more comfortable working with young children than supervising adults. The center director needs to insure that staff have the knowledge, skills, and time to collaborate with the other adults working in the classroom. Likewise, the custodians, food service staff, and clerical staff will need different levels and types of assistance.

When planning a staff training program, the director will have to assess the training needs of everyone, then make decisions about time, content, and training methods for the sessions. An experienced director can assess training needs by observing staff as they carry out their job responsibilities and by having conferences with them to discover more about their own analysis of needs and their interest in professional advancement. Assessment of staff training needs and professional development should flow from staff self-evaluation as well as directors' formal evaluation procedures and discussions from staff meetings. As directors glean insights into individual staff needs and interests, they can search for appropriate and challenging staff training and educational opportunities.

Time for Training

Finding a suitable time for training meetings is even more difficult than finding a suitable time for staff meetings. In the case of regularly scheduled staff meetings, the staff can plan ahead for the full year and schedule their other duties and commitments around the meeting times. However, training sessions that usually occur with less regularity often require a larger block of time than a staff meeting and have to be planned to coincide with the schedules of consultants or outside experts whose services are needed. If the director and center staff members are the only people involved in the training, scheduling difficulties are alleviated somewhat. Nonetheless, the problems of late afternoon or evening fatigue, and the inability of the staff to leave the classroom during the day, create special problems for the training of child care staff, unless the sessions can be planned for nap time or incorporated into the staff meetings. Because most training requires

larger time blocks, it may be necessary to discuss the possibility of a Saturday meeting or a weekend retreat. Half-day preschool programs that usually meet during the public school academic year often have training meetings in the early autumn before school begins or in the spring after school closes. In any case, if in-service training attendance is mandatory, this point must be included in the employee's job description and spelled out during orientation of new employees.

Mandatory Training

Decisions about whether attendance at training sessions should be mandatory or optional used to be decided by the director at the center level. Now licensing, state quality rating systems, and reimbursement policies often require a given number of hours of training each year. Individual teachers may be responsible for keeping track of and completing required training in order to maintain their teaching credential or eligibility. Because the stakes are very high (i.e., centers can lose funding, a quality rating, or accreditation if staff lack required training), the director needs to establish a process for tracking mandatory training and a vehicle for staff to be able to go to training during work hours when possible.

Training may be required by the center to maintain consistent programming or to address new challenges, opportunities, and program goals. This kind of training can be exciting to plan because it reflects what makes the program unique. Directors and interested staff can work together to create professional development opportunities that reflect the program's unique culture and goals. This training is important and requires whole staff involvement in order to gain buy in.

REFLECTION

Think about your personal feelings when you were told that you had to attend some function such as a meeting, a party, or a class, as opposed to the times when you were given a choice. When it was a matter of choice, what were the factors that motivated you to attend? Was it curiosity about who would be there or what would take place? Was it interest in what you expected would take place? Was it to please the person who requested you attend or who told you about the event? Can you analyze your feelings and reactions when you went someplace to please someone else as opposed to the times when you went because you were intrinsically motivated?

Place for Training

When there is a comfortable lounge or conference room at the center, the staff may prefer to stay in the building for the training sessions. The comfort and familiarity of the center will help create a feeling of openness, which could be very important if the success of the training is dependent on dialogue and exchanging ideas among staff members. If the training is a cooperative effort and several centers are involved, a space in a centrally located community building may be more convenient for the trainees. Sometimes, it is helpful to get away from the center. Regardless of the venue, the space should be comfortable, with adult-sized furniture including tables that provide a writing surface and an opportunity for interacting with colleagues.

Training Methods and Resources

The methods or strategies employed in the in-service training program will depend on the amount of time and the resources available and the nature of the content selected. For example, if one hour of a staff meeting is set aside for a refresher course in first aid, the best way to present that information may be in a lecture given by an approved trainer from the health department. If, on the other hand, there is more time to spend on the topic of first aid, it may be desirable to plan a full-day session with a Red Cross specialist. Enrolling some staff members who do not have first aid certificates in a Red Cross course that extends over several weeks and is available evenings or on Saturday is yet another alternative. First aid training can be expanded to include health, nutrition, and safety. The expansion of the program creates new training strategy possibilities. Group discussions led by the director would be an appropriate method to use in making the staff more aware of safety issues in the center. The program could include discussions about safety when using outdoor equipment, when planning cooking experiences, or when organizing field trips. The health or nutrition questions might be handled best by a nurse, physician, or a dietitian who would come for a seminar. A special educator might come to discuss health and safety issues as these relate to special-needs children. When outside consultants are brought in, the director's role is to sit in on the training in order to be able to do follow-up with the staff, thereby extending the new information to specific situations each teacher encounters in the classroom. There are any number of possible methods from which to choose, each one requiring different amounts of time and different resources and all individualized to meet the needs of the trainee. A list of training resources in the community as well as national opportunities should be available in the director's library at the center.

On-site workshops are useful mechanisms for encouraging direct involvement of the staff in a special content area. Implicit in the workshop

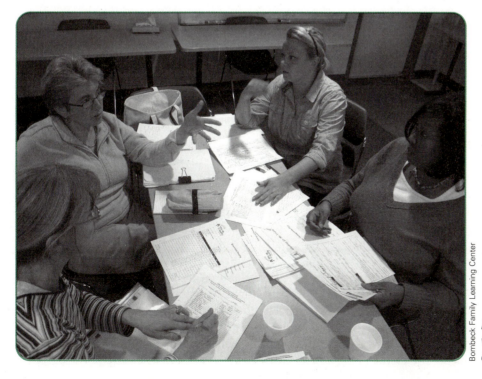

Bombeck Family Learning Center

Providing a comfortable room with tables and chairs facilitates collaboration between colleagues.

concept is the idea that those who attend participate actively in the program. Frequently, workshops are planned for a staff that expresses a need to know more about curriculum areas such as writing centers, math or science experiences for young children, or music in the classroom. Other areas, such as building skills for more effective conferences with parents or for ways to interact with volunteers, also can be handled in a workshop format that involves participants in a series of role-plays or simulation games. Workshops require active involvement from the participants and are more suitable for some training needs than are lectures, films, or seminars.

There should be planned follow-up for all types of training. Behavior change is not likely to follow a one-shot session or even a series of meetings unless there is follow-up by the director or supervisor at the center. Teachers need feedback and support to integrate new information into their day-to-day practice. It is helpful to follow up by periodically revisiting the ideas and information teachers have received, to discuss progress and/or problems they have had when attempting to implement new procedures or ideas, and to reaffirm each teacher's commitment to dealing with the challenges of change.

Visits to other centers are encouraged by some directors and can be a very helpful piece of the total staff training program. Watching other teachers and children is refreshing and interesting for some staff members. After such visits, they bring back program ideas, new and different ways to set up the physical environment, and sometimes a renewed interest in developing classroom materials such as math games or interactive charts. Some teachers who are able to move beyond the more obvious things like equipment or curriculum ideas may begin to compare and contrast classroom environments and teaching strategies, relating these differences to the differences in the stated philosophies of the programs. Follow-up group discussions will help teachers refine their understanding of how theory relates to practice. Why are the children in one program encouraged to negotiate with one another about dividing up the play dough, while the teacher controls amounts for each child in another center? The two strategies clearly reflect different program goals. Group discussions also may encourage teachers to reexamine the theoretical basis for the center program in which they work and reevaluate the curriculum to ascertain how closely it reflects the stated philosophy of the center, as well as their own philosophy of early childhood education.

Professional conferences and workshops provide excellent training opportunities for staff. Directors who commit to a personal program of professional

DIRECTOR'S CORNER

"One of the most helpful things we did in my administration class at college was role-playing. I especially remember role-playing a parent conference. Now I use that technique all the time with my staff. In staff training sessions, when we are discussing an issue like dealing with a difficult parent, I ask for a specific example and immediately turn it into a role-play. 'OK—now I'm the parent and here is my concern—you are the teacher,' and we play it out. Then we often reverse roles so I take the role of the teacher. It works very well for me as a director."

—Director, YMCA-sponsored center

development by attending professional meetings set a standard of excellence for their teachers to emulate. It is important to encourage staff to take advantage of these opportunities and to facilitate their attending conferences by allowing time off from work and subsidizing their travel and registration expenses if at all possible. Some child care programs not only subsidize conference attendance but also pay for teachers' memberships in professional organizations such as NAEYC, which includes membership in state and local affiliates, the Council for Exceptional Children (CEC), the Association for Childhood Education International (ACEI), the National Association of Child Care Professionals (NACCP), and the National Child Care Association (NCCA).

Staff members who express an interest in professional advancement are to be commended for their ambitious goals and encouraged to take courses toward a college degree in child development or early childhood education, or toward the Child Development Associate (CDA) or certified Child Care Professional (CCP) certificate in communities where these types of training programs are available. The availability of online courses offers easy access to educational opportunities for many. Some centers will help pay tuition for relevant courses as well as adjust work schedules to allow staff to attend daytime classes. Directors can lend further support to these part-time students by showing interest in what they are learning and guiding them to helpful resources available at the center.

More and more professional development training is expected to be credit based. In addition to not-for-credit or credit-based CDA programs, teachers are being encouraged to take course work that could lead to an associate or bachelor's degree in early childhood education or a closely related field. Some federally funded early childhood education programs, including Head Start, as well as a number of state licensing systems and NAEYC Accreditation Teachers Standards, have established criteria that require a certain minimum number of degreed staff before a program is approved. Therefore, more center directors are encouraging staff to take college credit courses, and the colleges and universities across the country are trying to meet that demand. At this time, there are also a number of opportunities for professional development training on the Internet. In some places, students are permitted to enroll in individual classes without matriculating in a degree program. Staff development course work for continuing education credit is also available online. Committing to any type of credit-based staff development work is very intimidating for some staff members. They have had little or no experience with any type of college-level work and they resist even the thought of taking courses because they are uneasy about their ability to do the work or have serious concerns about how time consuming it will be. Directors can help them by being available to talk through what they are experiencing and what they feel may help them succeed. When they are taking classes, it may be useful to suggest that they meet with other staff at break time to share concerns and seek help with assignments or study skills.

To provide on-site materials to support and enhance all aspects of the staff development program, it is the job of the director to establish a professional library and a teachers' resource center. The library books should cover information on child development, curriculum, classroom management, special-needs children, diversity, and working with other professionals and with families. Books on specific curriculum areas such as literacy, math, science, cooking, or music will help the staff plan for the children. Recent copies of professional journals and newsletters should be available in the teachers' library, along with a collection of audiovisual materials, including tapes, slides, videotapes, DVDs, and computers to provide a rich source of information on curriculum development and classroom management.

The teachers' resource center should be a space where teachers can make math games, charts, big books, and other teacher-made classroom materials. Supplies like paper, tagboard, paper cutter, scissors, glue, tape, plain die, marking pens, and so forth must be available in addition to a large working surface. It is a luxury to have things like a laminating machine or an Elison machine for stamping out letters and shapes for charts. When teachers have materials and space to work, they are more likely to develop individualized teacher-made classroom materials that will enrich the program for the children.

Training Content

A number of ideas for the professional development training program for staff already have been mentioned in the previous discussions on methods of training. Training needs will vary according to the previous training and experience of the center staff. Many teachers constantly are seeking new curriculum ideas and resource materials for the classroom; consequently, training in curriculum areas is usually welcomed. There is always interest in strategies for dealing with the difficult, challenging, disruptive child, or the withdrawn child. Furthermore, most teachers are interested in learning more about community resources where they can get advice about how to handle children with special needs, or about where to refer children and families for additional help. Although staff will rarely request it, directors are obligated to hold at least one staff meeting per year or set aside a time at a regularly scheduled staff retreat to review the NAEYC Code of Ethical Conduct and Statement of Commitment and the Code of Ethical Conduct Supplement for Early Childhood Program Administrators (see Appendix E). Although the orientation of new employees includes mention of the NAEYC Code of Ethics, yearly review of this important document will renew staff members' awareness of their professional commitment to ethical practice.

The director should determine if staff members need special coaching in conducting a home visit or a parent conference. These duties are taxing, produce anxiety, and require very special culturally sensitive communication skills that are suitable for the particular parent population being served. It is important to know that some families may be slow to accept a stranger and will draw back from a person whom they perceive as too intrusive. Attitudes about accepting newcomers, about education, and about child rearing vary among cultural, ethnic, and socioeconomic groups, and it is essential for staff to know what those differences are when they work with children and families. Staff members also find it helpful to have special guidance from the director in effective interpersonal communications.

There is a pressing need to assist staff with dealing with diversity in the classroom. Including children with disabilities and children from diverse cultural and ethnic groups into early childhood education programs means there must be training programs that focus on providing information about ways to meet the individual needs of children and families from these groups. Teachers may also need help handling issues regarding children of divorce, single-parent families, hospitalization of a parent or sibling, children who have been abused, and so forth.

When the staff is experienced and fully capable of coping with the day-to-day, here-and-now events in the classroom, staff development efforts can move on to the questions that challenge us in the twenty-first century. What do children need to know to survive in the twenty-first century? How will life change in the next 50 years, and what personality characteristics and thinking dispositions will be essential to function competently during those 50 years? The job of staff training is never complete because there are always new challenges.

STAFF SUPERVISION AND COACHING naeyc

The director, or the educational director in the case of large centers or some corporate chains, is responsible for supervision of classroom staff. (The director will be referred to as supervisor for the purposes of this discussion.) By observing, doing one-to-one mentoring and coaching, plus working in the classroom with the children and the staff, the supervisor gives support and guidance to each staff member and establishes a trusting relationship with each one. As a coach, the director's job is to "encourage and provide opportunities for defining and solving problems and for self-reflection and collaboration. It is important that you (the director) model the kind of behavior you want staff to use with children—providing for self-initiated learning, risk taking and exploration" (Carter & Curtis, 2010, p. 122). The trust and mutual respect that develop between coach and teacher provide the basis for building a

teaching-learning relationship that parallels the relationship between adult and child. Then the supervisor is able to create a favorable environment in which each staff member can gain new understandings of children, of self, and of the supervisor's expectations.

An experienced supervisor knows that sometimes growth and change take place slowly. Working together, talking together, and planning together will promote personal and professional competence on the part of classroom staff members, provided the supervisor is supportive and encouraging and is not perceived as being critical or threatening.

Principles of Supervision

You should keep in mind a number of basic principles or assumptions as you think about the director as staff supervisor. The same principles apply to the supervisory role, whether you are working with a new, inexperienced staff member or a mature, qualified, experienced teacher or are a new director moving into a fully staffed center.

- Supervision is a dynamic, evolutionary process that is based on trust.
- Supervision is individualized and adapted to the personality and teaching style of each staff member.
- Supervision provides a support system for each staff member.
- Supervision provides a framework within which the supervisor demonstrates professional skills for the entire staff.

However, an individualized model of staff development means you must use a developmental approach to supervision, and teachers who are at different stages in their careers will require qualitatively different supervisory strategies.

Supervisory Process

As classroom staff members grow and change, the thrust and focus of the supervisory process shifts accordingly. The process begins by providing support and guidance for a new staff member, who is integrating past learning experiences into a personal teaching style that is compatible with the center philosophy. The process changes as the staff member adjusts and develops into an accomplished teacher, who will, in turn, supervise assistants, aides, and student teachers, or be paired with a new teacher and become a mentor. If you think of this supervisory process on a continuum, it moves from a very directive approach for new teachers where the control is in the hands of the supervisor, to a collaborative model where an accomplished teacher and the supervisor share control of the process.

One-to-one coaching is the essential ingredient of the supervisory process, whether working with the beginning teacher or the accomplished professional who, in turn, will coach others in the center. Coaching includes encouraging, modeling, observing, and giving specific feedback. A coach is a cheerleader who watches and listens and shares skills, resources, and experience. Communicating with staff after an observation usually is handled in a conference, but when time is short, a brief note with some specific feedback may have to suffice.

The director must ensure that staff members engage in high-quality practices at all times. When there are questions and concerns about teacher performance, it always is a challenge to communicate those concerns in a way that addresses the issues but maintains program quality and does not compromise staff morale. Depending on the level of training and experience of the staff, you, as the director, will find that you will have to deal with questions and concerns about classroom practices on a regular basis. There may be issues about curriculum, classroom management, staff relationships, or interactions with parents. On any given day, you will see and hear things that must be addressed. Following are some examples:

- How should I approach Estella, who continues to call across the room to set limits for children who are not doing what she thinks they should be doing?

- I must talk with Consuelo about using positive redirection instead of the constant, "Stop running in the room" or "Don't spill your milk."

- Colin's group times are not rich or challenging these days. I must call him in and talk about that.

- What is the best way to tell Betsy that she and her assistant should be sitting with the children at lunch and eating what children eat? I also will have to tell them that they must wait until they are on break to have coffee or a Coke.

Dealing with questionable practices is especially distasteful for directors who prefer to avoid conflict and confrontations, but it is an important part of the supervisory process and goes to the core of what it takes to maintain the integrity of the program. Keep in mind that when you are responsible for supervision of staff, you will inevitably have to spend time and energy dealing with conflict (Sciarra & Dorsey, 2002).

REFLECTION

How do you feel about confrontation and conflict? Do you withdraw and avoid it like a turtle? Do you approach and attack like a shark? Do you wait and watch like an owl? What is your style of dealing with conflict and confrontation? How might that affect your performance as a supervisor? (Sciarra & Dorsey, 2002, p. 147)

Supervisory Cycle

The two pieces of the supervisory cycle, formative supervisory cycle and summative supervisory cycle, each include a discovery step, a conference step, and a planning and goal-setting step (Table 14-1). Ideally the director/supervisor and the teacher/supervisee began to build a relationship based on trust and mutual respect during the initial orientation sessions because that provided the foundation for a collaborative, ongoing supervisor/supervisee relationship.

The first step in the supervisory cycle is the discovery step for both the formative and summative segments of the cycle. The discovery step begins with a scheduled classroom observation that is followed by a scheduled conference with the teacher. Although making time and covering classrooms for regularly scheduled observations and conferences is not easy, it contributes significantly to the success of the teacher assessment/evaluation process. During the formative time period of the cycle, the emphasis for the observation and conference is reflection, discussion, and sharing of information and concerns about classroom events and practice. At the conference following the observation, the director and the teacher review and discuss events and actions observed. The formative conference is helpful for both participants if the director listens carefully and encourages the teacher to reflect, analyze, vent if needed, and evaluate events or issues that arose during the observation. A checklist for classroom observations is sometimes used to help supervisors focus on specific aspects of a teacher's performance. Sometimes asking open-ended questions will generate discussion that will be helpful for both the teacher and the director. For example, the director may ask the following:

- What was on your mind as you asked Tully what she was thinking about when she was repeatedly stabbing the play dough with the tongue blade?

TABLE 14-1 Supervisory process

Summative Supervisory Cycle	Formative Supervisory Cycle
Discovery Step	
Supervisor observes supervisee	Supervisor observes supervisee
Evaluation tool	Anecdotal records
Performance appraisal	Narrative records
	Checklists
	Casual notes and comments
Conference Step	
Supervisor reviews previously set goals	Supervisor empowers supervisee
Supervisor presents findings based on the performance appraisal	Nurturing and coaching
Supervisor and supervisee discuss results of the performance appraisal	Sharing information and concerns
Planning and Goal-Setting Step	
Supervisor states the decisions based on the performance appraisal	Supervisor and supervisee set mutually agreed upon goals
Raise	
Promotion	
No change in status	
Probation	
Dismissal	
Develop the action plan and put it in writing	Develop the action plan and put it in writing
Training	Readings
Course work	Training or course work
Reading	Observing peers or teachers in other programs
Conditions of the probationary period	
Steps to finalize dismissal	
Set the time for the next summative conference	Set the time for the next formative conference

Source: From Sciarra/Dorsey. Leaders and Supervisors in Child Care Programs, 1E. © 2002 Wadsworth, a part of Cengage Learning, Inc. Reproduced by permission. www.cengage.com/permissions

- Did you have a sense of what Farah was upset about in the bathroom before his "meltdown"?
- Did you realize that Perot had grabbed Lissa's doll baby away from her earlier in that dramatic play sequence—and that later she took his cowboy hat away from him and that is when you intervened?

The coaching and mentoring segment of the conference might include references to the center curriculum framework and books that are useful to support that, the NAEYC Accreditation Standards, the PAS, or licensing expectations. There may be times when sections of the job description or the performance appraisal can be used to support both the positive notations in the observation notes as well as those

items that may require special attention. The conference always ends with agreed-upon goals and plans to think about and act upon before the next scheduled observation. If it is time for the teacher to be evaluated, the planning time can be used to describe the summative steps in the process. It is an ideal time for the teacher and the director to review the performance appraisal tool so the teacher understands that the next steps will be related to performance appraisal and both the teacher and the director will be prepared for that step in the cycle. With this planning in place, the supervisory cycle continues.

The pattern of observation and conferencing for the summative segment of the supervisory cycle is also a scheduled observation followed by a scheduled conference. Programs differ in how and when summative evaluations are done. They may be done annually or semiannually or scheduled individually, based on hiring date. For the summative observation, the director uses the performance appraisal tool, summarizes the findings, and prepares to present these to the teacher at the conference. At this conference, the director takes the lead and presents the findings from the observation that was based on the performance appraisal. It is important to remember that this meeting comes after many casual contacts, a number of scheduled observations and conferences, and frequent communication between the director and teacher. Therefore, there are usually no surprises for the teacher at this time. If the information shared is critical or negative, the teacher may object or argue, but that has to be expected. However, if the director has coached, offered help, provided opportunities for training, and been up front about expectations during previous conferences, and if that has all been carefully documented with notes from conferences and previous encounters, the teacher should see that the results of the performance appraisal are fairly accurate. After discussion and clearly stated decisions based on the appraisal have been communicated, the conference ends with plans for the next step in the cycle, which is scheduling the coming series of formative observations and conferences to repeat the cycle (Sciarra & Dorsey, 2002).

Supervising New Teachers

New teachers need daily or even hourly support; therefore, the director/supervisor must plan to spend some time each day observing and teaching with the new teacher. If a new teacher is recently trained, that teacher will be developing a personal teaching style and will profit from the example that is set by an experienced supervisor. It is very important for a supervisor to work beside a new teacher with the children in the classroom. This supervisory procedure creates a rich learning environment for the new teacher and often provides a more favorable transition for the children and families who know the supervisor but are not yet well acquainted with the new teacher. As a supervisor, you must make sure to remove yourself gradually so that the new teacher can build a relationship with the children and families and begin to manage the classroom without your constant support. What you are doing, in effect, is providing hourly or daily support during the initial trust-building period but stepping back when the new teacher can function independently. You are scaffolding the experience for the teacher just as you would for a child in the classroom, gradually increasing the challenge as you stay nearby

> ### DIRECTOR'S CORNER
>
> "Since I am new here, I haven't developed a schedule for regular observations as yet, but I make the rounds at least twice a day, if only to let my teachers know I am available. Of course, I have a chance to catch things going on in each room—maybe a new chart or a teacher reading a book to a sleepy child. I make sure I leave a short note in each teacher's box, mentioning some little thing I noticed when I came by. If I see an activity or a procedure that concerns me, I mention it. 'I noticed you had the toddlers finger painting with chocolate pudding today. Drop by when you have a chance—I have some ideas about that that I would like to share with you.' It seems to work well for me."
>
> —Director, community-agency-sponsored center

because your ongoing support is still important when things do not go well.

Supervising Experienced Teachers

As teachers develop their skills and become more competent, they continue to profit from the supervisor's support. Positive reinforcement and constructive criticism from supervisors are excellent motivating factors. But experienced teachers also are ready for expansion and growth in new directions. They still are integrating and reorganizing what they have learned in the past, but they are now able to reach out for new learning opportunities. These teachers now are comfortable with their teaching style and can direct more attention to curriculum development. They are ready for the intellectual stimulation they can draw from taking course work, reading new publications, and attending professional meetings. Therefore, although the supervisor continues to observe these teachers and have conferences with them on a regular basis, emphasis now is placed on the supervisor as a resource person. The supervisor can supply new program ideas, new theoretical information, articles from professional journals and websites, research materials, and as many opportunities as possible for teachers to participate actively in professional organizations and conferences.

While experienced teachers are perfecting their teaching skills under the guidance of the supervisor, they also should be developing self-evaluation skills. With encouragement and help from a supervisor, experienced teachers feel secure enough to step back

Staff is used to informal drop-in visits where they are more likely to hear something good about what they are doing than a complaint. Having established a trusting relationship between staff and director is important when there is a need for constructive criticism.

Bombeck Family Learning Center

and evaluate their teaching. They can begin to ask themselves some of the questions a supervisor has been asking them and engage in some self-searching about their methodology. For example, one teacher might make the inquiry, "How could I have better handled the situation between those two children who had a conflict over the sand bucket? What I did was really not productive. I must find alternative ways of handling those two children." Another teacher might ask, "How can I adjust my questioning techniques for all the children in order to help them become better problem solvers? I heard you mention Rheta deVries. Maybe you could give me something she has written on that topic that will help me."

Supervising the Accomplished Teacher

The accomplished, long-term teacher still is perfecting teaching and self-evaluation skills and revising curriculum. However, having reached a new level of mastery, this teacher is ready to develop supervisory skills. While working with the teachers, the director/ supervisor has not only exemplified teaching and self-evaluation skills but also supervisory skills. In working with accomplished teachers, the director/ supervisor now turns to coaching them in supervisory skills. This teacher is preparing to assume responsibility for the supervision of assistants, aides, and, in some situations, student teachers. To serve in this capacity, the teacher will need instruction and support to develop the necessary skills for fulfilling supervisory responsibilities. The director/ supervisor still is observing and having conferences on a regular basis, giving attention to teaching strategies and self-evaluation. However, the new thrust is directed to this teacher's interaction with, and supervision of, other adults in the classroom.

Involving accomplished teachers with novice teachers in a mentoring program is an ideal way to offer the benefit of job enrichment for both. The director's role becomes one of modeling for the mentor by engaging in reflective practices and helping this teacher, who is very skilled at working with young children, learn more about the characteristics of the adult learner. The director models ways to use many of the same skills that teachers use when caring for young children, and now explores ways to "care for a fellow caregiver." Pairing mentors with novices is a challenge for the director who must observe, reflect, and confer with staff to ensure a "good fit" in each pairing. A successful peer mentoring program contributes to the well-being of staff and children alike. It is connected to both staff development and supervision, but, at the same time, is separate. It provides unique opportunities for both mentors and novices to learn from each other and grow professionally.

Supervision is one of the most difficult and anxiety-producing aspects of the director's job. It draws on every bit of professional skill the director has because it demands expertise in interpersonal communication, children's programming, teaching strategies, and self-evaluation. It also helps the director focus on the importance of being a model for the staff by making positive suggestions to coach and motivate and by using supportive, caring gestures and voice tone. This sets the tone for staff, who, in turn, are more likely to follow a similar pattern in their interactions with children and families.

Accomplished practitioners, like successful CEOs, give thoughtful attention to grooming their successors. Through ongoing encouragement and coaching that is fashioned to the talents and abilities of each accomplished teacher, the director guides them toward optimal professional growth. This prepares them to take on more responsibility and to advance their own professional careers. It is the talented and visionary center directors who can best bring along and groom the future leaders in the field.

REFLECTION

Think about the cooperating teacher who supervised your practicum. Did you receive support and constructive criticism? Did that person serve as a model of good supervisory skills for you? Think about how your cooperating teacher might have been more helpful. What do you feel you need before you can become a supervisor of a center classroom staff?

ASSESSING STAFF PROBLEMS

Assessing what the staff members view as work-related problems provides the basis for designing the staff development program and focusing individualized supervision activities. Once you have identified what teachers believe to be their major problems, you can take the first steps toward helping them solve those problems (Bloom, Sheerer & Britz, 2005). The expressed needs of staff can be addressed directly. If a teacher has problems handling the aggressive behaviors of a child, the director can respond in various direct ways, including offering relevant readings, observing or participating in the classroom, discussing various management strategies, calling in a consultant to observe and conference with the classroom staff, or discussing the general problem of dealing with aggression in a staff meeting. This direct response to an expressed need may motivate the staff member to become involved in a training plan offered by the director. On the other hand, when the selection of staff development activities is based on those issues the director views as problems, motivating staff interest will be more difficult. For example, if a new director finds the long-term staff using punitive and age-inappropriate techniques in response to unacceptable classroom behaviors, but the teachers are comfortable with their management methods, those teachers will resist making a commitment to any training designed to encourage them to use more positive management strategies. The new director will have

to spend time establishing a trusting working relationship with the professional staff before training related to the classroom management question will be accepted. Because the use of punitive management techniques can be hard on children, the new director may choose to bring in a consultant to work with individual staff members or may even consider making staff changes. A new director is well advised to design the initial staff development activities in response to the teachers' expressed needs.

Selection of staff development activities is often based on expressed needs of staff or is in response to new requirements that come down from funders or licensing or government agencies, but it also emerges from the interests and goals of a visionary director. The staff development program is often designed to guide the staff to make changes in what they think and in what they do. Response to change differs from one person to another—some are exhilarated and motivated by the opportunity to work with change, while others are anxious and immobilized. As individuals on the staff begin to respond to expectations or requirements presented to them, they need the director's support and encouragement. It is now critical that responsible directors keep a watchful eye on those who fail to progress. Documentation and regular observing and conferencing throughout the process are helpful to all staff but are essential for those whose failure to progress could be a problem that will require action on the part of the director in the future.

Expressed Teacher Concerns

Expressed teacher concerns cluster around a number of problem areas (Bloom, Sheerer & Britz, 2005). The director's task is to identify and then respond to these concerns. The areas of greatest concern include those points discussed in the following paragraphs.

Dealing with Assisting Staff

Teachers have a problem getting their assistants to follow through on assigned responsibilities and to work as a member of a cooperative team. In response to this problem, effective directing, evaluating, and giving feedback to subordinate staff would be appropriate areas to address in the staff training program for the teachers. The best way for the director to help teachers with this problem is to model exemplary supervisory skills.

Managing the Classroom

Teachers report problems with managing children's challenging behaviors. Behaviors on their list include aggression and violence, not picking up, not sharing, and not cooperating. In addressing the problem of working with these children, the director first might focus on developmental expectations for the specific age group in question, followed by ways to encourage prosocial behaviors. This is a sensitive problem area because the perceived problem sometimes results from teachers' unrealistic expectations. Directors must model developmentally appropriate responses to children's behaviors whenever they have encounters with children in the center. Managing children who present extremely oppositional or violent behaviors often requires the help of a mental health specialist.

Helping Children with Special Needs and Their Families

Teachers report that they do not know enough about how to deal appropriately with children with special needs. This becomes a serious problem when children with previously unidentified social-emotional problems join the group. Teachers suddenly realize that this child is, indeed, disturbed and in need of special help, but they are not prepared for the disruption and management challenges this new child presents. They want help on how to provide rich environments for these children as well as ways to work effectively with the family. Providing reading materials and planning special meetings on this topic will be helpful to teachers who are searching for better ways to help these special children. Directors also must watch for upcoming conferences and meetings on the topic and encourage staff to attend.

Because teachers and directors are seeing an increase in the number of children who exhibit challenging behaviors, some center directors are seeking funding for more mental health services or for a mental health specialist on the staff.

The role of the mental health specialist on staff is to plan regularly scheduled classroom observations, usually taking place in the morning and lasting from two to three hours. The conference to discuss the observation, with the director and the teachers in that room, should be on the same day, if possible, so the events of the day are still clear and fresh. Conferences can often be arranged for nap time. It is essential that directors attend these meetings because they must assume responsibility for curriculum and monitor all classrooms regarding curriculum matters. The conference time is devoted to discussing events of the day and highlighting those that precipitated anxiety and tension for the children. These notable events were often those that tended to pose problems for the more fragile children.

The role of the mental health specialist in the conference is to support staff as well as coach them as they all talk about the reactions of the children, what the children may have been trying to accomplish, or what they may have been thinking. With new insights into the effects of experiences on children and their reactions to those experiences, teachers begin to feel more competent about their ability to plan, evaluate, and work with them. The major thrust of the mental health specialist is to help center staff saturate the classroom, and eventually the entire center, with refined practices that will enhance the emotional well-being of all children in the program, not just those who have been called "challenging."

For the children who continue to require additional help, the mental health specialist can arrange to meet and work with them and their families for as long as needed. Clearly this approach is a departure from the more typical procedure in which the mental health specialist is called upon to observe a specific child. The expectation, in this case, is that the specialist will observe the child; identify the problem; and then offer help to the child, the child's teachers, and members of the family. This surely benefits all who participate and work with the specialist. The plan described previously puts the focus on all children in the classroom, knowing that everyone in the classroom is entitled to have the benefit of ongoing daily practice that has at its core the emotional well-being of young children.

Relating to Supervisors

Staff members often clash with directors. Teachers complain about not being treated fairly and not being respected as professionals. The response to this problem is clearly in the director's hands. Directors must work on their own professional development to enable them to become better staff managers.

Maintaining Parent Cooperation

Teachers have problems with parents who send a sick child to school; who are not prompt about picking their child up after school; and who do not cooperate with the teachers' efforts, such as when teachers encourage the use of messy materials. Here, the director can reinforce center policies by reviewing the parent handbook material with the parent, as well as participate in parent conferences when necessary, to mediate and to give support to both the teacher and the parent. In-service training focused on working with parents and becoming sensitive to their needs may help teachers feel more secure about handling difficult situations with parents.

Managing Time

Time to deal with nonteaching tasks like cleaning, planning, making materials, or doing other paperwork is a problem for teachers. Because time management is also a major problem for directors, it is something they have in common. Time management seminars under the guidance of an experienced trainer can be part of the staff development program.

It is especially important for the director to be a part of this training and to model good time management.

Although staff concerns always are situation specific, there is a common core of recurring problems that fall into the categories just listed. It can be reassuring to you, as a director, to know that your teachers' expressed needs are much like those of most teaching staffs.

SUMMARY

The staff development program contributes to both the personal and professional growth of the center staff. Through the planning and implementation of effective staff meetings, staff training programs, and staff supervision, the director creates an enriched learning environment for the staff. Given the benefits of an enriched environment and a director who demonstrates good interpersonal and professional skills, the staff members have the opportunity to enjoy the inevitable personal satisfaction and excitement that result from positive, individualized, professional growth experiences.

TRY IT OUT!

1. Role-play a child care center staff meeting and discuss one agenda item, "Timing for weekly staff meetings." It has been decided by the director that the entire staff (including the cook, the janitor, and the secretary) must meet every week. The question open for discussion is the day of the week on which the staff should meet, and when and how long the meetings should be. Assign the following roles to class members:
   a. Director: works Monday through Friday 9:00 a.m. to 5:00 p.m.
   b. Teacher A: works Monday through Friday 9:00 a.m. to 5:00 p.m.
   c. Teacher B: works Monday through Friday 6:00 a.m. to 2:00 p.m.
   d. Assistant teacher C: works Monday through Friday 10:00 a.m. to 6:00 p.m.
   e. Assistant teacher D: works Monday through Friday 6:00 a.m. to 2:00 p.m.
   f. Part-time teacher E: works Monday through Friday 10:00 a.m. to 2:00 p.m.
   g. Cook: works Monday through Friday 9:00 a.m. to 3:00 p.m.
   h. Janitor: works Monday through Friday 3:00 p.m. to 8:00 p.m.

   There are 35 children in the program who arrive on a staggered schedule between 6:15 a.m. and 9:30 a.m. and leave between 2:30 p.m. and 5:30 p.m. The children occupy two classrooms and two sleeping rooms. Sleeping rooms are adjacent to one another and to the outdoor area.

   The staff meeting discussion is to be led by the director, and the group is to come to some decision about when the regular staff meeting will be held. Use the blackboard or newsprint for note taking, if you need it. Practice good listening skills; make sure that everyone participates.

2. Role-play a special staff meeting that has been called by the director to discuss and reach a decision about allocation of classroom space at the child care center. There will be one additional classroom available beginning in September, and a new teacher, Mark, will be employed. The new classroom is larger than the others and opens directly to the playground.

   Sandra currently has the best classroom, which has its own bathroom. The other four rooms share a bathroom down the hall. Jean will be working with a new pilot program and will have many parents participating in her classroom. She was responsible for getting the pilot program funded, and it is a real asset for the center. Bob's classroom is far from the outside play area and from the storage room. Bob feels that this location is inconvenient. Sheila would like to keep her current classroom because she recently made curtains and painted the walls.

Barbara feels that her ten years of teaching qualify her for the new classroom.

Name	Years at Center	Degree	Current Classroom
Sandra	6	M.S.	Excellent
Barbara	10	B.S.	Very good
Sheila	4	B.S.	Very good
Bob	6	A.S.	Good
Jean	1	A.S.	Poor
Mark	0	B.S.	

The staff has allocated 30 minutes for making this decision. After the group has arrived at a decision, individually rate your level of satisfaction with the decision from 1 (low) to 5 (high). Also, rate your level of participation from 1 to 5.

Tally the results on the chalkboard. As a group, discuss the factors that contributed to the level of satisfaction or dissatisfaction. Was the level of participation a factor?

3 Think about a time when you were called in by a teacher or a boss for an appraisal of your performance (athletic performance, singing or dancing event, your work in a store or restaurant, and so forth). Reflect on how the teacher or boss handled the situation—how you felt about what she/he said, how you felt about yourself during the conference, how you feel about yourself now as you recall the incident, and so forth. Write a few paragraphs about why you think you had the feelings about yourself then as you experienced the conference as compared with how you feel about yourself now as you remember it, and why you think those feelings differ, if they do.

REFERENCES

Bloom, P. J. (2002). *Making the most of meetings: A practical guide*. Lake Forest, IL: New Horizons.

Bloom, P. J., Sheerer, M. & Britz, J. (2005). *Blueprint for action: Achieving center-based change through staff development*. Lake Forest, IL: New Horizons.

Carter, M. & Curtis, D. (2010). *The visionary director: A handbook for dreaming, organizing and improving*. St. Paul, MN: Redleaf Press.

Jones, E. (Ed). (1993). *Growing teachers: Partnerships in staff development*. Washington, DC: NAEYC.

Sciarra, D. J. & Dorsey, A. G. (2002). *Leaders and supervisors in child care programs*. Clifton Park, NY: Thomson Delmar Learning.

Tanner, D. & Tanner, L. (Eds.). (2007). *Curriculum development: Theory into practice* (4th ed.). Englewood Cliffs, NJ: Merrill.

Tanner, D. & Tanner, L. (Eds.). (1995). *Curriculum development: Theory into practice* (3rd ed.). Englewood Cliffs, NJ: Merrill.

Werner, S. (1996, May/June). Need a barometer for assessing the climate of your center? *Child Care Information Exchange, 109*, 29.

15

Evaluating CENTER COMPONENTS

© 2010 Cengage Learning

The director and staff members work together to participate in NAEYC accreditation by becoming familiar with accreditation materials prior to beginning their self-study.

Objectives

After reading this chapter, you should be able to:

- Explain the purpose of evaluation.
- Describe the director's role in evaluation.
- Describe how the center, the staff, and the director may be evaluated.
- List several methods of assessing children's progress.
- List criteria for selecting an assessment tool.

Standards Addressed in This Chapter

naeyc Professional Preparation Standard 3

naeyc Administrator Competencies Management Knowledge and Skills 3
Early Childhood Knowledge and Skills 3

naeyc Accreditation Standards 4, 10

Evaluation is an ongoing process. An evaluation can take the form of an analysis of a person's behavior, of an administrative policy or procedure, or of some other component of an early childhood education program or even of the whole program. Periodically, long-range planning should occur and the mission should be examined. Such an examination should provide data about usefulness or worth. Once an early childhood education program has been planned, the evaluation of that program should be designed immediately as part of the program's operational system.

Evaluation that is planned during the early stages of program development facilitates the process and notifies everyone from the start how the evaluation process will be conducted. The evaluator uses the mission statement or goals that were prepared prior to the opening of the center as the basis for making judgments about what is valuable in the program. These documents provide guidelines for assessing the center's program and the performance of individuals affiliated with that program.

Regular evaluation can indicate how successful the director and staff have been in adhering to their mission and in meeting their goals. Evaluation can help the director, board, and staff revise their goals as changes occur in the community and the world. This process also enables the director to make needed changes quickly before current practices have a negative effect on the program. Continuation of an ineffective aspect of the program is fruitless and frequently expensive. Inappropriate staff behavior may be detrimental to children's development or to staff relations. Desirable behavior, on the other hand, should be recognized, encouraged, and supported as a result of the evaluation process.

Assuming that the director has worked to create a "we" feeling rather than a "boss" approach, evaluation also will take on a collaborative tone. Rather than being threatening or punitive, evaluation will be a way to note and celebrate progress and to plan for the next stages. Then staff and director can support one another in reaching those revised or new goals.

Purpose of Evaluation

Early childhood center evaluation has often focused on classroom practices. However, current understandings of center effectiveness indicate that the overall administrative procedures and policies and the ways in which these are implemented ultimately relate to the quality of care and education that children receive at the center. The overriding purpose of evaluation of the center's administration is to ensure good-quality child care. Talan and Bloom (2011) have provided a tool for measuring leadership and management. Evaluation results should lead to examination of goals and their supporting policies and procedures.

Since a major purpose of evaluation is to determine whether the center's goals are being met and whether they or the program needs to be modified, the evaluators need to know what these goals are before gathering data. In effect, the evaluators must know who the clients are, what their needs are, and which of these needs the center is attempting to meet. For example, in a community where the local high school is expressing concern about the high number of dropouts due to pregnancy, a center director may decide to work with the school system to assess how many students could return to school if care were provided for their infants and toddlers. Together, the center and the school may be able to obtain funding to provide this service. In such a situation, particularly if tax dollars are to be used, community education would be important since many taxpayers may believe that the program would cause teen pregnancy rather than prevent school dropouts.

A further purpose of evaluation is to determine how effective the program is in meeting the needs of clients and how efficient it is in terms of cost, time, and energy. Are needs met to the satisfaction of the center and the clients? Are they partially met or not met at all? More important in our example, are significantly more teen parents returning to and staying in school when their babies receive child care? Even if needs are met, could the same job have been done for less money or by using less time or energy? Funding agencies, board members, and clients expect documentation that the center is doing what it has agreed to do. An evaluation provides the data for such documentation and possibly the basis for further funding.

A final reason for evaluation is the need to have a solid basis for future planning. The director uses the data from the current evaluation to determine the strengths and weaknesses of the program and to adapt the plan for the following year to correct any

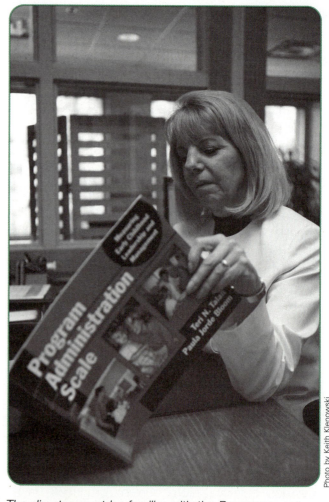

The director must be familiar with the Program Administration Scale as well as NAEYC Early Childhood Program Standards.

Photo by Keith Klenowski

deficiencies or to respond to newly perceived needs. For example, if one of the goals of the center is to provide a parent education program for all parents and the data show that only ten percent of the parents participated, then the director must determine whether the goal is inappropriate or whether the method of achieving it is not meeting the needs of the clients. If a thorough evaluation has been done, the director will have information from parents regarding how they felt about the parent program and why they did or did not attend. The information then can be used to plan changes in next year's program or to ascertain that this community does not need parent education from this particular center.

It would be easy to arrive at the conclusion that parents in the preceding example do not want or need parent education. But directors have to consider other factors and perhaps ask themselves the following questions:

- Have parents been involved in the planning so that they feel as though they are part of the program?

- Is there another parent education program already established in the community that is meeting these parents' needs?

- Is the timing, format, or content inappropriate for these parents?

- Has there been a breakdown in communication so that parents do not feel welcome or comfortable about coming?

- Are there other, more pressing matters confronting the parents?

- Are there ancillary problems such as babysitting or transportation?

Because one or more of these factors may have had a major effect on parent participation, the director should certainly address them to make sure that the evaluation is accurate.

REFLECTION

We have discussed the purpose of conducting an evaluation in early childhood centers and the people who conduct these investigations. Now think about the people who evaluate you. Who are they? Why do they evaluate you? Some of you may think of relatives or friends who evaluate your behavior on an ongoing basis. Others may immediately associate evaluation with teachers and employers. Do all these people see you in the same way? If not, why do some of them evaluate you in different ways? What is the purpose of their evaluation?

Evaluation Principles

Evaluation plans should be based on certain principles that reduce anxiety and increase cooperation among the individuals being evaluated.

1 The evaluation process is open; that is, the people or groups being evaluated know about the evaluation process in advance and have access to their own evaluation data. Furthermore, the people being evaluated have an opportunity to give input into their own evaluation.

2 Evaluation relates directly to program goals and objectives.

3 Each person being evaluated knows why, when, where, how, and by whom the evaluation is to be done.

4 Evaluation is conducted on an individual basis. However, for reporting purposes, the results are compiled and group data, rather than individual data, are presented.

5 The individual's evaluation is a confidential matter and is accessible only to those who need to know, such as an employee's supervisor or a child's teacher.

6 Evaluation is built into the program so that it occurs on a regular basis.

EVALUATION PLAN naeyc

As the director and staff work together to create an evaluation system, they consider what will be evaluated and why. They determine the intended audience for the evaluation plan. Will all or part of it be available to families, all staff, board members, funders, and the general public, or will it be available "in house" only? What does each of these groups need to know; what are they entitled to know? How will the information be used? Issues of confidentiality must be considered and must be specifically mandated in the center's policy manual. All who have access to information must agree to this overarching policy. Moreover, adopting the NAEYC Code of Ethical Conduct, its supplements, and Statement of Commitment will provide guidance when ethical dilemmas are encountered (see Appendix A).

Planners must give serious consideration to the appropriate amount of data to be collected. Keep in mind that someone has to prepare or select the evaluation tools. Someone has to see that the data are gathered and analyzed. And someone has to determine how the information will be used. Who will be

"The steering committee conducts an annual parent survey. One parent gathers all the information and then gives each classroom a printout of what the parents in their room specifically said. The parents' names aren't included, though. Parents seem willing to write things that they might not take time to say in person, and it's been real helpful to the staff to get this kind of feedback."

—Director, agency-sponsored early childhood center

responsible? Where will the information be kept and for how long? Specifying procedures to be used, including time lines, will facilitate the process and will help determine the optimum amount and type of information to be gathered.

The evaluation plan should include provisions for everyone connected with the center to participate. Staff members should be encouraged to participate in discussions about the center, its programs, policies, and procedures. The National Association for the Education of Young Children (NAEYC), in its Accreditation Criteria for Leadership and Management Standard, has the expectation that "At least annually, administrators, families, staff and other routinely participating adults are involved in comprehensive program evaluation that measures progress toward the program's goals and objectives. Valid and reliable processes are used to gather data and evidence" (Ritchie and Willer, 2005, p. 26).

Some directors or their boards may feel that a consultant is needed to help them develop tools for collecting information to ensure that these tools will provide the type of data that will be useful. In corporate systems, a national or regional staff member may plan and conduct some or all of the evaluation. When funds are received from a governmental or private agency, an employee of that agency may be assigned to perform an evaluation. When public schools operate preschool or child care programs, the principal usually is responsible for evaluating the staff.

An early childhood education evaluation plan involves three components: staff, children, and total program evaluation. A plan for each of these components includes delineating who will evaluate what, as well as how and when the evaluation will be conducted and for what purposes a particular evaluation is being done.

STAFF EVALUATION

Staff evaluation is a natural outgrowth of supervision, one of the basic duties of the director. Every staff member should be evaluated on a regular basis according to the procedure included in the policies and procedures manual.

Staff evaluation is conducted to enable the director and the staff member to analyze what the staff member is doing well and in what areas growth and change are desirable or required. This type of evaluation provides information to the funding agency and the board about how employees spend their time; it also validates the work of the employees.

The first form of evaluation is *employee selection*. In assessing an applicant's ability to work well with other employees, the director must be cautious, avoiding the selection of only those people who fit a mold. A successful choice is based on a careful evaluation of credentials and behavior, rather than on an overgeneralization of positive or negative traits. For example, the candidate who answers an early question to the interviewer's liking then may be regarded as being highly qualified, although he actually may be poorly skilled in working with young children. On the other hand, the candidate with an unusual style of clothing may be considered initially as incompetent when, in reality, that person might work quite well with young children. The director should avoid hiring only those applicants who are very similar to current employees, but still must consider whether or not the qualifications of a particular candidate will combine well with those of current employees to provide the total staff strength needed to meet center goals. In any case, the most important criterion is, "Is this the best person available to do the job?" Of course, the director will check the applicants' references and will require a documented background check.

Process and Procedures

Ongoing evaluation of staff members begins when they accept a position. At this time, the director and the new staff member go over the job description together carefully and make adjustments as needed to fit the circumstances, writing these changes (if any) into the job description. A comprehensive evaluation is based on this job description. The director makes it clear to employees from the beginning that they will be evaluated. However, another important component to be discussed with the employee is the support that will be provided to assist new staff members as they become acclimated to a new role. This support is particularly helpful for first-year teachers. They should also be informed that all staff are guided and supported so that they continue to grow professionally (Sciarra & Dorsey, 2002).

The director informs each employee why, when, where, and by whom the evaluation will be done; outlines the basis for the evaluation; and describes the method to be used. Often, a new employee is evaluated after a two- or three-month probationary period. If the employee's work is found to be satisfactory at this time, the employee and director then plan together for further growth by writing out what the employee expects to accomplish prior to the next evaluation. In this initial step in the evaluation cycle, the employee writes out goals and brings them to a meeting with the director, at which time both must agree on their importance and reasonableness. The goals must relate to the job description, and the subsequent evaluation is based on the mutually agreed-upon objectives.

For example, if one of the teacher's goals is to maintain a more orderly classroom, that teacher's procedural plan may include teaching the children to return things to the proper shelf, rearranging the classroom, or working with the classroom aide to develop a mutually agreeable plan for keeping materials in order. Sometimes, the director gives help at this stage, either by assisting the employee in finding ways of meeting an objective or by designating areas in which specific objectives should be defined. The primary goal at this step is to draw up a workable plan that the staff member can follow and that will enhance the overall program.

Next, the director and employee decide how data will be gathered. Will the director observe? Will parents be asked for their opinions? Will the teacher be asked to engage in a self-evaluation process? Will the teachers observe each other? Will children's behavior be used as a criterion? Again, both director and staff member reach agreement on what is the best plan to use. Some centers use checklists or rating scales. These tools are most useful in large centers in which a number of staff are working on comparable skills such as fostering a comfortable classroom atmosphere or preparing appropriate classroom materials.

The objectives and evaluation format are called a *work plan*, which is the formative component of staff evaluation. Once the plan has been written, the director and the staff member each receive a copy for reference as they work to achieve the objectives and to evaluate the progress that is made. They plan a specific time period for the next meeting: in a month, at the end of the semester, or whatever length of time fits their needs.

When a teacher is already doing an outstanding job, the director can support her in finding a new related interest and area for growth and development. Possibilities include offering to reschedule her hours so that she could participate in training on technology for children, or granting additional responsibilities for working with teachers new to the center and possibly even new to the field. If she is interested in administration, you may begin to involve her in work that would introduce her to that component of the early childhood field and would, at the same time, begin to prepare a successor for your role.

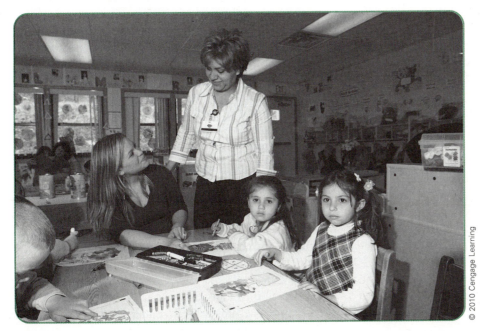

Teachers are aware that observation by the director is a regular component of the evaluation process.

© 2010 Cengage Learning

Obviously you will have to be able to replace her in the classroom during the time she is spending on these new endeavors and, of course, additional funds would be needed. However, when a teacher feels that she has outgrown her job, it is likely that she will search for new opportunities with other programs.

The Director's Role

The director's role in staff evaluation is to observe and analyze the work of a staff person, encourage the development of that person's strengths, and look for ways to promote growth in weaker areas. If the weak areas considerably outweigh the strong, then the director must terminate the employment of that individual because the director's role (except in special cases) is to promote growth rather than to provide total on-the-job training. The staff member's role is to work out the details of meeting the agreed-upon goals and to implement these plans.

In some centers, a standard form is used to evaluate each teacher. Although this may be seen as more equitable, it sets the same expectations for beginners as for experienced teachers. An alternative method is to evaluate all teachers with a standard form that addresses basic requirements. In addition, the director should provide individualized planning and evaluation for each teacher.

Some directors observe each teacher weekly, biweekly, or monthly and have a conference informally after making the observation. The director may take notes during the observation or write notes afterward, but any notes should be shared with the teacher because they are useful in helping to fulfill the specific objectives that have been set. It sometimes is easy to pick out and focus on the weak spots in a teacher's style, which leaves the teacher feeling incompetent. Other directors concentrate only on the positive aspects and are unable to address problem areas. The teacher who is aware of a problem knows that the director is not providing appropriate guidance; the teacher who is unaware of a problem receives unofficial sanction of the behavior when the director ignores it. In either case, some of the center's objectives are not met, and the observation and informal conference times are nonproductive.

Some directors make videotapes, DVDs, or audiotapes of teachers and review them with that teacher afterward. The advantage is that both are viewing the same situation during the conference. The disadvantage is that taping is intimidating to some staff. Of course, the tapes are confidential information and the subject's permission must be obtained if they are to be shown to others.

When the agreed-upon observations have been completed and other assessments have been made, the director meets with the staff member for a comprehensive evaluation of the work that is based on the work plan set up earlier. The staff member may bring a self-evaluation in a form preselected by the director to be completed by the employee, in a narrative form that is written by the employee, or in an unwritten form that the employee has planned to discuss with the director. During the conference, a work plan, including the objectives and an evaluation format, is drawn up again for the next evaluation cycle. This plan should also include opportunities for growth. The director summarizes the staff person's evaluation for the previous cycle in a written form that is dated. The staff member may add written comments if desired. Together they agree upon a development plan based on the staff member's needs and interests and the program needs. Then both the staff member and the director sign the evaluation form and the new work plan. Although this process is somewhat formal, the director's evaluation role becomes businesslike, as well as personal, if it is followed.

Professional Approach

In all staff evaluation situations, a professional approach must be taken. Such an approach conveys to each staff member the importance of the role and of the staff member's performance. Because this may seem difficult in the rather informal child care setting, the director may want to discuss with the staff what an important professional responsibility evaluation and planning should be.

Arranging unhurried, uninterrupted time and space for evaluation sessions is essential. Such procedures may seem superfluous in the majority of situations. However, establishing the pattern sets the stage for the occasional very difficult evaluation conference and should make it easier to proceed in a professional manner in those instances. Careful and thoughtful evaluation also sends a message to all staff that their work is indeed serious and can leave them feeling quite positive about what they have accomplished and ready to work toward continued development.

A similar evaluation process is followed for the director, and the board is usually responsible for its implementation. In a multisite corporate system, a regional representative may conduct the director's evaluation. Since the staff members in a well-run center may feel very close to one another and may consider the director a personal friend, it is wise to maintain structure in the evaluation process to allow

(A)   (B)

When teachers interact with individual children, their observations become important sources of data about each child's development.

everyone to be as objective as possible. Parents' perspectives on the director's performance are also significant and may be gathered by means of a survey.

Because the director is responsible for the overall quality of the center, logically, evaluation focuses on reaching quality indicators. These include low staff turnover, a low rate of staff absenteeism, high occupancy rates by clients, and sufficient resources in terms of teacher salaries, along with classroom equipment and supplies (Neugebauer, 1998).

Beyond that, however, managing the ever-changing needs of children, families, and staff requires tremendous organizational ability on the part of the director. Programs for children are complex, as evidenced by the fact that the director's day may involve developing new enrollment policies, assisting a struggling teacher in the classroom, and meeting with funders from a national organization. The complexity of the director's role reflects the unpredictable interconnectedness described by complexity theory. According to this theory, "the world is spontaneous, alive, and disorderly—in other words, complex. This results in organizations where there are no simple answers and where people and program continually interact with a constantly changing environment" (VanderVen, 2000). In evaluating directors, the complex nature of their role must be taken into account.

As director credentialing becomes more available, the board may want to require obtaining the credential as part of the evaluation. Currently, the credential is gaining in popularity as a way to improve center quality and to market the center to families. In at least one state, this credential is required. Many other states offer, or are developing, director credentials.

CHILD ASSESSMENT naeyc

Although the terms *assessment* and *evaluation* are often used as synonyms, Gullo offers the following definitions:

> *Assessment*: the process of gathering information about children in order to make educational decisions
>
> *Evaluation*: the process of making judgments about the merits, value, or worth of educational programs, projects, materials, or techniques (Gullo, 2005, pp. 159–160)

As was mentioned in Chapter 1, the curriculum plan is determined by the director in consultation with the teaching staff. The assessment plan is also the ultimate responsibility of the director. This plan should be designed to relate to the curriculum with emphasis on the needs and interests of each child. Because the major goals of an early childhood education center revolve around expectations about the development of children, the evaluation most commonly thought of to demonstrate the program's efficacy is child outcomes. Note that assessing young children's development has always been part of the responsibility of early childhood programs. Those assessments have focused on all aspects of development.

Directors help teachers understand the importance of writing notes about each child's strengths and needs.

Evaluation: Building an Effective Accountable System in Programs for Children Birth through Age 8. This joint statement reminds us to "Make ethical, appropriate, valid, and reliable assessment a central part of all early childhood programs. To assess young children's strengths, progress, and needs, use assessment methods that are developmentally appropriate, culturally and linguistically responsive, tied to children's daily activities, supported by professional development, inclusive of families, and connected to specific, beneficial purposes" (2003). Watch for newly developed position statements and updates of current statements on the NAEYC website.

More recently, and in response to a request from Congress, the National Research Council of the National Academies developed a report on assessment of young children. The report includes guidelines on instrument selection and implementation. For example, "Assessments should not be given without clear plans for follow-up steps that use the information productively and appropriately" and "Assessors should be trained to meet a clearly specified level of expertise in administering assessments, should be monitored systematically, and should be reevaluated occasionally. Teachers or other program staff may administer assessments if they are carefully supervised and if reliability checks and monitoring are in place to ensure adherence to approved procedures" (2008).

These strong, well-researched recommendations make it clear that assessment is a significant responsibility. The director's role is to ensure that the responsibility is met.

In some cases, child assessment has been haphazard or overlooked. When directors do not take responsibility for ensuring that assessment is a regular part of the program, it may not occur, or inappropriate assessment may be done.

Child assessment may involve an individual child, all the children enrolled in an early childhood center, or all the children funded by a particular organization or agency. The director must be sure there is a valid reason for the assessment, that the assessment process will not be detrimental to the child or children, and that parents have given consent.

Professional Recommendations

The NAEYC and the National Association of Early Childhood Specialists in State Departments of Education (NAECS/SDE) issued an important and informative joint statement in 2003 titled *Early Childhood Curriculum, Assessment, and Program*

Relation to Standards

The assessment issue is in the forefront today, in part because every state has created academic standards for K–12 programs. National standards have also been developed. Most states have also created academic standards for prekindergarten. Assessment related to those standards has assumed a prominent position in decision making by funders, families, the media, and even by early childhood educators.

A joint position statement of NAEYC and NAECS/SDE *Early Learning Standards: Creating the Conditions for Success* (2002), reiterates the long-held belief that early childhood programs must provide appropriate opportunities for *all* children to develop in all areas. The document encourages professionals to assume responsibility for recognizing the benefits and risks of the expanded standards movement and for ensuring that essential features of effective and appropriate standards be understood and delivered.

However, assessment for children in their early years must be quite different than that for school-age children. The National Research Council report emphasizes that "a primary purpose of assessing children or classrooms is to improve the quality of early childhood care and education…." Noting the differences between elementary-age and younger children, the report urges "extreme caution" when dealing with very young children and their programs (2008). Assessment results should then be used to modify, but not dictate, curriculum and teaching methods and to determine where additional resources and professional development may be needed. The goal is to improve programs for young children rather than to cast aspersions on children, families, teachers, or programs.

Center directors working with staff can help families, community members, and funders understand how the early childhood curriculum is designed to help each child learn. They can help dispel the myth that children are "just playing" by demonstrating how play contributes to broader cognitive development as well as to learning in the content areas (literacy, mathematics, science, and social studies). Directors and teachers can also focus on children's need to develop socially and emotionally. Certainly they should be aware of each child's progress in relating to one another in the classroom and beyond, and in continuing to develop as a socially, physically, and emotionally healthy human being.

Young children develop rapidly, so it is important that the progress they make in their normal development is not attributed solely to the center's program. Many other conditions affect the child's development, including parental behavior, cultural background, nutrition, and general health. Any one of these variables or combinations of them can affect the child's development positively or negatively, just as the center's program may have a positive or negative influence. The child's total development is a result of the interaction of many factors, which makes it difficult to evaluate the influence of one variable such as a specific child care or preschool experience.

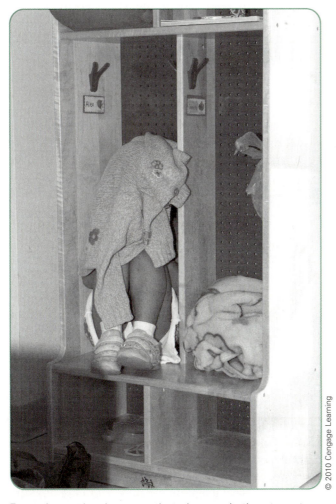

Poppy's teacher is aware that she needs time to get comfortable at school each morning.

© 2010 Cengage Learning

After a few minutes, Poppy peeks out.

© 2010 Cengage Learning

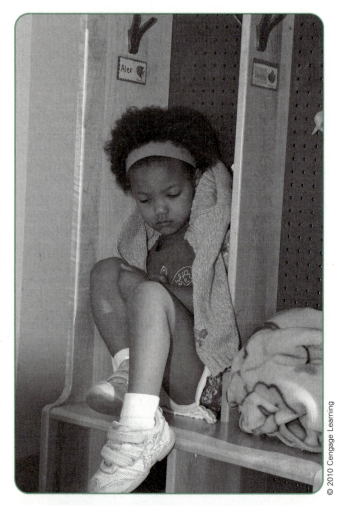

She's beginning to feel safe now. Her teacher makes a note to talk with the director about how to make Poppy feel more comfortable.

© 2010 Cengage Learning

Methods for Assessing Child Progress

Assessment of child progress is ongoing and is expected to inform the day-to-day curriculum, including teacher-child interactions. Professional recommendations delineate *criteria* for choosing and using assessment tools. For example, the tool must be valid and reliable and the assessor must be using the tool in a specified manner. The recommendations call for *appropriate methods* of assessing children. Therefore, directors must know which methods are appropriate and must ensure that only appropriate methods are employed.

Because teachers gather assessment information in their day-to-day teaching, directors must evaluate the methods based on the following criteria:

1 *Developmental appropriateness of the methods.* Does the teacher use appropriate questions to help understand the child's thinking? Is the

teacher aware of emerging knowledge and skills being exhibited by each child? Has a wide variety of related opportunities been provided to support children's interests? Is the level of materials appropriate so that every child's needs can be met? For a clear description of developmentally appropriate practice, see Copple and Bredekamp (2008).

2 *Cultural and linguistic responsiveness of the methods.* Is there evidence that the teachers are familiar with each child's culture and are using it as they plan curriculum? Is there at least one adult available who speaks the child's home language? If that is not possible, are teachers finding ways to communicate with each child?

3 *Connection of the methods to children's daily activities.* Do teachers plan and implement daily activities in ways that allow them to assess what children are learning? Do they use that information to plan additional or modified daily activities?

4 *Support of the methods by professional development.* Has the director provided opportunities for teachers to learn about the expected standards? Has professional development been provided to help teachers plan ways to help children meet the standards in meaningful ways?

5 *Inclusion of families.* Has the director provided opportunities for families to become acquainted with program goals? Have they had opportunities to observe in the classroom and to receive information about how the program is designed to meet goals? Does the director also have opportunities to develop this understanding?

6 *Connection of the methods to specific, beneficial purposes.* Are methods of assessment, particularly those using standardized assessment tools, designed to provide information that supports teachers as they modify curriculum for each child and for the group? Will the information obtained be helpful to families? Will the information demonstrate to funders the significance of the program?

Tools for Assessing Child Progress   **naeyc**

The director, in consultation with the teaching staff, decides on the tools to be used to document each child's progress. They discuss goals, time lines, and process. The assessment should also lead to planning to meet each child's needs. In cases involving researchers or funders who want or need to collect data, the director should consider whether this data collection presents an ethical dilemma. If so, the director must determine what course of action to take.

The first question to ask regarding any child assessment tool is, "Is it ethical to use this procedure?" Early childhood educators must be aware of and follow the Code of Ethical Conduct. The principle, *We shall do no harm to children*, supersedes all other principles in the code and can be used as a first consideration. (The code can be found in Appendix B, is on the NAEYC website, and can be purchased inexpensively from the NAEYC in brochure form. Providing a copy for each staff member and family helps everyone understand what is expected. The Code of Ethical Conduct addresses a breadth of principles related to early care and education and makes an excellent starting point for staff discussions of appropriate assessment.)

Important issues include the following:

- Will children be put in a stressful situation?
- Will individual children be evaluated unfairly because the test was normed on a specific population?
- Will children have had the opportunity to learn the material being assessed?
- Will the results of the assessment help the child by enabling families, teachers, and other professionals to plan for the child's continued progress?
- Will the use of the testing program or other assessment detract significantly from other important opportunities for the children (such as physical activity, arts, and opportunity to explore a wide range of materials)?

Preschool children may be assessed with screening instruments. These relatively brief tools identify children who need additional assessment because they *may* have a disability or a learning problem. Determining whether there actually is a problem and whether there is need for remediation then leads to a plan for the child and provision of an appropriate program and support. Input from parents is important. Children often behave differently at home than in a screening situation even when a parent is encouraged to be in the screening area. Children who have the advantage of early screening benefit from access to early program modifications to meet their needs whether in a preschool classroom or in a different setting.

Keep in mind that screening instruments are intended to provide information about an individual child's possible need for more thorough assessment and support. They are *not* intended to be administered twice to all children in a class to demonstrate the progress that a group has made by participating in that early childhood program.

Many other tools are available to be used by teachers. These include teacher observations, checklists, rating scales, portfolios, reports from other professionals, and standardized tests. The following sections take a brief look at each of these tools. Keep in mind the relationship between appropriate curriculum and appropriate assessment, but remember that assessment should not drive curriculum.

Teacher Observations

Throughout the year, the teacher may keep anecdotal and running records about each child. These notes, recorded on file cards or in a logbook, are summarized by the teacher periodically. Boehm and Weinberg (1997), Cohen, Stern, Balaban, and Gropper (2008), Genishi (1992), Jablon, Dombrom, and Dichtelmiller (2007), Nicolson and Shipstead (1998) and Nilsen (2008) are among the authors who describe general guidelines for observing children. The teacher notes the changes in developmental level and the specific objectives that the child has met or is working to develop. Using this method, the teacher is able to make statements about each child individually, placing emphasis on what the child's needs were, based on initial observations, and how the needs were met. She may modify her approach to working with the child, develop alternate play and learning opportunities, and use her developing understanding of each child to help each child continue to develop in a range of ways. This method uses subjective data provided by the teacher and is valuable only if the teacher is a skilled observer and collects data regularly. In a center that is minimally staffed, use of this method may be difficult. However, the NAEYC, in a brochure on testing of young children, states, "The systematic observations of trained

All teachers are expected to keep records of children's progress. Some teachers do this electronically.

Photo by Keith Klenowski

teachers and other professionals, in conjunction with information obtained from parents and other family members, are the best sources of information" (National Association for the Education of Young Children, 1988). Whether or not the NAEYC has updated that statement, it is still strongly supported by many knowledgeable educators. Professional teachers must know what to look for and how to recognize it. While many other persons may no longer agree with this primary reliance on systematic observations, the approach itself remains worthwhile and may uncover information not picked up by standard assessments.

Checklists

The director may find or create a checklist that names the behaviors toward which some of the center's objectives are aimed. Then teachers merely check whether or not the child exhibits the listed behavior based on their observations of that child. A question arises when the child sometimes does the task and sometimes does not, either because the task is just being learned, because the child chooses not to do it, or because no opportunity is made available. For example, an item might be "Buttons own coat." The child who does this occasionally may be in the process of learning and may not be ready to struggle with buttons on some days, or the child may be asking the teacher for help because he needs attention rather than help. Checklists generally focus on easily identifiable items, so additional assessments must also be used.

Rating Scales

The director may create or locate a rating scale that lists the behaviors closely paralleling the center's objectives. The rating scale alleviates the problem created by a checklist by providing a way for teachers to qualify their answers. The teacher rates each child at least at the beginning and the end of the school year and perhaps more frequently.

The rating may be based on numbers; for example:

Speaks clearly enough for a stranger to understand.

1   2   3   4   5

with an explanation of whether 1 or 5 is high.

The rating may involve descriptive words such as:

Participates in group activities:

never
seldom
occasionally
usually
always

The problems with rating scales are that each teacher may interpret the categories differently, and most teachers are reluctant to use the two ends of the scale (1 and 5, or never and always). Such scales, however, can be useful in pointing out general strengths and weaknesses in any child's development and in the functioning of the group. Rating scales are relatively quick to complete, and teachers can do them when the children are not present if they have been observing carefully.

Both checklists and rating scales are suitable for use if they are viewed as a particular teacher's assessment of an individual child instead of as a comparison of one child or class with another. In reporting data from checklists and rating scales, the teacher may comment on how many children recognize their names in print or play cooperatively in a group of two or more children. But this information must be placed in proper context by pointing out the children's ages and other factors that may influence the data. When space is provided on the form, the child's ratings at two or more widely spread times during a year can be included to show progress and areas in which additional support is needed.

Portfolios

One type of record keeping that can provide valuable information about each child is the portfolio. Some teachers use a two-part system with one folder in a locked cabinet and a second folder in the classroom readily accessible to the child. Folder one contains forms and information from families; the teacher's written observations such as anecdotal records; notes on plans for that child; progress reports; medical reports; and reports from previous teachers, agencies, or consultants who have worked with the child. This information is confidential and should be available only to those who have a legitimate right to it. The second folder provides the child with an opportunity to save products that he has created. The teacher may add photos, videos, notes, and audiotapes although the availability of these records depends on the center's budget and the time available to teachers to prepare these records. Periodically, the records must be sorted and decisions made about what is to be retained, since the record is intended to follow the child throughout school years. The child should participate in deciding what is to be retained, and the family, too, may want to be involved. Some records, however, must be retained by school policy or by law. See McAfee, Leong, and Bodrova (2004) and Nilsen (1997) for other ideas about portfolios.

Other Observers

The director may observe a particular child when a teacher has concerns about that child. Sometimes, an outside observer such as the director or a consultant brings a more objective analysis or may see factors in the environment or even in the teacher's behavior that appear to be influencing the child's behavior. After collecting data, the observer confers with the teacher, and together they design a plan for working with the child. When an individual child is being evaluated to an extent that is beyond the center's regularly scheduled observation plan, parental permission must be obtained. Parental participation in planning is preferable and sometimes required by law.

When a child with identified special needs is enrolled, the director, with written parental permission, contacts agencies familiar with the child to obtain previous evaluations. The director, parent, and representatives of other agencies also may meet to share information that would be useful in working with the child and family.

Reporting a child's behavior to parents usually is handled in a conference. Written information may be provided, but the use of checklists and rating scales for this purpose often is misleading. Parents may misunderstand the significance of this type of written report and categorize their child as a success or a failure. A more appropriate written evaluation

© 2010 Cengage Learning

Directors may encourage teachers to add photos to the children's portfolios. This photo represents two children's beginning ability to work cooperatively.

The director positions herself at the child's eye level so that she can talk with both child and parent.

for parents is a narrative report that describes the child's strengths and progress at school and discusses areas in which the child has difficulty (Horm-Wingard, 1992). The teacher also may confer with parents about ways to help the child continue progressing toward future educational goals.

Parents have the right to review information from their child's folder at any time. In some cases, they feel that it is damaging to the child to have certain information passed along to the next teacher. In other cases, they are eager for the new teacher to understand as much as possible about their child immediately so that the child does not have to endure a time period in which the teacher is discovering a hearing loss or some other condition for which an instructional plan should be designed. In any case, the teacher and parent discuss available information about the child and together determine which data should be sent forward to the next teacher. When a child has an individualized family service plan (IFSP) or an individualized education plan (IEP), the new teacher should have access to that plan and participate with the IEP team in updating the plan on a regular basis. Keep in mind that the family is an essential and required part of the team.

Standardized Tests

Until recently, little attention was paid to using standardized tests with young children. Several reasons are apparent. First, young children can't be tested in a group because they can write only in a limited way, if at all. In a group situation, they have trouble attending to the type of test form typically used in such standardized tests. Even if their task is to draw a circle around one of three pictures for each

question, they may be focused on an aspect of the question or of the pictures that is not related to the presumed correct answer.

For example, one kindergartner was asked to circle the picture of two characters from a story. The three choices were a picture of Jack and Jill falling down the hill, a picture of the three bears, and a picture of Little Red Riding Hood. After the test, the teacher talked with a child whom she was certain had well-developed concepts of twoness and threeness. She asked why he had circled the three bears. He replied, "Well, you see, there's two bears and one left over." She asked what he thought about circling Jack and Jill, and he quickly responded, "Jack and Jill is not a story; it's a poem." While that thinking may not be typical, we have no way of knowing why young children respond the way they do in a standardized testing situation. For this reason, standardized tests, if used at all with young children, must be carefully reviewed even when administered orally and individually.

When tests are administered to young children individually, results are often spurious. The answer a young child gives today may differ from the answer he provides a few days later. Children do not learn in small, isolated bits. As they examine their world, they form relationships with what they already know. Those relationships initially are not always accurate from an adult perspective but are meaningful to the child. As the child encounters additional situations, he creates new relationships, which may or may not be more realistic from an adult perspective. The information that a child learns by rote may be lost relatively quickly if it is meaningless to the child. It is this kind of information that is often assessed on standardized tests.

Even though directors must be sure the tests used in their centers are appropriate, funders may require inappropriate assessments. Such a situation presents an ethical dilemma: administering the test and the potential use of the results may be seen as inappropriate, while refusing to allow the testing may result in withdrawal of funds and loss of programs for children who are most in need of early education. In a critique of the Head Start National Reporting System (NRS), Meisels and Atkins-Burnett (2004) described this high-stakes achievement test for 4- and 5-year-olds as containing "items that are rife with class prejudice and are developmentally inappropriate." The authors presented a number of examples of NRS test items, explaining, in each case, the inadequacies of each. The authors concluded, "This test is not good early education practice. It is not good psychometric practice. It is not good public policy. And it is certainly not good for young children." Raver and Zigler (2004) argued that "the application of a strictly cognitive focus to assessments of school readiness runs counter to what the best developmental research tells us and what past policy experience has shown." After numerous discussions about the assessment among various constituents, the National Head Start Association reported, "With the recent enactment into law of the 'Improving Head Start for School Readiness Act for 2007,' the Head Start National Reporting System is terminated. Head Start programs are no longer required to administer the NRS" (National Head Start Association, n.d.).

REFLECTION

Find out what has replaced the National Reporting System since the Meisels and Atkins-Burnett and Raver and Zigler articles were written. Reflect on what you would have done and why if you had been a Head Start director when the National Reporting System was inaugurated.

The director's role is to understand and use an appropriate assessment program and to work to modify or eliminate high-stakes testing. In some cases, the director's ethical decision may be to refuse to allow such testing in his center. Such a decision may involve issues such as cessation of funding based on the refusal, thus impacting many children, families, and staff. A concerted effort over time, however, with supportive position statements by professional organizations and reasoned discussions with legislators, educators, funders, and other interested parties may prove more beneficial to children in the long run.

If tests are to be administered, the director is professionally responsible for determining whether the test in question is appropriate for the children to be assessed. The director should understand what the test measures, how it is to be administered, by whom, and for what purpose. What effect will it have on the curriculum and, more important, on the children? What provisions will be made for assessing children for whom the test is culturally inappropriate based on language, other aspects of culture, or special needs? The director is expected to know or learn about terms related to testing, such as what the scores mean, what different types of tests are designed to measure, what the results mean, and how they will be used. The

director is also responsible for ensuring that staff members understand these topics. A key component of the director's role is ensuring that, if standardized tests are administered, the results are not misused. A clear description of topics related to testing appears in Gullo's (2005) book on assessment and evaluation.

If we find that a particular test meets the criteria described earlier in this section, the next questions include the reliability and validity of the test.

- Would the results obtained by a particular data collector be similar enough to those of another trained data collector?
- If teachers are expected to test their own classes, what preparation will they receive?
- Who will teach the class while the teacher tests one child at a time?
- Does the test measure what it purports to measure?
- How will the results be reported?
- What do the results mean to teachers? To families?
- Will the people who receive the results know how to interpret them?
- What will be done with the results? Will they be used for the purpose for which the test was designed? Are the results beneficial to the children? If not, will the benefits to someone else outweigh the impact on the children and the program?

Some misuses of standardized tests of young children include the following:

- Keeping a child from entering kindergarten when he is chronologically eligible
- Rating a program
- Evaluating teachers
- Making curricular decisions based solely on specific test content
- Giving several tests two or more times per year.
- Teaching to the test.

Although a wide range of opportunities for assessment of children's progress has been mentioned, the more observant preschool teachers are, the more they will learn about each child. In combining brief teacher notes, parent comments, photos of the child engaged in the classroom, and anecdotal records, the teacher has a good understanding of a child. Bringing these observations together enables teachers to create a description of the child's development over the preschool enrollment period.

Before observing in classrooms, a program evaluator talks with the director about the procedures she will use.

Photo by Keith Klenowski

The director's knowledge and ability to support staff in implementing an appropriate child assessment plan is a major factor in its success. Using the results to meet children's needs is a significant part of the program's operational system. Such a plan demonstrates that laying out a detailed curriculum for the year is not appropriate, since it does not address children's particular needs and interests.

REFLECTION

Think about report card day when you were in elementary school. Can you recall any of your feelings about receiving a report card? If the experience was not always a good one for you, what might have made the experience better?

• Your own attitude or performance?

• Your classmates' behavior after report cards were distributed?

• Your parents' response when they saw your report card?

• Your teacher's comments on your report card?

• The grading system?

When you consider what you will include in a child's folder, try to remember your own grade-school days. Think about the effects that the inclusion of data about your behavior may have had on your relationships with teachers and your parents.

TOTAL PROGRAM EVALUATION

The program goals of the center, and the program itself, are designed to fulfill the particular needs that the center was established to meet. Consequently, at evaluation time, the needs, the goals, and the program are evaluated as part of the center's overall evaluation system.

At regular intervals, the community's needs must be assessed so that the center can plan for current and future populations. Because goals are closely tied to the philosophy of the center program, they change slowly. Nonetheless, they should be examined periodically, perhaps every few years, to determine whether they still are applicable. The objectives are more directly related to the individuals served at a given time. Therefore, they may change more rapidly than the goals. The objectives should be examined annually prior to the start of a new school or fiscal year.

In addition, the director or the board may prepare checklists or rating scales for the evaluation of the program. They can be distributed to staff members, parents, and community representatives; or these people may be asked to provide their evaluations in written or oral forms. Board members and funding agency representatives may contribute to the evaluation by reviewing aspects of the overall program such as the physical environment, curriculum, parent program, ancillary services, and board operations. They also may evaluate the staff performance in general, rather than individual, terms. Periodically, perhaps every few years, the policies and procedures manual, the job descriptions, and the board bylaws are reviewed. Even the evaluation plans and procedures are evaluated!

A widely used center evaluation tool is the *Early Childhood Environment Rating Scale* (Harms, Clifford, & Cryer, 2005). Seven areas are covered in separate subscales. These are personal care routines, furnishings and displays for children, language-reasoning experiences, fine and gross motor activities, creative activities, social development, and adult needs. After observing, the rater circles the appropriate category from 1 (inadequate) to 7 (excellent). Each subscale total rating is plotted on a profile sheet. Center staff then can decide in which areas they wish to make improvements. Profiles produced at different points in time can be used to determine changes in the center's program during that time period. Similar scales have been produced for rating infant-toddler programs, school age, and family child care. Instructional guides for observers are available in print and on videocassette.

Perhaps the most important evaluation a director can conduct is to look at quality of work life. Bloom points out that low morale, stress, and burnout soon affect commitment to the profession. When staff experience these tensions, it becomes very difficult for directors to maintain high-quality programs. Bloom (1996) recommends, therefore, that the director examine ten dimensions necessary to create a professional climate. Among these are supervisor support, opportunities for professional growth, and amount of staff autonomy in decision making. She further recommends surveying the staff, then using the resulting data to plan changes.

Staff surveys usually are anonymous, although in large centers, individuals may be asked to indicate age, job type, level of education completed, or any other category that will provide productive information. The purpose is to use the data for revising administrative practices and planning realistic changes in the center. Items that are obviously unattainable should, of course, not be included. For instance, one would not list "The center shall allow monthly unpaid mental health days" if such a policy would not be workable.

Many center directors and staff members are aware that they need to check the quality of their relations with parents, children, and staff members from a variety of cultures. Although it was not designed specifically for child care centers, the *Cultural Competence Agency Self-Assessment Instrument* (Child Welfare League of America, 2002) may help directors

provide leadership in analyzing areas of strength and areas where improvement is needed. This publication includes sections titled Valuing Diversity, Documents Checklist, Governance, Administration, Program and Policy Development, Service Delivery, Clients, and Interpreting Your Results.

Talan and Bloom (2011) have created a publication that provides guidance related to all aspects of early childhood program assessment, focusing on the leadership and management practices of center-based early childhood organizations. The format consists of ten categories of items, including center operations, fiscal management, program planning and evaluation, technology, and marketing and public relations. Each category is addressed on wide two-page spreads. A list of what to look for, such as needed documents, and questions to ask, appears on the left. The evaluator takes notes based on review of components of the category during the data-gathering phase. For example, when completing the section titled Assessment in Support of Learning, evaluators would probably ask the director how curriculum is planned. They would also determine whether reliable and valid assessments are being used. Next the evaluator completes the rating scale, allowing the rater to refer back to notes made during the data-gathering phase. Using a seven-point scale for each item assessed, the evaluator can create a profile depicting the center's leadership and management strengths and areas in which improvement can be considered. When completed, these documents provide valuable planning tools for directors.

DIRECTOR'S CORNER

A teacher asked if she could put a notice on the bulletin board saying she has an extra ticket to a show in town and wondering whether anyone wanted to join her. Another teacher said she'd love to go. Although they knew each other slightly at that point, after spending the evening together, they decided having opportunities to relax with other staff would be a great idea. "Join us at the outdoor rink for ice skating Saturday afternoon"; "Is anyone interested in checking out the free concert at the college next Friday? appeared on the board within the next few weeks. I'm noting collaboration in and across classrooms is really expanding as teachers find ways to get to know each other better."

—Director, agency-sponsored child care center

Accreditation

Accreditation in early childhood vocabulary refers to a type of center evaluation conducted by an outside agency, usually a professional organization. Several groups currently offer some type of early childhood education accreditation. These include the NAEYC, the National Association of Child Care Professionals (NACCP), and the National Child Care Association (NCCA). These organizations create descriptions of high-quality early childhood education and encourage center boards and directors to apply for accreditation. Programs such as the NAEYC's provide materials for self-study. If the center completes the self-study and decides to continue, it prepares the documents that will be reviewed and plans for a visit from trained assessors. More information can be found on the NAEYC's website and by contacting other organizations offering possible accreditation.

The Administration for Children and Families created a different type of system, the Quality Rating and Improvement System (QRIS), via the National Child Care Information and Technical Assistance Center (NCCIC). QRIS was designed to support states and communities as they work to improve the quality and availability of early care and education programs beyond the basic requirements needed for licensing. Often, Child Care and Development Funds are used for these activities. This approach provides opportunities for many programs to move at a pace that is realistic for them.

"A QRIS is not just about ratings or a stand-alone program to improve quality; it is a unique tool for system reform that has the potential to reach programs that serve a wide range of children and are financed by many public and private sources, including parent fees. Important components are relation to ECE program standards as well as technical assistance and coaching" (QRIS National Learning Network, 2011). In describing efforts to support high-quality early care and education, the NCCIC recognized that many parents need assistance in selecting this type of education for their children. This belief was reinforced by a study by the National Association for Child Care Resource and Referral Agencies (NACCRRA) that found that 96 percent of parents believe that all child care providers offer learning opportunities for children and 78 percent believe that all providers are trained in child development (NACCRA, 2009). Understandably, many parents do not know what kinds of questions to ask.

REFLECTION

Think about where you learned about young children, their behavior, and their interests. Maybe you have lots of older brothers and sisters, or maybe you did many hours of babysitting when you were younger. Since you are currently studying to be a Child Care Administrator, surely you must have studied Child Development.

Now think about parents who have not had those types of opportunities. Where might they have learned about child care and what is required in providing high-quality care for young children? Although many attempts to reach parents have been made, quite a few parents have not heard about them. They therefore choose child care based on location only or on what, from an adult perspective, looks fun. Many of us had no idea how important early childhood education, whether at home or away from home, is to a child's development.

Each state chooses standards based on research related to significant quality improvement. Although state funding is becoming more and more limited, the early childhood community works to help legislators and others understand the importance of early education. Funds are used to provide technical assistance and training to center directors and staff. As a center meets criteria and moves to the next level (designated by stars or other symbols), it may also receive increased subsidies to be used to further staff education or to provide additional classroom equipment. The ratings symbols are becoming familiar to families and help in decisions about child care. Currently, 25 states are engaged in QRIS, and most other states are considering this program.

In some areas, it appears that centers that already lead the community in quality and are accredited by the NAEYC are joining QRIS as a model to those centers who need to start more slowly and move up bit by bit. Some of them had supported each other as they completed requirements for NAEYC accreditation and/or renewal. This type of modeling can be significant in helping more and more programs move from licensure to accreditation directly or through a series of stars. (In some states, accreditation may be considered the top level of the system, while in others it may be a component of reaching the top step.)

The NAEYC's system for center accreditation includes lists of the values and evidence-based criteria to be used in decision making. In this system, early childhood programs are required to be in substantial compliance with all ten standards, all of which are considered to be reliable indicators of high quality. Under this plan, the public and staff of accredited centers will know that the centers have been assessed on criteria that lead to positive outcomes for children.

The process includes four steps:

❶ Enrollment. Engage in self-study (what you need to know in order to study what you do, what you need to think about as you study your program, and what you need to improve).

❷ Application. Submit application. Set time frame for completing formal self-assessment report.

❸ Enter candidacy. Submit self–assessment. Demonstrate that licensing, staffing, and health and safety requirements have been met.

❹ On-site visit.

NAEYC assessors visit and determine whether the program meets all ten NAEYC standards and selected components related to those standards.

The NAEYC views the self-study as an important way to begin program improvement whether or not the center decides to continue with the accreditation process. Materials for the accreditation process may be obtained from the NAEYC. Most directors find that when they take the time to read through the documents, the steps they need to take are all laid out for them and the procedures may no longer seem as intimidating. The director's role then is to obtain the support of the board and staff by letting them know what is expected, and that they will be engaging in a worthwhile team effort. Sharing the accreditation materials with confidence and being open to addressing staff members' questions and concerns will help everyone get started willingly.

Some changes will almost always be needed. Everyone involved may feel stressed as change is discussed. Here again, the director must listen to concerns and help the group decide how to address them. Making changes is less stressful when the group feels ownership. Some changes may be out of the question, often because of the finances involved. This does not necessarily mean that the center cannot become accredited, but the program report will have to describe how the staff has designed an appropriate alternate approach. In many cases, the staff will have to set priorities and create a schedule for working on various components within a certain time frame. Trying to tackle everything at once can be overwhelming and counterproductive.

Completing the accreditation self-study and the related paperwork takes time and resources. Often, successful directors find that the support of the board, parents, and colleagues makes a major difference. Preparing a time line and sticking to it also is helpful. One way to get staff involved is to begin with a discussion of the program's strengths. Encouraged by that discussion, your team will be ready to address areas that need to be improved and ways to accomplish that improvement (Eisenberg, 2000).

The board and the director must consider the cost of accreditation and the value to the children, families, and staff. In addition, the center may profit financially by being accredited as the community begins to recognize that the new process involves demonstration of quality in all aspects of the center's operation. If the decision is to move forward, the director submits the required documentation to the NAEYC Academy for Early Childhood Program Accreditation. The Academy will then review the documents and decide whether the program is ready for review.

Current information about the NAEYC accreditation process and procedures is available on the NAEYC website and in NAEYC publications.

Some directors may feel that they do not need to bother with accreditation because they have a long waiting list of children and their programs seem to be doing well. However, directors who take a professional approach will lead their staff in a self-study periodically, whether or not they choose to participate in a particular form of accreditation (Talley, 1997).

SUMMARIZING DATA

No matter what center evaluation process is chosen, the director is responsible for summarizing the data that are collected from all aspects of the evaluation process, showing the progress or regression since the last evaluation rather than focusing solely on the current performance level. The summary should provide a clear data picture for the reader and should reflect accurately the facts, ideas, and opinions provided by those who participated. Usually a comment that occurs frequently should receive more weight in the summary than an item that seldom appears in the data, no matter how striking or impressive that item appears. Furthermore, no new information should appear in the summary.

The summary is written, dated, and signed by the summarizer and should include a listing of sources used in its compilation. Some data may appear in graph or chart form, particularly if this format makes it easier to understand or more likely to be read. Appropriate computer software makes this task much easier.

Analyzing and Using the Data

The director or a designated committee uses the summary to cull out information. For example, in analyzing enrollment records, the dropout rate of children whose transportation is provided by the school may be compared with the dropout rate of those children who get to school by some other means.

In examining this information, it is necessary to keep other factors constant. For example, if all the children receiving transportation are from low-income families, and if some or all of the other children are from middle-income families, the dropout rate might be more closely related to income level than to mode of transportation. To clarify the situation, additional data would be needed.

Once the data have been analyzed, the director prepares a report for the funding agency, the board, and the other people or groups to whom the center is responsible. This type of report usually is prepared annually, although interim reports may be compiled. The report should be expressed clearly and should be easily comprehensible and professional in appearance. Current software simplifies this task and enhances the results.

Each board member receives a copy of the report, one or more copies are submitted to each funding agency that is involved, and one or more copies are filed at the center. The narrative may be enhanced and clarified by the addition of appropriate graphs, charts, or tables. A pie chart showing the use of the director's time, for example, can be more effective than a lengthy narrative that contains the same information. Graphs and charts can be computer generated and add an extra professional touch to a report. The fact that the report is read by people from a variety of backgrounds should be considered.

Usually, by the time the report for a given year is complete and is in the hands of board members, the planning process for the new year has been completed and put into operation. The report then is used primarily for future planning. The board looks at the report, which includes the director's recommendations, to determine the areas that need modification. For example, if there is a high rate of turnover among the teaching staff, the board looks further to see if the cause can be determined from the evaluation data. Perhaps the salaries at this center are much lower than those of other centers in the community, or perhaps the physical environment is poor. Decisions for change are based on available evidence that grows out of the total evaluation process.

SUMMARY

From the center's inception, an evaluation plan is an essential component of the total program. The purpose of the plan is to determine the value of the center's operation; to evaluate the individuals within it through an analysis of the progress and functioning of the staff, the children, and the overall program; and to provide a basis for future planning. The evaluation process must be open and ongoing and relate to the goals and objectives of the center. The process includes collecting, summarizing, analyzing, and using data according to a prespecified plan that lets everyone involved know how, when, where, why, and by whom an evaluation is being done.

TRY IT OUT!

1. Work with a partner and role-play a conference in which a teacher and a director set up a work plan for the next six months If you are assuming the role as teacher, try to use your own current classrooms skills and areas in which you need improvement as a basis for the objectives in your work plan. If you are playing the director, use your communication skills to find out what help this teacher seems to need and where his strengths lie. After the role-play, ask your classmates for a brief evaluation of the conference. Then have two other students repeat the role-play. Is the second role-play different from the one formulated in the first role-play?

2. You are a director responsible for evaluating each teacher. One teacher lives in the inner-city

community in which the center is located. She seems to be highly skilled at interacting with the children and at guiding them The teacher wants them to succeed in kindergarten, and as a consequence, even though the approach is not in keeping with the center's philosophy, frequently insists that they practice writing the alphabet and doing addition and subtraction problems. Role-play with a classmate a midyear evaluation conference you, as director, might have with this teacher.

First, use the information on the page labeled "Assessment in Support of Learning".

Write what you would look for in order to make your assessment in support of learning.

Would you need to speak with one or more people? What paper work would you need to confirm your assessment? What ratings will you give?

Repeat the process with "Accounting Practices".

If you were the director, how would you feel about this method of assessment? Why?

Note: Remember that these are two of several rating forms used in assessing the center.

Director's Resource 15-1

CHILD ASSESSMENT

Assessment in Support of Learning

Notes	Guiding Questions
* *Valid and reliable assessments* refers to research-based tools (e.g., High/Scope COR, Work Sampling System, or Teaching Strategies GOLD).	How do teaching staff assess children's learning and development?
	• What assessment tools are used? Are they teacher-made? Are they valid and reliable?
** *Standards* are published professional standards (e.g., NAEYC, NSACCA, or Head Start Child Development and Early Learning Framework) or individual state early learning standards.	• What age groups of children are assessed? • Are there any additional ways teachers assess children's learning and development?
Curriculum refers to a framework that guides the intentional implementation of activities in support of children's learning and development.	How is the curriculum planned? • How are standards considered? • How are individual child assessment results used by teachers in lesson or activity planning?
*** *Aggregated assessment results* are obtained when individual children's assessments are combined for the purpose of analysis (i.e., looking for trends to inform program improvement efforts).	• How are aggregated assessment results used to evaluate or make long-range plans for the program?

(continues)

Director's Resource 15-1 *(continued)*

Assessment in Support of Learning

	1	2	3	4	5	6	7
	Inadequate		**Minimal**		**Good**		**Excellent**

Inadequate	Minimal	Good	Excellent
__1.1 Teaching staff do not use an assessment tool to assess children's learning and development.	__3.1 Teaching staff D use an assessment tool to assess children's learning and development.	__5.1 Teaching staff D use a valid and reliable assessment tool to assess children, birth to 5 years of age.*	__7.1 Teaching staff D use additional measures to assess children's learning and development (e.g., portfolios of children's work, teacher's observation notes).
__1.2 Standards are not considered in curriculum planning.**	__3.2 Standards are D considered in curriculum planning.**	__5.2 Individual child D assessment results are utilized by teaching staff in lesson or activity planning.	__7.2 Aggregated D child assessment results are utilized by administrative staff in long-range planning and/or program evaluation.***

Rationale:

Circle the final score based on the scoring rules on pages 4–5.

1 2 3 4 5 6 7

Assessment in Support of Learning

You can download a full-size version of this form on the Education CourseMate website.

Director's Resource 15-2

FISCAL MANAGEMENT

Budget Planning

| Notes | Guiding Questions |

Notes

* Expenditures need to reflect the written goals; revenue needs to match or exceed expenditures.

** Use the following grid to determine when the fourth quarter begins:

Fiscal years begins	Fourth quarter begins
January 1	October 1
July 1	April 1
October 1	July 1

*** Quarterly cash-flow projections are developed from the operating budget and provide a summary of anticipated revenue and expenditures at three-month intervals.

Accepted practices that provide for adequate cash flow **may** include:

- ❐ the prompt deposit of income
- ❐ methods for informing parents about money owned
- ❐ clear written policies and procedures regarding the collection of delinquent tuition/fees
- ❐ clear written policies and procedures to maintain adequate attendance levels
- ❐ other _____

Guiding Questions

How is the program's operating budget prepared?

- Is the Administrator involved? How?
- Is a needs assessment conducted for the program?
- Are goals based on the needs assessment?
- Do the needs-assessment and goal-setting processes relate to the budgeting process? How?
- Does the budget reflect adequate resources to achieve program goals?

Does the Administrator have access to the program's current year operating budget? How detailed is the budget?

- Does it include both revenue and expenditures?
- Are there line-item breakdowns? How are these used?
- When is the projected operating budget for the next fiscal year available?

How effective is the budget in maintaining adequate cash flow?

- Are payroll, insurance, and taxes paid on time?
- Does the budget include a line item for deferred maintenance, equipment replacement, and/or capital improvements?
- How are cash-flow projections developed and used?
- What additional practices are in place to ensure adequate cash flow?

(continues)

Director's Resource 15-2 *(continued)*

Budget Planning

1	2	3	4	5	6	7
Inadequate		**Minimal**		**Good**		**Excellent**

__1.1 The Administrator is not involved in developing the program's operating budget.

__1.2 The current year operating budget, including revenue and expenditures, is not available.

__1.3 Payroll, insurance, and taxes are not always paid on time.

__3.1 The Administrator is involved in developing the program's operating budget.

__3.2 The current year operating budget, including revenue and expenditures, is available. **D**

__3.3 Payroll, insurance, and taxes are always paid on time. **D**

__5.1 Needs assessment and goals setting are an integral part of the program's budget-planning process. **D**

__5.2 The current year operating budget has line-item breakdowns to permit monitoring of revenue and expenditures. **D**

__5.3 The budget reflects deferred maintenance, equipment replacement, and/or capital improvements. **D**

__7.1 The operating budget includes sufficient resources to achieve the program's written goals.* **D**

__7.2 A projected operating budget for the next fiscal year is available by the beginning of the fourth quarter of the current fiscal year.** **D**

__7.3 Quarterly cash-flow projections and at least two other accepted practices provide for adequate cash flow.*** **D**

Rationale:

Circle the final score based on the scoring rules on pages 4–5.

1   2   3   4   5   6   7

Budget Planning

Source: Reprinted by permission of the Publisher. From Teri N. Talan and Paula Jorde Bloom, Program Administration Scale, 2e, New York: Teachers College Press © 2011 by Teri N. Talan and Paula Jorde Bloom. All rights reserved.

You can download a full-size version of this form on the Education CourseMate website.

REFERENCES

Bloom, P. J. (1996). *Improving the quality of work life in the early childhood setting*. Wheeling, IL.: The Early Childhood Professional Development Project, National Louis University.

Boehm, A. E. & Weinberg, R. A. (1997). *The classroom observer: Developing observational skills in early childhood settings* (3rd ed.). New York: Teachers College Press.

Child Welfare League of America. (2002). *Cultural competence agency self-assessment instrument* (revised). Washington, DC: Author.

Cohen, D., Stern, V., Balaban, N. & Gropper, N. (2008). *Observing and recording the behavior of young children* (5th ed.). New York: Teachers College Press.

Copple, C. & Bredekamp, S. (2008, January). Getting clear about developmentally appropriate practice. *Young Children*, 63(1), 54–55.

Eisenberg, E. (2000). Accreditation, strategies, benefits and practical tips. *Child Care Information Exchange*, 131, 70–73.

Genishi, C. (Ed.). (1992). *Ways of assessing children and curriculum: Stories of early childhood practice*. New York: Teachers College Press.

Gullo, D. F. (2005). *Understanding assessment and evaluation in early childhood education* (2nd ed.). New York: Teachers College Press.

Harms, T., Clifford, R. & Cryer, D. (2005). *Early Childhood Environment Rating Scale* (rev. ed.). New York: Teachers College Press. (Also available in Spanish.)

Horm-Wingard, D. (1992). Reporting children's development: The narrative report. *Dimensions of Early Childhood*, 21(1).

Jablon, J., Dombro, A. & Dichtelmiller, M. (2007). *The power of observation for birth through eight*. Washington, D.C.: Teaching Strategies, inc.

McAfee, O, Leong, D. & Bodrova, E. (2004). *Basics of assessment: A primer for early childhood educators*. Washington, D.C.: National Association for the Education of Young Children.

Meisels, S. & Atkins-Burnett, S. (2005). *Developmental screening in Early Childhood, A Guide (5th ed.)*. Washington, D.C.: National Association for the Education of Young Children.

Meisels, S. & Atkins-Burnett, S. (2004). The Head Start National Reporting System: A critique. *Young Children*, 59(1), 64–66.

National Association for Child Care Resource and Referral Agencies. (2009). Parents' Perceptions of Child Care in the United States: NACCRRA's National Parent Poll (November, 2009).

National Association for the Education of Young Children. (2008). *Stats and Facts*. Retrieved August 1, 2008, from http://www.naeyc.org.

National Association for the Education of Young Children. (1988). *Testing of young children: Concerns and cautions*. Washington, D.C.: Author.

National Association for the Education of Young Children and National Association of Early Childhood Specialists in State Departments of Education. (2003). *Early childhood curriculum, assessment, and program evaluation: Building an effective accountable system in programs for children birth through age 8*. Retrieved August 1, 2008, from http://www.naeyc.org/about/positions.asp.

National Association for the Education of Young Children and National Association of Early Childhood Specialists in State Departments of Education (2002). *Early learning standards: Creating conditions for success*. Retrieved August 1, 2008 from http://www.naeyc.org/about/positions.asp

National Head Start Association. (n.d.). *National Reporting System (NRS) terminated*. Retrieved January 24, 2008, from http://nhsa.org/announcements/announce_nrs_cancel.htm.

National Research Council. (2008). *Early childhood assessment: Why, what, and how?* Washington, DC: The National Academies Press. Retrieved August 8, 2008 from http://books.nap.edu/catalog/12446.html.

Neugebauer, R. (2009). Quality rating and improvement systems: A Strategic movement for defining quality. *Exchange*, 31, 66–68. Redmond, WA: Child Care Information Exchange.

Neugebauer, R. (1998). Out of the box ideas for evaluation. In R. Neugebauer & B. Neugebauer (Eds.), *The art of leadership: Managing early childhood organizations*, 2, 291–294. Redmond, WA: Child Care Information Exchange.

Nicolson, S. & Shipstead, S. G. (1998). *Through the looking glass: Observations in the early childhood classroom* (2nd ed.). Upper Saddle River, NJ: Merrill/Prentice Hall.

Nilsen, B.A. (2008). *Observation and assessment*. Clifton Park, NY: Thomson-Delmar Learning.

Nilsen, B. A. (1997). *Week by week: Plans for observing and recording young children*. Clifton Park, NY: Thomson Delmar Learning.

QRIS National Learning Network. (2011). Retrieved from http://qrisnetwork.org/our-framework, July 2, 2011.

Raver, C. & Zigler, E. (2004). Another step back? Assessing readiness in Head Start. *Young Children*, 59(1), 58–63.

Ritchie, S. & Willer, B. (Eds.). (2005). *Leadership and management: A guide to the NAEYC early childhood program standards and related accreditation criteria*. Washington, DC: National Association for the Education of Young Children.

Surr, J. (2004, March). Who's accredited? What and how the states are doing on best practices in child care. *Child Care Information Exchange, 156,* 14–19.

Talan, T. & Bloom, P. (2011). *Program administrators' scale: Measuring early childhood leadership and management* (2nd ed.) New York: Teachers College Press.

Talley, K. (1997). National accreditation: Why do some programs stall in self-study? *Young Children, 52*(3), 31–37.

Sciarra, D. J., & Dorsey, A. G. (2002). *Leaders and supervisors in child care programs.* Clifton Park, NY: Thomson Delmar Learning.

VanderVen, K. (2000). Capturing the breadth and depth of the job: The administrator as influential leader in a complex world. In M. Culkin (Ed.), *Managing quality in young children's programs: The leader's role,* 112–128. New York: Teachers College Press.

Warman, B. (1998). Trends in state accreditation policies. *Young Children, 53*(5), 52–55.

For additional references on assessment, see the January 2004 issue of *Young Children* published by NAEYC.

MARKETING *the* PROGRAM

Bombeck Family Learning Center

Brand the program by consistently using a logo on promotional materials, both in print and on the web.

Objectives

After reading this chapter, you should be able to:

- Identify the connection between a strategic plan and a marketing plan.
- Use a SWOT Analysis Chart to develop a marketing plan.
- Explain the connection between the age and life experience of the intended audience and how marketing materials are best developed and distributed.
- Identify the components of a well developed marketing tool kit.
- Design effective marketing materials for a variety of marketing tools.

Standards Addressed in this Chapter

naeyc Professional Preparation
Standards 2, 4, 6

naeyc Administrator Competencies
Management Knowledge
and Skills 6, 7, 8, 9, & 10
Early Childhood Knowledge
and Skills 7, 10

naeyc Accreditation Standards 8

An important part of the director's job in both new and ongoing programs is marketing and publicizing the center. The direction that marketing takes is based on competition in the area as well as identifying families that need to be reached in order to recruit children and promote the program. Obviously, young families are the first to come to mind, because most programs are set up to serve children from infancy to 5 years of age or primary school-age children in before- and after-school programs. However, there are other considerations. If program survival depends on tuition, the target population is clearly limited to those who can afford to pay for the service. On the other hand, if outside funding sources exist, it will be necessary to increase the scope of the publicity effort so that a greater portion of a diverse potential clientele can be reached. The marketing plan is also impacted by the program's sponsor, its location, and the geographic location in which potential families will likely live. Eligibility requirements also play a role: sometimes program sponsors limit the population to be served to university families, families who meet poverty eligibility requirements, children of hospital personnel, children of families who are employed by a particular business, children of club or church members, and so forth.

Marketing decisions require skillful analysis of circumstances specific to the center. For example, there will be minimal gains from marketing in an area where competing programs are limited to specific populations. Similarly, marketing will have a limited effect on families who choose a preschool program offered by an exclusive private school because that guarantees the child access to this private school's elementary school. What works for one center may not for another, and the director must be knowledgeable about the factors that impact how parents make decisions about where their children will receive early care and education. Centers might promote convenience, a flexible schedule, or a prime location as selling points for potential families.

A director who is skillful with marketing his or her center must have a keen understanding of the questions, concerns, and misconceptions that parents have. Marketing efforts shouldn't focus solely on attracting new children but should also seek to retain the children who are currently enrolled. Efforts to inform potential families about the benefits of a quality program for brain development and future school success can be key selling points for certain groups of parents, but this effort can be negated if a program allows currently served families to retain misperceptions and doubts about whether a play-based curriculum can prepare young children for kindergarten. A center may be at risk of losing a family whose goal is academic readiness for school success and who has doubts about whether academic skills can be developed within an emergent and developmentally appropriate play-based program. It is the job of the director and teachers to see opportunities in the day-to-day life of the center to demonstrate how the early childhood program addresses the goals of the families, which often includes the goal of school readiness.

Good marketing strategies are proactive and look for opportunities to communicate a consistent, clear, and positive message. Programs that identify and communicate a message consistently can avoid the misconceptions that crop up when there is a void of information. In the past, many early childhood programs have waited until the year before kindergarten to discuss school readiness. This timeline misses important marketing opportunities and often portrays the purpose of the prekindergarten year as a last ditch effort to prepare children for a kindergarten entry "event." Programs that convey an ongoing and consistent message about how children develop and learn can help parents come to understand that school readiness is a process that starts in infancy and that continues through kindergarten entry and into the primary grades.

There are many ways to market your program, but do not underestimate the value of "word of mouth" from parents who are enthusiastic about the quality of your program. A consistently communicated message can also positively impact "word of mouth" marketing as parents talk with other parents about their child's early learning program. It is also important for staff to understand that every time parents are in the center, they gather and interpret information about the program that impacts the "word of mouth" marketing message. Directors and staff should take regular "tours" of the center and their classrooms to examine the message that is being communicated. Arranging both

DIRECTOR'S CORNER

"One frustration that my teachers voiced centered on the parents' apparent lack of understanding about how an emergent and play-based curriculum could support the academic skills that children need to be ready for kindergarten. After lamenting this situation in several staff meetings, I asked my teachers what they could do to help parents better understand what their children were learning. We realized that parents didn't really want to know about the importance of play, and that our efforts to convert them were having a negative effect on their views of our program. After some brainstorming, the teachers decided to be proactive and started sharing evidence of the academic content that children learned in the context of play. While the children's experiences with a play-based and emergent curriculum remained the same, the way the program was framed for parents changed. We shifted our focus from selling the importance of play to showcasing what the children were learning during play. The weekly newsletter included examples of academic content learned. The parent communication board highlighted literacy and numeracy in the daily routine. The teachers changed the bulletin boards outside of their classrooms to documentation boards and included work samples and photographs with notations about what the children had learned. We were amazed by the impact that communicating this consistent message had on parent perceptions of what children were learning. It also had a positive effect on our word of mouth marketing."

—Director of a university-affiliated child care program

formal open house events and informal morning coffee conversations or afternoon snack gatherings that encourage parents to meet and chat are strategies that provide time for parents to hear a clear, consistent, and accurate message and also ask questions. But in the end, nothing sells better than offering a high-quality program worthy of accreditation and led by well-trained, qualified early childhood teachers.

BUILDING A MARKETING PLAN

Market Research

The first step in creating an effective marketing plan is to conduct market research. Once the values, beliefs, and needs of your market segment are better understood, then it is possible to identify strategies that are most likely to capture their attention and demonstrate how your program is well suited to address their needs.

Utilizing the results of the needs assessment and strategic planning process described in Chapter 2, program administrators will have collected important data to inform the marketing plan and will have completed the first steps in marketing the program. Knowing the needs of the customer and having a clearly articulated mission will help to target the message to an audience who will be most interested in the service that is being provided. Your first step is to revisit the needs

assessment data and mission and values statement from Chapter 2. This information will be helpful in developing a cost effective and targeted marketing plan. Directors will also be able to use this information to complete a *Strengths, Weaknesses, Opportunities,* and *Threats* (SWOT) Analysis for the program and proposed services.

SWOT Analysis

A SWOT Analysis is a simple but powerful framework for analyzing the SWOT program faces. The origins of the SWOT Analysis are somewhat sketchy, with some identifying the 1960s work of Albert Humphrey of Stanford University and others saying that the concept emerged from Harvard. Regardless of where the concept and acronym originated, it has evolved into a framework used by marketing experts that guides the user through an evaluation of internal and external factors that can impact the success of a business or a program. Environmental factors internal to the organization can usually be classified as strengths (S) or weaknesses (W), and those external to the organization can be classified as opportunities (O) or threats (T). The SWOT Analysis Process helps program administrators focus on strengths, minimize weaknesses and threats, and take the greatest possible advantage of opportunities.

Identify Stakeholders

The first step in conducting SWOT analysis is to identify your stakeholders and data that has already been collected. A *stakeholder* is defined as someone who is impacted by your program—the most obvious stakeholders are children, families, and staff. Less obvious stakeholders include your competitors, who strive to keep up with you, and the community, which benefits from your program's services. Each program will have a slightly different list based on the mission of the program.

Gather Existing Data

Stakeholders can provide important input for a well-developed marketing plan. A good place to start is to use information that has already been gathered as part of the strategic planning process. If completed within the last year or two, the needs assessment can provide important information. Think about other input from stakeholders that you might already have gathered. For example, if your program has chosen to be part of your state's quality rating system, has NAEYC accreditation, or has gone through a Head Start federal review, you will have already collected some information from your stakeholders.

TABLE 16-1   Sample SWOT analysis chart

Strengths	Weaknesses
Excellent staff	Staff turnover
Good facilities	Limited hours of operation
Prime location	Reduction in funding available from the county and state
Opportunities	**Threats**
Changing community demographics	Changing community demographics
New Quality Rating System can lead to additional funding	Competitors have achieved Stars on the Quality Rating System and your program has not

Source: © Cengage Learning, 2013.

Many programs collect data about the quality of their program through such devices as the *Early Childhood Environment Rating Scale Revised* (Harms, Clifford & Cryer, 1998) or the *Program Administration Scale* (Talan & Jorde Bloom, 2004). These tools provide data that are used by supervisors, administrators, and policy makers (all of whom are stakeholders) to identify the strengths and weaknesses of aspects of a program. Child assessment data can also be used to inform your SWOT Analysis.

Determine What Data are Missing

Once you have identified your key stakeholders and any existing data sources that you can refer to, discuss ways that you can find out more about what your stakeholders think are your program's strengths and weaknesses. What information is missing? Who do you need to hear from? How can you access that information?

Gather Internal and External Data

Most of the data that you have collected is most likely internal data from stakeholders who are part of or directly impacted by your organization. Some of you may have collected information from or about your competitors which would be the start of a review of the external data needed to determine the *threats* and *opportunities* in the SWOT Analysis. To complete a thorough external review, you need to become well grounded in the context of early care and education especially as it relates to quality and other trends that are impacting the market.

Construct a SWOT Analysis Chart

To construct an accurate SWOT Analysis chart, you will need to include the data that you have collected from stakeholders. You will use an internal focus to determine your program's *strengths* and *weaknesses*. To determine *threats* and *opportunities* you will look to factors that are external to your program. See Table 16-1 for a sample SWOT Analysis Chart.

Interpret the SWOT Analysis

Once completed, a SWOT Analysis Chart can help to identify areas where a marketing plan can have the most impact. Consider the completed sample in Table 16-1 and note how the information in the cells might be interpreted.

- **Strengths:** Note that any of the three identified strengths can become part of a marketing message that would attract new customers and retain the ones that already use the program's services.

- **Weaknesses:** It may be difficult to see how weaknesses can inform a marketing strategy until you also consider the opportunities. For example, the new Quality Rating System that is described as an opportunity can be used to offset the reduction in funding because programs in some states can earn additional funding while improving quality. Making the connection between these two elements is an important part of the analysis of this chart. You can also deal with the perceived weakness head on by considering such moves as increasing the hours of operation after completing a careful analysis of the financial impact.

- **Opportunities:** In addition to using opportunities to address areas of weakness, they can also stand alone. For example, changing demographics can be a true opportunity to broaden the target of your marketing strategies.

- **Threats:** Note how the same item can be both an opportunity and a threat. For example, changing demographics can provide opportunities for an expanded market. It can also force change and change can be uncomfortable. It is likely to be difficult to make decisions about how to address this factor without considering it as both an opportunity and a threat.

Developing a Marketing Plan

Once the SWOT Analysis is complete and interpreted, it is time to craft a marketing plan that can be communicated to others and that is in a format that can be followed by the people responsible for implementing the plan. Kalifeh (2011) suggests making a chart that includes the following when developing a marketing plan:

- Your strategies (a description of what you will do)
- A timeline for when you will undertake that strategy (remembering that marketing is a year-round endeavor)
- Materials and resources needed to accomplish the strategy
- A list of who is responsible or tasked with accomplishing the work
- A description of the costs.
- *Optional:* You might also want to create a column for evaluating the strategy, determining how you will measure success (p. 23).

The strategic planning process from Chapter 2 and the information from the SWOT Analysis should provide key information about your center and the potential market that will inform the marketing plan. This information will also help to decide where, how, and to whom to promote the program.

Who: Generational Factors

"Not everyone sees through the same eyes or hears through the same ears" (Wassom, 2004, p. 6). The perceptions of families who may be interested in the program and their process for making decisions vary based on a wide range of factors, including the generation that they are part of. Wasson goes on to state that a closer examination of generational tendencies "reveals valuable insight into why old marketing approaches are no longer as effective, and what changes you need to make to appeal to the majority of today's early care and education buyers" (p. 6). Wassom also identifies four generational groups in America today—Matures, Boomers, Generation X-ers, and Millennials—and describes how members of each generation are linked through shared life experiences. Those shared experiences cause them to view the world in unique ways, which extends to how

and when they make decisions about early care and education services. Today, the parents of young children tend to be Generation X-ers and Millennials, and their buying influences are very different from the Boomers of the past. (See Table 16-2.)

Where to Market Your Program

Traditionally, marketing a program and publicizing a center has been done through newspaper ads and radio announcements to reach a wide audience, while a more limited population is reached through direct mailing of brochures or circulars, displays of window placards, door-to-door solicitation, and advertisements in local newspapers, church bulletins, and military newsletters. In the past, telephone book advertising was also successful.

Because of the impact of technology, many of these traditional vehicles now have less of an impact. Young families today rely more on new media and the Internet for information. Consider taking advantage of Internet advertising—the Yellow Pages does not have the impact that it once did. *New media* refers to on-demand access to content anytime and anywhere using digital devices such as smart phones, iPods, iPads, and other tools. New media allows families to access just the information that they need at just the time they need it. The ability to have continuous and instant access to information through search engines and social networking sites makes such platforms as Google and Facebook important marketing tools.

New media also provides opportunities for interaction, so word of mouth marketing is an even more powerful tool. The directors who develop and maintain free Facebook sites for their centers are also providing a vehicle for families to talk about centers in ways that potential families are likely to interact with and trust. These new platforms can be frightening for many directors who would like to be more in control of the message that is being sent. However, like it or not, the advent of new media has shifted control to the consumer, who can provide feedback in a forum that is open for anyone to see. A director who is aware of how the program is being presented on Facebook or where the center appears on a Google search listing can impact the marketing message. By capitalizing on the everyday opportunities to communicate a consistent message during the day to day operations of the center, directors can impact how current families describe the program for potential families on Facebook or on other new media vehicles.

Regardless of the vehicle used to advertise, be sure to consider the ethnic and cultural makeup of the audience, as well as reading levels and language skills, as you write and design promotional materials.

TABLE 16-2   Characteristics of three generations

	Boomers	Generation X-ers	Millennials
Age	Born between 1946 and 1964	Born between 1965 and 1979	Born between 1980 and 2000
Early Life Experiences	Secure economic times Television The start of the Peace Corps and space exploration Civil rights Assassinations of John F. Kennedy and Martin Luther King Vietnam War	Recession and layoffs or double-digit interest and inflation Watergate and other well-publicized scandals Challenger exploded Berlin Wall fell End of the Cold War Rise of digital technology and the World Wide Web The Chernobyl nuclear disaster The Exxon Valdez oil spill	A time of economic change with the longest period of economic expansion as wealth and manufacturing moved outside of the United States Emergence of the global economy AIDS emerges The space shuttle program thrives Hubble Space telescope 24-hour news networks 9–11 and the War on Terror
Informed by	Newspapers Magazines Radio Network news Technology tends to augment the traditional way of doing things	Network and cable news Internet accessed through the personal computer Word of mouth	Peers Online news sources Widespread on-demand access to the Internet via new media
Group Demographics	80 million Married Boomers tend to live in dual earner families Better educated than their parents Trusting Impulsive buyers Emotional decision-makers Busy and hard working Value convenience Grant credibility based on proven history Few have young children but may influence how their grandchildren are raised.	49 million Many parents of young children needing child care are Generation X-ers Question authority Grew up with uncertainty Skeptical Resourceful Well educated Less trusting Not easily impressed Tend to plan and save until they can afford the best quality Take time to investigate, compare, and discuss before deciding	75 million The up and coming group of parents with young children are Millennials More optimistic and ambitious Are realistic about what is wrong with the world but believe they can make a difference Relationships with friends and family are highly valued Value parents' advice Value education as a means to success Less religious Inclusive and value diversity Very active and can be stressed

Childhood Technology Exposure	Color television	Cable TV	Interactive TV and streaming video
	Records, 8-tracks, and cassettes	Cassettes and CDs	MP3s and iPods
	Land lines	VCRs	DVDs and TiVo
		Personal computers	Laptops, Netbooks, and iPads
		Cell phones	Smart phones
Communication Preference Tendencies	Face to face	Cell phone calls	Text Messages
	Phone calls	Email	Facebook
Buying Influencers	Impacted by emotional benefits	Skeptical and focused on quality and value	Want to be a member of the crowd but yet stand out
	May not investigate thoroughly if they have good feelings	Will more likely rely on evidence and talk to others before making a decision	Hopeful about the future
	May want more flexible payment terms	Willing to pay top dollar but will demand the highest quality	Want to make a difference
	Education is important but happy children is more important	Likely to appreciate being able to use a credit card	Likely to consider recommendations from their peers and their parents
	Value feeling part of the center's community	Want good answers to questions about curriculum, policies, and procedures	
	Convenience and ancillary services are valued		
Advertising Approaches that Tend to Work	Use color and emotions in photos and taglines	Third party endorsements or testimonials	Interactive digital messages
	Include photos that they can relate to	Use bullets to outline specifics	Includes opportunities for peers to provide feedback
	Use bullets to communicate a quick message	Link to professional organizations or other unbiased sources so they can verify your claims	Easily accessed at a time convenient to them

Source: Howell & Strauss, 2001; Marston, 2011; Wassom, 2004; Wendover, 2007.

How to Construct the Message

It is also important to construct a message that resonates with the target audience. Marston (2011) reminds us that generational differences should impact how information is presented.

> Understand X-ers take nothing at face value and will seek out their own information and referrals. Look at your marketing as an introduction that directs them to further information. Make sure your website is stocked with data and product specifications. Want to further your credibility with X-ers? Point them to an unbiased resource and show them you've got nothing to hide. Remember, these are the folks who were born in the Watergate era and grew up in an age of highly publicized scandals. Honesty is unexpected yet highly treasured.

Likewise, Millennials are accustomed to relying on peer feedback for credibility. If Millennials are the targeted group, then an astute director might develop a center-sponsored Facebook site and encourage current families to provide feedback on the experiences that their children are having. By being proactive and knowledgeable about the benefits and pitfalls of new media, the director can capitalize on the benefits of the tools while laying ground rules that can overcome some of the disadvantages. For example, if the Facebook site is established by the director, then he or she can provide guidance about confidentiality and respectful interactions. The owner of the site can also remove inappropriate comments and add prompts that direct the kind of feedback that is provided. New media has changed the marketing landscape; directors can choose to take advantage of these inexpensive and powerful marketing tools or not. However, ignorance of how the center is being portrayed through new media platforms can be the downfall of a center.

Marketing Materials

Marketing materials are a collection of products designed to meet established marketing goals. The marketing plan will help to determine the kinds of marketing products that will work with the target audience. In most situations a variety of materials and platforms for dissemination is the most effective approach to achieve the desired outcome. With widespread availability of easy-to-use publishing software, many directors, even those with limited computer skills, can create attractive and professional marketing materials. Many of the products designed for print materials can be adapted to digital formats, including websites. Because of the shift to new media which requires immediate access to information, it is even more important to be proactive and have materials available to meet a variety of marketing needs. One strategy is to create a marketing tool kit that can be used to respond to a variety of marketing opportunities quickly and cohesively. Kalifeh (2011, p. 23) suggests the following as marketing resources that directors can cultivate to become part of a marketing tool kit.

- Print media (parent handbooks, business cards, brochures, press releases, advertisements, giveaways, etc.)
- Electronic media (website, social networking, email)

- Staff (an often overlooked marketing resource)
- Parents (some of your best public relations specialists)
- Events (employer partnerships, school transition partnerships, open house, Kids' Day, legislative tours, parent appreciation, etc.)

Brochures and Promotional Materials

The choice of words and the photographs used in the printed materials distributed by the center should reflect a subtle message of concern, respect, and appreciation for children and should express the philosophy behind the center's program. These materials project the image of the center and should exemplify your professionalism (Tiger, 1995).

Develop marketing materials that send a distinctive and powerful message. They must define your specialties and exactly what you offer that sets you apart from your competitors. The fundamentals of "quality care," "developmentally appropriate practice (DAP)," and "trained, caring staff" are descriptive but not distinctive. Brainstorm with staff, parents, board members, and consultants about how you are different, and put down some sample statements that will tell that story in the materials that you develop, such as:

- soft, cozy spaces in a homelike environment (use pictures if possible)
- innovative, cutting-edge social/emotional focus
- family-centered practice that treats family/child/teacher as a unit

Effective marketing requires that a program represents what it does well. This picture might be selected for marketing materials because it shows how children are engaged in a well-planned outdoor space with strong adult-child interaction, and that this center is a university-affiliated program.

Bombeck Family Learning Center

Find unique ways to identify your program with a logo that appears on all business cards, stationery, ads, and so on. Use of a particular "tagline" with the logo can become your mark of distinction. In marketing circles, this is called "branding." It is something potential clients recognize and remember. Taglines give a quick and easily remembered clip of what a program is about:

- "Where Every Child Is Special"
- "We Strengthen Children Emotionally and Academically"
- "Child Care That Nurtures Our Future"

Keep in mind that you are endeavoring to attract the attention of the current generation of young parents, many of whom are Generation X-ers or Millennials. Select techniques and content for the marketing materials that appeal to and entice this target generational group. For eye appeal and influence, consider:

- using color and emotion in taglines and photos
- mixing pictures and graphics (a photo of a teacher and child, a parent event, your accreditation credential)
- bulleting the benefits so there is a quick and easy way to sum up *what they will get from you*—a bit different from what you have to offer
- quoting testimonials from the current parent population
- using the talents of staff and parents to do creative marketing that will help you build your enrollment

The content and appearance of brochures or fliers make a statement to parents. The words should be informative and spell out the philosophy of the center's program; the photographs or some creative, clever artwork should convey, in less obvious ways, the fact that the staff of the center is professional and creative. It is the creative design of these materials that will attract attention, and attention is the first step to generating interest. The message for parents should be clear: any child who is sent to this center will share in the professionalism and creativity of the staff. When unsolicited letters from parents are available, using statements from those letters in brochures or publicity releases is an excellent way to get your message across. Every detail of any mailing piece to be used for initial advertising or in response to inquiries about the program should be carefully scrutinized.

The director is responsible for the preparation and the mailing of brochures, but other staff members as

DIRECTOR'S CORNER

"When it was time to make our logo more current, we worked very hard to choose one that communicated what we were about while also providing some brand recognition. We contacted a local university with a graphic design program and asked the program director if there was a class that was working on logo design. We were fortunate to be able to set up a competition in this class and had teams of students interview our center staff and examine our mission statement and handbooks. Teams designed a series of eight logos which were voted on by staff and families through a Facebook website. We had great buy-in from families and staff and ended up with a very attractive logo for the cost of the competition prize, which was a gift card to an art supply store for each member of the winning team. The process was a win for all involved."

—Director, private not-for-profit center

well as parents can contribute to the effort by providing artistic talents, access to a printer, or some other expertise. When a brochure is prepared, two major considerations are cost and content.

Costs vary depending on number, length, quality of paper, use of color, and use of photographs. Therefore, it is wise to discuss ideas for the brochure with a printer as soon as possible. Costs increase when the professionally done brochure includes photos or a logo that incorporates artwork, but it is these unique features that may be precisely what attracts the attention of prospective clients. The distinctive logo and tagline on every promotional piece becomes a familiar identifying symbol to potential customers. Money spent on an attractive brochure may be a good investment. Using a single color on heavyweight, standard-size paper will give a look of high quality yet keep the costs down. A brochure on standard-size paper in a three-fold format that can be addressed on one side is economical and efficient. Check the size and weight so that mailing costs will be within the minimal limit for first-class postage rates.

If the brochure is to be used over a long period of time, it is wise to avoid including items that are subject to change, such as the school calendar or the fee schedule. These variable items can be detailed in a short insert. The brochure itself should contain information that remains constant from year to year.

The following list includes some of the more stable items typically included in a brochure:

- name, address, and telephone number of the center
- a map showing location of the program
- description of the program
- sponsorship of the program
- enrollment procedures and children served (ages, inclusive program, diversity, and so forth)
- licensing and/or accreditation status of the center

It is important to include the hours, days, and months for the program. The stability of the operational schedule will determine whether such information should go into the brochure itself or be part of the insert.

Centers sell services to families who seek solutions to concerns and have questions about quality child care. It is helpful to them when promotional materials cover all the services available at the center. Prospective customers, especially those with more than one child, will want to have information about availability of services such as before- and after-school care, summer programs for school-age children, care for the mildly ill child, and backup care for older children on school holidays or for the baby cared for at home when the regular caregiver is ill.

Other selling points to cover in promotional materials might include the following:

- accreditation by NAEYC, NACCP, NECPA, or the state's quality rating system if available
- workshops
- lending library
- web address, to help keep potential clients up to date on all center activities
- email address, to keep in touch with administrators

Keep in mind that promotional materials are designed to tell prospective families that the center offers solutions for them and is there to help and support them and their children. Brochure space is limited, so details about program operation and range of services offered families can be described in pamphlets or booklets available for those who call for more information or visit the center. A well-planned open house provides a special opportunity to share these additional materials and publicizes the best features of the program.

PUBLIC RELATIONS

As a director, it behooves you to take advantage of opportunities to invite reporters to the center so that they can do newspaper or television pieces on your center. If you are affiliated with a large business or hospital, their public relations staff may help you. Television and newspaper reporters are interested in what is new at your center. If there is a new infant room opening or you have a new custom-designed playground, reporters and cameramen will come to you. Other newsworthy items might be a new teacher who signs for deaf children, installation of a ramp to accommodate children and adults with disabilities, or the use of senior citizen volunteers in the preschool classrooms.

Take your message to the local lodge or church gathering, PTA groups, or community meetings where it will reach parents whose busy lives may limit the time spent reading publications or listening to radio or television. To enrich your promotional materials, bring slides, videotapes, DVDs, or a PowerPoint presentation to these meetings to show what children and teachers do in child care centers. Always have an ample supply of business cards to distribute to your audience.

At community events that draw parents of young children, it is often useful to arrange to have a booth where a display of photos taken at the center and promotional materials will attract families who are interested in child care. Arrange for the director or a competent staff member who can answer questions and distribute admission applications to be available at these events. This is an excellent way to reach out to the community and capitalize on an opportunity to establish a personal contact with potential clients.

It is also worthwhile to get your message out to companies in the community, as well as to individuals and community groups. The first wave of companies interested in addressing the child care needs of their employees typically were attracted to setting up on-site child care centers. However, some companies are more inclined to look to existing community child care centers where they can purchase slots, buy priority status, or negotiate for corporate group rates for their employees. Developing a professional presentation that is designed for use with corporate clients and timely follow-up with appropriate contacts within the corporation will enhance your chances of attracting corporate clients (Duncan & Thornton, 1993).

The center's image is an important consideration in all aspects of the public information and public relations efforts. The appearance of the physical setting and the behavior of personnel in that setting are fundamental factors in creating good public relations and sound relationships with the children and with their parents. These factors are what convey professionalism and concern about children and families. The director serves as a model and encourages the staff to be mindful of their role as community advocates for children. Parents entering the building should see an interior prepared for use by children. Furthermore, parents should be greeted by a warm, caring person who expresses interest in them and in their children. A "Director's Coffee" once a month is a way to encourage parents to take a few minutes to chat before rushing off to work. When parents or others telephone the center, the person who answers must be pleasant, tactful, and knowledgeable.

An open house for parents who have made inquiries or have responded to your marketing efforts is a good way to expand the public relations program for the center. Remember to invite current parents, current staff members, and board members to these social events. An open house affords an opportunity for the staff to have an informal meeting with others who are interested in the center's activities. In the case of a new program, publicizing the open house can be part of the initial efforts at promotion. In the case of ongoing programs, staff and board members also will reap benefits from this kind of gathering, since it provides a time for interaction and communication among adults who have common concerns and share an interest in the children attending the program.

When the center is opened to visitors, the environment should be prepared just as it would be for the children. In this way, you can demonstrate how a well-planned environment should look and also provide an opportunity for parents to participate and use available materials. What better way to give parents a feeling for what happens each day than to have them use the materials in the classrooms! In addition, slides, a scrapbook of photos, or a videotape or PowerPoint presentation of children actively participating in the classroom can give parents further insights into what a quality program can offer their children.

Planning for the open house is done by people who understand the lifestyles and expectations of the clients who are likely to show interest in the event. Careful and sensitive planning regarding the time of the event and the level of informality communicates to members of the community that the people at the center understand and care about them and their children.

SUMMARY

The marketing plan for the program emerges from market research informed by the strategic planning process. Effective directors consider multiple factors when developing a marketing plan and can be informed by a carefully constructed SWOT Analysis as well as a sound understanding of the target audience. In today's technology enhanced society, marketing must include both traditional print strategies as well as new media. Marketing materials for the center must be drafted and directed to the population that the program is designed to serve. Successful recruitment of children and families will depend on the content and dissemination of the promotional materials about the program, as well as on the total public relations effort. While written materials advertising the center must be planned carefully to attract the families to be served, the role of word of mouth advertising cannot be overlooked.

TRY IT OUT!

❶ Think about a center you have been in on a regular basis. You are sitting outside in the parking lot as parents arrive. Is the building inviting? Does it really welcome children and families? Now imagine yourself inside, observing the way children are greeted. Do adults stoop down and extend a friendly welcome to the children? Are parents recognized and called by name? As you walk farther into the building, how does it look? What sounds do you hear? How does it smell? The impressions you are reliving are the same impressions parents and children experience each day that they enter the center. How do the answers to these questions impact the word of mouth marketing potential for this center?

❷ Work with a team to complete a SWOT Analysis using Working Paper 16-1. Consider a program that a member of the team works for or is familiar with and complete each of the four quadrants of your analysis and describe how you would address the following:

a. Identify strengths that you can capitalize on to promote the program.

b. Identify weaknesses that can be addressed or turned around and used as a marketing strategy.

c. Now look at the opportunities that you have identified. How can they be incorporated into a marketing plan?

d. Finally examine your threats. What marketing strategies can you use to reduce the threats?

Use these answers to identify what this center might include on a Facebook page.

Working Paper 16-1

(for use with Try It Out! 2)

SWOT ANALYSIS CHART

STRENGTHS	WEAKNESSES
OPPORTUNITIES	THREATS

INTERPRETATION Which aspects of the SWOT Analysis chart should be the focus of a marketing plan? Which are top priorities or can make the most impact on the success of the program?	HOW FINDINGS ARE ADDRESSED IN THE MARKETING PLAN
Strengths	
Weaknesses	
Opportunities	
Threats	

 You can download a full-size version of this form on the Education CourseMate website.

REFERENCES

Duncan, S., & Thornton, D. (1993, January). Marketing your center's services to employers. *Child Care Information Exchange*, 53–56.

Harms, T., Clifford, R. M., & Cryer, D. (1998). *The early childhood environment rating scale* (rev. ed.). New York: Teachers College Press.

Harms, T., Cryer, D. & Clifford, R. M. (2003). *Infant/toddler environment rating scale* (rev. ed.). New York: Teachers College Press.

Howell, N. & Strauss, B. (2001). Millennials rising: the next great generation. New York: Vintage Books.

Kalifeh, P. (2011, March/April). Marketing: No longer an afterthought. *Child Care Information Exchange*, 22–24.

Marston, C. (2011). Marketing to different generations: Choose your message wisely. International Association of Business Communicators. Retrieved April 16, 2011, from http://www.iabc.com/cwb/archive/2007/0807/Marston.htm.

Talan, T. N. & Jorde Bloom, P. (2004). Program Administration Scale. New York: Teachers College Press.

Tiger, F. (1995, March/April). The art of brochure design. *Child Care Information Exchange*, *107*, 24.

Wassom, J. (2004, March/April). Do they see what you see? Marketing to a new generation of child care buyers. *Child Care Information Exchange*, 6–8.

Wendover, R. W. (2007). *Crossing the generational divide: From boomers to zoomers*. Shawnee Mission, KS: National Press Publications,

NAEYC® Code of Ethical Conduct and Statement of Commitment

POSITION STATEMENT

A position statement of the National Association for the Education of Young Children

Revised April 2005, Reaffirmed and Updated May 2011

Endorsed by the Association for Childhood Education International

Adopted by the National Association for Family Child Care

Preamble

NAEYC recognizes that those who work with young children face many daily decisions that have moral and ethical implications. The **NAEYC Code of Ethical Conduct** offers guidelines for responsible behavior and sets forth a common basis for resolving the principal ethical dilemmas encountered in early childhood care and education. The **Statement of Commitment** is not part of the Code but is a personal acknowledgement of an individual's willingness to embrace the distinctive values and moral obligations of the field of early childhood care and education.

The primary focus of the Code is on daily practice with children and their families in programs for children from birth through 8 years of age, such as infant/toddler programs, preschool and prekindergarten programs, child care centers, hospital and child life settings, family child care homes, kindergartens, and primary classrooms. When the issues involve young children, then these provisions also apply to specialists who do not work directly with children, including program administrators, parent educators, early childhood adult educators, and officials with responsibility for program monitoring and licensing. (Note: See also the "Code of Ethical Conduct: Supplement for Early Childhood Adult Educators," online at www.naeyc.org/about/positions/pdf/ethics04.pdf. and the "Code of Ethical Conduct: Supplement for Early Childhood Program Administrators," online at http://www.naeyc.org/files/naeyc/file/positions/PSETH05_supp.pdf)

Core Values

Standards of ethical behavior in early childhood care and education are based on commitment to the following core values that are deeply rooted in the history of the field of early childhood care and education. We have made a commitment to

- Appreciate childhood as a unique and valuable stage of the human life cycle
- Base our work on knowledge of how children develop and learn
- Appreciate and support the bond between the child and family
- Recognize that children are best understood and supported in the context of family, culture,[1] community, and society
- Respect the dignity, worth, and uniqueness of each individual (child, family member, and colleague)
- Respect diversity in children, families, and colleagues
- Recognize that children and adults achieve their full potential in the context of relationships that are based on trust and respect

Conceptual Framework

The Code sets forth a framework of professional responsibilities in four sections. Each section addresses an area of professional relationships: (1) with children, (2) with families, (3) among colleagues, and (4) with the community and society. Each section includes an introduction to the primary responsibilities of the early childhood practitioner in

---

[1]The term *culture* includes ethnicity, racial identity, economic level, family structure, language, and religious and political beliefs, which profoundly influence each child's development and relationship to the world.

that context. The introduction is followed by a set of ideals (I) that reflect exemplary professional practice and by a set of principles (P) describing practices that are required, prohibited, or permitted.

The **ideals** reflect the aspirations of practitioners. The **principles** guide conduct and assist practitioners in resolving ethical dilemmas.[2] Both ideals and principles are intended to direct practitioners to those questions which, when responsibly answered, can provide the basis for conscientious decision making. While the Code provides specific direction for addressing some ethical dilemmas, many others will require the practitioner to combine the guidance of the Code with professional judgment.

The ideals and principles in this Code present a shared framework of professional responsibility that affirms our commitment to the core values of our field. The Code publicly acknowledges the responsibilities that we in the field have assumed, and in so doing supports ethical behavior in our work. Practitioners who face situations with ethical dimensions are urged to seek guidance in the applicable parts of this Code and in the spirit that informs the whole.

Often "the right answer"—the best ethical course of action to take—is not obvious. There may be no readily apparent, positive way to handle a situation. When one important value contradicts another, we face an ethical dilemma. When we face a dilemma, it is our professional responsibility to consult the Code and all relevant parties to find the most ethical resolution.

SECTION I: ETHICAL RESPONSIBILITIES TO CHILDREN

Childhood is a unique and valuable stage in the human life cycle. Our paramount responsibility is to provide care and education in settings that are safe, healthy, nurturing, and responsive for each child. We are committed to supporting children's development and learning; respecting individual differences; and helping children learn to live, play, and work cooperatively. We are also committed to promoting children's self-awareness, competence, self-worth, resiliency, and physical well-being.

Ideals

I-1.1—To be familiar with the knowledge base of early childhood care and education and to stay

informed through continuing education and training.

I-1.2—To base program practices upon current knowledge and research in the field of early childhood education, child development, and related disciplines, as well as on particular knowledge of each child.

I-1.3—To recognize and respect the unique qualities, abilities, and potential of each child.

I-1.4—To appreciate the vulnerability of children and their dependence on adults.

I-1.5—To create and maintain safe and healthy settings that foster children's social, emotional, cognitive, and physical development and that respect their dignity and their contributions.

I-1.6—To use assessment instruments and strategies that are appropriate for the children to be assessed, that are used only for the purposes for which they were designed, and that have the potential to benefit children.

I-1.7—To use assessment information to understand and support children's development and learning, to support instruction, and to identify children who may need additional services.

I-1.8—To support the right of each child to play and learn in an inclusive environment that meets the needs of children with and without disabilities.

I-1.9—To advocate for and ensure that all children, including those with special needs, have access to the support services needed to be successful.

I-1.10—To ensure that each child's culture, language, ethnicity, and family structure are recognized and valued in the program.

I-1.11—To provide all children with experiences in a language that they know, as well as support children in maintaining the use of their home language and in learning English.

I-1.12—To work with families to provide a safe and smooth transition as children and families move from one program to the next.

Principles

P-1.1—Above all, we shall not harm children. We shall not participate in practices that are emotionally damaging, physically harmful, disrespectful, degrading, dangerous, exploitative, or intimidating to children. *This principle has precedence over all others in this Code*.

---

[2]There is not necessarily a corresponding principle for each ideal.

P-1.2—We shall care for and educate children in positive emotional and social environments that are cognitively stimulating and that support each child's culture, language, ethnicity, and family structure.

P-1.3—We shall not participate in practices that discriminate against children by denying benefits, giving special advantages, or excluding them from programs or activities on the basis of their sex, race, national origin, immigration status, preferred home language, religious beliefs, medical condition, disability, or the marital status/family structure, sexual orientation, or religious beliefs or other affiliations of their families. (Aspects of this principle do not apply in programs that have a lawful mandate to provide services to a particular population of children.)

P-1.4—We shall use two-way communications to involve all those with relevant knowledge (including families and staff) in decisions concerning a child, as appropriate, ensuring confidentiality of sensitive information. (See also P-2.4.)

P-1.5—We shall use appropriate assessment systems, which include multiple sources of information, to provide information on children's learning and development.

P-1.6—We shall strive to ensure that decisions such as those related to enrollment, retention, or assignment to special education services, will be based on multiple sources of information and will never be based on a single assessment, such as a test score or a single observation.

P-1.7—We shall strive to build individual relationships with each child; make individualized adaptations in teaching strategies, learning environments, and curricula; and consult with the family so that each child benefits from the program. If after such efforts have been exhausted, the current placement does not meet a child's needs, or the child is seriously jeopardizing the ability of other children to benefit from the program, we shall collaborate with the child's family and appropriate specialists to determine the additional services needed and/or the placement option(s) most likely to ensure the child's success. (Aspects of this principle may not apply in programs that have a lawful mandate to provide services to a particular population of children.)

P-1.8—We shall be familiar with the risk factors for and symptoms of child abuse and neglect, including physical, sexual, verbal, and emotional abuse and physical, emotional, educational, and medical neglect. We shall know and follow state laws and community procedures that protect children against abuse and neglect.

P-1.9—When we have reasonable cause to suspect child abuse or neglect, we shall report it to the appropriate community agency and follow up to ensure that appropriate action has been taken. When appropriate, parents or guardians will be informed that the referral will be or has been made.

P-1.10—When another person tells us of his or her suspicion that a child is being abused or neglected, we shall assist that person in taking appropriate action in order to protect the child.

P-1.11—When we become aware of a practice or situation that endangers the health, safety, or well-being of children, we have an ethical responsibility to protect children or inform parents and/or others who can.

SECTION II: ETHICAL RESPONSIBILITIES TO FAMILIES

Families[3] are of primary importance in children's development. Because the family and the early childhood practitioner have a common interest in the child's well-being, we acknowledge a primary responsibility to bring about communication, cooperation, and collaboration between the home and early childhood program in ways that enhance the child's development.

Ideals

I-2.1—To be familiar with the knowledge base related to working effectively with families and to stay informed through continuing education and training.

I-2.2—To develop relationships of mutual trust and create partnerships with the families we serve.

I-2.3—To welcome all family members and encourage them to participate in the program, including involvement in shared decision making.

---

[3]The term *family* may include those adults, besides parents, with the responsibility of being involved in educating, nurturing, and advocating for the child.

I-2.4—To listen to families, acknowledge and build upon their strengths and competencies, and learn from families as we support them in their task of nurturing children.

I-2.5—To respect the dignity and preferences of each family and to make an effort to learn about its structure, culture, language, customs, and beliefs to ensure a culturally consistent environment for all children and families.

I-2.6—To acknowledge families' childrearing values and their right to make decisions for their children.

I-2.7—To share information about each child's education and development with families and to help them understand and appreciate the current knowledge base of the early childhood profession.

I-2.8—To help family members enhance their understanding of their children, as staff are enhancing their understanding of each child through communications with families, and support family members in the continuing development of their skills as parents.

I-2.9—To foster families' efforts to build support networks and, when needed, participate in building networks for families by providing them with opportunities to interact with program staff, other families, community resources, and professional services.

Principles

P-2.1—We shall not deny family members access to their child's classroom or program setting unless access is denied by court order or other legal restriction.

P-2.2—We shall inform families of program philosophy, policies, curriculum, assessment system, cultural practices, and personnel qualifications, and explain why we teach as we do—which should be in accordance with our ethical responsibilities to children (see Section I).

P-2.3—We shall inform families of and, when appropriate, involve them in policy decisions. (See also I-2.3.)

P-2.4—We shall ensure that the family is involved in significant decisions affecting their child. (See also P-1.4.)

P-2.5—We shall make every effort to communicate effectively with all families in a language that they understand. We shall use community resources for translation and interpretation when we do not have sufficient resources in our own programs.

P-2.6—As families share information with us about their children and families, we shall ensure that families' input is an important contribution to the planning and implementation of the program.

P-2-7—We shall inform families about the nature and purpose of the program's child assessments and how data about their child will be used.

P-2.8—We shall treat child assessment information confidentially and share this information only when there is a legitimate need for it.

P-2.9—We shall inform the family of injuries and incidents involving their child, of risks such as exposures to communicable diseases that might result in infection, and of occurrences that might result in emotional stress.

P-2.10—Families shall be fully informed of any proposed research projects involving their children and shall have the opportunity to give or withhold consent without penalty. We shall not permit or participate in research that could in any way hinder the education, development, or well-being of children.

P-2.11—We shall not engage in or support exploitation of families. We shall not use our relationship with a family for private advantage or personal gain, or enter into relationships with family members that might impair our effectiveness working with their children.

P-2.12—We shall develop written policies for the protection of confidentiality and the disclosure of children's records. These policy documents shall be made available to all program personnel and families. Disclosure of children's records beyond family members, program personnel, and consultants having an obligation of confidentiality shall require familial consent (except in cases of abuse or neglect).

P-2.13—We shall maintain confidentiality and shall respect the family's right to privacy, refraining from disclosure of confidential information and intrusion into family life. However, when we have reason to believe that a child's welfare is at risk, it is permissible to share confidential information with agencies, as well as with individuals who have legal responsibility for intervening in the child's interest.

P-2.14—In cases where family members are in conflict with one another, we shall work openly, sharing our observations of the child, to help all parties involved make informed decisions. We shall refrain from becoming an advocate for one party.

P-2.15—We shall be familiar with and appropriately refer families to community resources and professional support services. After a referral has been made, we shall follow up to ensure that services have been appropriately provided.

SECTION III: ETHICAL RESPONSIBILITIES TO COLLEAGUES

In a caring, cooperative workplace, human dignity is respected, professional satisfaction is promoted, and positive relationships are developed and sustained. Based upon our core values, our primary responsibility to colleagues is to establish and maintain settings and relationships that support productive work and meet professional needs. The same ideals that apply to children also apply as we interact with adults in the workplace. (Note: Section III includes responsibilities to co-workers and to employers. See the "Code of Ethical Conduct: Supplement for Early Childhood Program Administrators" for responsibilities to personnel (*employees* in the original 2005 Code revision), online at http://www.naeyc.org/files/naeyc/file/positions/PSETH05_supp.pdf.)

A—Responsibilities to co-workers

Ideals

I-3A.1—To establish and maintain relationships of respect, trust, confidentiality, collaboration, and cooperation with co-workers.

I-3A.2—To share resources with co-workers, collaborating to ensure that the best possible early childhood care and education program is provided.

I-3A.3—To support co-workers in meeting their professional needs and in their professional development.

I-3A.4—To accord co-workers due recognition of professional achievement.

Principles

P-3A.1—We shall recognize the contributions of colleagues to our program and not participate in practices that diminish their reputations or impair their effectiveness in working with children and families.

P-3A.2—When we have concerns about the professional behavior of a co-worker, we shall first let that person know of our concern in a way that shows respect for personal dignity and for the diversity to be found among staff members, and then attempt to resolve the matter collegially and in a confidential manner.

P-3A.3—We shall exercise care in expressing views regarding the personal attributes or professional conduct of co-workers. Statements should be based on firsthand knowledge, not hearsay, and relevant to the interests of children and programs.

P-3A.4—We shall not participate in practices that discriminate against a co-worker because of sex, race, national origin, religious beliefs or other affiliations, age, marital status/family structure, disability, or sexual orientation.

B—Responsibilities to employers

Ideals

I-3B.1—To assist the program in providing the highest quality of service.

I-3B.2—To do nothing that diminishes the reputation of the program in which we work unless it is violating laws and regulations designed to protect children or is violating the provisions of this Code.

Principles

P-3B.1—We shall follow all program policies. When we do not agree with program policies, we shall attempt to effect change through constructive action within the organization.

P-3B.2—We shall speak or act on behalf of an organization only when authorized. We shall take care to acknowledge when we are speaking for the organization and when we are expressing a personal judgment.

P-3B.3—We shall not violate laws or regulations designed to protect children and shall take appropriate action consistent with this Code when aware of such violations.

P-3B.4—If we have concerns about a colleague's behavior, and children's well-being is not at risk, we may address the concern with that individual. If children are at risk or the situation does not improve after it has been brought to the colleague's attention, we shall report the colleague's unethical or incompetent behavior to an appropriate authority.

P-3B.5—When we have a concern about circumstances or conditions that impact the quality of care and education within the program, we shall inform the program's administration or, when necessary, other appropriate authorities.

Section IV: Ethical Responsibilities to Community and Society

Early childhood programs operate within the context of their immediate community made up of families and other institutions concerned with children's welfare. Our responsibilities to the community are to provide programs that meet the diverse needs of families, to cooperate with agencies and professions that share the responsibility for children, to assist families in gaining access to those agencies and allied professionals, and to assist in the development of community programs that are needed but not currently available.

As individuals, we acknowledge our responsibility to provide the best possible programs of care and education for children and to conduct ourselves with honesty and integrity. Because of our specialized expertise in early childhood development and education and because the larger society shares responsibility for the welfare and protection of young children, we acknowledge a collective obligation to advocate for the best interests of children within early childhood programs and in the larger community and to serve as a voice for young children everywhere.

The ideals and principles in this section are presented to distinguish between those that pertain to the work of the individual early childhood educator and those that more typically are engaged in collectively on behalf of the best interests of children—with the understanding that individual early childhood educators have a shared responsibility for addressing the ideals and principles that are identified as "collective."

Ideal (Individual)

I-4.1—To provide the community with high-quality early childhood care and education programs and services.

Ideals (Collective)

I-4.2—To promote cooperation among professionals and agencies and interdisciplinary collaboration among professions concerned with addressing issues in the health, education, and well-being of young children, their families, and their early childhood educators.

I-4.3—To work through education, research, and advocacy toward an environmentally safe world in which all children receive health care, food, and shelter; are nurtured; and live free from violence in their home and their communities.

I-4.4—To work through education, research, and advocacy toward a society in which all young children have access to high-quality early care and education programs.

I-4.5—To work to ensure that appropriate assessment systems, which include multiple sources of information, are used for purposes that benefit children.

I-4.6—To promote knowledge and understanding of young children and their needs. To work toward greater societal acknowledgment of children's rights and greater social acceptance of responsibility for the well-being of all children.

I-4.7—To support policies and laws that promote the well-being of children and families, and to work to change those that impair their well-being. To participate in developing policies and laws that are needed, and to cooperate with families and other individuals and groups in these efforts.

I-4.8—To further the professional development of the field of early childhood care and education and to strengthen its commitment to realizing its core values as reflected in this Code.

Principles (Individual)

P-4.1—We shall communicate openly and truthfully about the nature and extent of services that we provide.

P-4.2—We shall apply for, accept, and work in positions for which we are personally well-suited and professionally qualified. We shall not offer

Glossary of Terms Related to Ethics

Code of Ethics. Defines the core values of the field and provides guidance for what professionals should do when they encounter conflicting obligations or responsibilities in their work.

Values. Qualities or principles that individuals believe to be desirable or worthwhile and that they prize for themselves, for others, and for the world in which they live.

Core Values. Commitments held by a profession that are consciously and knowingly embraced by its practitioners because they make a contribution to society. There is a difference between personal values and the core values of a profession.

Morality. Peoples' views of what is good, right, and proper; their beliefs about their obligations; and their ideas about how they should behave.

Ethics. The study of right and wrong, or duty and obligation, that involves critical reflection on morality and the ability to make choices between values and the examination of the moral dimensions of relationships.

Professional Ethics. The moral commitments of a profession that involve moral reflection that extends and enhances the personal morality practitioners bring to their work, that concern actions of right and wrong in the workplace, and that help individuals resolve moral dilemmas they encounter in their work.

Ethical Responsibilities. Behaviors that one must or must not engage in. Ethical responsibilities are clear-cut and are spelled out in the Code of Ethical Conduct (for example, early childhood educators should never share confidential information about a child or family with a person who has no legitimate need for knowing).

Ethical Dilemma. A moral conflict that involves determining appropriate conduct when an individual faces conflicting professional values and responsibilities.

Sources for glossary terms and definitions

Feeney, S., & N. Freeman. 2005. *Ethics and the early childhood educator: Using the NAEYC code.* Washington, DC: NAEYC.

Kidder, R.M. 1995. *How good people make tough choices: Resolving the dilemmas of ethical living.* New York: Fireside.

Kipnis, K. 1987. How to discuss professional ethics. *Young Children* 42 (4): 26–30.

services that we do not have the competence, qualifications, or resources to provide.

P-4.3—We shall carefully check references and shall not hire or recommend for employment any person whose competence, qualifications, or character makes him or her unsuited for the position.

P-4.4—We shall be objective and accurate in reporting the knowledge upon which we base our program practices.

P-4.5—We shall be knowledgeable about the appropriate use of assessment strategies and instruments and interpret results accurately to families.

P-4.6—We shall be familiar with laws and regulations that serve to protect the children in our programs and be vigilant in ensuring that these laws and regulations are followed.

P-4.7—When we become aware of a practice or situation that endangers the health, safety, or well-being of children, we have an ethical responsibility to protect children or inform parents and/or others who can.

P-4.8—We shall not participate in practices that are in violation of laws and regulations that protect the children in our programs.

P-4.9—When we have evidence that an early childhood program is violating laws or regulations protecting children, we shall report the violation to appropriate authorities who can be expected to remedy the situation.

P-4.10—When a program violates or requires its employees to violate this Code, it is permissible, after fair assessment of the evidence, to disclose the identity of that program.

Principles (Collective)

P-4.11—When policies are enacted for purposes that do not benefit children, we have a collective responsibility to work to change these policies.

P-4.12—When we have evidence that an agency that provides services intended to ensure children's well-being is failing to meet its obligations, we acknowledge a collective ethical responsibility

Statement of Commitment*

As an individual who works with young children, I commit myself to furthering the values of early childhood education as they are reflected in the ideals and principles of the NAEYC Code of Ethical Conduct. To the best of my ability I will

- Never harm children.
- Ensure that programs for young children are based on current knowledge and research of child development and early childhood education.
- Respect and support families in their task of nurturing children.
- Respect colleagues in early childhood care and education and support them in maintaining the NAEYC Code of Ethical Conduct.
- Serve as an advocate for children, their families, and their teachers in community and society.
- Stay informed of and maintain high standards of professional conduct.
- Engage in an ongoing process of self-reflection, realizing that personal characteristics, biases, and beliefs have an impact on children and families.
- Be open to new ideas and be willing to learn from the suggestions of others.
- Continue to learn, grow, and contribute as a professional.
- Honor the ideals and principles of the NAEYC Code of Ethical Conduct.

*This Statement of Commitment is not part of the Code but is a personal acknowledgment of the individual's willingness to embrace the distinctive values and moral obligations of the field of early childhood care and education. It is recognition of the moral obligations that lead to an individual becoming part of the profession.

to report the problem to appropriate authorities or to the public. We shall be vigilant in our follow-up until the situation is resolved.

P-4.13—When a child protection agency fails to provide adequate protection for abused or neglected children, we acknowledge a collective ethical responsibility to work toward the improvement of these services.

The National Association for the Education of Young Children (NAEYC) is a nonprofit corporation, tax exempt under Section 501(c)(3) of the Internal Revenue Code, dedicated to acting on behalf of the needs and interests of young children. The NAEYC Code of Ethical Conduct (Code) has been developed in furtherance of NAEYC's nonprofit and tax exempt purposes. The information contained in the Code is intended to provide early childhood educators with guidelines for working with children from birth through age 8.

An individual's or program's use, reference to, or review of the Code does not guarantee compliance with NAEYC Early Childhood Program Standards and Accreditation Performance Criteria and program accreditation procedures. It is recommended that the Code be used as guidance in connection with

implementation of the NAEYC Program Standards, but such use is not a substitute for diligent review and application of the NAEYC Program Standards.

NAEYC has taken reasonable measures to develop the Code in a fair, reasonable, open, unbiased, and objective manner, based on currently available data. However, further research or developments may change the current state of knowledge. Neither NAEYC nor its officers, directors, members, employees, or agents will be liable for any loss, damage, or claim with respect to any liabilities, including direct, special, indirect, or consequential damages incurred in connection with the Code or reliance on the information presented.

NAEYC Code of Ethical Conduct 2005 Revisions Workgroup

Mary Ambery, Ruth Ann Ball, James Clay, Julie Olsen Edwards, Harriet Egertson, Anthony Fair, Stephanie Feeney, Jana Fleming, Nancy Freeman, Marla Israel, Allison McKinnon, Evelyn Wright Moore, Eva Moravcik, Christina Lopez Morgan, Sarah Mulligan, Nila Rinehart, Betty Holston Smith, and Peter Pizzolongo (*NAEYC Staff*)

Code of Ethical Conduct

Supplement for Early Childhood Program Administrators

Adopted July 2006, **Reaffirmed and Updated May 2011**

A Position Statement Supplement of the National Association for the Education of Young Children

Adopted by the National Association for Family Child Care

Administrators of programs for young children are responsible for overseeing all program operations, serving as leaders in their programs, and representing the field to the community. Early childhood program administrators are called upon to sustain relationships with a wide variety of clients. They interact with and have responsibilities to children, families, program personnel, governing boards and sponsoring agencies, funders, regulatory agencies, their community, and the profession.

Program administrators deal with unique responsibilities and ethical challenges in the course of managing and guiding their programs and assume leadership roles within and beyond their programs. As managers and leaders, they are called upon to share their professional knowledge and expertise with families, personnel, governing boards, and others; demonstrate empathy for the families and children they serve; and communicate respect for the skills, knowledge, and expertise of teaching staff, other personnel, and families. Administrators accept primary responsibility for executing the program's mission as well as developing and carrying out program policies and procedures that support that mission. They also make a commitment to continue their own professional development and the continuing education of the personnel in the program they lead. Administrators also may be advocates for all children being able to gain access to quality programming. Some of the challenges faced by administrators involve balancing their obligations to support and nurture children with their responsibility to address the needs and safeguard the rights of families and personnel and respond to the requirements of their boards and sponsoring agencies.

Purpose of the Supplement

Like those in the field who work directly with young children, program administrators are regularly called upon to make decisions of a moral and ethical nature. The NAEYC Code of Ethical Conduct (revised 2005, reaffirmed and updated 2011) is a foundational document that maps the ethical dimensions of early childhood educators' work in early care and education programs. Program administrators share the ethical obligations assumed by all early childhood educators—obligations that are reflected in the core values, ideals, and principles set forth in the Code. Administrators embrace the central commitment of the early care and education field—and the Code—to ensure the well-being and support the healthy development of young children.

> **NOTE**
>
> This Supplement was reaffirmed by the NAEYC Governing Board in May 2011 and changes were made to Ideals and Principles that regard responsibilities to families to ensure alignment with current family engagement best practices in the field. In addition, references to the Code of Ethical Conduct, Section III, Part C: Responsibilities to Employees were deleted, as Section III, Part C was deleted in the May 2011 update of the Code.

Given the nature of their responsibilities, however, administrators face some additional ethical challenges. Conflicts often surface in the areas of enrollment policies; dealings with personnel; and relationships with families, licensors, governing boards, sponsoring agencies, and others in the community. The existing Code is a valuable resource that addresses many of the ethical issues encountered by administrators. However, it does not provide all of the guidance that they need to address the unique ethical issues that arise in their work. This Supplement offers additional core values, ideals, and principles related to the frequently recurring ethical issues encountered by administrators.

Core Values

In addition to the core values spelled out in the NAEYC Code of Ethical Conduct, early childhood program administrators commit themselves to the following additional core values.

We make a commitment to

- Recognize that we have many responsibilities—to children, families, personnel, governing boards, sponsoring agencies, funders, regulatory agencies, the community, and the profession—and that the well-being of the children in our care is our primary responsibility, above our obligations to other constituencies.

- Recognize the importance of and maintain a humane and fulfilling work environment for personnel and volunteers.
- Be committed to the professional development of staff.

Conceptual Framework

This document sets forth a conception of early childhood program administrators' professional responsibilities in five areas, some of which differ from those identified in the NAEYC Code. Each section addresses an area of professional relationships: (1) with children, (2) with families, (3) with personnel, (4) with sponsoring agencies and governing boards, and (5) with the community and society. The items in each section address the unique ethical responsibilities of administrators in early care and education settings.

Ideals and Principles

This Supplement identifies additional **ideals** that reflect exemplary practice (our aspirations) and **principles** describing practices that are required, prohibited, or permitted. The principles guide conduct and assist practitioners in resolving ethical dilemmas. Together, the ideals and principles are intended to direct practitioners to questions that, when responsibly answered, provide the basis for conscientious decision making. While the Code and this Supplement provide specific direction for addressing some ethical dilemmas, many others will require early childhood program administrators to combine the guidance of the Code and/or this Supplement with their best professional judgment.

The ideals and principles in the Code and this Supplement present a shared framework of professional responsibility that affirms our commitment to the core values of our field. The Code and the Supplement publicly acknowledge the responsibilities that early childhood professionals assume and, in so doing, support ethical behavior in our work. Practitioners who face situations with ethical dimensions are urged to seek guidance in the applicable parts of the Code/Supplement and in the spirit that informs the whole.

The ideals and principles in this Supplement are based on early childhood program administrators' descriptions of ethical dilemmas they have

encountered in their work. They are designed to inspire and guide administrators toward actions that reflect the field's current understanding of ethical responsibility.

The Supplement also includes items from the NAEYC Code that directly relate to the work of administrators—some are duplicates of Code ideals or principles, and some are adaptations. Items from the Code that are repeated or adapted for this Supplement are cross-referenced with their corresponding ideals and principles, with the Code references indicated in parentheses. Other items that expand and extend the NAEYC Code were written specifically for this Supplement. (*Note:* There is **not** necessarily a corresponding principle for each ideal.)

1. Ethical responsibilities to children

The early childhood program administrator's paramount responsibility is to ensure that programs for children provide settings that are safe, healthy, nurturing, and responsive for each child. Administrators are committed to establishing and maintaining programs that support children's development and learning; promote respect for individual differences;

and help children learn to live, play, and work cooperatively. Administrators are also committed to ensuring that the program promotes children's self-awareness, competence, self-worth, resiliency, and physical well-being.

Ideals

I-1.1 To ensure that children's needs are the first priority in administrative decision making, recognizing that a child's well-being cannot be separated from that of his/her family.

I-1.2 To provide a high-quality program based on current knowledge of child development and best practices in early care and education.

Principles

P-1.1 We shall place the welfare and safety of children above other obligations (for example, to families, program personnel, employing agency, community). **This item takes precedence over all others in this Supplement.**

P-1.2 We shall ensure that the programs we administer are safe and developmentally appropriate in accordance with standards of the field, including those developed and endorsed by NAEYC and other professional associations.

P-1.3 We shall have clearly stated policies for the respectful treatment of children and adults in all contacts made by staff, parents, volunteers, student teachers, and other adults. We shall appropriately address incidents that are not consistent with our policies.

P-1.4 We shall support children's well-being by encouraging the development of strong bonds between children and their families and between children and their teachers.

P-1.5 We shall support children's well-being by promoting connections with their culture and collaborating with communities to ensure cultural consistency between the program and families' childrearing practices.

P-1.6 We shall make every effort to provide the necessary resources (staff, consultation, other human resources, equipment, and so on) to ensure that all children, including those with special needs, can benefit from the program.

P-1.7 We shall ensure that there is a plan for appropriate transitions for children when they enter our program, move from one classroom to another within our program, and when they leave.

P-1.8 We shall apply all policies regarding our obligations to children consistently and fairly.

P-1.9 We shall review all program policies set forth by sponsoring agencies and governing bodies to ensure that they are in the best interest of the children.

P-1.10 We shall express our professional concerns about directives from the sponsoring agency or governing body when we believe that a mandated practice is not in the best interest of children.

P-1.11 If we determine that a policy does not benefit children, we shall work to change it. If we determine that a program policy is harmful to children, we shall suspend its implementation while working to honor the intent of the policy in ways that are not harmful to children.

2. Ethical responsibilities to families

The administrator sets the tone for the program in establishing and supporting an understanding of the family's role in their children's development. Administrators strive to promote communication, cooperation, and collaboration between the home and the program in ways that enhance each child's development. Because administrators provide the link between the family and direct services for children, they often encounter ethical issues in this area of responsibility.

Ideals

I-2.1 To design programs and policies inclusive of and responsive to diverse families.

I-2.2 To serve as a resource for families by providing information and referrals to services in the larger community.

I-2.3 To advocate for the needs and rights of families in the program and the larger community.

I-2.4 To support families in their role as advocate for their children and themselves.

I-2.5 To create and maintain a climate of trust and candor that fosters two-way communication and enables parents/guardians to speak and act in the best interest of their children.

Principles

P-2.1 We shall work to create a respectful environment for and a working relationship with all families, regardless of family members' sex, race, national origin, immigration status, preferred home language, religious belief or affiliation, age, marital status/family structure, disability, or sexual orientation.

P-2.2 We shall provide families with complete and honest information concerning program philosophy, educational practices, and the services provided.

P-2.3 We shall make every attempt to use two-way communication to convey information in ways that are accessible by every family served.

P-2.4 We shall establish clear operating policies and make them available to families in advance of their child entering the program.

P-2.5 We shall develop enrollment policies that clearly describe admission policies and priorities.

P-2.6 We shall develop policies that clearly state the circumstances under which a child or family may be asked to leave the program. We shall refuse to provide services for children only if the program will not benefit them or if their presence jeopardizes the ability of other children to benefit from the program or prevents personnel from doing their jobs.

P-2.7 We shall assist families in finding appropriate alternatives when we believe their children cannot benefit from the program or when their presence jeopardizes the ability of other children to benefit from the program or prevents personnel from doing their jobs.

P-2.8 We shall apply all policies regarding obligations to families consistently and fairly.

P-2.9 In decisions concerning children and programs, we shall draw upon our relationships with families as well as each family's knowledge of their child. (See also P-3.7 in this Supplement.)

P-2.10 We shall respond to families' requests to the extent that the requests are congruent with program philosophy, standards of good practice, and the resources of the program. We shall not honor any request that puts a child in a situation that would create physical or emotional harm. In such instances, we shall communicate with the family the reason(s) why the request was not honored and work toward an alternative solution.

P-2.11 We shall work to achieve shared understanding between families and staff members. In disagreements, we shall help all parties express their particular needs and perspectives. (*Note:* This is repeated in Section 3 [P-3.16] to emphasize the responsibility to both staff and family members.)

3. Ethical responsibilities to personnel

Early childhood program administrators are managers with the responsibility for providing oversight for all program operations, as well as serving as leaders in early care and education programs. They are responsible for creating and maintaining a caring, cooperative workplace that respects human dignity, promotes professional satisfaction, and models positive relationships. Administrators must exemplify the highest possible standards of professional practice both within and beyond the program. Ethical responsibilities to personnel include those that are related to working with staff they supervise and/or employ as well as the unions or groups that represent these staff. (*Note:* Administrators' ethical responsibilities to co-workers and employers are included in the Code of Ethical Conduct, Section III, Part A and Part B.)

Ideals

I-3.1 To create and promote policies and working conditions that are physically and emotionally safe and foster mutual respect, cooperation, collaboration, competence, well-being, confidentiality, and self-esteem.

I-3.2 To create and maintain a climate of trust and candor that enables staff to speak and act in the best interest of children, families, and the field of early care and education.

I-3.3 To coach and mentor staff, helping them realize their potential within the field of early care and education.

I-3.4 To strive to secure adequate and equitable compensation (salary and benefits) for those who work with or on behalf of young children.

I-3.5 To encourage and support continual development of staff in becoming more skilled and knowledgeable practitioners.

Principles

P-3.1 We shall provide staff members with safe and supportive working conditions that respect human dignity, honor confidences, and permit them to carry out their responsibilities through performance evaluation, written grievance procedures, constructive feedback, and opportunities for continuing professional development and advancement.

P-3.2 We shall develop and maintain comprehensive written personnel policies that define program standards. These policies shall be given to new staff members and shall be easily accessible and available for review by all staff members.

P-3.3 We shall apply all policies regarding our work with personnel consistently and fairly.

P-3.4 We shall be familiar with and abide by the rules and regulations developed by unions or other groups representing the interests or rights of personnel in our programs.

P-3.5 We shall support and encourage personnel in their efforts to implement programming that enhances the development and learning of the children served.

P-3.6 We shall act immediately to prevent staff from implementing activities or practices that put any child in a situation that creates physical or emotional harm.

P-3.7 In decisions concerning children and programs, we shall draw upon the education, training, experience, and expertise of staff members. (See also P-2.9 in this Supplement.)

P-3.8 We shall work to ensure that ongoing training is available and accessible, represents current understandings of best practice, and is relevant to staff members' responsibilities.

P-3.9 We shall inform staff whose performance does not meet program expectations of areas of concern and, when possible, assist in improving their performance.

P-3.10 We shall provide guidance, additional professional development, and coaching for staff whose practices are not appropriate. In instances in which a staff member cannot satisfy reasonable expectations for practice, we shall counsel the staff member to pursue a more appropriate position.

P-3.11 We shall conduct personnel dismissals, when necessary, in accordance with all applicable laws and regulations. We shall inform staff who are dismissed of the reasons for termination. When a dismissal is for cause, justification must be based on evidence of inadequate or inappropriate behavior that is accurately documented, current, and available for the staff member to review.

P-3.12 In making personnel evaluations and recommendations, we shall make judgments based on fact and relevant to the interests of children and programs.

P-3.13 We shall make hiring, retention, termination, and promotion decisions based solely on a person's competence, record of accomplishment, ability to carry out the responsibilities of the position, and professional preparation specific to the developmental levels of children in his/her care.

P-3.14 We shall not make hiring, retention, termination, and promotion decisions based on an individual's sex, race, national origin, religious beliefs or other affiliations, age, marital status/family structure, disability, or sexual orientation. We shall be familiar with and observe laws and regulations that pertain to employment discrimination. (Aspects of this principle do not apply to programs that have a lawful mandate to determine eligibility based on one or more of the criteria identified above.)

P-3.15 We shall maintain confidentiality in dealing with issues related to an employee's job performance and shall respect an employee's right to privacy regarding personal issues.

P-3.16 We shall work to achieve shared understandings between families and staff members. In disagreements, we shall help all parties express their particular needs and perspectives. (*Note:* This is repeated from Section 2 [P-2.11] to emphasize the responsibility to both staff and family members.)

4. Ethical responsibilities to sponsoring agencies and governing bodies

Programs providing early care and education operate under a variety of public and private auspices with diverse governing structures and missions. All early childhood program administrators are responsible to their governing and funding bodies. Administrators ensure the program's stability and reputation by recruiting, selecting, orienting, and supervising personnel; following sound fiscal practices; and securing and maintaining licensure and accreditation. Administrators are also responsible for overseeing day-to-day program operations and fostering positive relationships among children, families, staff, and the community.

Administrators' responsibilities to sponsoring agencies and governing bodies are optimally met in a collaborative manner. Administrators establish and maintain partnerships with sponsoring agency representatives, board members, and other stakeholders to design and improve services for children and their families.

Ideals

I–4.1 To ensure to the best of our ability that the program pursues its stated mission.

I-4.2 To provide program leadership that reflects best practices in early care and education and program administration.

I-4.3 To plan and institute ongoing program improvements.

I-4.4 To be ambassadors within the community, creating goodwill for program sponsors as well as for the program itself.

I-4.5 To advocate on behalf of children and families in interactions with sponsoring agency staff and governing body members for high-quality early care and education programs and services for children.

Principles

P-4.1 We shall ensure compliance with all relevant regulations and standards.

P-4.2 We shall do our jobs conscientiously, attending to all areas that fall within the scope of our responsibility.

P-4.3 We shall manage resources responsibly and accurately account for their use.

P-4.4 To ensure that the program's sponsoring agency and governing body are prepared to make wise decisions, we shall thoroughly and honestly communicate necessary information.

P-4.5 We shall evaluate our programs using agreed-upon standards and report our findings to the appropriate authority.

P-4.6 In presenting information to governing bodies we shall make every effort to preserve confidentiality regarding children, families, and staff unless there is a compelling reason for divulging the information.

5. Ethical responsibilities to community, society, and the field of early childhood education

Like those of all early childhood educators, administrators' responsibilities to the community include cooperating with agencies and professionals that share the responsibility for children, supporting families in gaining access to services provided by those agencies and professionals, and assisting in the development of community programs and services.

Early childhood program administrators often have the knowledge, expertise, and education to assume leadership roles. For this reason, they are responsible to the community, society, and the field of early childhood education for promoting the education and well-being of young children and their families.

Ideals

I-5.1 To provide the community with high-quality early care and education programs and services. (I-4.1)

I-5.2 To serve as a community resource, spokesperson, and advocate for quality programming for young children. To serve as a conduit between the community and programs by coordinating and collaborating with key community representatives.

I-5.3 To uphold the spirit as well as the specific provisions of applicable regulations and standards.

I-5.4 To increase the awareness of the public and policy makers about the importance of the early years and the positive impact of high-quality early care and education programs on society.

I-5.5 To advocate on behalf of children and families for high-quality programs and services for children and for professional development for the early childhood workforce.

I-5.6 To join with other early childhood educators in speaking with a clear and unified voice for the values of our profession on behalf of children, families, and early childhood educators.

I-5.7 To be an involved and supportive member of the early childhood profession.

I-5.8 To further the professional development of the field of early childhood education and to strengthen its commitment to realizing its core values as reflected in NAEYC's Code of Ethical Conduct and this Supplement. (I-4.8)

I-5.9 To ensure that adequate resources are provided so that all provisions of the Code of Ethical Conduct and this Supplement can be implemented.

Principles

P-5.1 We shall communicate openly and truthfully about the nature and extent of services that we provide. (P-4.1)

P-5.2 We shall apply for, accept, and work in positions for which we are personally well-suited and professionally qualified. We shall not offer services that we do not have the competence, qualifications, or resources to provide. (P-4.2)

P-5.3 We shall carefully check references and not hire or recommend for employment any person whose competence, qualifications, or character makes him or her unsuited for the position. (P-4.3)

P-5.4 When we make a personnel recommendation or serve as a reference, we shall be accurate and truthful.

P-5.5 We shall be objective and accurate in reporting the knowledge upon which we base our program practices. (P-4.4)

P-5.6 We shall be knowledgeable about the appropriate use of assessment strategies and instruments and interpret results accurately to families. (P-4.5)

P-5.7 We shall be familiar with laws and regulations that serve to protect the children in our programs and be vigilant in ensuring that these laws and regulations are followed. (P-4.6)

P-5.8 We shall hold program staff accountable for knowing and following all relevant standards and regulations.

P-5.9 When we become aware of a practice or situation that endangers the health, safety, or well-being of children, we have an ethical responsibility to protect children or inform parents and/or others who can. (P-4.7)

P-5.10 We shall not participate in practices in violation of laws and regulations that protect the children in our programs. (P-4.8)

P-5.11 When we have evidence that an early childhood program is violating laws or regulations protecting children, we shall report the violation to appropriate authorities who can be expected to remedy the situation. (P-4.9)

Workgroup for the Development of the 2006 NAEYC Code of Ethical Conduct Supplement for Program Administrators

Mary Ambery, Paula Jorde Bloom, Richard Cohen, Anne Dorsey, Stephanie Feeney, Nancy Freeman, Marla Israel, Ellie Kaucher, Eva Moravcik, Beatriz Otero, Julie Powers, Martha Staker, Todd Boressoff (NAEYC Board Liaison), Peter Pizzolongo (NAEYC Staff)

P-5.12 We shall be honest and forthright in communications with the public and with agencies responsible for regulation and accreditation.

P-5.13 When a program violates or requires its employees to violate NAEYC's Code of Ethical Conduct, it is permissible, after fair assessment of the evidence, to disclose the identity of that program. (P-4.10)

P-5.14 When asked to provide an informed opinion on issues, practices, products, or programs, we shall base our opinions on relevant experience, knowledge of child development, and standards of best practice.

The core NAEYC Code of Ethical Conduct is online at **www.naeyc.org/files/naeyc/file/positions/ PSETH05_supp.pdf**

National Association for the Education of Young Children 1313 L Street, NW, Washington, DC 20005-4101

Source: Reprinted with permission from the National Association for the Education of Young Children (NAEYC). Full text of all NAEYC position statements is available at www.naeyc.org/positionstatements.

NAEYC Standards for Early Childhood Professional Preparation Programs

The NAEYC Standards identify what early childhood educators are expected to know and do and establish criteria for determining excellence among teacher education candidates

Standard 1. Promoting Child Development and Learning

Students prepared in early childhood degree programs are grounded in a child development knowledge base. They use their understanding of young children's characteristics and needs and of the multiple interacting influences on children's development and learning to create environments that are healthy, respectful, supportive, and challenging for each child.

Key elements:

1a: Knowing and understanding young children's characteristics and needs, from birth through age 8.

1b: Knowing and understanding the multiple influences on early development and learning

1c: Using developmental knowledge to create healthy, respectful, supportive, and challenging learning environments for young children

Standard 2. Building Family and Community Relationships

Students prepared in early childhood degree programs understand that successful early childhood education depends upon partnerships with children's families and communities. They know about, understand, and value the importance and complex characteristics of children's families and communities. They use this understanding to create respectful, reciprocal relationships that support and empower families and to involve all families in their children's development and learning.

Key elements:

2a: Knowing about and understanding diverse family and community characteristics

2b: Supporting and engaging families and communities through respectful, reciprocal relationships

2c: Involving families and communities in young children's development and learning

Standard 3. Observing, Documenting, and Assessing to Support Young Children and Families

Students prepared in early childhood degree programs understand that child observation, documentation, and other forms of assessment are central to the practice of all early childhood professionals. They know about and understand the goals, benefits, and uses of assessment. They know about and use systematic observations, documentation, and other effective assessment strategies in a responsible way, in partnership with families and other professionals, to positively influence the development of every child.

Key elements:

3a: Understanding the goals, benefits, and uses of assessment – including its use in development of appropriate goals, curriculum, and teaching strategies for young children

3b: Knowing about assessment partnerships with families and with professional colleagues to build effective learning environments

3c: Knowing about and using observation, documentation, and other appropriate assessment tools and approaches, including the use of technology in documentation, assessment and data collection.

3d: Understanding and practicing responsible assessment to promote positive outcomes for each child, including the use of assistive technology for children with disabilities.

Standard 4. Using Developmentally Effective Approaches

Students prepared in early childhood degree programs understand that teaching and learning with young children is a complex enterprise, and its details vary depending on children's ages, characteristics, and the settings within which teaching and learning occur. They understand and use positive relationships and supportive interactions as the foundation for their work with young children and families. Students know, understand, and use a wide array of developmentally appropriate approaches, instructional strategies, and tools to connect with children and families and positively influence each child's development and learning.

Key elements:

4a: Understanding positive relationships and supportive interactions as the foundation of their work with young children

4b: Knowing and understanding effective strategies and tools for early education, including appropriate uses of technology

4c: Using a broad repertoire of developmentally appropriate teaching/learning approaches

4d: Reflecting on own practice to promote positive outcomes for each child

Standard 5. Using Content Knowledge to Build Meaningful Curriculum

Students prepared in early childhood degree programs use their knowledge of academic disciplines to design, implement, and evaluate experiences that promote positive development and learning for each and every young child. Students understand the importance of developmental domains and academic (or content) disciplines in an early childhood curriculum. They know the essential concepts, inquiry tools, and structure of content areas, including academic subjects, and can identify resources to deepen their understanding. Students use their own knowledge and other resources to design, implement, and evaluate meaningful, challenging curricula that promote comprehensive developmental and learning outcomes for every young child.

Key elements:

5a: Understanding content knowledge and resources in academic disciplines: language and literacy; the arts–music, creative movement, dance, drama, visual arts; mathematics; science, physical activity, physical education, health and safety; and social studies.

5b: Knowing and using the central concepts, inquiry tools, and structures of content areas or academic disciplines

5c: Using own knowledge, appropriate early learning standards, and other resources to design, implement, and evaluate developmentally meaningful and challenging curriculum for each child.

Standard 6. Becoming a Professional

Students prepared in early childhood degree programs identify and conduct themselves as members of the early childhood profession. They know and use ethical guidelines and other professional standards related to early childhood practice. They are continuous, collaborative learners who demonstrate knowledgeable, reflective, and critical perspectives on their work, making informed decisions that integrate knowledge from a variety of sources. They are informed advocates for sound educational practices and policies.

Key elements:

6a: Identifying and involving oneself with the early childhood field

6b: Knowing about and upholding ethical standards and other early childhood professional guidelines

6c: Engaging in continuous, collaborative learning to inform practice; using technology effectively with young children, with peers, and as a professional resource.

6d: Integrating knowledgeable, reflective, and critical perspectives on early education

6e: Engaging in informed advocacy for young children and the early childhood profession

Standard 7. Early Childhood Field Experiences

Field experiences and clinical practice are planned and sequenced so that candidates develop the knowledge, skills, and professional dispositions necessary to promote the development and learning of young children across the entire developmental period of early childhood–in at least two of the three early childhood age groups (birth–age 3, 3 through

5, 5 through 8 years) and in the variety of settings that offer early education (early school grades, child care centers and homes, Head Start programs).

Key elements:

7a. Opportunities to observe and practice in at least two of the three early childhood age groups (birth–age 3, 3–5, 5–8)

7b. Opportunities to observe and practice in at least two of the three main types of early education settings (early school grades, child care centers and homes, Head Start programs)

Source: Reprinted with permission from the National Association for the Education of Young Children (NAEYC).

NAEYC Program Administrator Definition and Competencies

I. PROGRAM ADMINISTRATOR DEFINITION

The program administrator is the individual responsible for planning, implementing, and evaluating a child care, preschool or kindergarten program. The role of the administrator covers both leadership and management functions. Leadership functions relate to the broad plan of helping an organization clarify and affirm values, set goals, articulate a vision, and chart a course of action to achieve that vision. Managerial functions relate to the actual orchestration of tasks and the setting up of systems to carry out the organization's mission.

Functions of the program administrator include the following:

- *Pedagogy*—Creating a learning community of children and adults that promotes optimal child development and healthy families

- *Organizational development and systems*—Establishing systems for smooth program functioning and managing staff to carry out the mission of the program; planning and budgeting the program's fiscal resources; managing organizational change and establishing systems to monitor and evaluate organizational performance

- *Human resources*—Recruiting, selecting, and orienting personnel; overseeing systems for the supervision, retention, and professional development of staff that affirm program values and promote a shared vision

- *Collaboration*—Establishing partnerships with program staff, family members, board members, community representatives, civic leaders, and other stakeholders to design and improve services for children and their families

- *Advocacy*—Taking action and encouraging others to work on behalf of high quality services that meet the needs of children and their families. The administrator may have different role titles depending on the program type or sponsorship

of the program. Common titles include director, site manager, administrator, program manager, early childhood coordinator, and principal.

II. CORE COMPETENCIES: RELEVANT INFORMATION FOR SELECTING ANNUAL PROFESSIONAL DEVELOPMENT OPTIONS

(Adapted with permission from the Illinois Director Credential)

The core competencies needed for effective early childhood program administration fall into two broad categories: management knowledge and skills and early childhood knowledge and skills. These are not discrete categories; they overlap conceptually and practically.

Management Knowledge and Skills

Administrators need a solid foundation in the principles of organizational management, including how to establish systems for smooth program functioning and how to manage staff to carry out the mission of the program.

1. Personal and professional self awareness

    - Knowledge and application of adult and career development, personality typologies, dispositions, and learning styles.

    - Knowledge of one's own beliefs, values, and philosophical stance

    - The ability to evaluate ethical and moral dilemmas based on a professional code of ethics

    - The ability to be a reflective practitioner and apply a repertoire of techniques to improve the level of personal fulfillment and professional job satisfaction

2 Legal and fiscal management

- Knowledge and application of the advantages and disadvantages of different legal structures
- Knowledge of different codes and regulations as they relate to the delivery of early childhood program services
- Knowledge of child custody, child abuse, special education, confidentiality, antidiscrimination, insurance liability, and contract and labor laws pertaining to program management
- Knowledge of various federal, state, and local revenue sources
- Knowledge of bookkeeping methods and accounting terminology
- Skill in budgeting, cash flow management, grant writing, and fund-raising

3 Staff management and human relations

- Knowledge and application of group dynamics, communication styles, and techniques for conflict resolution
- Knowledge of different supervisory and group facilitation styles
- The ability to relate to staff and board members of diverse racial, cultural, and ethnic backgrounds
- The ability to hire, supervise, and motivate staff to high levels of performance
- Skill in consensus building, team development, and staff performance appraisal

4 Educational programming

- Knowledge and application of different curriculum models, standards for high-quality programming, and child assessment practices
- The ability to develop and implement a program to meet the needs of young children at different ages and developmental levels (infant–toddler, preschool, kindergarten)
- Knowledge of administrative practices that promote the inclusion of children with special needs

5 Program operations and facilities management

- Knowledge and application of policies and procedures that meet state and local regulations as well as professional standards pertaining to the health and safety of young children
- Knowledge of nutritional and health requirements for food service

- The ability to design and plan the effective use of space based on principles of environmental psychology and child development
- Knowledge of playground safety design and practice

6 Family support

- Knowledge and application of family systems and different parenting styles
- Knowledge of community resources to support family wellness
- The ability to implement program practices that support families of diverse cultural, ethnic, linguistic, and socioeconomic backgrounds
- The ability to support families as valued partners in the educational process

7 Marketing and public relations

- Knowledge of the fundamentals of effective marketing, public relations, and community outreach
- The ability to evaluate the cost benefit of different marketing and promotional strategies
- The ability to communicate the program's philosophy and promote a positive public image to families, business leaders, public officials, and prospective funders
- The ability to promote linkages with local schools
- Skill in developing a business plan and effective promotional literature, handbooks, newsletters, and press releases

8 Leadership and advocacy

- Knowledge of organizational theory and leadership styles as they relate to early childhood work environments
- Knowledge of the legislative processes, social issues, and public policy affecting young children and their families
- The ability to articulate a vision, clarify and affirm values, and create a culture built on norms of continuous improvement and ethical conduct
- The ability to evaluate program effectiveness
- The ability to define organizational problems, gather data to generate alternative solutions, and effectively apply analytical skills in its solution

- The ability to advocate on behalf of young children, their families, and the profession

9 Oral and written communication

- Knowledge of the mechanics of writing, including organizing ideas, grammar, punctuation, and spelling
- The ability to use written communication to effectively express one's thoughts
- Knowledge of oral communication techniques, including establishing rapport, preparing the environment, active listening, and voice control
- The ability to communicate ideas effectively in a formal presentation

10 Technology

- Knowledge of basic computer hardware and software applications
- The ability to use the computer for program administrative functions

Early Childhood Knowledge and Skills

Administrators need a strong foundation in the fundamentals of child development and early childhood education to guide the instructional practices of teachers and support staff.

1 Historical and philosophical foundations

- Knowledge of the historical roots and philosophical foundations of early childhood care and education
- Knowledge of different types of early childhood programs, roles, funding, and regulatory structures
- Knowledge of current trends and important influences impacting program quality
- Knowledge of research methodologies

2 Child growth and development

- Knowledge of different theoretical positions in child development
- Knowledge of the biological, environmental, cultural, and social influences affecting children's growth and development from prenatal through early adolescence
- Knowledge of developmental milestones in children's physical, cognitive, language, aesthetic, social, and emotional development

- Knowledge of current research in neuroscience and its application to the field of early childhood education

3 Child observation and assessment

- Knowledge and application of developmentally appropriate child observation and assessment methods
- Knowledge of the purposes, characteristics, and limitations of different assessment tools and techniques
- Ability to use different observation techniques, including formal and informal observation, behavior sampling, and developmental checklists
- Knowledge of ethical practice as it relates to the use of assessment information
- The ability to apply child observation and assessment data to planning and structuring developmentally appropriate instructional strategies

4 Curriculum and instructional methods

- Knowledge of different curriculum models; appropriate curriculum goals; and different instructional strategies for infants, toddlers, preschoolers, and kindergarten children
- Ability to plan and implement a curriculum based on knowledge of individual children's developmental patterns, family and community goals, institutional and cultural context, and state standards
- Ability to design integrated and meaningful curricular experiences in the content areas of language and literacy, mathematics, science, social studies, art, music, drama, movement, and technology
- Ability to implement antibias instructional strategies that take into account culturally valued content and children's home experiences
- Ability to evaluate outcomes of different curricular approaches

5 Children with special needs

- Knowledge of atypical development, including mild and severe disabilities in physical, health, cognitive, social-emotional, communication, and sensory functioning
- Knowledge of licensing standards as well as state and federal laws (e.g., ADA, IDEA) as they relate to services and accommodations for children with special needs

- Knowledge of the characteristics of giftedness and how educational environments can support children with exceptional capabilities
- The ability to work collaboratively as part of a family-professional team in planning and implementing appropriate services for children with special needs
- Knowledge of special education resources and services

6 Family and community relationships

- Knowledge of the diversity of family systems; traditional, nontraditional, and alternative family structures as well as family life styles; and the dynamics of family life on the development of young children
- Knowledge of sociocultural factors influencing contemporary families, including the effect of language, religion, poverty, race, technology, and the media
- Knowledge of different community resources, assistance, and support available to children and families
- Knowledge of different strategies to promote reciprocal partnerships between home and center
- Ability to communicate effectively with parents through written and oral communication
- Ability to demonstrate awareness and appreciation of different cultural and familial practices and customs
- Knowledge of child rearing patterns in other countries

7 Health, safety, and nutrition

- Knowledge and application of practices that promote good nutrition, dental health, physical health, mental health, and safety of infants-toddlers, preschool, and kindergarten children
- Ability to implement practices indoors and outdoors that help prevent, prepare for, and respond to emergencies
- Ability to model healthful lifestyle choices

8 Individual and group guidance

- Knowledge of the rationale for and research supporting different models of child guidance and classroom management

- Ability to apply different techniques that promote positive and supportive relationships with children and among children
- Ability to reflect on teaching behavior and modify guidance techniques based on the developmental and special needs of children

9 Learning environments

- Knowledge of the effect of the physical environment on children's learning and development
- The ability to use space, color, sound, texture, light, and other design elements to create indoor and outdoor learning environments that are aesthetically pleasing, intellectually stimulating, psychologically safe, and nurturing
- The ability to select age-appropriate equipment and materials that achieve curricular goals and encourage positive social interaction

10 Professionalism

- Knowledge of laws, regulations, and policies that affect professional conduct with children and families
- Knowledge of different professional organizations, resources, and issues affecting the welfare of early childhood practitioners
- Knowledge of center accreditation criteria
- Ability to make professional judgments based on the NAEYC "Code of Ethical Conduct and Statement of Commitment"
- Ability to reflect on one's professional growth and development and make goals for personal improvement
- Ability to work as part of a professional team and supervise support staff or volunteers

Source: Reprinted with permission from the National Association for the Education of Young Children (NAEYC).

APPENDIX D

NAEYC Accreditation Standards for Early Childhood Programs

STANDARD 1 – RELATIONSHIPS

Topic 1.A: Building Positive Relationships Among Teachers and Families

Topic 1.B: Building Positive Relationships Among Teachers and Children

Topic 1.C: Helping Children Make Friends

Topic 1.D: Creating a Predictable, Consistent, and Harmonious Classroom

Topic 1.E: Addressing Challenging Behaviors

Topic 1.F: Promoting Self-Regulation

STANDARD 2 – CURRICULUM

Topic 2.A: Curriculum: Essential Characteristics

Topic 2.B: Areas of Development: Social-Emotional Development

Topic 2.C: Areas of Development: Physical Development

Topic 2.D: Areas of Development: Language Development

Topic 2.E: Curriculum Content Area for Cognitive Development: Early Literacy

Topic 2.F: Curriculum Content Area for Cognitive Development: Early Mathematics

Topic 2.G: Curriculum Content Area for Cognitive Development: Science

Topic 2.H: Curriculum Content Area for Cognitive Development: Technology
To avoid confusion in the numbering system, there are no criteria labeled 2.I.

Topic 2.J: Creative Expression and Appreciation for the Arts

Topic 2.K: Curriculum Content Area for Cognitive Development: Health and Safety

Topic 2.L: Curriculum Content Area for Cognitive Development: Social Studies

STANDARD 3 – TEACHING

Topic 3.A: Designing Enriched Learning Environments

Topic 3.B: Creating Caring Communities for Learning

Topic 3.C: Supervising Children

Topic 3.D: Using Time, Grouping, and Routine to Achieve Learning Goals

Topic 3.E: Responding to Children's Interests and Needs

Topic 3.F: Making Learning Meaningful for All Children

Topic 3.G: Using Instruction to Deepen Children's Understanding and Build Their Skills and Knowledge

STANDARD 4 – ASSESSMENT

Topic 4.A: Creating an Assessment Plan

Topic 4.B: Using Appropriate Assessment Methods

Topic 4.C: Identifying Children's Interests and Needs and Describing Children's Progress

Topic 4.D: Adapting Curriculum, Individualizing Teaching, and Informing Program Development

Topic 4.E: Communicating with Families and Involving Families in the Assessment Process

STANDARD 5 – HEALTH

Topic 5.A: Promoting and Protecting Children's Health and Controlling Infectious Disease

Topic 5.B: Ensuring Children's Nutritional Well-being

Topic 5.C: Maintaining a Healthful Environment

STANDARD 6 – TEACHERS

Topic 6.A: Preparation, Knowledge, and Skills of Teaching Staff

Topic 6.B: Teachers' Dispositions and Professional Commitment

STANDARD 7 – FAMILIES

Topic 7.A: Knowing and Understanding the Program's Families

Topic 7.B: Sharing Information between Staff and Families

Topic 7.C: Nurturing Families as Advocates for Their Children

STANDARD 8 – COMMUNITY RELATIONSHIPS

Topic 8.A: Linking with the Community

Topic 8.B: Accessing Community Resources

Topic 8.C: Acting as a Citizen in the Neighborhood and the Early Childhood Community

STANDARD 9 – PHYSICAL ENVIRONMENT

Topic 9.A: Indoor and Outdoor Equipment, Materials, and Furnishings

Topic 9.B: Outdoor Environment Design

Topic 9.C: Building and Physical Design

Topic 9.D: Environment Health

STANDARD 10 – LEADERSHIP AND MANAGEMENT

Topic 10.A: Leadership Topic

Topic 10.B: Management Policies and Procedures

Topic 10.C: Fiscal Accountability Policies and Procedures

Topic 10.D: Health, Nutrition, and Safety Policies and Procedures

Topic 10.E: Personnel Policies

Topic 10.F: Program Evaluation, Accountability, and Continuous Improvement

Source: Reprinted with permission from the National Association for the Education of Young Children (NAEYC).

Sources of Early Childhood Materials, Equipment, and Supplies

Achievement Products for Special Needs
P.O. Box 6013
Carol Stream, IL 60197-6013
(800) 373-4599
http://www.achievement-products.com

African American Images
P.O. Box 1799
Sauk Village, IL 60412
(800) 552-1991
http://www.africanamericanimages.com

Albert Whitman & Company
250 South Northwest Highway, Suite 320
Park Ridge, IL 60068
(800) 255-7675
http://www.albertwhitman.com

Angeles Corporation
9 Capper Drive
Daily Industrial Park
Pacific, MO 63069
(800) 346-6313
http://www.angelesstore.com

Becker's School Supplies
1500 Melrose Highway
Pennsauken, NJ 08110-1410
(800) 523-1490
http://www.shopbecker.com

Broderbund Software
Navarre Corporation
7400 49th Avenue North
Minneapolis, MN 55428
Broderbund Ordering:
(800) 395-0277
http://www.broderbund.com

Busy Kids LLC
937 139th Avenue NW
Andover, MN 55304-4124
(763) 757-4124
http://busy-kids.com

Candlewick Press
99 Dover Street
Somerville, MA 02144
(617) 661-3330
http://www.candlewick.com

Cengage Learning, Inc.
P.O. Box 6904
Florence, KY 41022-6905
(800) 487-8488
http://www.cengage.com/delmar

Child Care Manager
Personalized Software
118 S. Main St.
Phoenix, OR 97535-0359
(800) 553-2312
http://www.childcaremanager.com

Childforms
Charleston Drive, Suite 106
Mooresville, NC 28117
(800) 447-3349
http://www.childforms.com

Child Plus Software
Two Ravinia Drive
Suite 1300
Atlanta, GA 30346
(800) 888-6674
http://www.childplus.com

Clarion Books
Houghton Mifflin Harcourt
215 Park Avenue South
New York, NY 10003
(212) 420-5800
http://www.houghtonmifflinbooks.com/clarion

Community Playthings
2032 Route 213
Rifton, NY 12471
845-572-3410
http://www.communityplaythings.com

Custom Recreation
2190 North Cullen Avenue
Evansville, IN 47715
(888) 987-4477
http://www.customrecreation.com

Dick Blick Art Materials
P.O. Box 1267
Galesburg, IL 61402-1267
(800) 723-2787
http://www.dickblick.com

Didax Educational Resources Inc.
395 Main Street
Rowley, MA 01969
(800) 458-0024
http://www.didax.com

Discount School Supply
P.O. Box 6013
Carol Stream, IL 60197-6013
(800) 627-2829
http://www.discountschoolsupply.com

The Discovery Channel
One Discovery Place
Silver Spring, MD 20910
(240) 662-2000
http://www.discovery.com

Don Johnston Inc.
26799 West Commerce Drive
Volo, IL 60073
(800) 999-4660
http://www.donjohnston.com

Environments Inc.
P.O. Box 1348
Beaufort, SC 29901-1348
(800) 342-4453
http://www.eichild.com

Flagship Carpets
1546 Progress Road
P.O. Box 507
Ellijay, GA 30540
(800) 848-4055
http://www.flagshipcarpets.com

John R. Green
411 West 6th Street
Covington, KY 41011
(800) 354-9737
http://www.johnrgreenco.com

Growing Tree Toys
202 South Allen Street
State College, PA 16801
(800) 372-9982
http://www.growingtreetoys.com

Gryphon House Inc.
10770 Columbia Pike
Suite 201
Silver Spring, MD 20901
(800) 638-0928
http://www.gryphonhouse.com

Hachette Book Group
3 Center Plaza
Boston, MA 02108
(800) 759-0190
http://www.hachettebookgroup.com

HarperCollins Children's Books
10 East 53rd Street
New York, NY 10022
(800) 207-7000
http://www.harpercollinschildrens.com

Houghton Mifflin Harcourt Publishers
School Division
9205 SouthPark Center Loop
Orlando, FL 32819
(800) 225-5425
http://www.hmhco.com

Insect Lore
Box 1535
Shafter, CA 93263
(800) 548-3284
http://www.insectlore.com

International Playthings Inc.
75D Lackawanna Avenue
Parsippany, NJ 07054
(800) 445-8347
http://www.intplay.com

Johnson & Johnson Consumer Products Inc.
Johnson & Johnson Place
New Brunswick, NJ 08933
(800) 526-3967
http://www.jnj.com

Jonti-Craft Inc.
P.O. Box 30
171 Highway 68
Wabasso, MN 56293
(800) 543-4149
http://www.jonti-craft.com

Kaplan Early Learning Company
1310 Lewisville-Clemmons Road
Lewisville, NC 27023
(800) 334-2014
http://www.kaplanco.com

Lakeshore Learning Materials
2695 East Dominguez Street
P.O. Box 6261
Carson, CA 90895
(800) 778-4456
http://www.lakeshorelearning.com

Landscape Structures Inc.
601 7th Street South
P.O. Box 198
Delano, MN 55328-0198
(800) 438-6574
http://www.playlsi.com

Learning Resources Inc.
380 North Fairway Drive
Vernon Hills, IL 60061
(800) 333-8281
http://www.learningresources.com

Learning Station
165 Pilgrim Way
Fayetteville, GA 30214
(866) 532-7697
http://www.learningstationonline.com

Lego Education
P.O. Box 1707
Pittsburg, KS 66762-1707
(800) 362-4308
http://www.legoeducation.com

The Little Tikes Co.
2180 Barlow Road
Hudson, OH 44236-9984
(800) 748-2204
http://www.littletikes.com

Music for Little People
P.O. Box 1460
Redway, CA 95560-1460
(800) 409-2457
http://www.musicforlittlepeople.com

Music Together LLC
66 Witherspoon Street
Princeton, NJ 05842
(800) 728-2692
http://www.musictogether.com

Penguin USA
375 Hudson Street
New York, NY 10014-3657
(212) 366-2000
http://www.penguingroup.com

Playtime Equipment and School Supply Inc.
5310 North 99th Street, Suite 2
Omaha, NE 68134
(402) 571-1717
http://www.playtimeschoolsupply.com

Procare Software
3581 Excel Drive
Medford, OR 97504
(800) 338-3884
http://www.procaresoftware.com

Private Advantage
Child Care Management Software
Mt. Taylor Programs
716 College Avenue, Suite B
Santa Rosa, CA 95404
(800) 238-7015
http://www.privateadv.com

PRO-ED Inc.
8700 Shoal Creek Boulevard
Austin, TX 78757
(800) 897-3202
http://www.proedinc.com

Redleaf Press
10 Yorkton Court
St. Paul, MN 55117
(800) 423-8309
http://www.redleafpress.org

Rhythm Band Instruments Inc.
P.O. Box 126
Fort Worth, TX 76101
(800) 424-4724
http://www.rhythmband.com

S+S Worldwide
75 Mill Street
Colchester, CT 06415
(800) 288-9941
http://www.ssww.com

Scholastic, Inc.
557 Broadway
New York, NY 10012
(800) 724-6527
http://www.scholastic.com

School Specialty
W6316 Design Drive
Greenville, WI 54942
(888)388-3224
http://www.schoolspecialty.com

Seedlings Braille Books for Children
P.O. Box 51924
Livonia, MI 48151-5924
(800) 777-8552
http://www.seedlings.org

SofterWare Inc.
132 Welsh Road
Horsham, PA 19044
(215) 628-0400
(800) 220-4111
http://www.softerware.com

Sunburst Technology
1550 Executive Drive
Elgin, IL 60123-9979
(800) 321-7511
http://www.sunburst.com

Teachers College Press
P.O. Box 20
Williston, VT 05495
(800) 575-6566
http://www.teacherscollegepress.com

Terrapin Software
955 Massachusetts Avenue #365
Cambridge, MA 02139-3233
(800) 774-LOGO
http://www.terrapinlogo.com

Tom Snyder Productions
100 Talcott Avenue
Watertown, MA 02472- 5703
(800) 342-0236
http://www.tomsnyder.com

Toys to Grow On/Lakeshore Learning Materials
2695 East Dominguez Street
Carson, CA 90895
(800) 987-4454
http://www.ttgo.com

Tree Blocks
1187 Coast Village Road, #112
Santa Barbara, CA 93108
(800) 873-4960
http://www.treeblocks.com

Triarco Arts & Crafts
2600 Fernbrook Lane, Suite 100
Plymouth, MN 55447
(800) 328-3360
http://www.triarcoarts.com

Turn the Page Press Inc.
900 Church Street
Roseville, CA 95678
(800) 959-5549
http://www.turnthepage.com

U.S. Toy Company/Constructive Playthings
13201 Arrington Road
Grandview, MO 64030-1117
(800) 832-0224
http://www.ustoy.com

APPENDIX F

Early Childhood Professional Organizations and Information Sources

Administration for Children and Families
370 L'Enfant Promenade, SW
Washington, DC 20447
(202) 401-5324
http://www.acf.hhs.gov

Administration for Children, Youth and Families
Office of Head Start
8th Floor Portals Building
Washington, DC 20024
(866) 763-6481
http://www.acf.hhs.gov/programs/ohs

American Academy of Pediatrics
141 Northwest Point Boulevard
Elk Grove Village, IL 60007-0927
(847) 434-4000
http://www.aap.org

American Association for Gifted Children at Duke University
Box 90539
Durham, NC 27708-0539
(919) 783-6152
http://www.aagc.org

American Association of Families and Consumer Sciences
400 North Columbus Street, Suite 202
Alexandria, VA 22314
(703) 706-4600
http://www.aafcs.org

American Association of School Administrators
801 North Quincy Street, Suite 700
Arlington, VA 22203
(703) 528-0700
http://www.aasa.org

American Council on Education (ACE)
One Dupont Circle, NW, Suite 800
Washington, DC 20036
(202) 939-9300
http://www.acenet.edu

American Educational Research Association (AERA)
1430 K Street, NW
Washington, DC 20005
(202) 238-3200
http://www.aera.net

American Federation of Teachers (AFT)
555 New Jersey Avenue, NW
Washington, DC 20001
(202) 879-4400
http://www.aft.org

American Medical Association
515 North State Street
Chicago, IL 60654
(800) 621-8335
http://www.ama-assn.org

American Montessori Society (AMS)
281 Park Avenue South
New York, NY 10010
(212) 358-1250
http://www.amshq.org

American Speech-Language-Hearing Association
2200 Research Boulevard
Rockville, MD 20850-3289
(301) 296-5700
http://www.asha.org

The Annie E. Casey Foundation
701 Saint Paul Street
Baltimore, MD 21202
(410) 547-6600
http://www.aecf.org

Appalachian Regional Commission
1666 Connecticut Avenue, NW, Suite 700
Washington, DC 20009-1068
(202) 884-7700
http://www.arc.gov

Association for Childhood Education International (ACEI)
17904 Georgia Avenue, Suite 215
Olney, MD 20832
(800) 423-3563
http://www.acei.org

Association for Library Service to Children-American Library Association
50 E. Huron
Chicago, IL 60611
(800) 545-2433
http://www.ala.org/ala/mgrps/divs/alsc/index.cfm

Association for Supervision and Curriculum Development (ASCD)
1703 North Beauregard Street
Alexandria, VA 22311
(800) 933-2723
http://www.ascd.org

Association Montessori Internationale, USA
410 Alexander Street
Rochester, NY 14607
(800) 872-2643
http://www.montessori-ami.org

California Child Care Resource and Referral Agency
111 New Montgomery
San Francisco, CA 94105
(415) 882-0234
http://www.rrnetwork.org

Center for Child Care Workforce
555 New Jersey Avenue, NW
Washington, DC 20001
(202) 662-8005
http://www.ccw.org

Center for Nutrition Policy and Promotion
3101 Park Center Drive
Alexandria, VA 23202-1594
(703) 305-7600
http://www.cnpp.usda.gov

Centers for Disease Control and Prevention
1600 Clifton Road N.E.
Atlanta, GA 30333
(800) 232-4636
http://www.cdc.gov

Child Care Bureau
U.S. Department of Health and Human Services
Administration for Children and Families
Office of Family Assistance
370 L'Enfant Promenade, S.W.
5th Floor East
Washington, DC 20447
Phone Number: (202) 690-6782
http://www.acf.hhs.gov/programs/ccb/

Child Care Education Institute
3059 Peachtree Industrial Boulevard, NW, Suite 100
Duluth, GA 30097
(888) 418-5358
http://www.cceionline.com

Child Care Information Exchange
P.O. Box 3249
Redmond, WA 98073-2890
(800) 221-2864
http://www.ccie.com

Child Care in Health Care
c/o Rose Oliphant
2451 Blairs Landing Road
Uncertain, TX 75661
(903) 679-4166
http://www.childcareinhealthcare.org

Child Care Law Center
221 Pine Street, 3rd Floor
San Francisco, CA 94104
(415) 394-7144
http://www.childcarelaw.org

Child Care Services Association
1829 East Franklin Street, Building 1000
P.O. Box 901
Chapel Hill, NC 27514
(919) 967-3272
http://www.childcareservices.org

Child Trauma Academy
5161 San Felipe, Suite 320
Houston, TX 77056
(866) 943-9779
http://www.childtrauma.org

Children's Book Council Inc.
12 West 37th Street, 2nd Floor
New York, NY 10018-7480
(212) 966-1990
http://www.cbcbooks.org

Children's Defense Fund
25 E Street, NW
Washington, DC 20001
(800) 233-1200
http://www.childrensdefense.org

Children's Foundation
P.O. Box 1443
Loveland, CO 80539-1443
(888) 934-3733
http://www.childrensfoundationinc.com

Child Welfare League of America (CWLA)
2345 Crystal Drive, Suite 250
Arlington, VA 22202
(703) 412-2400
http://www.cwla.org

Community Development Institute-Head Start
10065 E. Harvard Avenue, Suite 700
Denver, CO 80231
(877) 789-4900
http://www.cdiheadstart.org

Council for Early Childhood Professional Recognition (CDA)
2640 16th Street, NW
Washington, DC 20009-3547
(800) 424-4310
(202) 265-9090
http://www.cdacouncil.org

Council for Exceptional Children (CEC)
1110 North Glebe Road, Suite 300
Arlington, VA 22201-5704
(888) CEC-SPED
http://www.cec.sped.org

Council for Indian Education
1240 Burlington Avenue
Billings, MT 59102
(406) 248-3465
http://www.cie-mt.org

Council of Chief State School Officers
One Massachusetts Avenue, NW, Suite 700
Washington, DC 20001-1431
(202) 336-7000
http://www.ccsso.org

Division for Early Childhood—Council for Exceptional Children
27 Fort Missoula Road, Suite 2
Missoula, MT 59804
(406) 543-0872
http://www.dec-sped.org

Early Childhood Leadership Program
Bank Street College of Education
610 West 112th Street
New York, NY 10025
(212) 875-4400
http://www.bnkst.edu/graduate-school/academics/
programs/leadership-programs-overview/early-
childhood-leadership/

Education Development Center (EDC)
55 Chapel Street
Newton, MA 02458
(617) 969-7100
http://www.edc.org

Eric Project c/o Computer Science Corp.
655 15th Street, NW, Suite 500
Washington, DC 20005
(800) LET-ERIC
http://www.eric.ed.gov

Families and Work Institute
267 Fifth Avenue, 2nd Floor
New York, NY 10006
(212) 465-2044
http://www.familiesandwork.org

The Feminist Press at the Graduate Center, CUNY
365 Fifth Avenue, Suite 5406
New York, NY 10016
(212) 817-7920
http://www.feministpress.org

Forum for Early Childhood Organization and Leadership Development
Midwest Center for Nonprofit Leadership
University of Missouri - Kansas City
Bloch School Room 310
5100 Rockhill Road
Kansas City, Missouri 64110
(816) 235-2305
http://www.bloch.umkc.edu/mwcnl/Forum/forum.htm

The Foundation Center
79 Fifth Avenue/16th Street
New York, NY 10003-3076
(212) 620-4230
http://foundationcenter.org

Foundation for Child Development
295 Madison Avenue, 40th Floor
New York, NY 10017
(212) 867-5777
http://www.fcd-us.org

Head Start-Johnson & Johnson Management Fellows Program
UCLA Anderson School of Management
110 Westwood Plaza, Suite B307
Los Angeles, CA 90095-1481
(310) 825-6306
http://www.anderson.ucla.edu/x320.xml

Head Start State Collaborative Project Center for Schools and Communities
275 Grandview Avenue, Suite 200
Camp Hill, PA 17011
(717) 763-1661
http://www.center-school.org

High/Scope Educational Research Foundation
600 North River Street
Ypsilanti, MI 48198-2898
(734) 485-2000
http://www.highscope.org

International Child Resource Institute
1581 Leroy Avenue
Berkeley, CA 94708
(510) 644-1000
http://www.icrichild.org

International Reading Association
800 Barksdale Rd.
P.O. Box 8139
Newark, DE 19714-8139
(800) 336-7323
http://www.reading.org

Kids and the Power of Work
1501 Broadway
New York, NY 10036
(212) 840-1801
http://www.kapow.org

McCormick Center for Early Childhood Leadership
National-Louis University
6310 Capitol Drive
Wheeling, IL 60090-7201
(800) 443-5522
http://www.cecl.nl.edu

National AfterSchool Association
8400 Westpark Drive, Suite 200
McLean, VA 22102
(730) 610-9028
http://www.naaweb.org/

National Association for Bilingual Education
1313 L Street, NW
Washington, DC 20005
(202) 898-1829
http://www.nabe.org

National Association for Family Child Care
1743 W. Alexander Street
Salt Lake City, Utah 84119
(800) 359-3817
http://www.nafcc.net

National Association for Gifted Children
1707 L Street, NW, Suite 550
Washington, DC 20036
(202) 785-4268
http://www.nagc.org

National Association for Sick Child Daycare
1716 5th Avenue North
Birmingham, AL 35203
(205) 324-8447
http://www.nascd.com

National Association for the Education of Young Children (NAEYC)
1313 L Street, NW, Suite 500
Washington, DC 20005
(202) 232-8777
(800) 424-2460
http://www.naeyc.org

National Association for the Education of Young Children
Accreditation of Programs for Young Children
1313 L Street, NW, Suite 500
Washington, DC 20005
(800) 424-2460
http://www.naeyc.org/academy

National Association of Child Care Professionals (NACCP)
National Accreditation Commission for Early Care and Education Programs
P.O. Box 90723
Austin, TX 78709
(800) 537-1118
http://www.naccp.org

National Association of Child Care Resource and Referral Agencies (NACCRRA)
1515 North Courthouse Road, 11th Floor
Arlington, VA 22201
(703) 341-4100
http://www.naccrra.org

National Association of Elementary School Principals
1615 Duke Street
Alexandria, VA 22314-3483
(703) 684-3345
(800) 386-2377
http://www.naesp.org

National Association of State Boards of Education
2121 Crystal Drive, Suite 350
Arlington, VA 22202
(703) 684-4000
http://www.nasbe.org

National Association of State Directors of Special Education (NASDSE)
1800 Diagonal Road, Suite 320
Alexandria, VA 22314
(703) 519-3800
http://www.nasdse.org

National Black Child Development Institute (NBCDI)
1313 L Street, NW, Suite 110
Washington, DC 20005-5110
(202) 833-2220
http://www.nbcdi.org

National Board for Professional Teaching Standards
1525 Wilson Blvd., Ste 500
Arlington, VA 22209
(800) 228-3224
http://www.nbpts.org

National Center for Children in Poverty
215 West 125th Street, 3rd Floor
New York, NY 10027
(646) 284-9600
http://www.nccp.org

National Center for Education in Maternal and Child Health
Georgetown University
Box 571272
Washington, DC 20057-1272
(202) 784-9770
http://www.ncemch.org

National Child Care Association (NCCA)
1325 G Street NW, Suite 500
Washington, DC 20004
(800) 543-7161
http://www.nccanet.org

National Child Care Information and Technical Assistance Center (NCCIC)
9300 Lee Highway
Fairfax, VA 22031-6050
(800) 616-2242
http://nccic.acf.hhs.gov

National Coalition for Campus Children's Centers
950 Glenn Drive, Suite 150
Folsom, CA 95630
(877) 736-6222
http://campuschildren.org

National Early Childhood Program Accreditation (NECPA)
c/o NECPA Commission Inc.
1150 Hungryneck Boulevard, Suite C305
Mount Pleasant, SC 29464
(800) 505-9878
http://www.necpa.net

National Early Childhood Technical Assistance Center
Campus Box 8040, UNC-CH
Chapel Hill, NC 27599-8040
(919) 962-2001
http://www.nectac.org

National Education Association (NEA)
1201 16th Street, NW
Washington, DC 20036
(202) 833-4000
http://www.nea.org

National Food Service Management Institute (NFSMI)
The University of Mississippi
6 Jeanette Phillips Drive
P.O. Drawer 188
University, MS 38677-0188
(622) 915-7658
http://www.nfsmi.org

National Head Start Association
1651 Prince Street
Alexandria, VA 22314
(703) 739-0875
http://www.nhsa.org

National Institute of Child Health and Human Development (NICHD)
Bldg 31, Room 2A32, MSC 2425
31 Center Drive
Bethesda, MD 20892-2425
(800) 370-2943
http://www.nichd.nih.gov

National Institute on Out-of-School Time
Wellesley Centers for Women, Wellesley College
106 Central Street Wellesley, MA 02481
(781) 283-2547
http://www.niost.org

National Latino Children's Institute
118 Broadway St, Suite 615
San Antonio, Texas 78205
(210) 228-9997
http://www.nlci.org

National League of Cities
1301 Pennsylvania Avenue, NW, Suite 550
Washington, DC 20004
(202) 626-3000
http://www.nlc.org

National Parent Teacher Association
541 North Fairbanks, Suite 1300
Chicago, IL 60611-3396
(312) 670-6782
http://www.pta.org

National Resource Center for Health and Safety in Child Care and Early Education
UCD-CON Campus Mail Stop F541
Education 2 North
13120 E. 19th Ave.
PO Box 6511
Aurora, CO 80045
(800) 598-KIDS (5437)
http://nrckids.org

National Women's Law Center
11 Dupont Circle, NW, Suite 800
Washington, DC 20036
(202) 588-5180
http://www.nwlc.org

North American Montessori Teachers Association (NAMTA)
13693 Butternut Road
Burton, OH 44021
(404) 834-4011
http://www.montessori-namta.org

Office of Minority Health
U.S. Department of Health and Human Services
The Tower Building
1101 Wootton Parkway, Suite 600
Rockville, MD 20852
(800) 444-6472
http://minorityhealth.hhs.gov

Office of Special Education Programs (OSEP)
Office of Special Education and Rehabilitation Services (OSERS)
U.S. Department of Education
400 Maryland Avenue, SW
Washington, DC 20202-7100
(202) 245-7459
http://www2.ed.gov/about/offices/list/osers/osep/index.html

Opportunity Finance Network
Public Ledger Building
620 Chestnut Street, Suite 572
Philadelphia, PA 19106
(215) 923-4754
http://www.opportunityfinance.net

Parent Cooperative Preschools International (PCPI)
National Cooperative Business Center
1401 New York Avenue, NW, Suite 1100
Washington, DC 20005
(800) 636-6222
http://www.preschools.coop

Puerto Rican Association for Hispanic Affairs
P.O. Box 8824
Port St. Lucie, FL 34985
(772) 621-6841
http://www.prafha.org

Save the Children Federation
54 Wilton Road
Westport, CT 06880
(800) 728-3843
http://www.savethechildren.org

Society for Research in Child Development (SRCD)
2950 St. State Street, Suite 401
Ann Arbor, MI 48104
(734) 926-0600
http://www.srcd.org

Southern Early Childhood Association (SECA)
P.O. Box 55930
Little Rock, AR 72215-5930
(800) 305-7322
http://www.southernearlychildhood.org

Southern Institute on Children and Families
P.O. Box 786
Lexington, SC 29071
(803) 779-2607
http://www.thesoutherninstitute.org

United Way of America
701 North Fairfax Street
Alexandria, VA 22314
(703) 836-7112
http://www.unitedway.org

U.S. Consumer Product Safety Commission
4330 East West Highway
Bethesda, MD 20814
(301) 504-7923
(800) 638-CPSC
http://www.cpsc.gov

U.S. Department of Agriculture
1400 Independence Avenue, SW
Washington, DC 20250
(202) 720-2791
http://www.usda.gov

USDA Food and Nutrition Service
3101 Park Center Drive, Room 926
Alexandria, VA 22302
(703) 305-2276
http://www.usda.gov

U.S. Department of Education
400 Maryland Avenue, SW
Washington, DC 20202
(800) USA–LEARN
http://www.ed.gov

U.S. National Committee of OMEP
World Organisation for Early Childhood Education
1314 G Street, NW
Washington, DC 20005-3105
(800) 424-4310
http://www.omep.org.gu.se/

Work/Family Directions Inc.
55 Chapel Street
Newton, MA 02458
(800) 447-0543
http://www.wfd.com

Zero to Three National Center for Infants, Toddlers and Families
2000 M Street, NW, Suite 200
Washington, DC 20036
(202) 638-1144
http://www.zerotothree.org

Early Childhood Periodicals and Media

PERIODICALS

Beginnings Exchange Press Inc.
P.O. Box 3249
Redmond, WA 98073-3249
(800) 221-2864
http://www.ccie.com
(Published as part of *Child Care Information Exchange*)

CDF Monthly eNewsletter
Children's Defense Fund
25 E Street, NW
Washington, DC 20001
(800) 233-CDF-1200
http://www.childrensdefense.org

Child Care Information Exchange
P.O. Box 3249
Redmond, WA 98073-2890
(800) 221-2864
http://www.ccie.com

Child Development
Society for Research in Child Development
Published by Wiley-Blackwell
http://www.wiley.com/bw/journal.asp?ref=
0009-3920

Childhood Education
Association of Childhood Education International
17904 Georgia Avenue, Suite 215
Olney, MD 20832
(800) 423-3563
http://www.acei.org/childhood-education

Children and Families
National Head Start Association
1651 Prince Street
Alexandria, VA 22314
(703) 793-0875
http://www.nhsa.org

Children Now
1212 Broadway, 5th Floor
Oakland, CA 94612
(510) 763-2444
http://www.childrennow.org

Children's Voice Online
Child Welfare League of America
2345 Crystal Drive
Arlington, VA 22202
(703) 412-2400
http://www.cwla.org/voice/default.htm

Dimensions of Early Childhood
Southern Early Childhood Association
PO Box 55930
Little Rock, AR 72215-5930
http://www.southernearlychildhood.org/
publications.php

Early Childhood Education Journal
Published by Springer
233 Spring Street
New York, NY 10013
(800) SPRINGER
http://www.springer.com/education+%26+
language/learning+%26+instruction/journal/
10643

Early Childhood Research Quarterly
Elsevier Publishing
360 Park Avenue South
New York, NY 10010-1710
(212) 633-3730
http://www.elsevier.com

Early Developments
Frank Porter Graham Child Development
Institute
University of North Carolina at Chapel Hill
CB 8180
Chapel Hill, NC 27599
http://www.fpg.unc.edu/products/
ed_products.cfm

Education Week
Editorial Projects in Education Inc.
Education Week
P.O. Box 3005
Langhorne, PA 19047-9105
(800) 445-8250
http://www.edweek.org/ew/index.html?intc=thed

Eric Project
c/o Computer Science Corporation
655 15th Street, NW, Suite 500
Washington, DC 20005
(800) LET–ERIC
http://www.eric.ed.gov

Exceptional Children
Council for Exceptional Children
1110 North Glebe Road, Suite 300
Arlington, VA 22201-5704
(888) 232-7733
http://www.cec.sped.org

Growing Child
P.O. Box 2505
Lafayette, IN 47996
(800) 927-7289
http://www.growingchild.com

InfoWorld
501 Second Street
San Francisco, CA 94107
(415) 572-7341
http://www.infoworld.com

Journal of Research in Childhood Education
Association of Childhood Education International
Published by Taylor & Francis
http://www.tandf.co.uk/journals/UJRC

MacWorld
501 2nd Street, 5th Floor
San Francisco, CA 94107
http://www.macworld.com

PC Magazine
Ziff-Davis Media Inc.
28 East 28th Street
New York, NY 10016
http://www.pcmag.com

PC World
PCW Communications Inc.
501 2nd Street, Suite 600
San Francisco, CA 94107
(415) 243-0500
http://www.pcworld.com

Reading Today and Reading Teacher
International Reading Association Inc.
800 Barksdale Road, Box 8139
Newark, DE 19714
(800) 336-7323
http://www.reading.org

Report on Preschool Programs
Business Publishers, Inc.
P.O. Box 17592
Baltimore, MD 21297
(800) 874-9180
http://www.bpinews.com/spec_rpp.htm

ReSource
High-Scope Educational Research Foundation
600 North River Street
Ypsilanti, MI 48198-2898
(734) 485-2000
http://www.highscope.org

SchoolAge Notes
P.O. Box 476
New Albany, OH 43054
(800) 410-8780
http://www.schoolagenotes.com

Teaching Pre K–8: The Magazine for Professional Development
40 Richards Avenue
Norwalk, CT 06854
(800) 249-9363
http://www.teachingk-8.com

Teaching Young Children
National Association for the Education of Young Children
1313 L Street, NW, Suite 500
Washington, DC 20005
(800) 424-2460
http://www.naeyc.org/tyc

Texas Child Care Quarterly
P.O. Box 162881
Austin, TX 78716
(512) 441-6633
http://www.childcarequarterly.com

Young Children
National Association for the Education of Young Children
1313 L Street, NW, Suite 500
Washington, DC 20005
(800) 424-2460
http://www.naeyc.org/yc/

Young Exceptional Children
Division for Early Childhood/Council for
Exceptional Children
27 Fort Missoula Road, Suite 2
Missoula, MT 59804
(406) 543-0872
http://www.dec-sped.org

Zero to Three
Zero to Three—National Center for Infants,
Toddlers and Families
2000 M Street, NW
Washington, DC 20036
(202) 638-1144
(800) 899-4301 (publications only)
http://www.zerotothree.org

MEDIA

Child Development Media, Inc.
5632 Van Nuys Boulevard, Suite 286
Van Nuys, CA 91401
(800) 405-8942
http://www.childdevelopmentmedia.com

Child Trauma Academy
5161 San Felipe, Suite 320
Houston, TX 77056
(281) 816-5604
http://childtrauma.org
The Child Trauma Academy is a nonprofit
research, service, and education collaborative
addressing the needs of children who have experienced or who are at-risk for maltreatment. They
make available both print and visual media, including many free resources, related to this issue.

CRM Learning
2218 Faraday Avenue, Suite 110
Carlsbad, CA 92008
(800) 421-0833
http://www.crmlearning.com
Videos related to communication and forming
positive interpersonal relationships.

Davidson Films Inc.
735 Tank Farm Road, Suite 210
San Luis Obispo, CA 93401
(888) 437-4200
http://www.davidsonfilms.com
Davidson Films supplies videos and DVDs featur-
ing many of the most well-known thinkers
who have influenced early childhood education.
Its "Giants" series includes Piaget, Elkind,
Montessori, Ainsworth, and Bandura.

**National Association for the Education of
Young Children**
1313 L Street, NW, Suite 500
Washington, DC 20005
(800) 424-2460
http://www.naeyc.org
NAEYC offers many videos, some in DVD format, that address nearly every aspect of early
childhood education including curriculum, developmentally appropriate practice, diversity, literacy, children with disabilities, play, and child
development.

Special Needs Project
324 State Street, Suite H
Santa Barbara, CA 93101
(800) 333-6867
http://www.specialneeds.com
The Special Needs Project provides videos,
DVDs, and books related to individuals with disabilities and inclusion.

Teachers College Press
P.O. Box 20
Williston, VT 05495
(800) 575-6566
http://www.teacherscollegepress.com/index.html

Appendix H

Director's Library

ADVOCACY

Children's Defense Fund. (n.d.). *Take action.* Available online at http://www.childrensdefense.org/take-action/.

> This webpage provides links to various resources that can inform advocacy efforts on behalf of young children and their families.

Kieff, J. (2009). *Informed advocacy in early childhood care and education: Making a difference for young children and families.* Upper Saddle River, NJ: Pearson/Merrill.

> This guide discusses the need for advocacy in early childhood and presents information on how to develop an advocacy plan. Six contexts for conducting advocacy are identified: individual child and family, the profession, program-based, the private sector, and the political and global arenas.

NAEYC. (2010). *Position statement on a call for vigilance and action by all policymakers on behalf of children and families.* Available online at http://www.naeyc.org/positionstatements/vigilance.

> This document presents NAEYC's position regarding the need to be mindful of the impact that legislation, laws, and regulations may have on young children's learning and development.

Robinson, A. & Stark, D. R. (2005). *Advocates in action: Making a difference for young children* (rev. ed.). Washington, DC: NAEYC.

> This book provides specific strategies for making change on behalf of young children and families. Included is information on the legislative process as well as examples of advocacy efforts throughout the country.

Washington, V. & Andrews, J. D. (Eds.). (2010). *Children of 2020: Creating a better tomorrow.* Washington, DC: Council for Professional Recognition.

> This book challenges readers to advance the field of early care and education through "smart improvisation." National leaders present analyses of progress as well as issues that must be addressed in the future. Discussion questions are provided that encourage discussion and taking action.

CHILD DEVELOPMENT

Charlesworth, R. (2011). *Understanding child development* (8th ed.). Clifton Park, NY: Delmar CengageLearning.

> This book introduces the reader to the unique qualities of the young child as distinguished from older children and demonstrates how to work with young children in ways that match their developmental level. The author also includes critical social and emotional factors that relate to and have an effect on development.

Puckett, M. B. & Black, J. K. (2008). *The young child: Development from prebirth through age eight* (5th ed.). Upper Saddle River, NJ: Pearson/Prentice Hall.

> A comprehensive coverage of child development written at a level appropriate for CDA programs and beyond.

CHILDREN WITH DISABILITIES

Allen, K. E. & Cowdery, G. E. (2012). *The exceptional child: Inclusion in early childhood education* (7th ed.). Clifton Park, NY: Thomson Delmar Learning.

> This text on inclusion in the early childhood environment emphasizes the fact that teachers of children with disabilities must have a thorough knowledge of typical growth and development. When teachers see developmental variations, they are able to judge where and how to work with each child and identify when there is a need for clinical evaluations and referrals. This book offers a comprehensive overview of early intervention and public policy, types and causes of developmental disabilities, working with parents, and "how to" strategies for classroom teachers.

Catlett, C., Winton, P. J. & Hamel, S. E. (2004). *Resource guide: Selected early childhood/early intervention training materials* (12th ed.). Chapel Hill, NC: The University of North Carolina, Frank Porter Graham Child Development Institute. Available online at http://www.fpg.unc.edu/~scpp/pdfs/rguide.pdf.

> This extremely helpful guide identifies more than 600 resources, including media and books related to nearly every aspect of teaching young children with disabilities. The guide is updated regularly and provides contact and ordering information.

Child Care Law Center. (2009). *ADA and out-of-school providers.* Available online at http://www.childcarelaw. org/pubs-audience.shtml.

Child Care Law Center. (2009). *Questions & answers about the Americans with Disabilities Act: A quick reference for child care providers.* Available online at http://www.childcarelaw.org/pubs-audience.shtml.

These updated documents provide an excellent overview of the requirements of the Americans with Disabilities Act. Written in question-and-answer format, information specific to child care providers is presented.

Council for Exceptional Children. (2005). *Universal design for learning: A guide for teachers and education professionals.* Upper Saddle River, NJ: Pearson/Merrill Prentice Hall.

This concise text offers education professionals a conceptual framework to create flexible, equitable, and accessible instructional techniques that accommodate individual learning differences in a classroom setting.

Deiner, P. L. (2010). *Inclusive early childhood education: Development, resources, and practice* (5th ed.). Clifton Park, NY: Cengage Delmar Learning.

This comprehensive resource contains information related to working with children with diverse abilities. It can be used as a reference book, but it also contains guidelines, vignettes and hands-on program planning ideas to prepare educators to successfully integrate *all* children into the early childhood program. Particularly useful for inexperienced teachers is the information related to translating IFSP/IEP goals into day-to-day classroom programming.

Division for Early Childhood/Council for Exceptional Children. *Young exceptional children monograph series.* Longmont, CO: Sopris West.

This series of monographs provides collections of articles on all aspects of educating children with disabilities. Topics include challenging behavior, natural environments, teaching strategies, assessment, family-based practices, collaborative teaming, early literacy, social-emotional development, and linking curriculum to child and family outcomes.

Gruenberg, A. M. & Miller, R. (2011). *A practical guide to early childhood inclusion: Effective reflection.* Upper Saddle River, NJ: Pearson/Merrill.

This text presents a developmental approach to including children with disabilities in the general early childhood classroom. A distinctive feature of this book includes the incorporation of a reflective decision-making model for practitioners.

Milbourne, S. A. & Campbell, P. H. (2007). *Cara's kit: Creating adaptations for routines and activities.* Arlington, VA: Council for Exceptional Children.

This kit provides guidance for adapting activities and routines in order to integrate young children with diverse abilities. The teacher version contains a booklet about adaptations and a CD-ROM with additional resources.

Roffman, L. & Wanerman, T. (2011). *Including one, including all: A guide to relationship-based early childhood inclusion.* St. Paul, MN: Redleaf Press.

This volume provides theoretical, conceptual, and practical information on inclusive early childhood programming. The authors present blueprints for organizing work with children and their families and addresses the challenges and rewards of inclusive environments for all children.

Watson, A. & McCathren, R. (2009). Including children with special needs: Are you and your early childhood program ready? *Young Children, 64*(2), 20–26.

This article presents information to help preschool and kindergarten administrators and teachers develop confidence in teaching children with disabilities.

Wolery, R. A. & Odom, S. (2000). *An administrator's guide to preschool inclusion.* Chapel Hill, NC: Frank Porter Graham Child Development Institute.

For many administrators working in early childhood programs, inclusion is filled with complex and puzzling issues. Administrators hold a powerful role in creating and maintaining inclusive classrooms for young children. This text provides insight into the administrative challenges and successes of inclusion. The document can be downloaded free of charge at http://www.fpg.unc.edu/~publicationsoffice/pdfs/AdmGuide.pdf.

COMPUTERS AND TECHNOLOGY

Carter, M. (2010). Helping teachers think about technology. *Exchange, 32*(1), 30–33.

In this article, the author discusses Information and Communication Technology (ICT) as a tool for supporting and facilitating learning in early childhood environments. When selecting technologies for use with young children, the reader is challenged to consider her values and philosophical beliefs and to reflect on how one's choices can enhance or undermine learning.

NAEYC. (1996). *Technology and young children—Ages 3 through 8: A position statement of the National Association for the Education of Young Children.* Available online at http://www.naeyc.org/files/naeyc/file/positions/PSTECH98.PDF.

This document presents the NAEYC perspective on the use of technology with young children. (At the time of this writing, the position statement is being revised.)

DIVERSITY/ANTI-BIAS CURRICULUM

Copple, E. (Ed.). (2003). *A world of difference.* Washington, DC: NAEYC.

This collection of readings provides a knowledge base and a thought-provoking discussion of issues relative to culture, language, religion, inclusion, and socioeconomic status. Emphasis is on building mutual respect and understanding between and among child care staff, children, and families.

Derman-Sparks, L. & Edwards, J. O. (2010). *Anti-bias education for young children and ourselves.* Washington, DC: NAEYC.

This volume, the successor to Derman-Sparks' classic *Anti-bias Curriculum*, provides updated information about creating early childhood environments that meet the needs of all children and their families. Tips are provided to help staff and children respect each other, themselves and those who have diverse backgrounds, experiences, families, abilities, cultures and language.

Espinosa, L. (2009). *Getting it RIGHT for young children from diverse backgrounds: Applying research to improve practice.* Upper Saddle River, NJ: Pearson/Prentice Hall.

This book provides research-based strategies that can be used to meet the challenges of teaching diverse children including those who are learning English and/or living in poverty.

Gonzalez-Mena, J. (2010). *Foundations of early childhood education: Teaching children in a diverse society.* Columbus, OH: McGraw-Hill.

This text provides an introduction to planning appropriate programming for young children with real-life examples, case studies, stories, and anecdotes. It incorporates discussions of cultural influences and identifies what staff members can do to meet every child's needs.

Gonzalez-Mena, J. (2008). *Diversity in early care and education programs: Honoring differences* (8th ed.). New York: McGraw-Hill.

This author describes an anti-bias approach to preschool curriculum through discussion of culture, adult relations, and conflicts in goals, values, expectations, and child-rearing practices.

Parlakian, R. (2004). *How culture shapes social-emotional development: Implications for practice in infant-family programs.* Washington, DC: Zero to Three Press.

Intended for leaders and practitioners, this book examines how culture shapes children's fundamental learning about themselves and their world and provides a framework for resolving cultural dilemmas.

ETHICS

Feeney, S. & Freeman, N. K. (2005). *Ethics and the early childhood educator: Using the NAEYC Code.* Washington, DC: NAEYC.

This companion to the NAEYC Code of Ethics presents a framework that can be used to help clarify key aspects of

the position statement and to encourage discussion on these important issues.

Feeney, S., Freeman, N. & Moravcik, E. (2008). *Teaching the NAEYC code of ethical conduct: Activity sourcebook* (2005 Code ed.). Washington, DC: NAEYC.

This book provides tools and techniques that can be used in college courses or staff trainings to introduce the use of the NAEYC Code of Ethical Conduct.

NAEYC. (2005). *Code of ethical conduct & statement of commitment.* A position statement of the National Association for the Education of Young Children (rev. ed.). Washington, DC: Author.

This document presents guidelines for ethical behavior for early childhood educators and presents a basis for resolving ethical dilemmas.

NAEYC. (2006). *Code of Ethical Conduct: Supplement for early childhood program administrators.* Available online at http://www.naeyc.org/files/naeyc/file/positions/PSETH05_supp.pdf.

This important document presents guidelines that can be used by program administrators as they face ethical challenges that are unique to their positions as leaders.

EVALUATION AND ASSESSMENT
The evaluation and assessment tools identified in this section represent no official endorsement of any practice, publication, or program by the authors.

Children
Dodge, D. T., Colker, L. & Heroman, C. (2001). *The creative curriculum developmental continuum assessment toolkit for ages 3–5.* Washington, DC: Teaching Strategies.

Dodge, D. T., Ruddick, S. & Berke, K. C. (2006). *The creative curriculum for infants, toddlers, and twos developmental continuum assessment toolkit.* Washington, DC: Teaching Strategies.

These toolkits provide assessment materials for infants, toddlers, and preschoolers that can be used in conjunction with The Creative Curriculum™ materials.

Grisham-Brown, J. & Frontczak, K. P. (2011). *Assessing young children in inclusive settings: The blended practices approach.* Baltimore, MD: P. H. Brookes.

This text presents a comprehensive model for the authentic assessment of young children, with and without disabilities, that can be used to inform planning and to ensure that program practices are aligned with both NAEYC and DEC guidelines. Classroom vignettes and examples are included along with other practical resources such as checklists and excerpts from selected assessment tools.

Gullo, D. (2004). *Understanding assessment and evaluation in early childhood education* (2nd ed.). New York: Teachers College Press.

> This volume provides a comprehensive overview of assessment strategies for young children. The author discusses developmental issues in testing and cautions against the inappropriate use of assessment. Attention is also given to the assessment of children with diverse cultures, languages, and abilities.

Johnson-Martin, N. M., Attermeier, S. M. & Hacker, B. J. (2004). *The Carolina curriculum for infants and toddlers with special needs* (3rd ed.). Baltimore: Brookes Publishing.

Johnson-Martin, N. M., Attermeier, S. M. & Hacker, B. J. (2004). *The Carolina curriculum for preschoolers with special needs* (2nd ed.). Baltimore: Brookes Publishing.

> These materials provide an integrated assessment and intervention program for young children with mild to severe disabilities. This criterion-referenced system permits observation of children in their natural environments playing with familiar materials, and supports collaboration among teachers, families, and service providers.

Linder, T. W. (2007). *Transdisciplinary play-based assessment* (2nd ed.). Baltimore: Brookes Publishing.

Linder, T. W. (2007). *Transdisciplinary play-based intervention* (2nd ed.). Baltimore: Brookes Publishing.

> These materials provide an integrated assessment and intervention program for children ages birth to 6 years. Children engage in natural play with a parent while four developmental domains are evaluated by a professional: sensorimotor, social and emotional, communication and language, and cognition. Interventions are based on results of the assessment.

Lynch, E. (2007). Authentic assessment in the inclusive classroom: Using portfolios to document change and modify curriculum. In E. Horn, C. Peterson, & L. Fox (Eds.), *Linking curriculum to child and family outcomes.* Longmont, CO: Sopris West.

> This article provides an overview of a developmentally appropriate assessment process that can be used with all children. Specific details on the benefits of the process as well as how to plan and implement portfolio assessment are included.

McLean, M., Wolery, M. & Bailey, D. B. (2004). *Assessing infants and preschoolers with special needs* (3rd ed.). Upper Saddle River, NJ: Pearson/Prentice Hall.

> This text provides an overview of issues related to assessing young children with disabilities. The focus is on planning effective, individualized learning environments with an emphasis on family-centered practices, environmental impact, and collaborative decision making.

Puckett, M. B., & Black, J. K. (2008). *Meaningful assessments of the young child: Celebrating development and learning* (3rd ed.). Upper Saddle River, NJ: Pearson/Prentice Hall.

> This text, based on the premise that curriculum, assessment, and teaching are intertwined, provides information on conducting informal and formal assessments and on developing an assessment system that draws information from a variety of sources.

Environment

Harms, T., Cryer, D., & Clifford, R. (2004). *Early Childhood Environment Rating Scale.* New York: Teachers College Press.

> There are four Harms, Cryer, and Clifford Rating Scales. They are: Infant/Toddler Environment Rating Scale, Revised Edition (ITERS-R) Early Childhood Environment Rating Scale. Revised Edition (ECERS-R) Family Child Care Environment Rating Scale, Revised Edition (FCCERS-R) School-Age Care Environment Rating Scale, Revised Edition (SACERS-R) These easy-to-use evaluation instruments answer many questions about the adequacy of early childhood settings. The ratings cover issues such as space, care routines, language, reasoning skills, social development, and adult needs.

Staff and Program

Bloom, P. J. (1996). *The early childhood work environment survey.* Wheeling, IL: National-Louis University.

> This tool assesses staff perceptions and attitudes about staff relations, administrative support, goal consensus and the physical setting of the program.

Bloom, P. J. (2010). *Measuring work attitudes in the early childhood setting: Technical manual for the Early Childhood Job Satisfaction Survey and the Early Childhood Work Environment Survey.* Wheeling, IL: McCormick Center for Early Childhood Leadership, National-Louis University.

> This technical guide and resource manual describes ten dimensions of organizational climate and provides many ideas for increasing job satisfaction and professionalism in early childhood programs.

Sylva, K., Srai-Batchford, I. & Taggarat, B. (2006). Assessing quality in the early years: Early childhood environment rating scale– extension (ECERS-E) (rev. ed.). Stoke on Trent, United Kingdom: Trentham Books. (Available through Stylus Publishing in the United States.)

> The ECERS-E has been developed to measure program quality in literacy, math, science and environment, and diversity. This revised edition clarifies and builds on the previous text, enabling programs to improve pedagogy and curriculum in preschool settings.

Talan, T. N. & Bloom, P. J. (2011). *The Program Administration Scale: Measuring leadership and management in early childhood.* (2nd ed.). New York, NY: Teachers College Press.

The instrument examines ten categories that include human resources development, personnel cost and allocation, center operations, child assessment, fiscal management, program planning and evaluation, family partnerships, marketing and public relations, technology, and staff qualifications.

Talley, K. L. (1997). How are you doing? A center director self-review tool. *Child Care Information Exchange, 177,* 17–23.

This article presents a tool for administrators that analyzes the program, work environment, budget and finance, public relations, family relations, planning and administration, and professionalism. The intent of the survey is to assist directors with their professional growth via a system of self-evaluation.

FINANCIAL MANAGEMENT, FUND-RAISING, AND MARKETING

Bray, I. (2008). *Effective fundraising for nonprofits: Real-world strategies that work.* Berkeley, CA: Nolo.

This volume presents information about working with individual donors, getting media coverage, soliciting grants from foundations and corporations, planning special events and using the Internet effectively. It addresses IRS rules and regulations and provides numerous planning worksheets.

Gross, M., Warshauer, W. & Shelmon, N. E. (2010). *Financial and accounting guide for not-for-profit organizations.* New York: Wiley.

This book provides detailed advice on cash, accrual, and fund accounting; financial statements; budgeting; internal control; tax requirements; and bookkeeping.

Jack, G. (2005). *The business of child care: Management and financial strategies.* Clifton Park, NY: Thomson Delmar Learning.

This volume focuses on managing enrollment, recruiting and retaining staff, budgeting, financial record keeping, and decision making. The accompanying CD-ROM provides financial spreadsheets that can be implemented in child care settings.

On-target marketing: Promotion strategies for child care centers. (1996). Redmond, WA: Child Care Information Exchange.

A compilation of articles that first appeared in *Child Care Information Exchange: The Director's Magazine.* Very helpful articles on courting the press, advertising your center, and handling parents' visits to your center.

FUNDING

Bergman, R. (2010). *Not just small change: Fund development for early childhood programs.* Redmond, WA: Child Care Information Exchange.

This book, written specifically for those involved with early childhood programming, covers numerous strategies related to fundraising and grant writing.

McDonough, B. (Ed.). (2009). *Annual register of grant support 2010: A directory of funding sources.*

A comprehensive guide to various types of grant support, both governmental and private.

National Child Care Information and Technical Assistance Center. (2009). *Starting and operating a child care business.* Available online at http://nccic. acf.hhs.gov/poptopics/startup.pdf.

This guide presents basic steps to consider in planning and operating an early childhood program. Included are links to sources that provide information on grant writing for child care programs. Additional resources on fund-raising, grants, and grant writing can be found at http://nccic.acf.hhs.gov/poptopics/fundraising.html.

GUIDANCE

Gartrell, D. J. (2004). *The power of guidance: Teaching social-emotional skills in early childhood classrooms.* Clifton Park, NY: Thomson Delmar Learning.

This book is well titled because it is, indeed, a powerful book as it explores age-appropriate and developmentally appropriate ways to teach social-emotional skills in the classroom through the use of thoughtful guidance practices. Gartrell has an informal, friendly writing style, and he uses many anecdotes to help the reader reflect on and apply his suggested approaches that promote the emotional well-being of young children.

Gartrell, D. J. (2011). *A guidance approach for the encouraging classroom* (5th ed.). Clifton Park, NY: Wadsworth Cengage Learning.

The first part of this excellent text explores the foundation of guidance and addresses issues such as conventional discipline versus guidance, mistaken behavior, the guidance tradition, and innovative theories about child development with guidance. Part two focuses on building an encouraging classroom. Of particular interest is the author's discussion of leadership communication that focuses on the importance of effective interaction with staff and parents.

Miller, D. F. (2010). *Positive child guidance* (6th ed.). Clifton Park, NY: Delmar Cengage Learning.

Child guidance is a challenging process of finding ways to help children become responsible, cooperative members of their group. This book is for caregivers who spend a great deal of time helping children become self-disciplined members of society. It is intended as a road map to guide adults as they work to meet the individual needs of children from infancy through early childhood.

HEALTH, SAFETY, AND SICK CHILD CARE

American Academy of Pediatrics, American Public Health Association, & Maternal and Child Health Bureau. (2011). *Caring for our children: National health and safety performance standards: Guidelines for out-of-home child care programs* (3rd ed.). Denver, CO: National Resource for Health and Safety in Child Care.

This edition offers nine comprehensive chapters of the latest information and program activities for child care providers, licensors, and policymakers in the early child care field. It covers healthy development, safe play facilities, supplies and equipment, infectious diseases, principles for including and caring for children with special needs, and much more. Updates to this volume can be found at: http://nrckids.org/CFOC/.

American Academy of Pediatrics, American Public Health Association, & National Resource Center for Health and Safety in Child Care and Early Education. (2010). *Preventing childhood obesity in early care and education programs.* Denver, CO: National Resource for Health and Safety in Child Care.

This booklet presents national standards that describe best practices in nutrition and physical activity for all types of early childhood programs. The document is available online at http://nrckids.org/CFOC3/PREVENTING_OBESITY/index.htm

Aronson, S. (2002). *Model child care health policies* (4th ed.). Washington, DC: NAEYC.

This booklet provides sample health care policies that can be used by early education programs. Included are reproducible forms, resource lists, and safety checklists.

Aronson, S. & Shope, T. (2009). *Managing infectious diseases in child care and schools: A quick reference guide* (2nd ed.). Elk Grove Village, IL: American Academy of Pediatrics.

This is a convenient, easy-to-reference guide specifically designed for use by child care teachers. It offers a quick resource to industry standards and proven policies for protecting the children in your care, the center staff, and the organization's liability.

Boise, P. (2009). *Go green rating scale for early childhood settings.* St. Paul, MN: Redleaf Press.

This research-based rating scale helps early childhood staff determine the level of environmental health and safety in their program and explains why particular scores are earned.

Marotz, L. R. (2012). *Health, safety and nutrition for the young child* (8th ed.). Clifton Park, NY: Delmar Cengage Learning.

This up-to-date, comprehensive text covers the essential aspects of health, safety, and nutrition for young children. It includes material on infant nutrition, AIDS, and sanitary procedures in group care facilities.

INFANT/TODDLER CARE

Gonzalez-Mena, J. & Widmeyer Eyer, D. (2008). *Infants, toddlers, and caregivers: A curriculum of respective, responsive care and education* (7th ed.). Columbus, OH: McGraw-Hill.

This book offers excellent coverage of infant/toddler development. It serves as a complete resource on attachment as well as infant and toddler care in group settings.

Greenman, J., Stonehouse, A., & Schweikert, G. (2007). *Prime times: A handbook for excellence in infant and toddler programs* (2nd ed.). St. Paul, MN: Redleaf Press.

The authors explore the topic of what makes for quality in infant and toddler programs, emphasizing the need for primary caregivers; small groups; responsive interactions; and environments that are safe, secure, and "filled with learning." This is a hands-on guide for practitioners.

Hast, F. & Hollyfield, A. (2002). *Infant and toddler experiences.* St. Paul, MN: Redleaf Press.

These authors differentiate between an activity and an experience. They describe experiences in detail, including materials needed and procedures to keep in mind that help caregivers promote healthy development for infants and toddlers.

Honig, A. (2001). *Secure relationships: Nurturing infant/toddler attachment in early care settings.* Washington, DC: NAEYC.

Based on knowledge of research and theory, Honig describes how loving, responsive, and consistent care from primary caregivers is the foundation for how children learn to form relationships.

Lally, D. (2008). *Caring for infants and toddlers in groups: Developmentally appropriate practice* (2nd ed.). Washington, DC: Zero to Three Press.

This book identifies research-based elements of quality care that support optimal development and learning of infants and toddlers in group care. Family- and center-based providers will learn research-based strategies to impact the lives of the children and the families they serve.

Parlakian, R. (2001). *The power of questions: Building quality relationships with infants and families.* Washington, DC: Zero to Three Press.

This book focuses on direct work with parents of very young children. It is a resource that explores reflective approaches and practices that staff can use to establish relationships with families. Strategies that define boundary-setting and managing one's reactions to families address the complex interpersonal situations that staff face every day when working in infant/toddler settings.

Raikes, H. H. & Edwards, C. P. (2009). *Extending the dance in infant and toddler caregiving: Enhancing attachment and relationships.* Baltimore, MD: Paul H. Brookes.

The authors provide a comprehensive blueprint for establishing and maintaining an early childhood program based on the formation of nurturing relationships and strengthening parent-child attachment.

LEADERSHIP

Bloom, P. J. (2002). *Making the most of meetings: A practical guide.* Lake Forest, IL: New Horizons.

A rich resource for guiding the planning and preparation of meetings, with helpful strategies for carrying out a successful meeting plus ways one can enhance effectiveness of meetings. This book will help directors preside over stimulating and inspiring staff and parent meetings.

Bloom, P. J. (2003). *Leadership in action: How effective directors get things done.* Lake Forest, IL: New Horizons.

This book includes discussion of many facets of leadership, including leadership roles, leadership as a way of thinking, knowing thyself, and becoming a facilitative leader. Bloom discusses the essential functions of a leader in early childhood education—to inspire, to inform, to motivate, and to serve as a symbol for the collective identity of the group.

Collins, J. C. (2001). *Good to great: Why some companies make the leap ... and others don't.* New York: Harper Collins.

While not a book written specifically for early childhood educators, this volume is considered to be an excellent discussion of how companies remain successful over time and how administrators and managers can attain sustained performance.

Collins, J. C. (2005). *Good to great and the social sectors: A monograph to accompany good to great.* New York: Harper Collins.

Collins applies the principles described in *Good to Great* to the not-for-profit sector. He calls himself a student of the social sector and explores the challenges facing social-sector leaders. Directors will discover ideas and inspiration from this interesting author.

Culkin, M. L. (Ed.). (2000). *Managing quality in young children's programs: The leader's role.* New York: Teachers College Press.

This book, which focuses on and acknowledges the importance of effective leadership in early childhood

programs, is one of the first of its kind. The articles, written by respected early childhood scholars and practitioners, cover the development of center directors and the director's credential. With growing interest in a credential for directors, this is a timely and much-needed source of information.

Gordon, T. (2001). *Leadership effectiveness training (LET).* E. Rutherford, NJ: The Penguin Group.

The basic skills for effective interpersonal communication, including active listening, "I" messages, and no-lose problem solving, are covered. These skills are analogues to those covered in Gordon's *Teacher Effectiveness Training* and *Parent Effectiveness Training*.

Neugebauer, B. & Neugebauer, R. (Eds.). (2003). *The art of leadership: Managing early childhood organizations* (Rev. ed.). Redmond, WA: Child Care Information Exchange.

The Neugebauers have carefully selected articles covering a wide range of topics of interest to directors. This is a collection of more than 90 articles written by respected specialists and covering leadership, organizational management, financial management, personnel management, program development, and community relations. Those directors who find *Child Care Information Exchange: A Magazine for Directors* helpful will find this compilation of informative articles assembled by the Neugebauers an excellent resource.

Sciarra, D. J. & Dorsey, A. G. (2002). *Leaders and supervisors in child care programs.* Clifton Park, NY: Thomson Delmar Learning.

The book is about leadership and supervision in the field of early child care and education. It is divided into three sections. Section I, Describing the Leader, draws on principles from business that leaders in early childhood can apply to the business of child care. Section II, Supervision 101, offers an in-depth discussion of supervision that will guide directors through the specific steps of an effective supervisory program. Section III considers other aspects of the leader's role. It addresses the issues faced by leaders as change agents and the leader's role as a professional in the field. This textbook has features similar to Sciarra and Dorsey's *Developing and Administering a Child Care Center* that make it a suitable companion for use in a college-level course as well as for working directors.

Winton, P. J., McCollum, J. A. & Catlett, C. (2007). *Practical approaches to early childhood professional development: Evidence, strategies, and resources.* Washington, DC: Zero to Three Press.

This book provides an organized format for building quality into professional development experiences. A CD-ROM includes handouts and activities as well as additional resources.

PLANNING SPACES

Curtis, D. & Carter, M. (2002). *Designs for living and learning: Transforming early childhood environments.* St. Paul, MN: Redleaf Press.

This book will inspire directors and teachers to create wonderful environments that are comfortable and inviting for children, families, and staff.

Greenman, J. (2005). *Caring spaces, learning places: Children's environments that work.* Redmond, WA: Exchange Press.

This is a helpful guide to planning spaces for young children. It is full of ideas and observations, as well as problems and solutions for those responsible for planning spaces for child care.

PROGRAM DEVELOPMENT AND CURRICULUM APPROACHES AND PACKAGES

The curricula identified in this section represent no official endorsement of any practice, publication, or program by the authors.

Albrecht, K. & Miller, L. G. (2000). *Innovations: The comprehensive infant curriculum: A complete interactive curriculum for infants from birth to 18 months.* Beltsville, MD: Gryphon House.

Albrecht, K. & Miller, L. G. (2001). *Innovations: The comprehensive toddler curriculum: A complete interactive curriculum for toddlers from 18 months to 36 months.* Beltsville, MD: Gryphon House.

Albrecht, K. & Miller, L. G. (2004). *Innovations: The comprehensive preschool curriculum.* Beltsville, MD: Gryphon House.

These three volumes by Albrecht and Miller offer a complete review of child development for each age group followed by sections on interactions, relationships, communicating, making friends, and age-appropriate activities. It is a very comprehensive series that presents a convincing position that curriculum is much more than well-arranged rooms and interesting activities.

Branscombe, N. A., Castle, K., Dorsey, A. G., Surbeck, E. & Taylor, J. B. (2003). *Early childhood curriculum: A constructivist perspective.* Boston and New York: Houghton Mifflin.

This comprehensive book explores the ways teachers can integrate constructivist principles in all areas of the curriculum, linking learning and development to the needs of children. It also invites the reader to become actively engaged in the construction of knowledge as it is presented in this book.

Copple, C. & Bredekamp, S. (Eds.). (2009). *Developmentally appropriate practice in early childhood programs: Serving children from birth through age 8* (3rd ed.). Washington, DC: National Association for the Education of Young Children.

This updated version of the contemporary early childhood education classic is accompanied by a supplementary CD containing readings on key topics plus video vignettes showing developmentally appropriate practice in action. Based on research, this volume helps teachers, directors, parents, and board members better understand sound practice that should reverse the current trend toward a narrow focus on academics for young children.

Crowther, I. (2003). *Creating effective learning environments.* Scarborough, Ontario, Canada: Thomson Nelson.

This author expresses the strong conviction that the fundamental truth about curriculum is that it must be based on the strengths and needs of children. She believes that the cornerstones of curriculum development are careful observation and documentation followed by planning and implementation. There are chapters covering areas of play, including sand and water play, block play, and dramatic play. Other specific learning environments addressed are creative arts, math/science, and manipulative experiences.

Curtis, D. & Carter, M. (2007). *Learning together with young children: A curriculum framework for reflective teachers.* St. Paul, MN: Redleaf Press.

This text presents a collaborative framework for thinking about curriculum. Teachers are challenged to consider their values and to explore how they can teach through observation, reflection, inquiry, and action. In addition, a discussion of how teachers can encourage children to represent their learning in multiple ways is provided.

Dodge, D. T., Colker, L. J. & Heroman, C. (2002). *The creative curriculum for pre-school.* Washington, DC: Teaching Strategies.

Dodge, D. T., Rudick, S. & Berke, K. (2006). *The creative curriculum for infants, toddlers and twos* (2nd ed.). Washington, DC: Teaching Strategies.

The Creative Curriculum™ materials present an environment-based approach to curriculum but also clearly define the teacher's role in connecting content, teaching, and learning. They apply recent research to the practice and strategies that help meet the needs of all children, including those with special needs as well as those who are second language learners.

Edwards, C., Gandini, L. & Forman, G. (Eds.). (1998). *The hundred languages of children: The Reggio Emilia approach—Advanced reflections* (2nd ed.). Stamford, CT: Ablex Publishing.

The book is a comprehensive overview of the Reggio Emilia approach to education, including its history and philosophy, teaching methods, parent perspectives, school organization, and attention to the planning of physical environments. The volume also discusses the role of adults in planning and implementing the curriculum as well as the inclusion of children with disabilities.

Frede, E. & Ackerman, D. J. (2007, March). *Preschool curriculum decision-making: Dimensions to consider.* NIEER policy brief. Available online at http://www.nieer.org/docs/?DocID=142.

> This document, published by the National Institute for Early Education Research, provides guidelines for decision makers responsible for evaluating and selecting the most appropriate curriculum for their specific early education program. Eight questions are posed and suggestions provided to assist in the selection process.

Gordon, A. M. & Williams Browne, K. (2010). *Beginnings and beyond* (8th ed.). Clifton Park, NY: Delmar-Cengage Learning.

> A comprehensive text covering many of the traditional questions that are of interest to early childhood educators, including What Is the Field of Early Childhood? Who Is the Young Child? Who Are the Teachers of the Young Child? What Is the Setting? What Is Being Taught? and How Do We Teach for Tomorrow?

Hohmann, M. & Weikart, D. P. (2002). *Educating young children: Active learning practices for preschool and child care programs* (2nd ed.). Ypsilanti, MI: High/Scope Press.

> This book provides the details of the High/Scope™ curriculum as well as a description of the adult's role in implementing the program. This approach to curriculum is based on the High/Scope Educational Research Foundation's longitudinal research on educating children in environments that support active and participatory learning.

Jackman, H. (2008). *Early education curriculum: A child's connection to the world* (3rd ed.). Clifton Park, NY: Thomson Delmar Learning.

> This third edition is designed for teachers who are looking for current early childhood education philosophies, fresh ideas, and new insight into curriculum planning. Interconnecting philosophies are underscored here, focusing not only on child-initiated curriculum but also on cultural context, learning by doing, physical activity and play, plus helpful discussions of interpersonal relationships.

Katz, L. G. & Chard, S. C. (2000). *Engaging children's minds: The project approach* (2nd ed.). Stamford, CT: Ablex Publishing.

> This volume provides an overview of an integrated approach to curriculum wherein children's interests are used as a basis for developing projects. Children identify a problem, brainstorm solutions, select and implement one solution, and evaluate the implementation. The role of the teacher in facilitating project development is also addressed.

Montessori, M. (1986). *The discovery of the child.* New York: Ballantine Books.

Montessori, M. (2002). *The Montessori method.* Mineola, NY: Dover Publications.

> Before educators explore the materials and methods of Montessori, they should first understand her basic philosophies, and these volumes provide a valuable introduction to the topic. In Montessori's own words, these books provide an overview of her approach to and theoretical basis for educating children as well as her understanding of the nature of the child.

Moomaw, S. (1997). *More than singing.* St. Paul, MN: Redleaf Press.

> This book, which includes a cassette recording, offers a wealth of wonderful musical experiences that teachers can plan, even though they may not be trained musicians. Teachers will learn to make resonant, inexpensive instruments as well as gain knowledge about how to select songs and rhythm activities and coordinate these with their whole language curriculum.

Moomaw, S. & Hieronymous, B. (1995). *More than counting: Whole math activities for preschool and kindergarten.* St. Paul, MN: Redleaf Press.

> An excellent resource for use by teachers and parents as they come to understand the "whole math" curriculum based on the constructivist model of cognitive development. The math games and materials described here in detail are not just additions to enrich the curriculum, they are the math curriculum for preschool and kindergarten.

Moomaw, S. & Hieronymous, B. (1997). *More than magnets.* St. Paul, MN: Redleaf Press.

> The science curriculum in early childhood classrooms has typically consisted of a classroom "display," usually with a plant/animal focus, or teacher-directed experiments. This book offers a comprehensive, developmentally appropriate approach to science education with young children, with special attention to physics and math. It has more than a hundred activities that engage children in interactive science explorations in many areas of the classroom.

Moomaw, S. & Hieronymous, B. (2001). *More than letters: Literacy activities for pre-school, kindergarten and first grade.* St. Paul, MN: Redleaf Press.

> This excellent book is an extensive compilation of emergent-literacy materials and activities that translate theory and research into a dynamic, effective literacy program for young children. The curriculum evolved following the emergence of the whole language movement and took shape as the authors explored their interest in how children construct literacy concepts.

Post, J. & Hohmann, M. (2000). *Tender care and early learning: Supporting infants and toddlers in child care settings.* Ypsilanti, MI: High/Scope Press.

> This book provides the details of the High/Scope™ curriculum for infants and toddlers. This approach to

curriculum is based on the High/Scope Educational Research Foundation's longitudinal research on educating children in environments that support active and participatory learning.

Sandall, S., Hemmeter, M. L., Smith, B. J. & McLean, M. E. (Eds.). (2005). *DEC recommended practices: A comprehensive guide for practical application in early intervention/early childhood special education.* Longmont, CO: Sopris West.

This collection of readings provides specific guidelines for early childhood programs that serve children with disabilities. Included are suggestions related to curriculum, child and program assessment, family-based practices, interdisciplinary teaming, and technology.

PROGRAM MANAGEMENT

Bloom, P. J., Hentschel, A. & Bella, J., (2010). *A great place to work: Creating a healthy organizational climate.* Lake Forest, IL: New Horizons

This text helps directors identify how ten dimensions of a center impact the work life for staff. These important dimensions include collegiality, opportunities for professional growth, supervisor support, reward systems, and goal consensus.

Cherry, C., Harkness, B., Kuzma, K. & Bates, D. (2001). *Child care center management: A hands-on resource* (3rd ed.). Grand Rapids, MI: Frank Schaffer Publications, Inc.

This guide provides information on many aspects of administering child care programs including budgeting, insurance, health issues, legal concerns and disaster preparedness.

Jack, G. (2005). *The business of child care: Management and financial strategies.* Clifton Park, NY: Thomson Delmar Learning.

This volume focuses on managing enrollment, recruiting and retaining staff, budgeting, financial record keeping, and decision making. The accompanying CD-ROM provides financial spreadsheets that can be implemented in child care settings.

RESEARCH

Eager to learn: Educating our preschoolers. (2000). Washington, DC: National Academy Press.

This booklet is about the education of children ages 2 to 5. It focuses on programs outside the home such as preschool, Head Start, and child care centers. It covers the major trends that will influence our thinking about the education of young children during the early part of the twenty-first century.

Gopnik, A., Meltzoff, A. & Kuhl, P. (1999). *The scientist in the crib: Minds, brains, and how children learn.* New York: William Morrow & Company.

This book tells the story of the new science of children's minds. These authors have united cognitive science with psychology, philosophy, linguistics, computer science, and neuroscience. Their research demonstrates that babies and young children know and learn more about the world than we ever imagined. It shows that very young children think, draw conclusions, and make predictions. This book lays out the science of babies' minds.

NICHD Early Child Care Research Network (Ed.). (2005). *Child care and child development: Results from the NICHD study of early child care and youth development.* New York: Guildford Press.

This text presents results from the most comprehensive scientific study to date of early childhood care and its impact on the development of the young child, including health and psychological adjustment. The researchers involved in this study are some of the most well-known names in the field of early childhood education scholarship.

Vandell, D., Belsky, J., Burchinal, M., Steinberg, L., Vandergrift, N. & NICHD Early Child Care Research Network. (2010). *Do effects of early child care extend to age 15 years? Results from the NICHD study of early child care and youth development.* Available online at http://nieer.org/docs/?DocID=293

This report provides outcomes of the longitudinal NICHD study on the impact of quality child care on children's development.

WORKING WITH STAFF, BOARD, COMMUNITY, AND PARENTS

Baker, A. C. & Manfredi/Petitt, L. A. (2004). Relationships, the heart of quality care: Creating community among adults in early care settings. Washington, DC: NAEYC.

This volume describes the concept of relationship-based child care, what attitudes support such care, and the policies required to implement this important approach to staff interaction and teaching.

Bloom, P. J. (2000). *Circle of influence: Implementing shared decision making and participative management.* Lake Forest, IL: New Horizons.

In this book, you learn that participative management is both a philosophy and a set of behaviors that define your interactions with people. You will explore techniques for managing the daily business of your center. If you implement these strategies and expand your staff's circle of influence over decision making, you will have true collaboration and commitment to shared goals.

Bloom, P. J. (2005). *Blueprint for action: Achieving center-based change through staff* development (2nd ed.). Lake Forest, IL: New Horizons.

This book is based on two basic assumptions, namely, that high-quality programs are distinguished by their willingness to deal with their imperfections and that organizational change can come about only through change in individuals. The blueprint Bloom presents in this excellent book serves as a guide for enhancing the professional development of all who work together to achieve changes that will move them toward their shared vision of excellence.

Bloom, P. J. (2007). *From the inside out: The power of reflection and self-awareness.* Lake Forest, IL: New Horizons.

Bloom speaks to personhood of early childhood educators in this book—ideas like self-mentoring, self-awareness, and being a self-reflective practitioner are just a few of her provocative words for those of us who spend our lives working with and thinking about young children.

Carter, M. & Curtis, D. (2009). *The visionary director: A handbook for dreaming, organizing and improvising in your center* (2nd ed.). St. Paul, MN: Redleaf Press.

The major thrust of this book is to help administrators develop their potential as leaders. Each principle presented in this book is accompanied by practical strategies that can guide the professional development of the administrator.

Caruso, J. J. & Faucett, M. T. (1999). *Supervision in early childhood education: A developmental perspective.* New York: Teachers College Press.

This book addresses supervisory issues pertinent to personnel in both public and private settings. The focus of this book is staff development, and it is both descriptive and practical.

Gonzalez-Mena, J. (2009). *50 strategies for communicating and working with diverse families* (2nd ed.). Upper Saddle River, NJ: Pearson/Prentice Hall.

This book presents culturally relevant ideas for working with families in today's diverse society. Included are strategies related to advocacy, nonverbal and written communication, handling conferences, transitions in the child's education, working with immigrant families, working with families of children with special needs, working with families referred for abuse or neglect, and many others.

Keyser, J. (2006). *From parents to partners: Building a family-centered early childhood program.* Washington, DC: NAEYC and St. Paul, MN: Redleaf Press.

This volume describes how directors can encourage parents to become involved in early childhood programs through the use of effective communication, newsletters, conferences, and special events. It also explores the reasons and methods for partnering with family members.

Note: Page numbers referencing figures are italicized and followed by an "*f.*" Page numbers referencing tables are italicized and followed by a "*t.*"